THE BIOPSYCHOLOGY OF DEVELOPMENT

CONTRIBUTORS

Frank A. Beach
C. G. Beer
Herbert G. Birch
Ernest Caspari
Paul Delost
René Dubos
Leon Eisenberg
Gilbert Gottlieb
Viktor Hamburger
Dale B. Harris

Williamina A. Himwich
R. A. Hinde
J. Křeček
Daniel S. Lehrman
Margaret Mead
Jay S. Rosenblatt
Mark R. Rosenzweig
B. F. Skinner
R. W. Sperry
C. H. Waddington

William F. Windle

THE BIOPSYCHOLOGY OF DEVELOPMENT

EDITED BY

ETHEL TOBACH, LESTER R. ARONSON,
and EVELYN SHAW

Department of Animal Behavior
The American Museum of Natural History
New York, New York

ACADEMIC PRESS   New York and London   1971

COPYRIGHT © 1971, BY ACADEMIC PRESS, INC.
ALL RIGHTS RESERVED
NO PART OF THIS BOOK MAY BE REPRODUCED IN ANY FORM,
BY PHOTOSTAT, MICROFILM, RETRIEVAL SYSTEM, OR ANY
OTHER MEANS, WITHOUT WRITTEN PERMISSION FROM
THE PUBLISHERS.

ACADEMIC PRESS, INC.
111 Fifth Avenue, New York, New York 10003

United Kingdom Edition published by
ACADEMIC PRESS, INC. (LONDON) LTD.
24/28 Oval Road, London NW1 7DD

LIBRARY OF CONGRESS CATALOG CARD NUMBER: 76-178218

PRINTED IN THE UNITED STATES OF AMERICA

CONTENTS

List of Contributors and Discussants — vii
List of Conference Participants — xi
Introduction — xv

I. Genetic Processes and Behavioral Development

Differentiation and Pattern Formation in the Development of Behavior
    ERNEST CASPARI — 3

Concepts of Development
    C. H. WADDINGTON — 17

II. Neural Developmental Processes

How a Developing Brain Gets Itself Properly Wired for Adaptive Function
    R. W. SPERRY — 27

Development of Embryonic Motility
    VIKTOR HAMBURGER — 45

Ontogenesis of Sensory Function in Birds and Mammals
    GILBERT GOTTLIEB — 67

Origin and Early Development of Neural Elements in the Human Brain
    WILLIAM F. WINDLE — 129

III. Biochemical Processes in Behavioral Development

Biochemical Processes of Nervous System Development
    WILLIAMINA A. HIMWICH — 173

Fetal Endocrinology and the Effect of Hormones on Development
    PAUL DELOST — 195

The Theory of Critical Developmental Periods and Postnatal Development of Endocrine Functions
    J. KŘEČEK — 233

Hormonal Factors Controlling the Differentiation, Development, and Display of Copulatory Behavior in the Ramstergig and Related Species
    FRANK A. BEACH — 249

Experiential Background for the Induction of
Reproductive Behavior Patterns by Hormones
    DANIEL S. LEHRMAN   297

Effects of Environment on Development of Brain and of Behavior
    MARK R. ROSENZWEIG   303

IV. Comparative Considerations of the Development of Socialization

Suckling and Home Orientation in the Kitten:
A Comparative Developmental Study
    JAY S. ROSENBLATT   345

Some Problems in the Study of the Development of Social Behavior
    R. A. HINDE   411

Diversity in the Study of the Development of Social Behavior
    C. G. BEER   433

V. Contemporary Issues in the Study of Behavior

Behavioral Science, Engineering, and Poetry
    DANIEL S. LEHRMAN   459

The Development of Human Behavior: Theoretical Considerations
for Future Research
    DALE B. HARRIS   473

Levels, Categories, and Methodological Assumptions in the Study
of Behavioral Development
    HERBERT G. BIRCH   503

Persistent Problems in the Study of the Biopsychology of Development
    LEON EISENBERG   515

VI. Societal Implications of the Study of Behavioral Development

Options Implicit in Developmental Styles
    MARGARET MEAD   533

A Behavioral Analysis of Value Judgments
    B. F. SKINNER   543

In Defense of Biological Freedom
    RENÉ DUBOS   553

Author Index   561

Subject Index   573

LIST OF CONTRIBUTORS AND DISCUSSANTS

Numbers in parentheses indicate the pages on which contributions begin.

LESTER R. ARONSON (525), Department of Animal Behavior, The American Museum of Natural History, New York, New York

FRANK A. BEACH (249), Department of Psychology, University of California, Berkeley, California

C. G. BEER (433), Institute of Animal Behavior, Rutgers University, Newark, New Jersey

HERBERT G. BIRCH (503), Albert Einstein College of Medicine, Bronx, New York

ERNEST CASPARI (3), Department of Biology, The University of Rochester, Rochester, New York

ALIA COHEN (229), Laboratoire de Physiologie Comparée, Faculté des Sciences, Paris, France

STANLEY M. CRAIN (43, 65), Department of Physiology, Albert Einstein College of Medicine, Bronx, New York

PAUL DELOST (195),* Laboratory of Animal Physiology, University of Claremont, Claremont, California

RENÉ DUBOS (553), The Rockefeller University, New York, New York

LEON EISENBERG (515), Department of Psychiatry, Massachusetts General Hospital, Boston, Massachusetts

GILBERT GOTTLIEB (67), Department of Mental Health, Psychology Laboratory, Dorothea Dix Hospital, Raleigh, North Carolina

---

* Present address: Department des Physiologie Faculté de Sciences, Clermont-Ferrand, France.

LIST OF CONTRIBUTORS AND DISCUSSANTS

VIKTOR HAMBURGER (45), Department of Biology, Washington University, St. Louis, Missouri

DALE B. HARRIS (473), Department of Psychology, Pennsylvania State University, University Park, Pennsylvania

WILLIAMINA A. HIMWICH (173), Thudichum Psychiatric Research Laboratory, Galesburg State Research Hospital, State of Illinois Department of Mental Health, Galesburg, Illinois

R. A. HINDE (411), Sub-Department of Animal Behavior, Cambridge University, Madingley, Cambridge, England

J. KŘEČEK (233), Institute of Physiology, Czechoslovak Academy of Sciences, Prague, Budejovicka, Czechoslovakia

DANIEL S. LEHRMAN (297, 459), Institute of Animal Behavior, Rutgers University, Newark, New Jersey

LEWIS P. LIPSITT (498), Department of Psychology, Brown University, Providence, Rhode Island

THOMAS E. MCGILL (43),* The Garden Cottage, Redford Road Estate, Edinburgh, Scotland

MARGARET MEAD (533), Department of Anthropology, The American Museum of Natural History, New York, New York

S. MILKOVIC (230), Laboratory of Experimental Medicine, University of Zagreb, Zagreb, Yugoslavia

RONALD OPPENHEIM (42), Department of Mental Health, Psychology Laboratory, Dorothea Dix Hospital, Raleigh, North Carolina

DOMINICK PURPURA (193), Department of Anatomy, Albert Einstein College of Medicine, Bronx, New York

JAY S. ROSENBLATT (345), Institute of Animal Behavior, Rutgers University, Newark, New Jersey

MARK R. ROSENZWEIG (303, 525), Department of Psychology, University of California, Berkeley, California

SHAWN SCHAPIRO (231),† Developmental Neuroendocrinology Laboratory, Veterans Administration Hospital, San Fernando, California

---

* Present address: Department of Psychology, Williams College, Williamstown, Massachusetts.
† Deceased.

B. F. SKINNER (543), Department of Psychology, Harvard University, Cambridge, Massachusetts

ROGER W. SPERRY (27, 527), Kerckhoff Laboratories, California Institute of Technology, Pasadena, California

C. H. WADDINGTON (17), Institute of Animal Genetics, Edinburgh, Scotland

WILLIAM F. WINDLE (129),* Institute of Rehabilitation Medicine, New York University Medical Center, New York, New York

PETER H. WOLFF (528), Department of Psychiatry, Harvard University Medical School, Boston, Massachusetts

* Present address: P.O. Box 302, Granville, Ohio.

LIST OF CONFERENCE PARTICIPANTS

ARMAND ABRAMOVICI, Tel-Aviv University, Tel-Aviv, Israel

RICHARD ANDREW, Sussex University, Sussex, United Kingdom

LESTER R. ARONSON, The American Museum of Natural History, New York, New York

P. P. BATESON, University of Cambridge, Cambridge, England

FRANK A. BEACH,* University of California, Berkeley, California

COLIN BEER,* Institute of Animal Behavior, Newark, New Jersey

MARTIN BERRY, The University of Birmingham, Birmingham, England

HERBERT G. BIRCH,* Albert Einstein College of Medicine, Bronx, New York

MARY A. B. BRAZIER, Brain Research Institute, Los Angeles, California

ERNEST W. CASPARI,† The University of Rochester, Rochester, New York

FRANCISCO COBOS, Harvard University School of Public Health, Bogota, Colombia

ALIA COHEN, Faculté des Sciences, Paris, France

MICHAEL CORNER, Netherlands Central Institute for Brain Research, Amsterdam, The Netherlands

STANLEY M. CRAIN, Albert Einstein College of Medicine, Bronx, New York

PAUL DELOST,* Faculté des Sciences, Clermont-Ferrand, France

* Presented papers published herein.
† Unfortunately, Dr. Caspari was unable to attend the Conference because of illness, and thus the Conference could not benefit from his participation in discussion. He was, however, able to submit his manuscript in time for its presentation at the meeting by Dr. Lehrman.

LIST OF CONFERENCE PARTICIPANTS

RENÉ DUBOS,* The Rockefeller University, New York, New York

LEON EISENBERG,* Massachusetts General Hospital, Boston, Massachusetts

ARIANE ETIENNE, University of Cambridge, Cambridge, England

ROSS EVANS, Columbia University, New York, New York

MICHAEL FOX, Washington University, St. Louis, Missouri

PETER S. GOLD, State University of New York, Buffalo, New York

PATRICIA S. GOLDMAN, National Institute of Mental Health, Bethesda, Maryland

GILBERT GOTTLIEB,* Dorothea Dix Hospital, Raleigh, North Carolina

VIKTOR HAMBURGER,* Washington University, St. Louis, Missouri

MAX HAMBURGH, Albert Einstein College of Medicine, Bronx, New York

DALE B. HARRIS,* Pennsylvania State University, University Park, Pennsylvania

MARIETA HEATON, Dorothea Dix Hospital, Raleigh, North Carolina

WILLIAMINA A. HIMWICH,* Thudichum Psychiatric Research Laboratory, Galesburg, Illinois

ROBERT A. HINDE,* University of Cambridge, Cambridge, England

MYRON HOFER, Montefiore Hospital and Medical Center, Bronx, New York

A. F. KALVERBOER, Academic Hospital, Groningen, The Netherlands

BERNARD KAPLAN, Clark University, Worcester, Massachusetts

HARRIET KAPLAN, Institute for Basic Research in Mental Retardation, Staten Island, New York

SEYMOUR KETY, Massachusetts General Hospital, Boston, Massachusetts

PETER KLOPFER, Duke University, Durham, North Carolina

JIRI KŘEČEK,* Institute of Physiology, Prague, Czechoslovakia

KNUT LARSSON, Göteborg University, Göteborg, Sweden

DANIEL S. LEHRMAN,* Institute of Animal Behavior, Newark, New Jersey

JEROME LETTVIN, Massachusetts Institute of Technology, Cambridge, Massachusetts

LIST OF CONFERENCE PARTICIPANTS   xiii

RITA LEVI-MONTALCINI, Washington University, St. Louis, Missouri

LEWIS P. LIPSITT, Brown University, Providence, Rhode Island

THOMAS E. MCGILL, Williams College, Williamstown, Massachusetts

MARGARET MEAD,* The American Museum of Natural History, New York, New York

GILBERT W. MEIER, George Peabody College, Nashville, Tennessee

DAVID R. METCALF, University of Colorado Medical School, Denver, Colorado

S. MILKOVIC, University of Zagreb, Zagreb, Yugoslavia

RONALD OPPENHEIM, Dorothea Dix Hospital, Raleigh, North Carolina

MICHAEL S. PLAUT, Galesburg State Research Hospital, Galesburg, Illinois

DOMINICK PURPURA, Albert Einstein College of Medicine, Bronx, New York

MARTIN RICHARDS, Unit for Research on Medical Applications of Psychology, Cambridge, England

WALTER H. RIEGE, University of California, Berkeley, California

J. S. ROSENBLATT,* Institute of Animal Behavior, Newark, New Jersey

MARK R. ROSENZWEIG,* University of California, Berkeley, California

GENE P. SACKETT, Macalester College, St. Paul, Minnesota

SHAWN SCHAPIRO,† Veterans Administration Hospital, San Fernando, California

J. SEDLECEK, Charles University, Prague, Czechoslovakia

EVELYN SHAW, The American Museum of Natural History, New York, New York

---

† Shawn Schapiro's untimely death as a result of an airplane accident on his way to another conference has deprived the scientific community of one of its most gifted investigators. Dr. Schapiro was an endocrinologist by training, but soon became interested in the development of endocrine systems and the relationship of such phenomena to behavior. He mastered several electroneurophysiological and biochemical techniques that permitted him and his colleagues to make many outstanding contributions to the study of behavioral development. We salute and honor him in this volume, and regret that we were forced to print only some of his contributions to the Conference because of space limitations.

B. F. SKINNER,* Harvard University, Cambridge, Massachusetts

MARVIN SNYDER, National Institute of Mental Health, Bethesda, Maryland

ROGER W. SPERRY,* California Institute of Technology, Pasadena, California

ETHEL TOBACH, The American Museum of Natural History, New York, New York

ARLENE TUCKER, New York Medical College, New York, New York

H. URSIN, Fysiologisch Institutt, Bergen, Norway

ELLIOT S. VALENSTEIN, Fels Research Institute, Yellow Springs, Ohio

MARGARET A. VINCE, University of Cambridge, Cambridge, England

C. H. WADDINGTON,* Institute of Animal Genetics, Edinburgh, Scotland

W. F. WINDLE,* New York University, New York, New York

PETER H. WOLFF, Harvard University Medical School, Boston, Massachusetts

ROCHELLE P. WORTIS, St. Mary's Hospital Medical School, London, England

INTRODUCTION*

An understanding of the historic causes for the recent acceleration in the study of development, and of behavioral development in particular, requires the perspective of time, as analyses of the trends in scientific pursuits are influenced by current theoretical controversy. The remarks that follow are limited largely by that consideration.

In the Department of Animal Behavior at The American Museum of Natural History, the impetus to study the development of behavior came from the writings and work of T. C. Schneirla. In the early stages of his scientific career, Schneirla became concerned about nonobjective theories of behavior that were based implicitly or explicitly on the assumption that much of behavior can be "explained" by "instincts." He criticized these on several grounds and in the classic book on comparative psychology written by him and N. R. F. Maier, alternative approaches to the study of the evolution of many different behavior patterns were offered systematically. In an article written for the volume honoring the renowned psychologist, Heinz Werner, in which Schneirla is ". . . skeptical of the instinct dogma . . . ," he proposed that the significant question about "instinctive behavior" is ". . . a set of problems concerning the evolutionary and ontogenetic origins of species-typical behavior." In the same paper, he later stated that "The fact cannot be emphasized too often that the central problem of instinctive behavior is one of development (Maier and Schneirla, 1935, Chapters VI and XI), working comparatively not just with higher mammals and a few other convenient types, but through the widest possible range." Implicit in this paper, and explicit in his other papers on development and on biphasic processes underlying approach and withdrawal, is the realization that development has to be studied on many different phyletic levels and on all intraorganismic levels as well. In his theoretical approach the role of biochemical processes, beginning with their expression in the "genome" and continuing through their contribution on the level

---

* The Conference was supported by a grant from the National Institute of Child Health and Human Development and funds from the Centennial Fund of The American Museum of Natural History. Preparation of this introduction by E. Tobach was supported by NIMH K3-MH-21867.

of physiological function (as in the endocrine system), was considered to continually integrate and fuse with effective internal and external stimulation, broadly defined on the molecular and molar level as "experience."

When called upon to appropriately celebrate the centennial of The American Museum of Natural History, it was natural that Dr. Schneirla and the organizers of this Conference, the proceedings of which comprise this book, immediately supported Lester Aronson's proposal that the study of the development of behavior was the most significant area in contemporary behavioral research and that a conference on the subject would be timely and appropriate. It is inevitable, therefore, that the planning of the Conference reflects the scientific concepts basic to the thinking and experimentation of Dr. Schneirla and the organizers. This, of course, in no way implies that a participant of the Conference necessarily agrees either with the principles underlying the Conference organization, or with the theoretical tenets of the organizers, as is very clear in several papers.

The participants who were asked to prepare papers for the Conference were by their work and interests representative of investigators at different levels of organization either within an organism, or at different phyletic levels. Behavioral development was considered from the molecular level (genetic processes), the systems level (endocrine and neural), and on the level of individual and social behavior. Time and other restrictions forced certain omissions—work with invertebrates and lower vertebrates was represented to a lesser extent than we hoped for. Similarly, an effort was made to deal with behavioral ontogeny at every major developmental stage but, again, logistics necessitated omitting papers on the process of aging. Although the Conference emphasized fundamental problems in development that are applicable to a greater or lesser extent to all animal life, the implications for human behavioral development were frequently raised in discussion and were considered systematically in the last two sessions.

In a way, the Conference was an experiment. Schneirla had proposed the "developmental" approach as an alternative to the pseudo-dichotomous conceptualization of "nature and nurture." Also, he had applied the concept of levels of organization to different behavioral patterns, such as social organization, to elucidate the relationships among the behavioral and physiological processes involved. With this in mind, we had suggested that the participants consider the usefulness of the concept of levels of integration for applying the knowledge of their disciplines to the fundamental questions of the development of behavior. Would it be possible by urging consideration of the relationships among different levels of organismic and phyletic organization to stimulate the participants to deal with the substance of the problems of the "evolution" and "ontogeny" of behavior—including species-typical behavior—without becoming embroiled in the kinds of debate that had marked the annals of behavioral science since its inception? As the reader can see from the papers, conference planners propose, but conference participants dispose. In the papers of Eisenberg, Birch, and Harris, the reader will find clues to the contemporary controversies that may have been responsible for the unplanned-for emphasis on the "heredity–environment" problem at the Conference. It should be noted, however, that several speakers and discussants called loudly and clearly for an end to the "fundamental-causes" aspect of the discussion, urging instead that developmental research be formulated so as to produce the greatest insight into the evolution and ontogeny of behavioral patterns.

Several other issues in experimental formulations were also given serious attention. The concept of the "critical period" is sharply different as discussed by Caspari, Křeček, and Rosenblatt. The relative merits of cross-sectional and longitudinal studies and the possible relationships between the two were heatedly debated at the Conference, and are treated in the papers by Birch, Harris, and Gottlieb. The fact that the different systems of any organism develop at different rates leads to many difficulties (Rosenzweig; Himwich): How is maturity defined (Himwich)? How can one make appropriate species comparisons and how do these comparisons affect the analysis of development on different levels of organization (Hinde)? Several participants emphasized the fact that information about behavioral development was frequently interpreted in the light of only partial information about other levels of organization—rarely do we have relevant information on the neurophysiological, anatomic, and molar behavioral levels for the *same* behavioral patterns. When such information is available, it is important, however, not to assume that any one level is sufficient in and of itself to explain behavioral development (Beach; Gottlieb). How can changes on the biochemical, anatomic, and behavioral levels be integrated to yield valid interpretations? How does one develop categories of behavioral analyses that can take into account these problems in developmental study (Hinde)?

Several speakers (e.g., Gottlieb, Himwich, Beer, Hinde, and Beach) pointed out that although all were concerned with responsivity to environmental stimulation, particularly within the theoretical framework of "instinctive behavior," there was still a great need for analyses of the physical characteristics of the sensory stimuli operative in species-typical developmental environments. Not only do the stimuli need to be physically analyzed, but as Beach pointed out, the changes in their meanings which take place as the state of the organism changes, and as development takes place, need to be studied (cf. Schneirla's papers on development).

Another important aspect of the Conference were the contributions made by some participants, particularly by Gottlieb, on the relation between ontogeny and phylogeny. A number of unanswered questions were posed in such a way as to lend themselves readily to experimental investigations that will yield important answers. Indeed, the Conference more than achieved one of its stated goals—the production of suggestions for future research by an historical, theoretical analysis of the discipline of behavioral development—as is evident in almost every paper.

In the course of the sessions, T. C. Schneirla's concept of a biphasic process underlying approach-withdrawal (A/W) as useful in behavioral analysis was challenged, and defended (Eisenberg; Rosenblatt and Aronson). Although this topic was considered only briefly during the formal session, it was discussed at some length during informal get-togethers. A survey of these discussions reveals potent arguments *pro* and *con*, as well as important misunderstandings as to the nature and potential value of the concept. It seems clear that some future conference on behavioral development could profit by a session devoted exclusively to Schneirla's formulation of the biphasic processes underlying A/W and their implications for development.

Other issues that aroused significant exchanges among the participants were the use of terms from one level of organization by investigators on another level; the use, misuse, and abuse of analogies from different levels of organization; the definition of "environment" at all stages of development; the problem of interspecies comparison of developmental patterns, e.g., should comparisons be based on the functional development of structural, motor, sensory, hormonal, or behavioral systems, or some integration of these? The most important of these arguments can be gleaned from the published proceedings herein, but one must bear in mind that this represents only a very small fraction of the extensive and lively discussions that took place throughout the Conference.

One should not overlook the effect of the setting of the Conference at the Museum and that T. C. Schneirla played an important role in the early stages of planning the Conference. His unfortunate death a year before the Conference took place deprived us of the contribution he had been planning to write with one of the Conference organizers (E.T.); the tentative title that he had in mind was "The Meaning of Cryptohomunculus."

The organizers of the Conference can only hope that at least one other of the original aims of the Conference has indeed been achieved: that the participants, auditors, and students at the Conference as well as the readers of this book will find much useful material and stimulating ideas in the papers and discussions reported herein.

ETHEL TOBACH
LESTER R. ARONSON

I. GENETIC PROCESSES AND BEHAVIORAL DEVELOPMENT

DIFFERENTIATION AND PATTERN FORMATION IN THE DEVELOPMENT OF BEHAVIOR

ERNEST CASPARI

In a discussion of the biopsychology of development it may be appropriate to review briefly the present state of the analysis of development and to speculate as to how it may apply to the development of behavioral characters. Our thinking about the problems of development has undergone some changes in the last decade, in part under the impact of the progress in molecular biology. It appears, however, that these changes are less profound than is frequently assumed and constitute rather an emphasis on different problems which are regarded as important and amenable to attack than a change in the fundamental nature of the analysis.

One aspect of development consists in the fact that an originally homogeneous population of cells becomes changed in such a way that different types of cells are being formed. This process is generally designated as differentiation. Differentiated cells differ from each other in their morphological appearance, their biochemical constitution, their physiological processes, and, particularly, their functions. The problem arises from the fact that differentiated cells do not differ in their genetic constitutions. It has been conclusively shown that differentiated plant cells can give rise to a complete new plant (Steward *et al.*, 1964) and that cell nuclei from the larval intestine of the frog *Xenopus* can sustain development into normal larvae if injected into enucleated eggs (Gurdon, 1966). These data show conclusively that differentiation does not necessarily imply loss of genetic information (even though loss of genetic information as one possible mechanism of differentiation is not excluded). The problem can therefore be stated in the form: how do cells which contain the same genetic information assume a number of different biochemical and morphological states?

In the process of differentiation certain types of proteins characteristic of the differentiated cell are formed. These proteins may be essential for the specific function of the cell, as, for example, hemoglobin in red blood cells, myosin in muscle cells, and lens protein in the lens of the eye. The same proteins are not formed by other types of cells at all, or only in minute quantities. The structure of proteins is dependent on information contained in the genes, and for some of the cell-specific proteins, particularly hemoglobin, these genes are known and have in part been localized. It must therefore be concluded that these genes, in cells in which their proteins are not formed, are inactive, insofar as production of the specific protein is concerned. The problem of regulation of genic activity emerges, therefore as a fundamental problem in differentiation.

Regulation of genic activity has been studied thoroughly in microorganisms, particularly in the β-galactosidase system in *E. coli*, and Jacob and Monod (1963) who investigated this regulatory system, have proposed to use it as a paradigm for gene regulation occurring in development. The system in *E. coli* consists of three components: (1) structural genes, which contain the information for the amino acid sequence of the proteins; (2) an operator gene, which is closely linked to the structural gene and has the ability to "turn it on," i.e., induce it to form its messenger RNA, which is then used in the synthesis of the protein; (3) a regulator gene, which is not linked to the operator but produces a protein which can combine with the operator and thus block it so that the structural gene remains "turned off." The regulator protein, in addition to combining with operator, can also combine with small molecules, among which is lactose, the normal substrate attacked by the enzyme produced by the structural gene. The regulatory protein is thus a bifunctional protein which has groups binding to the operator and to the inducer. In combination with the inducer the regulatory protein undergoes a change in conformation in such a way that it cannot combine with the operator; the structural gene is therefore turned on. Bifunctional proteins of this type have been called "allosteric proteins" by Jacob and Monod (1961), and biochemical evidence for the occurrence of such allosteric proteins is accumulating (Gerhard and Pardee, 1962; Koshland *et al.*, 1966). From our point of view it is important that proteins of this type can give rise to systems of negative feedback which can adapt a cell to its environment.

In the transfer of this concept of gene regulation to developmental processes, Jacob and Monod (1963) postulate interaction between two operator-controlled genes whose products may affect, according to some rule, the operator of the other gene. In this way, systems of positive and negative feedback can be constructed which may result in coordinate or alternative activation of the two genes involved, or in an oscillatory cycle of activity. These models are very attractive insofar as they can account for a number of processes actually occurring in differentiation. The search for developmental genetic systems which could bear on this hypothesis has, however, not been very successful. Since the operator initiates transcription in the attached structural gene, it must be expected, as expressly stated by Jacob and Monod (1961), that an operator mutation will affect a gene physically linked to it but not its homolog in the other chromosome. Cases of such "cis-trans" effects are very rare in higher organisms. The relation of the thalassemia gene to the structural gene for β-hemoglobin in man is the only case known to me (Motulsky, 1962).

The Jacob–Monod model assumes that regulation occurs at the level of transcription, i.e., the production of messenger RNA by the DNA of the structural gene. This is, however, not the only level at which regulation of genic activity is possible. The information transfer from messenger RNA to the polypeptide chain (protein), the so-called translation, is a complex process involving, in microorganisms, the activity of a small RNA which combines with amino acids (transfer RNA) and ribosomes, particles consisting of a third type of RNA and protein. Regulation of protein synthesis at the level of translation has been demonstrated to occur in bacteria (Hartman, 1965).

In higher organisms, additional levels of control seem to be possible. In recent years, considerable work has been done on problems of RNA and protein synthesis in developing cells of higher organisms. The intention of these studies is to describe developmental processes in terms familiar to us from molecular biology. While these investigations are still too much in a state of flux to be reviewed here, it is safe to state that information transfer in differentiating cells of higher organism [e.g., duck erythroblasts (Scherrer and Marcaud, 1968)] is a more complex process than it is in microorganisms, involving additional species of RNA. One of the main differences seems to be that the messenger RNA transcribed from the DNA does not immediately combine with ribosomes to be used in translation; there appears, in addition, a high molecular RNA in the nuclei which has a base composition similar to DNA and differs in this way from ribosomal RNA. Most of this "polydisperse" RNA has a short lifetime and is apparently soon destroyed. Only part of it combines with ribosomes and is used in the synthesis of proteins.

We obtain thus a hierarchical system of control of gene action in developing cells, at the level of transcription, insofar as only part of the DNA is transcribed, and at the level of polydisperse RNA, where only part of the transcribed RNA is used for the synthesis of proteins. Control at additional levels, biochemical as well as chromosomal, is possible, and evidence exists for its occurrence. But the relationship between the different control mechanisms known to exist is by no means clear.

Puffing observed in the salivary glands of *Diptera* is taken as evidence for the activity of individual genes, and one case is known where a particular puff has been identified with a particular gene controlling an intracellular secretion (Beermann, 1961). Basic proteins found in the chromosomes of higher organisms, the histones, are able to block the activity of genes and groups of genes (Bonner, 1965; Allfrey *et al.*, 1964). Heterochromatic regions of chromosomes are regarded as genetically inactive, and while certain chromosome regions are continually heterochromatic, other regions become permanently (or sometimes only temporarily) heterochromatized in the course of development, such as one X chromosome in female mammals (Lyon, 1961) and the paternal chromosome set in coccid males (Nur, 1966). Furthermore, controlling elements have been demonstrated in the chromosomes of corn (McClintock, 1967) and recently of *Drosophila* (Green, 1969); these control the activity of structural genes. Finally, in vertebrates as well as in insects, hormones are known to control protein and enzyme synthesis, and thus, presumably, gene action.

There is thus a wealth of regulatory mechanisms for gene action known at both the biochemical and the chromosomal level. Their relation to each other, their interaction at a particular step in differentiation, is at present completely unknown. But it appears that in higher organisms differentiation may be controlled by a variety of mechanisms, and it has been suggested that they are brought into play in sequence, and possibly in a hierarchical order. In this connection it should be recalled that differentiation does not involve a single switch from one steady state to another, as the induction of β-galactosidase in *E. coli* studied by Jacob and Monod, but rather a progressive series of changes, following each other in an orderly, progressive fashion over a considerable period of time and leading finally to the functional differentiated cell.

The process of differentiation has received much attention because it is relatively easy to fit into the conceptual framework of molecular biology. It deals with the developmental changes occurring in individual cells, and can therefore be compared to processes occurring in microbial cells. It is for this reason that developmental biologists frequently regarded differentiation as a secondary problem compared to morphogenesis. Morphogenesis has to account for the fact that the different events of differentiation occur in an orderly way, in specific places and at specific times, related to the organism as a whole. Goldschmidt (1927) first called attention to the fact that the problems subsumed under the term morphogenesis involve the formation of patterns, insofar as a uniform population of cells is divided into different groups of cells in an orderly spatial arrangement to each other which will undergo different paths of differentiation. I would like, therefore, to choose the term "pattern formation" for the fundamental developmental processes which lead to an orderly arrangement of differentiated cells in the organism.

As is true for many categorizing statements in biology, pattern formation cannot always be clearly distinguished from differentiation. It involves the "becoming different" of previously homogeneous cells and may therefore itself be regarded as a first step in differentiation. But, it is useful, conceptually, to distinguish it from the term differentiation as it is generally used because pattern formation involves the behavior of aggregates of cells rather than individual cells.

At the present state of biology, it is much harder to describe the behavior of cell aggregates than that of individual cells. Neither the concepts of molecular biology and cell physiology which draw on physical and chemical concepts nor the mathematical concepts of population biology are completely adequate, and therefore a specific set of concepts is being used in the description of pattern formation and morphogenesis. An example is the concept of the "embryonic field." This concept refers to the properties of aggregates of developing cells—or even individual cells of complex morphology—and to their organization not only in space but also with respect to time and to chemical and physical interactions and differentiations (Waddington, 1966). The characteristic property of an embryonic field is its ability to "regulate" (in the developmental, as opposed to the genetic-molecular, sense), i.e., to compensate for disturbances such as losses or gains of cellular material in such a way that an organized entity is formed in the course of its development. The properties of embryonic fields have been extensively studied experimentally, and attempts at a mathematical formulation of the properties of embryonic fields have been made. At the present time, however, the concept of the embryonic field, as well as other developmental concepts, appear more complex than those used at higher and lower levels of biological organization.

With respect to the mechanism of pattern formation Kühn (1965) distinguishes three fundamental mechanisms: unequal cell division, interaction between cells and cell groups and environmental stimuli. In his book, Kühn first discussed these mechanisms in lower organisms, algae and slime molds, but in later chapters, Kühn shows that these are the mechanisms by which organization is produced in the development of higher animals and plants.

In unequal cell division, the two nuclei arising from mitotic cell division come to lie in different cytoplasms which induce different types of differentiations. The mosaic development found in the cleavage divisions of many invertebrate phyla constitutes such an example. In later development, usually small organs consisting of a few cells are organized by unequal cell division, such as the scale apparatus of the Lepidoptera (Stossberg, 1938) and the stomatal apparatus of plants (Stebbins, 1967).

Interaction between different cells and cell groups of the same organism is the main mechanism of pattern formation in higher organisms. Most of the literature in experimental embryology deals with this specific aspect of development. I shall not deal with it further at this point, but some remarks should be made concerning induction by environmental conditions. As mentioned earlier, categorization of biological phenomena is not always clear-cut, and the category of environmental stimuli cannot always be sharply distinguished from interactions with other cells and cell complexes. These latter certainly involve stimuli external to the reacting cells such as hormones and other products of cellular activity. But it seems convenient to distinguish these stimuli from those originating outside the developing organism such as light and temperature. Kühn's own example for this mechanism is a colonial flagellate, *Celloniella palensis,* whose colonies assume different shapes depending on whether they grow in streaming water or under the ledges of rocks. Other examples would include the induction of polarity in the *Fucus* egg by light and the induction of flowering in higher plants by a variety of conditions. It should be noted that this mode of initiation of developmental processes is found, as far as I know, in plants only. It appears important to deal with this type of pattern formation here, because the question of environmental versus endogenous causation has been widely discussed for the origin of behavioral patterns. An example for induction of developmental patterns by environmental stimuli will therefore be briefly discussed.

In many flowering plants, a meristem may give rise either to a purely vegetative shoot or to a shoot carrying flowers. In some species flowering is induced by the relative duration of night and day, while in other species (biennials) exposure of the plant to low temperature is a prerequisite for flower formation. In both cases, the meristem carries, as a result of its genotype, its developmental history and its position on the plant, the potency to perform two different types of morphogenetic activities. It can become a vegetative or a flowering shoot. Which one of these is chosen depends on an environmental stimulus. This is in principle quite similar to the reaction of embryonic tissues on inductive stimuli derived from other cells in animal development. Here, again, a limited number of morphogenetic potentialities is present in the reacting tissue, determined by the genotype, the developmental history, and the position of the cells relative to other parts of the embryo. The inductive stimulus triggers one out of this limited number of potentialities. The specificity of the reaction is in both cases inherent in the reacting cells. The similarity between the two types of mechanisms becomes even more pronounced if it is considered that in the plant examples just given the environmental stimuli primarily induce the formation of hormone-like substances in the leaves which induce the meristems to produce flowers. There is thus no difference in principle between these two mechanisms of induction of morphogenetic processes. It is, however, worthwhile to point to this relationship because of its analogy to the heredity–environment problem.

One additional property of developmental systems should be mentioned: the existence of critical or sensitive periods. Many embryonic processes can be influenced before a particular developmental time, but will proceed uninterrupted, once this time has passed (Caspari, 1964). As an example we may mention the effect of the drug 5-fluorouracil (FU) on the development of the moth *Ephestia*. FU is an analog of the pyrimidine base uracil, and may be incorporated into RNA but not into DNA. It will therefore interfere with the function of newly synthesized RNA. Injection of FU into pupae of the moth *Ephestia* does not kill the animals, but stops development. More specifically, depending on the time of injection, a specific developmental process may either proceed to completion, or not proceed at all. For instance, the pigmentation of the accessory pigment cells does not take place at all if FU is injected on the third pupal day, while after injection of the drug at the fourth pupal day it starts at the normal time (seventh pupal day) and proceeds with normal strength and in the normal time (Muth, 1965). The differentiation process of pigment formation can therefore proceed in the presence of FU, and it must be concluded that the drug interferes with a process occurring previous to the onset of visible differentiation, in the critical period. The investigation of critical periods is a very sensitive means of distinguishing developmental processes, and Imberski (1967) has been able to demonstrate, in the development of the eye of *Ephestia,* 16 different processes, both differentiation and pattern formation, each characterized by a different sensitive period to FU. In addition, we have lately studied the appearance and disappearance of individual proteins in the pupal development of *Ephestia,* and we have found that the appearance, as well as the disappearance, of each protein has its own characteristic sensitive period.

If the general properties of developmental systems are applied to the development of behavioral characters, it does not appear as if any additional principles have to be invoked. Behavior is a functional concept, and it is therefore studied with different methods than those which are usually applied in developmental studies, in which the result of pattern formation or differentiation is usually observed by means of morphological or biochemical criteria. But we assume that behavior has a morphological and biochemical basis, the cells of the central nervous system and of the endocrine glands, and that the morphological and functional development of these cells is reflected in nervous and behavioral functioning.

Several of the papers in this conference are devoted to problems of differentiation of the nerve cells, the functional and biochemical maturation of the nerve cells. A greater number are concerned with problems of the origin of the functional pattern of the nervous system, particularly the interconnections of neurons with each other, and with sensory and effector structures. In these cases, pattern formation will involve interaction between cells and cell groups, as is usual in the processes of pattern formation in higher organisms. It is the nature of these interactions which is of particular interest.

One of the main problems which has concerned workers in the field of the development of behavior is the relation of functional activity of the interacting cells to the developing pattern, and to its function in the final differentiated organism. In this respect it is of importance to realize that in many developing organs complete organization and differentiation may proceed before any functional activity can be assumed. The lungs and the eyes of the mammalian embryo may be mentioned; at birth they are completely ready to function even though they have never been exposed to air or light, respectively. This does not, of course, exclude the possibility that functioning of cells may play a role in some cases of pattern formation, but in analogy to other developmental processes it is not necessary that any information in addition to that contained in the genes be supplied.

This principle can best be exemplified in the complex behavior patterns of insects, which are subject to relatively little modification as a result of environmental stimuli and previous behavioral activities. An example, involving social behavior, is the division of labor in the beehive. Individual bees go through all activities needed in the hive in series so that every bee performs all functions at some time in its life. The series is pretty well fixed, even though some variation in duration of the different periods of activity is possible, depending on the needs of the hive (Rösch, 1930). This series of behavioral activities is thus reminiscent of developmental process in which different periods follow each other in regular progression, the series of events being determined by the genotype.

The genetic basis is known, in the case of one behavior pattern, the so-called hygienic behavior of the honeybee (Rothenbuhler, 1964). Some strains of bees are resistant to the bacterial disease foulbrood, because the workers have the ability to open the cells in which dead larvae are present, remove them from the cells, and take them out of the hive. It has turned out that this behavior depends on the presence, in the worker bees, of two genes. One gene enables them to open up the cells containing dead larvae. The stimulus is presumably the absence of movement in the closed cells, the reaction, the opening of the cell. The second gene controls the removal of larvae from opened cells. The functional connection between these two activities is established by the fact that the result of the first activity is the stimulus initiating the second activity. There is thus no problem remaining in this system, except for the neuronal basis of the two activities and its establishment by the genes. In other words, the remaining problem is the problem of genetic control on pattern formation in space and time, the fundamental problem of gene action in development.

Rothenbuhler's work is a good example of the power of the method of genetic analysis of complex processes by resolving them into individual components controlled by single-gene loci. It may be suggested that this method can be widely applied to the study of behavior. Recent work on the chemotactic behavior of bacteria has shown that a limited number (at least five) of specific chemoreceptors is involved. In addition, mutants have been found which do not affect the chemoreceptors or the motility of the cells and are presumably involved in the control of information transfer from the receptor to the effector. These mutants map at three locations in the chromosome, suggesting that few genes are involved, and that the process is probably relatively simple (Adler, 1969; Armstrong and Adler, 1969). It is, of course, impossible to generalize from the behavior of a single-celled organism to that of a mammalian brain containing 10^{10} neurons. However, it is usually justified to assume that general principles can be more easily established in a smaller and simpler system than in large and complex ones. This consideration has led Benzer (1967) to start on a genetic analysis of the phototactic behavior of *Drosophila*, an animal containing about 10^5 neurons in its central nervous system.

One additional problem with which students of behavior have been particularly concerned is the modifiability of behavior, which is most strongly developed in mammals. Many behavior patterns can be modified by environmental stimuli, and by previous activities of the organism, and some behavior patterns found in higher vertebrates are dependent in their origin on learning. In other words, the development of a particular behavior pattern may be dependent on stimuli external to the organism. Such a situation is unusual in the development of other organ systems in animals, but, as stated earlier, has close analogies in plants. It has been pointed out on that occasion that such a process of determination is not in principle different from development controlled by stimuli originating from other cells. It should be stated explicitly that learning may be regarded as a developmental process which occurs at a later state of development.

The problem can therefore be stated in developmental terminology by asking whether learning involves differentiation processes or pattern formation, or both. This same question is usually asked using a different set of terms. Learning involves the storage of information, and the question has been raised whether the information is stored in the form of changes in the functional connection between neurons (facilitation or inhibition) or in the form of informational macromolecules. The former process would involve a change in the patterned relations of the cells to each other, while the latter hypothesis would imply a further differentiation, i.e., a specific intracellular change at the nucleic acid and protein level. The two models are of course not mutually exclusive; both types of processes might go on in the same system, as is the case for most developmental processes.

Neurons are actively metabolizing cells, and their activity is connected with protein synthesis which in turn depends on RNA synthesis. It is therefore not astonishing that drugs interfering with protein or nucleic acid synthesis affect neuronal functioning and, specifically, learning processes. More refined methods have been used which show that in a learning experiment specific cells in the central nervous system produce RNA. As examples, the experiments of Hydén and collaborators and of Glassman and collaborators may be mentioned. In the experiment by Hydén and Lange (1965), rats were trained to change their hand preference, and individual nerve cells and cell nuclei from the motor area of the cortex were tested for their content of RNA and the base ratio of this RNA. It turned out that in the early stages of training an increase in the production of nuclear RNA was observed, and this RNA had a base composition similar to that of DNA. It is therefore suggestive of the high molecular RNA which has been found to be produced in differentiating cells; if this suggestion is borne out, Hydén's findings would constitute the first demonstration of this type of RNA. In further progress of the learning process, an increase in the synthesis of ribosomal RNA is observed. Glassman and collaborators (Zemp *et al.,*

1966, 1967) subjected mice to avoidance conditioning and measured the uptake of labeled uridine in brain tissue. They found that conditioning results in increased RNA synthesis, that both nuclear and ribosomal RNA are involved, and that the increased RNA synthesis is restricted to a specific portion of the brain, the diencephalon.

All experiments agree that learning and conditioning proceeds under an increase in synthesis of several types of RNA, and that this increased synthesis is restricted to certain groups of nerve cells. There is no evidence for the existence of specific macromolecules which are involved in specific learning tasks, as might be expected in analogy to the formation of specific antibodies. For the time being, there thus appears no evidence for the involvement of informational macromolecules in learning, but the evidence suggests that in particular learning tasks particular neurons show activity, and that this activity involves RNA and presumably protein synthesis. Development of behavior by learning depends, therefore, on the preestablished pattern of the nervous system which has developed, at least in its early stages, without the influence of environmental stimuli.

It appears, therefore, that the problems of the development of behavior are in principle not different from those of other functions and organ systems. They proceed under the control of the genotype of the organism with respect to differentiation and pattern formation. In pattern formation interaction between cells of the nervous system, as well as with other organ systems, plays a determining role. The importance of environmental factors is probably different in different organisms and for different behavioral characters in the same organism. The main advantage of the behavioral system as compared to other developmental systems consists in the fact that it can be studied earlier and better at the functional level, because more sensitive methods for the study of neural function are available than for any other cell activity.

REFERENCES

Adler, J. (1969). Chemoreceptors in bacteria. *Science* Vol. 166, 1588–1597.
Allfrey, V. G., Faulkner, R., and Mirsky, A. E. (1964). Acetylation and methylation of histones and their possible role in the regulation of RNA synthesis. *Proc. Nat. Acad. Sci. U. S.* Vol. 51, 786–794.
Armstrong, J. B., and Adler, J. (1969). Complementation of nonchemotactic mutants of *Escherichia coli*. *Genetics* Vol. 61, 61–66.
Beermann, W. (1961). Ein Balbiani-Ring als Locus einer Speicheldrüsenmutation. *Chromosoma* Vol. 12, 1–25.
Benzer, S. (1967). Behavioral mutants of Drosophila isolated by countercurrent distribution. *Proc. Nat. Acad. Sci. U. S.* Vol. 58, 1112–1119.

Bonner, J. F. (1965). "The Molecular Biology of Development." Oxford Univ. Press, London and New York.
Caspari, E. (1964). The problem of development. *Brookhaven Lect. Ser.* No. 35.
Gerhard, J. C., and Pardee, A. B. (1962). The enzymology of control by feedback inhibition. *J. Biol. Chem.* Vol. 237, 891–896.
Goldschmidt, R. (1927). "Physiologische Theorie der Vererbung." Springer, Berlin.
Green, M. M. (1969). Mapping a *Drosophila melanogaster* "controlling element" by interallelic crossing over. *Genetics* Vol. 61, 423–428.
Gurdon, J. B. (1966). The control of gene activity during cell differentiation in higher organisms. *In* "Heritage from Mendel" (R. A. Brink, ed.), pp. 203–241. Univ. of Wisconsin Press, Madison, Wisconsin.
Hartman, P. E. (1965). Genetic control of enzyme production in bacteria. *Genet. Today, Proc. 11th Int. Congr., 1963* Vol. 2, pp. 123–128.
Hydén, H., and Lange, P. W. (1965). A differentiation in RNA response in neurons early and late during learning. *Proc. Nat. Acad. Sci. U. S.* Vol. 53, 946–952.
Imberski, R. B. (1967). The effect of 5-fluorouracil on the development of the adult eye in *Ephestia kühniella*. *J. Exp. Zool.* Vol. 166, 151–162.
Jacob, F., and Monod, J. (1961). On the regulation of gene activity. *Cold Spring Harbor Symp. Quant. Biol.* Vol. 26, 193–209.
Jacob, F., and Monod, J. (1963). Genetic repression, allosteric inhibition and cellular differentiation. *In* "Cytodifferentiation and Macromolecular Synthesis" (M. Locke, ed.), pp. 30–64. Academic Press, New York.
Koshland, D. E., Nemethy, G., and Filmer, D. (1966). Comparison of experimental binding data and theoretical models in proteins containing subunits. *Biochemistry* Vol. 5, 365–385.
Kühn, A. (1965). "Vorlesungen über Entwicklungsphysiologie," 2nd ed. Springer, Berlin.
Lyon, M. F. (1961). Gene action in the X-chromosome of the mouse, *Mus musculus* L. *Nature (London)* Vol. 190, 372–373.
McClintock, B. (1967). Genetic systems regulating gene expression during development. *In* "Control Mechanisms in Developmental Processes" (M. Locke, ed.), pp. 84–112. Academic Press, New York.
Monod, J., Wyman, J., and Changeux, J. P. (1965). On the nature of allosteric transitions: A plausible model. *J. Mol. Biol.* Vol. 12, 88–118.
Motulsky, A. G. (1962). Controller genes in synthesis of human hemoglobin. *Nature (London)* Vol. 194, 607–609.
Muth, W. (1965). The effect of 5-fluorouracil on the eye pigmentary system in *Ephestia kühniella*. *Exp. Cell Res.* Vol. 37, 54–64.
Nur, U. (1966). Nonreplication of heterochromatic chromosomes in a mealy bug *Planococcus citri* (Coccoidea: Homoptera). *Chromosoma* Vol. 19, 439–448.
Rösch, G. A. (1930). Untersuchungen über die Arbeitsteilung im Bienenstaat. 2. Die Tätigkeiten der Arbeitsbienen unter experimentell veränderten Bedingungen. *Z. Vergleich. Physiol.* Vol. 12, 1–71.
Rothenbuhler, W. (1964). Behavior genetics of nest cleaning in honey bees. IV. Response of F_1 and backcross generations to disease-killed brood. *Amer. Zool.* Vol. 4, 111–123.
Scherrer, K., and Marcaud, L. (1968). Messenger RNA in avian erythroblasts at the transcriptional and translational levels and the problem of regulation in animal cells. *J. Cell. Physiol.* Vol. 72, Suppl. 1, 181–212.
Stebbins, G. L. (1967). Gene action, mitotic frequency, and morphogenesis in higher

plants. *In* "Control Mechanisms in Developmental Processes" (M. Locke, ed.), pp. 113–135. Academic Press, New York.

Steward, F. C., Maper, M. O., Kent, A. E., and Holsten, R. D. (1964). Growth and development of cultured plant cells. *Science* Vol. 143, 20–27.

Stossberg, M. (1938). Die Zellvorgänge bei der Entwicklung der Flügelschuppen von *Ephestia kühniella. Z. Morphol. Oekol. Tiere* Vol. 34, 173–206.

Waddington, C. H. (1966). Fields and gradients. *In* "Major Problems in Developmental Biology" (M. Locke, ed.), pp. 105–124. Academic Press, New York.

Zemp, J. W., Wilson, J. E., Schlesinger, K., Boggan, W. O., and Glassman, E. (1966). Brain function and macromolecules. I. Incorporation of uridine into RNA of mouse brain during short-term training experience. *Proc. Nat. Acad. Sci. U. S.* Vol. 55, 1423–1431.

Zemp, J. W., Wilson, J. E., and Glassman, E. (1967). Brain function and macromolecules. II. Site of increased labeling of RNA in brains of mice during a short-term training experience. *Proc. Nat. Acad. Sci. U. S.* Vol. 58, 1120–1125.

CONCEPTS OF DEVELOPMENT

C. H. WADDINGTON

The greater part of biopsychological development takes place during periods of the life history much later than the embryonic. The concepts and theoretical approaches which have been worked out by students of early embyronic development are, therefore, useful to developmental psychologists mainly as analogies, which may offer them useful hints on their own model-building, rather than as an account of basic facts which bear directly on their interests. The group of embryological ideas which seem likely to be most suggestive in relation to later biopsychological development are those connected with the phenomena of embryonic regulation, which are so prominent in all the processes by which the fertilized zygote, whose dominating components are a collection of separable and discrete genes, develops into a mutually cooperating system of subunits which is so strongly characterized by *organization* that we commonly refer to the subunits as *organs* and the total entity as an *organism*.

Regulatory processes occur in very many different contexts during embryonic development, and some framework of classification, even a somewhat arbitrary one, must be used to arrange the material. One possible framework begins by dividing the subject matter into (i) changes in the (chemical) nature of the materials composing the developing system and (ii) changes in the spatial arrangement of these materials into ordered structures. Under each of these headings there is then a subdivision into (a) processes involving the elementary units and (b) processes affecting combinations of the units. It is, of course, clear that there are no really sharp boundaries between these categories, but typical examples of each class might be:

Category 1

a. The elementary chemical process of development is the specification by a single genetic locus of the constitution of a protein. The crucial point is the high degree of specificity; the basis of the whole system is the existence of many *individually distinct* genes.

b. It is typical of the development of all biological systems, except the very simplest, that gene activities are organized into "groups" or "batteries." In an organism containing some 10^5 genes, the theoretically possible number of combinations would be enormous, even if each gene had only two possible states of activity. In practice, any such organism contains only a few hundred different types of cells. This implies that only certain *constellations* of gene activities can occur.

Category 2

a. The elementary process of spatial arrangement (at the biological rather than the purely chemical level) is the association of active macromolecules into systems (such as cellular organelles, e.g., mitochondria and chloroplasts) in which they in some way fit together.

b. At a more complex level, large groups of cells, which include, when they first arise, up to a few thousand cells, exhibit properties of unity and organization, often referred to by the ill-defined phrase "the morphogenetic field."

From each of these categories, certain theoretical concepts have been developed.

From category 1 (change in chemical composition), perhaps the most illuminating point could be put, crudely, by the aphorism: *specificity arises much more from within the system than it is imposed from outside.*

This point began to emerge first in the context of changes in the complex constitution of cells (1b), with the theory of the autogenous, but "masked," evocator within embryonic cells, advanced some 30 years ago. It has recently been developed in a much more definite and precise form in the conceptual system of "regulator genes producing regulator substances which act on operator-structural genes," proposed by Jacob and Monod from their studies on the induced activities of single genes (a 1a context).

From these 1a investigations several concepts of great potential generality have been developed.

(a) In order to control the activity of a very specific agent (e.g., a specific gene), some other specific agent has to manufacture a controlling element (e.g., a "regulating substance") which has two properties— (i) it must have specificity for the agent which is to be controlled, (ii) it must react with other external factors in ways which modify or even destroy this specificity. The "element" which exerts the actual control must therefore be "bipotential." There is an interesting contrast here between the ideas of a quarter of a century ago and those of today. In the 1930's, we conceived of the regulating element as a specific agent (an "evocator") which was usually combined with some inactivating complement, forming a compound which could react with relatively unspecific external agents so as to break down the complex and release the active evocator. In the more recent formulation the regulating substance is conceived of as a large molecule which has two reactive sites; one of these specifically reacts with the gene it controls, but the specific properties of this site are altered when external, relatively unspecific agents act on some other site in the regulating molecule. The earlier view conceives of a specifically reacting substance the specificity of which can be obliterated by a reversible combination with something else; the later view envisages a single substance the molecules of which are flexible and changeable. This is certainly a more stimulating notion. Such molecules are referred to as "allosteric." The concept of a "bireactive" controlling element, with one highly specific reaction-capacity whose effectiveness is altered when something occurs in connection with another less specific reaction-capacity of the same element, seems to have wide application in many different contexts.

(b) A special situation, and one of general application, is likely to arise when there are circular relations between regulating and effective factors—in the simplest case, when gene A makes a regulator substance, which controls gene B, which in turn makes a substance which controls gene A. This is a classic situation of negative feedback. Like all such systems, it will have a tendency—which can be restrained by suitable damping—to go into oscillation. The implications of the concept that "the elementary entities in a developing system are fundamentally oscillatory" are far-reaching and as yet very little explored.

From studies of 1b phenomena (complex systems of chemical constitution) another set of concepts emerges.

(a) The basic point is that gene activities not only occur in "batteries" which comprise only a few out of the almost infinite number of theoretically conceivable combinations, but *each of the actually realized batteries has a property of self-stabilization.* Note first that any concept applicable to development must be one which involves progressive change as time passes; thus we are thinking not of a constellation of processes which just persists but of a "pathway of development." The characteristic of the pathways of development which actually occur in natural embryos is that the course they pursue is resistant to modification. If we act on such a system in a way which might tend to divert it from its normal course, we will find that it tends, after the initial fluctuation, to get back to the trajectory along which it had begun to travel. It is extremely difficult, if possible at all, to persuade a myoblast to produce myosin without also producing actin and the set of (as yet uncharacterized) substances which determine the cellular adhesiveness between muscle cells and other types of cells. The complex system of developing cells, involving perhaps a few hundred genes at a time, follows "chreods"—built-in alternative potential pathways, into one or the other of which the cell will go, and out of which it is very difficult to push it. This fact is the most obtrusive phenomenon of development in multicellular organisms. One of the most challenging problems of developmental biology today is how to explain it.

(b) One field to which appeal can be made is that concerned with the kinetic organization of cellular metabolism. We have, for instance, such phenomena as "end-product inhibition," in which the final product of a chain of enzymes inhibits the activities of one of the earlier enzymes in the sequence. This enzyme can also be considered as an "allosteric" molecule, with two reactive sites, one effective in bringing about the enzyme-controlled reaction and another which reacts with the "end product" and in so reacting alters the properties of the first site. Again, we have the straightforward, but still almost unexplored, properties of networks of enzyme-controlled processes, which, even if they do not involve end-product inhibition, may generate "system-properties" which are by no means obvious at first sight.

(c) Again, there are a number of possibilities for organizing "chreods" in more crudely material ways, e.g., by having a regulator substance which acts, equally or differentially, on a number of different structural genes; or by linking gene-controlled activities together materially at some other level, for instance, by the nature of the nuclear envelope, or of the endoplasmic reticulum, or possibly by variants of the activating enzymes or transfer RNA's.

(d) Perhaps the main point that has emerged is this: it may perhaps be the case that the fact that there are alternative developmental pathways, rather than an infinite gamut of possibilities, is an inherent property of developing biological systems; but the degree to which each pathway is canalized or self-establishing is dependent on the particular alleles of the genes involved in it; and it can be altered by selection of a population either for alleles which fit better into the canalized system (and thus increase the organism's resistance to modification) or for alleles which do not integrate so well with the others (and thus tend to decrease resistance to external influences). We are dealing with a system property, like the worth of a hand of cards at bridge; but that worth is itself dependent on some complex function of the values of each individual card.

From category 2a (morphogenesis by association of elementary particles) the two concepts of broadest application are probably:

(a) The association of complexes of structural units (e.g., protein molecules) into larger ordered aggregates is probably often a result of the interactions between the individual properties of the units, in a way formally similar to the manner in which chemical atoms may come together to form certain particular types of molecules—although the binding forces involved in the two situations are rather different. The interesting question that arises is the relation between the stability of the resulting complex and its efficiency in carrying out some coordinated set of functions. For instance, in mitochondria a set of enzymes appear to be associated together into an orderly spatial structure which is such that the whole complex functions very effectively in facilitating a certain path of metabolic change. Is the efficiency of the complex a necessary part of the system of interactions which stabilizes it? Or is it only natural selection which has preserved and made frequent those particular complexes which happen to be efficient, while there might be a vastly greater number, equally stable, but so inefficient that they scarcely ever persist in living systems? We know of some orderly molecular complexes of this kind which are probably metabolically inert (i.e., quite inefficient) such as "brochosomes" in the excretory glands of insects, scales on the surfaces of microscopic algae, empty heads of bacteriophage particles, etc. These suggest that metabolic efficiency is not a necessary factor in producing stability. At the same time, the question is interesting to ask in relation to more complex instances of developmental regulation, for instance in connection with psychological systems.

(b) Once a complex of units has come together into a stable configuration, the existence of this may greatly facilitate the formation of new similar structures. This is the principle generally known as "template action." Templates may certainly be one-dimensional, e.g., the linear sequence of nucleotides in nucleic acids. They may probably be two dimensional; such biological membranes as the nuclear envelope, the chloroplastal and mitochondrial lamellae, probably function in this way, though this is not certain. Even less well assured is the existence of three-dimensional (spatial) templates. Another possibility is the existence of temporal templates, e.g., an oscillator which "forces" a weakly oscillating source to resonate with it.

Template transmission of information in cellular systems may find an analogy in imitative or Gestalt learning of complexes of psychological items.

In category 2b [regulation in masses of material in which the individual units are unimportant, either because there are so many of them, or because they are badly defined (e.g., tissues or syncytia)] the concepts involved are:

(a) Embryonic development presents an enormous number of instances of the regulatory, unitary behavior of a mass of material ("field" behavior) in circumstances which make it extremely difficult to believe that recognizable, distinct spatial units are the operative elements whose interaction accounts for the effects observed. For instance, there is regulation within a developing vertebrate limb bud, but it contains too many cells for one to see how this regulation can be attributed to properties of the individual cells. Again, there may be regulation within masses, such as syncytia or even within single cells, in which no well-defined smaller spatial units can be clearly recognized. The nature of these "field" properties therefore remains one of the great mysteries of developmental biology.

A highly speculative hypothesis has been advanced, suggesting that possibly these properties emerge as the resultant of the interaction of many temporarily oscillating compartments in the system, the oscillations being essentially due to the inherent tendency of feedback-controlled systems to exhibit periodicity.

(b) One of the most provocative properties of "field systems" is the following: a "field" tends to develop into a complete unit more or less independently of its size, within a considerable range, but if this range is exceeded, it may produce two rather small twins, or if it is reduced below a certain limit, the field may produce one perhaps oversized section of the complete unit; for instance, instead of five very small fingers, one rather large third finger. The general point is the existence of a transition between regulation around a total entity to regulation around one subsection of that total entity.

Chreods

The most general of all these embryological notions is that of the chreod—a self-stabilizing time-trajectory of change in a multicomponent system (or multidimensional space). This is a purely descriptive concept. It does not in itself offer any suggestion as to how any particular chreodic process operates. Its importance is that it indicates the character of the phenomena we are trying to analyze and understand. Whether we are considering the appearance of a rather small number of different cell types in an organism whose genome contains tens of thousands of genes which might, theoretically, give rise to billions of different constellations of activities, or of a complex morphological structure, like the vertebrate pentadactyl limb, which develops into a very definite pattern in any given species, although the results of evolution show that it can become modified in an almost infinite number of ways; in both cases we are confronted by the self-stabilization of one out of an enormous range of potential variants. My (admittedly slender) acquaintance with psychological phenomena would suggest that many of them show similar characteristics; for instance, in visual perception, we can receive, on a continually wobbling retina, a pattern of light stimuli corresponding to a view of some small part of a face, seen from any angle, and illuminated from any direction, and still say confidently, "That's my mum." This means, or can be interpreted to mean, that the visual signals fell into the "field" (or the "basin of attractors" in more topological terminology) of the "mum" chreod. Again, turning to behavior, we run downstairs, and the "get downstairs" chreod is sufficiently self-stabilizing to accommodate a few minor stumbles. And I repeat the question I raised above: at the psychological level, what is the connection, if any, between the effectiveness of self-stabilization and efficiency in performing *some* function, whether useful or not?

II. NEURAL DEVELOPMENTAL PROCESSES

HOW A DEVELOPING BRAIN GETS ITSELF PROPERLY WIRED FOR ADAPTIVE FUNCTION*

R. W. SPERRY

Introduction

My title should be qualified with a further explanation that the following consists largely of what might be termed "some scattered views on the old nature/nurture controversy—as seen from a psychobiological standpoint." The questions raised are concerned generally with the extent to which the behavioral properties of the brain are inbuilt, i.e., predetermined by genetic, developmental, and maturational processes, or the other side of the coin, the extent to which the functional plasticity of the brain may be limited by developmental and maturational constraints. If we orient the discussion toward man and the relevant problems of the day, then the primary concern is with the general functional plasticity of human nature, its potentialities and its limitations. To what extent does our genetic endowment, i.e., our hereditary carry-over from the Stone Age, impose important or even limiting conditions on man's capacity to adapt, for example, to the very rapid changes in today's environment and to the even more rapid changes impending.

Functional Interchangeability among Nerve Connections

Thirty years ago when I started working on certain aspects of this general problem with experiments aimed at basic adaptation capacities of the central nervous system, it was the accepted doctrine of the day that the vertebrate brain is possessed of an extreme form of behavioral plasticity with an adaptation capacity almost without limitation. The followers of Pavlov in Russia and of J. B. Watson in this country were

---

* Work of the author and his laboratory is supported by funds from the National Institutes of Health, Grant No. MH 07332, and the F. P. Hixon Fund of the California Institute of Technology.

speculating that it should be feasible with conditioned reflexes and appropriate early training to shape human nature into more desired molds and into a more ideal society. Even the phylogenetically old organization of the spinal cord was thought to be intrinsically plastic and subject to adaptive reeducation. Neurosurgeons the world over were operating during the 1930's on the belief, seemingly supported by dozens of experimental and clinical observations, that they could rearrange the wiring diagram of the nervous system in almost any way desired within the bounds of surgical feasibility, even to the extreme of cross-connecting arm to leg nerves to reinnervate the paralyzed legs following spinal lesions. It was generally agreed that functional readjustment should soon restore proper function to such disarranged structures (Anokhin, 1935; Barron, 1934; Bethe and Fischer, 1931; Pollock and Davis, 1933). Having its wires crossed was no challenge to the brain of the 1920's and 1930's.

In his review of 1939 Kurt Goldstein concluded that it seemed immaterial what particular nerve connections exist; so long as any connections are present, correct function follows. It was about this time also that Karl Lashley was suggesting that if the surgery were feasible, the striate visual cortex could probably be cut free, lifted, rotated, and reconnected 180° out of phase without serious disruption of visual perception. Such was the thinking of the 1930's. (If you hadn't been there, you wouldn't believe it!) On the above terms, where the nerve fiber connections seemed to be functionally plastic and interchangeable, there was no problem in the developmental prewiring of the nervous system to provide for selective growth of proper connections. The general motto of the day was "Let function do it."

When I tried to find out experimentally more about the nature and location of these central reeducative adjustments following surgical transplantation of nerve–muscle and other nerve–endorgan relations, the predicted readjustments simply failed to occur (Sperry, 1940, 1943a,b). After further checks and experiments in rats, amphibians, and monkeys and a critical reexamination of the entire literature I was forced to arrive at a blanket contradiction of the whole plasticity concept as it had previously been applied to nerve–endorgan rearrangements. This whole story was summarized in detail at the time (Sperry, 1945a), and the conclusions still stand so far as I know. The revised interpretation stated that the interchange of nerve connections does in fact cause directly corresponding disturbances of function that are highly intractable to reeducation and in many cases impossible to correct.

The new picture that we emerged with implied a functionally specified system of wired-in behavioral nerve circuits, relatively implastic to rearrangement by function. The whole problem of developmental organization and the question of how a brain gets itself wired for adaptive function was, of course, markedly changed. We were now confronted with the question of how the proper nerve connections get established correctly in the first place: was this achieved through selective fiber growth or by early irreversible training, or by some combination of the two?

Selectivity in Growth of Nerve Connections

Back in the 1930's it seemed quite inconceivable that highly organized and precisely adjusted behavioral nerve nets could be grown into a brain prefunctionally. The authoritative word on nerve growth stated that the growth and termination of the nerve fibers is nonselective. Electrical and chemical theories for the orientation of growing nerve fibers had seemingly been ruled out during the 1920's and 1930's on the basis of tissue culture observations and a long series of experiments on growth and regeneration of peripheral nerves (Weiss, 1936, 1937, 1938).

When we began experiments to test for selectivity in the growth of central brain tracts, however, like the optic, the trigeminal, the vestibular, tectospinal, and other central nerve tracts, the outcome from the start supported just the opposite conclusion (Sperry, 1945b, 1951a,b). Repeatedly and consistently, the results indicated that nerve growth and connection within the brain and spinal cord proceeds with the utmost precision and selectivity. The most extensive findings were obtained on the visual or retino-tectal system of amphibians and fishes, and this system has come to serve as a simple model for investigation and illustration of many of the basic developmental phenomena now seen to underlie the ontogenetic patterning of brain pathways and fiber connections (Gaze, 1967; Jacobson, 1966; Sperry, 1965a; Sperry and Hibbard, 1968; Szekeley, 1966).

The critical experiments involved an inversion of visual perception produced by surgical rotation of the eye through 180°. This was combined with section and scrambling of the optic fibers that connect the eye to the brain. The objective was to see whether the regrowth of brain connections might restore a confusedly blurred or an orderly type of vision and, if orderly, whether the order would reflect functional adaptation (right-side-up vision) or prefunctional regulation by inherent growth mechanisms (upside-down vision).

The observed result of optic nerve regrowth with eyes rotated 180° was an unambiguous reestablishment of precisely ordered upside-down vision, inverted also from front to back. Behaviorally the inverted vision was highly maladaptive; nevertheless it was found to persist indefinitely without any significant correction by reeducation. It reverted promptly to normal, however, in an almost machinelike fashion, upon surgical rerotation of the eyeball back to its proper orientation. The result provided a direct answer to the long-standing nativist–empiricist controversy (Walls, 1951) as to whether spatial orientation in visual perception is something that is acquired by experience or something that is innately built into the nervous system.

On a bet that birds would be less rigidly wired than fishes and amphibians, Hess (1956) ingeniously devised a means to outfit newly hatched chicks with spectacles containing prisms that produced an illusory lateral deflection of the visual field 7° to right or left. This produced an initial lateral error of aim in pecking that was measured closely and was observed during the first week of experience to undergo a typical correction curve. The target closed in upon through practice, however, was not the real target but the illusory target displaced to one side. This result effectively put an end to the pages and pages of preceding controversy that had been accumulating in the literature as to whether the early improvement of aim and coordination in this much-studied research model for the nature/nurture issue should be attributed to learning or to maturation.

The new evidence supporting selective growth of nerve connections as the primary basis for functional organization in the visual and other central nervous systems reopened the question of chemical guidance in the growth and termination of nerve fibers. The electrical and mechanical contact guidance theories were clearly inadequate, even in combination, to account for the results. Accordingly, a chemoaffinity interpretation was invoked in which selective affinities at the molecular level were conceived to be operative in intercellular contacts to determine which nerve cells synapse with which. Subsequent experiments extended the concept to the patterning of fiber pathways as well as their terminations (Attardi and Sperry, 1963; Sperry, 1963). Thus the precise ordering of fiber pathways and connections in the prefunctional wiring of brain circuits came to be ascribed very largely to the operation of highly selective cytochemical affinities—an interpretation that still holds.

Scheme for Hereditary Prewiring of Behavioral Nerve Nets

In brief, as we now see it, the complicated nerve fiber circuits of the brain grow, assemble, and organize themselves through the use of intricate chemical codes under genetic control. Early in development the nerve cells, numbering in the billions, acquire individual identification tags, molecular in nature, by which they can be recognized and distinguished one from another.

As the differentiating neurons and their elongating fibers begin to form functional interconnections to weave the complex communication networks of behavior, the outgrowing fibers become extremely selective about the molecular identity of other cells and fibers with which they will associate. Lasting functional hookups are established only with cells to which the growing fibers find themselves selectively matched by inherent chemical affinities. In many cases the proper molecular match may be restricted further to particular membrane regions of the dendritic tree or soma of the target neuron.

The outgrowing fibers in the developing brain are guided by a kind of probing chemical touch system that leads them along exact pathways in an enormously intricate guidance program that involves millions, in the higher mammals presumably billions, of different, chemically distinct brain cells. By selective molecular preferences expressed through differential adhesivity the respective nerve fibers are guided correctly into their separate channels at each of the numerous forks or decision points which they encounter as they travel through what is essentially a three-dimensional multiple Y-maze of possible channel choices (Sperry, 1963).

Each fiber in the brain pathways has its own preferential affinity for particular prescribed trails in the differentiating surround. Both pushed and pulled along these trails, the probing fiber tip eventually locates and connects with certain other neurons, often far distant, that have the appropriate molecular labels. The potential pathways and terminal connection zones have their own individual biochemical constitution by which each is recognized and distinguished from all others in the same half of the brain and cord. Indications are that right and left halves are chemical mirror maps.

Essentially this amounts to a reinstatement in an extreme form of the old chemotaxis concept of Cajal. It extends the idea of neurospecificity as used earlier in the resonance principle of Weiss (1936) into new dimensions of refinement (Sperry, 1965b), and it extends chemotactic selectivity into areas of organization within the higher centers where the verdict even of Cajal had formerly been "Let function do it."

By tying the chemoaffinity concept of selective nerve growth to a crossed gradient scheme of cellular differentiation and to other basic morphogenetic principles from developmental biology (then called experimental embryology) we were able by the late 1940's to put together what had so long been needed so badly; that is, a fairly credible explanatory picture of the ontogenesis of behavioral nerve nets (Sperry, 1945b,

1951a,b, 1958). In general outline at least, one could now see how it would be entirely possible for behavioral nerve circuits of extreme intricacy and precision to be inherited and organized prefunctionally solely by the mechanisms of embryonic growth and differentiation. In addition to the patterning of fiber pathways and connections, the concept was applied as well to the innate determination of specific physiological properties in different neuronal types and glial elements. Application of this scheme to developmental organization of the human visual system along with other aspects of the general picture were recently reviewed in some detail (Sperry, 1965a).

The foregoing developments in neurogenesis were communicated promptly during the 1940's and early 1950's to the British and European schools of ethology, where they found immediate welcome. The new views in neurogenesis meant that interpretations in ethology where the evidence seemed to favor inheritance of behavior traits no longer need be inhibited by doctrine from the field of nerve growth and development saying, "It cannot be done." The way was now cleared for the much-abused concept of instinct to make its belated if somewhat qualified comeback.

The point of these historical flashbacks is to emphasize the fact that since the year 1940, there have occurred within the biological and closely related sciences, including ethology, profound upsets and polar revisions in our basic thinking relating to the nature/nurture problem. As yet the meaning and impact of these changes has only begun to permeate into areas outside biology and ethology. In the more human areas of behavioral science like clinical psychology, psychiatry, anthropology, education, and the social sciences generally, the prevailing conceptual approach on this subject remains today essentially unchanged or very little changed from where it stood 30 years ago.

Electric Field Theory and Individuality

Another theoretical movement of the 1940's tended to discourage attempts to ascribe inbuilt functional specificity to particular nerve connections. This was the electric field theory of cerebral integration developed in Gestalt psychology which emphasized the regulatory role at cortical levels of holistic pattern and field forces, at the same time deemphasizing the importance of individual neuronal connections (Köhler and Held, 1949). Experiments designed to test for the postulated electric field forces using cortical knife cuts, metallic implants to short-circuit the postulated force fields, and dielectric implants to distort them

(Lashley *et al.*, 1951; Sperry, 1947; Sperry and Miner, 1955; Sperry *et al.*, 1955) yielded results uniformly discouraging to the idea that any major regulative role is played by volume conduction and field effects as postulated in the Gestalt theory. The results favored instead a more traditional fiber circuit form of integration.

The turns taken by the evidence during the 1940's thus brought on all sides a general convergence in neurological thinking toward an ever closer correlation between behavior and brain mechanism, pointing in particular to dependence of brain function upon highly specialized and precisely ordered nerve circuitry patterned around a basic hereditary wiring diagram characteristic of the species. More than this, the hereditary brain structure underlying behavior came to be viewed by Lashley (1947) and others as extending beyond the species level to that of the individual brain. Experts who work intimately with brains in large numbers come to recognize in the surface fissuration of the cerebral cortex, for example, or in cross-sectional features of the thalamus and lower brain stem—whatever one's specialty—almost the same order of individual variation that the average person perceives in faces. Anatomical features of this kind are largely determined at birth. Presumably the inner microscopic and ultrastructural detail of the underlying circuitry is no less subject to individual variation. In general the available evidence along these lines suggests that the individuality we each carry around in the inherent configuration of our cerebral circuitry makes that found in fingerprint patterns grossly crude and simple by comparison.

Corpus Callosum and Organizational Plasticity

As we entered the early 1950's, there remained one further very substantial stronghold for nonconnectionistic theories favoring an extreme functional plasticity in cerebral organization. This was the literature on lesions of the corpus callosum in which complete surgical transection of this largest by far of all the fiber tracts in the brain, containing in man some 200,000,000 fibers, was reported to produce no important behavioral or mental impairments (Akelaitis, 1944). Correlations between brain function and fiber system morphology seemed at the cortical level to be remote to say the least. These observations were being widely used as theoretical ammunition against the role of specific fiber connections in favor of more plastic and in some cases almost mystical concepts of how cerebral organization is achieved. At this stage of our understanding it appeared entirely plausible that whereas fiber connectivity might be critical for orderly function in the sensory and motor pathways and in the lower centers, the same did not apply to the higher neocortical associations where new and much more plastic forms of integration seemed to prevail.

When we focused a series of experiments on this question beginning about 1952 (Myers and Sperry, 1953), the results failed to confirm the earlier callosum story. Specifically it proved possible with appropriate tests, first in animals and later in human patients, to demonstrate the presence of a large, and still growing, array of distinct functional deficits in interhemispheric integration produced by section of the corpus callosum and the other cerebral commissures (Sperry, 1961, 1968a; Sperry et al., 1969). Instead of opposing connectivity theory, the findings on the corpus callosum have now come to stand as some of the best evidence that we can point to for direct dependence of higher mental functions on specific fiber systems of the cerebral cortex.

Trends toward Nativism

Looking back now in perspective over the developments in psychobiology during the past 30 years, we see a progressive retraction in the claims for functional plasticity and experiential patterning in brain organization. Earlier doctrine on the functional interchangeability of nerve connections, on chemotaxis and the nonselectivity of nerve growth, on empiricist origins of perception, on electric field forces in cortical integration, and on the preservation of normal function after cerebral commissure section has in each case undergone major changes that now point collectively and with mutual reinforcement to a much closer dependence of behavior upon innate brain mechanisms. One may include also major developments within ethology that meantime have moved in the same direction. The gradually increased recognition and acceptance of the role of heredity in shaping behavior has amounted in respect to animal behavior to almost a complete about-face on the old instinct issue. Whereas the very term "instinct" was openly repudiated in professional circles during the 1930's, we find today wide acceptance of the general idea that an entire evolutionary tree can be constructed on the basis of hereditary behavior traits.

The major uncertainties that remain today in the nature/nurture arena are shifted very largely to aspects of human behavior, in which, of course, the environmental and experiential factors attain a sharply increased and paramount influence. Even here, the prevailing shift toward nativism is evident, with the lines between environment and heredity being much more finely drawn than formerly and the questions more narrowly focused. One need hardly mention that occasional efforts to simply dispense with the whole nature/nurture issue as merely a pseudo-problem have not been exactly helpful from the scientific standpoint.

In recent work with human commissurotomy patients where it is possible to compare the independent performance of the two surgically disconnected hemispheres working at the same task in seriatim, we find new evidence for the intrinsic differentiation of right and left hemispheres in man (Sperry et al., 1969; Bogen, 1969; Sperry and Levy, 1969), and a rationale is seen (Levy, 1969a,b) for the evolution of cerebral dominance and the lateral specialization of function in the human brain. The type of mental processing that one observes when the left hemisphere is in command has been characterized in recent experiments of Levy (1969a) as being verbal, sequential, analytic, logical, and computer-like, whereas that of the right hemisphere contrasts in being nonverbal, spatial, synthetic, insightful, and Gestalt-like. Correlations indicating mutual interference between the right and left forms of mental processing are evident in the test analyses. Thus, a distinct operational advantage can now be seen to having these two rather different and somewhat antagonistic mechanisms for the cerebral processing of information set apart in separate hemispheres.

Further support for this interpretation is found in the analysis of the WAIS subtest scores for left-handers as compared to right-handers (Levy, 1969a,b) and also in the test performance of patients with congenital absence of the corpus callosum (Sperry, 1970a,b). Recent studies of Geschwind (1970) confirm the presence of an anatomical asymmetry in the human brain that correlates with the lateralization of language and cerebral dominance. This anatomical asymmetry, according to Wada (1969), is already demonstrable at birth in stillborn infants—a severe blow to environmentalist theories of the origin of cerebral dominance. In the differential development and balance between the spatially focused faculties of the minor hemisphere, on the one hand, and the verbally focused faculties of the major hemisphere, on the other, one can see a range of possibilities for individual variation in the inherent structure of human intellect.

The infant chimpanzee studies are widely familiar in which attempts have been made to equate environmental factors for chimpanzee and human infants by raising chimpanzees in human households, sometimes along with human children. Attempts at teaching language, toilet training, and general table and house manners to these domiciled chimp youngsters have resulted in showing mainly that chimpanzees are chimpanzees and people are people. Recent work with manual sign language instead of speech (Gardner and Gardner, 1969) looks more promising and certainly offers a more sound approach to the assessment of chimpanzee intellect. At this date the results remain somewhat ambiguous, and may yet go down in the record as a monument to what a tremendous investment in time, money, and manpower is required to get into the chimpanzee brain a modest number of trained movements and cerebral associations that reflect an order of mental complexity relatively little above what might be expected from a trained dog. Much the same can already be said apparently for the efforts during the past decade to develop communication between people and porpoises.

Among the more relevant studies that deal with the development of intellect in human infants, one perceives today another important and growing trend toward nativism, based to a large extent on emerging evidence that infants and children undergo an orderly, preprogrammed sequence of maturational steps through different levels and kinds of mental achievement. It is commonly stated in human psychology that the first 4 to 6 years of life are the most important in determining the type of person an individual is to become. The implication generally has been that subtle events in the way the child is mothered, nursed, weaned, toilet trained, exposed to different experiences, and what-not make all the difference in shaping the end product during these tender, critical years. From the biopsychological standpoint one strongly suspects that the reason these first years appear to be so influential is not because of the experiential happenings primarily but because of the preprogrammed maturational processes that unfold with great rapidity during these first years. It is during these years that the particular array of genetic factors that shape the basic behavioral tendencies of each personality begin to unfold and gain behavioral expression.

The potency of learning and memory, by contrast, are at their minimum level during this same period. One wonders if it is not more in the deep recesses of questionable psychiatric theory than in the minds of infants that the Oedipus and other such complexes really thrive. Infants and very young children would seem by nature to be comparatively resistant to psychic damage. Much more than in later years, the tendency in ages 1 to 4 is to accept and forget. This applies to ordinary, average growth and experience, not to extremes of experiential deprivation and trauma. Nor does it at all follow from any of the foregoing that learning and experience are therefore unimportant. We assume throughout that all are in common agreement on a starting ground rule which recognizes that both learning and innate factors are critically involved, especially at the human level, and that we are therefore talking always about a balance of emphasis. We assume also that any statements must be appraised in the frame of reference of the questions being asked. Accordingly, it may be inferred from the preceding discussion that the role of heredity in the regulation of behavior has been generally underestimated during the past 50 years, and the role of experience has been correspondingly overrated.

Avid environmentalists may still prefer to believe that the morons, the Beethovens, the idiot savants, and the Leonardos, the mongoloids and the Einsteins, the Bachs, imbeciles, and Shakespeares, etc. among us (and the in between et ceteras) are distinctive primarily because of the environment and training. If so, they would do well to study the growing literature of behavioral genetics to which no more than this brief reference is included here. It now seems more difficult to find a human trait that is not significantly influenced by heredity than one that is (Fuller and Thompson, 1960; McClearn and Meredith, 1966). The kinds of behavioral traits that to date have been reported to show in man significant hereditary variation extend into quite complex, profound, and subtle personality and intellectual features involving the highest as well as the lowest levels of that complex we call human nature.

Geneticists take for granted that hereditary differences tend to increase as one goes from identical twins to siblings to near relatives to distant relatives to nonrelatives to species, genera, etc. We note that many of the hereditary behavioral differences reported for man have been demonstrated among offspring of the same parents where one would least expect the hereditary effects to be prominent. Some of the best studies involve comparisons between monozygotic twins and dizygotic twins based on the assumption that the monozygotic twins should be identical in innate constitution. There are slight complications in this assumption, one of which stems from the lateral dominance considerations referred to above. Identical twins tend to be one right-handed, the other left-handed, for developmental reasons. They are reported to show a reversed laterality in alpha activity (Fuller and Thompson, 1960), and in the extreme this mirror-image tendency may extend into hair whorls and even situs inversus of the heart. Where the twins happen to be genetically heterozygous with respect to handedness and cerebral dominance, the left-handed tendency is more labile and may be overcome by training pressures in this right-handed world. It has been mentioned above that the tendency toward cerebral ambivalence found statistically among left-handers appears to handicap somewhat against minor hemisphere functions, statistically speaking. These complications in laterality and cerebral dominance that tend to make identical twins not so identical in their innate cerebral constitution, if taken into account in the twin studies, should have the effect of making the hereditary influence appear stronger than it already does.

Plasticity of Neural Maturation

Pertinent evidence regarding the behavioral potency of cerebral plasticity has come from the kind of compensation achieved after early brain damage or after agenesis of specific brain structures like the cerebellum or corpus callosum. Compared to the fully developed brain, the still-growing or maturing brain exhibits significantly greater compensatory capacity. Special interest stems from the promise these anatomical situations hold for a direct approach to the structural and physiological basis of the observed plasticity.

We have been fortunate recently in having available for study an exceptionally asymptomatic case of callosal agenesis, a young woman with total congenital absence of the corpus callosum. We were able to make direct comparisons of her performance with that of patients in whom surgical disconnection of the hemispheres had been carried out in the adult (Saul and Sperry, 1968; Sperry, 1968b). This agenesis patient was a 19-year-old college girl who had maintained a scholastic average of about C or slightly above and who had always been presumed by herself and family to have been entirely normal until X-rays taken after a bout of headaches revealed a total absence of the corpus callosum. She recovered promptly with treatment, and during the following year she cooperated in taking the entire series of tests that we had previously worked out for demonstrating the symptoms of hemisphere disconnection in adult surgical patients.

The majority of the test tasks on which the surgical patients did poorly or failed completely, this agenesis patient passed without any apparent difficulty, performing essentially like a normal control. In particular the direct disruptions between basic right–left cross integrations that persist for years after operation in the surgical patients appeared to have been rather fully compensated. For example, she could readily and promptly read words flashed into either half field of vision or words extending across the midline, half in the left and half in the right visual fields, even when these were presented near the threshold for visual acuity. She also could respond promptly with the sum or product of two numbers flashed simultaneously, one in the left and one in the right visual field. These and related aspects of this case are reviewed elsewhere (Sperry, 1968b).

Further tests were then applied involving more complex and generalized tasks that call upon cooperation between the mental specialties of right and left hemispheres. The baseline for comparison here was obtained from normals rather than from the commissurotomy patients.

These later results indicate that compensation for absence of the corpus callosum is far from complete, leaving a definite handicap in the form of a mild minor hemisphere syndrome (Sperry, 1970a,b). Accordingly, we now distinguish between functions of the callosum that can, and those that cannot, be compensated for in agenesis. With regard to those that *are* compensated, we get some insight into the kind of basic plasticity of which the human brain is capable at best. I say, "at best," here because the defect is present from the early beginning, catching developmental, maturational, and functional forms of compensation from the start, and also because it is part of the neocortical system that is involved, presumably the most plastic in the brain.

At the behavioral level the compensatory achievements, like that for integration between right and left visual hemifields, appear remarkable indeed and are not easily explained with information at hand. The underlying factors that we consider most probably responsible include the following: (a) bilateral development of speech; (b) slight enlargement and reinforced use of the anterior commissure; and (c) slight enlargement and enhanced use of the ipsilateral sensory, motor, and associated interneuron systems of the brain. The ipsilateral components normally are weak but known to be substantially potentiated after birth injuries. The kind of neural compensation here envisaged thus consists mainly of the enhanced use of neural systems already present and provided for in development rather than the creation of entirely new neural systems under functional demand. Recent reports of increased collateral sprouting and even growth of novel connection patterns in the mammalian optic system after early brain damage (Goodman and Horel, 1966; Schneider and Nauta, 1969) look suggestive. It is easy to think of a persisting pressure for diffuse growth of new connections among late maturing microneurons that become ordered secondarily through functional reinforcement and/or disuse atrophy. One must remember, however, that it has yet to be demonstrated that the changes in circuit morphology effected by experience consist of more than an enhancement, maintenance, or neglect of connections that already are basically patterned by selective growth.

REFERENCES

Akelaitis, A. J. (1944). A study of gnosis, praxis and language following section of the corpus callosum and anterior commissure. *J. Neurosurg.* Vol. 1, 94–102.

Anokhin, P. (1935). "Reports on the Problem of Centre and Periphery in the Physiology of Nervous Activity." Gorky State Publ. House, Gorky, U.S.S.R.

Attardi, G., and Sperry, R. W. (1963). Preferential selection of central pathways by regenerating optic fibers. *Exp. Neurol.* Vol. 7, 46–64.

Barron, D. H. (1934). The results of peripheral anastomoses between the fore and hind limb nerves of albino rats. *J. Comp. Neurol.* Vol. 59, 301–323.

Bethe, A., and Fischer, E. (1931). Die Anpassungsfähigkeit (Plastizität) des Nervensystems. *Handb. Norm. Pathol. Physiol.* Vol. 15, 1045–1130.

Bogen, J. E. (1969). The other side of the brain. I: Dysgraphia and dyscopia following cerebral commissurotomy. *Bull. L.A. Neurol. Soc.,* Vol. 34, 73–105.

Fuller, J. L., and Thompson, W. R. (1960). "Behavior Genetics." Wiley, New York.

Gardner, R. A., and Gardner, B. T. (1969). Teaching sign language to a chimpanzee. *Science* Vol. 165, 664–672.

Gaze, R. M. (1967). Growth and differentiation. *Annu. Rev. Physiol.* Vol. 29, 59.

Geschwind, N. (1970). The organization of language and the brain. *Science,* Vol. 170, 940–944.

Goldstein, K. (1939). "The Organism." American Book Co., New York.

Goodman, D. C., and Horel, J. A. (1966). Sprouting of optic tract projections in the brain system of the rat. *J. Comp. Neurol.* Vol. 127, 71–88.

Hess, E. (1956). Space perception in the chick. *Sci. Amer.* Vol. 195, 71.

Jacobson, M. (1966). Starting points for research in the ontogeny of behavior. *Symp. Soc. Develop. Biol.* Vol. 25, 339–383.

Köhler, W., and Held, R. (1949). The cortical correlate of pattern vision. *Science* Vol. 110, 414–419.

Lashley, K. S. (1947). Structural variation in the nervous system in relation to behavior. *Psych. Rev.* Vol. 54, 325–334.

Lashley, K. S., Chow, K. L., and Semmes, J. (1951). An examination of the electrical field theory of cerebral integration. *Psych. Rev.* Vol. 58, 123–136.

Levy, J. (1969a). Information processing and higher psychological functions in the disconnected hemispheres of human commissurotomy patients. Thesis, California Institute of Technology.

Levy, J. (1969b). Possible basis for the evolution of lateral specialization of the human brain. *Nature (London)* Vol. 224, 614.

McClearn, G. E., and Meredith, W. (1966). Behavioral genetics. *Annu. Rev. Psychol.* Vol. 17, 515–550.

Myers, R. E., and Sperry, R. W. (1953). Interocular transfer of visual form discrimination habit in cats after section of the optic chiasma and corpus callosum. *Anat. Rec.* Vol. 115, 351–352.

Pollock, L. J., and Davis, L. (1933). "Peripheral Nerve Injuries." Harper (Hoeber), New York.

Saul, R., and Sperry, R. W. (1968). Absence of commissurotomy symptoms with agenesis of the corpus callosum. *Neurology* Vol. 18, 307.

Schneider, G. E., and Nauta, W. J. H. (1969). Formation of anomolous retinal projections after removal of the optic tectum in the neonate hamster. *Anat. Rec.* Vol. 163, 258 (abstr.).

Sperry, R. W. (1940). The functional results of muscle transposition in the hind limb of the rat. *J. Comp. Neurol.* Vol. 73, 379–404.

Sperry, R. W (1943a). Functional results of crossing sensory nerves in the rat. *J. Comp. Neurol.* Vol. 78, 59–90.

Sperry, R. W. (1943b). Effect of 180 degree rotation of the retinal field on visuomotor coordination. *J. Exp. Zool.* Vol. 92, 263–279.

Sperry, R. W. (1945a). The problem of central nervous reorganization after nerve regeneration and muscle transposition. *Quart. Rev. Biol.* Vol. 20, 311–369.
Sperry, R. W. (1945b). Restoration of vision after crossing of optic nerves and after contralateral transplantation of eye. *J. Neurophysiol.* Vol. 8, 15–28.
Sperry, R. W. (1947). Cerebral regulation of motor coordination in monkeys following multiple transection of sensorimotor cortex. *J. Neurophysiol.* Vol. 10, 275–294.
Sperry, R. W. (1951a). Mechanisms of neural maturation. In "Handbook of Experimental Psychology" (S. S. Stevens, ed.), pp. 236–280. Wiley, New York.
Sperry, R. W. (1951b). Regulative factors in the orderly growth of neural circuits. *Symp. Soc. Study Develop. Growth* Vol. 10, 63–87.
Sperry, R. W. (1958). Developmental basis of behavior. In "Behavior and Evolution" (A. Roe and G. G. Simpson, eds.), pp. 128–139. Yale Univ. Press, New Haven, Connecticut.
Sperry, R. W. (1961). Cerebral organization and behavior. *Science* Vol. 133, 1749–1757.
Sperry, R. W. (1963). Chemoaffinity in the orderly growth of nerve fiber patterns and connections. *Proc. Nat. Acad. Sci. U. S.* Vol. 50, 703–710.
Sperry, R. W. (1965a). Embryogenesis of behavioral nerve nets. In "Organogenesis" (R. L. DeHaan and H. Ursprung, eds.), Chapter 6. Holt, New York.
Sperry, R. W. (1965b). Selective communication in nerve nets: Impulse specificity vs. connection specificity. *Neurosci. Res. Program, Bull.* Vol. 3, 37–43.
Sperry, R. W. (1968a). Mental unity following surgical disconnection of the cerebral hemispheres. *Harvey Lect.* Ser. 62.
Sperry, R. W. (1968b). Plasticity of neural maturation. *Develop. Biol.* Suppl. 2, 306–327.
Sperry, R. W. (1970a). Perception in the absence of neocortical commussures. *Res. Publ., Ass. Res. Nerv. Ment. Dis.* Vol. 48, Chapter VII, pp. 123–138.
Sperry, R. W. (1970b). Cerebral dominance in perception. In "Early Experience in Visual Information Processing in Perceptual and Reading Disorders" (F. A. Young and D. B. Lindsley, eds.), Nat. Acad. Sciences, Washington, D. C.
Sperry, R. W., and Hibbard, E. (1968). Regulative factors in the orderly growth of retino-tectal connections. *Growth of Nerv. Syst., Ciba Found. Symp.* pp. 41–52.
Sperry, R. W., and Levy, J. (1969). Hemispheric specialization as reflected in the syndrome of the neocortical commissures. *Exerpta Med. Found. Int. Congr. Ser.* Abstr. No. 193, 176.
Sperry, R. W., and Miner, N. (1955). Pattern perception following insertion of mica plates into visual cortex. *J. Comp. Physiol. Psychol.* Vol. 48, 463–469.
Sperry, R. W., Miner, N., and Myers, R. E. (1955). Visual pattern perception following subpial slicing and tantalum wire implantation in the visual cortex. *J. Comp. Physiol. Psychol.* Vol. 48, 50–58.
Sperry. R. W., Gazzaniga, M. S., and Bogen, J. E. (1969). Interhemispheric relationships: The neocortical commissure, syndromes of hemisphere disconnection. In "Handbook of Clinical Neurology," Vol. 4, Chapter 14, pp. 273–290. North-Holland Publ., Amsterdam.
Székely, G. (1966). Embryonic determination of neural connections. *Advan. Morphog.* Vol. 5, 181.
Wada, J. 1969. Interhemispheric sharing and shift of cerebral speech function. *Exerpta Med. Found. Int. Congr.* Ser. Abstr. No. 193, 296.
Walls, G. L. (1951). The problem of visual direction. Part II. The tangible basis for nativism. *Amer. J. Optometry Arch. Amer. Acad. Optometry* Vol. 28, 115–146.

Weiss, P. (1936). Selectivity controlling the central peripheral relations in the nervous system. *Biol. Rev.* Vol. 11, 494–531.
Weiss, P. (1937). Further experimental investigation on the phenomenon of homologous response in transplanted amphibian limbs. *J. Comp. Neurol.* Vol. 66, 481–535.
Weiss, P. (1938). The selective relation between centers and periphery in the nervous system. *Collect. Net* Vol. 13, 29–32.

Discussion

R. Oppenheim: In the course of the discussion, Dr. Sperry stated that the remarkable differences often observed between early and late (i.e., young and adult) central nervous system lesions can be explained by the undamaged structure on the contralateral side of the nervous system assuming the function of its damaged counterpart. However, in many of these cases bilateral damage has been done. For example, in the Kennard study, the motor and premotor areas in both hemispheres were destroyed in young monkeys. They exhibited a profound recovery of motor function when compared to the effects of comparable damage to adults.

Results such as these, in my opinion, necessitate the postulation of a different kind of developmental mechanism than the highly specific one that Dr. Sperry has so elegantly worked out in the visual system and in the other long-fiber systems. The possibility of greater plasticity in the making or remaking of synaptic connections in both these longer fiber systems and especially in the shorter ones associated with interneurons or microneurons would seem to be called for on the basis of behavioral evidence such as the Kennard study.

I think there already exists in the literature models of possible mechanisms for the mediation of such plasticity in neuronal maturation. One such example is the phenomenon of collateral sprouting where partial denervation appears to trigger the growth of nerve sprouts from intact fibers in the denervated region. These sprouts then reinnervate the nerveless structure. This phenomenon has already been identified in peripheral motor, sensory, and autonomic systems after denervation and in normal neuromuscular systems.

Another example that is somewhat more speculative at present concerns the well-worked-out phenomenon of amphibian limb regeneration. Mature differentiated cells (muscle, bone, blood vessels, etc.) are somehow triggered by amputation to revert to a more embryonic undifferentiated state. They then redifferentiate into mature cells to form a new limb. At present it is not known to what extent the dedifferentiated cells regain their embryonic pluripotency. But, assuming that they do, and assuming that certain cell types in the central nervous system retain this capacity, such phenomena as recovery of function, differences between early and late lesions, etc., could be better understood. It would only be necessary that cells can make new and different kinds of synaptic connections upon injury to an adjacent part, not that they must undergo complete redifferentiation. However, the last possibility should not be ruled out at this time.

One other possible mechanism for explaining plasticity, especially regarding the so-called early experience effects, has been recently clarified by the work of Altman. He has shown that in certain cell types in the brain of various mammals nerve cell proliferation—and the subsequent stages of migration, growth, and differentiation—

continues well after birth. These findings at least raise the possibility that early experience, stimulation, etc., in one or more of these developmental stages could somehow modify or influence nerve cells, including the kinds of synaptic connections these cells make or accept upon their soma or processes.

There are other possible systems or mechanisms for explaining neural maturation and the making of synaptic connections than the one that Dr. Sperry has identified. Neither type of mechanism precludes the other. They both seem necessary to explain all the behavioral information available.

Dr. Sperry: Learning and the functional plasticity of neural maturation have certainly to be explained at the level you discuss. I think we agree on some of these points.

S. M. Crain: Jacobson (1969) recently published similar views to those suggested by Dr. Oppenheim, and he postulated that plasticity may be particularly characteristic of certain types of small interneurons that differentiate relatively late during central nervous system development. Now, couldn't the dichotomy that we've been discussing be related to a basic difference in the types of neurons that compose the central nervous system? The larger neurons, with long axons, appear to be clearly involved in point-to-point specificity relationships, as Dr. Sperry has so elegantly described. However, small interneurons, with short processes, many of which are still undergoing cell division late in development, may not begin to differentiate until a major portion of the central nervous system is already functioning, in the postnatal period. Perhaps these neurons are much more plastic than neurons which differentiate at an earlier stage, when relatively little function is occurring in neighboring neurons. Selective interference with the differentiation of these late developing neurons may lead to decreased plasticity in this modified central nervous system. It may be possible, for example, to utilize a mitotic inhibitor, e.g., colchicine, at critical stages in central nervous system development, just as this agent has been used by Beidler (1965) to selectively destroy taste cells—which continue to divide frequently even in the adult organism. Just as taste functions can be selectively blocked by systemic introduction of colchicine, we may find that immature animals injected with this drug, at a critical stage when these small interneurons are dividing at a maximal rate, may show less plasticity than normal, especially in higher mammals. I wonder if Dr. Sperry has any comments regarding such a neurocytologic basis to the wide variability in plasticity properties associated with different parts of the central nervous system.

Dr. Sperry: It is true that our direct evidence regarding the developmental patterning of neural connections comes primarily from observations on long-axon systems composed of Cajal's type I neurons. It is also an old speculation that continues to seem reasonable (Sperry and Hibbard, 1968) that the plastic changes imposed by function are located not in these long-axon systems but in Cajal's type II neurons. These latter are still maturing in man apparently at 12 years of age and later. Chemical, including drug, and nutritional, treatments to enhance the potentialities of the small interneuron system certainly hold exciting possibilities. None of this would alter the general point made above concerning our widespread underestimation in recent decades of the importance of genetic determinants.

T. E. McGill: My remarks concern only a minor point in Professor Sperry's presentation, but I should like to question the assumption that laterality is genetically determined. R. L. Collins (1968) has recently performed some very interesting experiments on paw preference in different inbred strains of mice and F_1 crosses between inbred strains. Collins measured paw preference by allowing hungry animals access to a small test tube into which they could reach for bits of food.

In interpreting Collins' results it is important to keep in mind that all members of a given inbred strain are, theoretically at least, genetically identical except for sex differences. This is also true for F_1 animals from a cross between two inbred strains.

Now, under the assumption of genetic determination of laterality, Collins' experiment has several possible outcomes. First, mice might not have a preferred paw, in which case the distribution for any genotype should show a modal value of about 50%. Second, all mice, regardless of genotype, might have the same lateral preference. And, third, some strains might be "right-pawed" and others "left-pawed." Considering the large number of behavioral characteristics for which strain differences have been reported, the latter result might be predicted.

None of these results occurred in Collins' experiment. Rather, for every genotype he studied, a distinct bimodal distribution of paw preference was found. Furthermore, the distributions tended to be symmetrical, with half the mice preferring the right paw and the other half preferring to use the left. The preferences were consistent over time and were correlated with "grip strength" within subjects.

Collins has also reanalyzed published data on the inheritance of laterality in humans and found no evidence for genetic determination of the trait.

Paw preference in mice and handedness in humans, then, may be determined by nongenetic factors, or at least by nonchromosomal factors.

Recent work by Williams (1969) using inbred strains of rats and monozygous quadruplet armadillos has shown very large intrastrain differences in many morphological and biochemical characters. Williams has speculated that these differences may be due to nonchromosomal, probably cytoplasmic, factors. It is possible that such characters as cerebral dominance and laterality are so determined.

Dr. Sperry: Is the tendency for one monozygotic twin to be left-handed, the other right-handed, inherited or not? The "steps-removed" between gene and adult character are often many and varied and the exact nature of the developmental mechanisms involved, while interesting of course to the developmental biologist, may or may not be critically relevant from the behavioral standpoint.

REFERENCES

Beidler, L., and Smallman, R. L. (1965). Renewal of cells within taste buds. *J. Cell. Biol.* Vol. 27, 263.

Collins, R. L. (1968). On the inheritance of handedness. I. Laterality in inbred mice. *J. Hered.* Vol. 59, 9–12.

Jacobson, M. (1969). Development of specific neuronal connections. *Science* Vol. 163, 543–547.

Sperry, R. W., and Hibbard, E. (1968). *Nerv. Syst., Ciba Found. Symp.* pp. 41–52.

Williams, R. J. (1969). Heredity, human understanding, and civilization. *Amer. Sci.* Vol. 57, 237–243.

DEVELOPMENT OF EMBRYONIC MOTILITY

VIKTOR HAMBURGER

The development of behavior in vertebrate embryos encompasses a multitude of problems. Embryos of different species develop under a great diversity of internal and environmental conditions. The duration of prenatal life and the degree of behavioral maturity at hatching or birth are very different even within the same class. While lower aquatic forms have to fend for themselves a week or so after fertilization, amniote embryos and fetuses live a sheltered life for weeks or months. All this is reflected in the type of motility performed by them. Another dimension of complexity in this area is added by the investigators themselves: they approach the subject matter from a variety of backgrounds and viewpoints, and they use different conceptualizations and terminologies. The conference would make a significant contribution if some of the semantic and terminological difficulties could be straightened out. This would facilitate communication between neuroembryologist, neurophysiologist, behaviorists and others who now begin to find common ground in this field.

In the relatively short history of our subject, a few key issues have been identified which will be listed (without any claim to completeness) :

1. The interrelations between the structural differentiation of the nervous system (neurogenesis) and the embryonic development of behavior

2. The relations of so-called spontaneous to stimulated or evoked activity

3. The role of information through sensory input in the prenatal development of behavior

4. The relations of prenatal to postnatal behavior patterns, or, viewed retrospectively, the question of embryonic antecedents to postnatal action patterns

5. Comparative and evolutionary aspects; generalizations and species-specific features of behavior development

These problems are intricately interwoven and could not be handled separately. Particularly, the first and last issues pervade all considerations. I shall deal with the interrelations of several of these problems and will begin with a consideration of the first topic and subsequently present some broader theoretical thoughts on the subject.

Neurogenesis and Behavior Development

ONSET OF MOTILITY

The relationship of the embryonic development of the nervous system and motility is unquestionably a central issue: historically, it was one of the first to be broached. The pioneer work of Coghill on the salamander *Ambystoma,* the work of Angulo y Gonzalez, and of Windle and his collaborators on mammalian fetuses, and, more recently, the work of T. Humphrey on human fetuses and of Bodian on the rhesus monkey, took this point of departure. In Russia, the school of Anokhin has followed the same line.

Nobody can argue with the basic tenet that the state of differentiation of the nervous system at a given stage of development delimits the behavioral capacities of the embryo at that stage. One cannot expect a flexion of the head or of the trunk, or eye movements, to occur until the appropriate motor neurons have matured sufficiently to conduct impulses and their axons have established provisional synaptic contacts with muscles. Reflexogenic responses are contingent upon the closure of the respective reflex circuits. Information storage is not possible until a neural structure capable of this faculty is available. These seem to be truisms; but they are not always respected. Of course, we do not imply that structural differentiation "explains" all behavioral performances of the embryo, but it delimits the range of its potentialities.

Unfortunately, our information in these matters is extremely limited. The earliest stages which mark the beginning of motility have been investigated most thoroughly in this respect. Motility begins remarkably early in vertebrate embryos. The inception of motility seems to follow a phylogenetic sequence. Salamanders and frogs perform the first movements (which are a bending of the head) in tail bud stages, long before limb buds have appeared. Chick embryos start in the same way, in limb bud stages, at $3\frac{1}{2}$ to 4 days of incubation. Rat and cat fetuses have paddle-shaped limb buds with indications of digits, and rhesus monkey and human fetuses are slightly more advanced when motility begins. In all instances, the onset of motility follows immediately upon completion of the first provisional neural connections. For instance, in the human fetus of 20–25 mm crown-rump length (7½ weeks menstrual age) Humphrey (1954, 1964) has found that the spinal tract of the trigeminal nerve has just reached the level of the second to the fourth cervical segments, and the tips of the cutaneous branches are still below the surface epithelium of the oral region, when stimulation of the perioral area elicits the first faint head-bending response. Motility always starts at the cranial and cervical levels and extends from there to trunk and tail, concomitant with the caudad growth of longitudinal fiber tracts and the craniocaudal sequence of neuromuscular maturation.

Practically all studies of this type have used silver-impregnation methods, which give particularly clear and beautiful pictures of nerve fibers in embryonic material. However, they are not quite adequate to demonstrate synaptic contacts. Reliable evidence, particularly for the crucial stages of the establishment of synapses, can be provided only by the electron microscope. The recent work of Bodian (1966) and Bodian et al. (1968) fulfills this requirement. In rhesus monkey fetuses of 20–22 mm crown-rump length (42–45 days ovulation age) neither spontaneous nor stimulated movements were observed, and no synapses were detected in the cervical motor neuropil. A few days later (24–28 mm), when the first local spontaneous and reflex movements occurred in the arms and neck, very primitive synaptic bulbs, all of one type, were found on dendrites of motor neuroblasts, though only in small numbers. At a slightly later stage (48–51 days, 32–41 mm), which marks the onset of considerably more complex intersegmental movements, including trunk, tail, and legs, large numbers of dendrites and axons were found in the motor neuropil; the synaptic bulbs were more numerous and of two types: axodendritic as well as axosomatic, on motoneurons. In this instance, then, the onset of overt motility coincides precisely with the first establishment of synaptic contacts on the motor neurons; and rapid progress in behavioral activity is paralleled by advances of differentiation on the ultrastructural level.

I have discussed this work in some detail, because it sets new standards for correlated neuroembryological–behavioral studies. It may force us to revise some earlier notions based on silver-impregnated material. For instance, the earlier work of Windle and collaborators (e.g., Windle and Baxter, 1936) on cat, rat, and chick embryos had shown a very suggestive time correlation between the influx of collaterals from sensory dorsal root fibers into the dorsal gray columns at the brachial level and the onset of forelimb movements. It had been inferred that the closure of the reflex arcs occurs at the point where these collaterals establish synaptic contacts with dorsal internuncials; and this notion has been generally adopted. Now, it seems to be in disagreement with the data of Bodian. The electron microscope evidence is incontrovertible, whereas the silver-impregnated material permits only inferences in this respect. Either reflex circuits are closed at different points in different mammalian species, or both investigators are right; the circuit may be closed at two points simultaneously. Bodian has not yet looked at the dorsal neuropil with the electron microscope. The case is an object lesson. It warns against premature generalizations, and it points out the need for the refinement of our tools.

Nevertheless, two main points hold true: inception of motility is nearly synchronous with the establishment of synaptic contacts; and very primitive neuroblasts and axons which are growing and differentiating are already capable of impulse conduction and functional activity. Gradually, more parts of the embryo go into action, and one is tempted to assume that each new activity, as, for instance, opening of the beak or eyelid, follows immediately upon the completion of the underlying structural pathways. However, no factual data are available concerning the latter point, and broad generalizations are not justified at this time. It is conceivable that in some instances inhibitory or other physiological processes delay the activation of a neural system.

PRECEDENCE OF MOTOR DIFFERENTIATION OVER SENSORY DIFFERENTIATION

In the spinal cord, the motor columns differentiate earlier than the sensory areas. This sequential order is manifested even before the columns make their appearance; it is reflected already in the chronology of mitotic activity which occurs prior to the neuroblast differentiation and to the formation of neuron patterns, such as columns or nuclei or strata. Quite generally, proliferation in the ventral basal plate (the future motor region) precedes that in the dorsal alar plate. For instance, in the chick embryo, the peaks of proliferative activity in the dorsal and ventral spinal cord are at least 4 days apart (Hamburger, 1948). This time difference is retained in the subsequent neuroblast migration and differentiation and in the formation of motor and sensory columns, respectively. As a result, the chick and most other embryos are motile before they can respond to tactile stimulation. The theoretical implications of this *prereflexogenic* or prestimulative period will be discussed later. (For the fishes and amphibians, a highly specialized type of intracentral, transient sensory cells, the Rohon–Beard cells, make very early sensitivity possible, apparently as an adaptive feature related to early hatching and swimming.) It is interesting that the same sequential order prevails in the brain. Usually, the effector systems differentiate in advance of the receptor systems. For instance, in the optic tectum of bird embryos, the basal stratum of effector cells differentiates first, and the sensory cells have to migrate across this layer to reach their more dorsal topographic positions (Fujita, 1964).

DEVELOPMENTAL MECHANICS OF NEUROGENESIS

A variety of mechanisms are at work to construct the exceedingly complex organization of the nervous system, including the patterns of nerve cell groups and the intricate circuitry on which its effective function depends. Specification of neuron types and regional structural differences in the central nervous system are determined very early by unknown factors, and progressive differentiation, formation of axons and dendrites and of fiber tracts and synaptic contacts proceed according to an intrinsic schedule. However, it would be quite erroneous to assume that each small part or unit proceeds on its own. On the contrary, interactions of cells and cell groups within the central nervous system and interactions with other embryonic, nonnervous structures play a vital role in the progressive structuration of the nervous system. The experimental methods and tools for the causal analysis of factors involved in neurogenesis were taken over from classic experimental embryology by pioneers in experimental neuroembryology, foremost among them Harrison and Detwiler. Of course, it is impossible to give even a cursory review of this field, but a few selected examples will illustrate the significant principle of interdependency.

The outgrowth of an axon from the embryonic nerve cell may appear to be a simple matter, but it is full of complexities. The machinery for the synthesis of axoplasmic material (mostly proteins) is located in the perikaryon which spins out the fiber. Once the delicate nerve fiber has emerged from the central nervous system or ganglion, it requires cues or signals from the substrate on which it is spun out to guide its growth and direct it toward its destination. It is now generally assumed that subtle biochemical interactions between the growing tip (growth cone) of an axon or dendrite and the substrates are at work, but the molecular basis of the path-finding process is unknown. At any rate, the stereotyped nerve patterns found in the adult are created during early embryonic, prefunctional periods through interaction of nerve fiber and substrate.

The establishment of the highly specific terminal synaptic contacts of one nerve cell with another requires an even more exacting mode of "recognition" between the two partners. The best information we have in this matter concerns the synaptic connections of retina fibers in the optic tectum of lower vertebrates (Sperry, 1951, 1965; Székely, 1966; Jacobson, 1970; Gaze, 1970). Neuroanatomical, electrophysiological, and behavioral data support the hypothesis of Sperry that the connections are established on the basis of highly selective biochemical affinities between the two contacting elements. Some basic experiments that lead to this conclusion take advantage of the capacity of the optic nerve of amphibians for complete functional regeneration. It can be shown that after optic nerve transection in frogs the regenerating fibers reestablish functional connections with precisely those cells of the optic tectum with which they had been connected before. Of course, this is not a one-to-one match of fiber and nerve cell; rather we are dealing with recognition within small areas; and gradient systems seem to play a role in the matching process. A certain element of trial and error may be involved, but strictly on the level of biochemical affinities. The following modification of the experiment shows that trial and error on the functional or behavioral level is not at all implicated. If optic transection is combined with 180° rotation of the eyeball, then the behavior response after functional recovery is misdirected. For instance, the aim at a food object presented to the frog behind it and below will be directed in the opposite direction, i.e., forward and upward, and this maladaptation is never corrected by experience. In earlier times, the possibility had been considered that synaptic contacts are established in a random fashion and that behavioral or functional trial and error selects the adaptive connections which become permanently fixed, while all others disappear. Obviously this notion is no longer tenable. A simple argument that neural structuration in the optic system is achieved by purely embryological, biochemical mechanisms is based on the fact that during embryonic development these synaptic contacts are completed before function begins.

Many other examples could be presented to illustrate a wide diversity of embryonic interactions. The term "maturation" hardly does justice to the highly dynamic "epigenetic" nature of neurogenesis; it does not convey the notion of a continuous interplay of subsystems during neurogenesis. Differentiation processes intrinsic to nerve cells are intricately interwoven with interactions between cells and units of the nervous system and between neural and nonnervous structures. The experimental analysis can unravel the different factors to some extent.

FUNCTIONAL ACTIVITY AND SENSORY INPUT AS FACTORS IN NEUROGENESIS

The causal analysis of neurogenesis would be incomplete unless the possible role of functional activity and sensory input were thoroughly scrutinized. We shall not be concerned here with the effects of these factors on the development and maintenance of nonnervous structures such as articulations and musculature. Such effects are well established and they will be dealt with briefly below. On the biopsychological level, two distinctly different problems are implied. Sensory input could play a dual role: as a factor in the progressive *structural* differentiation of the central nervous system or as a factor in the development of *behavior patterns* per se, without necessarily leaving structural traces of its impingement.

The first question was touched upon in the preceding section. In the case of the visual system the evidence is clearly against the implication of sensory input in the wiring of the optic tectum. Numerous experiments on other sensory systems support this conclusion (Sperry, 1951, 1965). On the motor side, the classic experiments of Weiss (1941, 1955) on amphibians demonstrate that action systems such as walking can develop without influence of sensory input. Teleosts proceed to the stage of perfect swimming in the prereflexogenic phase of development (Tracy, 1926). I think that most investigators today would agree with the assessment that the differentiation of the central and peripheral organization of the nervous system proceeds to advanced stages without the benefit of functional activity, sensory feedback, or environmental stimulation; that is, exclusively through the operation of embryological and concomitant biochemical mechanisms. Yet it is quite conceivable that in late stages and in the final perfection of the synaptic patterns sensory input may get involved. At present, our micromethods are hardly adequate to detect such effects, which one would expect to occur on the ultrastructural level. The question of the molecular basis of information storage is under vivid discussion. The important question of the role of sensory input in the development of behavior patterns will be discussed below.

Search for a Theoretical Framework

A large amount of descriptive material on embryonic motility in different forms has accumulated, but the theoretical interpretation lags behind rather sadly. Preyer, who inaugurated the study of behavior development in the 1880's, laid a very solid and substantial theoretical foundation which has not lost its validity to this day, though he had very little influence on the subsequent development of the field. Since then, we have had only one great theorist, E. G. Coghill, whose philosophical ideas and thinking had an impact on practically every worker in the field. His theory has many facets, some of which have stood the test of time very well. For instance, some of the ideas developed in the preceding chapter on neurogenesis were clearly enunciated in his writings. The basic tenet of his theory is the contention that motility is an integrated performance of the whole individual, from the first bending of the head of the early embryo, to the complex action patterns of later life, such as locomotion, food getting, etc. Local actions and reflexes of parts were thought to originate secondarily by emancipation, or, in his terminology, "individuation" from the total pattern. This is no longer tenable as an all-inclusive theory. It was built on too narrow a foundation. His notion is probably valid for his own material, the urodele amphibians, and for teleosts, but it breaks down when one tries to apply it to amniotes (see reviews by Hamburger, 1963, 1968). It is understandable that investigators now are reticent to entertain broad theoretical ideas, and, indeed, it would be unwise, at the present state of our knowledge, to try to formulate a general theory of embryonic development of behavior, particularly in view of the great diversities found in different forms. Nevertheless, I think, one should begin to search for a theoretical frame of reference and get an idea of the direction in which theoretical considerations should go.

Some important *generalizations* have emerged from the large body of investigations done in the past. As the broadest generalization, one can state the principle, inherent in all development, that neurogenesis as well as behavior development proceed from simple to complex patterns. But this does not imply that the two processes develop strictly in parallel. Not every step in neurogenetic differentiation finds its expression in the overt motility of the embryo. Whereas there is no doubt that neurogenesis is a continuous process, discontinuity has been observed in behavior development. For instance, we have not been able to observe a gradual buildup of the well-coordinated prehatching and hatching behavior in the chick embryo. The sequence of events, beginning at 17 days of incubation and ending in the escape from the shell, seems to be triggered off by changes in the internal milieu.

The principle of systemogenesis, established by Anokhin (1964) and his group, is another broad generalization. The responses of vertebrate embryos to tactile stimulation follow a pattern which seems to have validity over a wide range. One can distinguish three phases. In the first phase, local stimulation elicits only restricted local responses; e.g., stimulation of the perioral region, which in many forms is the first to become sensitive, results in head bending. The restriction of the movement to the cervical region is simply due to the immature condition of the neuromuscular apparatus in more posterior regions. In a second phase, the whole body responds with so-called total or mass movements. In the third phase, the response becomes restricted again, but now it consists of the specialized adaptive local action characteristic of that region, e.g., sucking or leg withdrawal. Dr. Gottlieb has given evidence for the universality of the sequential order in which sensory modalities originate in vertebrate embryos (see p. 67).

Such generalizations are important in relatively limited areas, but they do not add up to a general theory comparable in scope to that of Coghill. Altogether, one can say that direct observation and interpretation of the *form and pattern* of movements (an approach which is sometimes called "phenomenological," though not in the philosophical sense) has been disappointing in the search for directives for theoretical constructs.

There is a more promising and more fundamental approach to theory, namely, the *analytical approach;* that is, an inquiry into the causes or sources of embryonic motility. How do the movements originate? What are the underlying physiological mechanisms? To my knowledge, the only comprehensive attempt to come to an understanding of embryonic motility from this point of view has been made by Preyer, whose very substantial theoretical and observational contributions are embodied in his two books "Die Seele des Kindes" (1882) and "Specielle Physiologie des Embryo" (1885). His classification of the sources of animal and human motility, in general, though outdated in some respects, is of more than historical interest, because, in a modified form, it can serve as a starting point for a theoretical frame of reference.

Preyer distinguishes between six categories of motility "according to their causes." They are (1) *passive movements* (e.g., due to amnion or uterine contractions), (2) *irritative* (e.g., induced by endogenous humoral agents, drugs, asphyxiation, or by direct stimulation of nerves), (3) *reflexive* (i.e., mediated by sense organs and the sensory system), (4) *impulsive* (now usually called "spontaneous," that is, neither reflexogenic nor "irritative," usually uncoordinated, and probably caused by autonomous discharges of motor neurons), (5) *instinctive* (inherited, goal directed, integrated, e.g., sucking, caused either by stimulation or by endogenous agents), and (6) *ideational* (caused by mental images, essentially cortical).

Of these, category 1 is irrelevant for the present discussion and category 6 is not applicable to the embryo. Category 5 is not clearly definable as to causes and therefore of dubious status as an independent category. It also had better be omitted. This leaves categories 2, 3, and 4 for further consideration. I see the importance of this original effort on the part of Preyer to come to grips with a fundamental problem in two points: he takes as a starting point the underlying physiological mechanisms rather than forms or patterns of behavior; and, his scheme sets up "impulsive" (spontaneous) movements as a category in its own right, distinct from reflexogenic movements.

Following Preyer, and sharpening the definitions, we shall set up three categories of embryonic motility:

Category A. Motility resulting from autonomous discharges of nervous tissue, in a steady-state, relatively stable internal milieu *("spontaneous motility")*.

Category B. Motility resulting from discharges which are triggered, or caused, by humoral agents or other changes in the internal milieu *("endogenously stimulated motility")*.

Category C. Motility resulting from stimulation of the sensory system ("reflexogenous, or *"evoked motility"*).

Categories A and B are admittedly not as clearly demarcated against each other as are A and C. The reason for this is given below (see p. 60). Nevertheless, we maintain the distinction between A and B in the context of the present theoretical discussion, in order to set apart unambiguously category A as a special type of motility which derives explicitly from physiological processes generated within a group of neurons in the absence of internal milieu "stimuli." The capacity of many types of nerve cells to generate discharges autonomously is now widely recognized.

Some terminological questions have to be clarified. Preyer's term "impulsive" for category A is not acceptable because of its psychological undertones. The term "spontaneous" is not entirely satisfactory either. For one, it should not be used for both motility and electrical discharges of neurons. In the following discussion we shall use "spontaneous" strictly as a designation of a special mode of motility, and we shall speak of "autonomous" or "self-generated" discharges of neurons. Yet, there remains the further ambiguity that motility of both categories A and B appears as "spontaneous" on the behavioral level. In the absence of an obvious alternative term for either category, it is necessary to make an arbitrary decision. I shall use henceforth *"spontaneous* motility" strictly for category A and *"endogenously stimulated motility"* for category B. The latter term is provisional until a better substitute is found.

Spontaneous Motility as a Special Category of Motility (Category A)

Preyer established the category of "impulsive" (spontaneous) activity on the basis of observations which he had made on chick embryos, on a variety of mammalian fetuses, and on human infants (particularly his own son, who is the subject of his first book). He writes (1885, p. 453):

> When the newborn infant fidgets aimlessly in the air with his hands, when it performs completely uncoordinated leg movements without the least external provocation . . . then it performs impulsive movements. The newborn like the unborn moves the limbs without external stimuli out of an internal impulse, of which it is completely unaware. . . . It is the impulsive flexions and half-extensions of the extremities and not the much less pronounced reflex movements which characterize the behavior of the fetus and newborn. Very similar are the movements of mammals half awake from deep hibernation. Particularly the hamster then exhibits the same hardly describable uncoordinated and aimless movements of the limbs as does the mammalian fetus; sometimes slow and then again rapid or jerky.

He derived evidence for the nonreflexogenic nature of this type of movements from stimulation experiments on chick embryos. He discovered that while motility begins in the early part of day 5 (actually day $3\frac{1}{2}$–4), responses to tactile or other stimulation cannot be elicited until day 9 or 10 (actually day $7\frac{1}{2}$). He fully realized the theoretical importance of the prereflexogenic period, and he interpreted it correctly as resulting from the "unequal rate of development of motor and sensory columns of the spinal cord" (1885, p. 548) (see previous discussion, p. 48). He also anticipated the correct physiological mechanism underlying this type of motility. He writes (1882, p. 132): "Concomitant with the differentiation of the motor neurons in the spinal and cervical cord, there must be an accumulation of a certain quantity of potential energy, probably chemical in nature, which . . . can be transformed very readily into actual energy." Now, 87 years later, we have obtained the first evidence of spontaneous electrical discharges by embryonic nerve tissue (see below).

Our investigations of the motility in the chick embryo (in collaboration with Drs. Balaban; Decker; Narayanan; Oppenheim, and E. Wenger) have established a much broader basis for the recognition of spontaneous motility as a special category in its own right. As indicated, motility begins at $3\frac{1}{2}$ to 4 days with a slight bending of the head, performed once or several times in succession. Such episodes occur at first at long, irregular intervals of about 1 minute duration. Activity builds up gradually, and, up to about 13 days, shows a clear periodicity, activity phases alternating with inactivity phases. The former gradually increase in length, while the latter decrease. A plateau of maximal activity is attained at about 13 days, and maintained through 17 days, whereupon motility declines sharply. The form of movements is very much like that described for infants by Preyer (above). Movements up to 17 days are mostly unintegrated, aimless, jerky, convulsive in type, and sometimes smooth. During an activity phase, one observes a seemingly unpredictable combination of movements of parts, such as head, trunk, limbs, toes, eyeballs, eyelids, beak. We have designated these movements as type I (Hamburger and Oppenheim, 1967). Type II movements are so-called "startles," that is, rapid spasmodic movements passing through the whole body. They are relatively rare.

The adaptive significance of type I and type II motility is probably to guarantee the normal formation of articulations and the maintenance of muscle tissue. Nerveless limbs (Hamburger and Waugh, 1940) and embryos which have been paralyzed for varying periods (Drachman and Sokoloff, 1966) show severe joint abnormalities and muscle atrophy.

A very different type of movement makes its appearance around day 17: these are highly integrated body movements which lead to the attainment of the hatching position around day 19 and the subsequent pipping and hatching act. They have been designated type III movements. They are performed in episodes separated by shorter or longer intervals during which type I movements occur, though not very frequently (Hamburger and Oppenheim, 1967; Hamburger, 1968).

The existence of a prereflexogenic period in the chick embryo, first observed by Preyer, was confirmed by others. Hence, no experimental test of the nonreflexogenic nature of motility up to 7 days is required. Since the form of the movements does not change after 7 days, one suspects that they continue to be nonreflexogenic. However, rigorous experimental evidence is required to establish this point. Using the techniques of microsurgery on early embryos designed by classic experimental embryology, the following experiments were performed. Complete deafferentation of the leg level was achieved by a double operation in 2-day embryos: isolation of the lumbosacral spinal cord from cranial input by producing a gap in the thoracic cord, and simultaneous extirpation of the dorsal half of the lumbosacral spinal cord, whereby the neural crest, i.e., the material for spinal ganglia, is removed. In this way, both proprio- and exteroceptive sensitivity are eliminated, as well as any stimulation from more anterior levels. The motility of the experimental embryos was found to be the same as that of controls in which only the spinal cord gap had been made. The motility holds up well to the 15- to 17-day stage, when the residual spinal cord, which is inevitably exposed to the amniotic fluid, begins to deteriorate (Hamburger *et al.,* 1966). It is evident that type I leg motility can be performed in the absence of extero- and proprioceptive sensory input. In another experiment, the sensitivity of the head was eliminated by early embryonic removal of the two sources of the trigeminal ganglion, the preotic medullary neural crest, and the trigeminal placodes of both sides. Again, the motility of the experimental embryos was found to be normal up to 15 to 17 days (Hamburger and Narayanan, 1969). Both experiments dispose of the frequently stated contention that the brushing of the toes against the head provides a source of self-stimulation. Additional evidence against this particular mode of self-stimulation was obtained in an experiment in which both leg buds were extirpated in 4-day stages. Again, motility was not decreased (Helfenstein and Narayanan, 1969). In still another experiment, the embryos were deprived of the vestibular system by early embryonic extirpation of both otocysts. No change was observed in type I motility (Decker, 1970).

It is thus established conclusively that type I motility can be performed in the absence of sensory input from any source, including self-stimulation. (It should be noted that type I motility is the only kind performed up to 17 days.) The same claim cannot be made for type III behavior since none of the experimental embryos hatched. It remains to be seen whether this failure is due to the deficient sensory input or to neurological defects which were unavoidably present in the experimental animals.

On the basis of these findings, the hypothesis was proposed that spontaneous motility results from electrical discharges of neurons in the central nervous system, including the brain. Activity generated in the brain was postulated on the basis of findings that trunk and leg motility are reduced when a gap is made in the cervical cord (Hamburger et al., 1965).

The hypothesis was tested by direct recording of spike potentials from the embryonic spinal cord *in situ*. The considerable technical difficulties were overcome by Dr. Provine and Dr. Sharma, with the generous advice and aid of Dr. T. Sandel of the Psychobiology Laboratory of Washington University. So far, all recordings were made from the anterior end of the lumbosacral spinal cord of 14- to 17-day embryos. Extracellular recordings were made with glass micropipettes, 4–6 μ in diameter, filled with $3\,M$ KCl–agar solution. The cord was probed from dorsal to ventral. In the normal cord, the upper third (approximately the region of the dorsal columns) showed relatively little activity. Below this region is a narrow zone which is nearly silent. In contrast, the remainder of the cross section, including the motor region and the adjacent population of internuncial neurons, gives mostly discrete patterns of single-unit activity. Bursts were also observed rather frequently; they result probably from simultaneous discharges of several units. Continuously firing units with more or less regular interspike intervals were found particularly in the ventral region. Thus, for the first time, the existence of patterns of single-unit electrical activity was demonstrated in an embryo (Provine *et al.*, 1970).

Dr. Sharma has then taken up the crucial question of whether or not electrical discharges will continue after complete deafferentation. An acute preparation of a deafferented, isolated lumbosacral spinal cord was made, very much like the chronic preparation described above: the spinal cord was transected at the lower thoracic level, and all dorsal roots along the lumbosacral cord were cut at the same time. After recovery, the dorsal part of the cord showed only faint activity. The median and ventral regions continued to show single-unit activity, though at a lower level than normal. It is evident that although higher centers and sensory input contribute to the overall discharge level, neurons in the middle and ventral part of the spinal cord of 14- to 17-day embryos are capable of generating discharges autonomously. These discharges are in all probability the source of type I and type II motility. Thus, spontaneous motility, as defined on p. 54, seems to be well established as a special category (Sharma *et al.*, 1970).

The next question is whether or not our findings on the chick embryo can be generalized. If spontaneous motility is to be a building stone in a general theory of behavior development, one has to demonstrate that it is a universal phenomenon. Our evidence for the chick was obtained on three levels. On the observational level we have shown that unstimulated motility is actually performed at a high rate; next, its nonreflexogenic nature was affirmed by the demonstration of a prereflexogenic period in early stages and the deafferentation experiments for later stages. Finally, we have established its source as self-generated electrical discharges of spinal cord neurons. We have neither deafferentation experiments nor electrical recordings for any other form, and we have to rely largely on the existence of prereflexogenic periods. Hence our evidence regarding other forms is admittedly circumstantial and by far not as secure as that for the chick.

All vertebrate embryos which have been studied perform movements when undisturbed. In the following very brief survey, anamniotes and amniotes will be dealt with separately. In the turtle *Chelydra*, the form of movements is much like that of chick embryos: an early period of S-waves is followed by total body movements, during which "the activity of the head, neck, and tail as well as of the appendages appeared random and uncoordinated" (Decker, 1967). Motility in the turtle as well as in the lizard (Hughes *et al.*, 1967) is cyclic, activity phases alternating with inactivity phases. Both characteristics are suggestive of nonreflexogenic motility. Definite evidence for non-reflexogenic motility is derived from the existence of a prereflexogenic period both in the lizard and in the turtle (Hughes *et al.*, 1967). In mammals, a prereflexogenic period does not seem to exist. Altogether, in mammalian fetuses, motility begins at a much later stage of overall body development and spinal cord differentiation than in lower forms. This indicates a shift in the timetable of some neurogenetic process which remains to be elucidated. But the absence of a prereflexogenic period is no argument against the existence of category A; it merely deprives us of a piece of evidence in its favor. Spontaneous mammalian fetal movements have been described as mass movements and local movements. A reinvestigation of motility in rat fetuses (Narayanan et al., 1971) has confirmed the earlier findings of Angulo Y Gonzalez (1932) and Windle and Baxter (1936). In addition, we have found that the spontaneous movements are cyclic, as in the chick and in reptiles. They resemble those of these lower forms in another respect: they are aimless and uncoordinated. We consider these characteristics as indicative of the category A form of motility in the rat fetus. In this connection, it is of interest to note that action potentials were recorded from pieces of spinal cord and brain tissue of mouse and rat fetuses grown in organ culture (Crain, 1966). Such preparations give convincing evidence of self-generated electrical activity in mammalian neural tissue, since humoral agents are excluded.

To uphold the universality of category A motility, we have to include the lower vertebrates, which we have not considered up to this point, for a good reason. So far, we have associated spontaneous motility with unintegrated random motility as exemplified by type I in the chick embryo. In fact, this characteristic has attracted the attention of Preyer and others to this type of motility, and it was instrumental in setting up spontaneous movements as a special category. However, this association of spontaneity and lack of coordination is by no means obligatory. Teleosts and urodeles provide an illustration of an alternative combination, namely spontaneity and coordinated behavior. We have mentioned repeatedly the findings of Coghill (1929) that in the salamander *Ambystoma,* motility is integrated from the beginning up to swimming and later stages, and the same holds for teleosts (Tracy, 1926). In both instances, these integrated movements can be performed spontaneously. In teleosts, Tracy has found a prereflexogenic period lasting until after hatching. At later stages, spontaneous swimming continued after extirpation of eyes and olfactory organs and after spinal cord transection. Proprioception can also be excluded. Obviously, nonreflexogenic spontaneous motility does exist in teleosts. Tracy is inclined to assign this motility to our category B, since changes in the CO_2 content of the water modified motility. However, this experiment alone does not permit a distinction between categories A and B; moreover, this point is not important in the present context.

Coghill has not been explicit in his own writings concerning the nature of spontaneous motility in the salamander, except to point out that a brief prereflexogenic period exists. However, Herrick, who had an intimate knowledge of Coghill's theoretical thoughts, makes it abundantly clear in his biography (1949, p. 89) that Coghill considered the motility of *Ambystoma* essentially as autonomous and independent of sensory connections and that he placed much emphasis on the theoretical significance of these findings.

> As the anatomical inquiry advanced, Coghill was more and more impressed with the significance of the precocious development of the motor system, at first quite independent of any sensory connections, and of the dominant influence of motor patterns in both ontogenetic and phylogenetic development. This influence at its inception is autonomous, and the evidence clearly indicates that the primary factors in shaping the earliest patterns of behavior are not trial and error, use, or improvement by practice but intrinsic agencies not of stimulus-response type.

The occurrence of spontaneous coordinated motility has important implications for our theoretical considerations. It becomes clear that for the definition of category A only the physiological criterion of autonomous or self-generated bioelectrical activity is constitutive, but the pattern of overt motility is not distinctive. Category A includes both coordinated and uncoordinated behavior. More work will be required to establish the universality of category A on firm grounds. However, I believe that the data which we have summarized are strongly suggestive in this direction, and I do not know of any argument that would challenge the generalization.

Endogenously Stimulated Motility (Category B)

Although the distinction between categories A and B is clear-cut in the abstract definition (p. 54), there is in reality an interdependency between them, which does not set them apart as clearly as A is distinguished from C. It is evident that the performance of spontaneous motility requires a set of *permissive milieu conditions,* such as CO_2 and O_2 tension. A certain range of milieu conditions can be considered as the "normal" set for a given species and a given stage of development. "Normal" is defined in relation to the overt motility of the undisturbed embryo. The normal movements, performed in the normal constant internal milieu, can then be taken as a baseline for experimental work, such as deafferentation or brain extirpation. In this context, the distinction between A and B is meaningful. However, from the strictly physiological viewpoint, the distinction loses its significance, because each milieu factor represents a continuum in which the normal range is a more or less arbitrarily defined stretch. I do not wish to elaborate on this matter, except to point out that we are referring here to a much-neglected area. Detailed physiological investigations of the conditions under which normal motility occurs, as well as experimental manipulation of the internal milieu beyond the normal range, including drug effects, would probably yield valuable information. After all, we have learned a great deal about normal development from exposure of embryos to abnormal agents.

Stimulated Motility (Category C)

Stimulated motility is a unique and well-defined category, clearly distinct from categories A and B; it requires no special credentials. Since the sensory aspects of embryonic behavior have been handled expertly by Dr. Gottlieb (p. 67), I can be very brief and limit myself to a few aspects which have direct relevance to previously discussed topics.

There are several ways by which sensory input might conceivably influence embryonic motility: (1) as a patterning or structuring device. (2) it might have a "tonic" effect (on the physiological level); (3) it might have a "facilitating" effect (on the behavioral level); (4) it might trigger or "release" activity. All these types of influence have been identified in postnatal behavior.

Sources of stimulation can be provided (a) by the external environment of the embryo or (b) by stimuli emanating from the embryo itself, such as proprioceptive feedback, or tactile stimulation by its own movements, or its own vocalization. This latter category b is referred to as "self-stimulation."

Finally, we shall come back to the crucial question, raised above (p. 51): What is the role of sensory input in the normal process of behavior development in which the investigator does not interfere? To what extent does sensory input enter the picture as an actual cause of overt motility? Obviously, the environment of the embryo in the egg or uterus is much poorer in potential sources of information than the postnatal environment; but it could undoubtedly provide a limited number of stimuli. And the opportunity for self-stimulation is always present. Yet it seems that at least the chick embryo does not avail itself of any stimulation that might be accessible to it. Our experiments have shown that neither the absence of exteroceptive nor of proprioceptive stimulation, nor the prevention of self-stimulation, has an appreciable effect on the motility of the embryo up to 17 days. Amniotic contractions have been shown by Oppenheim (1966) to be ineffective in stimulating activity (it is of interest to note that the amnion in the turtle and the rat does not perform spontaneous contractions). Uterine contractions in the rat are equally ineffective (Narayanan *et al.*, 1971). This would imply that the many stimulation experiments that have been performed are not relevant to the actual performance of the embryo, although they may reveal a great deal concerning the response patterns and their gradual development. I should stress again that these remarks concern only type I motility up to 17 days of incubation. Around that time, behavior development makes a significant step forward. Preparations for hatching begin, and some of the higher sensory capacities such as vision develop to functional maturity. It is probably during this period that the sensory apparatus comes into its own as the guide for behavior performance (see Gottlieb, 1968).

It is obvious that one cannot generalize from our present limited set of data. However, the claims of those who attribute to sensory input a major role in embryonic behavior development have not been substantiated.

Concluding Remarks on Theory

If one accepts the premise that a theory of behavior development should be built preferably on physiological grounds rather than on the phenomenology of movements, then the three categories of motility, as defined above (p. 54), present themselves as the basic building blocks for a comprehensive theory. Because we know very little concerning category B, we shall deal only with A and C, in which the independent identities have been established. The question to be raised next concerns their relations to each other.

In all embryos, spontaneous and stimulated activity overlap over considerable periods. Both types emanate from a common substrate, the nervous system. The capacity for spontaneous electrical discharges seems to be a very elementary property of all or part of the embryonic and fetal nerve tissue. It finds an outlet either in uncoordinated total or "mass" movements or in coordinated behavior patterns. The former are apparently the result of massive discharges sweeping through the system, in the absence of inhibition, while in the latter case well-defined pathways are triggered. The stimulated motility is more specialized, based on specific receptors and sensory–motor connections. The response can be a poorly structured mass reaction in early embryos; but with increasing developmental progress, it becomes a neurally integrated, adaptive and coordinated response pattern. All embryos seem to share in all these forms of motility at one stage or another. I see no particular difficulty in visualizing that the same neural structures are activated at one time by self-generated discharges and at another time by sensory stimuli, or by changes in the humoral or gaseous internal milieu.

Finally, we raise the theoretically important question: What are the relations of categories A and C in the normal process of behavior development in vertebrate embryos? We have tried to build up a case for the importance and ubiquity of spontaneous motility (category A), whereas we have found no evidence that sensory stimulation plays a significant role in this process. Therefore, I suggest that any future theory of behavior development give serious consideration to the idea that *spontaneous activity takes precedence over stimulated activity in embryonic behavior development*. My arguments in favor of this notion can be summarized briefly:

1. The motor system differentiates in advance of the sensory system.
2. As a consequence, many embryos perform movements before they become sensitive to stimulation.
3. No influence of sensory input on embryonic motility could be detected in a well-analyzed test case, the chick embryo, at least up to 17 days of incubation.
4. All embryos perform spontaneous movements from the very onset of motility, but only mammalian embryos are sensitive to stimulation from the onset.
5. The capacity for autonomous electrical discharges which we assume underlies all spontaneous motility seems to be an elementary, primitive property of most or all nerve tissue.

In short, I believe that activity is the most elementary and basic characteristic of embryos: they are active before they become reactive. This position is the antithesis of the viewpoint expressed by Hooker at the end of his book (1952, p. 120): "Evidence so far gathered seems to indicate that the behavior of vertebrate animals, including man, has its genesis in the early exteroceptive responses exhibited during embryonic, larval, or fetal life." The primacy of action over response in animal behavior, in general, has been advocated by many, including Coghill (see quotation, p. 60). I now propose to apply this principle to the vertebrate embryo.

ACKNOWLEDGMENT

The work done in this laboratory was supported by Grant No. 5 RO1 NS 05721 from USPHS, National Institute of Neurological Diseases and Blindness.

REFERENCES

Angulo y Gonzalez, A. W. (1932). The prenatal development of behavior in the albino rat. *J. Comp. Neurol.* Vol. 55, 395–442.
Anokhin, P. K. (1964). Systemogenesis as a general regulator of brain development. *Progr. Brain Res.* Vol. 9, 54–86.
Bodian, D. (1966). Development of fine structure of spinal cord in monkey fetuses. I. The motoneuron neuropil at the time of onset of reflex activity. *Bull. Johns Hopkins Hosp.* Vol. 119, 129–149.
Bodian, D., Melby, E. C., and Taylor, N. (1968). Development of fine structure of spinal cord in monkey fetuses. II. Pre-reflex period to period of long intersegmental reflexes. *J. Comp. Neurol.* Vol. 133, 113–166.
Coghill, E. G. (1929). "Anatomy and the Problem of Behavior." Cambridge Univ. Press, London and New York.
Crain, S. M. (1966). Development of organotypic bioelectrical activities in central nervous tissues during maturation in cultures. *Int. Rev. Neurobiol.* Vol. 9, 1–43.
Decker, J. D. (1967). Motility of the turtle embryo. Chelydra serpentina (Linné). *Science* Vol. 157, 952–954.
Decker, J. D. (1970). The influence of early extirpation of the otocysts on the development of behavior in the chick. *J. Exp. Zool.* Vol. 174, 349–364.
Drachman, D. B., and Sokoloff, L. (1966). The role of movement in embryonic joint development. *Develop. Biol.* Vol. 14, 401–420.
Fujita, S. (1964). Analysis of neuron differentiation in the central nervous system by tritiated thymidine autoradiography. *J. Comp. Neurol.* Vol. 122, 311–328.
Gaze, R. M. (1970). "The Formation of Nerve Connections." Academic Press, London and New York.
Gottlieb, G. (1968). Prenatal behavior of birds. *Quart. Rev. Biol.* Vol. 43, 148–174.
Hamburger, V. (1948). The mitotic patterns in the spinal cord of the chick embryo and their relation to histogenetic processes. *J. Comp. Neurol.* Vol. 88, 221–284.
Hamburger, V. (1963). Some aspects of the embryology of behavior. *Quart. Rev. Biol.* Vol. 38, 342–365.
Hamburger, V. (1968). Emergence of nervous coordination. Origins of integrated behavior. *Symp. Soc. Develop. Biol.* Vol. 27, Suppl. 2, 251–271.
Hamburger, V., and Narayanan, C. H. (1969). Effects of the deafferentation of the trigeminal area on the motility of the chick embryo. *J. Exp. Zool.* Vol. 170, 411–426.
Hamburger, V., and Oppenheim, R. (1967). Prehatching motility and hatching behavior in the chick. *J. Exp. Zool.* Vol. 166, 171–204.
Hamburger, V., and Waugh, M. (1940). The primary development of the skeleton in nerveless and poorly innervated limb transplants of chick embryos. *Physiol. Zool.* Vol. 13, 367–380.
Hamburger, V., Balaban, M., Oppenheim, R., and Wenger, E. (1965). Periodic motility of normal and spinal chick embryos between 8 and 17 days of incubation. *J. Exp. Zool.* Vol. 159, 1–14.
Hamburger, V., Wenger, E., and Oppenheim, R. (1966). Motility in the chick embryo in the absence of sensory input. *J. Exp. Zool.* Vol. 162, 171–204.
Helfenstein, M., and Narayanan, C. H. (1969). Effects of bilateral limb-bud extirpation on motility and prehatching behavior in chicks. *J. Exp. Zool.* Vol. 172, 233–244.
Herrick, C. J. (1949). "George Ellett Coghill, Naturalist and Philosopher." Univ. of Chicago Press, Chicago, Illinois.
Hooker, D. (1952). "The Prenatal Origin of Behavior." Univ. of Kansas Press, Lawrence, Kansas.

Hughes, A., Bryant, S., and Bellairs, A. (1967). Embryonic behaviour in the lizard, Lacerta vivipara. *J. Zool.* Vol. 153, 139–152.

Humphrey, T. (1954). The trigeminal nerve in relation to early human fetal activity. *Res. Publ., Ass. Res. Nerv. Ment. Dis.* Vol. 33, 127–154.

Humphrey, T. (1964). Some correlations between the appearance of human fetal reflexes and the development of the nervous system. *Progr. Brain Res.* Vol. 4, 93–135.

Jacobson, M. (1970). "Developmental Neurobiology." Holt, Rinehart and Winston, New York.

Narayanan, C. H., Fox, M. W., and Hamburger, V. (1971). Prenatal development of spontaneous and evoked activity in the rat. *Behavior*, in press.

Oppenheim, R. (1966). Amniotic contraction and embryonic motility in the chick embryo. *Science* Vol. 152, 528–529.

Preyer, W. (1882). "Die Seele des Kindes." Grieben, Leipzig.

Preyer, W. (1885). "Specielle Physiologie des Embryo." Grieben, Leipzig.

Provine, R. R., Sharma, S. C., Sandel, T. T., and Hamburger, V. (1970). Electrical activity in the spinal cord of chick embryos *in situ. Proc. Nat. Acad. Sci. U. S.* Vol. 65, 508–515.

Sharma, S. C., Provine, R. R., Hamburger, V., and Sandel, T. T. (1970). Unit activity in the isolated spinal cord of chick embryo *in situ. Proc. Nat. Acad. Sci. U. S.* Vol. 66, 40–47.

Sperry, R. W. (1951). Mechanisms of neural maturation. *In* "Handbook of Experimental Psychology" (S. S. Stevens, ed.), pp. 263–280. Wiley, New York.

Sperry, R. W. (1965). Embryogenesis of behavioral nerve nets. *In* "Organogenesis" (R. L. DeHaan and H. Ursprung, eds.), pp. 161–186. Holt, New York.

Székely, G. (1966). Embryonic determination of neural connections. *Adv. Morphogen.* Vol. 5, 181–219.

Tracy, H. C. (1926). The development of motility and behavior reactions in the toadfish (Opsanus tau). *J. Comp. Neurol.* Vol. 40, 253–369.

Weiss, P. (1941). Self-differentiation of the basic patterns of coordination. *Comp. Psychol. Monogr.* Vol. 17, 1–96.

Weiss, P. (1955). Nervous system. *In* "Analysis of Development" (B. H. Willier, P. Weiss, and V. Hamburger, eds.), pp. 346–401. W. B. Saunders Co., Philadelphia.

Windle, W. F., and Baxter, R. E. (1936). Development of reflex mechanism in the spinal cord of albino rat embryos. Correlations between structure and function, and comparisons with the cat and the chick. *J. Comp. Neurol.* Vol. 63, 189–204.

Discussion

S. M. Crain: The patterns of spontaneous motility which have been observed in embryos may not be a significant indicator of the behavioral repertoire which has actually developed since important components may remain "latent," under "normal" environmental conditions, due to the presence of inhibitory synaptic circuits. During growth of a chick embryo in a tightly packed shell, *active inhibition* of motor activity may be a more pertinent manifestation of behavioral development than the occurrence of spontaneous motility. Appearance of random, uncoordinated type I movements in the early chick embryo does not necessarily contradict Coghill's concept (1928) that "behavior develops from the beginning through the progressive expansion of a perfectly integrated total pattern. . . ." Demonstration of an orderly development of patterned inhibition of motor activity, which may become much more dominant in embryos of higher vertebrates, might reconcile the apparent dichotomy emphasized by Dr. Hamburger, between principles of behavior development in the amphibian versus the chick embryo. Support for this view will require systematic electrophysiological studies of the entire central nervous system during embryological development using selective pharmacological agents, in conjunction with electric stimuli, to clarify the complex inhibitory systems which probably play an important role in determining the behavior of the embryo from the earliest stages of synaptic network formation (Purpura, 1969; Crain, 1969; Crain and Peterson, 1967), but which may involve drastically different patterns, depending upon the specific survival requirements of each species [as emphasized in Anokhin's concept (1964) of "systemogenesis"].

Furthermore, in view of Dr. Hamburger's strong emphasis on the primacy of *spontaneous* motor activity in the development of embryonic behavior, it would be of interest to clarify the functional significance of this activity. Is it involved mainly in maintenance of joints and muscles (Hamburger, 1968) or does it also play a role in the development of patterned synaptic systems underlying behavior? This could be analyzed by a selective block of *all* spontaneous discharges during chronic exposure of the early embryo to selective pharmacological agents, as we have done in our tissue-culture model system [during the development *in vitro* of synaptic networks in embryonic brain and spinal cord explants (Crain *et al.*, 1968)]. Would the organized central nervous bioelectric activities associated with integrated type III patterns of hatching behavior still occur after removal of the blocking drug at 17 days *in ovo*, just as relatively normal swimming behavior appeared within minutes after removal of chronic anaesthetics in the classic studies with developing amphibian larvae (Harrison, 1904; Carmichael, 1926; Matthew and Detwiler, 1926)? Or would some types of functional deficits be detected by careful analysis, as suggested by Dr. Gottlieb (see his chapter)?

REFERENCES

Anokhin, P. K. (1964). Systemogenesis as a general regulator of brain development. *Progr. Brain Res.* Vol. 9, 54–86.

Carmichael, L. (1926). The development of behavior in vertebrates experimentally removed from the influence of external stimulation. *Psychol. Rev.* Vol. 33, 51–58.

Coghill, E. G. (1929). "Anatomy and the Problem of Behavior." Cambridge Univ. Press, London and New York.

Crain, S. M. (1969). Electrical activity of brain tissue developing in culture. *In* "Basic Mechanisms of the Epilepsies" (H. H. Jasper, A. A. Ward, and A. Pope, eds.), pp. 506–516. Little, Brown, Boston, Massachusetts.

Crain, S. M., and Peterson, E. R. (1967). Onset and development of functional interneuronal connections in explants of rat spinal cord-ganglia during maturation in culture. *Brain Res.* Vol. 6, 750–762.

Crain, S. M., Bornstein, M. B., and Peterson, E. R. (1968). Maturation of cultured embryonic CNS tissues during chronic exposure to agents which prevent bioelectric activity. *Brain Res.* Vol. 8, 363–372.

Hamburger, V. (1968). Emergence of nervous coordination. Origins of integrated behavior. *Devel. Biol. Suppl.* Vol. 2, 251–271.

Harrison, R. G. (1904). An experimental study of the relation of the nervous system to the developing musculature in the embryo of the frog. *Amer. J. Anat.* Vol. 3, 197–219.

Matthew, S. A., and Detwiler, S. R. (1926). The reaction of Amblystoma embryos following prolonged treatment with chloretone. *J. Exp. Zool.* Vol. 45, 279–292.

Purpura, D. P. (1969). Factors in stability and seizure susceptibility of immature brain. *In* "Basic Mechanisms of the Epilepsies" (H. H. Jasper, A. A. Ward, and A. Pope, eds.), pp. 481–505. Little, Brown, Boston, Massachusetts.

ONTOGENESIS OF SENSORY FUNCTION IN BIRDS AND MAMMALS

GILBERT GOTTLIEB

Introduction

By synthesizing the research results of many different laboratories representing various disciplines, it has been possible to derive the probable sequence in which the sensory systems develop in certain vertebrate species. The sequence in which the sensory systems become functional is important for comparative and evolutionary purposes, and it also provides a testing ground for our most basic conceptions of the epigenesis of behavior. In this paper the sequence of sensory development will be portrayed in birds and mammals, and the ontogenetic and phylogenetic significance of this sequence will be discussed with special reference to current conceptions of the development of the nervous system and behavior.

Whereas my last review on this topic was restricted to birds (Gottlieb, 1968), in the present essay the literature coverage is extended to a number of disparate mammalian forms. The present review is intended to supplement the recent reviews of this subject by Volokhov (1968) and Scherrer (1968). Volokhov has summarized a number of important behavioral studies, conducted in Russia by himself and his collaborators, on various mammals—principally rabbits, dogs, cats, and rats—and the sequence of sensory development, whether it is based on rudimentary behavior or more complicated perceptual and learning performances, is in complete agreement with the present sequence derived from a more extensive analysis of the literature. Scherrer's review is confined to the cortical electrophysiology of the somesthetic, auditory, and visual systems in neonatal cats and rabbits, and it, too, is in agreement with the present picture.

The mammals covered in the present survey are opossums, rats, house mice, deermice, rabbits, cats, man, guinea pigs, and sheep. These nine forms vary greatly in degree of precocity at birth, ranging from the fetus-like newborn opossum to the highly mobile and almost self-sufficient guinea pig and sheep. The choice of these particular mammalian forms was dictated by comparative requirements as well as the information available on them relative to other forms. However, a few species were included in which the picture is incomplete, and they may possibly represent exceptions to the recurrence of the sequence of sensory development evident in other species. For the present purpose it happens to be useful that marsupials (opossum), rodents (rat, mouse, guinea pig), lagomorphs (rabbit), carnivores (cat), artiodactyls (sheep), and primates (man) each represent evolutionary lines which have been independent of each other for at least the last 70 million years or so (Hodos and Campbell, 1969).

To the extent that the sequence of sensory development in mammalian forms coincides with the sequence found in birds, the temporal order of sensory development would transcend particular divergent evolutionary pathways and the varying social and ecological factors which are peculiar to each species. Since birds and mammals have evolved along entirely separate courses from their reptilian ancestors, one would suppose the sequential order of sensory development in certain reptiles to conform to that of birds and mammals, to the extent that the latter two groups show a similar pattern of development in the systems under review. Since the foregoing statements may seem a bit presumptuous, it would be well to point out that we already know certain neurological processes do show a great degree of similarity in the order in which they develop, in disparate groups of mammals at least. For example, Langworthy's study (1933) of the sequence of myelinization in opossums, cats, and man led him to conclude that there is a definite ontogenetic march of myelinization in opossums, cats, and man that holds true for all three species. The present purpose is to determine whether such an analogous regularity holds for the much broader question of the functional development of certain sensory systems in birds and mammals and, if so, to discuss the phylogenetic significance of such a regularity and, finally, to describe the various theoretical explanations which can be put forth to account for it on an ontogenetic basis. Accordingly, in the first part of the paper data on the sequential development of the mammalian sensory systems are reviewed, and in the final sections of the chapter the phylogenetic and ontogenetic issues are discussed.

Sequential Development of the Sensory Systems

While the significance of sensory function must or should ultimately be tied to behavior, electrophysiological and histological research have much to offer in reconstructing the probable sequence of sensory development. Figure 1 shows the temporal order of development in four afferent systems based on the electrophysiological, histological, and behavioral evidence available from work on bird embryos (primarily the chick embryo). If the sequence evident in the avian embryo (tactile–vestibular–auditory–visual) also holds for mammalian forms, it may not be erroneous to think of it as a rather general pattern among vertebrates. The temporal relationship between the vestibular and proprioceptive systems represents the most problematical reconstruction, so proprioception has been omitted from the present review. Very little developmental work has been done on proprioception, and these two systems are more difficult to assess than the somesthetic, auditory, and visual systems. Gustation and olfaction are not dealt with at all, and the unconventional sensitivities demonstrated in the chick embryo [nonvisual photic sensitivity (Bursian, 1965) and nonauditory acoustic sensitivity (Sviderskaya, 1967)] are also omitted from the present review.

The avian data upon which Fig. 1 rests have been presented fully

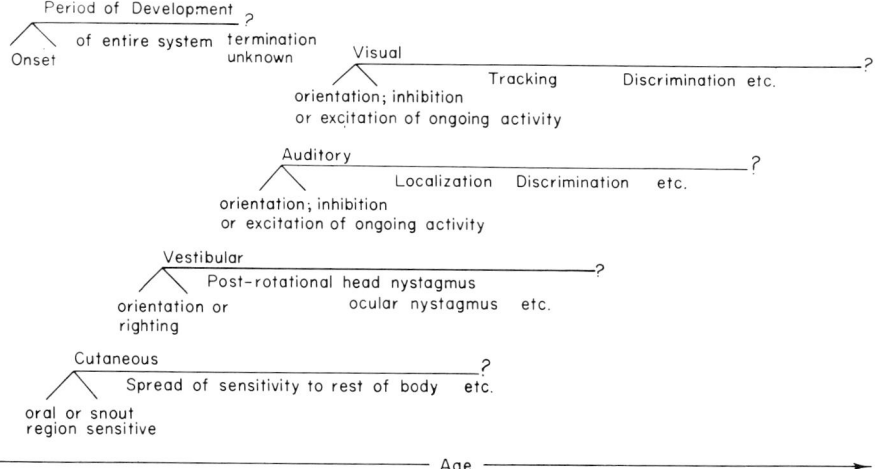

FIG. 1. The ontogenetic sequence of development of four sensory systems derived from research on the chick embryo (Gottlieb, 1968). Reading from left to right, the chart indicates some of the behavioral phenomena which would be present as each system becomes functional in mammalian species. The initial behavioral response in each modality is usually a species-characteristic change in bodily orientation or attitude, or a cessation or increase in ongoing activity, immediately following stimulation. Other kinds of behavior appear later in the development of each system. (The "discrimination" behavior mentioned in the auditory and visual spheres refers to the young animal's ability to form conditioned responses based on reward or punishment. In light of current evidence, this kind of ability appears to develop some time after the onset of a system.)

elsewhere (Gottlieb, 1968), so they will not be recapitulated here. With the exception of work on the onset of tactile sensitivity in mammals, very little comprehensive behavioral research has been conducted on the question of onset of function in the various sensory systems. Much of the evidence for functional differences comes from electrophysiological and histological studies. In attempting to assign functional priority to one sensory system over another on the basis of electrophysiological and histological data, it is important to consider the status of the systems at the presumed onset of function and the age at which the systems reach complete or adult stature (rate of development after onset of function). In the kitten, for example, evoked cortical responses to certain auditory and visual stimuli (clicks and bright flashes of light) are first recorded at about the same age (day 5 postnatally). In terms of latency and waveform, however, the aurally evoked response is more mature at the outset and it matures more rapidly than the visually evoked response (Ellingson and Wilcott, 1960). It is highly probable that microelectrode recordings from the auditory nerve or cochlear potentials would reveal an earlier onset of auditory sensitivity than evoked cortical responses. Generally speaking, the peripheral ganglia and nerves mature earlier than the centers inside of the nervous system, and these in turn mature before the higher levels of the brain such as the cortex. Consequently, comparisons of the onset of the sensory systems, in order to be really valid, must be based on approximately the same functional level of the nervous system.

Although it is difficult with the behavioral findings to be certain that one is always dealing with approximately the same functional central neural level, wherever possible this approach has been maintained in the present work. The problem is very much simplified in the case of neurophysiological recordings or histological information where, for example, auditory receptor can be compared to visual receptor, auditory electrocortical response to visual electrocortical response, etc. In the latter instance, however, there is the problem of comparing the effects and significance of such totally artificial stimuli as clicks and bright flashes of light. When tones are used instead of clicks, for example, the onset of the aurally evoked cortical response occurs on day 2 in kittens (Pujol and Marty, 1968). While these and other methodological problems will not be discussed in detail here, the reader should be alerted to the highly tentative character of the day of onset given for a sensory system when it is derived solely from physiological and histological evidence. At the moment, getting a picture of the correctness of the *sequence* in which the sensory systems develop is more important than the specific day of onset of each system.

Finally, the fact that few investigators have examined the onset of sensory function in more than one or two modalities in a given species means that, in most instances, it has been necessary to utilize Investigator A's information for the onset of one system and Investigator B's information for the onset of another system in the same species. In the case of species in which, for example, two systems appear to develop within 1 or 2 days of each other, there is the distinct possibility that the picture has been clouded by the fact that we do not have information on the sequential development of the two systems in the same animals. The ideal way to study the sequence of sensory development, one which takes into account individual variability, is to study the sequence in the same individual. This information would be extremely valuable, but no studies of the sequence of sensory development have been conducted in that fashion.[1]

OPOSSUM

Of all the animals treated here, the opossum (*Didelphys virginiana*) is clearly the most immature at birth (Fig. 2). It has a fetal appearance when it emerges from the birth canal after 12 to 13 days of gestation and makes its short journey to the maternal pouch. It remains in the pouch for the next 70 days or so with the maternal teat well down its throat for the majority of this period. Indeed, Langworthy (1933) notes that it is extremely difficult to disengage the very young opossum from the teat without doing damage to its mouth.

From Hartman's observations (1920) of parturition in opossums, it is possible to conclude that tactile sensitivity is present in the foremost part of the body at birth. The alternate grasping reactions of each of the forelimbs propel the neonate to the pouch, and the continuous side-to-side movements of the neonate's head facilitate localization of the teat inside the pouch. Hartman writes (1920, p. 256): "With each turn of the head the snout is touched to the mother's skin as if to test it out, and

---

[1] Before turning to the review, I would like to remark on one of the more obvious problems in evaluating research which derives from many disciplines. Namely, besides the fact the reviewer is not an expert in all the areas under consideration, standards of evidence are different for various disciplines, and such standards change within a discipline over the course of years. I think it is reasonable to say, however, that at the very least, a review like this one can give us an impression of whether or not the sequence for birds is valid for mammals. If the vast majority of the work, good and dubious, leads to the same conclusion, it seems to me that is significant and worthy of some credence. By way of reaching a compromise between a tedious critique and a complete suspension of criticism, I have cited procedural failings only when they could substantially alter the conclusions or results of certain studies.

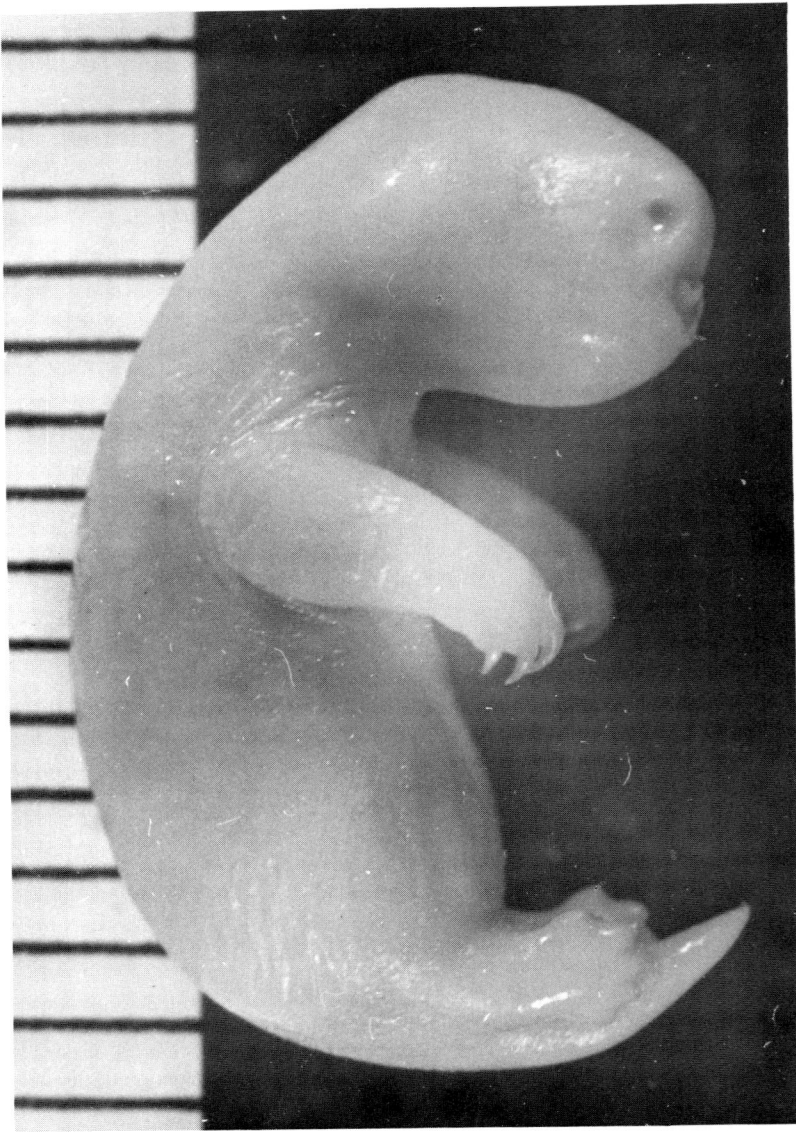

FIG. 2. Newborn opossum (*Didelphys virginiana*). Opossums are very small and have a fetal appearance at birth. Note the absence of eyes and ears. The barely developed pit in the nasal area is the early stage of the right nostril. In contrast to the eyes, ears, and nose, the oral orifice is relatively well developed, as are the front limbs in comparison to the hind limbs. The scale at left is in 1-mm divisions. (Right lateral view of specimen No. 68406 from the Laboratory of Comparative Neurology, Michigan State University. Reproduced with the kind permission of J. I. Johnson, Jr.)

if the teat is touched, the embryo stops and at once takes hold." Based on Hartman's incidental observations, olfaction or gustation would not seem to be involved in the localization of the teat by the newborn. First, by tilting the mother, the opossum can be made to crawl away from the pouch and, second, almost any protuberance on the skin may be seized orally in the same way the teat is taken. The fact that newborn opossums crawl upward (against gravity) upon birth, as well as their response to a tilted surface, would seem to indicate that they are negatively geotropic and that the vestibular system is functional at birth. In the absence of systematic observations on this question, however, the more usual evidence for vestibular function (below) will have to be accepted at the moment.

It is not known if cutaneous sensitivity is present in the opossum before birth, but it would seem highly likely that the snout and the forelimbs would be sensitive to such stimulation prenatally. In 7-day-old pouch young, Langworthy (1928) observed definite responses to tactile stimulation over the whole body, with the oral (trigeminal) region being especially sensitive. At this time the eyes are not open, there is no response to sound, and, as far as could be determined, the vestibular system is not yet functional. Langworthy (1928, p. 214) found that the righting reflex begins to develop around 41 days: "When made to stand upon its legs the young animal could balance and take two or three steps. . . ." In substantial agreement, Larsell et al. (1935) observed the onset of the righting reflex at about 43 days. These same authors observed the onset of "startle responses" to sound (definite spasmodic contraction of trunk musculature) in 50-day-old specimens. The correlative neuroanatomy for vestibular and auditory function has been well worked out by Langworthy (1928) and Larsell et al. (1935, 1944). From the work of these investigators and Schmidt and Fernandez (1963), it is known that the auditory mechanism is complete structurally and functionally by 77 to 80 days.

There is no firm evidence on the onset of visual sensitivity in the opossum. Langworthy (1928, pp. 226–227) observed that the eyes first open around 62 days and that the animal is easily detached from the nipple at that time. In connection with the onset of visual sensitivity, it is perhaps relevant to note that opossums do not leave the pouch until about 70 days (Reynolds, 1954). However, Tansley (1933, p. 89) observed that the retina of marsupial eyes is well developed before the eyes are opened. Unfortunately, she does not mention which one of the many marsupial species she studied. While the external auditory canal opens around day 48–50, and overt startle responses to certain sounds occur on day 50, the opossum's eyelids do not separate until about day 62. Therefore, it seems reasonable to tentatively conclude that auditory

TABLE 1
Ontogenetic Sequence of Sensory Function in the American Opossum

Gestation period (approximate)	Neonate's condition at birth	Approximate day of onset of function and type of evidence			
		Tactile	Vestibular	Auditory	Visual
12.5 days	Extremely altricial (fetus-like)	Postnatal day 1 or earlier Behavior: Hartman, 1920 Postnatal day 7 or earlier Behavior: Langworthy, 1928	Postnatal day 41–43 or earlier Behavior: Langworthy, 1928; Larsell et al., 1935 Histology: Langworthy, 1928; Larsell et al., 1935	Postnatal day 50 Behavior: Larsell et al., 1935 Histology: Larsell et al., 1944	Postnatal day 62 or earlier Behavior: Langworthy, 1928 (incidental observation only) Histology: Langworthy, 1928

development is somewhat in advance of visual development in the opossum. Obviously, an ontogenetic behavioral study is required to document this conclusion.

While the earliest onset of tactile, vestibular (negative geotropism?), and visual sensitivity is not known in the American opossum, the available evidence (summarized in Table 1) indicates that the sequence of sensory development is tactile–vestibular–auditory–visual.

Because of its very immature state at the time of birth, the opossum, like other marsupials, makes an excellent mammalian subject for behavioral embryology. Further recommendations are that these animals readily breed in captivity if given the proper space and materials (Reynolds, 1954), and they appear to show the more general brain–behavior relationships characteristic of other mammals (W. W. Roberts et al., 1967).

DOMESTIC RAT

According to Angulo y González (1932), tactile sensitivity is first overtly manifested by the albino rat fetus on day 15–17. Lane (1917) found the first behavioral evidence of vestibular sensitivity (righting reflex) in a roughly 21-day-old rat fetus. (Lane's procedure for studying the prenatal behavior of rat fetuses is definitely unsatisfactory—he killed the pregnant mother-to-be and excised the fetuses for study in a warm air chamber—so it is entirely possible that vestibular function develops earlier than day 21.) According to Lane's histological study, structural development of the semicircular canals is almost complete, sensory and supporting cells are clearly differentiated, and neural connections can be traced to the medulla and cerebellum at this age. According to Wada (1923), the nerve cells of the vestibular ganglion are very highly developed in the newborn rat (day 22), both in terms of size and histological structure.

Domestic rats are born around 21.5 days, and audition and vision become functional after birth (Fig. 3). Volokhov (1968) reports the presence of a "primitive orienting reflex" to auditory stimulation as early as day 5, while the more mature "orienting-exploring reflex" is not evident until day 10–12. Wada (1923) reports the first Preyer reflex (characteristic twitching movement of the pinnae of the ears in response to sound) on day 9, while Crowley and Hepp-Reymond (1966) record the first cochlear potentials in response to pure tones on day 8. Wada (1923) found that the tectorial membrane had reached the outermost row of the outer hair cells and that the tunnel of Corti was open in all its turns only in the one rat of a litter which responded to sound on day 9. The

76   G. GOTTLIEB

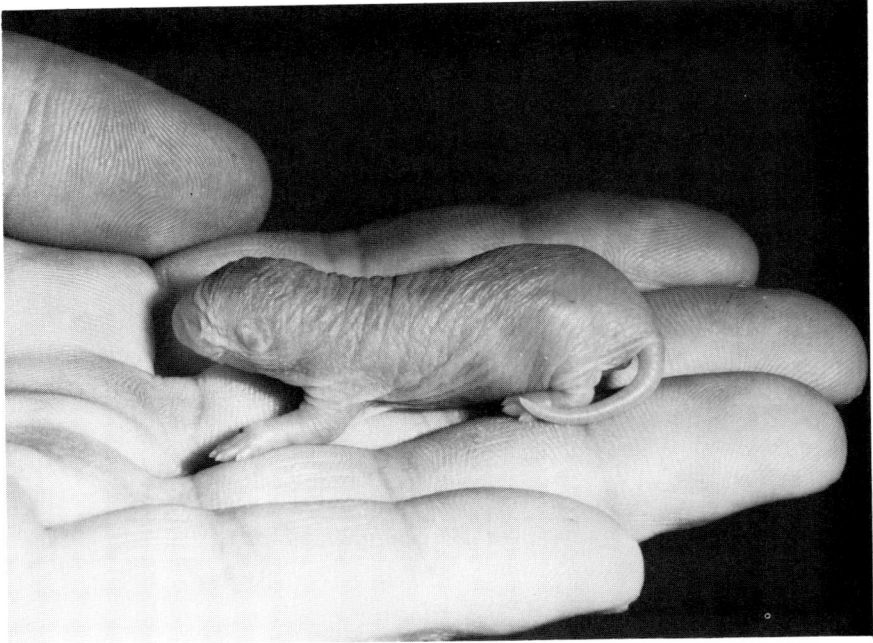

FIG. 3. Newborn rat (black-hooded strain). All domestic rats look essentially alike after birth. This rat was 7 hours old when the picture was taken. (Photograph by Rainer Foelix.)

ears of this rat's nonresponding littermates had not achieved this state of anatomical development, and Wada notes that it is more usual to obtain the first overt auditory response on day 10.

It is important to note that in white rats the external auditory meatus does not open until around day 12–13 after birth. While auditory sensitivity is evident before the external auditory canal opens, it also happens that visual sensitivity develops before the eyes are open (the neonate's eyelids are very thin). Crozier and Pincus (1937) observed an ill-coordinated negative phototropism as early as day $8\frac{1}{2}$ in a "dark-eyed, black-hooded" strain of domestic rat. Since the eyes of these particular rats do not open until day 14—albino rats' eyes open on day 15–17—the behavior observed by Crozier and Pincus presumably represents brightness discrimination. Crozier and Pincus used an uninsulated 200-foot-candle light which radiates considerable heat. In a belated defense of this procedure, they point out that young rats typically move toward a heat source but away from a source of bright light. In his experimental histological studies of the neonate rat visual system,

TABLE 2
Ontogenetic Sequence of Sensory Function in the Domestic Rat

Gestation period (approximate)	Neonate's condition at birth	Approximate day of onset of function and type of evidence			
		Tactile	Vestibular	Auditory	Visual
21.5 days	Altricial	Prenatal day 15–17 Behavior: Angulo y González, 1932 Histology: Lane, 1917	Prenatal day 21 (?) Behavior: Lane, 1917 Histology: Lane, 1917; Wada, 1923	Postnatal day 5 Behavior: Volokhov, 1968 Postnatal day 9–10 Behavior: Wada, 1923 Histology: Wada, 1923 Postnatal day 8–9 Physiology: Crowley and Hepp-Reymond, 1966	Postnatal day 8.5–9 Behavior: Crozier and Pincus, 1937; Detwiler, 1932 Postnatal day 10 Physiology: Rose, 1968 Postnatal day 10–12 Histology: Crozier and Pincus, 1937; Detwiler, 1932

Detwiler (1932, p. 490) incidentally observed what he described as a definite avoiding reaction to light as early as day 8. By day 8 the rat retina is completely developed with the exception of the rods, which are still quite small (Detwiler, 1932; Tansley, 1933). While domestic rats appear to be behaviorally responsive to light on day 8, the earliest electrophysiological and histological evidence for visual function is obtained on day 10–12 at the receptor as well as the cortex (Crozier and Pincus, 1937; Detwiler, 1932; Rose, 1968). Thus, the question remains whether the behavioral response on day 8 is visually mediated or not. If so, the discrepancy between the physiological data and the behavioral data probably is attributable to limitations of technique in the former. For example, while Detwiler could not find any visual purple in the rat retina earlier than day 11, based on his behavioral observations (and those of others), he believed it to be present in dilute amounts as early as day 8. Though this is a rather unsatisfactory way of resolving the discrepancy, the matter must rest here.

While there is definitely an overlap in the development of auditory and visual sensitivity in domestic rats, the first overt response to sound occurs on day 5 and the first overt response to light occurs on day 8, so domestic rats adhere to the sequence of sensory development evident in the chick embryo and the opossum (tactile–vestibular–auditory–visual). The available evidence for the onset of sensory function in domestic rats is summarized in Table 2.

HOUSE MOUSE

I have been unable to locate any studies which deal with the onset of tactile or vestibular function in house mice, and the functional priority of the auditory and visual systems is also in doubt. Domestic house mice (*Mus musculus*) are born after approximately 20.5 days of gestation (Fig. 4), and the first overt manifestations of auditory and visual sensitivity develop around 9 to 10 days after birth.

Using a microscope to observe the Preyer reflex in response to a handclap in awake neonates, Alford and Ruben (1963) found the earliest onset of auditory sensitivity to be on day 9. Alford and Ruben studied a number of different litters of the CBA-J strain of house mouse, and they noted a great deal of intra- and interlitter variability in the onset of the Preyer reflex. One litter did not show the Preyer reflex until day 14. The reflex was not found in two animals at 13 days of age. All animals evinced the Preyer reflex by day 14. In terms of cochlear microphonic potentials, Alford and Ruben report that all of the animals which showed the reflex also manifested cochlear potentials. However, of

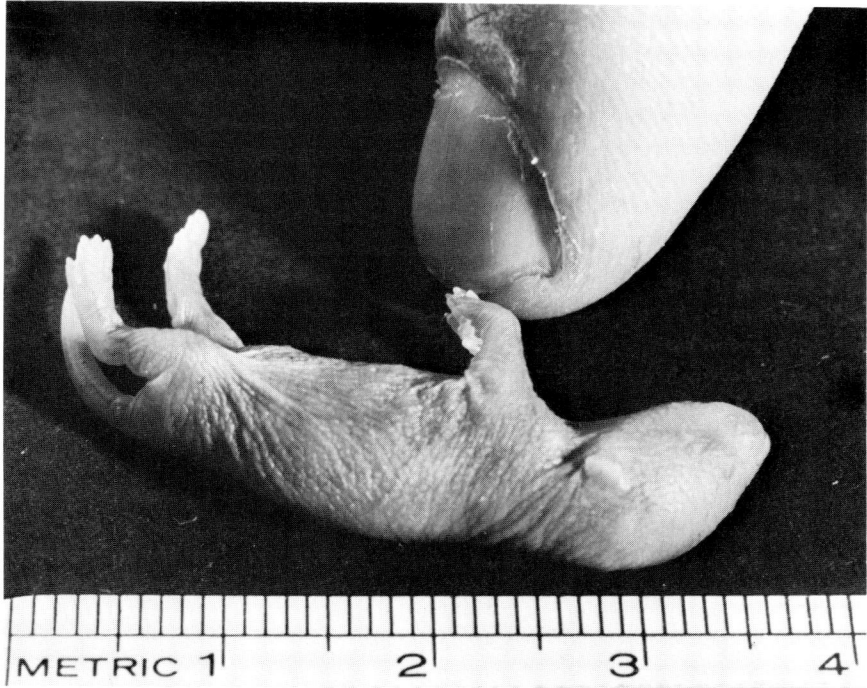

FIG. 4. Newborn house mouse (albino strain). All strains of house mice have much the same appearance after birth. This one was about 1 hour old at the time of the photograph. Note the similarity in size and appearance to the newborn deermouse (Fig. 5) and rat (Fig. 3). (Photograph by Rainer Foelix.)

14 neonates which did not show the reflex, five manifested cochlear potentials. The earliest cochlear potentials in response to a click occurred on day 9. It is of methodological interest to note that none of the neonates responded to the click with the Preyer reflex. That is, the behavioral reaction required a more intense (or a different) stimulus than did the physiological response. Alford and Ruben examined the organ of Corti in behaviorally responsive and unresponsive animals and could not find any gross differences in the organ which would account for the presence or absence of the Preyer reflex.

In a subsequent study by Mikaelian and Ruben (1965), involving seven litters of CBA-J mice, the Preyer reflex was present in some animals on day 9 and in all animals by day 10. In the latter study the investigators utilized more highly controlled auditory stimuli than in the first study. As documented by Änggard (1965) in his elegant study of cochlear function in rabbits, as well as by Pujol and Marty (1968) with cats, the use of certain kinds of stimuli may lead to an erroneous conclusion about the onset of auditory function. To be specific, mixed tones may elicit a response when clicks do not.

With respect to visual sensitivity, Crozier and Pincus (1937), using a heat-filtered light this time, found behavioral evidence (negative phototropism) for the onset of this modality on day 10. (They identify their strain only as "chocolate.") While Keeler *et al.* (1928) were unable to record evoked retinal potentials until day 13 or 14, more recently, Noell (1958) has recorded such potentials on day 11 in C57 black mice. The histological evidence from several strains of house mice (Noell, 1958) indicates that the house mouse retina is capable of some function around day 10.

On anatomical grounds, Gyllensten (1959) believes it is almost impossible for visual stimulation to be transmitted from the retina to the higher brain areas before day 15 in house mice. This particular issue could be clearly answered by recording evoked electrocortical responses at various ages in young house mice. Alternatively, it is possible that the negative phototropism is not mediated through the cortex or, less likely, that the phototropism is not visually mediated. [There is evidence for nonvisual photic sensitivity in birds (Gottlieb, 1968).] It will be recalled that in their experiment on mice Crozier and Pincus used a heat-shielded light source, so, in the present instance, the possibility of a response to heat alone (i.e., excessive heat) can probably be discounted.

While there is some overlap in the first overt signs of auditory and visual sensitivity in house mice, the first signs of function are reported for audition on day 9 and for vision on day 10. The auditory system can also be tentatively assigned temporal priority on the basis of the physiological and histological evidence. The auditory receptor (organ of Corti) apparently reaches its adult size and configuration by day 10 (Mikaelian and Ruben, 1965), whereas it is doubtful if the visual receptor (retina) even has its full complement of rods at that time (Keeler *et al.,* 1928, p. 812; Noell, 1958). Obviously, more study is required before the question of temporal priority of auditory and visual sensitivity in house mice can be answered satisfactorily.

There are numerous strains of house mice, and it is plausible that the day of onset of the various sensory functions might show strain-specific differences. On the basis of the information available on various species and subspecies of deermice (below), however, changes in day of onset do not necessarily result in a change in the sequence of sensory development within a strain or subspecies.

By way of concluding, as shown in Table 3, in house mice no data are available on the onset of tactile and vestibular sensitivity, and the

TABLE 3
Ontogenetic Sequence of Sensory Function in the House Mouse

Gestation period (approximate)	Neonate's condition at birth	Approximate day of onset of function and type of evidence			
		Tactile	Vestibular	Auditory	Visual
20.5 days	Altricial			Postnatal day 9–14 Behavior, Histology, and Physiology: Alford and Ruben, 1963 Postnatal day 9–10 Behavior, Histology, and Physiology: Mikaelian and Ruben, 1965	Postnatal day 10 Behavior: Crozier and Pincus, 1937 Postnatal day 10–11 Physiology and Histology: Noell, 1958 Postnatal day 13–14 Physiology: Keeler et al., 1928 Postnatal day 15 or later Histology: Evidence reviewed by Gyllensten, 1959

temporal priority of the auditory system over the visual system is tentative.

DEERMOUSE

A number of workers have been interested in the behavior and early postnatal development of deermice, and from the various studies reviewed by Layne (1968), it is possible to determine the sequence of vestibular, auditory, and visual function rather precisely in the genus *Peromyscus*. As shown in Table 4, six species and subspecies of *Peromyscus* deermice show a consistent pattern in the temporal relationship between the first appearance of the righting response, opening of the auditory canal, startle response to sound, opening of the eyes, and visually mediated optokinetic response. In all cases but one (*P. polionotus*), the sequence is clearly vestibular–auditory–visual. In the instance of *polionotus,* the possible exception is the relationship between the onset of auditory and visual sensitivity, where Layne (1968) notes the startle response occurring on day 11 and the eyes opening on day 13–14, while Vestal and King (1968) observe eye-opening and the optokinetic response on day 11. Unfortunately, Vestal and King did not record the day of ear-opening or the startle response in their population. It is known

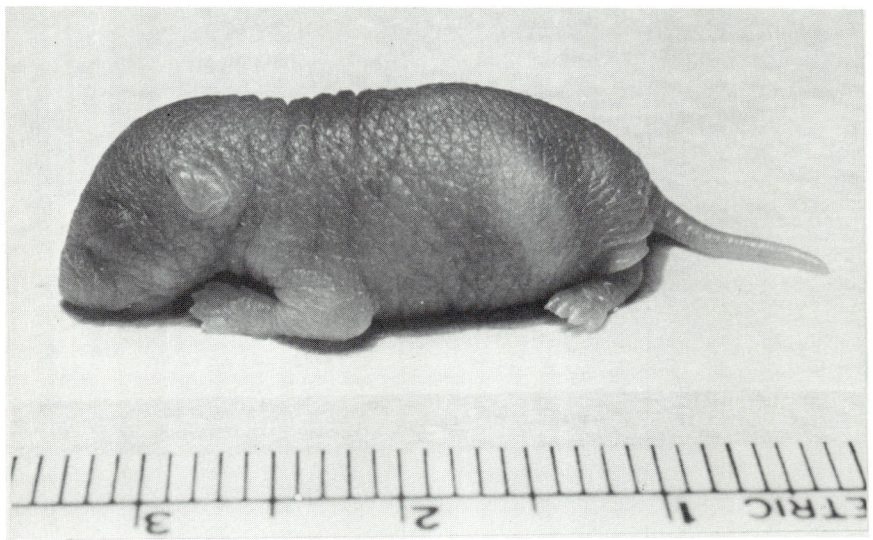

FIG. 5. Newborn deermouse (*Peromyscus maniculatus bairdi*). At birth, deermice bear a striking similarity to certain other altricial rodents such as house mice (Fig. 4) and domestic rats (Fig. 3). (Photograph by Kristi Dege and Paul Heron).

TABLE 4
Ontogenetic Sequence of Sensory Function in Deermice (*Peromyscus*)[a]

Species	Approximate postnatal day of onset of function				
	Righting response (vestibular)	External auditory canal open	Startle response (auditory)	Eyes open	Optokinetic response (visual)
P. floridanus	5	12	13	14–16	
P. polionotus	4–5	10–11*	11	13–14 11†	11†
P. leucopus noveboracensis	7	10	10	13	
P. megalops auritus	8	17	18	22	
P. maniculatus bairdi	7	10*		9–13†	11–13†
P. maniculatus gracilis	9	12*		14–15†	14–15†

[a] The figures come from Layne's review (1968), except the numbers marked with superior asterisks, which are previously unpublished figures tallied by J. A. King (1969) from observations made by Dr. Edward O. Price on 24 *P. polionotus*, 22 *P. m. bairdi*, and 24 *P. m. gracilis*, and the numbers marked with superior daggers, which were taken from Vestal and King's study (1968) of the optokinetic response. Professor King writes that the onset of the startle response occurs no later than 24 hours after the external auditory canal opens in these species of deermice.

that there are local variations in the same form of deermice due to selection and other procedural factors which differ between laboratories, or which differ in the same laboratory at different times (for example, see p. 32 of the Vestal–King article).

Thus the behavioral and anatomical evidence (ear and eye-opening) indicate that six forms of deermouse conform to the ontogenetic pattern of sensory development observed in other mammalian and avian species (Table 4). The exact onset of tactile sensitivity in deermice is not known, but it almost certainly is present on the day of birth or earlier (Fig. 5), as it is in other animals which suckle. If that supposition is confirmed experimentally, deermice would show the complete tactile–vestibular–auditory–visual sequence of sensory development.

DOMESTIC RABBIT

According to the available behavioral evidence, domestic rabbits evince tactile sensitivity to the head region prenatally on day 16 (Pankratz, 1931; Volokhov, 1968), the vestibular righting reflex prenatally on day 27–28 (Obraztsova, 1961, cited by Volokhov, 1968), a primitive orienting response to sound on day 7 after birth (Volokhov, 1968), and an optokinetic response to visual stimulation between 10 and 16 days postnatally (Warkentin, 1937) (Fig. 6). On the physiological and histo-

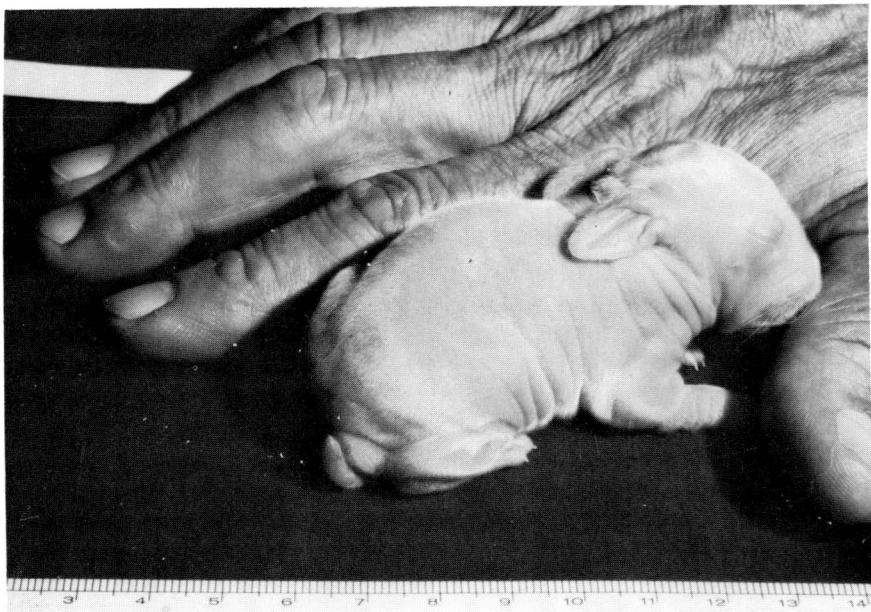

FIG. 6. Newborn rabbit (albino New Zealand strain). The external bodily characteristics of rabbits are more advanced at birth than mice or rats. This one was about 18 hours old when the photograph was taken. (Photograph by Rainer Foelix.)

logical side, auditory function begins as early as day 5 postnatally (Änggård, 1965; Klyavina and Obraztsova, 1968), while visual function begins on day 7 or day 8 postnatally (various investigators; see Table 5). The postnatal electrophysiological investigations of the rabbit's somesthetic, auditory, and visual systems by Marty and Scherrer (1964) very neatly substantiate the present picture. The cortical latencies for tactile, auditory, and visual stimulation reached their minimum by day 6, day 10, and day 21, respectively. Thus, in domestic rabbits the available behavioral, physiological, and histological evidence is in accord with regard to the sequence of sensory development, and the sequence is tactile–vestibular–auditory–visual.

DOMESTIC CAT

Cat fetuses show overt tactile sensitivity on day 24 (Coronios, 1933; Windle and Griffin, 1931) and the vestibular righting response around day 51–54 (Windle and Fish, 1932). Kittens are born about 63 days after conception. Eight days after birth they show an overt response to

TABLE 5
Ontogenetic Sequence of Sensory Function in the Domestic Rabbit

Gestation period (approximate)	Neonate's condition at birth	Approximate day of onset of function and type of evidence				
		Tactile	Vestibular	Auditory	Visual
32 days	Altricial	Prenatal day 16 Behavior: Pankratz, 1931; Volokhov, 1968	Prenatal day 27–28 Behavior: Volokhov, 1968	Postnatal day 7 Behavior: Volokhov, 1968 Postnatal day 5 Physiology and Histology: Änggård, 1965; Klyavina and Obraztsova, 1968	Postnatal day 10–16 Behavior: Warkentin, 1937 Postnatal day 7 Physiology and Histology: Hunt and Goldring, 1951; Marty and Scherrer, 1964; Volokhov, 1968 Postnatal day 8 Physiology and Histology: Noell, 1958

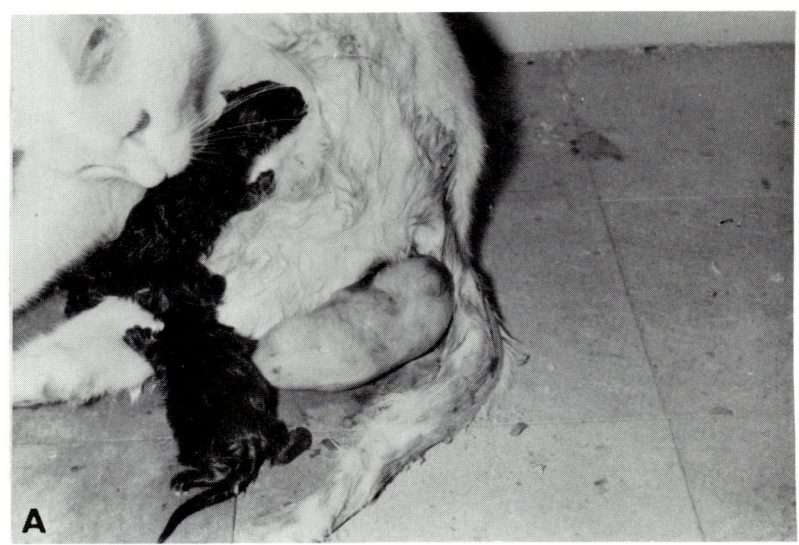

FIG. 7. Newborn kittens. Based on the presence of fur and their relative agility, kittens appear to be more advanced at birth than mice or rats, though all of these species are regarded as altricial. A. A litter in the process of birth. The third kitten (near mother's tail) has just been born and is still inside the birth sac. B. A close-up view of a newborn kitten. (Photograph A by Robert Woll; photograph B by Marieta B. Heaton.)

sound (Volokhov, 1968) and 12 to 17 days after birth they evince an optokinetic response to visual stimulation (Warkentin and Smith, 1937). Thus, the behavioral evidence indicates that the tactile–vestibular–auditory–visual progression of sensory development is present in domestic cats (Fig. 7).

Numerous investigators have recorded evoked auditory and visual potentials in kittens on days 4 and 5, but the earliest physiological signs of auditory and visual function are not yet known. The earliest auditory evoked cortical potentials are reported for day 2–3 (Pujol and Marty, 1968), while the earliest visual evoked cortical responses are reported for day 4 (Rose and Lindsley, 1968). The importance of the stimulus is shown by Pujol and Marty, who used tones rather than clicks; the earliest auditory potentials evoked by clicks is on day 5 (Ellingson and Wilcott, 1960; Marty and Scherrer, 1964). While it has become conventional for electrophysiologists to use clicks and light flashes to evoke auditory and visual responses, neither of these stimuli is very meaningful in terms of the auditory and visual stimuli typically encountered by animals.

Since many technical difficulties (type of stimulation as well as recording problems) have to be overcome in order to record the onset of sensory function, most developmental electrophysiologists tend to emphasize characteristic differences or changes in waveforms, latency, etc., as a consequence of age, rather than the functional onset of a system. For example, Ellingson and Wilcott (1960) recorded both auditory and visual evoked potentials from the cortex of kittens beginning on day 5. They conclude (pp. 374–375):

> The evidence we have presented indicates that in the cat the visual afferent system is less mature at birth and attains maturity at a later age than the auditory system by the following criteria: (i) time of appearance of evoked responses in the cortex, (ii) wave form of earliest responses, . . . (iii) latency of earliest responses relative to adult latency, (iv) age at which adult latency is attained, and (v) magnitude of individual differences of earliest responses.

Thus, based on these conclusions, which are similar to the conclusions of Marty and Scherrer (1964) on auditory and visual electrophysiology, it seems safe to conclude that the physiological evidence, as well as the behavioral evidence, indicates the temporal priority of development of the auditory system over the visual system.

With regard to tactile sensitivity in relation to auditory and visual sensitivity, Marty and Scherrer (1964) compared the "definitive latencies" of the three systems in young kittens and concluded that a chronological hierarchy exists, with somesthesia occupying first place, audition second, and vision third. Marty and Scherrer account for these differences

TABLE 6

Ontogenetic Sequence of Sensory Function in the Domestic Cat

Gestation period (approximate)	Neonate's condition at birth	Approximate day of onset of function and type of evidence			
		Tactile	Vestibular	Auditory	Visual
63 days	Altricial	Prenatal day 24 Behavior: Coronios, 1933; Windle and Griffin, 1931	Prenatal day 51–54 Behavior: Windle and Fish, 1932	Postnatal day 8 Behavior: Volokhov, 1968 Postnatal day 2–3 Physiology: Pujol and Marty, 1968 Postnatal day 5 or earlier Physiology: Ellingson and Wilcott, 1960; Marty and Scherrer, 1964	Postnatal day 12–17 Behavior: Warkentin and Smith, 1937 Postnatal day 4 Physiology: Rose and Lindsley, 1968 Postnatal day 5 or earlier Physiology: Ellingson and Wilcott, 1960; Marty and Scherrer, 1964 Histology: Marty and Scherrer, 1964; Tilney and Casamajor, 1924 Postnatal day 6 Physiology: Zetterström, 1956

in terms of receptor differences, specifically onset of function and rate of development of each kind of receptor. In this respect it is pertinent that Zetterström (1956) was unable to record the electroretinogram in kittens until day 6, which happens to be the time when all of the rods in the kitten retina have become segmented. Before that time only rods in the central region of the retina have formed distinguishable outer segments (Sidman and Wislocki, 1954). According to the morphological differentiation of the retina (Donovan, 1966) and visually evoked electrocortical responses (Rose and Lindsley, 1968), the kitten's visual system is completely mature at about 2 months after birth. In contrast to the relative immaturity of the auditory and visual systems, the somesthetic system of the newborn kitten is in many anatomical and physiological respects comparable to the adult (Rubel, 1969).

In summary (Table 6), the presently available prenatal and postnatal behavioral and physiological evidence are in accord that sensory development in domestic cats follows the tactile–vestibular–auditory–visual sequence.

MAN

All of the four sensory systems under review become capable of function before birth in man. An overt response to tactile stimulation is present in the human fetus around day 49 after fertilization, consisting of bending the head away from the site of stimulation when the oral region is touched lightly (Hooker, 1952).[2] The correlative trigeminal anatomy of this and other cutaneous responses has been worked out in detail by Humphrey (1964, 1968). Sometime between day 90–120 Minkowski (1928, p. 565) observed what he presumed to be vestibular righting reflexes in human fetuses, and Humphrey (1965) holds that the lateral vestibular nucleus is almost certainly functional between 12 to 16 weeks of prenatal development. Since the human newborn is barely able to right its head (Peiper, 1963), Humphrey (1965, pp. 54–55) points out that the increase in the size of the head prior to birth may not be matched by a comparable increase in muscle tonus, so, vestibular righting reflexes might be absent in the newborn for this reason rather than insufficient vestibular development. The question of vestibular onset in human fetuses definitely requires more study since it is entirely possible that the responses observed by Minkowski—he observed the fetus' overt

[2] This fetus had a crown–rump length of 20.7 mm. Similarly, Fitzgerald and Windle (1942) report a response in a 20.0-mm fetus whose oral zone they stimulated "strongly" with a needle. Hooker (1952, p. 61) used a series of delicately calibrated hairs to stimulate his subjects, and this is a much more precise way to study tactile sensitivity (i.e., avoiding deep pressure stimulation).

response to rapid changes in bodily position—could have been solely the result of proprioceptive stimulation. However, there is little doubt that the vestibular system is highly developed at birth—newborn infants show ocular nystagmus in response to rotation (Galebsky, 1927; Heck, 1952; Lawrence and Feind, 1953; McGraw, 1941), and this particular vestibular response typically develops well after the development of vestibular righting reflexes in other mammals. Based on the most recent analyses of the motion pictures of fetuses other than the one shown in Fig. 8, Professor Humphrey (1969) now feels confident that vestibular function is present at 80 days of age and earlier, but she would acknowledge the difficulty in definitively separating reflexes due to proprioceptive stretch stimuli from vestibular responses to quick changes in bodily position. The fetus' earliest observed response to the latter is described as a slow side-to-side head movement. Proprioceptive stretch reflexes are usually brisk, as indicated in the rapid snapping shut of the mouth seen in Fig. 8. Tactile sensitivity of the perioral region, as reported by Hooker (1952) and Humphrey (1964, 1968), is present in an approximately 49-day-old fetus. Based on the most recent motion picture evidence, Professor Humphrey now considers that vestibular function is probably present in an approximately 59-day-old fetus (34.3 mm crown–rump length), which is considerably earlier than the older published evidence cited above and in Table 7.

At about 6 months the human fetus is capable of responding to auditory stimulation. At this time the organ of Corti is comparable to the adult (Bredberg, 1968) and Wedenberg (1965), in collaboration with Johansson and Westin, has recorded fetal heart rate changes to sound stimulation *in utero*, taking apparently adequate precautions against instigation of the response by the expectant mother. (An earlier report of human fetal tachycardia in response to sound stimulation was made by Murphy and Smyth in 1962.) During the seventh month the fetus' bodily reaction to sound is of sufficient magnitude so that objective behavioral recordings can be made via a pneumograph attached to the mother's body (Fleischer, 1955). Actually, 2 to 7 weeks before term, it is frequently possible to indirectly observe the fetus' response to sound by merely watching the maternal abdomen and noting the extent to which strong abdominal deformations coincide with repeated applications of the stimulus (e.g., Wedenberg, 1965), and Fleischer's technique, or ones similar to it, take advantage of this opportunity and place the observations on a firm footing. As intrauterine recording techniques become more sophisticated, it will become possible to delineate more precisely the onset of auditory sensitivity in human fetuses. Since we know that auditory function, as well as other sensory functions, can occur prior to the complete maturation of the receptor, there is a good reason to be-

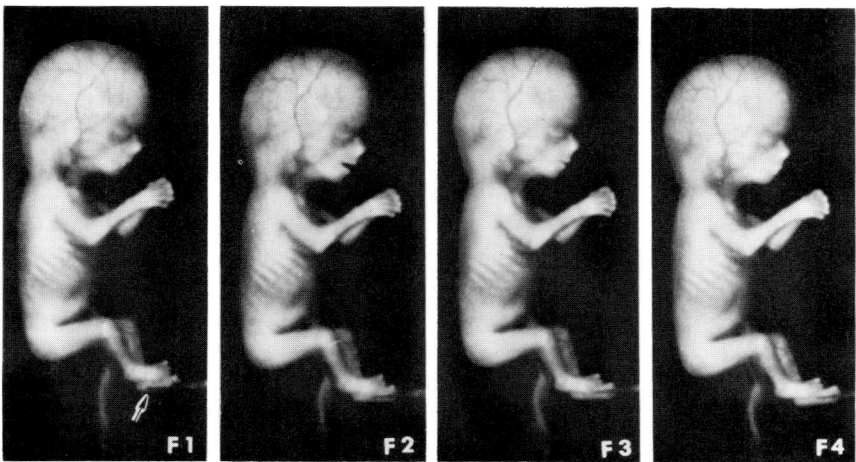

FIG. 8. An approximately 80-day-old human fetus (70 mm crown–rump measurement). The pictures were taken from successive frames of a 16-mm motion picture made after a medically supervised abortion and show the fetus responding to tactile stimulation of the sole of its left foot (arrow in F1) by rapidly opening and closing its mouth. The four frames span 0.25 seconds. The observations were made with the fetus immersed in an isotonic bath at normal body temperature. As indicated in the text, 49-day-old fetuses (20–21 mm long) are responsive only to stimulation about the oral region, but by this age tactile sensitivity has spread to many other surfaces of the body. The photographs are reproduced at about 0.8 of the fetus' size. (Reproduced from Humphrey, 1968, Fig. 11, with permission of the author and publisher.)

lieve that human auditory sensitivity may begin earlier than presently indicated. This supposition is supported by the very recent report of auditory evoked cortical responses in human infants born prematurely after 21 to 27 weeks of gestation (Weitzman and Graziani, 1968). Since a response was obtained from the youngest infant tested (21 weeks), the onset of auditory sensitivity in man is still not known.

While the earliest onset of the capacity for visual function in the human fetus is not known, Ellingson (1960) recorded evoked cortical responses to light flashes in a premature infant as early as day 182 (26 weeks) or thereabouts, and Engel (1964) recorded such a response in a premature infant around day 154 (22 weeks). Ellingson reports that the evoked response in the youngest prematures has an initially negative waveform and a longer latency than full-term babies. Older prematures are more likely to show an initially positive waveform than is the full-term infant. In the present context it is important to note that the initially negative waveform is regarded as "a primitive form of primary cortical evoked response" (Ellingson, 1960, p. 667). In comparison with the auditory receptor (organ of Corti), which is completely differentiated several months before birth, the human visual receptor (retina) is not completely developed even at birth. Zetterström (1955), for example, could not record a measurable electroretinogram from infants until 2 or 3 days after birth, even though she used stimulating intensities of almost 100 lux. On the behavioral side, it is uncertain whether the newborn is capable of an optokinetic response to visual stimulation (e.g., Galebsky, 1927). According to histological evidence (Mann, 1964), the macula of the retina is not completely differentiated until around 4 months after birth. Other evidence for the protracted period of maturation of the human retina are the changes which continue to occur in the electroretinogram up to about 6 months of age (Zetterström, 1951). Implicit in this discussion is the idea that, developmentally speaking, the receptor is the limiting factor in the assumption of sensory function and, at least in the visual modality, there is ample evidence on this point both in birds (Gottlieb, 1968) and in mammals (Marty and Scherrer, 1964). Many years ago, in a little-known publication, Lane (1917) emphasized that from the standpoint of the onset of function, the receptor is the last element to be formed in *every* sensory system.

Several studies of newborn infants help to clarify the picture of early visual and auditory development. Directly after birth (Wertheimer, 1961), the neonate is capable of making localizing responses to sound, as evidenced by head-turning and eye movements in the direction of the sound source (Turkewitz et al., 1966; Waltan, 1921). With respect to vision, however, the newborn can focus his eye on targets only at a particular distance (about 19 cm)—accommodation begins to approximate the adult range at around 4 months (Haynes et al., 1965). In a conditioning experiment cited by Razran (1933), Denisova and Figurin (1929) found that auditory conditioned responses are formed earlier (33–56 days) than visually conditioned responses (56–77 days) in the same infants. [Kasatkin and Levikova (1935) also found that an auditory conditioned response could be formed in human infants between 34 and 43 days after birth.] Lipsitt and Kaye (1964) report the possibility of auditory conditioning as early as day 3 or 4, but they note that their results could have been a consequence of sensitization or pseudoconditioning. On the anatomical side, Langworthy (1933) and Yakovlev and Lecours (1967) observed that the auditory system is more completely myelinated than the visual system before birth and until several months after birth. Also, myelinated auditory projection fibers reach the cerebral cortex earlier than the optic fibers (Langworthy, 1933; Yakovlev and Lecours, 1967). After birth, the optic fibers myelinate very rapidly, whereas the auditory and even the somesthetic fibers have a protracted period of postnatal myelinization (Yakovlev and Lecours, 1967).

In conclusion, based on the available behavioral evidence, in the human fetus tactile sensitivity is evident around the seventh week after fertilization, vestibular function may develop during the third or fourth month (if not earlier), and auditory sensitivity is evident in the seventh month (and probably earlier). No comparable behavioral evidence is available for visual function, but the histological evidence suggests that the capacity for visual function develops rather late in human prenatal development. The physiological evidence (evoked electrocortical responses) suggests that auditory function can begin earlier than visual function, but that is merely fortuitous, being based solely on the age at which individual premature infants have become available for study. With these qualifications in mind, as far as is known at present (Table 7), the sequential development of tactile, vestibular, auditory, and visual competence in man conforms to that of other unrelated mammals as well as birds.

DOMESTIC GUINEA PIG

At the time of birth after a 68-day gestation period, these animals are already in a very advanced stage of development. They are highly mobile and all of their sensory systems would appear to be functional. Though several monographs have been published on the prenatal behavior of guinea pigs, there is a surprising paucity of information on the onset of the various sensory systems in this form. Carmichael (1934) has investigated thoroughly the prenatal development of tactile sensitivity in a large number of guinea pig fetuses of various ages, and he also made some incidental observations on other sensory systems. The founder of behavioral embryology, Preyer (1885), made several significant observations on prenatal auditory and visual function in guinea pig fetuses, and Avery (1928) extended these observations and made a number of other general observations of prenatal activity. Otherwise the information is rather sketchy in a mammal which is otherwise very advantageous for behavioral embryological study, especially for establishing possible relationships between prenatal sensory function and postnatal perception. The technique for studying behavior in externalized fetuses has been well worked out and fully described by Carmichael (1934), while Bergström *et al.* (1961) and Rosen and McLaughlin (1966) have performed the same service for intrauterine electrophysiological investigation.

Overt responsiveness to tactile sensitivity first manifests itself on day 31–32 (Carmichael, 1934). As is in all other embryonic or fetal vertebrates, the first sensitive area to evoke an overt motor response is a highly localized spot in the head region. From that point cutaneous

94 G. GOTTLIEB

TABLE 7
Ontogenetic Sequence of Sensory Function in Man

Gestation period (approximate)[a]	Neonate's condition at birth	Approximate day of onset of function and type of evidence			
		Tactile	Vestibular	Auditory	Visual
265 days	Altricial	Prenatal day 49 Behavior: Hooker, 1952 Histology: Humphrey, 1964	Prenatal day 90–120 Behavior: Minkowski, 1928 Histology: Humphrey, 1965; Langworthy, 1933	Prenatal day 210 or earlier Behavior: Fleischer, 1955 Prenatal day 180 or earlier Physiology: Wedenberg, 1965 Physiology and Histology: Evidence reviewed by Bredberg, 1968 Prenatal day 147 or earlier Physiology: Weitzman and Graziani, 1968 (one premature infant)	Prenatal day 182 or earlier Physiology: Ellingson, 1960 (one premature infant) Prenatal day 154 or earlier Physiology: Engel, 1964 (one premature infant)

[a] Some researchers age the human fetus from the first day of the last menstrual period of the expectant mother, whereas others take into account that conception probably occurred around 2 weeks after that date. The first procedure is based on a "gestation" period of 280 days, while the second procedure, being based on a 265-day gestation period, is more nearly correct with respect to the fetus' age. Therefore, the latter procedure has been used here. In the very young fetuses, crown-rump measurements are usually included along with menstrual age. In the present instance, the approximate age of the fetus at the onset of tactile sensitivity and vestibular sensitivity (see legend for Fig. 8) has been verified in correspondence with Tryphena Humphrey. In the older fetuses (under auditory and visual sensitivity), age has been specified in the table on the basis of a 265-day gestation period, and this has resulted in a figure 2 weeks younger than that published by Weitzman and Graziani, Ellingson, and Engel. The European investigators (Fleischer, Wedenberg, and Bredberg) appear to have based their age estimates on a 265-day gestation period, so the figures here coincide with their published figures.

sensitivity radiates discontinuously to other portions of the body in what is usually described as a cephalo-caudal progression, but that is only a very rough and imprecise characterization (cf. Carmichael, 1934; Hooker, 1952; Humphrey, 1964).

While vestibular function develops prenatally in the guinea pig, it is not known how early it develops. Avery (1928) reports some observations of vestibular function in three 61-day-old guinea pig fetuses. He placed them on a rotating table on which they were revolved ten times to the left, ten times to the right, and ten times to the left in immediate succession. All of the fetuses responded with compensatory head and eye movements (nystagmus) only after the third series of revolutions. Avery notes that it is difficult to assess vestibular sensitivity in this manner earlier than day 61 because of the inability of younger fetuses to maintain an upright position of the head and body. Carmichael (1934) placed several air-breathing fetuses (day 65) on a turntable and observed compensatory head and trunk movements during rotation. Carmichael (p. 421) states that observations were not made systematically and that the responses require further study. To show the reactions observed by Avery and Carmichael, the guinea pig fetus must lift its head off the underlying surface. Vestibular sensitivity might be demonstrated earlier if the fetus were free to move in a liquid medium where elevation of the head was not a requisite factor.

The information is also unclear for the onset of auditory sensitivity in the guinea pig fetus. The external auditory canal opens around day 45 (Avery, 1928), and the organ of Corti appears completely differentiated between day 46–48 (Chodynicki, 1968). According to Chodynicki, at this same age the spaces in the scala vestibuli and scala tympani are fully formed, and the tunnel of Corti is open in all its four turns. In addition, there is an increase in the activity of respiratory enzymes in the sensory cells and in the stria vascularis, and an increase in glycogen grains in the hair cells. Further, Nissl bodies appear in the spiral cells between days 46 and 48. Whereas Chodynicki was able to record the first cochlear microphonic response (33–140 μV) via bone conduction around the 46th to the 48th day of gestation (80-mm fetuses), he was unable to record such a response for airborne sounds (reported as 75 dB without a reference level). Chodynicki's fetuses were heavily sedated and, thus, were precluded from reacting overtly to the sound stimulation. A very small evoked cochlear potential (1–2 μV) in response to airborne sound has been recorded from one 52-day-old fetus which also reacted overtly to the sound [reported as 600 Hz at 100 dB above the human threshold at the animal's ear (Rawdon-Smith *et al.*, 1938)]. Avery (1928, p. 289) reports that overt responses to "high pitched" and "clang" sounds could not be elicited before day 60. At that time a slight twitch of the ear (pinna or Preyer reflex) was observed, and a few days later the fetuses sometimes also jumped (startle response) when aurally stimulated. Avery's auditory work was hampered by inadequate equipment for delivering the sounds, and he does not give an estimate of the intensity of the sounds, but from his description it is doubtful that his sounds were as intense as those employed by Rawdon-Smith *et al.* The possible difference in intensity and frequency (in Hertz) of the stimulation in the Avery and Rawdon-Smith studies could account for the discrepancy in the behavioral evidence for onset of auditory function. However, Rawdon-Smith *et al.* obtained their results with only one fetus, so the issue is not clear.

Despite the various discrepancies and complications on signs of auditory function, it would appear that auditory sensitivity is definitely present around day 60–62 (if not before) in guinea pig fetuses. Namely, Avery observed gross startle responses (and the pinna reflex) at this time, while Rawdon-Smith *et al.* recorded rather clear evoked cochlear potentials (100 μV or more) in response to airborne sound at that age. Although the anatomical and histochemical evidence suggests that the inner ear may be functional as early as day 46-48 (Chodynicki), the extent to which auditory sensitivity may be present before day 60 is a bit unclear. Avery's observations are the most extensive and would be more conclusive on this point were it not for the fact that the large majority of his fetuses were 60 days old or more at the time of study. (Apparently he studied relatively few fetuses younger than 60 days.)

Whereas the external auditory meatus opens around day 45, the guinea pig fetus' eyelids first separate around day 59. Visual perception is apparently highly developed by day 63. Avery writes that these fetuses avoid obstructions, artificial barriers, and partitions at that time. However, he does not describe the exact nature of the tests and the actual behavior of the fetuses. Preyer (1885) noted that fetuses closed their eyes when exposed to sunlight during the eighth week of gestation. (Due to the great morphological and behavioral variability he observed within and between litters, Preyer summarized his observations according to weeks rather than days of development.) Avery observed the pupillary reflex in response to exposure to bright sunlight on day 59. Since the eyes first open on day 59, and no observations are mentioned for earlier ages (i.e., Avery appears not to have artificially separated the eyelids earlier than day 59), the earliest onset of the pupillary reflex is not known. During the final week of gestation, by the use of atropine, which abolishes a neurally mediated response, Preyer demonstrated that the pupillary reflex was neurally mediated.

Carmichael reports an "iris reflex" between 41 and 45 days. Whether this latter observation represents a neurally mediated response or not is unclear (the atropine test was not used nor was the eye excised and exposed to light). It is known that the eyes of dead animals will sometimes show pupillary constriction, and it is necessary to explore this response in a number of different ways to determine whether or not it is a visual (neural) response in young fetuses. If application of atropine to the eye blocks the response, or if the freshly excised eye does not make the response, visual function can be inferred. It is important to avoid the erroneous conclusion of a neurally mediated response when non-neural photochemical processes in the iris [(or in the retina, Weale, 1956)] are solely responsible for the reaction to the light source. In any event the value of the pupillary reflex for the present purpose is dubious owing to the fact that it is a smooth muscle reflex, whereas all the reflexes surveyed in the other sensory modalities have involved skeletal musculature. Smooth muscle reflexes generally are mediated at a different (lower) level of the nervous system than skeletal muscle responses.

With respect to the sequence of sensory development in the guinea pig fetus, tactile sensitivity rather definitely shows the earliest onset of the systems under review. The sequence of vestibular, auditory, and visual development is not clear. According to the behavioral evidence, vestibular sensitivity is evident on day 61, auditory sensitivity on day 52 or 60, and visual competency on day 63. Avery (1928) could not evaluate vestibular function by his method prior to day 61; one fetus aged 52 days showed an overt response to auditory stimulation (Rawdon-Smith *et al.,* 1938); and it seems likely that the capacity for visual function (other than the pupillary reflex) develops earlier than day 63. Because of the degree of functional overlap in these three systems around day 60, and our inability to estimate the probable onset of function in each of these systems, no firm conclusions can be drawn on the sequential aspect of vestibular, auditory, and visual development in the precocial guinea pig (Fig. 9).

The presently available studies concerning the onset of sensory function in guinea pigs are summarized in Table 8.

Perhaps this is a good place to raise certain methodological issues which have been suppressed in the preceding portion of the review. Assuming that further work might be done on prenatal sensory function in the guinea pig, it should be realized that it is essential that the functions which are to be assessed in comparing the systems should be roughly if not precisely analogous ones. For example, one could examine the latency of electrocortical evoked responses to auditory and visual stimulation. [According to preliminary observations, both auditory and

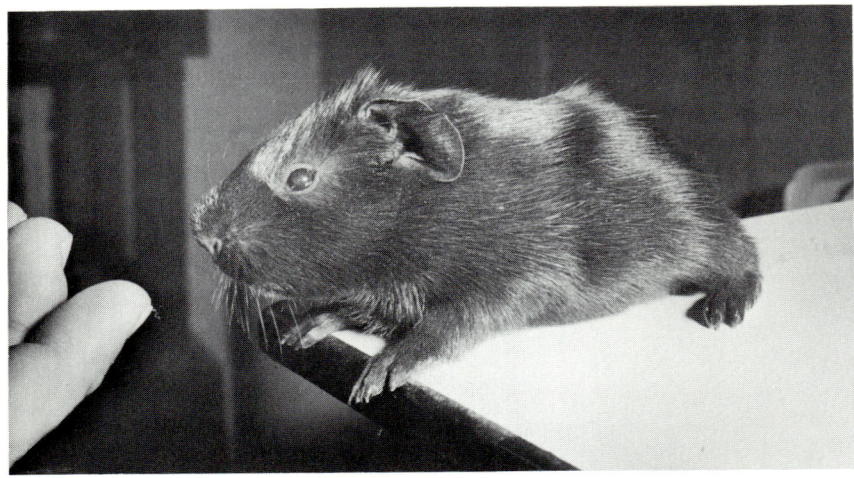

FIG. 9. Two views of a newborn guinea pig (approximately 18 hours old). These rodents are precocial, being able to locomote and survive without maternal care (other than nourishment) soon after birth. All of the sensory systems become capable of function prior to birth in the guinea pig. (Photograph by Rainer Foelix.)

visual electrocortical responses are present on day 60 (Jasper et al., 1937).] The same sort of analysis could be done at the receptor level. The histology of the receptors or the afferent pathways could be compared as an index of maturation. While physiological and anatomical studies between modalities are relatively straightforward when the parameters of stimulation are varied, behavioral comparisons between audition and vision are not simple to devise. One supposes simple orientations, auditory localization and visual fixation or pursuit, are basic in

TABLE 8

Ontogenetic Sequence of Sensory Function in the Domestic Guinea Pig

Gestation period (approximate)	Neonate's condition at birth	Approximate day of onset of function and type of evidence				
		Tactile	Vestibular	Auditory	Visual
68 days	Precocial	Prenatal day 31-32 Behavior: Carmichael, 1934	Prenatal day 61 or earlier Behavior: Avery, 1928	Prenatal day 60 Behavior: Avery, 1928 Prenatal day 52 Behavior: Rawdon-Smith et al., 1938 (one fetus) Physiology: Rawdon-Smith et al., 1938 Prenatal days 46-48 Physiology and Histology: Chodynicki, 1968	Prenatal day 63 Behavior: Avery, 1928 Prenatal day 65 (?) or earlier Behavior: Preyer, 1885, pp. 484-485 Prenatal day 59 or earlier Physiology: Avery, 1928 (pupillary reflex) Prenatal day 41-45 Physiology: Carmichael, 1934 ("iris reflex")

the development in each of these modalities. More advanced abilities would involve perceptual discrimination tasks in which one might employ the procedures of animal psychophysics (e.g., a comparison of difference limens in the auditory and visual modalities at similar ages).

The onset of vestibular sensitivity can be determined unequivocally by the presence of what neurologists call "labyrinthine righting reflexes," which probably develop earlier than the head and eye movement responses to rotation studied by Avery and Carmichael. For the outcome of such studies to be conclusive, however, it is necessary that such responses be abolished by destruction of the peripheral vestibular apparatus, or otherwise rendering it nonfunctional, because certain of these early reflexes may be entirely proprioceptive in nature. The course of development of vestibular sensitivity can be determined (1) by observing the fetus' response to rapid changes in bodily position, (2) by noting the onset of head- or body-righting, (3) by observing head nystagmus in response to systematic rotation, and, finally, (4) by noting the occurrence of ocular nystagmus in response to rotation. This sequence may in fact represent the main stages of vestibular development in many animals (in this connection, see Fish and Windle, 1932).

DOMESTIC SHEEP

Despite the popularity of the large, slow-growing sheep fetus as a subject for prenatal electrophysiological and histological study, there are very little data available on the onset of the sensory systems in this highly precocial animal. The sheep's gestation period is around 147 days, and at birth all of the lamb's sensory systems are highly functional.

Overt responses to tactile stimulation of the snout region (trigeminal nerve) occur around day 40 of prenatal development (Barcroft and Barron, 1939). While Molliver (1967) has conducted a careful electrophysiological investigation of tactile sensory development in sheep, he did not report on the response of fetuses less than 55 days old. (A long-latency evoked cortical response to snout stimulation was present at 55 days.) More recently, Meyerson and Persson (1969) have recorded evoked cortical responses to snout stimulation (trigeminal area) on day 48, which was the age of the youngest fetuses they studied.

Åström (1967) performed an extensive histological study of cortical development in sheep fetuses, and Bernhard et al. (1967) have synthesized the anatomical and physiological findings of Molliver and Åström with their own work on the fetal somesthetic cortex. From the present standpoint, it is of some interest that all these workers seem to agree that the cortex of the day 62 sheep fetus (about 40% of the gestation period) is comparable to the newborn kitten's cortex. With reference to stage of development at birth, of course, the precocial sheep would be significantly advanced over that of the altricial cat. Åström (1967, p. 51) also compares the approximately 62-day-old fetal sheep cortex to that of newborn mice, rats, and rabbits. In the present context, this is by way of emphasizing how accelerated the prenatal development of a precocial form is relative to altricial ones.

According to the anatomical–behavioral findings, vestibular sensitivity is not present in the sheep fetus until some time after day 50–52. Barcroft and Barron (1939, p. 489) destroyed the labyrinths of two fetuses at this age and observed that they could still right their heads after the operation. These investigators concluded that the ability to right the head at this age is probably mediated by tonic neck reflexes (proprioception). However, the earliest electrophysiological evidence for proprioception is day 60 (Änggård et al., 1961). Thus, the precise time

FIG. 10. Two-day-old lambs. These precocial animals are born in a very advanced stage of development. It is not known how early in prenatal development they are capable of vestibular, auditory, and visual function. (Photograph courtesy of Lester C. Ulberg.)

TABLE 9
Ontogenetic Sequence of Sensory Function in the Domestic Sheep

Gestation period (approximate)	Neonate's condition at birth	Approximate day of onset of function and type of evidence			
		Tactile	Vestibular	Auditory	Visual
147 days	Precocial	Prenatal day 40 Behavior: Barcroft and Barron, 1939 Prenatal day 48 or earlier Physiology: Meyerson and Persson, 1969 Prenatal day 55 or earlier Physiology: Molliver, 1967 Histology: Åström, 1967 (cortical)	After prenatal days 50–52 Behavior and Anatomy: Barcroft and Barron, 1939	Prenatal day 100 or earlier Physiology: Bernhard et al., 1959	

of onset of proprioceptive and vestibular sensitivity in sheep fetuses is in doubt.

Auditory sensitivity is evident in 100-day-old sheep fetuses, as indicated by evoked cortical potentials (Bernhard *et al.*, 1959).

From observations of newborn sheep (Fig. 10) it is certain that vestibular and visual competency develop before birth; however, I have been unable to locate any studies on the prenatal development of these sensory systems. Within several hours after birth, sheep are capable of visual depth perception (Lemmon and Patterson, 1964), and it seems highly likely that the capacity for other aspects of visual function (including depth perception) begins before that time.

In conclusion, as summarized in Table 9, tactile sensitivity is manifested around day 40 in the sheep fetus, vestibular sensitivity is not evident by day 52, auditory function is evident on day 100, and the prenatal onset of visual competence is not known.

Summary of the Sequential Development of the Sensory Systems in Nine Mammalian Species: Phylogenetic Significance

The currently available evidence indicates that the sequence of sensory development is tactile–vestibular–auditory–visual in opossums, rats, deermice, rabbits, cats, and man. In house mice, no data are available on the somesthetic and vestibular systems, and the auditory system may or may not have functional priority over the visual system. In guinea pigs, tactile sensitivity is the first to develop, but the priority of the other three systems is in doubt. In sheep, vestibular sensitivity develops later than tactile sensitivity, but it is not known when vestibular, auditory, or visual sensitivity actually begin to function.

Thus, six of the nine species seem to conform to the sequence of sensory development evident in the avian embryo and, while there is insufficient evidence on the other three species, there are at present no marked contradictions of the sequence in these other species. It is tentatively concluded, therefore, that the particular sensory systems under review probably develop in the same sequence in many if not all mammalian species. This sequence is apparently a very stable if not invariant feature of diverse phylogenies, being present in birds and in the oldest (opossum) and the youngest of the altricial mammals (man). (Figure 11 shows the main lines of evolutionary descent of birds and mammals.)

Finally, it should be noted that the mammalian lines under review—marsupials, rodents, lagamorphs, carnivores, artiodactyls, and primates—have evolved independent of each other for at least the last 70 to

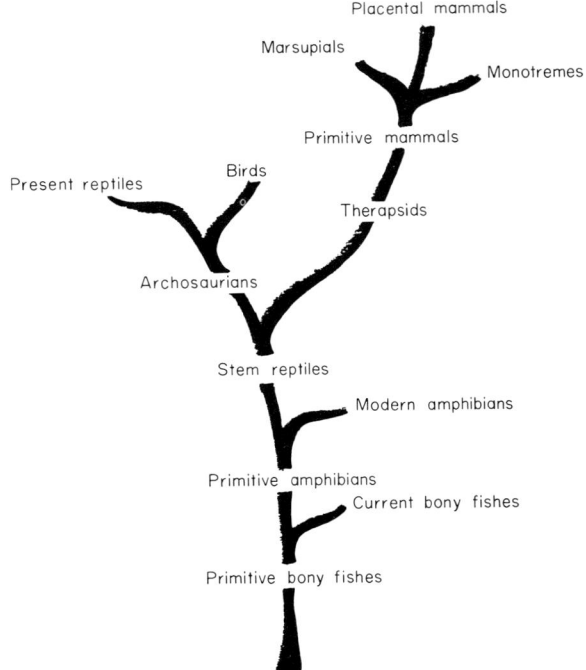

FIG. 11. The main lines of evolutionary descent of birds and mammals. Based on the available evidence, the ontogenetic sequence of development of the sensory systems would appear to be the same in mammals and birds. If that is true, then the same sequence was likely present in the extinct stem reptiles if not earlier. This inference follows from the fact that the ancestors of modern birds (archosaurian reptiles) and mammals (therapsid reptiles) both arose from the stem reptiles.

100 million years, and none of these particular species can be considered ancestral to any of the other species. The ancestors of all mammals were therapsid (upright-walking) reptiles, which are extinct. Egg-laying mammals—the monotremes[3]—retain many more reptilian characteristics than marsupial or placental mammals, so it would be of great interest to determine whether the sequence of sensory development is tactile–vestibular–auditory–visual in that group because it would shed considerably more light on the phyletic origin of the sequence. With regard to birds—they arose from extinct archosaurian reptiles—the present-day crocodilians would be of interest because they also descended from archosaurians

---

[3] As mentioned by Romer (1966, p. 198), the living monotremes (the duckbill and spiny anteater of Australia) are very primitive and highly specialized, and they may represent a line of descent from mammal-like reptiles entirely separate from that of other living forms.

and apparently have not changed very much. Since turtles share a remote common ancestor with birds and mammals in the stem reptiles, they would also be of interest in the present context.

By this approach—namely, examining the sequence of sensory development in egg-laying mammals, crocodiles, alligators, and turtles—the generality of the sequence could be determined and the inference that the same sequence was present in the extinct ancestors of birds and mammals could be better evaluated. While the information on current reptilian forms is sparse, it is known that tactile sensitivity develops before vestibular sensitivity in loggerhead turtles (Smith and Daniel, 1946), and that terrapin embryos evince tactile sensitivity very early in development, when they are about 6 mm in length (Tuge, 1931). Otherwise, the field seems to be entirely open for inquiry. Future research could place the origin of the sequence of sensory development in the extinct stem reptiles, or perhaps even earlier in phylogeny. With regard to the sequence of sensory development in amphibians, for example, Youngstrom (1938) has examined the onset of tactile sensitivity, ocular movement (nystagmus?) in response to rotation, and bodily reaction to rotation in the larvae of seven species of frogs and toads. The reactions developed in that particular order in all seven species, but it was not possible for Youngstrom (p. 359) to discern whether the nystagmus-like ocular response reflected a sheerly vestibular reaction or whether it represented ". . . an effort to maintain fixation of the field of vision." Very young larvae of certain species frequently move away from an object which is made to approach them in the frontal plane, but, as Youngstrom observes, the larvae are also very sensitive to mechanical jarring and to currents in the water at this stage, so they could be responding simply to perturbations in the water produced by movement of the object. There are obvious ways in which the onset of vestibular and visual sensitivity can be sorted out, so the problem is by no means insuperable. Hibbard (1964), in connection with his labyrinth transplantation experiments, examined tactile, vestibular, and auditory sensitivity in amphibian larvae, but, unfortunately, he does not report the day or stages at which the larvae were tested, so no conclusion can be reached on the sequence of sensory development in amphibians based on the available literature.

Ontogeny, Phylogeny, and Evolution

It is interesting to note that man is the only one of the altricial species reviewed in which all of the sensory systems are capable of function prior to birth. This sensory precocity is usually reserved for motorically precocious species (e.g. guinea pig and sheep). While man happens to have the longest gestation period of the seven altricial species surveyed, length of gestation cannot be the sole determining factor for his sensory precocity, otherwise cats (63-day gestation period) would show some auditory or visual precocity over mice and rats (20- to 24-day gestation period), but they don't (cf. Tables 2, 3, and 6).

It should be mentioned, incidentally, that the legendary motor primacy of behavioral embryology, first enunciated by Preyer (1885) in connection with the early motility of the chick embryo, later observed by Coghill (1929) in his studies of amphibian larvae and by Tracy (1926) in his study of fish embryos, is not a conspicuous feature of human prenatal behavior in which the sensorimotor reflexes have been greatly accelerated in appearance in ontogeny, even when compared to other primates (Bodian, 1968). The essential ideas of motor primacy are that the early motility of embryos is independent of sensory influences or that the differentiation and growth of the primary motor mechanism occurs independent of its relations with the sensory systems, both of which lead to a relatively late "entrapment" of the motor systems by the sensory systems. This would not appear to be true in human prenatal behavior.

From an ontogenetic point of view, man and the other primates are unique in having combined the precocial pattern of sensory development with the altricial pattern of motor development. One supposes that this combination has significant ramifications for perceptual, intellectual, and social development, and that it has played an important role in the neurological and behavioral evolution of primates. While it would be very difficult, perhaps, to establish this as a causal proposition, it does serve to alert us to the dependence of evolution on alterations in ontogeny, rather than regarding evolution or phylogeny as the "cause" of altered ontogenies. On logical grounds, evolution is a consequence of nature's more successful experiments in ontogeny. In de Beer's words (1951, p. 139): "Phylogeny plays no causal part in determining ontogeny except insofar as past external factors have been responsible for exerting selection and preserving those internal factors which are operative in the ontogeny of the descendants." Thus, as observed by de Beer, during evolution three things happen. (1) Certain sequences or stages in the remote ancestral ontogeny are retained in the ontogeny of the descendants (e.g., the sequence in which the sensory systems develop). I would propose the term homochrony for such instances. (2) Certain quantitative novelties appear in ontogeny (e.g., in primates the onset of the sensory systems is accelerated so sensory function begins before birth). These are instances of heterochrony in de Beer's terminology. Heterochrony denotes changes in the timing of sequences or stages in the ontogeny of the descendants. Such changes must, of course, be based on genetic changes, otherwise the basis for them would be incapable of transmission from generation to generation, and they would have no evolutionary significance. (3) Qualitative novelties arise in ontogeny (e.g., thumb–forefinger apposition, erect posture, and language). It is only the first of these three events (1) for which the remote ancestors are directly responsible; (2) and (3) are new items, and it is the new items in ontogeny which represent evolution, not the old ones. For this reason it is appropriate to say that evolution, or that which is new in phylogeny, is a consequence of alterations in ontogeny.

For clarification of the relationship between homochronous and heterochronous features in ontogeny, the ontogenetic stability of the sequence of sensory development may be contrasted to the heterochronic neural phenomena described by Anokhin (1964) in his theory of systemogenesis. Anokhin holds (1964, p. 66) that during the prenatal ontogeny of different species there is a selective acceleration of maturation of those neural substrates which, in the future, ". . . combine to create a fully developed and arborized functional system with positive adaptive effect for the newborn." He goes on to say (p. 85):

> It is true that the systemogenetic type of . . . maturation . . . is the most marked for those functional systems of the organism which must be mature exactly at the moment of birth. They are evidently inborn, the preparation for their consolidation is preformed, and in fact, in the process of . . . ontogenesis, they correspond demonstrably to the ecological factors of that species of animal. . . .

In light of the present results, it would appear that certain aspects of neural ontogeny (e.g., homochrony of the sensory systems) transcend the systemogenetic principle, while other aspects adhere to it. That is, as illustrated by Anokhin, (1) some neural structures in each species show a differential rate of maturation which is specific to that species, (2) such differences in structural maturation may have positive adaptive effects for the neonate, and (3) they may also correspond to the ecology of the species. The sequence in which the sensory systems develop, however, does not follow these rules. Systemogenetic or heterochronic phenomena are species-specific, while a homochronic pattern such as the sequence of sensory development is species-general. While heterochrony incorporates something new or different in ontogeny and thereby provides the ontogenetic material which is essential for evolution and speciation, homochrony is a phylogenetic heritage which has little or no immediate value for speciation. Thus, the heterochronic or systemogenetic phenomena represent species differences in ontogeny and are the essential concomitants of progressive evolution, while the homochronic or species-general phenomena, being merely repetitions of ancestral ontogenetic stages in the ontogeny of descendants, represent affinities between species and are the conservative features of evolution. While heterochrony may indeed result in a "positive adaptive effect" for the neonate, homochrony may only offer developmental constraints which are neutral with respect to the adaptation of the newborn. Whereas heterochrony may be directly related to the ecology of the species, homochrony would appear to be indifferent to ecological differences between species. Although there can be little doubt about the importance of heterochrony in the adaptive economy of each species, it should be noted that instances of marked heterochrony may sometimes tend to obscure the homochronic or otherwise homologous aspects of neural and behavioral ontogenesis. Application of the concept of homology to behavior is a very complicated affair (Atz, 1970), and the pervasiveness of heterochrony undoubtedly contributes to the problem by making it far easier to detect species differences than to detect similarities between species.

Ontogenetic Regulation of the Sequence of Sensory Development in Birds and Mammals

When particular morphological, neurological, or behavioral patterns are observed to recur invariably in related species, it is common to regard such patterns as phylogenetic heritages. While this description is quite appropriate as far as it goes, it does not describe or explain the ontogenetic development of the pattern. When a particular pattern such as the sequence in which the sensory systems develop is present in closely related as well as distantly related species, however, there is a strong temptation to regard it as ontogenetically predetermined, in the sense that the pattern must be under very strict genetic control. In this context "very strict" means not only that there are multiple genes responsible for the pattern but that the pattern is so narrowly and steeply buffered that it will manifest itself under all but lethal developmental conditions. One assumes that the strongest kind of developmental buffering results from multiple genes which can act in alternative combinations to increase the likelihood of the same end result.

While there can be no quarrel over the importance of evolutionary and genetic considerations in the study of the nervous system and behavior, I do think it is possible to overestimate the self-realizing potency of the genetic and cytoplasmic material with regard to neural and behavioral development. Since, in what follows, I may seem to underestimate the potency of inherited factors, as well as the self-differentiating prowess of the nervous system, at the outset I would like explicitly to state certain working assumptions. (1) Genetic and cytoplasmic inheritance play an essential role in establishing the ontogenetic limits of structural and physiological variation. [Presumptive evidence for the role of cytoplasm is provided in Storrs and Williams (1968).] (2) The presence of certain genetic combinations substantially increases the probability that certain events will occur later in development. (3) Intrinsic chemical processes carry the maturation (that is, the proliferation, migration, differentiation, and growth) of sensory cells up to a certain as yet unknown point in development. Whereas many developmental biologists and behaviorists would agree on the general correctness of these first three assumptions, the validity of the following two assumptions remains to be documented. (4) Cellular function plays a role in regulating the species-typical rate of structural maturation and in completing sensory development, especially with respect to fully adaptive or adjustive behavior. (5) Sensory stimulation also plays a role in regulating the species-typical rate of maturation and in completing sensory development, especially in perfecting perceptual development.

The importance of the fourth and fifth assumptions is to call attention to the possibility that the invariant sequence of sensory development observed in mammalian and avian species may represent a probabilistic outcome of the joint operation of genetic, biochemical, functional, and sensory stimulative conditions which occur during the normal course of ontogeny in the intact animal. This is in contrast to the idea that molecular and biochemical processes are solely responsible for the complete and orderly structural maturation of the nervous system. At the earliest stages of ontogeny molecular and biochemical processes give an indispensable impetus to maturation, whereas it is suggested that later on function and sensory stimulation also play an active role in regulating the maturation process.

There can be no doubt from *in vitro* studies that sensory, internuncial, or motor cells can mature to the point where they become capable of evoked electrical activity without the benefit of prior function or sensory stimulation (e.g., Crain *et al.,* 1968). If stimulation normally plays a role in the intact animal, however, then deficits would be present in systems which are deprived of normally occurring function or stimulation, and improvements would result in systems which receive augmented stimulation. Specifically, if the amount of normally occurring function or stimulation does affect the maturation of a system, then deprivation should lead to a later onset, a higher threshold, or imperfections in the final development of the system, whereas augmentation should lead to an earlier onset, a lower threshold, or a more rapid and highly developed competence of the system. Since it is now possible to explant fetal mammalian neural tissue prior to synaptic formation and observe the activity of such cells after synapses have been formed (Crain et al., 1968), ultimately, it should be possible to determine how far a neural system can mature without function and stimulation, and the specific kinds of deficits which occur under such conditions. Up to now the tremendous technical obstacle has been to get the cells to live and grow successfully in a culture medium—now that problem has been solved, and perhaps a more sophisticated analytic approach can be made on the activity of such cells.

In the study in question (Crain et al., 1968), fetal rodent cortical and spinal cord cells were explanted and exposed to blocking agents so they could not fire spontaneously. After 5 to 30 days the cells showed no spontaneous or evoked complex activity, but in some cases simple action potentials could be triggered by extremely high stimulating currents. When the blocking agent was removed from the culture medium, the very first electrical stimulation often produced complex, long-lasting discharges, indicating that functional synaptic networks had formed in the culture in the absence of prior functional activity. This is an ingenious demonstration that the early maturation of neural cells can be accomplished without the benefit of prior activation or function, much like the experiments which show that amphibians become capable of swimming in the absence of prior muscular movement (Carmichael, 1926; Harrison, 1904; Matthews and Detwiler, 1926). While there can be no doubt that cells can mature and amphibians can swim without prior function or exercise, it is entirely possible that there are imperfections in the activity of such cells and in the swimming behavior of the previously paralyzed amphibia. The latter has in fact been documented—Fromme (1941) found previously undetected quantitative deficiencies in the swimming behavior of the embryos after they were released from the anesthetic. As reported by the previous investigators, there were no qualitative differences in the swimming behavior of the anesthetized and unanesthetized embryos. Thus, withholding the normal opportunity for prior exercise (neuromuscular function) led to a quantitative imperfection in later neuromuscular function, a result which is in keeping with the present point of view.

Assuming that it can be documented that appropriate function or stimulation does affect the onset, rate of development, or perfection of a system, the next question is whether the sequence of sensory development can be altered by withholding or augmenting normally occurring function or stimulation. To the extent that each system develops relatively independently, acceleration or deceleration of one system would not affect the rate of development of another system. If there is an interdependence between certain systems, acceleration or deceleration of one system would alter the rate of development of another system (either in a compensatory way or in a positively correlated way). If compensation holds, one system might completely outstrip the other, whereas, if the systems are positively correlated, no alteration in the sequence of development would occur because any retardation or acceleration in one system would be matched in the other system. Thus, even if a certain developmental interdependence exists between the sensory systems, as it very likely does in mammals, the kind of change which may occur in related systems is not entirely predictable, so the overall effect on the sequence of sensory development itself is not predictable.

While we are not now in a position to answer the question of the extent to which normally occurring function and stimulation play a role in regulating the otherwise invariant ontogenetic sequence of sensory development in mammals or birds, there are bits and pieces of evidence on the possible effects of function and stimulation on organic maturation and behavioral development, and they will now be cited. The assumption which is basic to the present point of view is that during the maturation of a system there is a bidirectional or reciprocal relationship between structure and function, whereby each affects the other (structure $\leftrightarrow$ function). The more traditional view of maturation, one which has not been discarded in all quarters, is that there is a unidirectional relationship between structure and function, wherein there is no reciprocity or regulative feedback during the maturation process (structure $\rightarrow$ function).

FUNCTION PRIOR TO COMPLETE MATURATION

Certain neurons in a system may be functional without necessarily being responsive to sensory stimulation or being stimulated, so function and stimulation are regarded as separate items. The unanswered question is whether the emission of spontaneous activity affects the maturation of such cells (or neighboring cells). Maturation is defined as the formative period of structural development during which cells are in the process of proliferation, migration, differentiation, and growth.

While we do not yet know whether function itself plays a role in maturation, we now have evidence that at least certain neural cells can become functional while they are still immature. In a recent study

Woodward et al. (1969) were able to record from Purkinje cells in the process of migration in the neonate rat's cerebellum. Specifically, these investigators recorded intermittent spontaneous action potentials from these motor cells several hours after birth when the cells were still in the process of migration from the dorsal rhombencephalic lip. (The characteristic layering of the Purkinje cells is not completed until 2 to 3 days of age.) At the time the recordings were made the Purkinje cell also is still undergoing growth and differentiation (Woodward et al., 1969, pp. 129–131): "The cell bodies enlarge rapidly during the second week; the fine processes disappear; and the apical dendritic tree begins to develop. The Purkinje cell appears mature by 3 weeks of age." While there is as yet no evidence of the occurrence of spontaneous activity in immature *sensory* cells, it seems likely that sensory neurons also have this capability.

An example of a sensory system becoming functional before maturation is complete is furnished by the auditory system, in which electrophysiological responses to sound stimulation are obtained from the opossum and mouse cochlea before the fluid spaces are fully developed (Larsell et al., 1944; Mikaelian and Ruben, 1964). At the time the peripheral part of the auditory system begins functioning, it is responsive only to certain frequencies (Larsell et al., 1944; Mikaelian and Ruben, 1965). The same holds true for the other sensory systems. When the somesthetic system first becomes functional, sensitivity is restricted to one zone of the body (usually that part of the snout or oral region innervated by the trigeminal nerve). The early evoked neural or behavioral activity in the vestibular and visual systems (reviewed in the first part of the chapter) shows them to be functional prior to complete maturity. From these studies, however, it is not known (1) whether function of the mature parts of a system affects the maturation of the immature parts of the system or, in case of the possibility of function in immature sensory cells, (2) whether function affects their own rate of maturation.

A recent study by Hogg and Bryant (1969) adds considerable substance to the notion that immature neural tissue is capable of function. According to their findings, at the time the rat fetus first evinces an overt response to tactile stimulation, the tips of the still growing sensory nerve fibers are well below the surface epithelium and, more importantly, there are no recognizable receptors on the nerve endings at the time stimulation is effective. The same statements apparently hold for the first tactile response of the human fetus (Humphrey, 1964). The means by which the neural impulse is initiated at this time is not known; possibly it is activated by pressure or mechanical deformation of the nerve fiber (Hogg and Bryant, 1969).

Since we have indications that immature (motor) cells are capable of spontaneous activity, and function can be evoked in sensory systems prior to maturity, it is not entirely implausible to assume that normally occurring function and sensory stimulation may play some role in regulating the rate of maturation of neural networks. We will now turn to the very limited body of evidence on this point.

DECELERATION OF MATURATION IN THE VISUAL SYSTEM AS A CONSEQUENCE OF LIGHT DEPRIVATION

The visual system is an easy one to deprive or to augment, and almost all of the studies of the effect of normally occurring sensory stimulation on maturation have been performed on the visual system. For the present purpose, certain studies involving prolonged deprivation are of little value because the deficits evident in these studies merely show the importance of stimulation for maintaining a system rather than for influencing maturation (e.g., Wiesel and Hubel, 1963). While the present concern is the effect of stimulation on the maturation of avian and mammalian sense organs, it is interesting to note parenthetically that even larval arthropod photoreceptor cells show a dependence on light for their normal development (White, 1968).

Zetterström (1956) has studied the functional maturation of the visual receptor in kittens by means of the electroretinogram (ERG). The developing kitten ERG assumes its completely adult form at 9 to 10 weeks in normally reared litters. Kittens reared in light begin to show an ERG between 6 to 10 days after birth, whereas dark-reared kittens show a delay up to 28 days in the first appearance of the ERG. After 28 days kittens maintained in the dark show an ERG which is normal for their age, with the exception of a longer latency of the very first response.

The various parts of the visual system react differently to light deprivation. In house mice, the rate of maturation is decelerated in the retina, lateral geniculate body, and visual cortex, while the size and composition of the optic nerve fibers (except myelinization) are unaffected by deprivation (Gyllensten and Malmfors, 1963; Gyllensten *et al.*, 1965, 1966a,b). While the myelin sheaths and visual cortex eventually reach their normal size and composition in the absence of light, the retina and the lateral geniculate body remain slightly hypotrophied. From the biochemical point of view, in rats light deprivation results in a decrease in acetylcholinesterase in the superior colliculi and lateral geniculate bodies, whereas no change in enzymic activity occurs in the visual cortex (Maletta and Timiras, 1967). What is most interesting from the present standpoint is the compensatory growth which occurs in the auditory cortex as a consequence of light deprivation (Gyllensten *et al.,* 1966a). The mechanism for this enhancement, whether it occurs from increased reliance on audition or for some other reason, is not known. The change is a rather complicated one. Early in development both the auditory and visual cortex show hypotrophy (though there is less hypotrophy in the auditory cortex), whereas later on, beginning at 4 months of age, the auditory cortex shows hypertrophy.

Many years ago a dispute arose over the necessity of myelinization for function and, in that context, a large number of light-deprivation studies were conducted on various mammalian forms (most of which are reviewed by Warkentin and Smith, 1937). While it is no longer disputed that function can occur prior to, or without, myelinization, those studies are pertinent in the present context because they indicate a deceleration in rate of myelin deposition in the visual system as a consequence of light deprivation. Since the presence of myelin does accelerate neural transmission time, a decrement of myelin deposition at any age probably would cause prolonged latencies in visual responsiveness, and that would affect the rate at which the visual system becomes functionally perfected. While visual stimulation can accelerate myelin deposition in the optic nerve (and thereby shorten transmission time), it is important to know that myelinization of the optic nerve eventually becomes normal in the absence of visual stimulation (Gyllensten *et al.,* 1966b). Thus, while sensory stimulation is not essential to the ultimate formation of myelin, stimulation does affect the rate at which myelin is formed. And thus, the experimental evidence shows that the rate of anatomical and functional maturation in the visual system is regulated by exposure to light.

Though proprioception is not one of the systems reviewed here, it is pertinent to mention in passing that muscular movement may play a role in the functional maturation of the brain of chick embryos. While spontaneous electrical potentials are present around day 13 (the precocial chick hatches on day 20), additional bursts of cerebral electrical activity accompany motor movement that is of especially long duration, and this electrical activity (as well as the spontaneous electrical activity) ceases when the motor system is paralyzed at any time between day 13 and day 17 (Bogdanov, 1963). After day 17 motor paralysis does not abolish the ongoing electrical activity, a situation which Bogdanov interprets as indicating the effectiveness of other sensory modalities in maintaining the tonus of the central nervous system. As a form of control, Bogdanov reports that direct application of the paralytic substance to the brain (in a dosage ten times greater than the experimental concentration) did not significantly alter the electrical activity. Also, sectioning the spinal cord below the medulla abolished or suppressed the cerebral electrical activity before day 17 but not thereafter. Thus, the possibility is open that motor movement may generate proprioceptive impulses which contribute to the functional activity of the chick embryo's brain between day 13 and day 17 of development. [This suggestion in no way contradicts the capacity of the chick embryo to move in the absence of proprioceptive or other stimulation, as demonstrated by Hamburger et al. (1966); nor does the chick's capacity for autogenous motility contradict the possibility that muscular movement in the intact embryo contributes to the functional development of the nervous system.]

Since the visual system is the last one to develop, studies which show a delay in visual maturation as a consequence of deprivation are much less relevant to the question of the invariance of the sequence of sensory development than ones which show an acceleration as a consequence of augmentation.

ACCELERATION OF MATURATION IN THE VISUAL SYSTEM AS A CONSEQUENCE OF AUGMENTED LIGHT STIMULATION

One has the impression that the rate of sensory maturation is much more readily retarded by deprivation than it is accelerated by augmentation. There have been very few attempts to accelerate sensory maturation by precocious or increased stimulation, however.

In chick embryos, Peters et al. (1956) incidentally observed an acceleration in the evoked cerebral response to flashes of light as a consequence of prior exposure to a few light flashes. In a controlled follow-up of that study, using duck embryos, Paulson (1965) found that 24 hours of prior light exposure (1) lowered the age at which 100% of the embryos responded to photic stimulation, (2) decreased the latency of the a-wave of the ERG, and (3) decreased the latency of the evoked response at the optic lobe.

While exposure to continuous illumination significantly shortens the incubation period in various strains of chickens (Gold, 1969; Lauber and Shutze, 1964; Siegel et al., 1969), this effect is primarily nonvisual, operating, as it does, most strongly during the first week of incubation when the visual system is in a very rudimentary stage of development. It is pertinent, however, that the right eye of illuminated embryos becomes larger than their left eye on six indices of growth, a condition which does not exist in nonilluminated embryos (Lauber and Shutze, 1964). Due to the embryo's position in the egg during the final half of incubation, the right eye is exposed to more light than the left eye. Thus, light may stimulate biochemical or hormonal activity which affects metabolic and growth processes in certain parts of the nervous system.

While the connection (if any) between sensory stimulation and the release of growth hormones is not known, it is of interest that, in rats, prenatal administration of bovine pituitary growth hormone or somatotropin itself causes an increase in proliferation of cortical neurons which leads to a higher cortical neuron density (Zamenhof et al., 1966) and an acceleration in reflexive development prior to weaning (Clendinnen and Eayrs, 1961; Ray and Hochhauser, 1969). Since some of the neurosecretory organs (hypothalamus and pineal body in particular) are responsive directly or indirectly to light cycles, it is not beyond the realm of possibility that light could affect metabolic and maturational processes mediated by the release of hormones during the embryonic period in birds and the neonatal period in mammals. [Since it may be relevant to the very early stages of avian embryonic development, mention is made of the light sensitivity of melanophores in neural crest explants in amphibia (Bagnara and Obika, 1967).]

One of the main problems of investigating the effects of precocious or increased amounts of stimulation on sensory maturation is that excessive stimulation can be deleterious as well as beneficial. Chronic exposure to light, for example, can cause retinal atrophy or damage, as shown by studies of newborn chicks and rats (Lauber et al., 1961; Noell et al., 1966). For certain kinds of early stimulation studies, it is also most important to control for litter effects (D. L. King, 1969).

DECELERATION OF MATURATION IN THE AUDITORY SYSTEM AS A CONSEQUENCE OF SOUND DEPRIVATION

Behavioral evidence indicates that duck embryos are capable of hearing at least 5 days before hatching. In the normal course of events, the embryos begin vocalizing 3 days before hatching. If the embryos are deprived of hearing their own vocalizations and the vocalizations of sibs, they show a 24-hour delay in the appearance of their usual ability to distinguish the maternal call of their own species from that of other species after hatching (Gottlieb, 1971).

Thus, withholding normally occurring auditory stimulation causes a deceleration in the rate of maturation of the auditory system in ducklings.

ACCELERATION OF MATURATION IN THE AUDITORY SYSTEM AS A CONSEQUENCE OF SOUND AUGMENTATION

Duck embryos first respond overtly to the maternal call of their species on day 22 (5 days before hatching), at which time they show an inhibition of bill-clapping in response to the maternal call. They begin vocalizing on day 24, and the kind of bill-clapping response they make to the maternal call changes at that time; beginning on day 24, they show an excitation of bill-clapping to the maternal call. While it has not yet been possible to either accelerate or decelerate the onset of the initial overt (bill-clapping) response to the maternal call on day 22, it is possible, by precocious exposure to the vocalizations of sibs, to accelerate the change in bill-clapping response which normally occurs on day 24 (Gottlieb, 1971). Namely, the precociously stimulated embryos show an excitation of bill-clapping to the maternal call on day 23 instead of day 24, indicating that a more advanced aurally mediated response has been brought about by the prior stimulation. Thus, precocious exposure to normally occurring auditory stimulation accelerates the sequence of changes in the maturation of an aurally mediated response in duck embryos.

DECELERATION AND ACCELERATION OF MATURATION OF THE REPRODUCTIVE SYSTEM AS A CONSEQUENCE OF SENSORY STIMULATION

To return momentarily to the question of sensory stimulative effects on glandular secretion, it has been demonstrated that 9-month-old virgin male budgerigars (parakeets) show normal development of testicular activity only if they have been able to hear themselves produce typical budgerigar vocalizations (the "loud warble" in particular). Partially devocalized males do not develop full testicular activity (compared to sham-operated and nonoperated birds), even when they are exposed to the normal vocalizations of other males of the same age (Brockway, 1967). This is the first direct evidence that auditory self-stimulation plays a role in regulating the maturation of species-typical neuroendocrine or reproductive physiological activity.

In house mice, Vandenbergh (1969) has demonstrated that exposure of young female mice to the odor of adult males prior to weaning regulates sexual maturation (vaginal opening and first estrus). When they are not exposed to any males or male odors, or when they are exposed to castrated males, females come into first estrus at about 54 days after birth. However, when the females are exposed to an intact male or simply the soiled bedding from the cage of an intact male, first estrus occurs at 39 to 45 days after birth. Thus, the rate of sexual maturation in female mice is accelerated or decelerated depending on exposure to normally occurring odoriferous stimulation during the first 21 days after birth.

Summary and Conclusions

The ontogenetic sequence in which the sensory systems develop in the chick embryo is tactile–vestibular–auditory–visual. That same sequence is present in opossums, rats, deermice, rabbits, cats, and man. For reasons of insufficient evidence, it is not known definitely whether the sequence also holds for house mice, guinea pigs, and sheep; however, no marked or obvious contradictions are present in those species. Thus, the sequence of development of these sensory systems transcends particular divergent evolutionary pathways and the varying social and ecological factors which are peculiar to each species. Since birds and mammals have evolved along entirely separate courses from their extinct reptilian ancestors, the sequence of sensory development in reptiles very likely conforms to that of birds and mammals.

Since none of the avian or mammalian species under consideration is ancestral to any of the other species, it seems quite possible that the tactile–vestibular–auditory–visual sequence of sensory development was present in the extinct ancestors of birds (archosaurian reptiles) and in the extinct ancestors of mammals (therapsid reptiles). This inference could be placed on a very firm foundation if current monotremes (egg-laying mammals which retain many more reptilian characteristics than placental or marsupial mammals) and crocodilians (which are descended from archosaurians) also show the same sequence of sensory development. Such an outcome would point to the presence of the sequence in the stem reptiles (if not earlier in phylogeny), and this eventuality could, in turn, be assessed by an analysis of the sequence in turtles (descended from stem reptiles). The sparse information available on the ontogenesis of sensory function in turtle embryos indicates that they may indeed show the tactile–vestibular–auditory–visual sequence. If all of these species show the same sequence of sensory development, it would seem improbable that we are dealing with innumerable instances of convergent evolution, but, rather, that the sequence has remained unchanged from the earliest ancestral reptile groups and perhaps originated even earlier in phylogeny. Although the sequence per se is the same in extant birds and mammals, the specific time of onset of each sensory system does show interspecific variation (heterochrony), and this would appear to be related to species-specific ecological and other factors.

From an ontogenetic point of view, man and the other primates are unique in having combined the precocial pattern of sensory development with the altricial pattern of motor development. Namely, man is the only one of the altricial species in which all of the sensory systems become capable of function prior to birth. This sensory precocity is usually reserved for motorically precocious species such as guinea pigs and sheep. Along this line, we are reminded of the dependence of evolution on alterations in ontogeny. While the sequence in which the sensory systems develop is a homochronous phenomenon, the acceleration of sensory function in man is a heterochronous phenomenon. Instances of homochrony are merely repetitions of ancestral ontogenetic stages in the ontogeny of descendants. Thus, they are phylogenetic heritages which represent affinities between species, but being a conservative feature of evolution, they have little or no immediate value for speciation. Heterochrony, however, incorporates something new or different in ontogeny and thereby provides the ontogenetic material which is essential for evolution and speciation. While heterochronic phenomena are species-specific, a homochronic pattern such as the sequence of sensory development is species-general. While, as Anokhin (1964) suggests, heterochrony may result in a positive adaptive effect for the neonate and may be directly related to ecological differences between species, homochrony would appear only to offer developmental constraints which are neutral with respect to the adaptation of the newborn and ecological differences between species. Although there can be little doubt about the importance of heterochrony in the adaptive economy of each species, it should be noted that instances of marked heterochrony may sometimes tend to obscure the homochronic or otherwise homologous aspects of neural and behavioral ontogenesis. Application of the concept of homology to behavior is a very complicated affair (Atz, 1970), and the pervasiveness of heterochrony undoubtedly contributes to the problem by making it far easier to detect species differences than to detect similarities between species.

Although the homochrony of the somesthetic, vestibular, auditory, and visual systems does not illuminate mechanisms of evolution—where species differences in ontogeny are more germane than similarities—the pervasiveness of the sequence poses an excellent testing ground for our most basic conceptions of the ontogeny of the nervous system and behavior. Namely, while genetic, cytoplasmic, and other biochemical factors undoubtedly play an indispensable role in the maturation process, the possibility is raised that cellular function and sensory stimulation also play a role in regulating the species-typical rate of structural maturation and in completing sensory development, especially with respect to fully adaptive or adjustive behavior. The ontogenetic question is this: Does the invariant sequence of sensory development observed in mammalian and avian species represent a probabilistic outcome of the joint operation of genetic, biochemical, functional, and sensory stimulative conditions which occur during the normal course of development in the intact animal? This is in contrast to the idea that molecular or intrinsic biochemical processes are solely responsible for the complete and orderly structural maturation of the nervous system.

While there are relatively few experiments on this topic, it is known that certain nerve cells are capable of spontaneous function while they are undergoing the terminal phases of migration, differentiation, and growth (that is, before maturation is complete). It is not known whether cellular function itself, independent of sensory stimulation, plays a regulative role in the maturation process. Acceleration and deceleration of maturation does occur as a consequence of sensory augmentation and deprivation. However, it is too soon to say whether the sequence of sensory development is altered by these changes, especially since the only studies available deal exclusively with visual and auditory maturation.

In the future it should prove profitable to examine the effects of function or sensory stimulation on systems other than the one being directly manipulated. There is some evidence for developmental interdependence between the sensory systems, so that changes occurring in one system can cause changes in the rate of development or ultimate perfection of other systems. In this regard it might be enlightening to examine the effects on auditory and visual development caused by manipulations of the somesthetic and vestibular systems.

Finally, I think it would repay us to be more sensitive to the limits placed on our conceptualizations by the now current ideas of "function," as defined by histology, electrophysiology, and behavior. We have seen in this review that a behavioral response to stimulation sometimes occurs prior to the time when there is histological or physiological evidence for the functional capability of the system, and vice versa. This circumstance emboldens me to repeat a suggestion I have made before in the case where there is no immediate behavioral, physiological, or histological evidence of function: if the later behavior or physiology of a system is affected by withholding or augmenting stimulation during a supposed prefunctional stage, then that system can be regarded as in fact having been functional at the time of stimulus deprivation or augmentation. It is in this way that we can overcome preconceptions or limitations imposed on us by strictly technical deficiencies or, even more important, our current ignorance about the developmental conditions under which function is possible.

Along the lines of unconventional functions, it is enlightening to learn that electrical impulses of a nonneural and nonmuscular origin are present in the skin of toad larvae (A. Roberts, 1969). Activity in this "ectodermal conducting system" is evoked by tactile stimulation. Since this capability arises during the transition to the free-swimming stage, it could possibly play some role in the behavior of the larvae, but that has not been documented. From the present point of view, the main importance of Roberts' finding is the implication that parts of an immature organism can be sensitive to sensory stimulation in advance of conventional neural innervation. While it is not known whether a similar capability is present in avian and mammalian forms, when the rat fetus and the human fetus first respond to tactile stimulation, the growing tips of the trigeminal nerve fibers are well below the surface epithelium and the fibers possess no specialized nerve endings at that time (Hogg and Bryant, 1969; Humphrey, 1964). Light affects the ongoing motility of the chick embryo during the first week of incubation (Bursian, 1965), and embryos exposed to light at this time also hatch precociously (Lauber and Shutze, 1964; and others), but the mechanism of action of photic stimulation during this period is unknown.

ACKNOWLEDGMENTS

I appreciate the helpful comments of Tryphena Humphrey, Ronald W. Oppenheim, and Marieta B. Heaton on an earlier draft of this paper.

I am indebted to Rainer Foelix for photographic assistance; he made the pictures of the neonatal house mouse, rat, rabbit, and guinea pig which appear in this chapter. Acknowledgment is also made to Robert Woll and Marieta B. Heaton, Paul Heron and Kristi Dege, Tryphena Humphrey, Lester C. Ulberg, and Philip S. Ulinski and John Johnson for graciously allowing me to reproduce their pictures of kittens, deermice, human fetuses, lambs, and opossums, respectively.

This review was written in connection with research activities supported by the National Institute of Child Health and Human Development (Research Grant HD-00878).

REFERENCES

Alford, B. R., and Ruben, R. J. (1963). Physiological, behavioral and anatomical correlates of the development of hearing in the mouse. *Ann. Otol., Rhinol., & Laryngol.* Vol. 72, 237–247.

Änggård, L. (1965). An electrophysiological study of the development of cochlear functions in the rabbit. *Acta Oto-Laryngol.* Suppl. 203, 1–64.

Änggård, L., Bergström, R., and Bernhard, C. G. (1961). Analysis of prenatal spinal reflex activity in sheep. *Acta Physiol. Scand.* Vol. 53, 128–136.

Angulo y González, A. W. (1932). The prenatal development of behavior in the albino rat. *J. Comp. Neurol.* Vol. 55, 395–442.

Anokhin, P. K. (1964). Systemogenesis as a general regulator of brain development. *Progr. Brain Res.* Vol. 9, 54–86.

Åström, K.-E. (1967). On the early development of the isocortex in fetal sheep. *Progr. Brain Res.* Vol. 26, 1–59.

Atz, J. W. (1970). Application of the idea of homology to behavior. *In* "Development and Evolution of Behavior" (L. R. Aronson *et al.*, eds.), pp. 53–74. Freeman, San Francisco, California.

Avery, G. T. (1928). Responses of foetal guinea pigs prematurely delivered. *Genet. Psychol. Monogr.* Vol. 3, 248–331.

Bagnara, J. T., and Obika, M. (1967). Light sensitivity of melanophores in neural crest explants. *Experientia* Vol. 23, 1–6.

Barcroft, J., and Barron, D. H. (1939). The development of behavior in foetal sheep. *J. Comp. Neurol.* Vol. 70, 477–502.

Bergström, R. M., Hellström, P. E., and Stenberg, D. (1961). An intrauterine technique for recording of EEG in animals. *Ann. Chir. Gynaecol. Fenn.* Vol. 50, 430–433.

Bernhard, C. G., Kaiser, I. H., and Kolmodin, G. M. (1959). On the development of cortical activity in fetal sheep. *Acta Physiol. Scand.* Vol. 47, 333–349.

Bernhard, C. G., Kolmodin, G. M., and Meyerson, B. A. (1967). On the prenatal development of function and structure in the somesthetic cortex of the sheep. *Prog. Brain Res.* Vol. 26, 60–77.

Bodian, D. (1968). Development of fine structure of spinal cord in monkey fetuses. II. Pre-reflex period to period of long intersegmental reflexes. *J. Comp. Neurol.* Vol. 133, 113–166.

Bogdanov, O. V. (1963). The significance of proprioceptive input for functional maturation of the central nervous system in the chick embryo. *Sechenov Physiol. J. USSR* Vol. 49, 701–705 (translated from Russian).

Bredberg, G. (1968). Cellular pattern and nerve supply of the human organ of Corti. *Acta Oto-Laryngol.* Suppl. 236, 1–135.

Brockway, B. F. (1967). The influence of vocal behavior on the performer's testicular activity in budgerigars (*Melopsittacus undulatus*). *Wilson Bull.* Vol. 79, 328–334.

Bursian, A. V. (1965). Primitive forms of photosensitivity at early stages of embryogenesis in the chick. *J. Evol. Biochem. Physiol.* Vol. 1, 435–441 (translated from Russian).

Carmichael, L. (1926). The development of behavior in vertebrates experimentally removed from the influence of external stimulation. *Psychol. Rev.* Vol. 33, 51–58.

Carmichael, L. (1934). An experimental study in the prenatal guinea pig of the origin and development of reflexes and patterns of behavior in relation to the stimulation of specific receptor areas during the period of active fetal life. *Genet. Psychol. Monogr.* Vol. 16, 338–491.

Chodynicki, S. (1968). Embryogenesis of the auditory part of the inner ear in the guinea pig. *Acta Theriol.* Vol. 13, 219–260.

Clendinnen, B. G., and Eayrs, J. T. (1961). The anatomical and physiological effects of prenatally administered somatotrophin on cerebral development in rats. *J. Endocrinol.* Vol. 22, 183–193.

Coghill, G. E. (1929). "Anatomy and the Problem of Behavior." Cambridge Univ. Press, London and New York.

Coronios, J. D. (1933). Development of behavior in the fetal cat. *Genet. Psychol. Monogr.* Vol. 14, 283–383.

Crain, S. M., Bornstein, M. B., and Peterson, E. R. (1968). Development of functional organization in cultured embryonic CNS tissues during chronic exposure to agents which prevent bioelectric activity. *In* "Ontogenesis of the Brain" (L. Jílek and S. Trojan, eds.), pp. 19-25. Charles Univ. Press, Prague.

Crowley, D. E., and Hepp-Reymond, M.-C. (1966). Development of cochlear function in the ear of the infant rat. *J. Comp. Physiol. Psychol.* Vol. 62, 427-432.

Crozier, W. J., and Pincus, G. (1937). Photic stimulation of young rats. *J. Gen. Psychol.* Vol. 17, 105-111.

de Beer, G. R. (1951). "Embryos and Ancestors," rev. ed. Oxford Univ. Press (Clarendon), London and New York.

Denisova, M. P., and Figurin, N. L. (1929). The problem of the first associated food reflexes in infants. (See Razran, 1933.)

Detwiler, S. R. (1932). Experimental observations upon the developing rat retina. *J. Comp. Neurol.* Vol. 55, 473-492.

Donovan, A. (1966). The postnatal development of the cat retina. *Exp. Eye Res.* Vol. 5, 249-254.

Ellingson, R. J. (1960). Cortical electrical responses to visual stimulation in the human infant. *Electroencephalogr. Clin. Neurophysiol.* Vol. 12, 663-677.

Ellingson, R. J., and Wilcott, R. C. (1960). Development of evoked responses in visual and auditory cortices of kittens. *J. Neurophysiol.* Vol. 23, 363-375.

Engel, R. (1964). Electroencephalographic responses to photic stimulation, and their correlation with maturation. *Ann. N. Y. Acad. Sci.* Vol. 117, 407-412.

Fish, M. W., and Windle, W. F. (1932). The effect of rotatory stimulation on the movements of the head and eyes in newborn and young kittens. *J. Comp. Neurol.* Vol. 54, 103-107.

Fitzgerald, J. E., and Windle, W. F. (1942). Some observations on early human fetal activity. *J. Comp. Neurol.* Vol. 76, 159-167.

Fleischer, K. (1955). Untersuchungen zur Entwicklung der Innenohrfunktion (Intrauterine Kindsbewegungen nach Schallreizen). *Z. Laryngol. Rhinol.* Vol 34, 733-740.

Fromme, A. (1941). An experimental study of the factors of maturation and practice in the behavioral development of the embryo of the frog, *Rana pipiens*. *Genet. Psychol. Monogr.* Vol. 24, 219-256.

Galebsky, A. (1927). Vestibular nystagmus in new-born infants. *Acta Oto-Laryngol.* Vol. 11, 409-423.

Gold, P. S. (1969). Effects of prehatching stimulation on growth and behavior in a domestic chick. *Amer. Zool.* Vol. 9, 1074 (abstr.).

Gottlieb, G. (1968). Prenatal behavior of birds. *Quart. Rev. Biol.* Vol. 43, 148-174.

Gottlieb, G. (1971). "Development of Species Identification in Birds: An Inquiry into the Prenatal Determinants of Perception." Univ. of Chicago Press, Chicago, Illinois.

Gyllensten, L. (1959). Postnatal development of the visual cortex in darkness (mice). *Acta Morphol. Neer.-Scand.* Vol. 2, 331-345.

Gyllensten, L., and Malmfors, T. (1963). Myelinization of the optic nerve and its dependence on visual function—a quantitative investigation in mice. *J. Embryol. Exp. Morphol.* Vol. 11, 255-266.

Gyllensten, L., Malmfors, T., and Norrlin, M.-L. (1965). Effect of visual deprivation on the optic centers of growing and adult mice. *J. Comp. Neurol.* Vol. 124, 149-160.

Gyllensten, L., Malmfors, T., and Norrlin, M.-L. (1966a). Growth alteration in the auditory cortex of visually deprived mice. *J. Comp. Neurol.* Vol. 126, 463-470.

Gyllensten, L., Malmfors, T., and Norrlin-Grettve, M.-L. (1966b). Developmental and functional alterations in the fiber composition of the optic nerve in visually deprived mice. *J. Comp. Neurol.* Vol. 128, 413–418.

Hamburger, V., Wenger, E., and Oppenheim, R. (1966). Motility in the chick embryo in the absence of sensory input. *J. Exp. Zool.* Vol. 162, 133–160.

Harrison, R. G. (1904). An experimental study of the relation of the nervous system to the developing musculature of the frog. *Amer. J. Anat.* Vol. 3, 197–220.

Hartman, C. G. (1920). Studies in the development of the opossum *Didelphys virginiana* L. V. The phenomena of parturition. *Anat. Rec.* Vol. 19, 251–261.

Haynes, H., White, B. L., and Held, R. (1965). Visual accomodation in human infants. *Science* Vol. 148, 528–530.

Heck, W. E. (1952). Vestibular responses in the newborn. *Arch. Otolaryngol.* Vol. 56, 573.

Hibbard, E. (1964). Selective innervation and reciprocal functional suppression from grafted extra labyrinths in amphibians. *Exp. Neurol.* Vol. 10, 271–283.

Hodos, W., and Campbell, C. B. G. (1969). *Scala Naturae:* Why there is no theory in comparative psychology. *Psychol. Rev.* Vol. 76, 337–350.

Hogg, I. D., and Bryant, J. W. (1969). The development of sensory innervation in the mouth and pharynx of the albino Norway rat (*Mus norvegicus albinus*). *J. Neurol.* Vol. 136, 33–56.

Hooker, D. (1952). "The Prenatal Origin of Behavior." Univ. of Kansas Press, Lawrence, Kansas.

Humphrey, T. (1964). Some correlations between the appearance of human fetal reflexes and the development of the nervous system. *Progr. Brain Res.* Vol. 4, 93–133.

Humphrey, T. (1965). The embryologic differentiation of the vestibular nuclei in man correlated with functional development. *Int. Symp. Vestibular Oculomotor Problems, 1965* pp. 51–56.

Humphrey, T. (1968). The development of mouth opening and related reflexes involving the oral area of human fetuses. *Ala. J. Med. Sci.* Vol. 5, 126–157.

Humphrey, T. (1969). Personal communication.

Hunt, W. E., and Goldring, S. (1951). Maturation of evoked response in the visual cortex in the postnatal rabbit. *Electroencephalogr. Clin. Neurophysiol.* Vol. 3, 465–471.

Jasper, H. H., Bridgman, C. S., and Carmichael, L. (1937). An ontogenetic study of cerebral electrical potentials in the guinea pig. *J. Exp. Psychol.* Vol. 21, 63–71.

Kasatkin, N. I., and Levikova, A. M. (1935). On the development of early conditioned reflexes and differentiations of auditory stimuli in infants. *J. Exp. Psychol.* Vol. 18, 1–19.

Keeler, C. E., Sutcliffe, E., and Chaffee, E. L. (1928). A description of the ontogenetic development of retinal action currents in the house mouse. *Proc. Nat. Acad. Sci. U. S.* Vol. 14, 811–815.

King, D. L. (1969). The effect of early experience and litter on some weight and maturational variables. *Develop. Psychol.* Vol. 1, 576–584.

King, J. A. (1969). Personal communication.

Klyavina, M. P., and Obraztsova, G. A. (1968). The influence of the sound stimulus intensity on the time and amplitude characteristics of the cerebral cortex evoked potentials in early postnatal ontogenesis of a rabbit. *In* "Ontogenesis of the Brain" (L. Jílek and S. Trojan, eds.), pp. 395–400. Charles Univ. Press, Prague.

Lane, H. H. (1917). The correlation between structure and function in the development of the special senses of the white rat. *Univ. Okla. Bull., Univ. Stud.* No. 8, New Ser. No. 140, 1–88.

Langworthy, O. R. (1928). The behavior of pouch-young oppossums correlated with the myelinization of tracts in the nervous system. *J. Comp. Neurol.* Vol. 46, 201–247.

Langworthy, O. R. (1933). Development of behavior patterns and myelinization of the nervous system in the human fetus and infant. *Carnegie Inst. Contrib. Embryol.* No. 139, 1–65.

Larsell, O., McCrady, E., and Larsell, J. F. (1944). Development of the organ of Corti in relation to the inception of hearing. *Arch. Otolaryngol.* Vol. 40, 233–248.

Larsell, O., McCrady, E., and Zimmerman, A. A. (1935). Morphological and functional development of the membranous labyrinth in the opossum. *J. Comp. Neurol.* Vol. 63, 95–118.

Lauber, J. K., and Shutze, J. V. (1964). Accelerated growth of embryo chicks under the influence of light. *Growth* Vol. 28, 179–190.

Lauber, J. K., Shutze, J. V., and McGinnis, J. (1961). Effects of exposure to continuous light on the eye of the growing chick. *Proc. Soc. Exp. Biol. Med.* Vol. 106, 871–872.

Lawrence, M. M., and Feind, C. R. (1953). Vestibular responses to rotation in the newborn infant. *Pediatrics,* Vol. 12, 300–306.

Layne, J. N. (1968). Ontogeny. In "Biology of Peromyscus (Rodentia)" (J. A. King, ed.), Am. Soc. Mammalogists. Spec. Publ. No. 2, pp. 148–253.

Lemmon, W. B., and Patterson, G. H. (1964). Depth perception in sheep: Effects of interrupting the mother-neonate bond. *Science* Vol. 145, 835–836.

Lipsitt, L. P., and Kaye, H. (1964). Conditioned sucking in the human newborn. *Psychon. Sci.* Vol. 1, 29–30.

McGraw, M. B. (1941). Development of rotary-vestibular reactions of the human infant. *Child Develop.* Vol. 12, 17–19.

Maletta, G. J., and Timiras, P. S. (1967). Acetylcholinesterase activity in optic structures after complete light deprivation from birth. *Exp. Neurol.* Vol. 19, 513–518.

Mann, I. (1964). "The Development of the Human Eye," 3rd ed. Grune & Stratton, New York.

Marty, R., and Scherrer, J. (1964). Critères de maturation des systèmes afférents corticaux. *Progr. Brain Res.* Vol. 4, 222–236.

Matthews, S. A., and Detwiler, S. R. (1926). The reactions of Amblystoma embryos following prolonged treatment with chloretone. *J. Exp. Zool.* Vol. 45, 279–292.

Meyerson, B. A., and Persson, H. E. (1969). Evoked unitary and gross electric activity in the cerebral cortex in early prenatal ontogeny. *Nature* Vol. 221, 1248–1249.

Mikaelian, D., and Ruben, R. J. (1965). Development of hearing in the normal CBA-J mouse. Correlation of physiological observations with behavioral responses and with cochlear anatomy. *Acta Oto-Laryngol.* Vol. 59, 451–461.

Minkowski, M. (1928). Neurobiologische Studien am menschlichen Foetus. In "Handbuch der biologischen Arbeitsmethoden" (E. Abderhalden, ed.), Sect. V, Part 5B, No. 5, Sr. No. 253, pp. 511–618. Urban & Schwarzenberg, Berlin.

Molliver, M. E. (1967). An ontogenetic study of evoked somesthetic cortical responses in the sheep. *Progr. Brain Res.* Vol. 26, 78–92.

Murphy, K. P., and Smyth, C. N. (1962). Response of foetus to auditory stimulation. *Lancet* Vol. 5, 972–973.

Noell, W. K. (1958). Studies on visual cell viability and differentiation. *Ann. N. Y. Acad. Sci.* Vol. 74, 337–361.

Noell, W. K., Walker, V. S., Kang, B. S., and Berman, S. (1966). Retinal damage by light in rats. *Invest. Ophthalmol.* Vol. 5, 450–473.

Pankratz, D. S. (1931). A preliminary report on the fetal movements in the rabbit. *Anat. Rec.* Suppl. 48, 58–59 (abstr.).

Paulson, G. W. (1965). Maturation of evoked responses in the duckling. *Exp. Neurol.* Vol. 11, 324–333.

Peiper, A. (1963). "Cerebral Function in Infancy and Childhood." Consultants Bureau, New York.

Peters, J. J., Vonderahe, A. R., and Powers, T. H. (1956). The functional chronology in developing chick nervous system. *J. Exp. Zool.* Vol. 133, 505–518.

Preyer, W. (1885). "Specielle Physiologie des Embryo. Untersuchungen über die Lebenserscheinungen vor der Geburt." Grieben, Leipzig.

Pujol, R., and Marty, R. (1968). Structural and physiological relationships of the maturing auditory system. *In* "Ontogenesis of the Brain" (L. Jílek and S. Trojan, eds.), pp. 377–385. Charles Univ. Press, Prague.

Rawdon-Smith, A. F., Carmichael, L., and Wellman, B. (1938). Electrical responses from the cochlea of the fetal guinea pig. *J. Exp. Psychol.* Vol. 23, 531–535.

Ray, O. S., and Hochhauser, S. (1969). Growth hormone and environmental complexity effects on behavior in the rat. *Develop. Psychol.* Vol. 1, 311–317.

Razran, G. H. (1933). Conditioned responses in children: A behavioral and quantitative critical review of experimental studies. *Arch. Psychol.* Vol. 148, 73–75. [Citation of Denisova and Figurin experiment (1929).]

Reynolds, H. C. (1954). Studies on reproduction in the opossum (*Didelphis virginiana virginiana*). *Univ. Calif., Berkeley, Publ., Zool.* Vol. 52, 223–283.

Roberts, A. (1969). Conducted impulses in the skin of young tadpoles. *Nature (London)* Vol. 222, 1265–1266.

Roberts, W. W., Steinberg, M. L., and Means, L. W. (1967). Hypothalamic mechanisms for sexual, aggressive, and other motivational behaviors in the opossum, *Didelphis virginiana*. *J. Physiol. Comp. Psychol.* Vol. 64, 1–15.

Romer, A. S. (1966). "Vertebrate Paleontology," 3rd ed. Univ. of Chicago Press, Chicago, Illinois.

Rose, G. H. (1968). The development of visually evoked electrocortical responses in the rat. *Develop. Psychobiol.* Vol. 1, 35–40.

Rose, G. H., and Lindsley, D. B. (1968). Development of visually evoked potentials in kittens: Specific and nonspecific responses. *J. Neurophysiol.* Vol. 31, 607–623.

Rosen, M. G., and McLaughlin, A. (1966). Maternal and fetal electroencephalography in the guinea pig. *Amer. J. Obstet. Gynecol.* Vol. 95, 997–1000. [Further details in Rosen, M. G., & McLaughlin, A. (1966). Fetal and maternal electroencephalography in the guinea pig. *Exp. Neurol.* Vol. 16, 181–190.]

Rubel, E. W. (1969). A comparison of somatotopic organization in sensory neocortex of newborn kittens and adult cats. Ph.D. Thesis, Michigan State University, East Lansing, Michigan.

Scherrer, J. (1968). Electrophysiological aspects of cortical development. *Progr. Brain Res.* Vol. 22, 480–489.

Schmidt, R. S., and Fernandez, C. (1963). Development of mammalian endocochlear potential. *J. Exp. Zool.* Vol. 153, 227–235.

Sidman, R. L., and Wislocki, G. B. (1954). Histochemical observations on rods and cones in retinas of vertebrates. *J. Histochem. Cytochem.* Vol. 6, 413–433.

Siegel, P. B., Isakson, S. T., Coleman, F. N., and Huffman, B. J. (1969). Photo-acceleration of development in chick embryos. *Comp. Biochem. Physiol.* Vol. 28, 753–758.

Smith, K. V., and Daniel, R. S. (1946). Observations of behavioral development in the loggerhead turtle *(Caretta caretta)*. *Science* Vol. 104, 154–156.

Storrs, E. E., and Williams, R. J. (1968). A study of monozygous quadruplet armadillos in relation to mammalian inheritance. *Proc. Nat. Acad. Sci. U. S.* Vol. 60, 910–914.

Sviderskaya, G. E. (1967). Effect of sound on the motor activity of chick embryos. *Bull. Exp. Biol. Med. (USSR)* Vol. 63, 24–28 (translated from Russian).

Tansley, K. (1933). Factors affecting the development and regeneration of visual purple in the mammalian retina. *Proc. Roy. Soc., Ser. B* Vol. 114, 79–103.

Tilney, F., and Casamajor, L. (1924). Myelinogeny as applied to the study of behavior. *Arch. Neurol. Psychiat.* Vol. 12, 1–66.

Tracy, H. C. (1926). The development of motility and behavior reactions in the toadfish *(Opsanus tau)*. *J. Comp. Neurol.* Vol. 40, 253–369.

Tuge, H. (1931). Early behavior of the embryos of the turtle, *Terrapene carolina* (L.). *Proc. Soc. Exp. Biol. Med.* Vol. 29, 52–53.

Turkewitz, G., Birch, H. G., Moreau, T., Levy, L., and Cornwell, A. C. (1966). Effect of intensity of auditory stimulation on directional eye movements in the human neonate. *Anim. Behav.* Vol. 14, 93–101.

Vandenbergh, J. G. (1969). Male odor accelerates female sexual maturation in mice. *Endocrinology* Vol. 84, 658–660.

Vestal, B. M., and King, J. A. (1968). Relationship of age at eye opening to first optokinetic response in deermice *(Peromyscus)*. *Develop. Psychobiol.* Vol. 1, 30–34.

Volokhov, A. A. (1968). Comparative studies of the functional development of analyzer systems in animals in the process of ontogenesis. *Progr. Brain Res.* Vol. 22, 527–540.

Wada, T. (1923). Anatomical and physiological studies on the growth of the inner ear of the albino rat. *Amer. Anat. Mem.* No. 10, 1–174.

Waltan, O. (1921). L'audizione nei neonati. *Policlinico* Vol. 28, 1010–1012.

Warkentin, J. (1937). An experimental study of the ontogeny of vision in the rabbit. *Psychol. Bull.* Vol. 34, 542–543 (abstr.).

Warkentin, J., and Smith, K. U. (1937). The development of visual acuity in the cat. *J. Genet. Psychol.* Vol. 50, 371–399.

Weale, R. A. (1956). Observations on the direct effect of light on the irides of *Rana temporaria* and *Xenopus laevis*. *J. Neurophysiol.* Vol. 132, 257–266.

Wedenberg, E. (1965). Prenatal tests of hearing. *Acta Oto-Laryngol.* Vol. 206, 27–32.

Weitzman, E. D., and Graziani, L. J. (1968). Maturation and topography of the auditory evoked response of the prematurely born infant. *Develop. Psychobiol.* Vol. 1, 79–89.

Wertheimer, M. (1961). Psychomotor coordination of auditory and visual space at birth. *Science* Vol. 134, 1692.

White, R. H. (1968). The effect of light and light deprivation upon the ultrastructure of the larval mosquito eye. III. Multivesicular bodies and protein uptake. *J. Exp. Zool.* Vol. 169, 261–277.

Wiesel, T. N., and Hubel, D. H. (1963). Single cell responses in striate cortex of kittens deprived of vision in one eye. *J. Neurophysiol.* Vol. 26, 1003–1017.

Windle, W. F., and Fish, M. W. (1932). The development of the vestibular righting reflex. *J. Comp. Neurol.* Vol. 54, 85–96.

Windle, W. F., and Griffin, A. M. (1931). Observations on embryonic and fetal movements of the cat. *J. Comp. Neurol.* Vol. 52, 149–188.

Woodward, D. J., Hoffer, B. J., and Lapham, L. W. (1969). Postnatal development of electrical and enzyme histochemical activity in Purkinje cells. *Exp. Neurol.* Vol. 23, 120–139.

Yakovlev, P. I., and Lecours, A.-R. (1967). The myelinogenetic cycles of regional maturation of the brain. *In* "Regional Development of the Brain in Early Life" (A. Minkowski, ed.), pp. 3–65. Blackwell, Oxford.

Youngstrom, K. A. (1938). Studies on the developing behavior of Anura. *J. Comp. Neurol.* Vol. 68, 351–379.

Zamenhof, S., Mosley, J., and Schuller, E. (1966). Stimulation of the proliferation of cortical neurons by prenatal treatment with growth hormone. *Science* Vol. 152, 1396–1397.

Zetterström, B. (1951). The clinical electroretinogram. IV. The electroretinogram in children during the first year of life. *Acta Ophthalmol.* Vol. 29, 295–304.

Zetterström, B. (1955). Flicker electroretinography in newborn infants. *Acta Ophthalmol.* Vol. 33, 157–166.

Zetterström, B. (1956). The effect of light on the appearance and development of the electroretinogram in newborn kittens. *Acta Physiol. Scand.* Vol. 35, 272–279.

ORIGIN AND EARLY DEVELOPMENT OF NEURAL ELEMENTS IN THE HUMAN BRAIN

WILLIAM F. WINDLE

Strange as it may seem, we have little exact knowledge about the origin and sequential growth of intrinsic structures—the tracts and nuclei—in the brain of man, certainly not enough to fully appreciate development of his behavior. Many of us who should have contributed the knowledge have been content to "conceptualize" on the basis of little information. Some of us have neglected our search for facts and have wasted time seeking confirmation of time-honored theories. Others have lost sight of early goals and turned to different, seemingly more exciting, endeavors.

Knowledge of development of the human brain attained a stability long ago with respect to its gross features. Little has been added to the morphological textbook accounts of formation of the central nervous system since the classic works of Minot (1892) and Keibel and Mall (1912) at the turn of this century. To be sure, there have been more recent studies of one aspect or another of neuroembryology, few of them, however, employing human embryos stained by methods capable of revealing intrinsic structures that were invisible to such pioneer neuroembryologists as His (1904) and Streeter (1904, 1906, 1908). Recently there has been a resurgence of interest in neuroembryology. The experimenter has entered the field and brought new techniques, notably, electron microscopy (Bodian *et al.*, 1966) and autoradiography with tritiated thimadine (Angevine, 1965). Nevertheless, the human embryo can be employed experimentally to only a limited extent, and there are still wide gaps in our knowledge of morphological development.

Early human embryos had been in short supply, abortion laws being what they were, but it was my good fortune to come into possession of a number of living human embryos of 4 to 8 weeks gestation that could be processed by a reduced-silver method (Ranson's pyridine–silver). Table 1 lists those up to the end of the sixth week. Most of them were obtained

TABLE 1
Human Embryos at 4–6 Weeks of Gestation Stained by the Pyridine–Silver Method[a]

Embryo	Greatest length (mm)	Estimated age[b]	
		Menstrual (day)	Morphological (day)
727	~3	28	26–27
821	~4	—	27–28
466	5	51	28
693	6	14	31
828	6	47	31
924	6	—	31
926	6.5	56	32
H-II	7	42	32
813	8	44	34
864	8	50	34
912	8.5	— (36.5)	35
661	9	—	36
810	9	65 (41.5)	36
819	9+	—	37
920	9.5	64	39
H-III	10	—	39
867	10	62	39
484	10	—	39
713	11	49	40
808	11+	64 (40.5)	41
733	11+	49	41
836	12	56	42
809	12	—	42

[a] Twelve embryos of the seventh week (12.5–18 mm) were studied in addition to those listed.
[b] Coital ages in parentheses.

at hysterotomy and sterilization. This was before "The Pill." The patients were advised not to become pregnant, but should they miss a period, they were urged to report to the surgeon immediately. Photographs of several of these specimens are shown in Fig. 1.

There is always uncertainty about the age of a human embryo. Dates of the last menstruation are notoriously inaccurate. Recollection of the time of intercourse can be erroneous, but if it is not, the exact time of fertilization may be hours or even days later. There are several among the embryos in my collection that were obtained from patients who declared a single intercourse, and in three instances this took place on an easily recalled holiday (Table 2). But for most specimens, about the best one can do is to estimate embryonic age from the state of development of certain clearly evident structures, following standards accepted

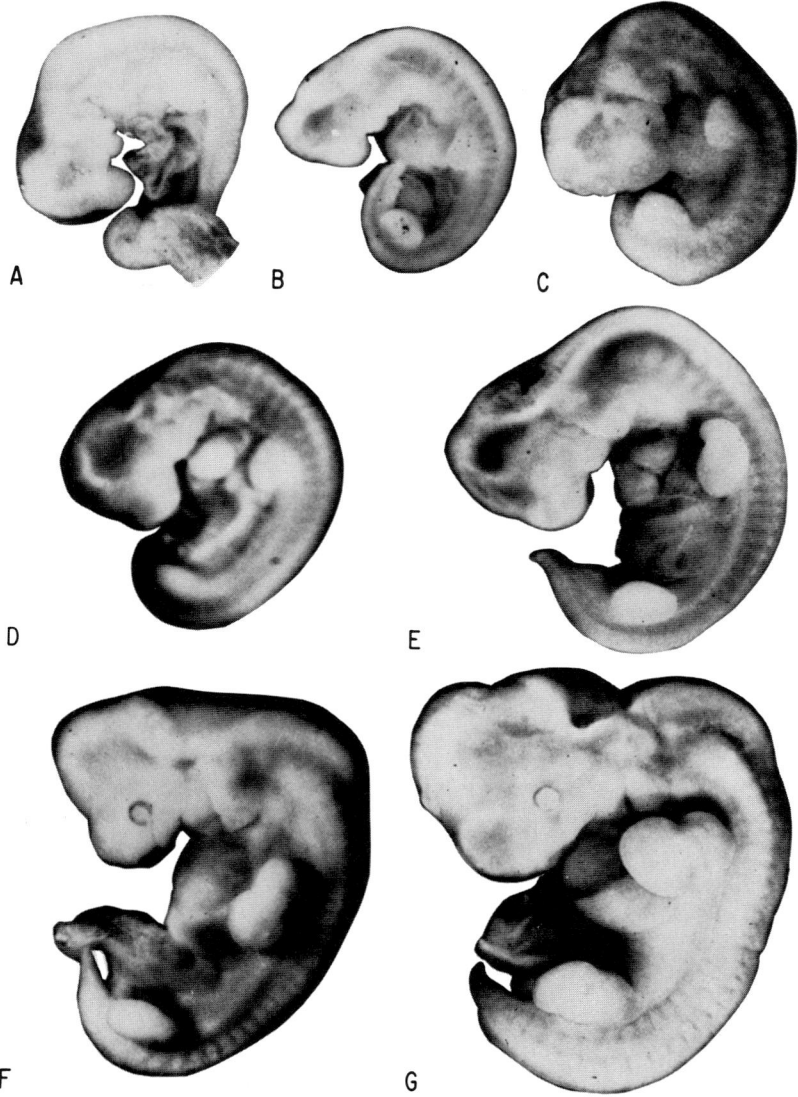

FIG. 1. Human embryos. A, 828 (6 mm); B, 924 (6 mm); C, 864 (7 mm); D, H-II (7 mm); E, 912 (8.5 mm); F, 920 (9.5 mm); G, 867 (10 mm). Photographed before preparation for pyridine–silver staining.

by mutual agreement among embryologists. Streeter's "horizons" (1942, 1945, 1948, 1951) provide excellent standards, but most readers will find it difficult to substitute them for the customary age classifications.

Size also serves as a poor criterion of age. The youngest embryos

TABLE 2
Human Embryos from Reliably Dated Intercourses

Number	Conception date	Abortion date	Age[a] (days)	Size[b] (mm)
912	12–31–41	2–6–42	36.5	8.5
810	2–14–38	3–29–38	41.5	9
808	2–4–38	3–17–38	40.5	11+
731	12–25–35	2–10–36	46.5	15
699	3–18–36	5–25–35	66.5	35

[a] These are coital ages, i.e., number of days between intercourse and surgery.
[b] Sizes are crown–rump length measured in physiological saline solution before fixation.

are usually twisted and their greatest length expressed in millimeters may be quite meaningless. Measurements obtained in the fresh state differ considerably from those taken after fixation. Furthermore, size differs with the kind of fixing fluid used. Fixation of embryos in ammoniated absolute ethyl alcohol, as required by the pyridine–silver staining technique, resulted in gross distortion, and the specimens became brittle, which led to fractures in cutting the sections, as is revealed by some of the accompanying photomicrographs.

The courses of developing tracts of nerve fibers were hard to follow, even in the best series of sections. Therefore, models were constructed of cardboard of a thickness proportional to that of the sections. Each section was projected onto the cardboard and cut out. These were stacked loosely, and the position of each group of axons indicated with colored crayons. Only in this way was it possible to separate some of the tracts of the forebrain.

Neurons or neuroblasts at early stages are the only elements with which I am concerned in this report. They are recognizable when neurofibrils appear in the cytoplasm and processes begin to grow out. Ramón y Cajal (1960, trans.) studied their formation in detail. Cowdry (1914) noted their first appearance in chick embryos of 15 somites on either side of the floor plate of the rhombencephalon. Similarly, in rat and cat embryos neurofibrillar differentiation begins in that location (Rhines and Windle,

FIG. 2. Photomicrographs of sections through the neural tube of human embryos stained by the pyridine–silver technique. A. Embryo 821 (4 mm), level of X and XII. 40 ×. B. Embryo 828 (6 mm), level of X and XII. 20 ×. C. Detail of B. 80 ×. D. Embryo 819 (9+ mm), level of X and XII. 20 ×. E. Embryo 693 (6 mm), upper spinal cord. 20 ×. F. Embryo 867 (10 mm), level of IV. 20 ×. For abbreviations in this and subsequent figures, see Appendix, pp. 168–169.

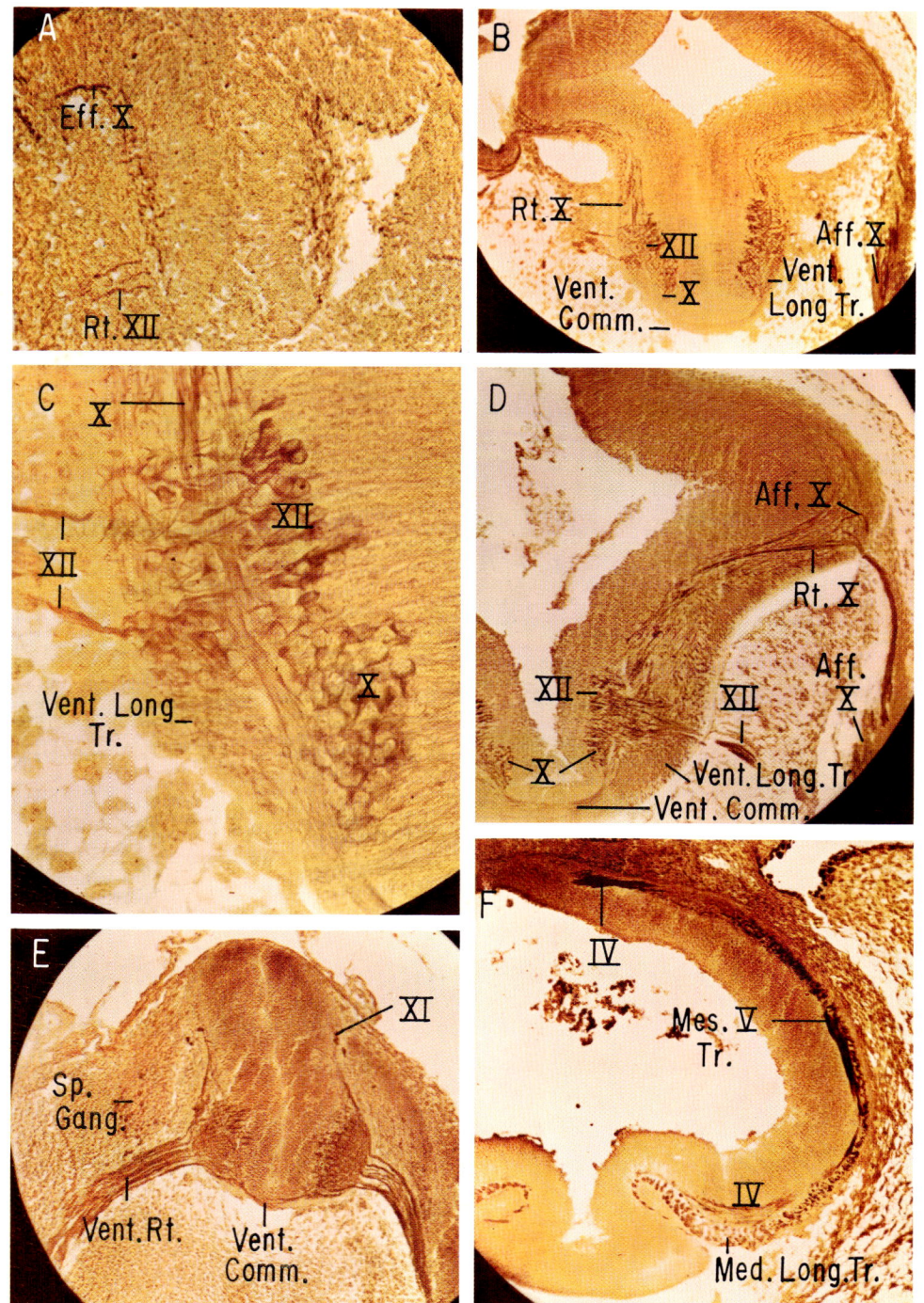

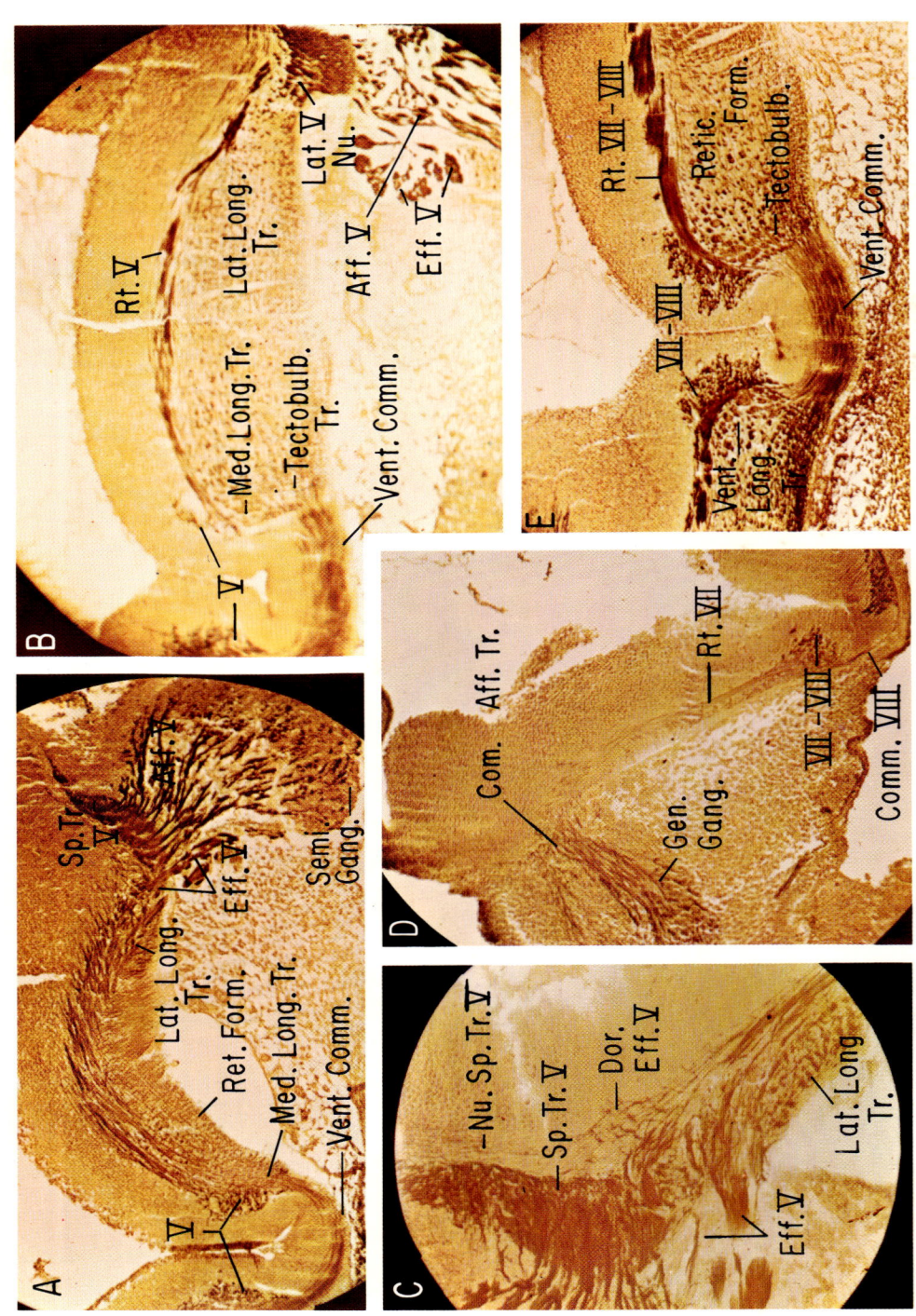

1941). It had already started in one human embryo nearly 4 weeks old.[1] No photograph of the specimen was obtained, and since this is the youngest human embryo in which I have seen silver-stained neural elements, a description of it follows.

The greatest length of the embryo before placing it in fixing fluid was about 4 mm; after fixation it measured slightly more than 3 mm. Optic vesicles were present. Lens placodes were visible as uninvaginated epithelial thickenings. Indistinct olfactory placodes were identified. Otocysts had formed, but retained their attachments to the surface epithelium. There were no limb buds. Somites could not be counted. The specimen resembles 30-somite embryo No. 836 of Bartelmez and Dekaban (1962), but its development may have been slightly less advanced.

The Primary Efferent Nuclei and Nerves

FOURTH WEEK

Primary efferent neuroblasts are among the first elements of the human brain to be stainable by the pyridine—silver method (Figs. 2 and 3). They occupy a medial position on either side of the floor plate of the 4-mm embryo, forming an interrupted ventral column. The cranial nerve nuclei of III, IV, V, VI, VII, IX-X-XI and XII, and some upper spinal nuclei[2] are recognizable, but the nerve roots of IV and VI are lacking. The lower rhombencephalon is more advanced in development than other regions (Figs. 2A, 4, and 9). Efferent fibers of XI form the only compact nerve there and in upper spinal segments.

Comparison with embryos of other species, especially the cat, leads

---

[1] A smaller embryo of the fourth week (727) showed no neurofibrillar differentiation, but postmortem changes may have rendered neuroblasts unstainable. A slightly larger one (466), though living when placed in fixing fluid, contained no stained neural elements.

[2] Roman numerals will be used for the cranial nerves to conserve space. The word "tract" (in the spinal cord, "funiculus") will be used instead of "fascicle" and "bundle" for longitudinally coursing clusters of axons.

FIG. 3. Photomicrographs of sections through the neural tube of human embryos stained by the pyridine–silver technique. A. Embryo 819 (9+ mm), level of V. 20 ×. B. Embryo 809 (12 mm), level of V. 20 ×. C. Embryo 867 (10 mm), detail of V nerve roots. 40 ×. D. Embryo 828 (6 mm), level of VII-VIII. 20 ×. E. Embryo 807 (12.5 mm), level of VII-VIII. 20 ×. (See Appendix for abbreviations.)

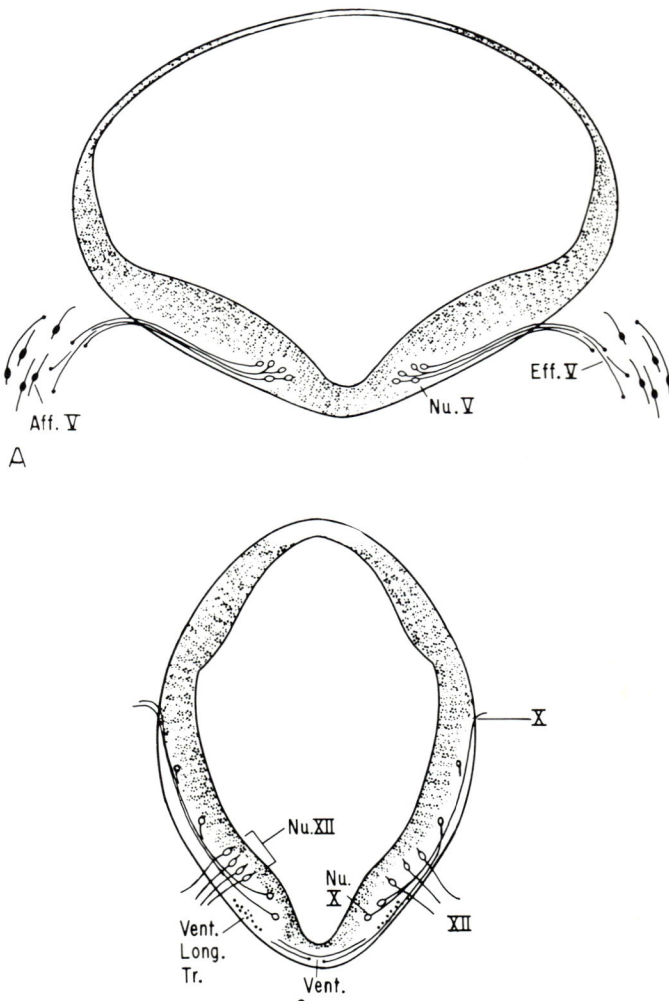

FIG. 4. Diagrammatic representation of three levels of the neural tube of human embryo at 4 weeks. A. Level of V. B. Level of X and XII. C. Upper spinal cord. (See Appendix for abbreviations.)

to the belief that human neurofibrillation may be initiated in primary efferent neuroblasts before the 30-somite stage (horizons xii-xiii of Streeter), but as in other species, this can vary from specimen to specimen. Neurofibrillar development in the 4-mm human embryo is similar to that in 22-somite cat embryos (Rhines and Windle, 1941).

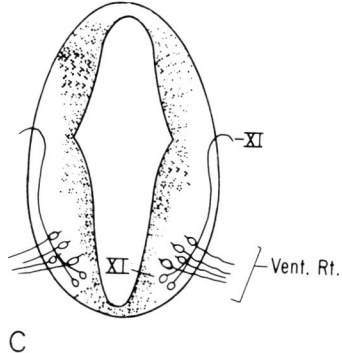

FIG. 4. (continued)

FIFTH WEEK

The primary efferent column of neuroblasts in embryos measuring 6 mm greatest length is divisible into two series of nuclei which I have designated ventrolateral and ventromedial. Neuroblasts of the ventrolateral column send axons directly out of the neural tube to form cranial nerves III, VI, XII, and the spinal nerves (Fig. 5). Those of the ventromedial column, comprising nuclei of cranial nerves IV, V, VII-VIII, and IX-X-XI, send them dorsolaterad through the ventrolateral nuclear column toward the sulcus limitans. The two columns are illustrated in photomicrographs (Figs. 2B and 3D).

The nuclei of nerves III, VI, and XII, forming the ventrolateral column, are distinctly separate, one from the other. The nucleus of III at this stage has no medial component and is isolated at the cephalic flexure about 200 μ above the rostral end of IV. That of XII merges caudally with spinal C1. Axons from neuroblasts in nuclei of III, VI, XII, and the spinal nerves, emerging from the basal plate ventrally, form small rootlets which quickly disperse in the adjacent mesenchyme.

The ventromedial neuroblasts form a continuous column from the isthmus to the upper part of the spinal cord. The nucleus of IV is joined with that of V by a thin scattering of neuroblasts (at least one per section). Those of VII and VIII are inseparable, as are those of IX, X, and XI. The combined primary efferent nucleus VII-VIII forms the largest mass of neuroblasts in the neural tube of 6-mm human embryos.

The ventromedial column is characterized, not only by its position, but by the course its axons take, all of which pass toward the sulcus limitans. Axons of IV continue on toward the roof plate, where a few decussate at the 6-mm stage. Most of those of efferent VIII arise on the

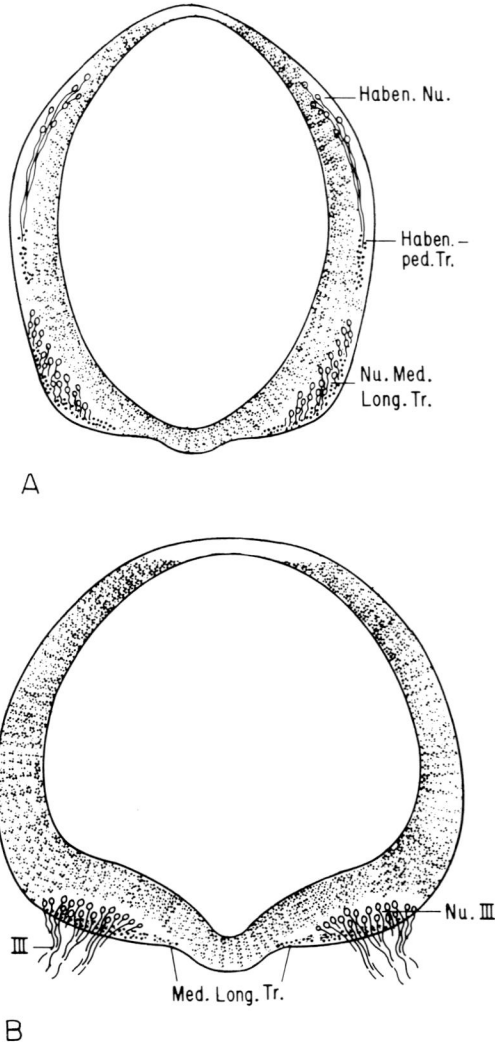

FIG. 5. Diagrammatic representation of sections through the neural tube of human embryos in the first half of the fifth week. A. Diencephalon at the level indicated in Fig. 10. B. Mesencephalon at the level of nucleus III. C. Level of nucleus IV and its commissural axons. D. Metencephalon at the most caudal level of IV. (See Appendix for abbreviations.)

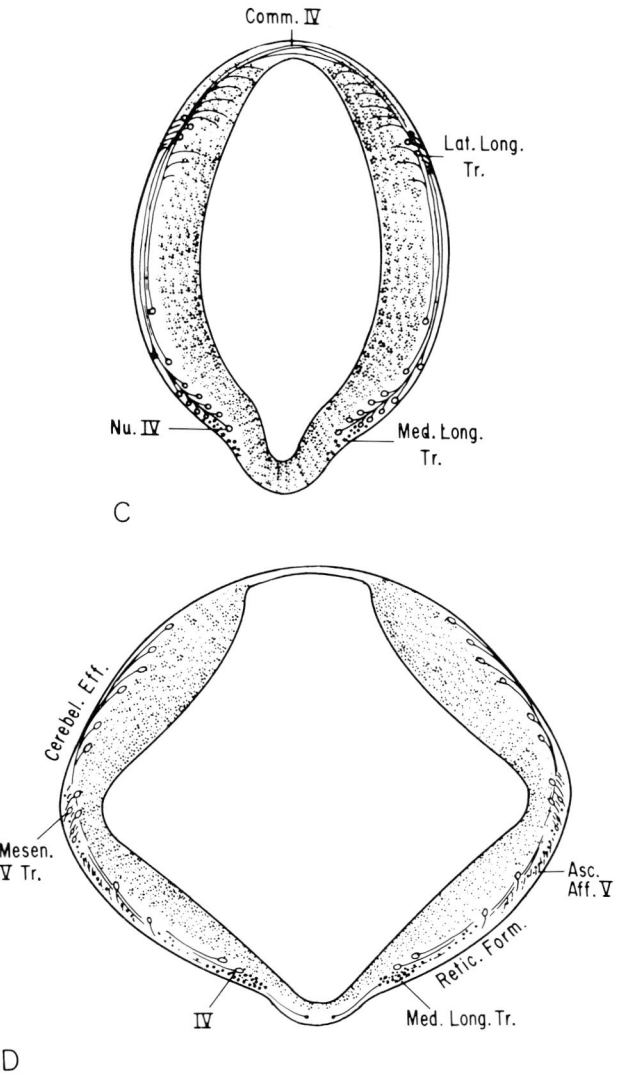

FIG. 5. (continued)

opposite side and cross in the floor plate, forming a darkly stained commissure dorsal to, and more prominent than, the ventral commissure formed by arcuate second-order neuroblasts (Fig. 3D). All axons except those of IV emerge from the ventrolateral aspect of the neural tube just before reaching the level of the sulcus limitans (Fig. 4A). The most compact extramedullary nerve roots are those formed by V, VII, and XI; multiple rootlets are formed by IX and X.

Another feature characterizes the ventromedial nuclei of 6-mm embryos. Cells are seen along the intramedullary course of their rootlets. These are efferent neuroblasts which have one process extending mesad toward the nucleus and another one running laterad to join the emerging nerve. Such neuroblasts occur along intramedullary rootlets of IV and V, but few are seen along those of the other nerves. Occasionally, the dendrite of a neuroblast can be traced all the way back into the ventromedial cell group. In addition to the cells along the rootlets, there is a small accumulation of cells, medial and dorsal to the point of entrance of the afferent V root, from which a few axons can be traced into the efferent V root. This small "general visceral efferent" nucleus results from lateral migration of neuroblasts along the intramedullary course of efferent V axons, beginning in the early part of the fifth week.

The ventrolateral nuclei of III, VI, XII, and the spinal nerves are larger in embryos of 8 mm than in those of 6 mm. The nucleus of III is almost continuous with that of IV, but the latter lies more medially and its neuroblasts have a different orientation. The nucleus of VI resembles that of II but is smaller; lying lateral to the ventromedial column at the level of VII-VIII, its caudal neuroblasts intermingle with the rostral ones of IX. The axons of VI enter the mesenchyme in 8-mm embryos and turn sharply rostrad to form the nerve. A few separate rootlets emerge between the nuclei of VI and XII and enter neither nerve. The nucleus of XII merges imperceptibly with the cervical spinal efferent column. Extramedullary nerve roots of XII pass ventrolaterad, the upper ones tending to form dorsal divisions, resembling spinal nerves. It is on one of these that the ganglion of Froriep, still undifferentiated at the 8-mm stage, will be located.

The ventromedial column in 8-mm embryos is represented, as before, by nuclei of IV, V, VII-VIII, and IX-X-XI nerves. Nuclei of IV and V lie directly dorsal to the medial longitudinal tract; the more caudal members of the column bear a similar relation to the ventral longitudinal tract.

Migrating neuroblasts are found in 8-mm embryos along the intramedullary rootlets of IV, V, and the IX-X-XI complex, but not along those of VII-VIII. Some of migrating cells of V form a small "general visceral efferent" nucleus among developing second-order neuroblasts at the point where the efferent V root emerges from the neural tube. Axons of a few neuroblasts of this dorsal nucleus can be traced into the emerging efferent V root. No similar accumulations of neuroblasts are found in relation to IV or VII, but there are a few cells migrating along the

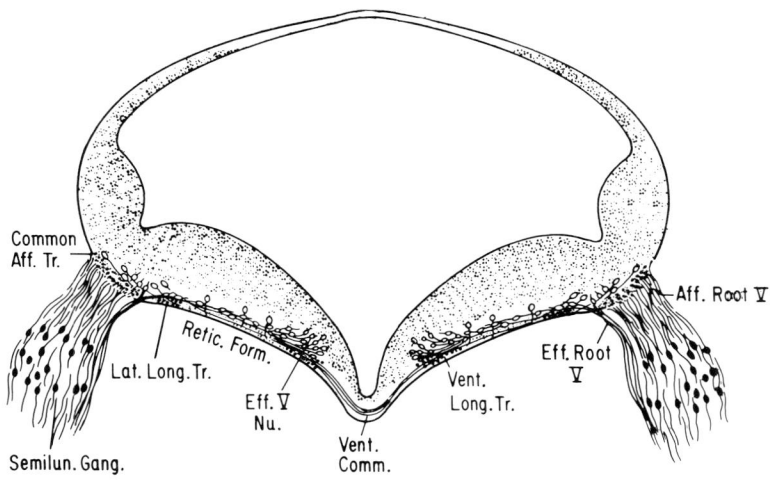

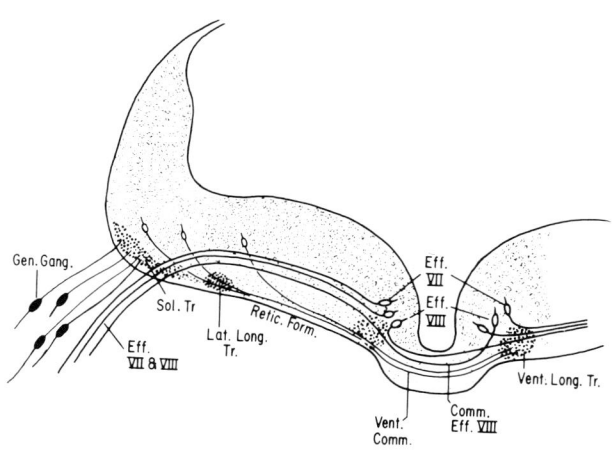

FIG. 6. Diagrammatic representation of two sections through the rhombencephalon of human embryos. A. Early fifth week, level of V. B. Early sixth week, level of VII-VIII. (See Appendix for abbreviations.)

rootlets of IX-X-XI, which will become aggregated and may foretell the development of comparable nuclei (e.g., the dorsal motor X) associated with these nerves.

The combined efferent nucleus of VII-VIII (Fig. 6B) is the largest one in the ventromedial column; it is beginning to elongate at 8 mm, and some of the neuroblasts in its caudal portion send their axons rostrad before they turn laterad to help form intramedullary rootlets. Thus, the first step has been taken at the 8-mm stage toward formation of the genu of VII.

A crossed component forms a prominent darkly stained commissure in the dorsal part of the floor plate. This is efferent VIII, the cells of which are with those of efferent VII in the ventromedial column.[3] At the site of emergence of the efferent VII root, a group of fibers, which because of their dark stain seem to belong to efferent VIII, leaves the rhombencephalon more laterally and joins the lightly stained afferent VIII root. I cannot follow the efferent axons throughout their entire course, but darkly stained fibers are seen again more peripherally, entering the ventrolateral wall of the otocyst at the junction of vestibular and cochlear pouches. Probably the dark fibers are the same at both locations and may be efferent terminations of VIII. If so, they comprise the first primary efferent nerve ending in the human embryo.

SIXTH WEEK AND LATER

No changes except increase in size occur in the ventrolateral nuclei of III, VI, XII, or the spinal nerves of embryos measuring 9–10 mm greatest length (horizons xv-xvi of Streeter). The photomicrograph in Fig. 2D illustrates structures at the level of XII comparable with those in Fig. 2B at 6 mm.

The ventromedial column remains substantially as it was at the end of the fifth week. A few neuroblasts are present along the intramedullary course of IV and the upper rootlets of V, but their migration to the dorsal site in V (i.e., general visceral efferent) has nearly ended (Fig. 3C). No neuroblasts are identifiable at the comparable location in VII, and few in IX and X. The main nuclei of IV, V, VII-VIII, and IX-X-XI are still in the ventromedial column.

A few axons from neuroblasts in the small dorsal efferent V nucleus can be followed into the emerging efferent root, but others, arising from similarly placed neuroblasts, pass into the afferent root. The neuroblasts contributing the latter belong to the mesencephalic V nucleus, which seems to arise from migrated neuroblasts from the efferent cell

[3] Before Rasmussen (1960) demonstrated its efferent character in adult animals by experimental methods, this group of axons puzzled neuroembryologists, who variously considered it an afferent VII, a crossed efferent VII, or an afferent VIII component. Kimmel (personal communication) and I agree that, accepting the long-held dictum that cranial nerve VIII is exclusively afferent, it did not occur to us that an efferent component could be present in it.

column or from cells in the mantle layer at the junction of the roots of V, or from both.

The main lateral migration of neuroblasts from the ventromedial column has not begun to form definitive nuclei in embryos of 10 mm (Windle, 1949). However, the nucleus of VII has elongated, with lengthening of the rhombencephalon, thus forming the ascending portion of the genu of VII. This occurs in no other nuclei of the ventromedial column at this stage; perhaps the reason is anchorage of efferent VII by the contralateral efferent VII component and its prominent commissure.

Embryos measure 11–12 mm greatest length in the latter part of the sixth week (horizon xvii of Streeter). No significant changes take place in the ventrolateral column. A crossed component of III was found in cat embryos of comparable developmental stages, but it cannot be identified in the human specimens. If there is a general visceral nucleus, it is indistinguishable from the other components of III.

The most noteworthy advance in development occurred in the ventromedial column with formation of definitive lateral (the so-called special visceral) efferent nuclei by migration of neuroblasts. There is no migration in nucleus IV, which remains at the ventromedial site. However, a second migration does take place in V (Fig. 3B) at the end of the sixth or early in the seventh week (12.5 mm); all ventromedial neuroblasts change their orientation, turn about, and, pointing their dendrites along the course of their axons, as it were, move to a position medial to the afferent V tract and ventral to the small dorsal efferent V nucleus (Windle, 1949). This results in the formation of a thin, darkly

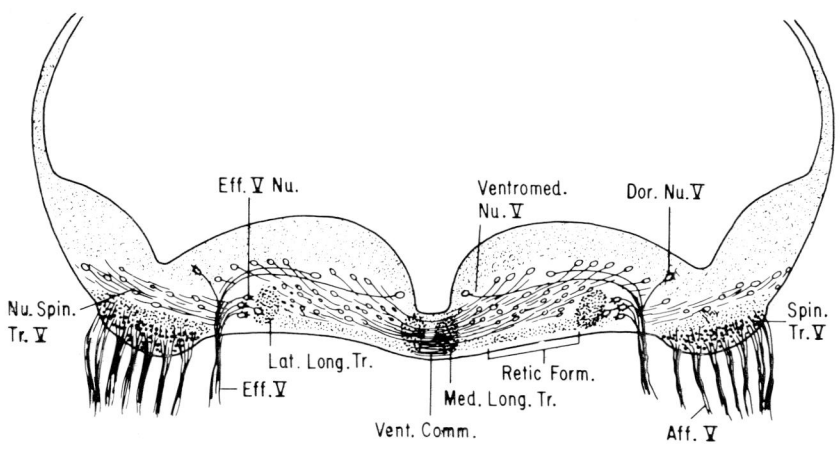

FIG. 7. Diagrammatic representation of a section through the rhombencephalon at the level of V in human embryos of 11–12 mm. (See Appendix for abbreviations.)

stained genu of V (Fig. 7), similar to, but less prominent than, that encountered in cat embryos (Windle, 1933).

The genu of VII is incomplete at 6 weeks, because neuroblasts in the ventromedial nucleus of VII have not begun to migrate laterad from the caudal end of the nucleus. This migration will be the last to occur; it takes place late in the seventh week. Nuclei of the IX-X-XI complex remain in the ventromedial position until the seventh week, when their lateral migration is accomplished.

SUMMARY

Neurofibrils begin to differentiate in primary efferent neuroblasts in the medial part of the basal plate of the lower rhombencephalon and upper spinal cord during the latter part of the fourth week. Their formation slightly precedes that of primary afferent and second-order elements.

Two columns of nuclei, ventrolateral and ventromedial, are formed, the former by III, VI, XII, and spinal neuroblasts, the latter by IV, V, VII-VIII, and the IX-X-XI complex. Axons of the ventrolateral nuclei pass directly out of the basal plate into the mesenchyme. Those of the ventromedial nuclei course laterad toward the sulcus limitans before emerging. The intramedullary axons of IV continue past the sulcus limitans and decussate in the roof plate. A substantial number of efferent axons of VIII form a commissure in the floor plate and accompany the axons of VII on the opposite side.

Some of the neuroblasts of the ventromedial column migrate laterad along the course of their intramedullary axons during the fifth and sixth weeks. Those of V, and to lesser extent IX, X, and XI, reach a dorsolateral position in the angle between efferent and afferent roots, forming the first elements of dorsal efferent nuclei. I could not identify a component of VII at this time. Neuroblasts which may belong to salivatory nuclei could not be separated from those of X.

A second migration of neuroblasts occurs in the latter part of the sixth and during the seventh weeks. That of V is the first to be completed by a sudden shifting of the entire remnant of the ventromedial nucleus to definitive special visceral efferent site, leaving a few of its axons spun out in a thin genu. The nucleus of VII begins its migration at the 8-mm stage, when its neuroblasts shift caudad, causing it to elongate. However, seemingly held close to the floor plate by the crossed efferent component of VIII, the nucleus of VII does not effect its migration to the definitive lateral site until after the other efferent nuclei (IX, X, and XI—i.e., nucleus ambiguus) have done so. With the lateral migration of VII in the latter part of the seventh week, presumably accompanied by VIII, the genu of VII is completed. Thus, all primary efferent nuclei of the human brain are laid down at their definitive sites before the eighth week of gestation, which is the critical time for initiation of motor behavior in the human fetus.

The Primary Afferent Ganglia and Tracts

FOURTH WEEK

A few neuroblasts have differentiated in cranial but none in spinal ganglia of the 4-mm embryo. Silver-stained elements are present only in the semilunar (V), geniculate (VII), and inferior ganglia of IX and X. There are more in the geniculate ganglion than the others. Very few axons leave the ganglia, and none enters the neural tube. Consequently, no primary afferent tract is present.

FIFTH WEEK

Neurofibrillar differentiation is under way actively in cranial and spinal ganglia of 6-mm embryos, but the semilunar, geniculate, and inferior ganglia of IX and X are more advanced than the superior of IX and X, the accessory, hypoglossal (Froriep), and spinal ganglia (Compare Figs. 2E and 3D). The vestibular ganglion (VIII) contains smaller lightly stained neuroblasts, distinguishing it from the geniculate (VII) ganglion, with which it is closely associated. The semilunar ganglion is the largest one, but it is less compactly filled with silver-staining neuroblasts than the geniculate or inferior ganglia of IX and X. All these ganglia are connected with the brain by afferent nerve roots formed by the central processes of their bipolar neuroblasts. The root of V is the largest.

Maximum development in spinal ganglia is found in the cervical region, diminishing caudally. Some embryos show more advanced development than others. Although cervical dorsal root fibers are present, they do not reach the spinal cord in all specimens. No dorsal funiculus is found in the spinal cord of one 6-mm embryo (Fig. 2E), but a few dorsal root fibers do reach the cord of another specimen, and a very small dorsal funiculus appears in the cervical regions of a 7-mm embryo. Peripheral processes are larger than central processes of spinal afferent neuroblasts and join the efferent axons to form short peripheral nerves.

Above the first cervical segment of some embryos 6 and 7 mm long, a few neuroblasts occur along rootlets of XI; a little ganglion is present in one embryo, and scattered cells in another. The superior ganglion of X contains few silver-stained neuroblasts; about 25 are present on one side, mainly along the rostral border of the ganglion. The left superior ganglion of IX of one specimen is entirely devoid of silver-stained neuroblasts, but that on the right side contains an occasional one.

Central processes of the primary afferent neurons of V, VII, VIII (vestibular); IX, and X form a primordial common afferent tract in the rhombencephalon (Tello, 1934). This diminutive group of axons lies on the surface of the neural tube near the sulcus limitans (Fig. 3D). It consists, at its rostral end, solely of afferent V axons, some passing rostrad for a few sections, but most descending as the thin peripheral spinal V tract. The afferent root of V is much larger than the sum of its two divisions in the brain, but few if any of its fibers entering the neural tube go farther caudally than the level of VII-VIII.

The afferent component of VIII adds little to the dorsal part of the common afferent tract in embryos of 6–7 mm because most of its fibers end immediately upon entering the neural tube. Primary afferent VII fibers (nervus intermedius) enter the common afferent tract ventral to, although not entirely separate from, those of VIII and course caudad in diminishing number until joined by afferent components of IX and X. The common afferent tract, over most of its course, is composed of axons from the ganglia of VII, IX (inferior), and X (inferior), and this part of it is, therefore, the solitary tract, superficially placed at this stage in its development. As it descends, the tract diminishes in size but can be followed caudally almost as far as the first cervical segment. No contribution is made by XI.

The very beginning of a mesencephalic V component is visible in the embryos of 6–7 mm. The tract is formed just rostral to the point of entrance of the afferent V root by axons of a few neuroblasts that do not resemble other primary afferent elements but are indistinguishable from secondary afferent or even primary dorsal efferent V neuroblasts.

Development of primary afferent neurons is confined to ganglia associated with the rhombencephalon and spinal cord until the latter part of the fifth week, when neurofibrils appear in a few neuroblasts located in the unindented medial border of the olfactory placode of 8-mm embryos. A few of these first olfactory neuroblasts send processes into the mesenchyme. Other neuroblasts, located in the mesenchyme nearby, belong to the terminal nerve. No axons from either source reach the brain.

The semilunar ganglion of 8-mm embryos is a relatively large mass of cells, only a small percentage of which have begun to differentiate into neurons. Nevertheless, the actual total number of silver-stained neuroblasts is great, and the root is much the largest one entering the neural tube. The three peripheral divisions of V are distinct, the opthalmic being the longest. Central processes of the bipolar neuroblasts of V enter the neural tube, those from the ophthalmic division a little rostral and medial to those from other parts of the ganglion. In addition to the axons from the semilunar ganglion, the ascending division of the afferent V root contains fibers from the mesencephalic V tract. This makes it impossible to determine precisely where the primary afferent V fibers to the primordium of the main afferent nucleus of V end. Most primary afferent fibers of the root turn caudad upon entering the brain and form the spinal V tract. Many of these end within 30 μ, but a few continue to the level of VII. There they lose their identity in the common afferent tract when joined by the few descending afferent fibers of VII.

The well-formed geniculate ganglion, compactly filled with differentiating neuroblasts in embryos of 8 mm, gives rise to a large central afferent VII root. This enters the rhombencephalon between descending VIII and spinal V tracts, joining the latter immediately and contributing descending fibers to the resulting common afferent tract. As the afferent VII root, incompletely separated from VIII, enters the neural tube, it lies dorsolateral to the efferent VII root and ventromedial to VIII.

The ganglion of VIII (vestibular), lying medial and caudal to the geniculate ganglion, can be distinguished readily from the latter because its smaller cells of uniform size stain more lightly. Most of its root fibers, upon entering the neural tube, end at once, although a few of them form a short ascending tract just lateral to the spinal V tract and others descend in the dorsolateral part of the common afferent tract. The former, representing the vestibulocerebellar tract, run less than halfway toward the entrance of the afferent root of V; the latter, comprising the spinal vestibular root, descend for about the same distance. Some peripheral fibers of VIII (vestibular) enter the ventrolateral wall of the otocyst between vestibular and cochlear pouches.

A few cells of the superior ganglion of IX have developed neurofibrils, but the primary afferent IX root is still formed entirely by axons of neuroblasts in the inferior ganglion of IX in 8-mm embryos. The IX root enters the common afferent tract, which is enlarged at the point of its entrance but becomes small just caudal to that. A well-formed peripheral IX trunk passes to the third branchial arch.

The superior ganglion of X at 8 mm has neurofibrils in only a few neuroblasts, mainly along its medial border, but the inferior ganglion of X is large and filled with silver-stained neuroblasts.

The superior ganglionic mass of X contributes a few axons to the common afferent tract, but the nodose ganglion is the main contributor. The tract, actually the primordium of the solitary tract at this level, is enlarged by each X rootlet entering it, diminishing sharply in size between rootlets. It cannot be traced as far caudally as the first spinal dorsal root. Peripherally, nerve X can be traced along the pharynx to the stomach.

A ganglion (Froriep) is present in XII, but no neurofibrils are differentiating in its cells at 8 mm. Efferent fibers of XII wander through the ganglion and some of these fibers turn dorsad toward the neural tube lateral to the XI ramus, giving a false appearance of being dorsal rootlets.

Dorsal rootlets of spinal ganglia enter the spinal cord to form a diminutive dorsal funiculus in embryos at the end of the fifth week. These are present as far caudally as the lumbar region.

SIXTH WEEK AND LATER

New developments in embryos measuring 9–10 mm greatest length are mainly quantitative. More neuroblasts of the terminal and olfactory nerves are present, but connections with the brain are lacking.

The ganglia of cranial and spinal nerves contain more silver-stained neuroblasts and greater numbers of fibers in the roots than at earlier stages. The superior ganglia of IX and X are still appreciably less advanced in development than their respective inferior ganglia. Those of XII (Froriep) and Cl are small.

The common afferent tract has increased in size, but its definitive components have not become separated (Figs. 2, 3, and 8). It contains primary afferent fibers from V, VII, VIII (vestibular), IX, X, and now even a few from XI, which may be transient.

Neuroblasts are beginning to differentiate in the spiral ganglion of VIII (cochlear), but their processes are short and no nerve has formed. The primary afferent root of VIII still consists entirely of vestibular axons. Some of the peripheral fibers pass into the developing vestibular labyrinth to end in the epithelium. Nowhere else at 6 weeks do neurons have telodendria in epithelium.

The mesencephalic V cells can be identified in the mesencephalon at this stage. A few near the entering afferent V root are unipolar.

Late in the sixth week, embryos 11–12 mm long present few noteworthy new developments in the primary afferent systems. Olfactory or terminal nerve fibers (or both) enter the wall of the telencephalon.

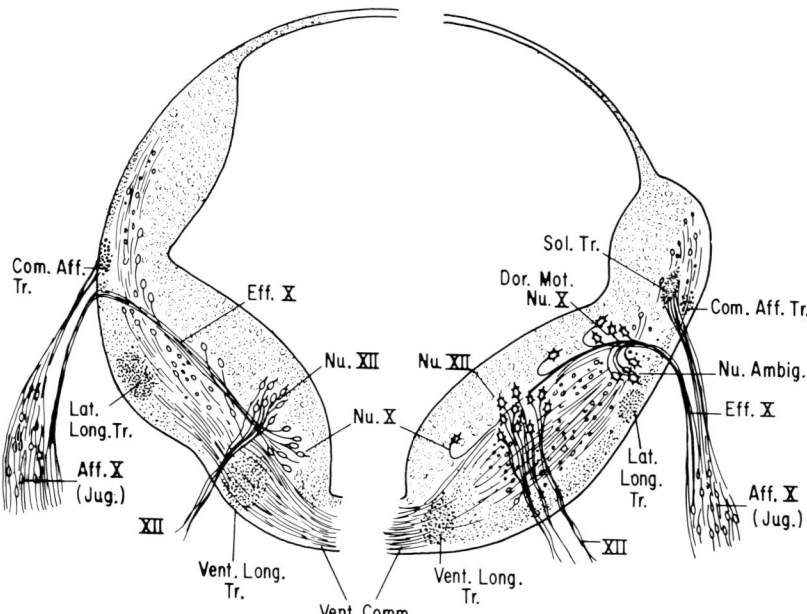

FIG. 8. Diagrammatic representation of sections through the rhombencephalon at the level of X and XII in human embryos of the sixth week (left) and early part of the seventh week (right). (See Appendix for abbreviations.)

Cochlear axons reach the brain, but their nuclei of termination are indistinct.

The solitary tract at the end of the sixth week begins to separate from other components of the common afferent tract below the level of VII. This may be due to new primary afferent contributions of V and VIII (vestibular) to the superficial layer, and to increased numbers of second-order neurons the axons of which, on their way to the reticular formation, stream ventrolaterad at right angles to longitudinal fibers of the common afferent tract. Thus, the solitary tract begins to occupy a position deep to, although not completely separate from, the spinal V and spinal VIII tract (Fig. 8). The caudal end of the solitary tract reaches upper cervical segments. The spinal V tract is lost near the level of C1. A prominent spinal dorsal funiculus ascends and overlaps the spinal V tract in embryos of 12 mm. The lower limit of spinal VIII axons cannot be determined.

A previous study (Wilson et al., 1941) demonstrated that the solitary tract becomes more deeply situated at later stages of development.

In the seventh week (16-mm embryos), a few of its terminal fibers pass mesad toward the midline just caudal to the open part of the fourth ventricle; these form a dorsal commissure, first described by Strong (1938) in fetuses of about 9 weeks gestation.

The mesencephalic V tract at the end of the sixth week is visible throughout the mesencephalon (Fig. 2F). It courses caudad and, crossing the intramedullary root of IV, comes to lie lateral to the dorsal one-third of that root. Some of the mesencephalic V axons pass to the opposite side with those of IV in older fetuses. Nerve fibers of the mesencephalic V tract give off collateral branches to the definitive (special visceral) efferent V nucleus in embryos of the seventh week (16 mm), as noted previously (Wilson et al., 1941).

The spinal dorsal funiculus attains prominence during the sixth week, appearing as a crescent-shaped tract on the dorsal aspect of the spinal cord. It contains fewer axons from the first cervical than from other spinal ganglia. A minute contribution from XII (Froriep) joins it. The funiculus at the junction of spinal cord and rhombencephalon is actually more dorsal than the spinal V tract; it becomes incorporated in the common afferent tract. Its fibers separate from the latter in embryos of 7 weeks gestation and extend rostrally as a separate fasicle into the rhombencephalon where they end near second-order neuroblasts of the primordial gracile and cuneate nuclei.

The more lateral of the spinal V tract fibers enter the spinal cord in proximity to neuroblasts of the future substantia gelatinosa, recognizable in embryos of 16 mm. Their course and termination in the spinal cord were described by Humphrey (1952). Some of them reach the level of C2 at 8 weeks (22 mm) and C3 or C4 at 8.5 weeks (26.5 mm). The maxillary-mandibular fibers form a separate and longer fascicle than the ophthalmic fibers.

The first collaterals of the dorsal funiculus axons are forming in the spinal cord in human fetuses of 7 weeks gestation (Windle and Fitzgerald, 1937). These increase in number in fetuses measuring 16–20 mm crown-rump length; i.e., in the eighth week. They will make the connections required for spinal reflexes. Similarly, elements required for trigeminal reflexes are laid down at about the same time. However, neuromuscular development and intraspinal neuronal connections are incomplete at the end of the seventh week. The seventh week is a period of rapid growth of primary efferent telodendria and an elaboration of the connections between primary afferent neurons and the second-order nerve cells located in their nuclei of termination. Collaterals of the primary afferent axons undergo marked development at the brachial spinal level in fetuses 20 mm long (eighth week). Similarly, collaterals of spinal

V tract fibers (maxillomandibular) enter the substantia gelatinosa in 8-week-old fetuses of 25 mm. Reflexes have been elicited in human fetuses of comparable ages (Fitzgerald and Windle, 1942; Hooker, 1939a,b, 1954; Windle and Fitzgerald, 1937). The first reflexes appear to involve two-neuron arcs, both at brachial and cervical levels.

SUMMARY

Neurofibrillar development begins during the fourth week in ganglia of V, VII, and inferior ganglia of IX and X. It extends to superior ganglia of IX and X, as well as VIII (vestibular) and the upper spinal ganglia, early in the fifth week. Axons reach the rhombencephalon, and a common afferent tract appears during the fifth week. There is a diminutive dorsal spinal funiculus at that time.

The afferent V root soon becomes the largest one entering the rhombencephalon, and some of its axons turn slightly forward to find the primordium of the main afferent V nucleus, while others descend in the common afferent tract superficial to secondary neuroblasts, which will become the nucleus of spinal V tract in the brain and substantia gelatinosa in the spinal cord. However, no functional reflex connections are made until 8 weeks. The mesencephalic V tract is formed during the fifth week from cells in the wall of the neural tube; origin of its neurons is unlike that in the ganglia of primary afferent nerves.

Primary afferent roots of VII, IX, and X contribute to the part of the common afferent tract that will become the solitary tract. That tract does not begin to separate from V and VIII components until the latter part of the sixth week and is never completely isolated from these components in its rostral end. A spinal dorsal funiculus ascends and overlaps the descending common afferent tract components during the seventh week. Its fibers send collaterals into the primordium of the spinal gray column during the seventh week, completing reflex connections in the brachial region by 8 weeks.

Cells of the spiral ganglion of VIII (cochlear) begin to differentiate during the early part of the sixth week, but the axons of VIII entering the brain at that time are mainly vestibular; they turn rostrad and caudad, initiating the vestibulocerebellar tract and spinal VIII tract, respectively. Some peripheral vestibular fibers enter the otocyst wall. Cochlear nuclei are indistinct at 7 weeks, but vestibular nuclei can be identified.

A few neuroblasts of the terminal and olfactory nerves make their appearance between the fifth and sixth weeks.

Two commissures of primary afferent neurons are formed during the seventh week or later. These are a component of the mesencephalic V tract, crossing with axons of IV, and a commissure of the solitary tract at the level of the future obex.

The Secondary Nuclei and Tracts

The secondary nuclei and tracts of the human embryo are of two main types. There are those developing from mantle layer neuroblasts of both alar and basal plates, constituting the nuclei of termination of primary afferent neurons. They give rise to the secondary afferent tracts. The first neuroblasts of such nuclei make their appearance before telodendria of the respective primary neurons reach them.

Secondary nuclei of the second type, most of which are located more rostrally in the neural tube, give rise to interneuron systems of higher order, such as the medial longitudinal and medial forebrain tracts and the anterior and posterior commissures. No afferent connections with these systems are effected in embryos younger than 7 or 8 weeks.

FOURTH WEEK

The stage of development of second-order neurons of the 4-mm human embryo is about equivalent to that of cat embryos of 22 somites (Rhines and Windle, 1941; Windle, 1932a,b, 1933, 1935). The first few cell bodies of neuroblasts are visible. Their arcuate axons curve ventrad and cross in the floor plate at upper spinal and lower rhombencephalic levels, but form no longitudinal tract there. A little farther rostrally, at the level of efferent X and XII nuclei, a few, having formed a ventral commissure, turn rostrad to initiate a ventral longitudinal tract.[4] There is no other tract at 4 weeks. Although neurofibrillar differentiation has started in a few cells at the rostral end of the mesencephalon, constituting the interstitial nucleus (Cajal), no axons of the medial longitudinal tract are present (Fig. 9).

FOREBRAIN OF EMBRYOS OF THE FIFTH WEEK

Neurofibrillar differentiation is in progress in the prosencephalon early in the fifth week of gestation. For convenience, I shall describe

[4] Three tracts occupy the same position relative to the floor plate. They are the uncrossed descending axons from the interstitial nucleus, which I designate "medial longitudinal," the crossed ascending axons from arcuate interneurons of the rhombencephalon, which I designate "ventral longitudinal," and the spinal "ventral funiculus."

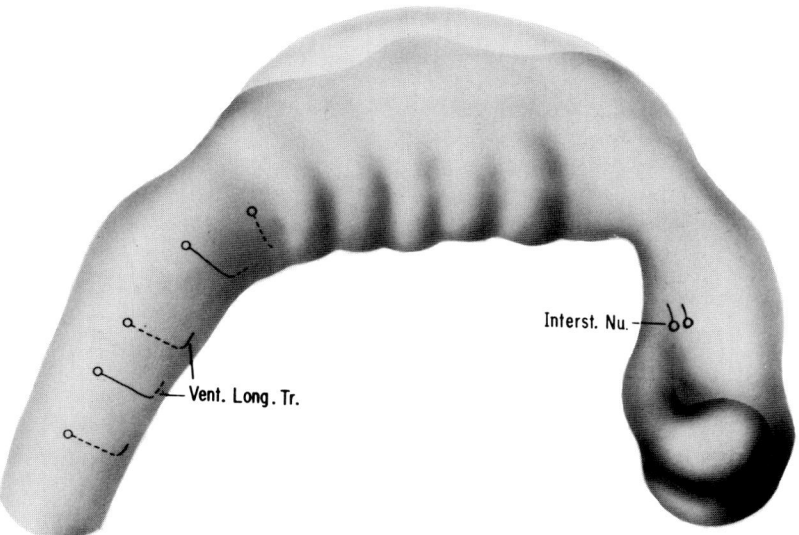

FIG. 9. Locations of neural elements at 4 weeks. The brains of human embryos in Figs. 9 to 13 were redrawn from illustrations in Hochsletter's book (1919). Locations of some of the principal neurons of the second order and their tracts have been superimposed upon the drawings as closely as possible to the positions they occupy in pyridine–silver stained specimens of the present series. (See Appendix for abbreviations.)

events in 6–7-mm and in 8-mm embryos separately, proceeding from rostral to more caudal regions.

It is impossible to be certain of the identity of the earliest forebrain nuclei and tracts. A few neuroblasts appear around the optic stalk of 6-mm embryos, sending thin axons ventral to it in a caudal direction toward the mamillary recess. They are joined by a few others from above and just behind the stalk, as shown diagrammatically in Fig. 10. A few fibers of this thin peripheral tract course caudally as far as the interstitial nucleus. They comprise a diffuse system containing the first components of the medial forebrain tract and, more rostrally, a preopticohypothalamic tract.

There are many more axons in this system at the 8-mm stage (Fig. 11). Two groups of fibers are separated by the optic stalk. Those above it are traceable into the caudal diencephalon. Those below and in front of the stalk form a less prominent tract with a slightly different trajectory. Some of the fibers of the latter tract are preopticohypothalamic, destined later to become the preopticohypophyseal tract. Others are designated noncommittally as olfactohypothalamic. A few axons of the

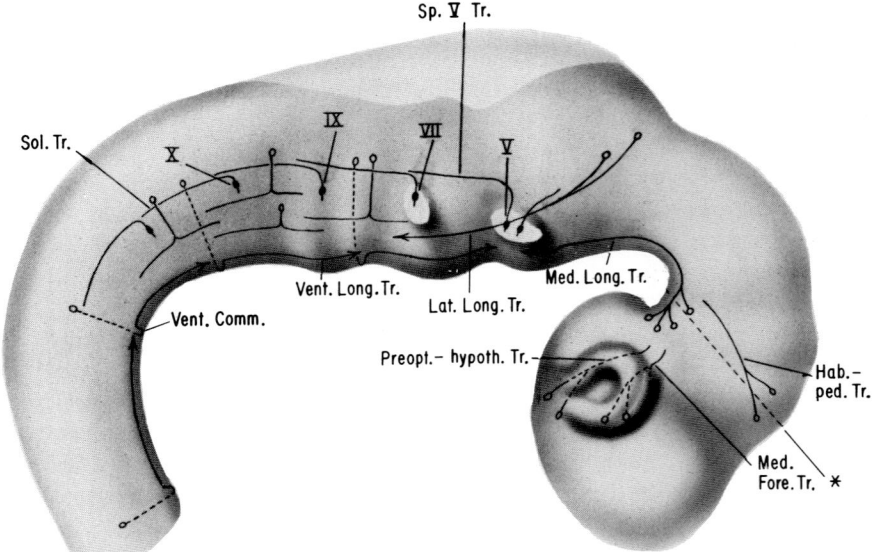

FIG. 10. The main second-order neurons and tracts in human embryos at the early 5-week stage (6 mm). The primary afferent elements of V, VII, IX, and X are included. (See Appendix for abbreviations.)

most rostral neuroblasts comprise the first elements of an olfactory tract.

Axons of the medial forebrain tract, or closely related ones, pass toward the mamillary recess, and one or two cross to the other side, initiating a supramamillary commissure in 8-mm embryos. There are a few neuroblasts in the caudal part of the forebrain that send axons into the ventral diencephalon, forming what may be called a striatosubthalamic tract. Others, passing forward below the optic stalk, form a minute commissure, probably the primordium of dorsal supraoptic and anterior commissures. Between these fibers and those of the medial forebrain tract there is a small group of axons with different orientation, which pass toward the hypothalamus and may represent the fornix primordium. It is not easy to separate one of these tracts from another during the fifth week. They are represented diagrammatically in Figs. 10 and 11.

Structures in the caudal diencephalon are easier to identify. The interstitial nucleus is fully as large as the nucleus of cranial nerve III in 6-mm embryos. It lies in the ventrolateral wall in front of the cephalic flexure, extending rostrally almost to the mamillary primordium. It forms the medial longitudinal tract, which passes ventral to nuclei III and IV, diminishing in size and ending before reaching the ventromedial efferent V nucleus. This tract is larger at 8 mm, but it still cannot be

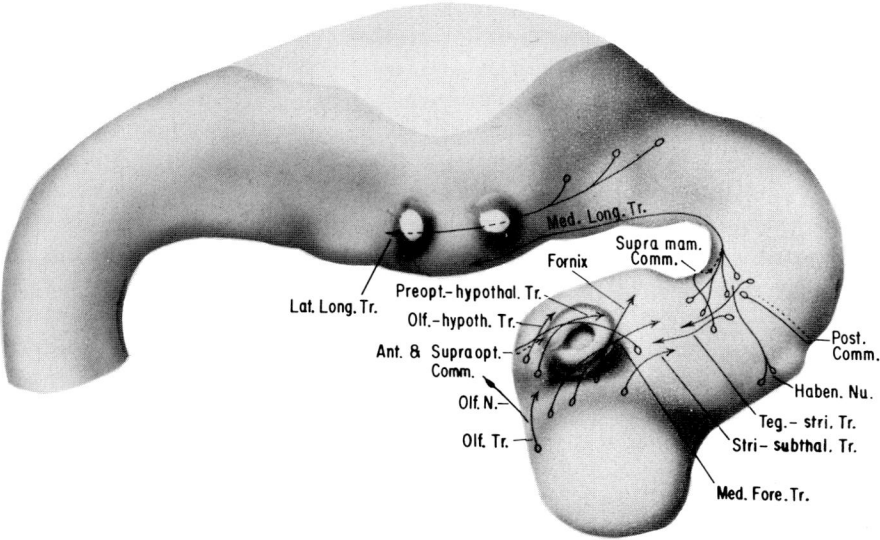

FIG. 11. Locations of the principal nuclei of the second order and their tracts and commissures in the rostral parts of the neural tube of human embryos at the end of the fifth week (8 mm). (See Appendix for abbreviations.)

traced much farther caudally than efferent V or the upper part of VII, where it is overlapped by ascending fibers.

Neuroblasts lateral to those of the interstitial nucleus comprise the nucleus of the posterior commissure (Darkschewitsch). The decussating axons of these are first seen in 8-mm embryos.

A small group of neuroblasts lateral to the diencephalic roof is the primordium of the habenular nucleus. Their axons course ventrad in 6-mm embryos toward the interstitial nucleus, forming the habenulo-peduncular tract, which gains in prominence at the 8-mm stage (Fig. 11).

MESENCEPHALON AND ISTHMUS REGIONS OF EMBRYOS OF THE FIFTH WEEK

There are few neuroblasts, other than those of cranial nerve nuclei III and IV, in the mesencephalon of 6- to 8-mm embryos. The interstitial nucleus and that of the posterior commissure occupy the junction with the diencephalon. The medial longitudinal tract is the only one in the mesencephalon at 6 mm. It lies very close to the floor plate, with a few fibers even coursing caudad in the floor plate. By the 8-mm stage, a few lateral longitudinal second-order axons are visible in the vicinity of nucleus IV, i.e., at the caudal end of the mesencephalon. These are the first elements of tectobulbar tracts.

Neurofibrillar differentiation is encountered in the alar plate at the isthmus. Certain neuroblasts there send axons into the thin marginal zone to course ventrad and caudad. These form a descending tract on the periphery at the sulcus limitans, closely associated with ascending V root, shifting mesad as it descends, and disappearing ventromedial to the entrance of V. The tract, first clearly visible at 8 mm, diminishes in size more caudally, where it lies close to the lateral longitudinal tract. Since the rhombic lip of the metencephalon caudal to the isthmus will become the primordium of the flocculus of the cerebellum, the axons in question appear to constitute a cerebellobulbar tract. More ventral neuroblasts may represent the primordium of the locus ceruleus. This complex was described in connection with development of the mesencephalic V tract in the cat and in other species (Windle and Fitzgerald, 1942). The cerebellobulbar tract is easily mistaken for the mesencephalic V tract, which was identified in 6-mm embryos.

LOWER RHOMBENCEPHALON AND SPINAL CORD OF EMBRYOS OF THE FIFTH WEEK

Differentiating neuroblasts are encountered in alar and basal plates of 6-mm embryos adjacent to the ascending V root. Their axons course ventromesad into the marginal zone of the same side, where they turn longitudinally to form the primordial reticular formation between emergence of the efferent V root and the medial longitudinal tract. The lateral part of this formation is more compact than the medial part, and constitutes the lateral longitudinal tract. The more caudal fibers of the cerebellobulbar tract pass into it in 8-mm embryos.

Other secondary neuroblasts send arcuate axons into the floor plate to form the ventral commissure of 6-mm embryos. The most rostral commissural fibers are found at the level of entrance of primary afferent V. Some fibers of the commissure contribute to the medial part of the reticular formation of the opposite side, but others turn rostrad and join the few remaining descending fibers of the medial longitudinal tract.

The ventral longitudinal tract of 6-mm embryos becomes prominent in the lower rhombencephalon, where many fibers cross the floor plate in the ventral commissure and ascend. The size of the commissure and the size of the ventral longitudinal tract are related to the number of secondary neuroblasts and arcuate axons, varying from region to region. Their numbers increase at points where primary afferent nerve roots enter the neural tube and decrease in the regions between roots. Their neuroblasts constitute primordia of nuclei of termination of the primary afferent neurons. There are more arcuate neurons at the level of VII-VIII (vestibular) nerves than at any other location.

Axons of other basal-plate neuroblasts pass directly into the reticular formation to form a loose grouping of longitudinal fibers between the common afferent and ventral longitudinal tracts. The more compact lateral longitudinal tract ends in the lower rhombencephalon, and the reticular formation proper does not course more than one or two segments into the spinal cord, where second-order neurons appear to be concerned almost entirely with the formation of the ventral commissure and ventral funiculus. The latter, like the ventral longitudinal tract, is an ascending secondary afferent system at the 6-mm stage.

Two distinct tracts and many loosely arranged fibers (reticular formation) are present in 8-mm embryos. A lateral longitudinal (central tegmental) tract arises from neuroblasts in the alar plate of the rostral part of the rhombencephalon. The most dorsal neuroblasts at this level give rise to ascending secondary vestibular fibers. Other alar-plate neuroblasts send their axons caudad and ventrad in the marginal zone mesial to the spinal V component of the common afferent tract. The cerebello-bulbar tract is incorporated in this system. The mesencephalic V tract is related to the upper part of this tract but leaves it to join with the primary afferent V root. The lateral longitudinal tract is predominately a descending one in 8-mm specimens. More ventrally and medially, there are a few scattered fibers comprising the reticular formation proper. Some of these arise from local basal plate neuroblasts.

Most interneurons of the alar and dorsal part of the basal plate caudal to the entrance of afferent V in 8-mm embryos give rise to arcuate fibers which stream through the reticular formation to decussate in the floor plate. Above the level of V this commissure is very small and is not seen beyond a point just caudal to the nucleus IV. Fibers turn into the ventral longitudinal tract from the commissure. The medial longitudinal tract drops out at the upper level of VII in 8-mm embryos. Increase in size of the ventral commissure at the lower end of the rhombencephalon is related to increase in number of interneurons in the dorsal part of the alar plate, where neuroblasts form the primordia of the nuclei gracilis and cuneatus. The spinal dorsal funiculus has not reached this level at 8-mm. The ventral longitudinal tract of the lower rhombencephalon may include the first part of the medial lemniscus, although this cannot be identified with certainty at 5 weeks. The interneurons adjacent to the common afferent tract form primordia of the following secondary afferent nuclei: main trigeminal nucleus, spinal tract nucleus, solitary tract nucleus, and medial vestibular nucleus. The ascending longitudinal fibers of the rhombencephalon constitute, for the most part, common secondary tracts at the 8-mm stage.

FOREBRAIN OF EMBRYOS OF THE SIXTH WEEK

Neuroblasts in the forebrain of embryos 9–12 mm long (Fig. 12) can be more clearly identified with definitive systems than previously. The group in front of the eye, sending axons caudad after swinging ventral to the optic stalk, does not belong to the rhinencephalon proper, as it appeared to at 5 weeks. Due to a shifting with enlargement of the pallium and thickening of the tuber cinereum, these cells now appear to occupy a more ventral position, relatively, than at earlier stages. This assemblage of neuroblasts lies in the rostral part of the tuber cinereum and many of their axons form the preopticohypothalamic tract. Some pass caudad uncrossed, but others cross in a supraoptic commissure, closely associated with the anterior commissure. A few wander ventrad into the infundibulum (the posterior lobe of the hypophysis is a simple pouch) and constitute the beginning of the preopticohypophyseal tract.

The olfactory lobe is beginning to form in front of the optic stalk in the sixth week. Its medial part is filled with neuroblasts whose axons

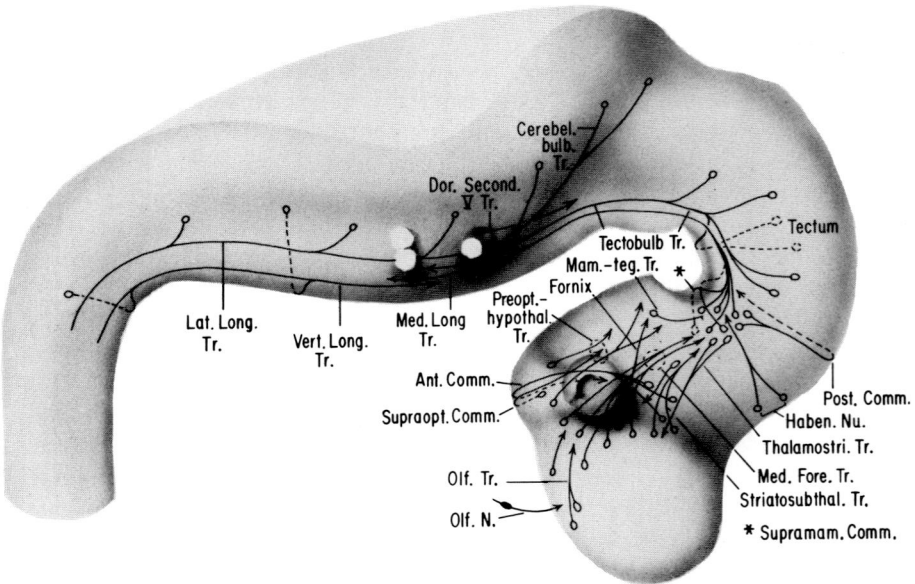

FIG. 12. Locations of the principal second-order neurons in rostral parts of the neural tube of human embryos early in the sixth week (10 mm). (See Appendix for abbreviations.)

have a plexiform arrangement at the very front of the brain. Most of the fibers pass ventrad and caudad toward the optic stalk, the more rostral ones constituting the olfactory tract. Into the rostral end of this system, pass fibers of the terminalis–olfactory nerve complex, which arise from a few cells in the medial wall of the olfactory pit, the vomeronasal pouch, and the mesenchyme between the olfactory pit and telencephalic wall.

Many neurons arise from the thickened lateral wall of the olfactory lobe and the olfactory striatum. These pass ventrocaudad and collect in a tract located between the optic stalk and the corpus striatum, which constitutes an olfactosubthalamic system. Behind the eye, many of these fibers sweep over the postoptic ridge and come to lie deep to the supraoptic tract with descending preopticohypothalamic fibers. Here they come to occupy the wide medial forebrain tract.

A few neuroblasts in the more caudal and lateral part of the olfactory striatum send their axons into a more ventral region. These fibers approach the lateral wall of the mamillary pouch in its more rostral part and appear to constitute the fornix. A few fibers arise from the dorsolateral wall of the mamillary body more caudally. These pass into the medial forebrain tract, some coursing caudad along its ventral border and others apparently passing dorsad to represent the beginning of a mamillothalamotegmental system in 10-mm embryos.

The corpus striatum give rise to another outflow of axons in 10-mm embryos, the striatosubthalamotegmental tract, which occupies the more dorsal part of the medial forebrain tract. Descending fibers of all tracts decrease in number at the level of the rostral end of the interstitial nucleus, but a few fibers continue on past the diencephalon to enter the mesencephalon lateral to the medial longitudinal tract.

Many neuroblasts are found in the lateral diencephalic wall. Some of these appear to contribute axons to the medial forebrain tract, but most of them are ascending fibers that pass ventral to the eye to reach the lamina terminalis. There they decussate in a small compact bundle representing the supraoptic and anterior commissures. The fibers returning through the decussation can be followed for only a short distance.

Other ascending fibers arise laterally in the more caudal diencephalic wall and pass to the corpus striatum as a thalamostriatal tract, seen clearly at 10 mm.

The first few (about a dozen) neuroblasts of the optic nerve arise from the optic cup early in the sixth week, and the commissure (chiasma) appears by the end of the week. Optic tracts are not seen until the seventh week.

Other neuroblasts in the lateral diencephalon send axons ventrad caudal to the mamillary body. They decussate in the floor and several prominent (more caudal) groups of them pass into the medial part of the opposite medial longitudinal tract. These constitute the supramamillary commissure (Forel), first identified in an embryo of 8 mm.

Accompanying the medial forebrain tract, but a little more deeply placed and dorsal to it, is an ascending bundle of fibers, the subthalamostriatal tract, arising from the group of cells dorsolateral to the interstitial nucleus at the end of the sixth week.

The habenulopeduncular tract, arising near the roof of the diencephalon behind the pallium, becomes prominent in embryos of the sixth week. Some of its fibers cross in the roof as the habenular commissure. The tract courses caudad, then swings ventrocaudally to occupy a deep position at the point where it is crossed by the medial forebrain tract in the region of the nucleus of the posterior commissure.

The interstitial nucleus is the more ventral part of a large group of neuroblasts. That of the posterior commissure is located more dorsally in this cell group. Possibly the dorsomedial part of the red nucleus is included in it. The posterior commissure is a wide tract in the roof between the diencephalon and mesencephalon in embryos of the sixth week. Rostral to the posterior commissure nucleus and the habenulopeduncular tract, a few neuroblasts of the dorsolateral diencephalic wall give rise to axons coursing ventrad. These decussate in the floor of the diencephalon to form the subthalamic commissure.

MESENCEPHALON OF EMBRYOS OF THE SIXTH WEEK

The medial longitudinal tract, arising from the interstitial nucleus at the junction of the diencephalon with the mesencephalon, descends uncrossed. It is joined at its upper end by a few fibers that crossed in the posterior commissure and by others from the supramamillary commissure coursing in a ventral position. Merging laterally with the medial longitudinal tract in the rostral mesencephalon are a few descending uncrossed fibers arising in the caudal part of the diencephalon, descending fibers of the medial forebrain tract, including some of striatal origin (striatosubthalamic tract), and a few from the lateral primordium of the mamillary body (mamillotegmental tract).

At least two groups of neurons take origin in the lateral mesencephalic wall and form descending tracts during the sixth week. Axons from the dorsolateral and rostral wall of the tectum pass ventrad and cross the floor plate just caudal to the supramamillary commissure to descend on the opposite side ventral and ultimately a little lateral to the medial longitudinal tract. These constitute the crossed tectobulbar tract. In the caudal part of the mesencephalon, the ventral commissure is represented by only an occasional stray axon. Cells in the lateral mesencephalic wall give rise to coarser fibers, which pass caudad and shift ventrad as they descend. These form the uncrossed or lateral tectobulbar tract; they join the lateral longitudinal tract.

A few ascending axons are found peripheral to the descending tracts, but only in the caudal part of the mesencephalon. The more dorsal ones arise in secondary neuroblasts located at the level of the main secondary afferent V nucleus and, therefore, constitute the primordium of a dorsal secondary trigeminal tract. Other ascending fibers shift lateral out of the ventral longitudinal tract of the rostral rhombencephalon and go forward along the lateral wall of the mesencephalon. They are the vanguard of a crossed ascending common secondary afferent system of crossed origin.

METENCEPHALON (ISTHMUS TO TRIGEMINAL REGION) OF EMBRYOS OF THE SIXTH WEEK

Just caudal to nerve IV, before it crosses in the roof of the isthmus, a group of alar-plate neuroblasts gives rise to axons which course ventrad and caudad to join the descending uncrossed tectobulbar tract. They assume a ventrolateral position in the basal plate rostral to the ascending ramus of the primary afferent V tract. This is the tract that was designated the "angular bundle" in a recent article (Windle and Fitzgerald, 1942). Other fibers cross it diagonally, ascending into the mesencephalon from the region of the main secondary afferent V nucleus. These constitute the dorsal secondary trigeminal tract.

At the level of V, the ventral commissure contains fibers of basal-plate origin as well as those from the secondary afferent V neuroblasts. Some of these fibers turn rostrad lateral to the medial longitudinal tract. The latter tract becomes much smaller at the level of V and contains ascending as well as descending components of local origin in its ventral and lateral parts.

The mesencephalic V tract occupies a deep position medial to the dorsal secondary afferent V tract. It arises from large unipolar cells, found almost as far forward as IV in the sixth week. More medial fibers arise from locus ceruleus neuroblasts and become associated with mesencephalic V tract.

The lateral longitudinal tract at the level of V contains the following: (a) descending neurons from the locus ceruleus, (b) descending neurons from the primordium of the cerebellum (flocculus and nodulus), (c) direct descending tectobulbar neurons from the inferior colliculus, (d) a few fibers from diencephalon and upper mesencephalon (possibly a thalamoolivorubral tract), (e) ascending secondary afferent neurons (dorsal secondary trigeminal tract), and (f) some ascending tegmental neurons in the reticular formation adjacent to the lateral longitudinal tract.

LOWER RHOMBENCEPHALON AND SPINAL CORD OF EMBRYOS OF THE SIXTH WEEK

The two most conspicuous groups of second-order axons throughout the rhombencephalon constitute the ventral and lateral longitudinal tracts. Both are located in the basal plate. The former is predominantly an ascending pathway; the latter, for the most part, a descending one. The descending medial longitudinal tract from the interstitial nucleus merges with the ventral longitudinal tract and cannot be followed farther caudally than the level of VII. At the point of entrance of each primary afferent nerve root, groups of second-order, alar-plate neuroblasts contribute arcuate fibers through the ventral commissure to the ventral longitudinal tract of the opposite side. The commissural neuroblasts of the alar plate occupy a more dorsal position in the lower rhombencephalon than they do at higher levels. Some of these form the primordium of the medial lemniscus at the end of the sixth and in the early part of the seventh weeks.

The lateral longitudinal tract and reticular formation of the rhombencephalon receive some commissural and additional uncrossed associational axons from alar and lateral basal plate neuroblasts. The lateral longitudinal tract is largest at the VII-VIII and IX-X levels and becomes smaller below the level of X. It extends caudally into the upper spinal cord and becomes incorporated into the lateral funiculus.

Embryos of the first part of the sixth week present few qualitative advances in neurofibrillar differentiation over those of the fifth, but by the end of the sixth week, the wall of the rhombencephalon has increased notably in thickness (compare Figs. 3D and 3E). Its mantle layer is the site of rapid growth which contributes greatly from this stage onward to development of second-order afferent nerve nuclei and their pathways to the thalamus and associated centers. The secondary afferent V tracts and initial components of the medial lemniscus can be recognized, but the nucleus of the solitary tract and its projection pathway cannot be separated from other elements of mantle and marginal layers at 12 mm. Second-order vestibular neuroblasts are numerous, but neuroblasts of cochlear nuclei and their axons are unidentifiable.

The spinal cord at the end of the sixth and the beginning of the seventh weeks has both ventral and lateral funiculi. Like the ventral longitudinal tract in the lower rhombencephalon, the ventral spinal funiculus is formed by commissural axons; the neuroblasts of these occupy a dorsomedial position adjacent to the most dorsomedial part of the funiculus. The lateral funiculus, comparable with the lateral longitudinal tract and reticular formation of the rhombencephalon, springs mainly from neuroblasts of the mantle layer nearer the lateral border of the dorsal funiculus. The lateral funiculus has a mixed population, containing uncrossed descending axons as well as some ascending ones, whereas the ventral funiculus consists of crossed ascending fibers (Rhines and Windle, 1941).

A relationship between the association neurons of second-order and collateral branches of primary afferent neurons from the dorsal funiculus is established at 7 to 8 weeks (Windle and Fitzgerald, 1937). This provides the basis for the first ipsilateral spinal reflexes. Contralateral reflexes appear later, when primary afferent collaterals emerge from the more medial part of the dorsal funiculus adjacent to the cell bodies of arcuate neuroblasts whose axons traverse the ventral commissure.

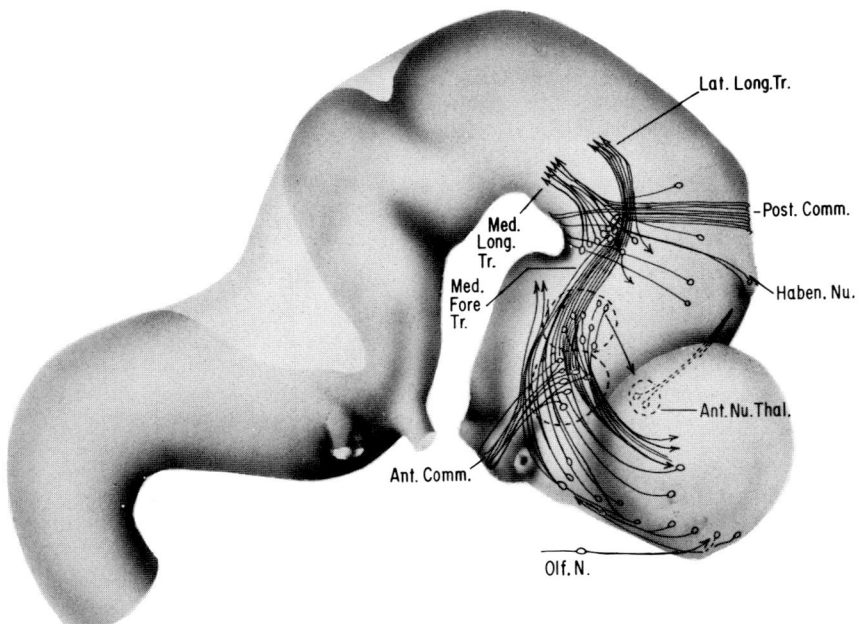

FIG. 13. The rostral part of the brain of embryos during early part of the seventh week (12.5–13 mm). The great increase in number of neurons of previously initiated tracts made detailed study of their course and termination impossible with the technique used. (See Appendix for abbreviations.)

SUMMARY

The nuclei and tracts of secondary neurons undergo such a rapid differentiation and on so complicated a template—the embryonic forebrain—that one's efforts to sort them out, especially in embryos larger than 12.5 mm, are usually frustrated. Figure 13 illustrates the picture at the beginning of the seventh week. Simpler patterns exist in the more caudal parts of the brain and the spinal cord.

Second-order neuroblasts appear at 4 weeks in the lower rhomb-

TABLE 3
Tracts Identified in Human Embryos

Name of tract	Length of embryo (mm)					Direction of initial fibers[a]
	4	6	8	10	12	
Ventral longitudinal	+	+	+	+	+	A
Medial longitudinal	−	+	+	+	+	D
Ventral funiculus	−	+	+	+	+	A
Lateral longitudinal	−	+	+	+	+	A and D
Reticular formation	−	+	+	+	+	A and D
Medial forebrain	−	+	+	+	+	D
Preopticohypothalamic	−	+	+	+	+	D
Mesencephalic V	−	+	+	+	+	C
Habenulopeduncular	−	+	+	+	+	D
Supraoptic	−	−	+	+	+	D
Tectobulbar	−	−	+	+	+	D
Cerebellobulbar	−	−	+	+	+	D
Olfactohypothalamic	−	−	+	+	+	D
Olfactory	−	−	+	+	+	D
Striatosubthalamic	−	−	+	+	+	D
Fornix	−	−	+	+	+	D
Vestibulocerebellar	−	−	+	+	+	A
Spinal vestibular	−	−	+	+	+	D
Secondary V	−	−	+	+	+	A
Preopticohypophyseal	−	−	−	+	+	D
Olfactosubthalamic	−	−	−	+	+	D
Mamillothalamotegmental	−	−	−	+	+	D
Striatosubthalamotegmental	−	−	−	+	+	D
Thalamostriatal	−	−	−	+	+	A
Subthalamostriatal	−	−	−	−	+	A
Optic	−	−	−	−	+	C
Medial lemniscus	−	−	−	−	+	A
Vestibulospinal	−	−	−	−	+	D

[a] Abbreviations are: A, ascending; C, commissural; and D, descending.

encephalon and upper spinal cord, where their arcuate axons form a crossed ascending tract. Differentiation proceeds both rostrally and caudally, and by the end of the sixth week most secondary afferent systems of the brain have been laid down. The spinal dorsal-column nuclei and most of those of the cranial nerves are present; only the cochlear nuclei are lacking. Few if any fibers of the secondary afferent tracts have reached their destinations in thalamus or cerebellum by 6 weeks and, of course, there is no cerebral cortex.

The tracts that descend into the brain stem proper from the diencephalon, cerebellar primordium, and mesencephalon are the uncrossed medial longitudinal tract (from interstitial nucleus), the uncrossed cerebellobulbar tract, and the crossed and uncrossed tectobulbar tracts. A vestibulobulbar component is present at 6 weeks, but no central auditory tracts have appeared.

Neurofibrillar differentiation in the forebrain leads to formation of tracts that are difficult to separate from one another. The main groups comprise a primordial system containing, for the most part, descending and commissural axons. At five weeks, the medial forebrain tract is the most prominent one, and there are a few other uncrossed descending axons. The olfactory tract joins this system. Another group of axons represents the hypothalamohyphophyseal system, and this, too, is initiated during the fifth week. Finally, axons coursing forward in the fore-

TABLE 4
Commissures Identified in Human Embryos

Name of commissure	Length of embryo (mm)				
	4	6	8	10	12
Ventral	+	+	+	+	+
Motor VIII	−	+	+	+	+
Motor IV	−	+	+	+	+
Supramamillary	−	−	+	+	+
Supraoptic (dorsal)	−	−	+	+	+
Anterior	−	−	+	+	+
Posterior	−	−	+	+	+
Tectobulbar	−	−	+	+	+
Secondary V and VIII	−	−	+	+	+
Habenular	−	−	−	+	+
Subthalamic	−	−	−	+	+
Optic	−	−	−	−	+
Medial lemniscus	−	−	−	−	+

brain are recognizable in the fifth week. These are concentrated mainly in supraoptic and tegmentostriatal tracts. The former crosses in front of the optic stalk with the anterior commissure. Table 3 lists all tracts identified in embryos up to the end of 6 weeks of gestation. The commissures of all types that appear between the fourth and sixth weeks are shown in Table 4.

Discussion

Initiation of neurofibrillar differentiation in the lower rhombencephalon and upper spinal cord in the human embryo of the fourth week is consonant with the findings in other mammalian species (Kimmel, 1941; Pearson, 1946, 1947; Tello, 1934) and in the chick embryo (Cowdry, 1914; Windle and Austin, 1936). The sequence of appearance of cranial nerve nuclei that was reported by Bok (1915), and on which he based his theory of "stimulogenous fibrillation" to support ontogenetically Ariens–Kappers' "neurobiotaxis," was not confirmed in this study, or in previous ones, for that matter.

If "ontogeny recapitulates phylogeny," it seems strange that such nuclei as V, VII, and IX-X-XI, customarily designated as "general visceral efferent" or "special visceral efferent," should be situated medial to III, VI, and XII, which are called "somatic efferent." Then too, a parasympathetic (visceral efferent) component of III, if present, must occupy the somatic column; and nucleus IV, always classified as somatic, at first presents features similar to those of visceral nuclei in human as well as other mammalian development. Furthermore, how are we to classify primary efferent VIII, which innervates a "special somatic" sense organ and differentiates in the visceral efferent column?

We should no longer try to make embryology of the mammalian brain fit theories based on structure and function of lower vertebrates. Even though all vertebrates do pass through primitive three- and five-vesicle stages, the early development of the brain of a mammal is intrinsically different from that of a fish or an amphibian. The developmental basis for mammalian behavior, especially human, appears to be quite different from that for behavior in the lower vertebrates.

What does the embryonic brain have to do with development of behavior? Certainly, it is concerned with sensory input and motor functions, but it is hard to say just when either has its beginning. Perhaps we should time it with the initiation of muscle contractions. There are no intrinsic neural elements when contractions of the human heart muscle begin at 3 to 4 weeks of gestation. Furthermore, other types of muscle are capable of contraction before nerves reach them—smooth muscle of the intestines by 7, and skeletal muscle before 8 weeks.

Neuronally controlled skeletal movements and reflexes have been observed at 8 weeks (Bergström, 1968; Fitzgerald and Windle, 1942; Hooker, 1939a,b, 1954). The structural basis for the neural mechanisms of reflex action precedes the appearance of reflexes. The elements of reflex arcs are seen in human embryos as young as 6 to 7 weeks of gestation. I have described the sequences of this structural development in the present report. Movements of the arms have been obtained in nonanesthetized 8-week human fetuses 20 mm in crown-rump length (Fitzgerald and Windle, 1942). Movements of the head have been elicited in specimens 25 mm long (Humphrey, 1952). The truly reflex nature of responses to stimulation in monkey fetuses has been demonstrated by Bodian and his colleagues (1966) electron microscopically. As gestation proceeds from 8 to 12 weeks, these simple reflexes become incorporated into more complex activities.

Early behavior clearly relates to establishment of vital functions, notably, circulation of blood, suckling, swallowing and digestion of food, elimination of wastes, and in higher vertebrates, air breathing. Most of these functions are common to all species, and neural development to support them may present similarities. However, fishes and larval amphibians have no need to anticipate pulmonary respiration in their embryonic stages, though it is of prime importance to mammals to have mechanisms for air breathing in good order well in advance of birth. Breathing movements are present at least as early as the twelfth week in the human fetus (Windle, 1940). The first reflexes of human embryos of 8 weeks appear to become incorporated into breathing movements by 11 or 12 weeks (Hooker, 1954, discussion; Windle, 1940). This is long before viability.

Fetal respiratory movements should not be thought of as spontaneous prenatal functions. They represent behavioral capabilities that come into play when intrauterine conditions place the life of the fetus in jeopardy; placental separation and the concomitant asphyxia bring them about. Indeed, the first manifestations of human somatic behavior, except the early limb reflexes, have been demonstrated only after removal of the fetus from the uterus.

The course of human development has not been followed throughout intrauterine life. It may never be. However, we have raised the curtain and have seen the first act, as it were. Interpretations of what was viewed have not always been harmonious. Perhaps it will help reconcile points of view to deal strictly with factual observations, regardless of their relevance to theories of development based on lower forms of life.

ACKNOWLEDGMENT

The research article on which this report was based appeared as Part II of *Experimental Neurology Supplement* 5, 1970. Completion of the research and preparation of the illustrations were made possible by a grant from the National Institute of Child Health and Human Development (HD 03417). Cost of the color plates was defrayed by a supplementary grant.

REFERENCES

Angevine, J. B., Jr. (1965). Time of neuron origin in the hippocampal region. *Exp. Neurol. Suppl.* 2, 1-70.
Bartelmez, G. W., and Dekaban, A. S. (1962). The early development of the human brain. *Carnegie Inst. Wash. Publ.* No. 621; Contrib. Embryol. Vol. 37, 13-32.
Bergström, R M. (1968). Development of EEG and unit electrical activity of the brain during ontogeny, pp. 61-71. *In* "Ontogenesis of the Brain" (L. Jílek and S. Trojan, eds.), Charles Univ. Press, Prague.
Bodian, D., Melby, E. C., Jr., and Taylor, N. (1966). Development of fine structure of spinal cord in monkey fetuses. I. The motoneuron neuropil at the time of onset of reflex activity. *Bull. Johns Hopkins Hosp.* Vol. 119, 129-149.
Bok, S. T. (1915). Die Entwicklung der Hirnnerven und ihrer zentralen Bahnen. *Die stimulogene Fibrillation. Folia Neurobiol.* Vol. 9, 475-565.
Cowdry, E. V. (1914). The development of the cytoplasmic constituents of the nerve cells of the chick. *Amer. J. Anat.* Vol. 15, 389-429.
Fitzgerald, J. E., and Windle, W. F. (1942). Some observations on early human fetal movements. *J. Comp. Neurol.* Vol. 76, 159-167.
His, W. (1904). "Die Entwickelung des menschlichen Gehirns während der ersten Monate." Hirzel, Leipzig.
Hochstetter, F. (1919). "Beitrage zur Entwicklungs geschichte des menschlichen Gehirns," Vol. 1. Deuticke, Vienna.
Hooker, D. (1939a). "A Preliminary Atlas of Early Human Fetal Activity." Privately printed.
Hooker, D. (1939b). Fetal behavior. *Res. Publ., Ass. Res. Nerv. Ment. Dis.* Vol. 19, 237-243.
Hooker, D. (1954). Early human fetal behavior, with a preliminary note on double simultaneous fetal stimulation. *Res. Publ., Ass. Res. Nerv. Ment. Dis.* Vol. 33, 98-113.
Humphrey, T. (1952). The spinal tract of the trigeminal nerve in human embryos between $7\frac{1}{2}$ and $8\frac{1}{2}$ weeks of menstrual age and its relation to early fetal behavior. *J. Comp. Neurol.* Vol. 97, 143-209.
Keibel, F., and Mall, F. P. (1912). "Manual of Human Embryology," Vol. 2. Lippincott, Philadelphia, Pennsylvania.
Kimmel, D. (1941). Development of the afferent components of the facial, glossopharyngeal and vagus nerves in the rabbit embryo. *J. Comp. Neurol.* Vol. 74, 447-474.

Minot, C. S. (1892). "Human Embryology." Wm. Wood & Co., New York.

Pearson, A. A. (1946). The development of the motor nuclei of the facial nerve in man. *J. Comp. Neurol.* Vol. 85, 461–476.

Pearson, A. A. (1947). The roots of the facial nerve in human embryos and fetuses. *J. Comp. Neurol.* Vol. 87, 139–159.

Ramón y Cajal, S. (1960). "Studies on Vertebrate Neurogenesis." Thomas, Springfield, Illinois. (Translation of L. Guth, "Etudes sur la Neurogénese de quelques Vertébrés," 1929.)

Rasmussen, G. L. (1960). Efferent fibers of the cochlear nerve and cochlear nucleus. *In* "Neural Mechanisms of the Auditory and Vestibular Systems" (G. L. Rasmussen and W. F. Windle, eds.), pp. 105–115. Thomas, Springfield, Illinois.

Rhines, R., and Windle, W. F. (1941). The early development of the fasciculus longitudinalis medialis and associated neurons in the rat, cat and man. *J. Comp. Neurol.* Vol. 75, 165–189.

Streeter, G. L. (1904). The development of the cranial and spinal nerves in the occipital regions of the human embryo. *Amer. J. Anat.* Vol. 4, 83–116.

Streeter, G. L. (1906). On the development of the membranous labyrinth and the acoustic and facial nerves in the human embryo. *Amer. J. Anat.* Vol. 6, 139–166.

Streeter, G. L. (1908). The peripheral nervous system in the human embryo at the end of the first month (10 mm). *Amer. J. Anat.* Vol. 8, 285–301.

Streeter, G. L. (1942, 1945, 1948, 1951). Developmental horizons in human embryos (horizons xi to xxiii). *Carnegie Inst. Wash. Publ.* Nos. 541, 557, 575, and 592; *Contrib. Embryol.* Vol. 30, 211–245; Vol. 31, 27–63; Vol. 32, 133–203; Vol. 34, 165–196.

Strong, R. M. (1938). Further observation on the f. solitarius and its nucleus in the human brain. *Anat. Rec.* Vol. 70, Suppl. 3, 77.

Tello, J. F. (1934). Les différenciations neurofibrillaires dans le prosencéphale de la souris de 4 à 15 mm. *Trav. Lab. Invest. Biol. Univ. Madrid.* Vol. 19, 339–395.

Wilson, E. E., Windle, W. F., and Fitzgerald, J. E. (1941). Development of the tractus solitarius. *J. Comp. Neurol.* Vol. 74, 287–307.

Windle, W. F. (1932a). The neurofibrillar development of the 7-mm cat embryo. *J. Comp. Neurol.* Vol. 55, 99–138.

Windle, W. F. (1932b). The neurofibrillar development of the five-and-one-half-millimeter cat embryo. *J. Comp. Neurol.* Vol. 55, 315–331.

Windle, W. F. (1933). Neurofibrillar development in the central nervous system of cat embryos between 8 and 12 mm long. *J. Comp. Neurol.* Vol. 58, 643–723.

Windle, W. F. (1935). Neurofibrillar development of cat embryos: Extent of development in the telencephalon and diencephalon up to 15 mm. *J. Comp. Neurol.* Vol. 63, 139–171.

Windle, W. F. (1940). "Physiology of the Fetus." Saunders, Philadelphia, Pennsylvania.

Windle, W. F. (1949). Trigeminal efferent neurons of silver-stained 4–7 weeks human embryos. *Anat. Rec.* Vol. 103, 106–107.

Windle, W. F., and Austin, M. F. (1936). Neurofibrillar development in the central nervous system of chick embryos up to 5 days' incubation. *J. Comp. Neurol.* Vol. 63, 431–463.

Windle, W. F., and Fitzgerald, J. E. (1937). Development of the spinal reflex mechanism in human embryos. *J. Comp. Neurol.* Vol. 67, 493–509.

Windle, W. F., and Fitzgerald, J. E. (1942). Development of the human mesencephalic trigeminal root and related neurons. *J. Comp. Neurol.* Vol. 77, 597–608.

Appendix

Abbreviations Used in Illustrations

Aff.	Afferent
Aff. X (Jug.)	Jugular ganglion X
Ant. Comm.	Anterior commissure
Ant. Nu. Thal.	Anterior nucleus of the thalamus
Asc. Aff. V	Ascending primary afferent V
Cerebel.-bulb. Tr.	Cerebellobulbar tract
Cerebel. Eff.	Cerebellar efferent neuroblasts
Com. Aff. Tr.	Common afferent tract
Comm.	Commissure
Comm. IV	Commissural IV axons
Comm. Eff. VIII	Commissural efferent VIII axons
Dor. Eff. (Nu.) V	Dorsal nucleus V (general visceral)
Dor. Mot. Nu. X	Dorsal motor nucleus X
Dor. Second. V Tr.	Dorsal secondary V tract
Eff.	Efferent
Eff. V Nu.	Efferent nucleus V (special visceral)
Gen. Gang.	Geniculate ganglion VII
Haben. Nu.	Habenular nucleus
Haben.-ped. (Hab.-ped.) Tr.	Habenulopeduncular tract
Interst. Nu.	Interstitial nucleus (Cajal)
Lat. Long. Tr.	Lateral longitudinal (tegmental) tract
Lat. V Nu.	Lateral nucleus V (special visceral)
Mam.-teg. Tr.	Mamillotegmental tract
Med. Fore. Tr.	Medial forebrain tract
Med. Long. Tr.	Medial longitudinal tract
Mes. V Tr.	Mesencephalic V tract
Nu.	Nucleus
Nu. Ambig.	Nucleus ambiguus
Nu. Med. Long. Tr.	Interstitial nucleus (Cajal)
Nu. Sp. Tr. V	Nucleus spinal V tract
Olf.-hypothal. Tr.	Olfactohypothalamic tract
Olf. N.	Olfactory nerve
Olf. Tr.	Olfactory tract
Post. Comm.	Posterior commissure
Preopt.-hypothal. Tr.	Preopticohypothalamic tract
Ret. (Retic.) Form.	Reticular formation
Rt.	Rootlet
Semi. Gang.	Semilunar ganglion V
Sol. Tr.	Solitary tract
Sp. Gang.	Spinal ganglion
Sp. Tr. V	Spinal V tract
Stri.-subthal. Tr.	Striatosubthalamic tract
Supramam. (Supra mam.) Comm.	Supramamillary commissure
Supraopt. Comm.	Supraoptic commissure
Tectobulb. Tr.	Tectobulbar tract

Teg.-stri. Tr.	Tegmentostriatal tract
Thalamostri. Tr.	Thalamostriatal tract
Vent. Comm.	Ventral commissure
Vent. Long. Tr.	Ventral longitudinal tract
Vent. Rt.	Ventral rootlets
Ventromed. Nu. V	Ventromedial nucleus V

III. BIOCHEMICAL PROCESSES IN BEHAVIORAL DEVELOPMENT

BIOCHEMICAL PROCESSES OF NERVOUS SYSTEM DEVELOPMENT

WILLIAMINA A. HIMWICH

Certain concepts of the development of the brain are fundamental to the interpretation of biochemical data obtained in relation to function, to the various methods of measuring brain development that may be applicable to experiments on animals, and, in some cases, to studies of human beings. To illustrate our present grasp of the situation, I would like to paraphrase a sentence of Garrigan and Chargaff (1963): In trying to reflect on the biochemistry of development, we may come to the conclusion that even our power of formulating the problems is still in a developmental stage.

Basic Patterns of the Development of the Brain

The brain, as we have all become increasingly aware, works as an integrated single organ, the specific function of its parts being demonstrable especially in the presence of pathological changes. From the standpoint of biochemical studies of brain, this complexity presents an enormous problem of sampling and of functional interpretation of data. If we analyze the brain as a whole, on one hand, then the changes which occur in a part, and which may be the crucial ones responsible for specific behavioral responses, may be masked. If, on the other hand, we subdivide the brain, the physical problem of taking samples so that they are comparable not only from one experiment to another but also from one laboratory to another is of great importance. The obvious answer to this problem is the use of anatomical landmarks in dividing the brain. This solution, however, results in only a relatively few areas being sampled. These areas, moreover, are mixed regions of white and gray matter including many nuclei with undoubtedly different functions. In the biochemical field, some progress is being made in the development of methods which will allow the preparation of much more specific smaller fragments (Graham et al., 1967; S. P. R. Rose, 1967; Whittaker, 1968; Hydén and Hartelius, 1948; Salganicoff and De Robertis, 1965). However, even as we accomplish this, we are faced with the problem of the quantitative, reproducible isolation of cellular parts. Even with the use of the best available method, the uncertainty of the exact proportions of dendrites, of synaptosomes, or of mitochondria present in a subcellular preparation of the brain is an illustration of the difficulties encountered in this field. Similar difficulties are met in separating neurons and glia reliably. However, only to the extent that we can approach the biochemistry of the synapse as opposed to that of the cell as a whole can we hope to obtain the data necessary to establish the biochemical substrata required for brain function. Much of our confusion in biochemistry as it relates to function arises from the fact that we cannot reach the actual functioning area with any degree of reproducibility (for example, the confusion attending γ-aminobutyric acid (GABA) concentrations and function; Roberts and Kuriyama, 1968). As these problems are attacked by those investigators who have developed the elegant methods for separation, and as their methods of fractionating brain continue to be revised, we hope to be better able to deal with these relations. The influence of the compartmentation of various compounds will be discussed later.

In the past, attempts to relate biochemical development to function have been based upon various concepts of the way in which the brain develops. Their use has led to the rich interpretation of the data and has served to add immeasurably to our knowledge of functional development as related to the biochemical and the electrophysiological patterns (H. E. Himwich, 1951). It must, however, be kept in mind at all times that none of these theories of development is an absolute. Each has been called upon when its use gave the most productive interpretation of specific experimental results. As we obtain more knowledge, we must move toward a better understanding of the way in which the brain develops and the relation between biochemistry and behavior.

In terms of chronological age perhaps the oldest theory of brain development is neurophylogenesis which postulates that the brain matures from caudad to cephalad; that is, that the pons medulla matures earlier than the cerebral cortex and is illustrated (Fig. 1) by the oxygen consumption of parts of dog brain during development (H. E. Himwich and Fazekas, 1941). This theory may be referred to as the horizontal picture of development. Hughlings Jackson (1884a,b,c) developed this concept to explain behavior after trauma to the brain in man. Its basic ideas have been widely used for the interpretation of data and have

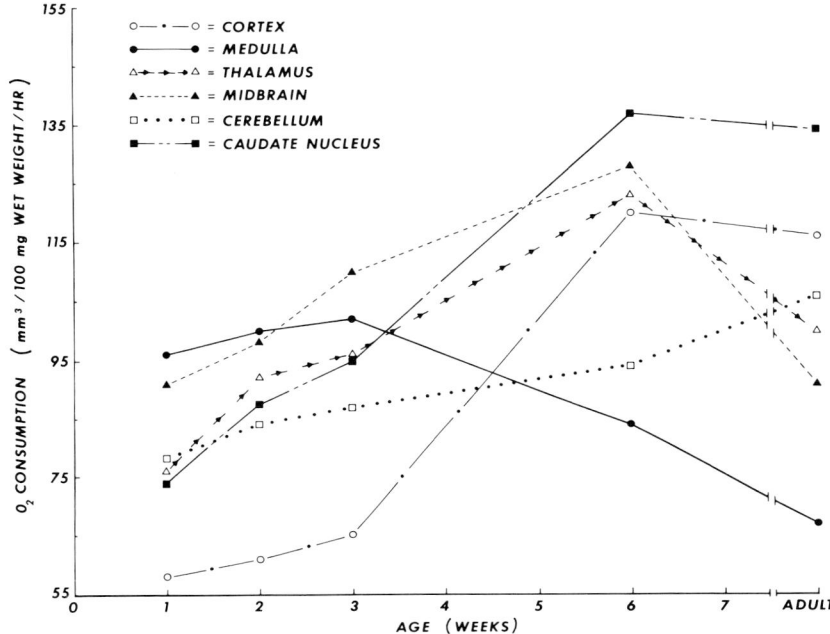

FIG. 1. Oxygen consumption of dog brain parts at various ages. (From H. E. Himwich and Fazekas, 1941.)

permitted correlations of studies of the effects of anoxia (Fischer and Jílek, 1958; H. E. Himwich and Himwich, 1962), of hypoglycemia (H. E. Himwich, 1951; Chesler and Himwich, 1944), of Jacksonian epilepsy (Jackson, 1884a,b,c) and of developmental biochemistry (W. A. Himwich, 1969).

The second theory, which has not been so widely used but which also has many possibilities, is the concept of vertical development. This concept was put forward originally by Magoun and his colleagues (Moruzzi and Magoun, 1949) and was further emphasized by Livingston et al. (1954). H. E. Himwich (1960) points out:

> The central nervous system may be regarded as divided into three vertical columns extending throughout the entire length of the central nervous system: the first includes ascending spinal pathways carrying sensory impulses that are relayed by the thalamus to specific sensory areas of the cortex. The second column consists of the descending motor pathways of the corticospinal tracts. Between these two is a third composed of indirect connections: association areas of the cerebral cortex, the reticular formation of the brainstem and the extrapyramidal motor tracts descending to the anterior horn cells of the spinal cord.

> The third column also possesses ascending functions in the two parts of the activities of the reticular formation (Rinaldi and Himwich, 1955a,b) which are continued by the diffusely projecting thalamacortical unspecific projections.

The application of this theory for biochemical interpretation is hindered by the very gross divisions of the central nervous system, thus making it impossible to pinpoint what has happened in a particular nucleus or connecting system. Nor has this theory been of much use in determining biochemical correlations because of the difficulties of accurate dissection of the systems involved. However, in a situation where dissection is relatively simple, such as in studies of the visual tract including retina, geniculate bodies, superior colliculi, and visual cortex, this concept may be used (W. A. Himwich et al., 1967b; W. A. Himwich, 1968; Davis et al., 1969; Callison and Spencer, 1968).

A third theory developed so beautifully by Professor Anokhin and his colleagues (Anokhin, 1964) is that of systemogenesis. Fundamentally this theory holds that irrespective of their location, those brain nuclei which are essential for the survival of the young in its particular environmental situation are those which develop first. This concept requires a careful study of the environmental situation of the young of any given species, or, in some cases, even of subspecies, if we are to make the necessary interpretations. Again this theory, in terms of its relation to biochemical development, has not been widely used, and again the difficulty lies in the dissection of the necessary material for the study. So far only histochemical methods have been available, but as methods develop, I am sure, we will be in a better position to correlate biochemical data. I would like to give just one or two illustrations taken from Professor Anokhin's work. In mammals the neurons controlling sucking mature earlier than the other neurons of the facial nucleus. Vision develops late in those young born in dark caves or burrows and kept there until they can protect themselves to some extent. In such young, smells and sounds are more important stimuli.

A fourth viewpoint is that of Vogt (1925), whose studies revealed that injurious substances may affect the various cerebral areas in such a selective manner as to indicate that some are especially susceptible to a given toxic substance. They suggested a physiochemical basis to explain the greater sensitivity exhibited by some brain structures in comparison with others. More recently the histochemical researches of Cammermeyer and Swank (1951) and Swank and Cammermeyer (1949) revealed additional evidence for the third type of stratification of cerebral functions, for example, anesthesia with barbiturates and convulsions due to picrotoxin produce selective injuries in the cerebral neurons of dogs.

Measures of Brain Development

Let us look first at what we know about the biochemical aspects of brain development. I prefer here to restrict my comments to biochemistry since that is my area of competence. The facets of behavior, electrophysiology, and anatomy I study are only used to permit correlation with the basic biochemistry.

We know certain fundamental facts of brain development which, if the time element is ignored, can be applied to all species. The brain grows in weight, in length, and in volume as it matures. At the same time the water is replaced by dry matter, especially lipid and protein (Fig. 2). Some free amino acids increase in concentration (Fig. 3) (Agrawal et al., 1966), others decrease and still others maintain their original concentrations. In general these events appear to occur first in the caudad areas and later in the cephalad ones. Some areas such as the hippocampus appear to be relatively mature at birth, thus being exceptions to a neurophylogenetic concept and fitting better into the theory

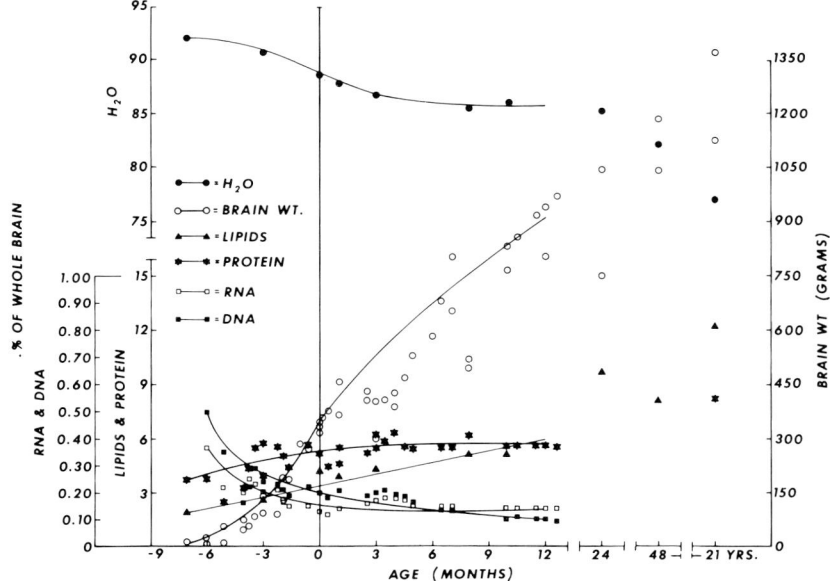

FIG. 2. Development of the human brain. (From W. A. Himwich et al., 1963; MacArthur and Doisy, 1918–1919; Tilney and Rosett, 1931; Scammon, 1933; Winick, 1968.)

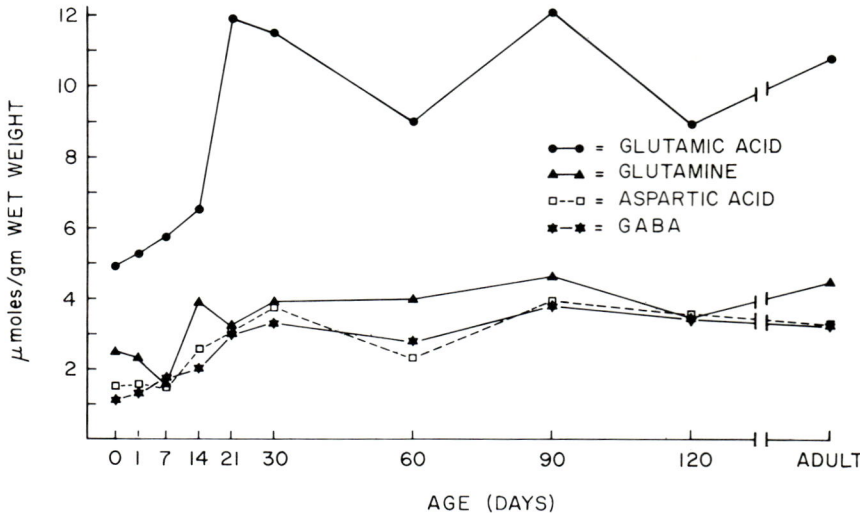

FIG. 3. Postnatal changes in the free amino acid pool of rat brain (whole brains used). (From Agrawal et al., 1966.)

of systemogenesis (W. A. Himwich and Dravid, 1967; Purpura and Papas, 1968; Schwartz et al., 1968). The free amino acid pattern as well as that of amino acids in protein appear to be characteristic of the area studied, even though there are changes with maturation (Davis and Himwich, 1971). Glutamic acid dominates the free amino acid picture to a high degree in rostral areas, but to a lesser degree in the midbrain, since the concentrations of GABA are higher in this area (Fig. 4) (Dravid et al., 1965). Differences in DNA, RNA, and protein (Fish and Winick, 1960; Winick, 1968; Chanda and Himwich, 1970) in brain parts are well documented.

GENERAL FACTORS AFFECTING THE VALIDITY OF THE MEASUREMENTS

In any measurement of the influence of environmental factors upon brain development we must constantly attempt to separate the secondary effects of the experimental conditions upon the brain mediated through primary changes in the total organism from effects which occur directly upon the brain. For example, in our laboratory, puppies (dogs) loaded with phenylalanine from birth weighed slightly less but not significantly so than the littermate controls (Fig. 5) (W. A. Himwich et al., 1967a). The experimental animals, however, seemed lethargic and less alert than the controls. When both groups were tested in a problem solving maze,

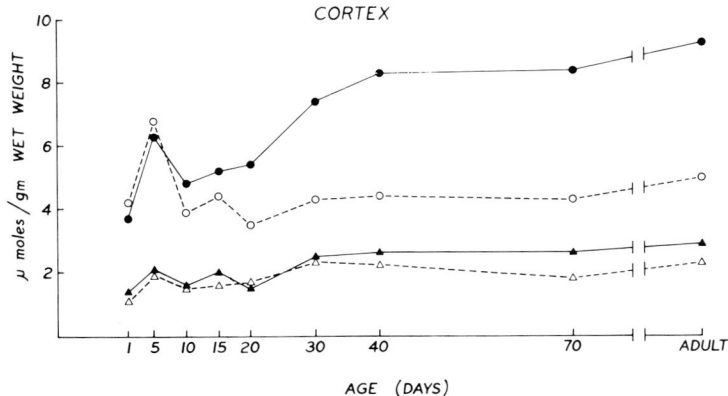

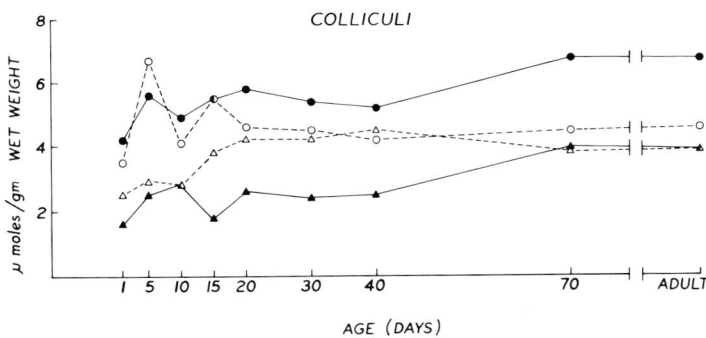

FIG. 4. Amino acid concentrations in dog brain parts. ●, glutamic acid; ▲, aspartic acid; △, GABA; ○, glutamine. (From Dravid et al., 1965.)

the experimental animals performed less well. But we could not determine whether this was due to the effects of phenylalanine upon intelligence, to a lower level of motor activity, or to less motivation in the experimental animals.

Some biochemists have been prone to believe that the brain is the last organ affected biochemically under changed environmental conditions. But the brain in terms of its chemistry, may be more susceptible than we have realized. The almost immediate response that follows a change in environment is an example of the dynamic state of many brain constituents (W. A. Himwich, 1969). The direction and amount of these changes, however, are dependent upon the part being studied (Fig. 6). It is also inevitable that in many experimental situations we cannot isolate satisfactorily the effects of the variable we are studying from other

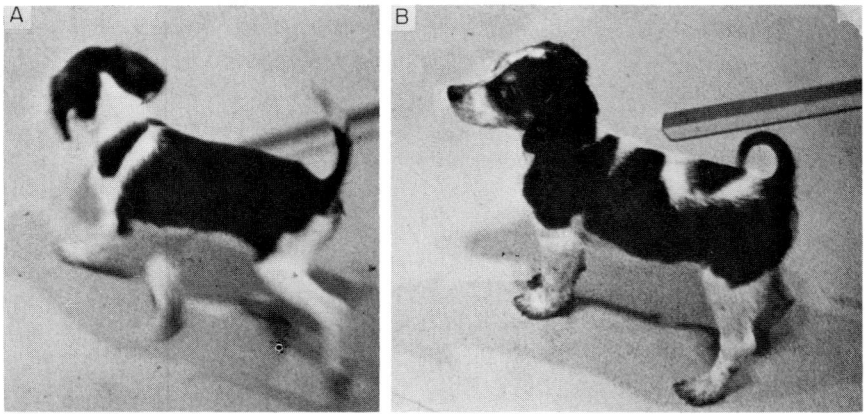

FIG. 5. Littermate puppies. A. Control. B. Dog given phenylalanine (1 mg/kg at 1 to 5 days of age; 3 mg/kg each day thereafter).

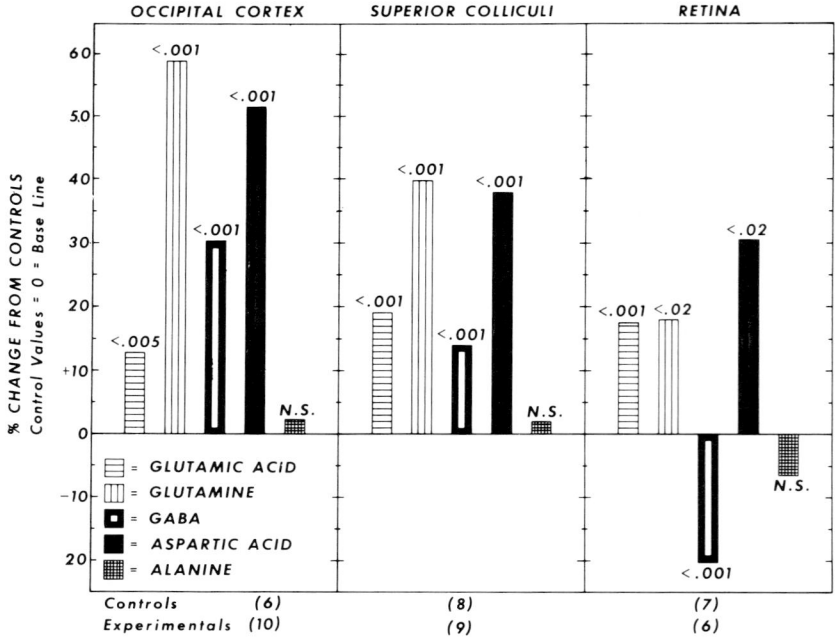

FIG. 6. The effect of visual deprivation for 3 days on amino acids in discrete areas of the visual system of rabbits. (From W. A. Himwich, 1968.)

environmental factors to which the animal is exposed. Nothing occurs in a vacuum. Such separation can never be complete, but we need to work toward experimental designs in which the effects of the various factors are analyzed individually insofar as it is practical. In general, psychologists have been much more active in this area than have biochemists.

Young animals must be provided with warmth and with maternal care and all that term implies as continuously as possible up to the instant they are tested or sacrificed for analysis. Data obtained on animals exposed to adverse conditions are worthless except to measure the effects of the adverse conditions. Data from such studies are not good background material for studies of normal development.

Although recent developments in electrophysiological techniques permit measurements in freely moving animals, it is still often necessary to use anesthesia, either local or general, to prevent discomfort or

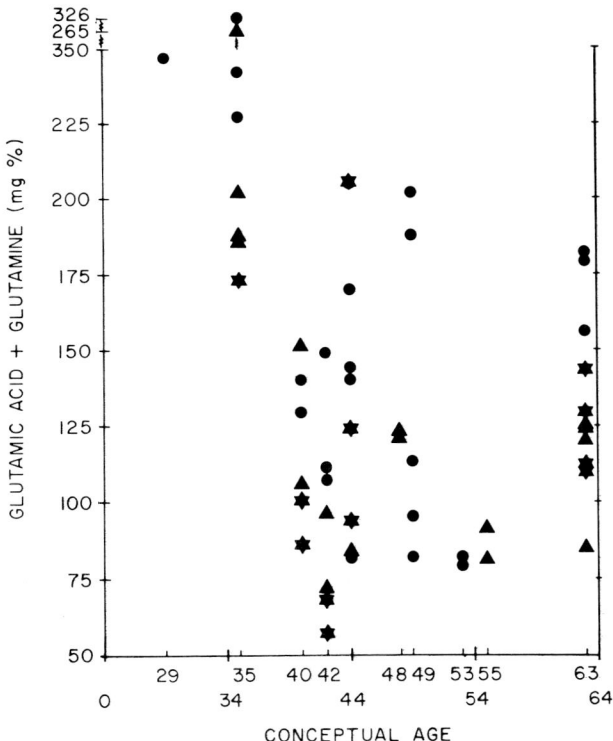

FIG. 7. Glutamic acid plus glutamine concentrations in individual members of guinea pig litters. Each litter is represented by the same symbol on any given day. (From W. A. Himwich, 1962.)

anxiety in the experimental situation (G. H. Rose and Ellingson, 1970). I would not expect to find normal electrophysiological responses in such animals nor if our biochemical methods are capable of determining small enough changes would I expect to find the neurochemistry normal.

Another important problem that arises is that of circadian rhythm. Although not all possible parameters have yet been explored, it seems probable that virtually all biochemical constituents, behaviors, and physiological parameters have definite rhythms (Halberg, 1969). These inherent rhythms are each different, and it is not yet possible to generalize as to which are synchronized. The rhythms undoubtedly affect the animals' responses to drugs (Friedman and Walker, 1969) and to stimuli (Ader, 1967), to mention only two examples. I suspect that much of the apparently unavoidable variation that has appeared in biological experiments is due to the fact that experimenters ignore this factor.

Other difficulties are inherent—for example, members of the same litter are not identical biochemically (Fig. 7) or even in size, weight, and vigor. In all experimental animals, events occur with relative rapidity. From a management point of view, it may be practical to take animals at 1, 5, 10, 15, etc., days of age, but if events are occurring rapidly, even scheduling for every consecutive day may not give the most meaningful information (Fig. 8).

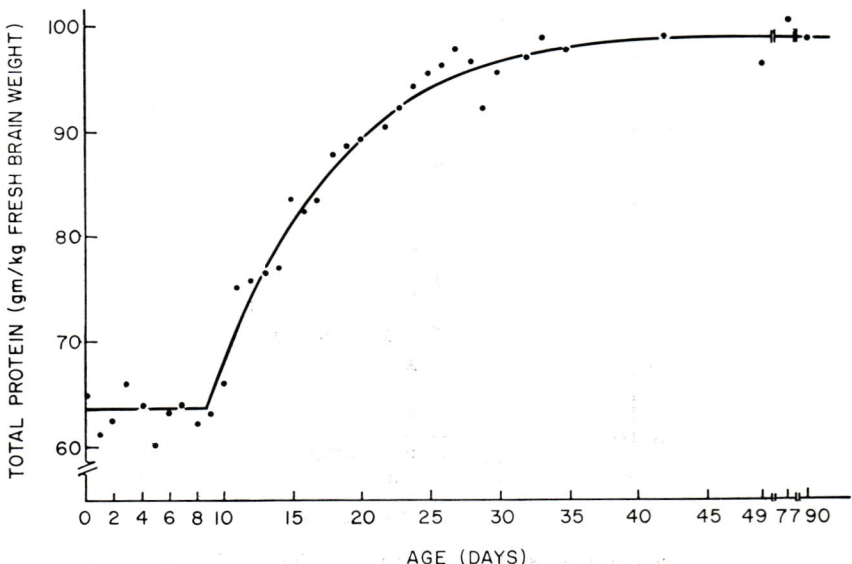

FIG. 8. Total brain protein and rat age in days. (From Pitts and Quick, 1967.)

ANATOMICAL MEASURES OF BRAIN DEVELOPMENT

There are many anatomical measures of brain development which have been widely used. Probably the most sophisticated is the measurement of dendritic spines used by Valverde and his colleagues at the Instituto de Cajal (Valverde, 1966), and also by Scheibel and Scheibel (1964) in California. The least sophisticated, but perhaps equally productive, is the measurement of brain size in terms of weight and length. In both cases there is the problem of directly relating the changes that have been observed to the behavior of the animal. Except as it may denote an earlier degree of maturation, is an increase in size of any importance in terms of function? Are the dendritic spines essential for visual function? For what kind and degree of function? These questions can and must be answered. In between these two extremes there are many anatomical measures. Schadé and his group (Schadé, 1959; Schadé and Pascoe, 1964) have studied the arborization of dendrites in cubes of cortical tissue. The appearance of basilar dendrites on the neurons appears to have a close correlation with certain electrophysiological events. The arborization of the dendrites appears to be of importance also (Berl and Purpura, 1966). Unfortunately, no chemical methods are available to measure such microscopic but specific cellular areas.

BEHAVIORAL TESTING

The problems of behavioral testing are enormous. To reproduce under laboratory conditions a behavior which is an *adequate* measure of the global behavior is difficult, if not impossible. In the laboratory we can reproduce only small fragments of function, and in some species these fragments appear to be stereotypes rather than meaningful measures of normal behavior. In our laboratory, we have studied dogs more than any other animal because in this species we seem to have an opportunity to relate the spontaneous behavior induced by a total situation to the experimental conditions. This approach has some advantages, but also some disadvantages, the chief one being the inability to quantify the observations in a satisfactory fashion. Also, we often wish to study specific behavioral responses, just as in neurochemistry we wish to analyze specific regions of the brain.

ELECTROPHYSIOLOGICAL TESTING

The measurement of the development of the brain by studies of the spontaneous EEG has yielded a huge volume of data. The changes that appear with maturation in the various species of animals have been

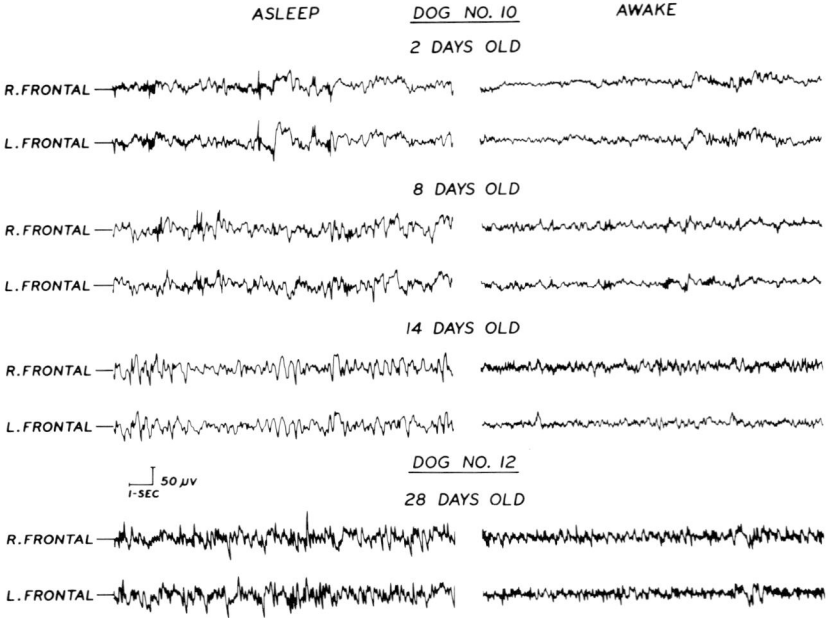

FIG. 9. Electroencephalographic records obtained from unanesthetized dogs during the first 4 weeks of life. (From Petersen et al., 1964.)

thoroughly discussed by Ellingson and Rose (1970) (Fig. 9). Even more productive have been studies made with the evoked potential to various stimuli. In these studies we are dealing in most cases with measurements made under essentially artificial conditions. However, much progress is being made with chronically implanted electrodes and more normal experimental circumstances (G. H. Rose and Ellingson, 1970). The development of the visual evoked potential in the dog has been thoroughly studied by Mysliveček (1970) and by Fox (1968) (Fig. 10). Similar data are available for the rat and cat (G. H. Rose and Ellingson, 1970). The nature of the stimulus—e.g., a flashing light for visual responses—requires more control of experimental circumstances than does the recording of the spontaneous EEG. Again considerable progress has been made. We still, however, are dealing in the case of a flashing light with an artificial stimulus which may be relatively unimportant to the animal in his normal habitat. The work on the response of frogs to a small stationary stimulus as compared to a small object moving in the visual field is a good example, as is the study of response in the rabbit visual cortex to movement and contrast (Arden et al., 1967). It is difficult to believe that a flash of light is really meaningful to an animal such as the rabbit. Possibly, in the olfactory field it would be possible to use odors which are similar if not identical to those which occur in the normal environment. The use of auditory stimuli other than clicks is also promising.

The problem of environmental control which permits normal functioning of the brain is an important one and one that we can solve only by carefully defining our aims and evaluating our methods.

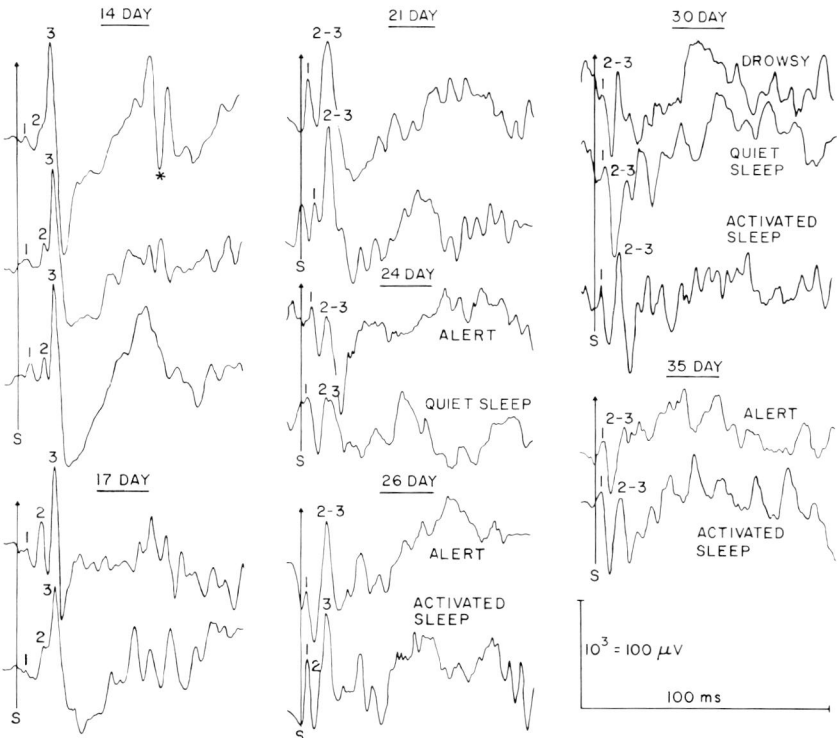

FIG. 10. Longitudinal study of visually evoked potentials in dog QB (chronic electrode L.D., C.A.T. recordings of 1 stimulus, all at 10^3); numbers 1, 2, and 3 signify the peaks of negative components. Note gradual merging of second negative peak (2) with ontogenetically older negative peak (3) to form a single peak 2-3. The positive wave preceding 2-3 increases in amplitude with age, while the negative wave 2-3 decreases. The consistent negative wave (1) recorded at all ages may be an onset phenomenon. The major qualitative change during quiet sleep is increased amplitude of afterdischarge; evoked potentials are similar during wakefulness and activated (REM) sleep. The asterisk in the 14-day-old subject refers to a secondary evoked potential, which is occasionally seen after an initial evoked response to a single stimulus.

CHEMICAL MEASUREMENT

In the field of chemical measurement during development, our problem is somewhat simpler in that the brain can be removed at a predetermined time under controlled conditions. The work from our laboratory over the last few years has illustrated that some substances are very easily influenced by changes in environment, while other substances are very resistant to change (W. A. Himwich *et al.,* 1968; W. A. Himwich, 1969). Is there an immediate and functional response to changes in the concentrations of those substances which are so easily influenced? So far we are not sure. It may be that these substances are those that respond quickly to changes of hormone secretion such as might be expected to occur during stress and that they have little or no functional relationship in terms of brain activity. They may represent an enlargement of the "margin of safety" in the concentration of substances such as acetylcholinesterase.

The problems of compartmentalization also complicate the picture. I would like to illustrate this with two schemes of compartmentation: one arising from the work of Heinrich Waelsch and his colleagues (Van den Berg *et al.,* 1969) suggests that there are two compartments for glutamic acid each of which proceeds on a separate metabolic pathway; the other from the work of Salganicoff and De Robertis (1965) suggests that there are two pools of GABA, one at the synapse where GABA functions as an inhibitory transmitter and the other in the cytoplasm itself where it functions merely as a member of the metabolic pool. How do we separate the two glutamic acid compartments? How do we differentiate between the two sites for GABA in biochemical analyses?

Our data would suggest to us that among the compounds that respond rapidly to stress, especially in the cortex, are certain amino acids: glutamic acid, glutamine, GABA, aspartic acid, and acetylcholinesterase (W. A. Himwich, 1969; W. A. Himwich *et al.,* 1968). It has been shown previously by Saunders (1966) that changes in acetylcholinesterase can be easily demonstrated in response to behavioral and environmental manipulation. We are inclined to believe that this response may follow any environmental change. Dr. Rosenzweig (personal communication) tells me that their attempts to change AChE by manipulation of formal training or by many changes in environment have been negative. This question is therefore still open. If we study animals at two different periods of time after a change in the environment, we find an initial change in these substances followed by a return to normal even though the environmental change persists (early weaning and shielding eyes)

(W. A. Himwich *et al.,* 1968; W. A. Himwich, 1969). This, however, is only one possible explanation, and other studies may bring additional ones.

So far the most rewarding substances to follow in studying chemical maturation are the free amino acids and those substances such as lipids and proteins which are part of the basic structure of the brain. On the basis of changes in these substances, we can plot dates of chemical maturation which are helpful in our studies. They, however, are not the entire answer. We do not know, for instance, when we study changes in the free amino acid pool, if these changes are reflected in or compensated by the amino acids incorporated into proteins.

MULTIDISCIPLINARY APPROACHES—THEIR PITFALLS AND ADVANTAGES

In theory, correlations in the same experimental animals of behavior or function with biochemistry, anatomy, and electrophysiology should yield the greatest amount of information for the least expenditure of time, effort, and money. Having tried for some 15 or 16 years to arrive at the millennium where it would be possible to do such multidisciplined studies, I find myself in the position of being far better able to discuss the pitfalls rather than the advantages of this approach. Many of the pitfalls are obvious—one is the problem of obtaining equally competent personnel for all of these fields at the same time so that you can work on the same animals under exactly the same experimental conditions. Another problem which is even more basic is the fact that our methods of measurement are not yet good enough in any of these fields to give us the kind of one-to-one correlation we would like. However, I feel that as many facets as possible of the multidisciplined approach are well worth doing simultaneously. Some successful multidisciplined teams can be named; e.g., Rosenzweig–Krech–Diamond–Bennett. Any basic data, carefully obtained and reported with careful descriptions of all of the basic environmental and contributing conditions, are always of value. It is unfortunate that only recently have we come to understand a bit more about the influence of environment. In the past we have not described in the necessary detail the environmental conditions under which our animals were reared and under which the samples were taken. It seems to me that we should attempt to expand this background knowledge consistently and uniformly in the next decade so that we will have as much information as possible about all of the environmental conditions of any experimental animal. Such information would make a multidisciplined approach in a single laboratory of less importance.

Species Differences

Because our ultimate interest lies in the development of man, it seems to me essential that we talk somewhat about species differences and those relationships which can be traced between various species. We know that there are certain basic general rules which govern the development of the brain from the formation of the neural streak to maturity in somewhat the same fashion in all species. For example, in all mammalian species there is a time when cells are crowded together, when neurons are forming and migrating. This period is followed by one of development of dendrites, their arborization, the laying down of myelin, the concomitant decrease of water and increase in size. At the same time these events are occurring, there are increases of protein (Pitts and Quick, 1967; Clouet and Gaitonde, 1956).

However, we cannot generalize freely from species to species as to which changes occur before gestation and which occur after birth. The rates of growth of the brain in the two periods may differ widely in the same species, and they differ again from species to species (W. A. Himwich, 1962). As we go to the other chemical constituents which are perhaps more specialized, for example, the biogenic amines, we see even among the members of this group of compounds marked differences in the rates at which they reach mature levels after birth (Agrawal and Himwich, 1970).

In terms of electrophysiological development there are marked differences in the development of responses to stimuli. The response to auditory stimuli differs from the visual response in terms of maturation (Scherrer, 1968; Scherrer et al., 1970). If one is studying the development of the auditory evoked response, for example, the situations would be quite different in the rabbit and in the cat (Fig. 11). This perhaps is an excellent example of systemogenesis: the rabbit, due to his environmental situation, needs to be able to hear at an earlier time than does the cat. Another way to compare species is to determine the length of time after puberty required for the evoked potential to mature (Ellingson and Rose, 1970). We must sooner or later develop from all these isolated data generalized rules of development which then can be brought to bear upon a species close to man that shows at least the same outward developmental patterns. The chimp is of course a prime candidate for this type of study.

In conclusion, I have raised more questions than I have answered. I feel these questions must be answered in any developmental experimental work irrespective of which basic discipline is studied. There are

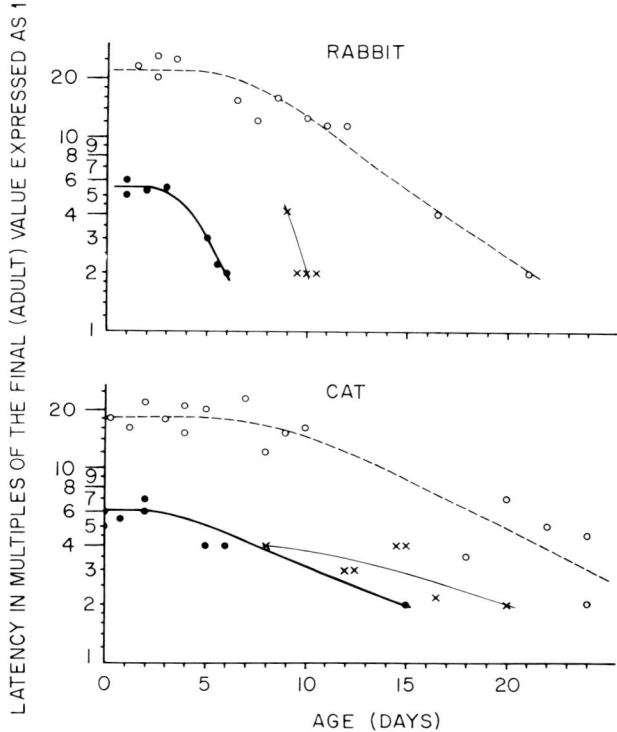

FIG. 11. Evoked potentials in the rabbit and cat at various ages. ●, somesthetic; ○, visual; X, auditory. (From Scherrer et al., 1970.)

other questions that I have not considered, such as: What do we mean by maturity in the central nervous system? What is the relationship between maturity of the central nervous system and maturity of the organism as a whole? We also need to know the factors that accelerate or delay brain development. The obvious one of nutrition still needs more exploratory work to be useful for application to human development.

REFERENCES

Ader, R. (1967). Behavioral and physiological rhythms and the development of gastric erosions in the rat. *Psychosom. Med.* Vol. 29, 345–353.

Agrawal, H. C., Davis, J. M., and Himwich, W. A. (1966). Postnatal changes in free amino acid pool of rat brain. *J. Neurochem.* Vol. 13, 607–615.

Agrawal, H. C., and Himwich, W. A. (1970). Amino acids, proteins and monoamines of developing brain. *In* "Developmental Neurobiology" (W. A. Himwich, ed.), pp. 287–310, Thomas, Springfield, Illinois.

Anokhin, P. K. (1964). Systemogenesis as a general regulator of brain development. *Prog. Brain Res.* Vol. 9, 54–86.

Arden, G. B., Ikeda, H., and Hill, R. M. (1967). Rabbit visual cortex: Reaction of cells to movement and contrast. *Nature (London)* Vol. 214, 909–912.

Berl, S., and Purpura, D. P. (1966). Regional development of glutamic acid compartmentation in immature brain. *J. Neurochem.* Vol. 13, 293–304.

Callison, D. A., and Spencer, J. W. (1968). Effect of chronic undernutrition and/or visual deprivation upon the visual evoked potential from the developing rat brain. *Develop. Psychobiol.* Vol. 1, 196–204.

Cammermeyer, J., and Swank, R. L. (1951). The effect of anaesthetics and picrotoxin on the tissue phosphatases in the cerebellum and olivary nucleus of the dog. *Acta Pharmacol. Toxicol.* Vol. 7, 65–82.

Chanda, S., and Himwich, W. A. (1970). Unpublished data.

Chesler, A., and Himwich, H. E. (1944). Effect of insulin hypoglycemia on glycogen content of parts of the central nervous system of the dog. *A.M.A. Arch. Neurol. Psychiat.* Vol. 52, 114–116.

Clouet, D. H., and Gaitonde, M. K. (1956). The changes with age in the protein composition of the rat brain. *J. Neurochem.* Vol. 1, 126–133.

Davis, J. M., and Himwich, W. A. (1971). Unpublished data.

Davis, J. M., Himwich, W. A., and Agrawal, H. C. (1969). Some amino acids in the developing visual system. *Develop. Psychobiol.* Vol. 2, 34–39.

Dravid, A. R., Himwich, W. A., and Davis, J. M. (1965). Some free amino acids in dog brain during development. *J. Neurochem.* Vol. 12, 901–906.

Ellingson, R. J., and Rose, G. H. (1970). Ontogenesis of the electroencephalogram. *In* "Developmental Neurobiology" (W. A. Himwich, ed.), pp. 441–474. Thomas, Springfield, Illinois.

Fischer, J., and Jílek, L. (1958). The response of the organism to cerebral ischaemia in the course of ontogenesis. III. Morphological changes of the CNS after ligature of the carotids in the course of postnatal life in the rat. *Sb. Lek.* Vol. 60, 346–354.

Fish, I., and Winick, M. (1960). Cellular growth in various regions of the developing rat brain. *Pediat. Res.* Vol. 3, 407–412.

Fox, M. W. (1968). Neuronal development and ontogeny of evoked potentials in auditory and visual cortex of the dog. *Electroencephalogr. Clin. Neurophysiol.* Vol. 24, 213–226.

Friedman, A. H., and Walker, C. A. (1969). Rat brain amines, blood histamine and glucose levels in relationship to circadian changes in sleep induced by pentobarbitone sodium. *J. Physiol. (London)* Vol. 202, 133–146.

Garrigan, O. W., and Chargaff, E. (1963). Studies on the mucolipids and the cerebrosides of chicken brain during embryonic development. *Biochim. Biophys. Acta* Vol. 70, 452–464.

Graham, L. T., Jr., Shank, R. P., Werman, R., and Aprison, M. H. (1967). Distribution of some synaptic transmitter suspects in cat spinal cord: Glutamic acid, aspartic acid, γ-aminobutyric acid, glycine, and glutamine. *J. Neurochem.* Vol. 14, 465–472.

Halberg, F., (1969). Chronobiology. *Annu. Rev. Physiol.* Vol. 31, 675–725.

Himwich, H. E. (1951). "Brain Metabolism and Cerebral Disorders." Williams & Wilkins, Baltimore, Maryland.

Himwich, H. E. (1960). Functional organization of the brain, past and present. *J. Nerv. Ment. Dis.* Vol. 130, 505–519.

Himwich, H. E., and Fazekas, J. F. (1941). Comparative studies of the metabolism of the brain of infant and adult dogs. *Amer. J. Physiol.* Vol. 132, 454–459.

Himwich, H. E., and Himwich, W. A. (1962). Anoxia and cerebral metabolism. *Int. J. Neurol.* Vol. 3, 413–427.

Himwich, W. A. (1962). Biochemical and neurophysiological development of the brain in the neonatal period. *Int. Rev. Neurobiol.* Vol. 4, 117–158.

Himwich, W. A. (1968). Multi-disciplined studies of the visual system in developing rabbits. *In* "Ontogenesis of the Brain" (L. Jílek and S. Trojan, eds.), pp. 269–276. Charles Univ. Press, Prague.

Himwich, W. A. (1969). The effect of environment upon the developing brain. *In* "The Future of the Brain Sciences" (S. Bogoch, ed.), pp. 237–255. Plenum Press, New York.

Himwich, W. A., Davis, J. M., and Agrawal, H. C. (1967b). Biochemical substrates for the development of the matured evoked potential. *Recent Advan. Biological Psychiat.* Vol. 9, 271–279.

Himwich, W. A., Davis, J. M., and Agrawal, H. C. (1968). Effects of early weaning on some free amino acids and acetylcholinesterase activity of rat brain. *Recent Advan. Biol. Psychiat.* Vol. 10, 266–270.

Himwich, W. A., and Dravid, A. R. (1967). Amino acid content of various brain parts as related to neurophysiological and behavioural maturation. *In* "Regional Development of the Brain in Early Life" (A. Minkowski, ed.), pp. 257–271. Blackwell, Oxford.

Himwich, W. A., Dravid, A. R., and Berk, T. J. C. (1967a). Phenylalanine loading in the new-born puppy: Techniques. *In* "Regional Development of the Brain in Early Life" (A. Minkowski, ed.), pp. 221–242. Blackwell, Oxford.

Himwich, W. A., Pennelle, D. K., and Tucker, B. E. (1963). Comparative biochemical development of fetal human, dog, and rabbit brain. *In* "Recent Advances In Biological Psychiatry" (J. Wortis, ed.), Vol. 5, pp. 293–308, Plenum Press, New York.

Hydén, H., and Hartelius, H. (1948). Stimulation of the nucleoprotein-production in the nerve cells by malononitrile and its effect on psychic functions in mental disorders. *Acta Psychiat. Neurol.* Suppl. 48, 1–117.

Jackson, J. H. (1884a). Evolution and dissolution of the nervous system. Lecture I. *Lancet* Vol. 1, 555–558.

Jackson, J. H. (1884b). Evolution and dissolution of the nervous system. Lecture II. *Lancet* Vol. 1, 649–652.

Jackson, J. H. (1884c). Evolution and dissolution of the nervous system. Lecture III. *Lancet* Vol. 1, 739–744.

Livingston, W. K., Haugen, F. P., and Brookhart, J. M. (1954). Functional organization of the central nervous system. *Neurology* Vol. 4, 458–496.

MacArthur, C. G., and Doisy, E. A. (1918–1919). Quantitative chemical changes in the human brain during growth. *J. Comp. Neurol.* Vol. 30, 445–486.

Moruzzi, G., and Magoun, H. W. (1949). Brain stem reticular formation and activation of the EEG. *Electroencephalogr. Clin. Neurophysiol.* Vol. 1, 455–473.

Mysliveček, J. (1970). Electrophysiology of the developing brain—Central and Eastern European contributions. *In* "Developmental Neurobiology" (W. A. Himwich, ed.), pp. 475–527. Thomas, Springfield, Illinois.

Petersen, J., Di Perri, R., and Himwich, W. A. (1964). The comparative development of the EEG in rabbit, cat and dog. *Electroencephalogr. Clin. Neurophysiol.* Vol. 17, 557–563.

Pitts, F. N., Jr., and Quick, C. (1967). Brain succinate semialdehyde dehydrogenase. II. Changes in the developing rat brain. *J. Neurochem.* Vol. 14, 561–570.

Purpura, D. P., and Pappas, G. D. (1968). Structural characteristics of neurons in the feline hippocampus during postnatal ontogenesis. *Exp. Neurol.* Vol. 22, 379–393.

Rinaldi, F., and Himwich, H. E. (1955a). Alerting responses and actions of atropine and cholinergic drugs. *A.M.A. Arch. Neurol. Psychiat.* Vol. 73, 387–395.

Rinaldi, F., and Himwich, H. E. (1955b). Cholinergic mechanism involved in function of mesodiencephalic activating system. *A.M.A. Arch. Neurol. Psychiat.* Vol. 73, 396–402.

Roberts, E., and Kuriyama, K. (1968). Biochemical-physiological correlations in studies of the γ-aminobutyric acid system. *Brain Res.* Vol. 8, 1–35.

Rose, G. H., and Ellingson, R. J. (1970). Ontogenesis of evoked potentials. In "Developmental Neurobiology" (W. A. Himwich, ed.), pp. 393–440. Thomas, Springfield, Illinois.

Rose, S. P. R. (1967). Preparation of enriched fractions from cerebral cortex containing isolated, metabolically active neuronal and glial cells. *Biochem. J.* Vol. 102, 33–43.

Salganicoff, L., and De Robertis, E. (1965). Subcellular distribution of the enzymes of the glutamic acid, glutamine and γ-aminobutyric acid cycles in rat brain. *J. Neurochem.* Vol. 12, 287–309.

Saunders, V. F. (1966). Effect of behavioral and environmental manipulations on central cholinesterase activity in the rat. *Fed. Proc., Fed. Amer. Soc. Exp. Biol.* Vol. 25, 385.

Scammon, R. E. (1933). White House Conference on Child Health and Protection, quoted by E. Boyd (1941) in "Outline of Physical Growth and Development," Table 27, Burgess Publishing Co., Minneapolis, Minn.

Schadé, J. P. (1959). A histological and histochemical analysis of the developing cerebral cortex. *Proc., Kon. Ned. Akad. Wetensch., Ser. C* Vol. 62, 445–460.

Schadé, J. P., and Pascoe, E. G. (1964). Maturational changes in cerebral cortex. III. Effects of methionine sulfoximine on some electrical parameters and dendritic organisation of cortical neurons. *Progr. Brain Res.* Vol. 9, 132–154.

Scheibel, M., and Scheibel, A. (1964). Some structural and functional substrates of development in young cats. *Progr. Brain Res.* Vol. 9, 6–25.

Scherrer, J. (1968). Electrophysiological aspects of cortical development. *Progr. Brain Res.* Vol. 22, 480–489.

Scherrer, J., Verley, R., and Garma, L. (1970). A review of French studies in the ontogenetical field. In "Developmental Neurobiology" (W. A. Himwich, ed.), pp. 528–549. Thomas, Springfield, Illinois.

Schwartz, I. R., Pappas, G. D., and Purpura, D. P. (1968). Fine structure of neurons and synapses in the feline hippocampus during postnatal ontogenesis. *Exp. Neurol.* Vol. 22, 394–407.

Swank, R. L., and Cammermeyer, J. (1949). The selective effect of anesthetics and picrotoxin on the cerebral cortex of the dog: An electro-encephalographic and histochemical study. *J. Cell. Comp. Physiol.* Vol. 34, 43–70.

Tilney, F., and Rosett, J. (1931). The value of brain lipoids as an index of brain development. *Bull. Neurol. Inst. New York* Vol. 1, 28–71.

Valverde, F. (1966). The pyramidal tract in rodents. A study of its relations with the posterior column nuclei, dorsolateral reticular formation of the medulla oblongata, and cervical spinal cord (Golgi and electron microscopic observations). *Z. Zellforsch. Mikrosk. Anat.* Vol. 71, 297–363.

Van den Berg, C. J., Krzalić, I.J., Mela, P., and Waelsch, H. (1969). Compartmentation of glutamate metabolism in brain. Evidence for the existence of two different tricarboxylic acid cycles in brain. *Biochem. J.* Vol. 113, 281–290.

Vogt, O. (1925). Der Begriff der Pathoklise. *J. Psychol. Neurol.* Vol. 31, 245–255.

Whittaker, V. P. (1968). Synaptic transmission. *Proc. Nat. Acad. Sci. U. S.* Vol. 60, 1081–1091.

Winick, M. (1968). Changes in nucleic acid and protein content of the human brain during growth. *Pediat. Res.* Vol. 2, 352–355.

Discussion

D. Purpura: It is appropriate at the juncture to discuss several points brought out by Dr. Himwich, particularly factors which can provide data on correlations of structure and function and indices of brain maturation. A major question to be raised is: What criteria can be applied to assess cortical maturation?

Ontogenetic studies carried out in our laboratory for the past decade have emphasized the importance of different patterns of synaptogenesis in the feline cerebral cortex. It is clear that the earliest synaptic relations in the cortex are established by axodendritic synapses located on apical dendritic trunks. This may be considered a primitive type of synaptic relationship that is effected in the antenatal period prior to the onset of obvious neocortical function. During the early postnatal period a second synaptic receptor zone is elaborated in relation to the cell bodies and basilar dendrites of cortical neurons. Finally, synapses are established on dendritic spines during the second and third postnatal weeks. It is a remarkable finding that, at least from the standpoint of the fine structure of neurons and synapses, the cerebral cortex of the cat attains morphological maturation by the end of the first month.

Electrophysiological studies, including intracellular recording from immature cortical neurons, have revealed important features of synaptogenesis. It has been observed that postsynaptic potentials (PSPs) of immature cortical neurons are generally of much longer duration than PSPs of mature cortical elements. Perhaps the most intriguing finding in these studies relates to the extraordinary precocious development of inhibitory synaptic pathways in the immature neocortex and hippocampus. In fact insofar as inhibition is concerned, the immature cortex is as mature as it will ever be! Suffice it to say that unlike the mature hippocampus, it is clear that in the immature hippocampus such inhibition is largely if not exclusively generated at axodendritic synapses.

Several years ago, in studies with Dr. S. Berl, Department of Neurology, College of Physicians and Surgeons, it was found that of the various free amino acids in neonatal kitten brain, GABA was found in concentrations similar to those found in the adult animal, whereas glutamic acid was significantly reduced in concentration. These observations are in agreement with subsequent findings reported by Dr. Himwich. Perhaps the relatively high levels of GABA in the cortex of neonatal kittens points to a role of this amino acid in the production of the prominent and prolonged inhibitory postsynaptic potentials observed in the immediate neonatal period.

There are additional maturational factors to be considered other than those related to the morphogenesis of neurons, synapses, and neuron–glia interactions. Our studies have also indicated that dendrites of some immature cortical neurons have electrogenic properties that differ from those observed in mature neurons. Specifically dendrites of immature cortical neurons may exhibit spike generation and propagation under appropriate conditions of activation. Evidently, since such dendritic spike electrogenesis is not observed in neocortical neurons of mature animals, it is not unlikely that maturational processes operate to "suppress" excitability of dendrites. Here then is a late maturational event that could not have been detected by the usual morphological or biochemical "criteria" of brain maturation.

The significance of the foregoing findings for the study of the development of behavior is as yet unexplored. Surely the fact that there is a differential and precocious development of inhibition in the hippocampus, a cortical structure implicated in learning, memory, and other complex behavioral activities, should be of considerable interest to behaviorists. Perhaps inhibition is a major factor in the orderly elaboration of cortical neuronal organizations, providing some sort of protective function that might be highly susceptible to antenatal or postnatal insults. Hopefully the basic information supplied by the developmental neurobiologist will continue to provide important clues to the development of behavior in its broadest sense.

FETAL ENDOCRINOLOGY AND THE EFFECT OF HORMONES ON DEVELOPMENT

PAUL DELOST

Introduction

The prenatal development of mammals is brought about by numerous extremely complex phenomena which lead to the establishment of normal structures and physiological functions in the newborn and thus to a proper unfolding of postnatal life. Various genetic, nutritional, and hormonal factors are involved in prenatal development. The merit of modern endocrinology has been to point out the very important role of fetal hormones. Although their role has not been established definitively, fetal hormones may affect the development of the fetus by at least four mechanisms: by the direct stimulation of the general somatic development of tissues and skeleton; by bringing about the differentiation and development of specific receptors; by indirectly activating some metabolic processes necessary for prenatal development; or by participating in fetal homeostasis, chiefly in transplacental exchange, the regulation of which appears to be essential for normal development.

It is obvious that the study of fetal endocrine function presents numerous and difficult problems. The following data deal with the three problems I think are essential.

1. To prove that peripheral endocrine glands—gonads, thyroid gland, adrenal gland, parathyroid glands, pancreas—become active during fetal life and that they are eventually regulated by the hypophysis; accordingly, to determine the periods during which fetal hormones are secreted and the periods during which tissues are receptive to these hormones; to establish the various actions of fetal endocrine glands on development.

2. To test the concepts that there is transplacental passage of maternal hormones; that hormones are produced by the placenta itself;

and that the fetal tissues are receptive to maternal and placental hormones; accordingly, to determine whether the female or the placenta supply hormones to the fetus, by the removal of fetal endocrine glands or by producing a deficiency in their activity.

3. To view fetal endocrinology as a problem of the reciprocal regulation of the placenta and the fetus; one, or both, may be able not only to secrete specific hormones, but also to metabolize extraneous hormones as well as their own hormones. In prenatal development, the homeostasis of the fetoplacental unit is probably more important than the production of the fetal hormones themselves. The homeostatic mechanism may function either by opening the placental barrier to maternal or placental hormones in the case of fetal endocrine gland deficiency, or by closing it to extraneous hormones in the case of excesses, which may be noxious. Among the research areas of fetal endocrinology, one of the most interesting is certainly that concerning the production of irreversible congenital malformations, and of disorders of prenatal and postnatal somatic development after injection of exogenous hormones into the fetus or into the female during pregnancy. These experiments are of interest for two reasons: to specify the limits of the fetoplacental barrier, and to emphasize the dangers of hormonal therapy for the pregnant female.

The problems that we propose to examine here are made even more difficult because they must be studied comparatively. Indeed, fetal endocrinology presents important differences among species, and it is difficult to extrapolate information about the physiology of the human fetus from that of other mammals. Furthermore, although morphological, histological, cytological, and biochemical techniques have contributed considerably to fetal endocrinology, it is certain that the new data derived from dosage studies and fetoplacental hormonal metabolism must be taken into account.

We shall summarize briefly the first two points, for they already have been reviewed excellently: the role of hormones in fetal development by Moore (1950) and Jost (1954, 1961a); the function of the fetal hypophysis by Jost (1966a); the transplacental passage of hormones by Snoeck (1958); the comparative physiology of the secretion of fetoplacental hormones by Diczfalusy (1962); and the physiology and pathology of the human fetus by Liu (1966). We shall especially stress developmental disorders induced by exogenous hormones, because they have not yet been the subject of a general review and because they have been extensively studied in my laboratory by Drs. Boucher, Carteret, Cl. Jean, Ch. Jean and others, including myself.

Activity of Fetal Endocrine Glands and the Role of Fetal Hormones in Prenatal Development

Numerous observations have shown that the endocrine glands and the hypophysis are active at various stages all through fetal life. This appears to be a general phenomenon in mammals which has been demonstrated well experimentally and by the presence of hormones in the endocrine glands themselves. It is known, in some species, at least, that the hypophysis plays a role in the development of peripheral endocrine glands and that complex hypothalamo-hypophyseal relations are established with some endocrine glands at certain stages of fetal development. There is little evidence of fetal hormone action on somatic growth, on specific tissues, or on metabolism during prenatal development. We have little knowledge concerning the chemical structure of hormones elaborated by fetal endocrine glands and their secretions. We shall only touch upon the principal discoveries without discussing them; the reader should refer to the special reviews cited.

FETAL GONADAL HORMONES AND SEXUAL STRUCTURES

The essential stages of sexual differentiation in the vertebrates are now well known. Complete information is given in the following works: Raynaud, 1942a; Jost, 1947a; Ponse, 1949; and Young, 1961.

There are three important periods in sexual development: first, a period of differentiation of the gonads into ovary or testis; second, a period of differentiation of the genital tract in conformity with the genetic sex and by the regression of heterologous anlagen; third, a period of growth of the established sexual structures until birth. The mechanisms of these morphological modifications are still incompletely understood. Following the observation of natural freemartinism, the role of gonadal hormones in the genital organogenesis of the fetus was clarified by experiments on the effects of injecting sex hormones and by embryonal castration. (Raynaud and Frilley, 1947a,b, 1948; Wells, 1947; Jost, 1947b,c,d.)

In the male fetus, castration interrupts the masculinization of the fetus and induces a type of female sexual differentiation with feminization of the urogenital sinus and the external sexual organs and of the development of the Müllerian ducts. Apparently, fetal testis secretions stimulate the Wolffian ducts, masculinize the urogenital sinus and genital tubercule, and inhibit the Müllerian ducts. Cases of gonadal dysgenesis in the human fetus (Diczfalusy, 1962; Grumbach et al., 1955) show an identical action of the testis in humans. Furthermore, the Jost experiments on the rabbit and observations made of human fetal development favor an interpretation of a local action of the fetal testis upon the genital ducts.

Castration of the male fetus does not resolve the problem concerning fetal testicular secretion. Although it was shown that embryonic human testicular tissue is able to convert precursors into dehydroepiandrosterone, androst-4-ene-3, 17-dione, and testosterone (Acevedo et al., 1961), fetal hormonal secretion perhaps cannot be ascribed to a synthetic androgen or to an androgen produced by the adult male, as the development of the male structure is stimulated and the development of the Müllerian ducts is inhibited. It is not clear whether the fetal testis elaborates two distinct hormones responsible for these very different actions, or whether adrenocortical androgen plays a role in these mechanisms.

In the female fetus, castration brings about little modification of sexual development, confirming the nonhormonal theory of Wiesner (1934). Furthermore, *in vitro* cultures of Müllerian ducts show that they are able to develop autonomously. However, it is not possible to dismiss the possibility of estrogenic activity by the fetal ovaries, for Rosa (1955) has demonstrated a typical estrogenic action of the ovary in the human fetus at the eighth month of pregnancy. Also, the possibility of estrogenic intervention from the mother or the placenta cannot be excluded, as a great deal of estrogen is found in the placenta and in the amniotic fluid (Parkes, 1954). Finally, as we shall discuss later, exogenous estrogen injected into the fetus or the mother has a typical feminizing action.

Is the *hypophysis* involved in fetal gonadal function? Although gonadotropic hormone has been detected in the embryonic pituitary gland in the pig, horse, and human, information about prenatal gonadotropic function is derived mainly from the effects of embryonal hypophysectomy in rodents. Hypophysectomy produces only very little alteration of sexual organogenesis in the mouse and the rat (Raynaud, 1959b). However, certain experimental results indicate that the fetal hypophysis plays a significant role. In the rat the embryonic testis grafted in the adult exerts an androgenic activity only in the presence of gonadotropic hormone (Jost, 1953). In human male fetuses lacking an adenohypophysis, or in anencephalics, a reduction of some sexual structures is sometimes seen (Jost, 1966a). In the female fetus there is a correlation between the number of chromophil cells in the fetal pituitary and the histological development of the ovary. In the rabbit fetus, decapitation done before sexual differentiation produces important anomalies of the male genital tract, which are secondary to interstitial gland deficiency of the fetal testis (Jost, 1951a,b). In this species, as in the human, the hypophysis is necessary only at a very specific stage of sexual differentiation, between days 22 to 24, the stage corresponding to maximal activity of the testis and of the PAS-positive cells of the hypophysis.

In conclusion, the control of the fetal testis by the hypophysis seems to exist in the rabbit. It is probable that in other species the gonadotropic hormones of maternal or placental origin supply the fetal hypophysis, at least in the case of fetal hypophysectomy. This is particularly clear in the human, in which it seems that the testicular fetal interstitial cells are stimulated both by fetal hypophysis and placenta (Jost, 1966a).

FETAL ADRENOCORTICAL AND ADRENOMEDULLARY HORMONES

These questions have been analyzed in detail in recent reviews (Diczfalusy, 1962; Jost, 1966b), and we shall give only a brief summary of the issues. Complementary data concerning corticosteroid production by the fetal adrenal cortex will be found in reviews of Bloch (1965) and of Villee and Villee (1965).

1. The development of the adrenal cortex and the production of adrenocortical hormones during prenatal life have been demonstrated by morphological, physiological, and biochemical proofs. The adrenal weight increases from day 16 in the rat (Cohen, 1963), and the cortical zones begin to grow significantly from day 20 in the rabbit (Jost, 1966b). It seems that in the sheep, the fetal adrenal gland is able to secrete its corticosteroids into the bloodstream, as cortisol and corticosterone have been found in the adrenal vein (Chester-Jones et al., 1964). In the human fetus many histological and histochemical works attest to fetal adrenal cortex activity (Ross, 1962). It has been found that there is an increase of cholesterol concentration from the nineteenth week; an ability to synthesize some estrogens (Diczfalusy et al., 1961), androgens (Bloch et al., 1956), and cortisol and corticosterone from progesterone (Hillman et al., 1962); presence of progestational steroids (Hoffmann, 1947) and cortisol in the newborn adrenal (Gardner and Tice, 1957). Villee's studies suggest that the human fetal cortex is the center of qualitative and quantitative changes of steroid production simultaneously with and in proportion to gestational progress, that is, in favor of a gradual development of various enzymic systems (Villee et al., 1961). On the contrary, the level of corticosterone in fetal rat adrenal glands rises until day 18.5 and then decreases suddenly (Kamoun et al., 1964).

2. Hypothalamic–pituitary–adrenal cortex relationships in the fetus are indicated by many facts. Removal of the fetal hypophysis, by decapi-

tation or by X-rays, produces cortical involution in the mouse, in the rabbit, and in the rat. ACTH counteracts the effects of decapitation, and unilateral adrenalectomy is followed by compensatory hypertrophy (Jost et al., 1962; Jost, 1966a). ACTH has been identified in the human fetal hypophysis (Taylor et al., 1953; Ghilain and Schwers, 1957). It seems that the hypophysis stimulates the fetal cortex during a limited period only, e.g., days 18 to 20 in the rat and days 20 to 24 in the rabbit (Jost, 1966b). Hypophyseal stimulation decreases at birth in these species, as in the mouse (Eguchi, 1960). From observations done in anencephalic human fetuses (Schwers, 1959; Diczfalusy, 1962; Tuchmann-Duplessis and Mercier-Parot, 1963) and from encephalectomy experiments done in the rat fetus (Jost et al., 1966), a corticotropin-releasing factor seems to exist in the hypothalamus of the fetus. It would appear that a true feedback system between the hypothalamic–pituitary complex and the adrenal cortex of the fetus has been demonstrated (Jacquot, 1959).

3. The adrenomedullary hormones are certainly produced by fetal medullary tissue, as epinephrine and norepinephrine have been discovered in the fetal adrenal glands of various species: rabbit, guinea pig, rat, sheep, human (Hokfelt, 1951; Shepherd and West, 1951). They are probably excreted, as they have been found in the adrenal vein of the fetal sheep (Comline and Silver, 1961) and in the heart, kidney, lung, and brain of the human fetus (Greenberg and Lind, 1961). Recent research by Roffi (1968) has shown that in the rat and rabbit, at least, there is a critical period in medullary development and in the metabolism of the adrenomedullary hormones at the end of pregnancy, and that there are important relationships between the medulla and the adrenal cortex in the fetus.

4. Effects of fetal adrenocortical and adrenomedullary hormones on target organs and their metabolism are not very well known. It seems that the adrenocortical hormones have an inhibitory action on the fetal thymus gland (Bearn, 1960; Angervall and Lundin, 1964). Experiments using adrenalectomy and decapitation on rat and rabbit fetuses have shown that glycogen storage in the fetal liver is dependent in part at least on fetal adrenocortical hormones; the hepatic glycogen increases corresponding with the increase of fetal adrenal secretions stimulated by the hypophysis. In addition, rat fetal adrenocortical hormone activity can be supplied by the mother (Jacquot, 1956, 1959). In the rabbit, fetal corticosteroids act upon the liver only in synergy with a hypophyseal or placental metabolic hormone (Jost and Jacquot, 1958; Jost, 1961a). In the same way, the fetal adrenocortical hormones play an important role in the glycogen regulation in the fetal heart (Picon and Bouhnik, 1966).

Fetal adrenomedullary hormones seem to act in the hemodynamic regulation of the fetus in sheep (Dawes et al., 1956), in the rabbit, and in the guinea pig (Dornhorst and Young, 1952), and probably participate in the control of placental circulation (Jost, 1966b).

In conclusion, although there is evidence of fetal adrenal activity and of adrenal regulation by the fetal hypophysis, various physiological actions of fetal adrenal hormones in prenatal development remain to be discovered.

FETAL THYROID HORMONES

Publications concerning fetal thyroid functioning are very numerous (Waterman, 1959; Jost, 1961b; Diczfalusy, 1962; Dieterlen-Lievre, 1963; Myant, 1964; Geloso, 1967). Only principal issues will be discussed here.

Differentiation of the fetal thyroid tissue occurs in several successive stages, identical in all species, leading to the formation of follicles, which appear in the course of the second half of pregnancy in species with short gestation periods and in the first third of pregnancy in the sheep, the calf, the monkey, and the human. It has been shown that thyroxine, triiodothyronine, monoiodotyrosine, and diiodotyrosine exist in the fetal thyroid of many species (Geloso, 1967) and that some of these hormonal compounds are present with iodures in the fetal plasma (Gorbman et al., 1951, 1952; Verain and Verain-Pinoy, 1960; Jost and Vigouroux, 1965).

Although these hormones could come from the mother also, Geloso recently proved that the fetal thyroid of the rat is capable itself of synthesizing and of liberating this hormone into the circulation (Geloso, 1964, 1967). Hormonal synthesis begins in the fetal thyroid generally when the follicular structure is formed. Nevertheless, it can begin before the complete differentiation of thyroid tissue in some species: the rat (Geloso, 1967), the rabbit (Waterman and Gorbman, 1956), the pig (Rankin, 1941), and the calf (Wolff et al., 1949). Fetal thyroid hormonogenesis then increases until term, although it seems to show maximal activity between day 16 and 18 in the rat (Geloso, 1967). It is interesting to note that in the rat, at least, the fetal thyroid is the main source of thyroid hormones in fetal plasma, the placenta allowing only a small quantity of the hormones to pass through (Geloso and Bernard, 1967).

The relationships between the hypophysis and the fetal thyroid are now clearly established (Deanesly, 1961; Jost, 1966a). The appearance of thyrotropic cells in the fetal hypophysis is simultaneous with the onset of fetal thyroid activity (rabbit and rat); TSH is present in the human fetal hypophysis (Mizusawa, 1966; Levina, 1966). Goiter appears in the fetus after the hypophysectomized mother is treated with antithyroid drugs, unless the fetus has been hypophysectomized. The fetal thyroid reacts to TSH injection *in vivo* and *in vitro* (Nataf, 1968). Fetal thyroidectomy accelerates the development of thyrotropic cells. Anencephalic human fetuses have a differentiated thyroid gland, but it is reduced in size. Destruction of the fetal hypophysis by X-ray (Raynaud and Raynaud, 1956) and by decapitation (Jost, 1966a) does not inhibit differentiation of the thyroid nor the establishment of thyroxinogenesis (basic development); it does reduce the level of fetal thyroid activity considerably, which shows that when the fetal thyroid has become functional, it is dependent strictly on the fetal hypophysis (Jost, 1966a; Geloso, 1967). It appears that the maternal hypophysis does not play a role in fetal thyroid function.

Comparatively little is known about the role of fetal thyroid hormones in prenatal development. Thyroid hormone deficiency produces serious perturbations of the nervous system (Eayrs, 1961; Legrand, 1965), of thermoregulation (Hamburgh *et al.*, 1964), and of skeletal maturation (Geloso *et al.*, 1968) all through postnatal development. This does not seem to be the case during prenatal development. Some authors believe that fetal thyroid hormones are not indispensable to fetal development, because the maternal hormones may function, as in the case of the human (Myant, 1963), or because the lack of thyroid fetal hormones is compensated for by other hormones, particularly growth hormone (Hamburgh, 1968). However, certain facts indicate that fetal thyroid hormones probably participate in the somatic development of the fetus: congenital cretinism resulting from athyroidism in the human (Wilkins, 1959); an increase of fetal lipids after thyroidectomy in the fetus of the rabbit (Jost and Picon, 1958), and difficulties of histological differentiation of bone in rat fetuses hypothyroidized by decapitation (Geloso *et al.*, 1968).

FETAL PARATHYROID AND PANCREATIC HORMONES

The physiology of the parathyroid is largely unknown in the fetus. It appears that the fetal parathyroids do not secrete significant quantities of hormone. Nevertheless, parathormone injection produces a hypercalcemia in the dog fetus, and women with hyperparathyroidism may have hypoparathyroid infants (Diczfalusy, 1962).

There are various indications of pancreatic endocrine activity in the fetus: histological and cytochemical differentiation of the islets of Langerhans in the rat (Hard, 1944), the rabbit (Bencosme, 1955), and the mouse (Golosow and Grobstein, 1962); appearance of an insulin-like activity before histochemical differentiation of β cells in the hamster (Sak et al., 1965); presence of both insulin and glucagon in fetal pancreatic tissue (Gonet, 1961); and indications of β cell activity in the human fetus beginning in the third month and the presence of insulin in the fetal pancreas in the fourth month (Rosa, 1955).

The fetal pancreas is probably able to secrete large amounts of hormones, but their roles in prenatal development are unknown. However, the possibility of insulin transfer from fetus to the mother and from the mother to the fetus (Knobil and Josimovich, 1959) and the pathology of diabetes in pregnant women leading to giant fetuses and hypertrophy of the islets of Langerhans in neonates indicate complex relationships between the mother and the pancreas of the fetus (Diczfalusy, 1962).

GROWTH HORMONE, FETAL HORMONES, AND PRENATAL SOMATIC DEVELOPMENT

The action of fetal hormones in somatic development is not known. It is certain that fetal gonadectomy, thyroidectomy, and adrenalectomy do not modify the growth of the fetus, but we cannot deduce that the fetal hormones of these glands do not affect fetal growth. Indeed, functional deficiency of these glands can be compensated for by the maternal glands or the placenta, and it is known, as we shall see below, that exogenous gonadal, thyroid, or corticosteroid hormones, injected into the fetus or the mother, can reduce prenatal and postnatal growth. We have shown that fetal growth of the mouse remained normal after injecting prolactin into the fetus or the mother (Ch. Jean and Delost, 1969b).

The question of the role of fetal growth hormone remains—is it necessary for fetal growth? From various observations (Diczfalusy, 1962; Jost, 1966b), it seems that it does not play an important role, as witnessed by the normal somatic development of anencephalic human monsters; by very little reduction in fetal growth in the mouse, the rat, and the hamster after fetal hypophysectomy; and by a lack of exogenous STH action on fetal growth of the rat (Tuchman-Duplessis and Mercier-Parot, 1955) and of the mouse (Ch. Jean and Delost, 1968; Ch. Jean, 1968a). However, some facts favor the concept that they do play a role: the detection of growth-promoting activity in the fetal pituitary glands of various animals; the stimulation of fetal growth by the administration of extraneous growth hormone to the decapitated rat fetus (Heggestad, 1955; Jost, 1966a); and the development of mammary gland by the direct injection of extraneous STH into the mouse fetus (Ch. Jean and Delost,

1968; Ch. Jean, 1968a). Furthermore, it is clear that the placenta produces a growth hormone factor in the rat and in the human and that, in certain species, as in the mouse, STH is able to cross over the placenta (see later discussion).

In conclusion, it is clear that the endocrine glands and hypophysis become active and produce hormones and that relationships between the hypophysis and peripheral glands are established in the fetus. There is evidence that certain fetal hormones may act upon target organs and their metabolism, but the role of fetal and hypophyseal hormones in fetal growth is not well known. Some results, particularly the effects of ablation of the fetal endocrine glands, must be carefully interpreted, as the transplacental passage of hormones and the hormonal metabolism of the fetoplacental unit are not thoroughly understood.

Transplacental Passage of Hormones and the Metabolism of Hormones by the Fetoplacental Unit

A thorough discussion of this problem is not relevant here; readers should refer to specialized reviews (Snoek, 1958; Diczfalusy, 1962; Liu, 1966). We will make some remarks only about the transplacental passage of hormones, and about the way the mother–fetus and the fetoplacental units metabolize hormones.

The transplacental passage of hormones from the mother to the fetus should be considered in two respects: the normal physiological passage of hormones produced by the placenta or the maternal endocrine glands and the passage of exogenous hormones injected into the mother. In both cases, the fetoplacental unit may play an important regulatory role, either by opening the placental barrier to endogenous hormones when they are necessary for fetal physiology or by blocking any excess of exogenous hormones which might injure the fetus.

There is evidence for the normal physiological passage of some maternal or placental hormones to the fetus. It has been shown that maternal corticosteroids (Jacquot, 1959) and maternal thyroxine (Geloso, 1967) do pass through the placenta. It is possible that in certain circumstances the following hormones are also able to pass through: maternal or placental estrogens, placental progesterone, prolactin-like and growth-hormone-like factors of the placenta in the rat and the human, placental gonadotropin in the human (Jost, 1966a), and maternal androgens (Diczfalusy, 1962). It is not certain whether maternal insulin crosses the placenta (Diczfalusy, 1962; Knobil and Josimovich, 1959). However, prolactin and ACTH and TSH from the mother or placenta are not able to cross the placenta normally. The possibility of gonadotropin passage is not contraindicated, as fetal hypophysectomy does not disturb sexual development in the mouse and rat.

Numerous facts show that exogenous hormones injected into the mother reach the fetus. Such is the case with androgens and estrogens (Raynaud, 1942b), corticosteroids (Jost, 1966b), thyroid hormones (London et al., 1963; Pickering, 1964; Carteret and Delost, 1964; Carteret, 1965; Geloso, 1967), adrenalin (Snoeck, 1958), and possibly insulin (Diczfalusy, 1962). Passage of hypophyseal hormones seems more doubtful; ACTH, TSH, and the gonadotropins probably do not go through. Nevertheless two observations show that placental passage of exogenous prolactin and growth hormones to the fetus is possible. Sonenberg et al. (1951) injected the pregnant mother with marked LTH and found it again in the fetus. Recently, we have shown that STH injected into the pregnant mouse produces modifications of the fetus mammary glands similar to those obtained by direct injection into the fetus (Ch. Jean and Delost, 1968; Ch. Jean, 1968a).

It is obvious that the problem of placental permeability to hormones remains to be solved. It is necessary to know the permeability throughout gestation, the percentage of hormone passing over the placenta, the circulation and distribution of hormones in the fetus, the sites of fixation in the fetus, and, more particularly, the passage of hormones from the fetus to the mother. The very interesting work done on the human fetus by Diczfalusy (1962) and Liu (1966) strongly indicates that the fetus and placenta should be considered an integrated endocrine unit able to produce and metabolize hormones. It is certain that the fetus is able to metabolize and to conjugate estrogen, progesterone, corticosteroids, and probably androgens and other steroids. The fetal metabolites may then be returned to the placenta where they are hydrolyzed or further metabolized. It is possible that some of these metabolites are necessary for fetal development, but it is more likely that an important role of the fetoplacental unit is to let hormones cross over in the case of fetal endocrine gland deficiency, or to close the placental barrier in cases of excess extraneous hormones. In this last instance, the fetoplacental unit seems to be limited, as shown by the development of fetal disorders when exogenous hormones are injected into the mother.

Developmental Disorders after Prenatal Treatment with Hormones

The protective role of the human fetoplacental unit against exogenous hormones must be studied by comparative fetal endocrinology.

Indeed, exogenous hormones injected directly into the fetus or into the pregnant mother act not only upon specific receptors by affecting their differentiation but also upon somatic development, which can be partially or totally inhibited. Furthermore, exogenous hormones can interrupt the pregnancy or produce significant congenital malformations. Their effects may become apparent during the fetal period, especially at the time of birth, or sometimes during neonatal and postnatal development. They often result in irreversible lesions. We shall report the disorders produced by sexual hormones, thyroid hormones, and corticosteroids.

DISORDERS OF GESTATION AND OF PRENATAL GROWTH

Exogenous hormones injected during gestation are able to produce abortion and a deceleration of fetal growth rate. Sexual hormones and corticosteroids are particularly noxious; thyroid hormones are noxious to a lesser degree.

Thyroid hormones rarely produce abortion and reduce fetal growth only slightly. In the mouse, thyroxine injected into the mother, even in high doses, never induces abortion and does not modify the duration of gestation. However, mortality can be increased from 10 to 90% with prolonged thyroxine treatment; newborn weight is reduced 13%; triiodothyronine and diiodothyronine are without effect (Carteret, 1965). A decrease in the weight of newborn rabbits (Lesinski, 1949) and of the body size in fetal rats (Tusques, 1955) are noticed after treatment of the mother with thyroxine.

Numerous observations have shown that corticosteroids, particularly cortisone and hydrocortisone, disturb the pregnancy and affect the fetus, leading to abortion, resorption, debilitation or mortality of neonates, and inhibition of fetal development to a greater or lesser degree. Sensitivity to corticosteroids differs according to species and according to whether the injection is made into the mother or into the fetus.

Gestation disorders induced by sexual hormones are now classic, so we shall be brief. In various species estrogens are able to produce total interruption of gestation, high embryonal mortality, and delay or suppression of parturition. Male hormones or certain synthetic progestational steroids (Vokaer, 1963) may have similar effects on gestation. When the fetus survives in spite of treatment by sexual hormones, its growth often is stunted or greatly reduced. This inhibition is typical with estrogen administration (Raynaud, 1942b), as when estradiol dipropionate injected into a pregnant mouse produces a decrease from 13 to 33% in live neonatal weight, whenever the dose is between 100 and 5000 μg (Cl. Jean, 1967).

Androgens have similar effects. Recently, we have shown that testosterone propionate injected into a pregnant mouse produces a decrease of 45% in the weight of the neonates. Various synthetic androgens also greatly reduce the body size and the weight of the rat fetus (Jost, 1960). Numerous mechanisms have been proposed about the actions of these sexual hormones, which we cannot discuss here. We would like to mention, however, that in the case of estrogens, we notice in the mouse a decrease of placental weight at the time of birth which varies from 20 to 40%, according to the dose (Ch. Jean, 1968c).

DISORDERS OF NEONATAL AND POSTNATAL GROWTH

An important discovery in fetal endocrinology is that prenatal treatment with exogenous hormones can affect postnatal growth ultimately. One of the most surprising facts is that corticosteroids or thyroid hormones injected into the pregnant mother greatly inhibit the growth of the offspring even though the ponderal deficiency at the time of birth is not very great. By using cesarean techniques we have been able to obtain in our laboratory live descendants from pregnant females treated with estrogens and so have been able to study the postnatal effects of such treatment.

Corticosteroids

The experiments of Mercier-Parot (1957) on the rat have shown that the administration of cortisone to pregnant females disturbs parturition in only 30% of the cases and inhibits prenatal growth very slightly, the newborn appearing normal. However, it injures neonatal and postnatal development significantly, a fact not foreseen during prenatal development. Indeed, at birth the offspring are very fragile; they die in large numbers soon after birth, and survive no more than 20 days. During intrauterine life, the growth curve of these fetuses is similar to that of the fetuses of untreated females, but the growth rate decelerates rapidly after birth, and later on clearly shows almost a total inhibition of postnatal growth (a decrease of 50% on day 6 and 70% on day 10).

Thyroid Hormones

Thyroxine or triiodothyronine injected into the pregnant mouse produces an inhibition of postnatal development in the descendants (Carteret and Delost, 1961, 1962, 1963a,b; Carteret, 1964, 1965). The delay in the appearance of the effect of this treatment on the growth of the offspring is all the more significant, as the treatment with thyroxine is given late in the pregnancy. The effect is not augmented by increasing the dose, or with repeated injections, as only one injection of 50 μg of thyroxine is responsible for the maximal delay. This delay in growth

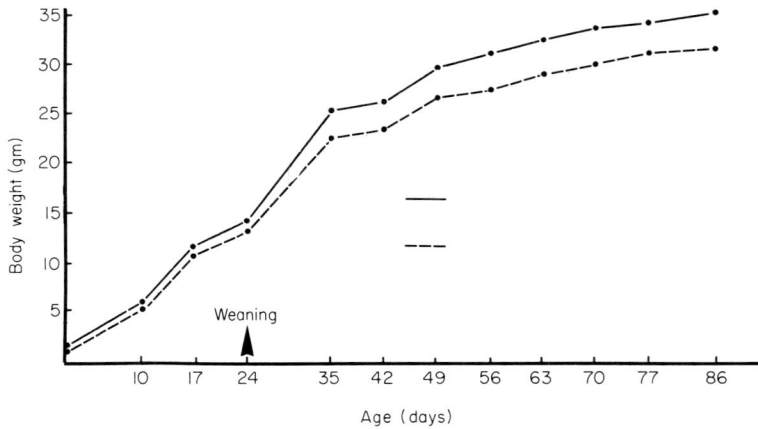

FIG. 1. Postnatal growth of male descendants of mice born of control mothers and of mothers treated with 50 μg of thyroxine on the 18th day of pregnancy, after interchange of mothers at the time of birth. ———, offspring of controls fed by treated mothers; - - - -, offspring of treated mice fed by control mothers.

only appears between day 17 and day 24 at weaning time. It is not a total cessation of growth, but a partial inhibition of the somatic development of the descendants, which affects the skeletal and ponderal growth of the body and its various organs. This inhibition, which varies from 10 to 20%, is not transitory but is definitively acquired by the adult (Fig. 1).

Sexual Hormones

Thus far, we have studied estrogens only (Cl. Jean, 1967; Cl. Jean and Delost, 1968). A study of 1820 mouse fetuses (Swiss strain) has shown that after estradiol injections into pregnant females in dosages ranging between 100 and 5000 μg, although there was embryonal mortality, a significant percentage (59 to 71%) of the newborn are alive at birth, if they are delivered by cesarean section (Table 1). Nursed by substitute mothers, 27 to 55% reach adulthood; the others die during the first day of life (Fig. 2). The mortality, proportional to dose (49% with 100 μg; 73% with 5000 μg), is brought about by respiratory difficulty, probably as a secondary effect of the vascular action of the estrogens. Disorders of postnatal growth in the surviving descendants are a function of dose level: with doses between 100 and 500 μg a decrease in skeletal growth and in ponderal body and organ growth is permanent from birth to puberty and varies between 10 and 25%; with 1000 μg, inhibition is more marked. However, with a dose of 5000 μg the neonatal body weight

TABLE 1
Effect of Estrogens Injected Into the Pregnant Mouse on Fetal and Postnatal Mortality[a]

Estradiol Dose (µg)	100	200	500	1000	5000
Number of treated litters	22	30	17	26	149
Number of embryos	181	277	123	224	1015
Resorption Nodules					
Number of embryos	28	17	15	30	139
Percent	15.5	6.1	12.2	13.4	13.7
Lysed neonates					
Number of embryos	5	17	11	16	150
Percent	2.8	6.1	8.9	7.1	14.8
Dead neonates					
Number of embryos	20	46	20	40	131
Percent	11.0	16.6	16.3	17.9	12.9
Live neonates[b]					
Number of embryos	128	197	77	138	595
Percent	70.7	71.1	62.6	61.6	58.6
Died within 0–24 hours[b]					
Number of embryos	63	89	48	69	433
Percent	49.2	45.1	62.3	50.0	72.7
Reached adulthood[b]					
Number of embryos	65	108	29	69	162
Percent	50.8	54.9	37.7	50.0	27.3

[a] From Cl. Jean, and Delost (1968).
[b] Neonates obtained by cesarean technique.

deficit is rapidly compensated for beginning at 10 days of age, and by day 35 the rate of growth of the experimental subjects is greater than that of the controls. The fact that estrogens inhibit postnatal growth with low doses, while they stimulate it with high doses, results perhaps from the paradoxical effects of different concentrations of various substances upon biological systems (Schatz et al., 1964). Without entering into the details of the mechanisms of the disturbances produced by the injection of exogenous hormones into the pregnant female, it is probable that the inhibition of the postnatal growth of the descendants is the consequence of a direct action by hormones on the fetus prenatally, perhaps on the hypothalamo-hypophyseal complex, but is probably not the result of an action upon the mother, since the descendants have been nursed by substitute mothers. It is interesting to note that similar postnatal growth disorders in descendants have been obtained after injection of antibiotics into pregnant mice: penicillin (Boucher and Delost, 1964a), streptomycin (Boucher and Delost, 1964b), and tetracycline (Boucher and Delost, 1967).

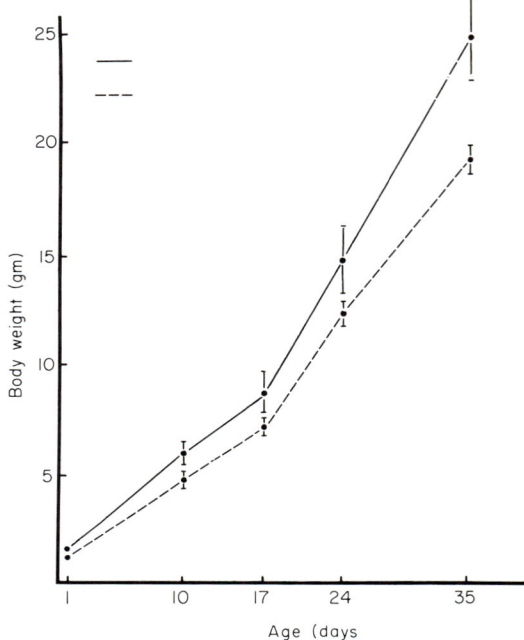

FIG. 2. Postnatal growth of male mice born of mothers treated with 1000 μg of estradiol on the 14th day of pregnancy and fed by substitute control mothers. ●——●, controls; ●--●, experimental male mice (Cl. Jean, 1967).

CONGENITAL MALFORMATIONS

In addition to the action we have just described, hormones injected into the fetus or into the pregnant mother may have no specific teratogenic effects or may produce congenital malformations of target organs, as is the case for sex hormones.

1. Teratogenic Effects

Thyroxine. Embryonic cataract in the rat; deformation of the head and eyes, coelosomie, and ocular malformations in blindworm (Raynaud and Raynaud, 1965).

Cortisone. Anomalies of the extremities and cleft palate in the rat, the mouse, and the rabbit.

Epinephrine and vasopressin. Anomalies of limbs, tongue, mandibles, and tail; amputations.

Estrogens. Central nervous system degeneration in the mouse (Raynaud, 1942b) and in the rat (Ch. Jean, 1968c).

2. Gonadal and Mammary Malformations

It has been well known for 25 years that estrogens and androgens injected into the fetus or into the pregnant female induce gonadal and mammary malformations in the fetus and in the newborn. Therefore, we shall review them briefly. We shall, however, emphasize our interest in the postnatal development of these malformations, which stimulated intensive and extensive research in our laboratory.

Malformations of the Fetus and of the Newborn

Numerous investigations have been made in various species, and only some of them will be mentioned here.

Androgens induce masculinization of the female fetus by the development of a more or less complete male genital tract near the ovaries and sometimes by slightly modifying the female tract (Raynaud, 1942b). Androgens masculinize the mammary anlagen of female mouse fetuses as well (Raynaud, 1947, 1949; Raynaud and Raynaud, 1956). In our laboratory, androgens also produced an important regression of mammary gland in the male rat (Ch. Jean and Delost, 1969a; Ch. Jean and Cl. Jean, 1969).

Estrogens have a pronounced effect on the male fetus: inhibition of the male genital tract and persistence of certain female structures (Raynaud, 1942b, 1950, 1959a) and transformation of testis into ovotestis or into ovary in the opossum (Burns, 1956). In the female fetus estrogens can produce hypertrophy of the Müllerian ducts and metaplasia of the urogenital sinus. Estrogens affect mammary embryogenesis adversely in both sexes in the mouse: partial or total inhibition of mammary anlagen, nipple hypertrophy, and serious malformations of the mammary area (Raynaud and Raynaud, 1956). Recently, these malformations have been confirmed in the rat (Delost *et al.,* 1962, 1963; Ch. Jean and Delost, 1965b; Ch. Jean, 1968b,c).

Postnatal Malformations

It was important to know the postnatal development of animals born with sexual and mammary malformations as a result of prenatal treatment with sex hormones. This problem was particularly difficult to resolve because research with estrogens and androgens resulted in a lack of normal spontaneous parturitions. We were able to work with prenatal estrogen treatment in our laboratory by obtaining through the cesarean technique a sufficient number of descendants to permit good statistical analyses.

In the mouse and rat intersexual females, the male genital tract persists after birth and reacts to androgens, while a permanent estrus takes place, probably as a result of LH deficiency. Disorders of sexual behavior appear in the adult in both sexes (Raynaud, 1938; Kobayashi, 1967).

Hoshino (1965) has produced a large number of 3-week-old mice lacking nipples and mammary glands by giving the mother testosterone on day 12 of pregnancy.

Systematic studies of the development of both the gonads and the mammary gland from birth to adulthood were done on the offspring of pregnant mice treated with estrogens in our laboratory.

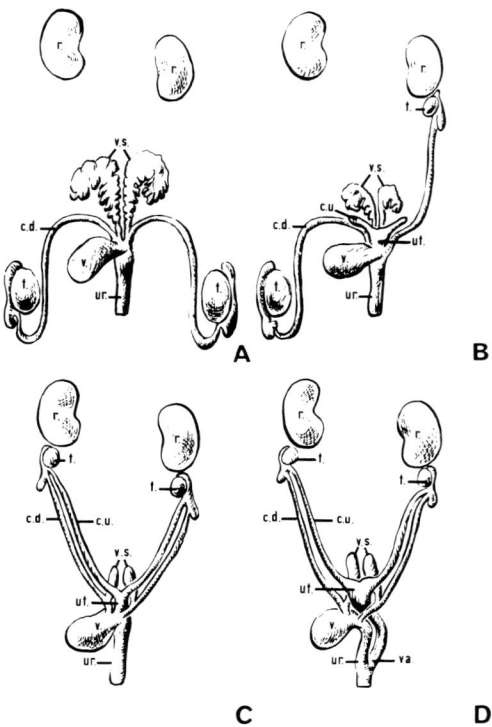

FIG. 3. Schematic reproduction of some examples of cryptorchidism, modifications of the seminal vesicles, and the persistence of female genital structures in male intersexes born of mice treated with estradiol during pregnancy. A. Thirty-five-day-old control. B. Thirty-five-day-old intersex. Very often, one testis remained under the kidney. A complete uterus persisted, as well as the caudal parts of the uterine horns. The mother was treated with 200 μg of estradiol. C. Thirty-five-day-old intersex. Both testes remained in an ectopic position, under the kidneys. The cranial bending of the seminal vesicles, as well as their lobulation, are inhibited. Persistence of two complete uterine horns, of the uterus, and of the cranial part of the vagina is evident. The mother was treated with 5000 μg of estradiol. D. Certain 90-day-old intersexes presented a complete vagina which opens into the urethra, besides the malformations described above. The mother was treated with 5000 μg of estradiol. (c.d.) Vas deferens; (c.u.) uterine horn; (r.) kidney; (t.) testis; (ur.) urethra; (ut.) uterus; (v.) vesica; (va.) vagina; (v.s.) seminal vesicles. (Cl. Jean, 1968a.)

Estrogens injected into the mouse on day 14 of gestation induced characteristic disorders of postnatal sexual development in the offspring. Pseudohermaphroditism was produced in the male, as evidenced by cryptorchidism, inhibition of the male genital tract, and persistence of female genital structures (Fig. 3). The frequency of these abnormalities increased with the dose of estradiol injected. The alterations in seminiferous tubules and the interstitial glands of the ectopic testis are extremely significant, as the position of the testis is higher (Fig. 4). Many of the intersexes are sterile at adult age. Between puberty and adulthood the male genital tract undergoes a certain amount of development, which never makes up, however, for the inhibition observed at puberty. The female genital structures of the male pseudohermaphrodites may constitute a complete female genital tract, well differentiated and functional, with Fallopian tubes, uterine horns, uterus, and vagina; low doses of estradiol are sufficient to obtain these female structures near a normal male genital tract (Fig. 5). Between puberty and adulthood, the female genital tract is able to react to exogenous estrogens and to show a spontaneous hypertrophy, probably under the estrogenic influence of the ecotopic testis (Cl. Jean and Delost, 1964, 1965a,b; Cl. Jean, 1968a).

In the female, unexpected significant disorders appear in postnatal sexual development, which are expressed by an inhibition of postnatal development of the female genital tract which persists definitively in the adult female after prenatal treatment with doses of estradiol between 100 and 1000 μg (Fig. 6); and such typical malformations of the female genital structures as absence of uterine body, bifid vagina, uretrovaginal fistule, and hypospadias, which were obtained with doses ranging from 100 to 5000 μg. Male genital structures remain well developed in many adult females as Wolffian rudiments and Cowper's glands (Fig. 7). Disorders of ovarian functioning are especially pronounced with high doses of estradiol (5000 μg): early luteinization of the ovaries at puberty and persistent estrus in adulthood (Fig. 8). Malformations of the genital tract and disorders of the ovaries are secondary to perturbations of the hypothalamo-hypophyseal system, which appear in the course of postnatal development and remain into adulthood (Cl. Jean and Delost, 1966, 1967a,b; Cl. Jean, 1968b).

In the mouse, anomalies in the mammary gland and the nipple in both sexes at birth are induced by estradiol injection into the pregnant female. In regard to the mammary gland, we noticed either a congenital amastia or a rudimentary state of mammary anlage. At puberty the mammary gland was still very involuted; but, between puberty and adulthood, the rudimentary glands of the descendants were stimulated, and by day 80 the mammary development of the experimental females was not different from that of the control females, and the experimental

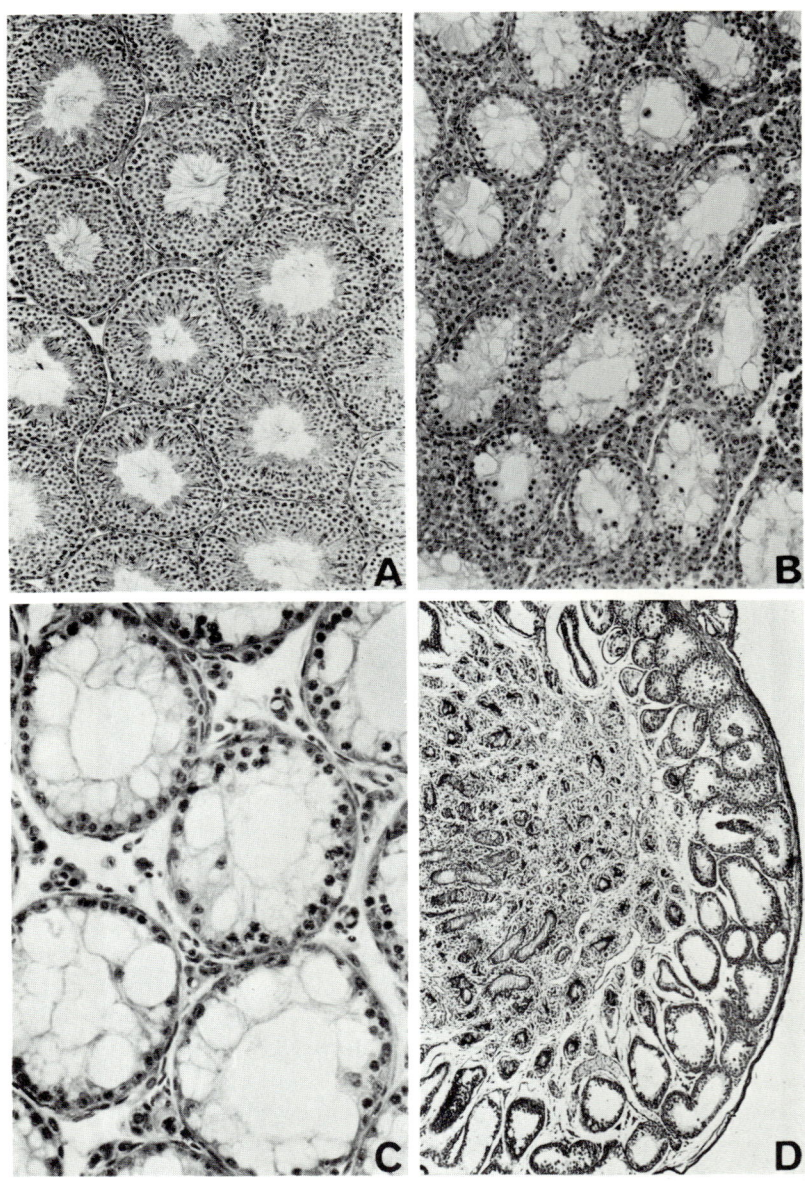

FIG. 4. Alterations of the ectopic testis in 35-day-old male intersexes born of mice treated with different doses of estradiol (from 200 to 5000 μg) on the 14th day of pregnancy. A. Control; normal spermogenesis. 125 ×. B. Seminiferous tubules degenerating; hyperplasia of the interstitial gland. 125 ×. C. Semniferous tubules degenerating; interstitial gland atrophied. 320 ×. D. Seminiferous tubules and interstitial gland completely degenerated. 50 ×. (Cl. Jean and Delost, 1964.)

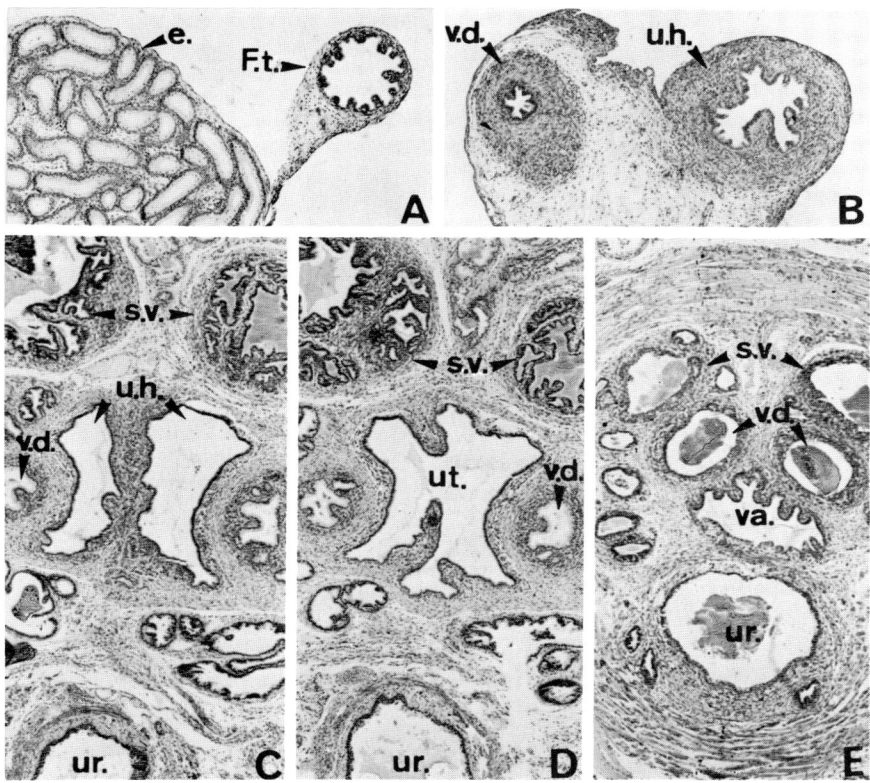

FIG. 5. Persistence of the female genital structures in 35-day-old male intersexes born of mice treated with estradiol on the 14th day of pregnancy. A. Fallopian tube near the epididymis (1000 μg). 50 ×. B. Uterine horn near the vas deferens (1000 μg). 32 ×. C. Caudal parts of the two uterine horns between the vas deferens (1000 μg). 50 ×. D. The two uterine horns join to form a uterine body between the vas deferens (5000 μg). 50 ×. E. The uterine body is followed by a vagina placed between the vas deferens and the urethra (5000 μg). 50 ×. (e.) Epididymis; (F.t.) Fallopian tube; (ur.) urethra; (ut.) uterine body; (u.h.) uterine horn; (va.) vagina; (v.d.) vas deferens.

males were not different from the controls of the same age. Therefore, the atrophy observed at birth is not irreversible, and even very rudimentary glands are able to grow after puberty and to form a normal mammary gland able to secrete milk at adulthood. Only total amastia at birth remains irreversible (Fig. 9).

The following anomalies were evident in the development of the nipple at birth: athelia, nipple raising, various endothelial abnormalities, feminization in the male, etc. These were present at puberty and

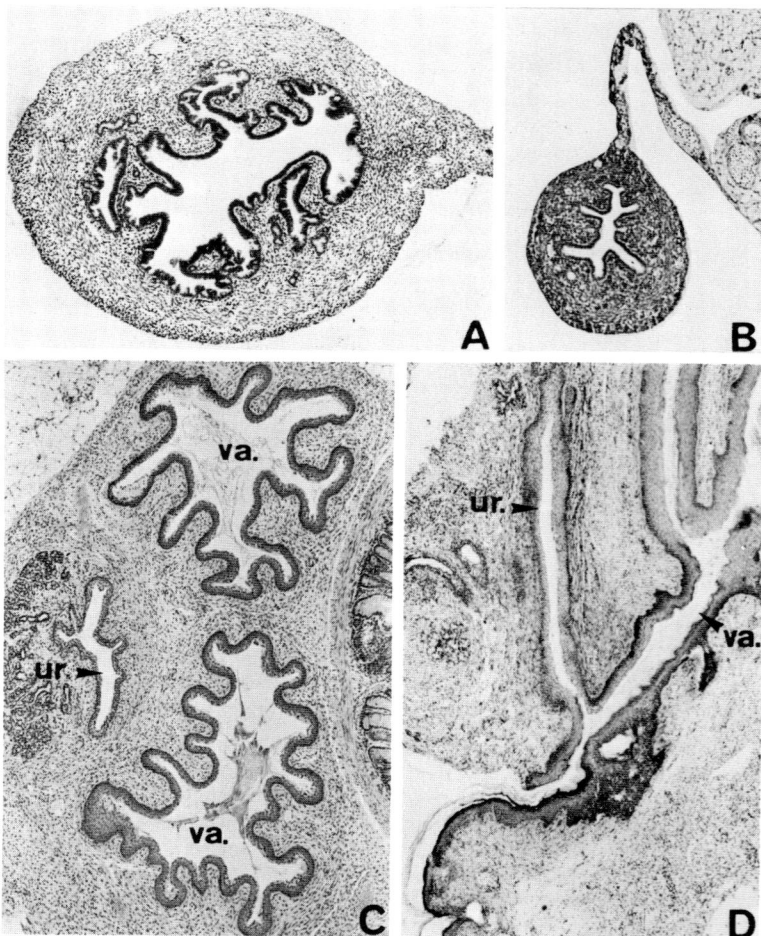

FIG. 6. Malformations of the urogenital tract in 35-day-old females born of mice treated with estradiol on the 14th day of pregnancy. A. Control; uterine horn. 50 ×. B. Uterine horn atrophied (100 μg). 50 ×. C. Bifid vagina (1000 μg). 50 ×. D. Urethrovaginal fistula (1000 μg). Sagittal section, 50 ×. (ur.) Urethra; (va.) vagina.

adulthood with some structural modifications. These frequently occurring anomalies are opposed to milk ejection in adult females. The frequency of these mammary gland and nipple malformations is proportional to the estradiol dose injected into the mother. They appear predictably at a dose level of 100 μg (Ch. Jean and Delost, 1964, 1965a,b; Ch. Jean, 1969a,b) (Fig. 10). Doses of less than 1.0 μg only produce a small percentage of athelia (Hoshino and Connolly, 1967).

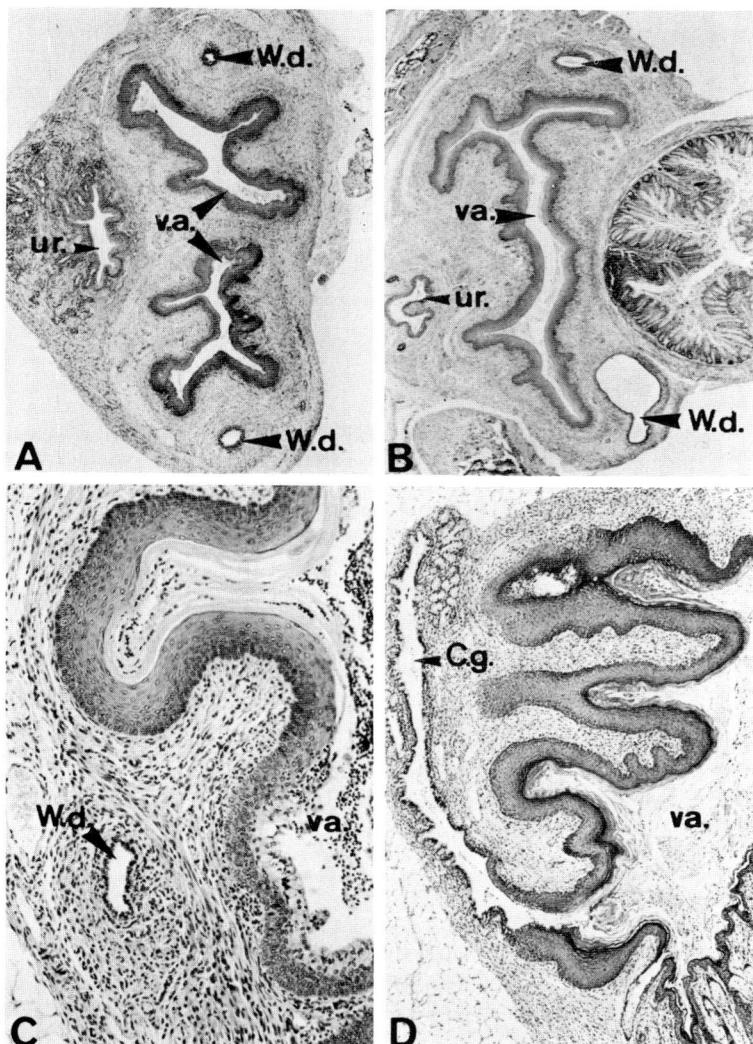

FIG. 7. Persistence of the male genital structures in females, born of mice treated with 1000 μg of estradiol on the 14th day of pregnancy. A. Bifid vagina; persistence of the two Wolffian ducts (35 days old) . 32 ×. B. Persistence of the two Wolffian ducts (80 days old) . 125 ×. C. Wolffian duct near the vagina (35 days old) . 125 ×. D. Cowper's gland opening into the vagina (35 days old) . 50 ×. (C.g.) Cowper's gland; (ur.) urethra; (va.) vagina; (W.d.) Wolffian duct.

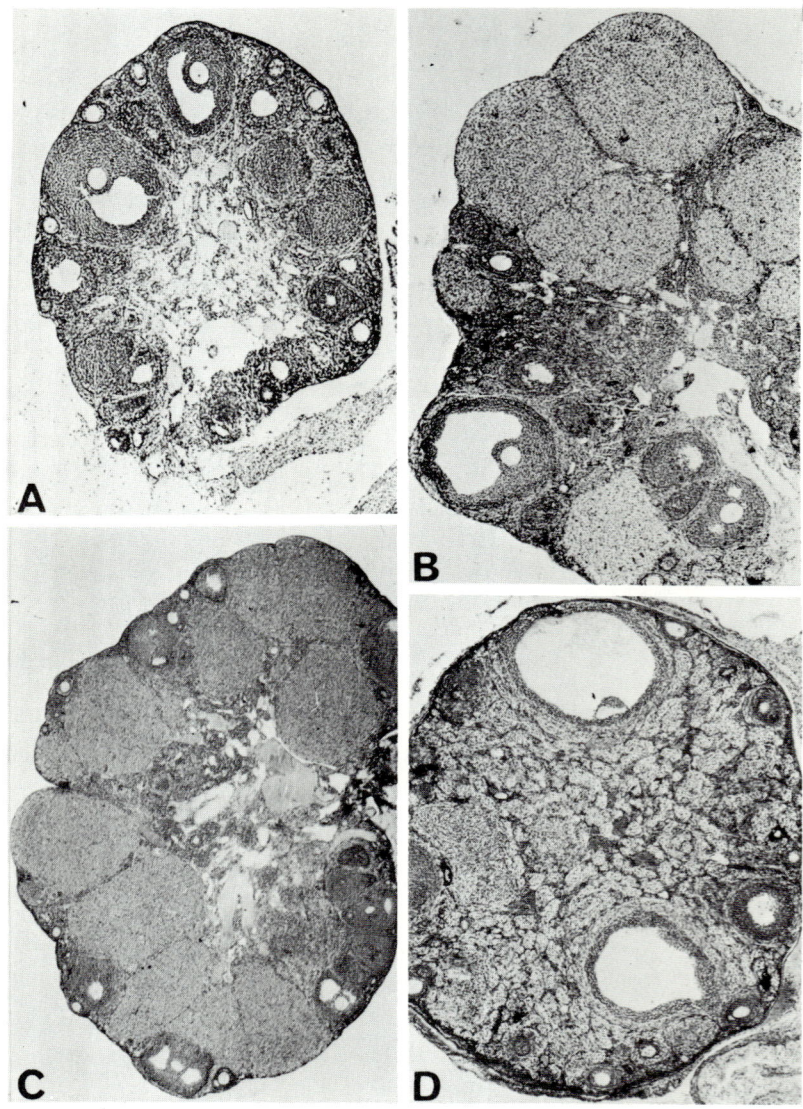

FIG. 8. Disorders of ovarian functioning in 35-day-old and 80-day-old females born in mice treated with different doses of estradiol (from 200 to 5000 µg) on the 14th day of pregnancy. A. Thirty-five-day-old controls; prepuberal ovary. The cyclic luteinization has not yet appeared. 50 ×. B. Early luteinization in a 35-day-old female. 50 ×. C. Eighty-day-old control; normal cyclic luteinization. 32 ×. D. Absence of cyclic luteinization and hyperplasia of the interstitial gland in an 80-day-old female. 50 ×. (Cl. Jean, 1968b).

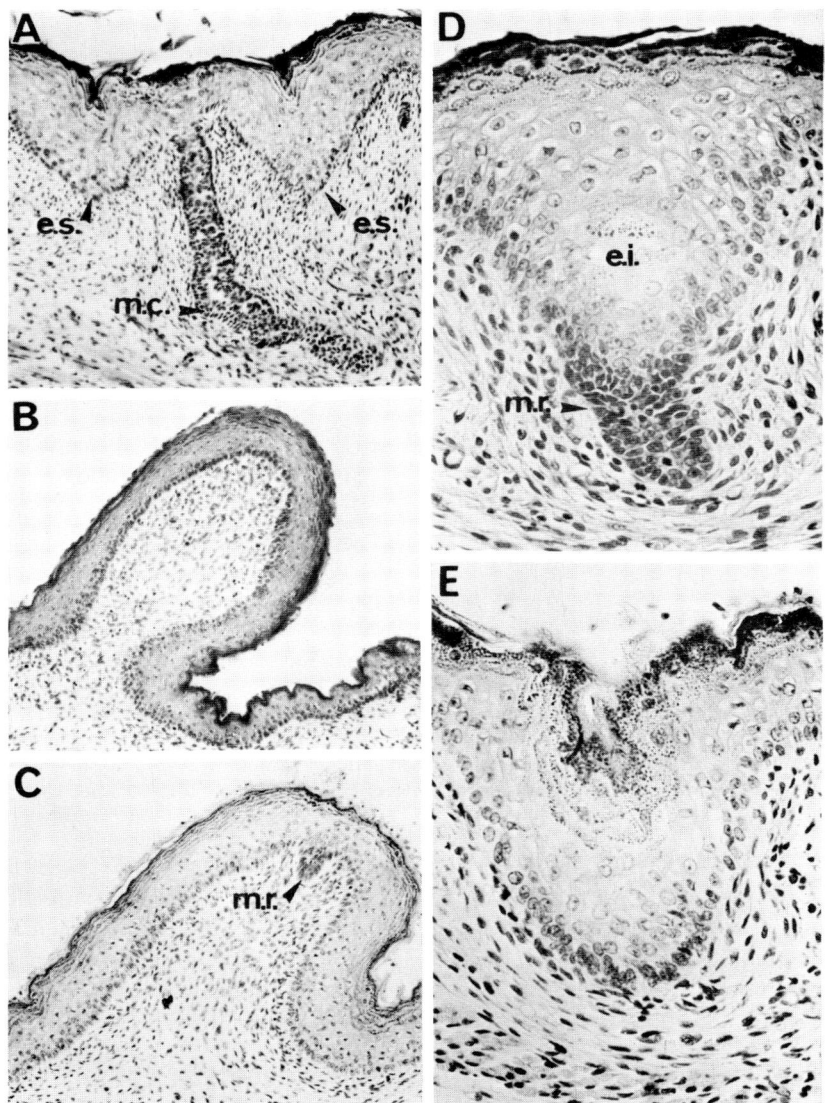

FIG. 9. Types of mammary malformations in newborn rats of both sexes whose mothers received one injection of 10 mg of estradiol on the 14th day of pregnancy. A. Control female; the mammary anlage are represented by a mammary cord which opens at the apex of the future nipple and by epithelial invaginations which delimit the nipple and represent the anlage of the nipple sheath. 125 ×. B. Female; prominent nipple and absence of mammary anlage. 125 ×. C. Female; prominent nipple and persistence of a mammary rudiment. 125 ×. D. Female; mammary anlagen made up of an ectodermal base associated with a mammary rudiment. 320 ×. E. Male; coelomastia (skin pocket). 320 ×. (e.s.) Epithelial sheath; (e.i.) epidermal invagination; (m.c.) mammary cord; (m.r.) mammary rudiment.

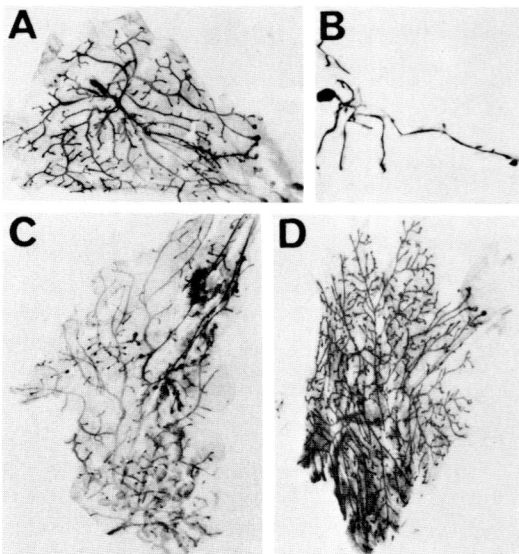

FIG. 10. Postnatal growth of mammary glands in females born of mice treated with estradiol, on the 14th day of pregnancy. A. Thirty-five-day-old control. 3.3 ×. B. Atrophy of the mammary gland in a 35-day-old female. The mother was treated with 500 µg of estradiol. 3.3 ×. C. Eighty-day-old control. 3.3 ×. D. Between puberty and maturity, in 80-day-old females, some mammary glands achieve a normal development spontaneously. The mother was treated with 1000 µg of estradiol. 3.3 ×. (Ch. Jean, 1969b.)

In conclusion, developmental disorders are extremely frequent after the injection of hormones into the fetus or into the pregnant female. It is remarkable that some of them appear only later during postnatal development, and that sometimes only histological examination can show them. Generally, there is a particular dosage level at which they are produced. The frequency of their appearance is proportional to the hormone dose injected. This fact shows that the protection afforded by the fetoplacental unit against exogenous hormones is limited. This may occur because either the fetus metabolizes only low doses or the placental barrier becomes permeable at certain dose levels. The discovery of these disorders once more points out the dangers of hormone treatment of the human species during pregnancy. Although this problem is heatedly debated by clinicians, more and more congenital malformations are being described in descendants after hormonal treatment of the mother (Wilkins, 1959). It is not possible to predict the possibility of teratogeny in the human on the basis of animal experiments in which only pharmacological doses are used; the techniques of comparative physiology need to be used if the hormonal function of the fetoplacental unit is to be understood.

Concluding Remarks

Only a few aspects of fetal endocrinology have been treated here; the mechanisms cannot be discussed in this limited space. All the endocrine glands are active in the fetus, all of them evidencing a sensitive period of activity. Many are under the control of a hypophyseal feedback process; maternal or placental hormones sometimes are able to compensate for deficiencies of the fetal endocrine glands.

Although the fields of experimental morphology and physiology have contributed greatly to our knowledge, many questions remain to be answered concerning fetal hormonal structure, secretion, and the role of fetal hormones in prenatal somatic growth and in the physiology of the fetus. Moreover, fetal endocrinology should be based on the concept of the fetoplacental unit, the study of which appears to be more and more necessary for the understanding of fetal homeostasis. Hormonal exchange between the mother, the placenta, and the fetus certainly plays a very important role in prenatal development. It is obvious that our interest in the human species makes it desirable for us to be able to specify the limits of the fetoplacental unit's protective function against exogenous hormones, because of the prenatal and postnatal growth disorders and because of the congenital malformations induced by hormone administration to the mother during pregnancy.

REFERENCES

Acevedo, H. F., Axelrod, L. R., Ishikawa, E., and Takari, F. (1961). Steroidogenesis in the human fetal testis: The conversion of pregnenolone-7α-H^3 to dehydroepiandrosterone, testosterone and 4-androstene-3, 17-dione. *J. Clin. Endocrinol. Metab.* Vol. 21, 1611–1613.

Angervall, L., and Lundin, P. M. (1964). Corticosteroid action on the fetal thymus and spleen. *Endocrinology* Vol. 74, 986–989.

Bearn, J. (1960). Le rôle de la glande surrénale foetale dans le développement du thymus foetal du Lapin. *C. R. Acad. Sci.* Vol. 250, 198–199.

Bencosme, S. A. (1955). The histogenesis and cytology of the pancreatic islets in the rabbit. *Amer. J. Anat.* Vol. 96, 103–151.

Bloch, E. (1965). Hormone production by the foetal adrenocortical gland. *Proc. 2nd Int. Congr. Endocrinol., 1964* Int. Congr. Ser. No. 83, Symp. No. 32, Part II, pp. 785–789.

Bloch, E., Benirschke, K., and Rosenberg, E. (1956). C_{19} Steroids, 17α-Hydroxycorticosterone and a sodium retaining factor in human fetal adrenal glands. *Endocrinology* Vol. 58, 626–633.

Boucher, D., and Delost, P. (1964a). Développement post-natal des descendants issus de mères traitées par la pénicilline au cours de la gestation chez la Souris. *C. R. Soc. Biol.* Vol. 158, 528–532.

Boucher, D., and Delost, P. (1964b). Développement post-natal des descendants issus de mères traitées par la streptomycine au cours de la gestation chez la Souris, *C. R. Soc. Biol.* Vol. 158, 2065–2069.

Boucher, D., and Delost, P. (1967). Développement post-natal de la Souris après traitement de la mère gestante et des descendants par les tétracyclines. *C. R. Soc. Biol.* Vol. 161, 300–305.

Burns, R. K. (1956). Transformation du testicule embryonnaire de l'opossum en ovotestis ou en "ovaire" sous l'action de l'hormone femelle, le diproprionate d'oestradiol. *Arch. Anat. Microsc. Morphol. Exp.* Vol. 45, 173–202.

Carteret, P. (1964). Sur le ralentissement du développement de la première génération après injection de thyroxine à la mère à divers stades de la gestation. *C. R. Soc. Biol.* Vol. 158, 2332–2338.

Carteret, P. (1965). Les troubles du développement post-natal des descendants après traitement de la Souris gestante par les hormones thyroïdiennes. Doctorate of Sciences Thesis, University of Clermont.

Cartaret, P., and Delost, P. (1961). Influence d'une dose unique de thyroxine injectée à la mère au 18ᵉ jour de la gestation sur la croissance post-natale des descendants chez la Souris. *C. R. Soc. Biol.* Vol. 155, 2334–2337.

Carteret, P., and Delost, P. (1962). Action de la thyroxine sur la croissance de la Souris. *J. Physiol. (Paris)* Vol. 54, 309–310.

Carteret, P., and Delost, P. (1963a). Croissance post-natale des descendants issus de mères traitées par une dose unique de thyroxine au cours de la gestation chez la Souris. *J. Physiol. (Paris)* Vol. 55, 218–219.

Carteret, P., and Delost, P. (1963b). Les effets de la thyroxine injectée à la mère à différentes périodes de la gestation sur la croissance et les glandes endocrines des descendants chez la Souris. *Gen. Comp. Endocrinol.* Vol. 3, Abstr. 19, 690–691.

Carteret, P., and Delost, P. (1964). Premiers résultats de l'étude du passage transplacentaire de la thyroxine marquée chez la Souris. *J. Physiol. (Paris)* Vol. 56, 542–543.

Chester-Jones, I., Jarrett, I. G., Vinson, G. P., and Potter, K. (1964). Adrenocorticosteroid production of foetal sheep near term. *J. Endocrinol.* Vol. 29, 211–212.

Cohen, A. (1963). Corrélations entre l'hypophyse et le cortex surrénal chez le foetus de rat. Le cortex surrénal du nouveau-né. *Arch. Anat. Microsc. Morphol. Exp.* Vol. 52, 277–407.

Comline, R. S., and Silver, M. (1961). The release of adrenaline and noradrenaline from the adrenal glands of the foetal sheep. *J. Physiol. (London)* Vol. 156, 424–444.

Dawes, G. S., Mott, J. C., and Rennik, B. R. (1956). Some effects of adrenaline, neoadrenaline and acetylcholine on the foetal circulation in the lamb. *J. Physiol. (London)* Vol. 134, 139–148.

Deanesly, R. (1961). Foetal endocrinology. *Brit. Med. Bull.* Vol. 17, 91–95.

Delost, P., Jean, Ch., and Jean. Cl. (1962). Production expérimentale de malformations mammaires chez le foetus de rat par injection d'oestradiol à la mère au 14ᵉ jour de la gestation. *C. R. Soc. Biol.* Vol. 156, 2048–2052.

Delost, P., Jean, Ch., and Jean, Cl. (1963). Malformations de la glande mammaire et du mamelon chez le foetus produites par l'oestradiol injecté à la Ratte gestante. *J. Physiol. (Paris)* Vol. 55, 237–238.

Diczfalusy, E. (1962). Endocrinology of the foetus. *Acta Obstet. Gynecol. Scand.* Suppl. 41, 45–85.

Diczfalusy, E., Cassmer, O., Alonso, C., and Miquel, M. (1961). Oestrogen metabolism in the human foetus. I. Tissue levels following the administration of 17β-oestradiol and oestradiol. *Acta Endocrinol.* Vol. 37, 353–375.

Dieterlen-Lievre, F. (1963). Le rôle de la thyroïde dans le développement embryonnaire des oiseaux et des mammifères. *Ann. Biol.* Vol. 2, 17–33.

Dornhurst, A. C., and Young, I. M. (1952). The action of adrenaline and noradrenaline on the placental and foetal circulations in the rabbit and guinea-pig. *J. Physiol. (London)* Vol. 118, 282–288.

Eayrs, J. T. (1961). Age as a factor determining the severity and reversibility of the effects of thyroid deprivation in the rat. *J. Endocrinol.* Vol. 22, 409–419.

Eguchi, Y. (1960). Experimental studies on the adrenal cortex of the mouse fetus. I. Effects of maternal adrenalectomy on the adrenal of the fetus based on histology and volume determination. *Embryologia* Vol. 5, 206–218.

Gardner, L. I., and Tice, A. A. (1957). Cortisol and three less polar substances in adrenal tissue from the human newborn. *Helv. Paediat. Acta* Vol. 12, 147–154.

Geloso, J. P. (1964). Corrélations thyréo-hypophysaires chez la foetus de rat en fin de gestation. *J. Physiol. (Paris)* Vol. 56, 358–359.

Geloso, J. P. (1967). Fontionnement de la thyroïde et corrélations thyréohypophysaires chez le foetus de rat. *Ann. Endocrinol. (Paris)* Vol. 28, 1–80.

Geloso, J. P., and Bernard, G. (1967). Effets de l'ablation de la thyroide maternelle ou foetale sur le taux des hormones circulantes chez le foetus de rat. *Acta Endocrinol.* Vol. 56, 561–566.

Geloso, J. P., Hemon, P., Legrand, J., Legrand, C., and Jost, A. (1968). Some aspects of thyroid physiology during the perinatal period. *Gen. Comp. Endocrinol.* Vol. 10, 191–197.

Ghilain, A., and Schwers, J. (1957). Réaction *in vitro* sur la surrénale foetale humaine à l'ACTH. Pp. 1443–1445. Extraction et dosage de l'ACTH dans l'hypophyse foetale humaine. *C. R. Soc. Biol.* Vol. 151, 1606–1608.

Golosow, N., and Grobstein, C. (1962). Epitheliomesenchymal interaction in pancreatic morphogenesis. *Develop. Biol.* Vol. 4, 242–255.

Gonet, A. (1961). Correction du diabète expérimental du rat par la greffe pancréatique foetale. *Acta Endocrinol. (Copenhagen)* Suppl. 62, 1–32.

Gorbman, A., Lissitzky, S., Michel, O., Michel, R., and Roche, J. (1951). Métabolisme de radioiode par le foetus de boeuf au voisinage du terme. *C. R. Soc. Biol.* Vol. 145, 1642–1644.

Gorbman, A., Lissitzky, S., Michel, O., Michel, R., and Roche, J. (1952). Metabolism of radioiodine by the near-term bovine fetus. *Endocrinology* Vol. 51, 546–561.

Greenberg, R. E., and Lind, J. (1961). Catecholamines in tissues of the human fetus. *Pediatrics* Vol. 27, 904–911.

Grumbach, M. M., Van Wyk, J. J., and Wilkins, L. J. (1955). Chromosomal sex in gonadal dysgenesis (ovarian agenesis): Relationship to male pseudohermaphroidism and theories of human sex differentiation. *J. Clin. Endocrinol. Metab.* Vol. 15, 1161–1193.

Hamburgh, M. (1968). An analysis of the action of thyroid hormone on development based on *in vivo* and *in vitro* studies. *Gen. Comp. Endocrinol.* Vol. 10, 198–213.

Hamburgh, M., Lynn, E., and Weiss, E. P. (1964). Analysis of the influence of thyroid hormone on prenatal and postnatal maturation of the rat. *Anat. Rec.* Vol. 150, 147–162.

Hard, W. L. (1944). The origin and differentiation of the alpha and beta cells in the pancreatic islets of the rat. *Amer. J. Anat.* Vol. 75, 369–403.

Heggestad, C. B. (1955). Retardation of ponderal growth in hypophysectomized fetal rats and its prevention by means of an injected growth hormone. *Anat. Rec.* Vol. 121, 399–400 (abstr. 298).

Hillman, D. A., Stachenko, J., and Giroud, C. O. P. (1962). In vitro studies of the human newborn adrenal cortex. *In* "Conference on the Human Adrenal Cortex" (A. R. Currie, T. Symington, and J. K. Grant, eds.), pp. 596–607. Livingstone, Edinburgh and London.

Hoffmann, F. (1947). Untersuchungen üher die Progesteronbildung in der föetolen Nebenniere, *Zentralbl. Gynaekol.* Vol. 69, 43–48.

Hokfelt, B. (1951). Noradrenaline and adrenaline in mammalian tissues. *Acta Physiol. Scand.* Vol. 25, Suppl. 92.

Hoshino, K. (1965). Development and function of mammary glands of mice prenatally exposed to testosterone propionate. *Endocrinology* Vol. 76, 789–794.

Hoshino, K., and Connolly, M. T. (1967). Development and growth of mammary glands of mice prenatally exposed to estradiol benzoate. *Anat. Rec.* Vol. 157, 262.

Jacquot, R. (1956). Surrénale et fonction glycogénique du foie chez l'embryon de rat. *C. R. Soc. Biol.* Vol. 150, 2137–2140.

Jacquot, R. (1959). Recherches sur le controle endocrinien de l'accumulation de glycogène le fois chez la foetus de rat. I. Expériences de décapitation du foetus *in utero. J. Physiol. (Paris)* Vol. 51, 655–692.

Jean, Ch. (1968a). Influence sur l'embryogenèse de la glande mammaire de l'hormone somatotrope injectée à la mère gravide ou au foetus. *C. R. Soc. Biol.* Vol. 162, 1473–1477.

Jean, Ch. (1968b). Nature et fréquence des malformations mammaires du rat nouveau né en fonction de la dose d'oestradiol injectée à la mère gravide. *C. R. Soc. Biol.* Vol. 162, 1144–1149.

Jean, Ch. (1968c). Les malformations mammaires du Rat nouveau-né après traitement de la mère gestante par les oestrogènes. Doctoral Thesis, University of Clermont.

Jean, Ch. (1969a). Evolution post-natale des anomalies mammaires produites chez les descendants par un traintment oestrogénique de la Souris gestante. *C. R. Soc. Biol.* Vol. 163, 1126–1131.

Jean, Ch. (1969b). Evolution post-natale de l'atrophie de la glande mammaire produite chez la Souris nouveau-née par injection d'oestrogènes à la mère gravide. *C. R. Soc. Biol.* Vol. 163, 1747–1754.

Jean, Ch., and Delost, P. (1964). Atrophie de la glande mammaire des descendants adultes issus de mères traitées par les oestrogènes au cours de la gestation chez la Souris, *J. Physiol. (Paris)* Vol. 56, 377.

Jean, Ch., and Delost, P. (1965a). Actions des oestrogènes sur la morphogénèse de la glande mammaire. *Gen. Comp. Endocrinol.* Vol. 5, Abstr. 50, 687–688.

Jean, Ch., and Delost, P. (1965b). Oestrogènes et malformations congénitales expérimentales de la morphologenèse mammaire. *C. R. Soc. Biol.* Vol. 159, 2357–2362.

Jean, Ch., and Delost, P. (1968). Action de l'hormone somatotrope sur l'embryogenèse mammaires de la Souris. *J. Physiol. (Paris)* Vol. 60, Suppl. 2, 471.

Jean, Ch., and Delost, P. (1969a). Androgènes et embryogénèse mammaire. *J. Physiol. (Paris)* Vol. 61, Suppl. 1, 139–140.

Jean, Ch., and Delost, P. (1969b). Prolactine et embryogénèse mammaire. *J. Physiol. (Paris)* Vol. 61, Suppl. 2, 323-324.

Jean, Ch., and Jean, Cl. (1969). Action des androgènes sur la différenciation des ébauches mammaires du Rat noveau-né. *C. R. Soc. Biol.* Vol. 163, 1754-1758.

Jean, Cl. (1967). Action des oestrogènes sur la gestation et sur la croissance des descendants. Doctorate of Sciences Thesis, University of Clermont.

Jean, Cl. (1968a). Malformations génitales induites chez la Souris adulte par une action oestrogène prénatale. 1. Le mâle (Pseudo-hermaphrodisme mâle). *Arch. Anat. Microsc. Morphol. Exp.* Vol. 57, 121-166.

Jean, Cl. (1968b). Malformations génitales induites chez la Souris adulte par une action oestrogène prénatale. II. La femelle. *Arch. Anat. Microsc. Morphol. Exp.* Vol. 57, 191-226.

Jean, Cl., and Delost, P. (1964). Cryptorchidie congénitale par injection d'oestrogènes à la Souris gestante. *C. R. Soc. Biol.* Vol. 158, 2321-2324.

Jean, Cl., and Delost, P. (1965a). Les anomalies de développement du testicule des descendants après injection d'oestrogènes à la mère gestante. *J. Physiol. (Paris)* Vol. 57, 634-635.

Jean, Cl., and Delost, P. (1965b). Oestrogènes et malformations sexuelle congénitales. *Gen. Comp. Endocrinol.* Vol. 5, Abstr. 51, 688.

Jean, Cl., and Delost, P. (1966). Les anomalies de l'appareil génital des descendants femelles après injection d'oestrogènes à la mère gestante. *J. Physiol. (Paris)* Vol. 58, 238-239.

Jean, Cl., and Delost, P. (1967a). Lesions of the gonads and of the genital tract in adult mice after estrogen treatment of the pregnant mother. *4th Conf. Eur. Comp. Endocrinol., 1967,* Abstr. 87.

Jean, Cl., and Delost, P. (1967b). Stimulation par un traitement oestrogénique postnatal des structures génitales femelles obtenues chez la Souris mâle adulte par injection d'oestradiol à la mère gravide. *J. Physiol. (Paris)* Vol. 59, 246-247.

Jean, Cl., and Delost, P. (1968). Mortalité foetale après traitement de la mère gestante par les oestrogènes. *J. Physiol. (Paris)* Vol. 60, Suppl. 1, 264.

Jost, A. (1947a). Recherches sur la différenciation sexuellet de l'embryon de lapin. *Arch. Anat. Microsc. Morphol. Exp.* Vol. 36, 151-200.

Jost, A. (1947b). Sur les effets de la castration précoce de l'embryon mâle de Lapin. *C. R. Soc. Biol.* Vol. 141, 126-129.

Jost, A. (1947c). Recherches sur la différenciation sexuelle de l'embryon de lapin. 3. Role des gonades foetales dans la différenciation sexuelle somatique. *Arch. Anat. Microsc. Morphol. Exp.* Vol. 36, 271-315.

Jost, A. (1947d). Sur le rôle des gonades foetales dans la différenciation sexuelle somatique de l'embryon de lapin. *C. R. Soc. Biol.* Vol. 34, 255-263.

Jost, A. (1951a). Recherches sur la différenciation sexuelle de l'embryon lapin. IV. Organogenèse sexuelle masculine après décapitation du foetus. *Arch. Anat. Microsc. Morphol. Exp.* Vol. 40, 247-281.

Jost, A. (1951b). La physiologie de l'hypophyse foetale. *Biol. Med. (Paris)* Vol. 40, 205-229.

Jost, A. (1953). Problems of fetal endocrinology: The gonadal and hypophyseal hormones. *Recent Progr. Horm. Res.* Vol. 8, 379-418.

Jost, A. (1954). Hormonal factors in the development of the fetus. *Cold Spring Harbor Symp. Quant. Biol.* Vol. 19, 167-181.

Jost, A. (1960). Action de divers stéroïdes sexuels et voisins sur la croissance et la différenciation sexuelle des foetus. *Proc. 1st Int. Congr. Endocrinol., 1960* in *Acta Endocrinol.* Vol. 34, Suppl. 50, 119–123 (1960).

Jost, A. (1961a). The role of fetal hormones in prenatal development. *Harvey Lect.* Ser. 55, 201–226.

Jost, A. (1961b). Physiologie des hormones thyroïdiennes chez la foetus. *In* "Colloquio sobre a Tireoide" (C. Chagas and L. C. Lobo, eds.), pp. 81–112. Inst. Biofis., Rio de Janeiro.

Jost, A. (1966a). Anterior pituitary function in foetal life. *In* "The Pituitary Gland" (G. W. Harris and B. T. Donovan, eds.), pp. 299–323. Univ. of California Press, Berkeley, California.

Jost, A. (1966b). Problems of fetal endocrinology: The adrenal glands. *Recent Progr. Horm. Res.* Vol. 22, 541–574.

Jost, A., and Jacquot, R. (1958). Influence de la thyroïdectomie du foetus de Lapin sur le teneur de son corps en lipides et en azote. *C. R. Acad. Sci.* Vol. 246, 1281–1283.

Jost, A., and Picon, L. O. (1958). Sur le rôle de l'hypophyse, des surrénales et du placenta dans la synthèse de glycogène par le foie foetal du lapin et du Rat. *C. R. Acad. Sci.* Vol. 247, 2459–2462.

Jost, A., and Vigouroux, E. (1965). Données sur les composés iodés organiques du plasma chez le lapin adulte et chez le foetus. *Ann. Endocrinol.* Vol. 26, 691–704.

Jost, A., Jacquot, R., and Cohen, A. (1962). Pituitary control of the foetal adrenal cortex. *In* "Conference on the Human Adrenal Cortex" (A. R. Currie, T. Symington, and J. K. Grant, eds.), pp. 569–579. Livingstone, Edinburgh and London.

Jost, A., Dupouy, J. P., and Monchamp, A. (1966). Fonction corticotrope de l'hypophyse et hypothalamus chez le foetus de rat. *C. R. Acad. Sci.* Vol. 262, 147–150.

Kamoun, A., Mialhe-Voloss, C., and Stutinsky, F. (1964). Evolution de la teneur en corticostérone de la surrénale foetale de rat. *C. R. Soc. Biol.* Vol. 158, 828–832.

Knobil, E., and Josimovich, J. B. (1959). Placental transfer of thyrotropic hormone, thyroxine, triiodothyronine, and insulin in the rat. *Ann. N. Y. Acad. Sci.* Vol. 75, 895–904.

Kobayashi, F. (1967). Prenatal effect of testosterone propionate on the differentiation of sexual functions in rats. II. Effects on the estrus cycles, copulatory ability and other sexual functions. *Folia Endocrinol. Jap.* Vol. 43, 30–42.

Legrand, J. (1965). Influence de l'hypothyroïdisme sur la maturation du cortex cérébelleux. *C. R. Acad. Sci.* Vol. 261, 544–547.

Lesinksi, J. (1949). The influence of thyroxine on the size of the foetus. *Excerpta Medica.* Part III, p. 449.

Levina, S. E. (1966). Development of hypothalamic, pituitary and placental endocrine function in human embryogenesis. *Symp. Funct. Regul. Develop. Endocrines, 1966,* Institute of Endocrinology, Slovak Academy of Sciences, Bratislava, Abstr., p. 18.

Liu, N. (1966). Some aspects of endocrinology in the fetus and the newborn. *Pediat. Clin. N. Amer.* Vol. 13, 1047–1076.

London, W. T., Money, W. L., and Rawson, R. W. (1963). Placental transport of I^{131} labeled thyroxine and triiodothyronine in the guinea pig. *Endocrinology* Vol. 73, 205–209.

Mercier-Parot, L. (1957). Influence de la cortisone et de l'hormone corticotrope sur la gestation et le développement post-natal du Rat. Doctorate of Sciences Thesis. University of Paris.

Mizusawa, S. (1966). Fetal thyrotropin. *Folia Endocrinol. Jap.* Vol. 42, 69–81.
Moore, C. R. (1950). The role of the fetal endocrine glands in development. *J. Clin. Endocrinol.* Vol. 10, 942–985.
Myant, N. B. (1963). La thyroïde et le développement foetal. *Postepy. Biochem. Polska* Vol. 9, No. 1, 19–34
Myant, N. B. (1964). The thyroid on reproduction in mammals. *In* "The Thyroid Gland" (R. Pitt-Rivers and W. R. Trotter, eds.), Vol. 1, pp. 283–302. Butterworth, London and Washington, D. C.
Nataf, B. M. (1968). Fetal rat thyroid gland in organ culture. *Gen. Comp. Endocrinol.* Vol. 10, 159–173.
Parkes, A. S. (1954). Some aspects of the endocrine environment of the fetus. *Cold Spring Harbor Symp. Quant. Biol.* Vol. 19, 3–8.
Pickering, D. E. (1964). Maternal thyroid hormone in the developing fetus. Observations on monkeys (*Macaca mulatta*). *Amer. J. Dis. Child.* Vol. 107, 567–573.
Picon, L., and Bouhnik, J. (1966). Evolution de la teneur du coeur en glycogène au cours de la vie foetale et néonatale chez la Rat. pp. 249–252. Action de la corticosurrénale sur la teneur du coeur en glycogène chez la foetus de Rat et le Rat nouveau-né. *C. R. Soc. Biol.* Vol. 160, 288–291.
Ponse, K. (1949). "La Différenciation du Sexe et l'Intersexualité chez les Vertébrés" Rouge, Lausanne.
Rankin, R. M. (1941). Changes in the content of iodine compounds end in the histological structure of the thyroid gland of the fetal pig during fetal life. *Anat. Rec.* Vol. 80, 123–135.
Raynaud, A. (1938). Développement et différenciation des diverses parties du tractus génital male des Souris femelles intersexuées recevant après la naissance des injections de propionate de testostérone. *C. R. Soc. Biol.* Vol. 129, 1033–1038.
Raynaud, A. (1942a). Recherches embryologiques et histologiques sur la différenciation sexuelle normale de la Souris. *Bull. Biol. Fr. Belg.* Suppl. 29.
Raynaud, A. (1942b). Modification expérimentale de la différenciation sexuelle des embryons de Souris par action des hormones androgènes et oestrogènes. *Actual. Sci. Ind.* Vol. 925 and Vol. 926.
Raynaud, A. (1947). Effet des injections d'hormones sexuelles a la Souris gravide sur le développement des ébauches de la glande mammaire des embryons. I. Action des substances androgènes. *Ann. Endocrinol.* Vol. 8, 248–253.
Raynaud, A. (1949). Nouvelles observations sur l'appareil mammaire des foetus de Souris, provenant de mères ayant recu des injections de testosterone pendant la gestation. *Ann. Endocrinol.* Vol. 10, 54–62.
Raynaud, A. (1950). Recherche expérimentales sur le développement de l'appareil génital et le fonctionnement des glandes endocrines des foetus de Souris et de mulot. *Arch. Anat. Microsc. Morphol. Exp.* Vol. 39, 518–576.
Raynaud, A. (1959a). Quelques effets des hormones oestrogènes chez la foetus de Souris. *Arch. Anat. Microsc. Morphol. Exp.* Vol. 48 (bis), 245–260.
Raynaud, A. (1959b). Effects of destruction of the fetal hypophysis by X-rays upon sexual development of the mouse. *Comp. Endocrinol., Proc. Columbia Univ. Symp., 1958* pp. 452–478.
Raynaud, A., and Frilley, M. (1947a). Effets sur le développement du tractus génital des embryons de Souris, de la destruction des ébauches de leur glandes génitales, par une irradiation au moyen des rayons X, à l'âge de 13 jours. *C. R. Soc. Biol.* Vol. 141, 1134–1137.
Raynaud, A., and Frilley, M. (1947b). Destruction des glandes génitales de l'embryon

de Souris, par une irradiation au moyen des Rayons X, à l'âge de treize jours. *Ann. Endocrinol.* Vol. 8, 400–419.

Raynaud, A., and Frilley, M. (1948). Effet sur le développement des diverses glandes annexes du tractus génital des embryons de Souris, de la déstruction au moyen des Rayons X, des glandes génitales des embryons. *C. R. Soc. Biol.* Vol. 142, 422–426.

Raynaud, A., and Raynaud, J. (1956). La production expérimentale de malformations mammaires chez les foetus de Souris, par l'action des hormones sexuelles. *Ann. Inst. Pasteur, Paris* Vol. 90, 39–91 and 187–220.

Raynaud, A., and Raynaud, J. (1965). Malformations oculaires observées chez les embryons d'orvet (*Anguis fragilis* L.) traités par la thyroxine. *C. R. Soc. Biol.* Vol. 159, 11–15.

Roffi, J. (1968). Evolution des quantités d'adrénaline et de noradrénaline dans les surrénales des foetus et des nouveau-nés de Rat et de lapin. *Ann. Endocinol.* Vol. 29, 277–300.

Rosa, P. (1955). "Endocrinologie Sexuelle du Foetus Féminin." Masson, Paris.

Ross, M. H. (1962). Electron microscopy of the human foetal adrenal cortex. In "Conference on the Human Adrenal Cortex" (A. R. Currie, T. Symington, and J. K. Grant, eds.), pp. 558–569. Livingstone. Edinburgh and London.

Sak, M. F., Macchi, I. A., and Beaser, S. B. (1965). Postnatal development of beta cells and ILA section in the pancreatic islets of the golden hamster. *Anat. Rec.* Vol. 152, 25–34.

Schatz, A., Schlscha, E. B., and Schatz, V. (1964). Soil organic matter as a natural chelating material. Part 2. The occurrence and importance of paradoxical concentration effects in biological systems. *Compost Sci.* Vol. 5, 26.

Schwers, J. (1959). L'hypophyse foetale. *Bull. Soc. Roy. Belge Gyn. et Obst.* Vol. 29, 157–163.

Shepherd, D. M., and West, G. B. (1951). Noradrenaline and the suprarenal medulla. *Brit. J. Pharmacol.* Vol. 6, 665–674.

Snoeck, J. (1958). "Le placenta humain, Aspects morphologiques et fonctionnels." Lab. Gynecol. Exp. Univ. Libre de Bruxelles. Clin. gynecol. obstet. hosp. Saint-Pierre. Masson, Paris.

Sonenberg, M., Money, W. L., Keston, A. S., Fitzgerald, P., and Godwin, J. T. (1951). Tracer studies with radioactively labeled prolactin preparations. *J. Clin. Endocrinol.* Vol. 11, 747.

Taylor, N. R. W., Loraine, J. A., and Robertson, H. A. (1953). The estimation of ACTH in human pituitary tissue. *J. Endocrinol.* Vol. 9, 334–341.

Tuchmann-Duplessis, H., and Mercier-Parot, L. (1955). Hypophyse et développement prénatal. L'hormone somatotrope est-elle responsable du gigantisme foetal? *Presse Med.* Vol. 63, 1831–1834.

Tuchmann-Duplessis, H., and Mercier-Parot, L. (1963). Etude comparative de la structure de l'hypophyse et de la surrénale des anencéphales et des hydrocéphales humains. *C. R. Soc. Biol.* Vol. 157, 977–981.

Tusques, J. (1955). Effet toxique (cataracte) sans effet morphogénétique de la thyroxine injectée *in utero*, chez les foetus de Rat blanc, avant le développement des sensibles locales. *C. R. Soc. Biol.* Vol. 149, 1170–1173.

Verain, A., and Verain-Pinoy, A. (1960). Métabolisme du radioiode par le foetus de chat au voisinage du terme. *C. R. Acad. Sci.* Vol. 251, 3079–3081.

Villee, D. B., and Villee, C. A. (1965). Synthesis of corticosteroids in the fetal placental unit. *Proc. 2nd Int. Congr. Endocrinol., 1964* Int. Congr. Ser. No. 83, Symp. No. 30, Part II, pp. 709–714.

Villee, D. B., Engel, L. L., Loring, J. M., and Villee, C. A. (1961). Steroid hydroxylation in human fetal adrenals: formation of 16α-hydroxyprogesterone, 17-hydroxyprogesterone and deoxycorticosterone. *Endocrinology* Vol. 69, 354–372.

Vokaer, R. (1963). La progestérone et les progestatifs de synthèse. *In* "l'insuffisance lutéale," pp. 245–285. VIIème Réunion des Endocrinologistes de Langue Francaise, Beyrouth, 1963. Publication des *Ann. Endocrin.*, Paris Masson, Paris.

Waterman, A. J. (1959). Development of the thyroid-pituitary system in warm-blooded amniotes. *Comp. Endocrinol. Proc. Columbia Univ. Symp., 1958* pp. 351–367.

Waterman, A. J., and Gorbman, A. (1956). Development of the thyroid gland of the rabbit. *J. Exp. Zool.* Vol. 132, 509–538.

Wells, L. J. (1947). Progress of studies designed to determine whether the fetal hypophysis produces hormones that influence development. *Anat. Rec.* Vol. 97, 409 (abstr. 197).

Wiesner, B. P. (1934). The post-natal development of the genital organs in the albino rat. *J. Obstet. Gynecol.* Vol. 41, 867–922.

Wilkins, L. (1959). Masculization of the female fetus due to the use of certain synthetis oral progestins during pregnancy. *Arch. Anat. Microsc. Morphol. Exp.* Vol. 48, 313–329.

Wolff, J., Chaikoff, I. L., and Nichols, C. W. (1949). The accumulation of thyroxine-like and other iodine compounds in the fetal bovine thyroid. *Endocrinology* Vol. 44, 510–519.

Young, W. C. (1961). "Sex and Internal Secretions." Williams & Wilkins, Baltimore, Maryland.

Discussion

A. Cohen: It seems to be of interest from a general point of view to know by which process the endocrine glands of fetal animals may act on target organs. There is now some evidence that the fetal endocrine glands are able to influence functional development of target organs by controlling the activity of one or several enzymes in these organs.

To support this idea there is an interesting work concerning the action of corticoids on the epinephrine content of the adrenal of the developing fetal rat (review in Roffi, 1968). If rat fetuses are deprived of their pituitary gland by decapitation at a stage which impairs the normal development of adrenocortical glands, the epinephrine content of adrenal medulla is at term one-fourth of the normal adrenal content either in normal or in adrenalectomized mothers.

By contrast norepinephrine accumulates in above-normal levels after fetal decapitation. The developmental increase in the activity of the enzyme that methylates norepinephrine to epinephrine [phenylethanolamine-N-methyl transferase (PNMT)] is prevented by decapitation of rat fetuses. Injection of ACTH or cortisol to decapitated fetuses raises this activity to near control levels.

These experiments show that corticoids may act on epinephrine synthesis in fetal adrenals by controlling the activity of the methylating enzyme of norepinephrine.

These findings give evidence that fetal hormones are, at least in this experiment, more important than maternal hormones for the normal process of epinephrine synthesis in the adrenal medulla during fetal life.

REFERENCE

Roffi, J. 1968. Influence des corticosurrénales sur la synthèse d'adrénaline chez le foetus et le nouveau-né de rat et de lapin. *J. Physiol.*, Vol. 60, 455–494.

S. Milković: Undoubtedly the results reported by Dr. Delost warn us of the danger involved in the treatment of the pregnant female, but to what extent are the results obtained in this way applicable to the interpretation of physiological processes and their regulatory mechanisms?

First of all we have to distinguish between two, at the first sight identical, questions: (1) whether, during prenatal development, when the maternal organism and the placenta are involved in a growing process of the developing fetus, the fetal organs are capable of functioning (provoked, e.g., by an external stimulus) and (2) whether, in fact, there is such a natural spontaneous functioning without any external instigation.

Let us consider whether the growing fetus needs its own "functioning" systems, or whether they only play a relatively passive role during prenatal growth, the fetus being, in a way, the mother's parasite. If we suppose, and I believe it is quite reasonable to do so, that the developing fetuses are not forced to take care of homeostasis, etc., because the mother and the placenta do this task for them, then we may assume that the functioning capacity should be developed during prenatal life, but real function need not necessarily start at that time.

For the sake of clarification, a few examples from our work will be given. Fetal adrenocorticotropic function begins before day 18, but after day 17 of intrauterine development. Extreme differences in fetal plasma corticosterone concentration (mothers with huge, hypersecreting adrenal glands versus adrenolectomized mothers) cannot influence the onset of the adrenocorticotrophic activity, but when this activity has already been established, then specific influences of maternal corticoids are easy to demonstrate. However, fetal liver glycogen deposition, highly dependent on corticoids in adult organisms, are essentially the same, both as regards their appearance and concentration, in spite of the very much different function of the maternal and fetal pituitary–adrenocortical system. It is true, although some relevant enzymic activities (glycogen synthetase, phosphorilase) as well as glucose 6-phosphate concentration were found to be influenced by this treatment of pregnant mothers. Therefore, the fetal liver glycogen deposition seems to be primarily a result of the chronological age of the fetus rather than of corticosterone concentration in the circulating blood.

Truth, to say, ligation of the tuba uterina before pregnancy will make it possible to reduce the normal litter size by half. At birth only slightly increased body weight as compared to the offsprings of normal intact mothers is found. However, body weight increase after birth is quite different in favor of the offsprings whose number has been reduced, which is not possible to demonstrate if reduction of litter size is made after birth. Furthermore, the blindness phase in these physically better-developed newborns is shortened from 15 to 13 days.

In summary, the intrauterine development seems to be quite stable in spite of hormonal and probably some other influences; however, such hardly detectable intrauterine changes may influence postnatal development.

It is to be regretted that the behavior of such rats has never been observed. Had we done so, a great deal of information clarifying our standpoint would have been collected.

S. Schapiro: I believe a syndrome has been described (Kohn, 1914) in which female children at birth occasionally have enlarged mammary glands and vaginal bleeding, indicating that progesterone and estrogens can get across the placental barrier and exert effects on the developing young *in utero*. In addition, Saxonova has reported (1963) that giant infants are frequently born to severely acromegalic mothers.

REFERENCES

Kohn, A. (1914). Synkainogenese. *Wilhelm Ronx' Arch. Entwicklungsmech. organismen* Vol. 39, 113-130.

Saxonova, N. S. (1963). The effect of disturbed function of the hypophysis during pregnancy (acromegaly) on the prenatal and postnatal development of the child's brain. *Probl. Endokrinol. Gormonoter.* Vol. 3, 87-92.

THE THEORY OF CRITICAL DEVELOPMENTAL PERIODS AND POSTNATAL DEVELOPMENT OF ENDOCRINE FUNCTIONS

J. KŘEČEK

Developmental physiology is a young topic, a young branch of the very, very old tree of physiology. It was only in the 19th century that the basis was set for understanding the developmental aspects of physiology. And so, the first pioneers of evolutionary physiology appeared at the turn of this century, and among them was a Czech professor named Edward Babák. At present, there is no general theory in this field but the amount of information continues to increase.

The concept of "critical periods" has appeared more and more frequently in papers on developmental psychology and developmental physiology in recent years. The term refers to the postnatal periods of sudden developmental changes, analogous to those well known in embryology. But only experimental psychologists have attempted to formulate a more general theory of critical periods.

According to Scott (1962) postnatal growth and development depend on so-called organizing processes. Generally, the significance of this concept is expressed in the following way: what has been organized during individual development can be reorganized only with difficulty, as organization inhibits reorganization. The organizational process can be influenced only at the time it is occurring, that is, during the critical developmental period.

King, in 1958, tried to delineate these postnatal "phases of organization" in mammals with respect to the age of the individual. He divided postnatal development into three stages. First, the infantile stage: from birth to weaning; second, the juvenile stage: from weaning up to sexual maturity; and third, adulthood: after sexual maturity. Beyond doubt, in each of these developmental stages characteristic peculiarities of the organism become evident. It is also evident that each of these stages has really been initiated by a developmental change. So, birth precedes the infantile stage, weaning the juvenile one, and sexual maturation precedes adulthood. In Scott's terminology, these three phases can be denoted as organizational phases, and so can, perhaps, be considered "critical periods."

I would like to comment on "stages" and "critical periods." The infantile or the suckling stage is a period of relative stability, during which the child is nourished by the mother. The juvenile stage, between weaning and sexual maturity is similarly fairly stable.

The periods of weaning and of sexual maturation are, however, accompanied by very basic changes in functions, in reactivity, and in ecological conditions. I think it would be useful for methodological purposes to distinguish between these two kinds of developmental phases—the stable stages and the instable critical periods.

There are some new results in developmental physiology that, at present, can hardly be applied to constructing a new theory, but that may help us to explain ontogenetic development in more or less physiological terms.

The applicable data have been attained mostly by the study of the development of laboratory rats. It appears that in these mammals individual developmental phases can be timed according to the age of the individual. A very simple diagram of the relation between the age of the rat and its developmental stage is shown in Fig. 1. The developmental stages of the rat are plotted according to King's scheme.

After birth, an infantile stage of about two weeks follows which should, however, be denoted as a "suckling" period, because this term means quite clearly that during this period the young animal is nourished exclusively with milk. The weaning period takes about 14 days, and is followed by a short stability stage—the juvenile one. The interval

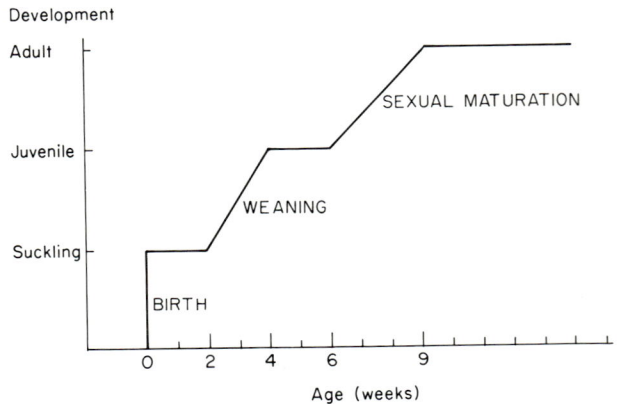

FIG. 1. Stages in the development of the rat.

between this stage and that of adulthood—sexual maturation—passes relatively slowly, and most probably lasts from the 6th to the 9th week of age, because toward the beginning of the interval the vaginae of the female rats start to open, and toward the end their reproductive ability develops fully.

This timing of developmental stages can help us in searching for the mechanisms of organization and in attempting to influence this organization, as it establishes these stages on the basis of mere determination of age. The experimenter is not entirely dependent on vague definitions, but can base his work on quantitative data.

The timing of periods of relative stability and of periods of changes is in perfect correlation with the development of interrelationships between the developing mammal and other members of the species, especially between the young and their mothers, as is shown in Fig. 2. The ecological changes refer to relations between the developing individual and its mother. Birth cancels the close relationship that existed during pregnancy, but up to weaning the mother and her young still form an ecological unit. Only after weaning do young animals become completely independent of their mother, and sexual maturity creates a new interindividual relationship—a coupling of the male and female.

Parallel with ecological changes, functional stepwise development also takes place, as is shown in Fig. 3. During and immediately after birth, anatomical and functional changes in the circulatory, respiratory, and digestive systems take place, and weaning is accompanied by qualitative digestive changes (Hahn and Koldovský, 1966), as well as by the

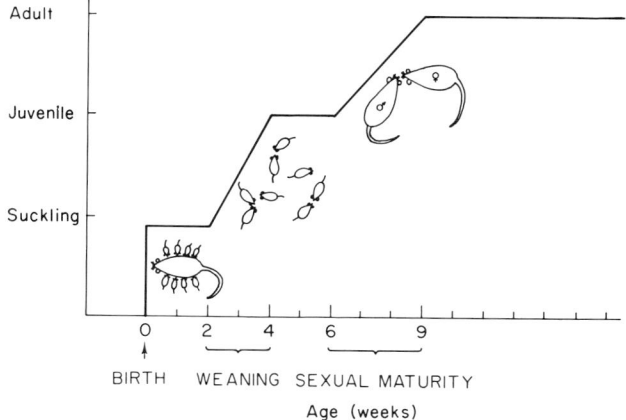

FIG. 2. Critical periods in the development of the rat; ecological changes during development.

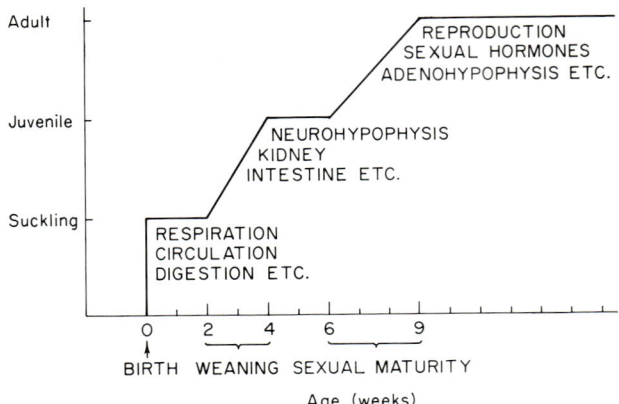

FIG. 3. Critical periods in the development of functions in the rat.

transformation of the structure and function of the kidneys and their regulation (Křeček, 1962). As is generally known, the start of reproductive ability during sexual maturation is connected with the morphological and functional reorganization of reproductive and sexual organs.

It is especially important to note that by external manipulation the further development of the individual can be influenced in at least two of the periods of functional change characterized by Scott as critical periods. (Fig. 4). A great number of authors have shown that handling the newborn not only alters the development of its behavior, but also permanently influences endocrine mechanisms (Denenberg, 1964; Levine, 1957, 1962; Levine and Lewis, 1959).

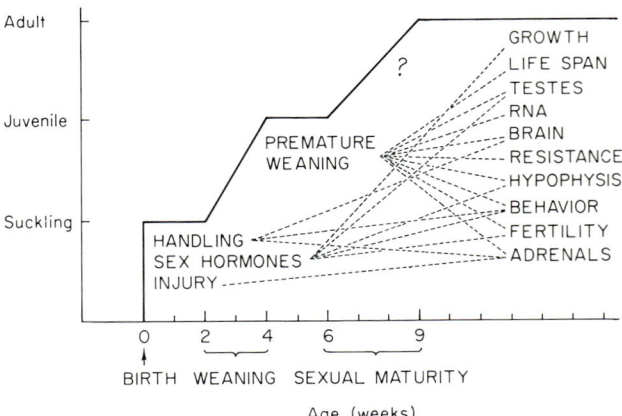

FIG. 4. Critical periods in the development of the rat; high sensitivity to environmental stimuli.

A single small dose of androgenic or estrogenic hormones injected into newborn rats causes an endocrine disturbance which manifests itself after long latent periods or only after sexual maturation, and results very often in an entire loss of reproductive function, as shown by Bradbury (1941), Gorsky and Barraclough (1963), and others.

Interference with weaning has also very similar late consequences. Premature weaning, for example, shortens life, causes disturbances in reproductive capacity, in higher nervous activity, in reactivity to pathogenic stimulation and in behavior (Kraus et al., 1961; Nováková et al., 1962; Koldovský et al., 1963).

It can therefore be taken as proved that during postnatal development there exist certain special periods of change in natural interindividual relations, transformation of structure and function, and a susceptibility to external influences in terms of the further development of the individual. There is no reason why the term "critical periods" cannot be used to specify these periods.

Endocrinology has contributed many interesting facts to elucidate these critical periods. Ontogenetic development and endocrinology are not new themes. Medical science knows very well that endocrine disturbances have an entirely different clinical picture according to the age at which they take place. Diabetes mellitus is a more severe disease for the young organism than for the adult one; hypothyroidism leads to cretinism in infants, whereas it does not damage mental activity in adulthood.

At the beginning of this century Foà wrote:

> L'ovaire embryonnaire, greffé en substitution d'un des ovaires de femelles très jeunes impubères, ou de femelles adultes arrivées à la maturité sexuelle, peut prendre dans un cas comme dans l'autre: toutefois, dans le premier cas, il conserve à peu près la même structure et le même degré de développement que lorsqu'il a été greffé; dans le second cas, au contraire, il atteint bientôt la structure d'un ovaire adulte, accelerant de beaucoup son évolution normale. L'ovaire embryonnaire, greffé en substitution d'un ovaire appartenant à de vieilles femelles arrivées à l'age de la ménopause, dégenère très rapidemente et est resorbé sans laisser de trace."[1]

It has been known for at least 60 years that sexual maturation substantially changes endocrine functions. In his paper, Dr. Delost showed the dependence of fetal endocrine functions on the functions of the mother, and it is logical that after birth, during the perinatal critical

---

[1] "An embryonic ovary grafted in place of one of the ovaries of very young prepubertal females or sexually mature females is not rejected in either case: however, in the first case it retains nearly the same structure and degree of development as when it was grafted; in the second case it very quickly attains the structure of an adult ovary, at a rate greatly accelerated over the normal rate. An embryonic ovary grafted in place of one of the ovaries of an old menopausal female rapidly degenerates and is resorbed without leaving a trace."

period these relationships change. Thus, two of the three critical periods under consideration are known to be accompanied by changes in endocrine function. What about endocrinology of the weaning period?

Some time ago, we investigated this problem and found that during the weaning period functional changes essential for water and electrolyte metabolism take place. This finding is not surprising, if we take into account that during the weaning period fluid intake changes from obligatory milk feeding to a separated regulation of fluid and food intake. A suckling animal always has an abundant water supply and does not activate mechanisms responsible for water retention. In agreement with that, no vasopressin, a hormone which activates water reabsorption in the kidney and thus decreases its excretion, was found in the blood of suckling animals. This is shown in the upper part of Fig. 5.

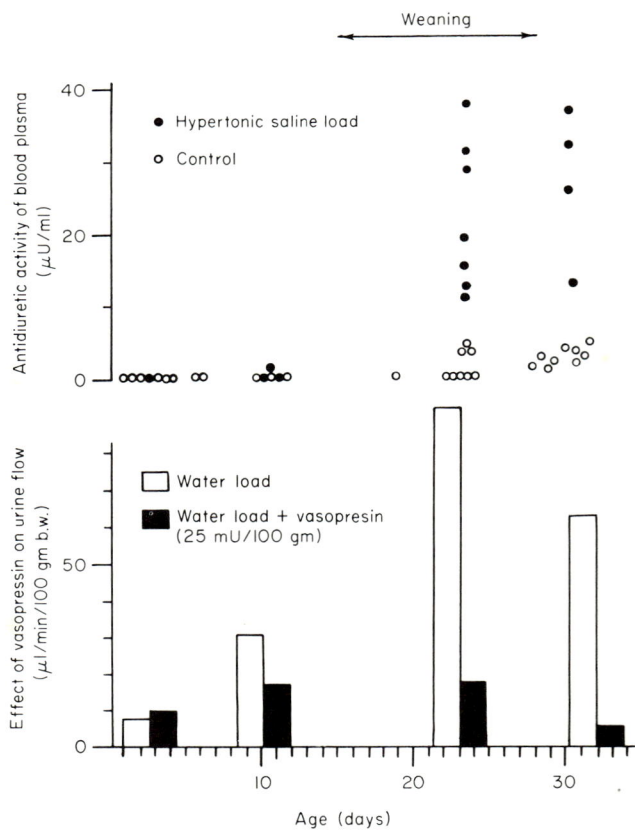

FIG. 5. The development of osmoregulatory function by the neurohypophysis.

Vasopressin begins to be detectable in the blood during weaning, and, toward the end of this period, blood values reach the level of those found in adult animals; the osmotic load begins to increase its level as well. Even the kidney starts to react to vasopressin at that time. These changes are not the result of the maturation of the pituitary, which is probably finished just before birth, as evidenced by the fact that you can find a significant amount of vasopressin in the neurohypophysis of newborn animals. Thus all the three "critical periods" are accompanied by changes of endocrine functions. During these developmental periods some of the endocrine functions disappear while others are either newly established or their significance changes. The appearance of vasopressin in the blood is dependent on weaning. It is probably not induced by weaning, because premature weaning does not accelerate the development of the values of antidiuretic activity in the plasma. I am referring to the natural change in the relationship between pup and mather, not to the separation of the two carried out by laboratory routine. Weaning does not take place in 1 day. When we removed the mothers from the young rat pups, at the age of 15 days, we were able to keep more than 80% of the animals alive. If we did this with 14-day-old animals, only 20% were able to survive. At 16 or 17 days of age, 100% of the animals were able to survive. We explain this as follows. The micturation reflex is not present in suckling animals and the mother produces the urine flow, stimulating the area around the genital organ. If the animals die when separated from their mothers at an age less than 14 days, it is usually not due to hunger, but due to this disruption of bladder function. The end of the weaning period is between 27 and 29 days and the distribution is very narrow. I am speaking only about this particular strain of Wistar rats. I have not come across any case of weaning at 21 days. We had good evidence that milk was taken by the young rat up to the age of 28 or 29 days. This was proved by the injection of radioactive strontium into the mother and looking for the presence of this strontium in the offspring; it appeared only up to the age of 29 days. After that no strontium passed from the mother to the young one. The beginning of weaning was demonstrated by the measurement of labeled barium sulfate which was put into the nutriment. Only after the 14th or 15th day can you find this material in the stomach of the baby. Thus, we are able to say that weaning occurs between 14 and 28 days (A. Babický *et al.*, 1970).

It seems to me that from the point of view of developmental endocrinology, the most remarkable are those discoveries showing some long-lasting changes produced by manipulations in the critical periods. Such evidence was developed for the perinatal and weaning periods.

In regard to the neonatal period, Pfeiffer in 1936, and afterward many other authors, showed that in the rat there is a very short period after birth during which endocrine influences markedly interfere with the development of reproductive functions. Also, in the experiments of Barraclough and Leath (1954), a single injection of testosterone given to 5-day-old female rats was enough to bring about changes that were evident in adulthood. In these rats, nonovulating ovaries with corpora lutea were found, estrous cycles were suppressed, and they were completely sterile. Gorski and Barraclough (1962) demonstrated an effect with a single 10 μg dose of the hormone only in rats younger than 10 days of age, however. Much higher doses of the same hormone were ineffective if injected into older animals. According to Gorski and Arai (1968), the full effect of the hormone appears to act for at least 3 hours.

The critical nature of the weaning period was investigated by a slightly different method, but the results are compatible in many respects.

As stated earlier, the process of weaning is gradual, and lasts about a fortnight. Nevertheless, young rats at the age of 15 to 16 days are able to survive if the mother rat is suddenly removed; but, this artificial intervention results in many changes of various functions at a later age (Kraus *et al.*, 1961; Koldovsky *et al.*, 1963). At least two of the affected functions are involved in endocrine regulations, namely the activity of the gonads and of the adrenal glands.

Together with Palaty (1967), we investigated the effect of premature weaning on the development of androgenic hormone production in the male rat (Fig. 6). Androgenic activity was estimated indirectly by means of the seminal vesicle weight, and by the determination of its citric acid content. Until sexual maturation no significant difference was found between animals that were normally weaned and animals prematurely weaned. Only after day 60, after sexual maturation, were the differences in seminal vesicle weight and citric acid content apparent. Premature weaning either decreased the plasma level of androgenic hormones or decreased the sensitivity of the target organs. This difference is also observed in animals 100 days old.

This effect is very complicated. We believe that the effect of premature weaning can be explained by the role of nutrition and social factors. If you provide the animal with high fat nutriment that is similar to the mother's milk, you can to some degree prevent the negative effect.

Dr. Ader at Rochester (1962) has described some pathological changes on the gastric mucosa in prematurely weaned rats. He was able to suppress those changes by leaving the mother with cauterized nipples in the cage of premature weaned baby rats. We have reproduced his results. Dr. Nováková (1966) in my department showed that the presence

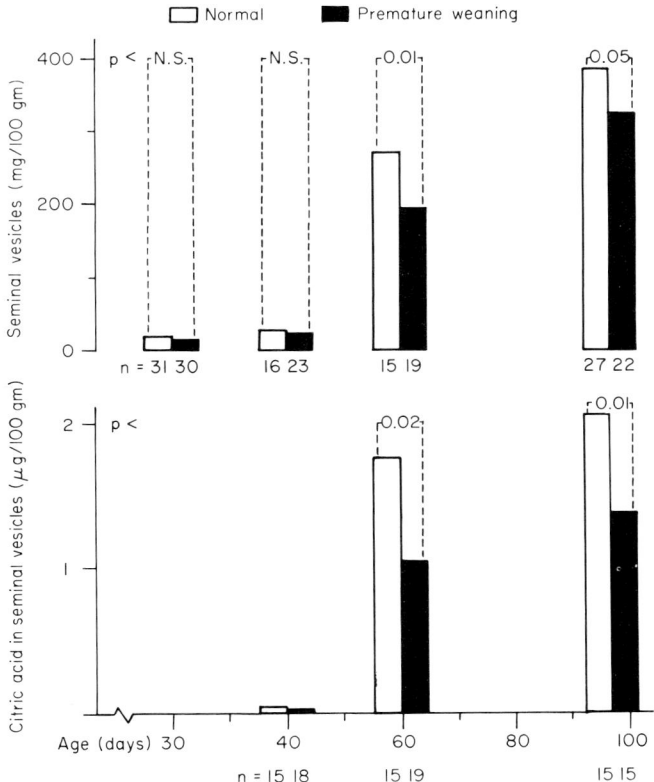

FIG. 6. The effect of premature weaning on androgenic activity in the rat (weight and citric acid content of the seminal vesicles).

of a nipple-cauterized mother plus high fat diet prevented the occurrence of behavioral disturbances in prematurely weaned rats.

These results with androgens resemble in certain respects those obtained during our investigation of adrenal function. Together with Kraus (1968) we investigated the *in vitro* production of corticosterone by the adrenals of normally and prematurely weaned rats. It should be noted that the adrenals of prematurely weaned rats can be stimulated by ACTH in the same way as of normally weaned animals. The effect of premature weaning could be detected earlier than in the previous experiments, because corticosterone production was decreased, as shown in Fig. 7, at the age of 23 days. But only after sexual maturation did long lasting effects appear, that is, corticosterone production was decreased only in females.

The appearance of delayed effects depending on sexual maturation

242   J. KŘEČEK

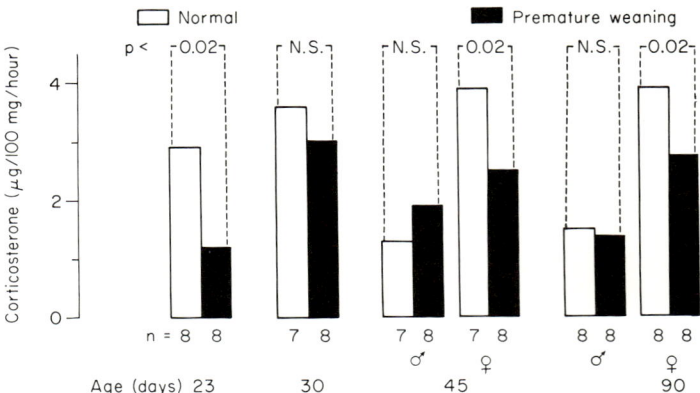

FIG. 7. The effect of premature weaning on the *in vitro* production of corticosterone by the adrenals in the rat.

seems to be a common feature for both the production of androgens and glucocorticoids. The delayed effects appear to justify the use of the expression "critical" for the period of sexual maturation, but in an unusual way. An organism, the development of which has been modified during previous critical periods, reaches the stage of sexual maturation; during this period a substantial reorganization of endocrine reproductive functions takes place. This genetically timed event, however, does not catch up with the normal organism, only with the deeply altered one. Therefore, the establishment of new functions does not proceed normally in the modified animal.

This hypothesis is supported by two results obtained from adrenal gland investigations. Apart from glucocorticoids, the adrenal gland produces another group of steroids, mineralocorticoids, the most familiar being aldosterone. When investigating with Kraus (1970) the relation between the pineal gland and aldosterone, we accidentally discovered that a change in aldosterone production induced by perinatal traumatisation depended on sexual maturation. Pinealectomy is a rather serious surgical intervention in the skull cavity of the experimental animal. For technical reasons we performed the surgery in neonatal rats, i.e., in the perinatal critical period. Our study included also a group of sham-operated animals and it turned out that the sham-operations per se affected the production of aldosterone. We compared the production of aldosterone in 30-day-old and adult rats. No effect of the sham-operation was observed in immature rats; it appeared only in adults, in which production of aldosterone was decreased (Fig. 8).

The importance of sexual maturation for the appearance of late ef-

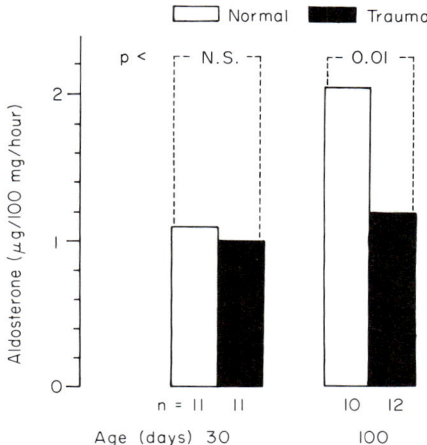

FIG. 8. The effects of neonatal injury on the *in vitro* production of aldosterone by the adrenals in the rat.

fects in aldosterone production was also observed in studies on prematurely weaned rats (Fig. 9). In contrast to corticosterone, the effect of premature weaning on aldosterone production disappeared during sexual maturation (Kraus, 1970). In order to analyze corticosterone production in prematurely weaned animals we investigated gonadectomized rats. To make the study complete, we also investigated aldosterone production (Fig. 10). It was shown that in the absence of sex glands a difference in aldosterone production between normally and prematurely

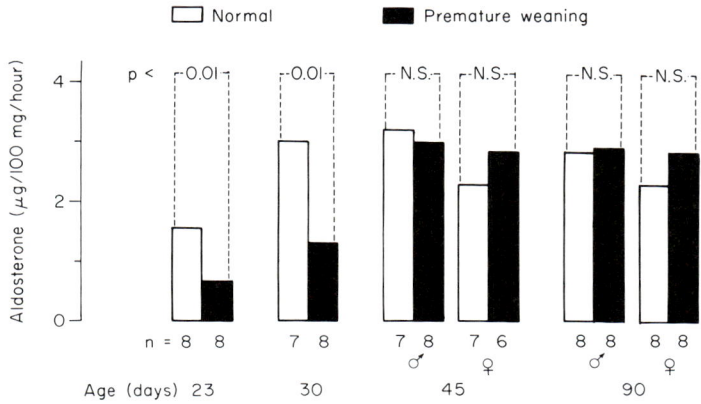

FIG. 9. The effect of premature weaning on the *in vitro* production of aldosterone by the adrenals in the rat.

244   J. KŘEČEK

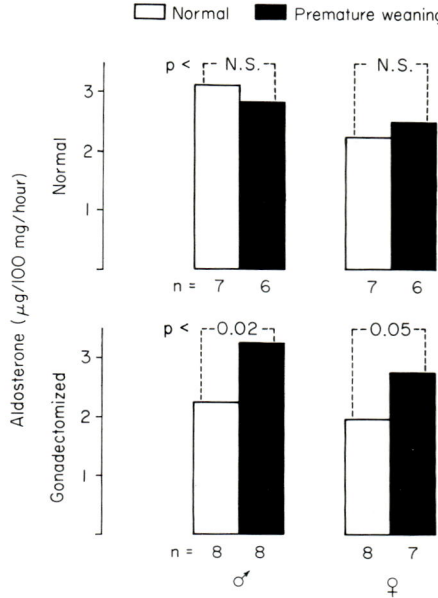

FIG. 10. Gonadectomy and the effect of premature weaning on aldosterone in 45-day-old rats.

weaned rats became detectable at the age of 45 days, in other words, at the stage of sexual maturation. Both gonadectomized prematurely weaned males and females produced more aldosterone than gonadectomized but normally weaned animals.

Hence, sexual maturation disclosed a disorder in aldosterone production caused by perinatal traumatization, but sexual maturation caused the delayed effect of premature weaning to disappear. It seems feasible to say that in some critical periods the sensitivity to environmental stimulation is more pronounced while in others the genetically coded developmental program is more accentuated.

In the female, the beginning of sexual maturation could be taken to be the time of the opening of the vagina which is at the age of about 40 days, but this is not sexual maturation as such. You can find very marked endocrine changes in the hypophysis before this period of vaginal opening, but this does not mean the animal is able to reproduce.

Reproductive capacity begins some three weeks later, at about 60–65 days. But you can alter this so that it can begin earlier or later, by differential feeding. If the animals are well fed, the vagina opens at 40 days. If they are undernourished, the time of opening differs. It is an environmental development process and can therefore not be measured only by days.

The delayed effects of intervention in the perinatal and weaning critical periods can be characterized in general as nonspecific. Osťádalová (1967) showed for example that a perinatal injection of sexual steroid hormones affects irreversibly not only reproductive functions but also body growth, bone metabolism, and other functions. Recently we were able to demonstrate that injection of testosterone at 2 days of age affects even the behavior of animals. If rats were offered a free choice of 3% NaCl solution or water, they consumed such quantities of those fluids as to maintain a defined, relatively stable ratio of salt and water intake. A reasonable indicator of this behavioral regulation is the overall concentration of NaCl in the ingested fluid. This value undergoes changes during postnatal development. After sexual maturation there is an apparent difference between males and females, the concentration being higher in females (Fig. 11). This difference was not abolished by gonadectomy, but did disappear if the rats received an injection of testosterone propionate perinatally. The effect of premature weaning on the behavioral regulation of water intake was also observed by Nováková et al. (1962). It was shown by means of conditioned reflexes elaborated

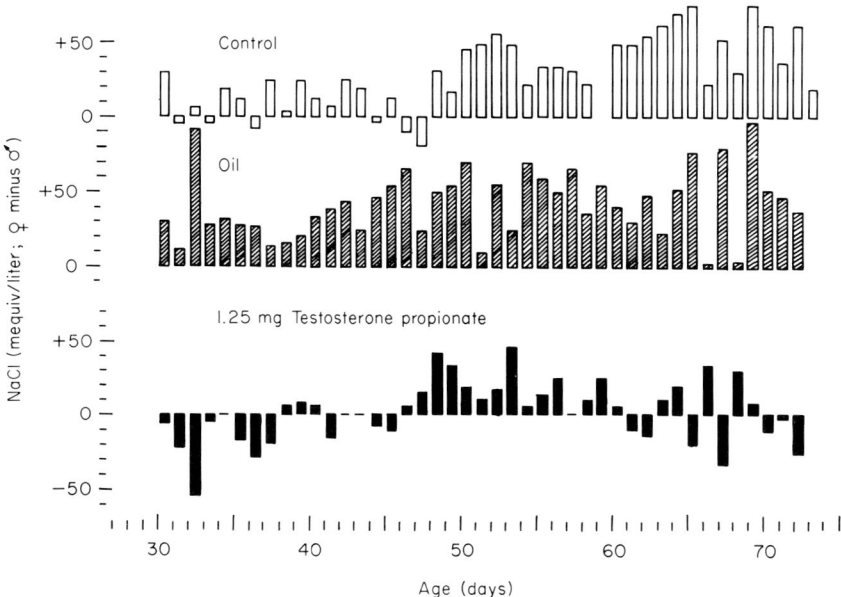

FIG. 11. The delayed effect of neonatal administration of testosterone propionate on sex differences in salt intake in the rat.

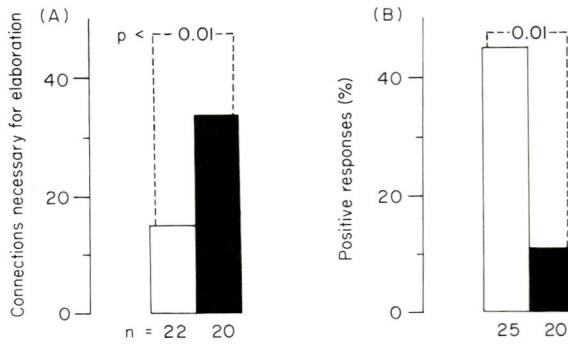

FIG. 12. The effect of premature weaning on higher nervous activity of adult rats. Elaboration of conditioned reflexes (A); retention of elaborated conditioned reflexes (B).

on the basis of water intake that prematurely weaned rats required more connections for the establishment of conditioned reflexes than those weaned normally and that the conditioned reflex extinguishes more quickly in prematurely weaned rats (Fig. 12). The intensity of the effect is dependent on the age of premature weaning.

Nováková (1969) further investigated this phenomenon by looking for changes in cerebral cells. She found that in prematurely weaned rats the concentration of ribonucleic acid in Purkinje cells and in cells of the hippocampus was decreased. Both groups of cells are tetraploid. In the diploid cell population similar changes were observed only in the hypothalamus (Fig. 13).

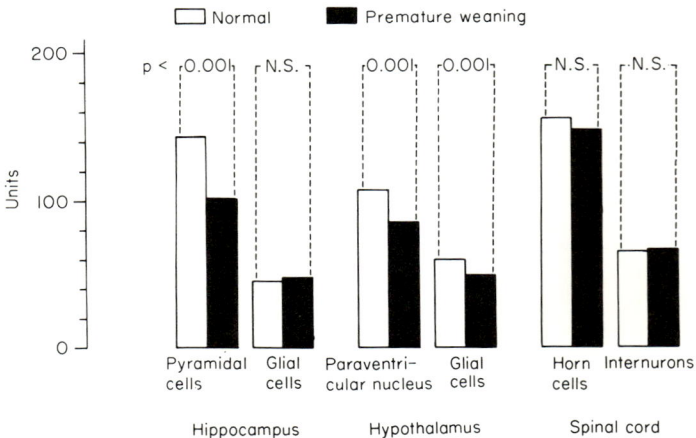

FIG. 13. The effect of premature weaning on RNA content in different neural cells in the rat.

It was shown by Harris (1964) that a perinatal injection of steroid hormones affects hypothalamic functions as well. It seems, therefore, that the reason for the nonspecific delayed effects of interventions in the critical periods may be found in hypothalamic damage. This may also explain why intervention in critical periods so often influences not only endocrine functions, but also the behavior of animals.

I have tried to integrate some findings of our and other laboratories studying the development of endocrine functions by the use of the theory of critical periods. Unfortunately, we know very little in this field, but we are now able to ask questions which we were not able to ask 20 years ago. I hope that future research can help us to answer some of these questions.

REFERENCES

Ader, R. (1962). Social factors affecting emotionality and resistance to disease in animals III. Early weaning and susceptibility to gastric ulcers in the rat. A control for nutritional factors. *J. Comp. Psychol.* Vol. 55, 600.

Babický, A., Ošťádalová, I., Parízek, J., Kolář, J., and Bibr, B. (1970). Use of radioisotope techniques for determining the weaning period in experimental animals. *Physiol. Bohemoslov.* Vol. 19, 457–467.

Barraclough, C. A., and Leathem, J. H. (1954). Infertility induced in mice by a single injection of testosterone propionate. *Proc. Soc. Exp. Biol. Med.* Vol. 85, 673.

Bradbury, J. T. (1941). Permanent after-effects following masculinisation of the infantile female rat. *Endocrinology* Vol. 28, 101.

Denenberg, V. H. (1964). Critical periods, stimulus input and emotional reactivity: A theory of infantile stimulation. *Psychol. Rev.* Vol. 71, 335.

Gorski, R. A., and Arai, Y. (1968). Critical exposure time for androgenisation of the developing hypothalamus in the female rat. *Endocrinology* Vol. 82, 1010.

Gorski, R. A., and Barraclough, C. A. (1962). Studies on hypothalamic regulation of FSH. Secretion in the androgen-sterilized female rat. *Proc. Soc. Exp. Biol. Med.* Vol. 110, 298.

Gorski, R. A., and Barraclough, C. A. (1963). Effects of low dosage of androgen on the differentiation of hypothalamic regulatory control of ovulation in the rat. *Endocrinology* Vol. 73, 210.

Hahn, P., and Koldovský, O. (1966). "Utilisation of Nutrients during postnatal Development." Pergamon Press, Oxford.

Harris, G. W. (1964). The Upjohn lecture of the endocrine society. Sex hormones, brain development and brain function. *Endocrinology* Vol. 75, 627.

King, J. A. (1958). Parameters relevant to determining the effect of early experience upon the adult behaviour of animals. *Psychol. Bull.* Vol. 55, 46.

Koldovský, O., Anděl, J., Dlouhá, H., Faltin, J., Flandera, V., Hahn, P., Kraus, M., Křeček, J., Křečková, J., Kubát, K., Novák, V., and Nováková, V. (1963). The late effects of early weaning. *Proc. 5th Congr. Czech. Physiol. Soc., 1963* p. 133.

Kraus, M. (1970). Individual history and the development of aldosterone regulation. "The Postnatal Development of Phenotype," pp. 151–160. Academic, Prague.

Kraus, M., Anděl, J., Dlouhá, H., Flandera, V., Křeček, J., Křečková, J., and Rokos, J.

(1961). The development and length of life of rats weaned normally and prematurely and living on a free choice of electrolyte solutions. "The Development of Homeostasis," p. 117. Academic Press, New York.

Kraus, M., Křeček, J., and Popp, M. (1967a). The development of corticosterone production by the adrenal gland of normal and prematurely weaned rats. *Physiol. Bohemoslov.* Vol. 16, 120.

Kraus, M., Křeček, J., and Popp, M. (1967b). The development of aldosterone production in normal and prematurely weaned rats. *Biol. Neonatorum* Vol. 11, 338.

Křeček, J. (1962). "The Weaning Period and Water Metabolism." Státní Zdrav. Naklad., Prague (in Czech).

Křeček, J., and Palatý, V. (1967). The effect of premature weaning on the development of androgenic activity in male rats. *Physiol. Bohemoslov.* Vol. 16, 501.

Levine, S. (1957). Infantile experience and resistance to physiological stress. *Nature (London)* Vol. 126, 405.

Levine, S. (1962). Plasma free corticosteroid response to electric shock in rats stimulated in infancy. *Science* Vol. 135, 795.

Levine, S., and Lewis, G. W. (1959). Critical period for effects of infantile experience on maturation of stress response. *Nature (London)* Vol. 129, 42.

Nováková, V. (1966). Role of the mother during the suckling period of newborn rats on subsequent adult learning. *Physiol. Behav.* Vol. 1, 219.

Nováková, V., Faltin, J., Flandera, V., Hahn, P., and Koldovský, O. (1962). Effect of early and late weaning on learning in adult rats. *Nature (London)* Vol. 193, 280.

Nováková, V., Schlütter, G., and Sandritter, W. (1969). RNS-Gesamtmenge der Ganglienzellen des Zentralnervensystems bei normal und frühentwöhnten Ratten. *Virchows Arch., B* Vol. 4, 1.

Oštádalová, I. (1967). On some late effects of administration of estrogen in early postnatal period. Dissertation, Prague (in Czech).

Pfeiffer, C. A. (1936). Sexual differences of the hypophysis and their determination by the gonads. *Amer. J. Anat.* Vol. 58, 195.

Scott, J. P. (1962). Critical periods in behavioral development. *Science* Vol. 138, 949.

HORMONAL FACTORS CONTROLLING THE DIFFERENTIATION, DEVELOPMENT, AND DISPLAY OF COPULATORY BEHAVIOR IN THE RAMSTERGIG AND RELATED SPECIES

FRANK A. BEACH

Introduction

The ramstergig (*Iurasequens sexualis*)[1] is a hitherto undescribed species of rodent belonging to the order *Myostrichomorpha*. The species is unique in that all relationships between its anatomical, physiological, and behavioral characteristics are completely known and never subject to controversy. This applies to every stage of the ramstergig's life from formation of the zygote to death.

The ramstergig is a monotypic species, but it shares many characteristics with the rat, the hamster, and the guinea pig, three species which also have served as subjects in numerous experiments on the development of sexual functions, including mating behavior. It is the purpose of this paper to compare the established facts concerning the ramstergig with our less perfect knowledge of development and behavior in the other three species. To anticipate one of our conclusions concerning the epigenesis of brain mechanisms mediating coital behavior, it can be said that the neurontogeny of the ramstergig follows precisely current theories describing the "organizational" action of gonadal hormones. The same statement cannot be made with equal confidence when we consider the rat, the hamster, or the guinea pig.

---

[1] The anonymous zoologist who first described the ramstergig was an indifferent classicist. Intending to name it "Follower of sexual laws," he actually applied the designation "Sexual follower of laws." This doesn't appear to have made any lasting difference.

Normal Development of the Reproductive System

Epigenesis of the reproductive system follows much the same course in all of the species with which this paper is concerned. Three consecutive stages are involved.

FIRST STAGE

The gonads have not yet differentiated, and both males and females possess a Wolffian duct system and a Müllerian duct system. Within the central nervous system of the ramstergig the cells or cell systems which eventually will mediate copulatory behavior are as yet undifferentiated, and there is still no variation between the sexes. The situation with respect to the other three rodent species is less clear-cut. There is a possibility that the brains of both males and females contain anlagen for two systems, one capable of developing into mechanisms for mediation of masculine responses and the other having the potential for developing into mechanisms for feminine responses. If they do, indeed, exist, these presumptive neural systems might be considered analogous, but only generally so, to the Wolffian and Müllerian systems.

SECOND STAGE

As a consequence of differences in the chromosomal constitution of males and females, the gonads of XY individuals differentiate into testes, while those of XX individuals give rise to ovaries. The fetal ovary produces no secretions, but the embryonic testis releases into the bloodstream a fetal morphogenetic testicular substance (FMTS) which has effects upon both of the associated duct systems. In the presence of FMTS the Wolffian duct system differentiates and develops, giving rise to the vas deferens, seminal vesicle, and epididymis. At the same time FMTS may act to prevent development of the Müllerian duct, which, as a consequence, degenerates and eventually disappears altogether. In the absence of FMTS, i.e., in the genetic female, the Wolffian system is not stimulated but degenerates and finally disappears, whereas the Müllerian system develops into Fallopian tubes, uterus, and upper vagina.

The FMTS has no known effects upon the central nervous system of the ramstergig. In the rat, hamster, and guinea pig only one thing is certain. If the anlangen for duplicate or bisexual mechanisms exist, they do not respond to FMTS as do the Wolffian and Müllerian systems. That is to say tissues capable of giving rise to neural circuits for mediation of the masculine coital pattern do not degenerate in the female, and those with a potential for producing feminine mechanisms in the brain are not eliminated in the male.

THIRD STAGE

At birth in the ramstergig, rat, and hamster, and earlier in development of the guinea pig, males and females possess a genital tubercle which is not yet differentiated into either a masculine or feminine genital structure. In the normal course of events the genital tubercle of the male undergoes differentiation to form a penis and scrotum. These changes depend in part upon stimulation by androgen, which is available in the form of testosterone secreted by the testes. This is quite different from the FMTS, which operates earlier in ontogeny. In females, where testosterone is lacking, the tubercle gives rise to a clitoris and external vagina, including the major and minor labia. It is important to note that since the masculine and feminine structures are derived from the same original, undifferentiated tissues, it is impossible for the same individual to possess both a clitoris *and* a penis, or a scrotum *and* an external vagina. The alternatives are mutually exclusive.

"ORGANIZATIONAL" EFFECTS ON THE NERVOUS SYSTEM

The third stage in the development of the reproductive system is of special importance in connection with the eventual display of copulatory behavior because in the ramstergig differentiation or organization of brain mechanisms controlling masculine or feminine mating responses is governed by the same processes which direct differentiation of the external genitalia. In the male, testicular androgen induces the organization of central nervous system circuits specialized for the mediation of mounting, thrusting, intromitting, and ejaculating. Absence of testosterone in the female prevents the organization of the aforementioned mechanisms but permits the development of alternative circuits suited to the mediation of feminine receptive responses, including lordosis. As in the case of genital development, these two alternatives are mutually exclusive in ramstergigs, and therefore the ramstergig is what is known technically as a "straight" species. Males always engage exclusively in masculine sexual behavior and females display only the feminine mating pattern.

We have indicated that in the male ramstergig androgen exerts an "organizing action" on the nervous system, and particularly upon the brain. When applied to other species, this type of effect is carefully discriminated from the "activating action" that the same hormone exerts upon fully developed neural mechanisms in the adult animal (Phoenix *et al.*, 1959). As applied to the ramstergig, the concept of hormones as organizers is derived directly from a theory generated by early experiments in embryology.

Spemann (1938) and his contemporaries noted that one of the first steps in the development of the vertebrate central nervous system consists of formation of a neural tube from ectodermal tissue situated near the dorsal lip of the blastopore. Operating on blastocysts of various species, these early workers removed ectodermal tissue from other regions of the embryo and grafted it into place adjacent to the dorsal lip. If this was done at precisely the right time in development, the transplanted cells gave rise to a neural tube. In other words, cells which normally would have become skin of the back or belly could be caused to develop into part of the nervous system. Many comparable experiments with other tissues and other presumptive organs provided evidence supporting the theory that certain regions in the developing embryo produce chemical substances which were named "organizers" because of their apparent ability to induce organization of specialized structures from previously undifferentiated tissues irrespective of the normal end product or presumptive "fate" of that tissue.

In the male ramstergig endogenous testosterone functions as an organizer, acting upon previously undifferentiated neural tissue to induce development of a specialized mechanism which in adulthood will be responsive to androgen and will mediate the execution of exclusively masculine coital responses. Because testosterone is lacking in the female ramstergig, her brain develops in the opposite direction and gives rise to a mechanism which in adulthood will be sensitive to ovarian hormones and will mediate exclusively the feminine mating pattern.

Some of the investigators who have studied sexual development in the rat and guinea pig have published statements which could be interpreted to mean that central nervous system development in these species follows the same course as it does in the ramstergig. For example, after examining the mating responses of female guinea pigs exposed prenatally to androgen, Gerall (1966, p. 367) reached the following conclusion.

> The hypothesis to which the data of the present study primarily relate has been outlined by Young and his co-workers (Phoenix *et al.*, 1959; Young *et al.*, 1964), Harris (1964), and Levine and Mullins (1964). Essentially it is suggested that, as in the case of somatic tissue development, neural regions pass through an undifferentiated stage during which they possess bisexual potentiality. Whether a neural region develops into a female or male behavior integrating unit is determined primarily by the presence of an androgenic substance which, whether elaborated by the embryonic testes or injected, "organizes" or induces the undifferentiated sexual neural areas to develop into a center regulating male be-

havior. In the absence of such a substance, the intrinsic tendency in mammals is for the relevant neural tissue to be organized into female behavior controlling regions.

A related point of view was expressed by Phoenix et al. (1968, p. 35) in an article summarizing a great deal of experimental work done by W. C. Young and his colleagues.

> We viewed the action of the gonadal hormones on central nervous tissue in the developing fetus as analagous to their action on genital tract tissue, including those tissues constituting the external genitalia.

Elsewhere in the same review these authorities recorded their conclusions (Phoenix et al., 1968, p. 36).

> ... androgens, or some particular androgens [were] the hormone responsible for determining the organization of the neural tissues that mediated sexual behavior.

Twenty-three years before publication of the foregoing conclusions the present author had written as follows (Beach, 1945, p. 400).

> The sex hormones are best regarded not as stimuli or as organizing agents but as chemical sensitizers which alter the stimulability of critical mechanisms within the central nervous system.

We shall now proceed to review the evidence which has given rise to this type of interpretation. We will begin by concentrating on experiments and observations dealing with the domestic rat, temporarily bypassing results obtained with hamsters and guinea pigs but examining studies of these two species later. If we can first establish clearly the most important differences between rats and ramstergigs this will provide a useful starting point for examination of differences and similarities between the remaining rodent species.

Bases for Current Theories Concerning "Mechanisms" Mediating Copulatory Behavior

During the first two decades of the current century biologists were intensely interested in problems of sexual differentiation and its possible control by endocrine factors. Partly as a result of Lillie's classic analysis of the freemartin (1917) considerable emphasis was placed upon the notion that testicular secretions had the capacity to "induce" masculine characters, whereas ovarian secretions "induced" feminine attributes.

Some experimentalists reported that appropriate manipulation of the endocrine system at the proper stage of development could induce reversal of behavioral as well as morphological characters. Steinach (1912) and Moore (1919) claimed that they had produced feminine mating responses in male rats by ovarian transplants. A few contemporary investigators felt that the reported findings were not conclusive proof of sex reversal. Stone (1924) argued against the position that an individual's behavior was of necessity exclusively either masculine or feminine, and he described untreated and morphologically normal male rats which mated with receptive females in male fashion and reacted to mounting by other males with adoption of the feminine copulatory pattern. Another male rat of the same type was later reported by the present writer, who also described the execution of portions of the masculine coital pattern by normal females of the same species (Beach, 1938). These observations led to the following conclusion (p. 334).

> The specificity of the mating patterns for the two sexes, although probably inherited, is not rigidly dictated by the innately organized substratum. . . . it is obvious that in a few individuals at least, there exists the innate organization essential to the mediation of the mating pattern of either sex. The presence or absence of such duplicate arrangement within all individuals is a matter for speculation.

A study by Pfeiffer in 1936 included no data regarding behavior, but he was the first to show that testicular secretion during the first few days of life had a permanent effect upon certain pituitary functions in adult rats. Normally in this species the female pituitary functions cyclically, first inducing the growth of ovarian follicles, then stimulating the occurrence of ovulation, and later inducing another phase of follicular growth to be followed again by ovulation. When ovaries were implanted in male rats castrated in adulthood, follicles were stimulated to grow, but ovulation did not occur. Pfeiffer's contribution was to demonstrate that if males were castrated at birth and given ovarian transplants in adulthood, the ovaries underwent regular cycles of folliculogenesis and ovulation in the characteristic female rhythm. To this extent genetic males deprived of testicular secretions from birth have been "feminized."

Twenty years later, after much additional research, G. W. Harris concluded that the essential difference between pituitary gonadotropic function in male and female rats rested upon differences in the hypothalamus, and that the establishment of a masculine acyclic pattern of hormone secretion (lacking the ovulation phase) depended upon stimulation of the hypothalamus by testis hormone during the first few days of life. Harris wrote as follows (1955), ". . . it seems likely that some neural structure in the male animal becomes differentiated and fixed in its function under the influence of androgens in early life."

Harris' point of view assumed particular importance for interpretations of behavior when, in 1962, he and Levine reported that female rats injected with androgen at 5 days of age did not ovulate in adulthood and furthermore *would not copulate with males* even when they were supplied with normally adequate amounts of exogenous ovarian hormones. It began to appear that the neural structures which are "differentiated and fixed . . . under the influence of androgens in early life" might include mechanisms responsible for the mediation of copulatory performance.

This conclusion had already been reached independently by Phoenix *et al.* (1959) as a result of experiments in which pregnant guinea pigs were injected with testosterone propionate. The female offspring of treated mothers displayed varying degrees of masculinization of the external genitalia plus reduction or elimination of the tendency to display feminine copulatory behavior when treated with estrogen and progesterone in adulthood. Prenatal exposure to androgen also increased the tendency for masculinized females to execute mounting responses after the administration of testosterone in adult life. Phoenix *et al.* interpreted these findings as evidence for an "organizing effect" of androgen upon the developing brain (1959). "The embryonic and fetal periods are periods of organization and differentiation in the direction of masculinization or feminization."

The current theoretical position of many writers with regard to effects of gonadal hormone during early development can be stated in condensed form as follows.

1. Presence of androgen during a limited period of high sensitivity in the central nervous system affects the individual in such a way that later in life androgen tends to increase the probability that behavior typical of the genetic male (mounting, thrusting, intromitting, and ejaculating) will occur in response to appropriate external stimulation. A qualitatively similar effect can be induced to a greater or lesser degree in genetic females by exposing them to androgenic stimulation during the sensitive period.

2. In the absence of androgen during the sensitive period of central nervous system growth the individual tends to develop in such a manner that during adulthood there is an increased probability of the occurrence of such feminine responses as lordosis under the influence of ovarian hormones and appropriate exteroceptive stimulation. This state of affairs comes about normally in genetic females since they lack endogenous testosterone during development. Because of the absence of androgen the development of mechanisms for masculine behavior is prevented. A

similar condition can be produced to varying degrees in genetic males by prenatal treatment with antiandrogens or by castration at birth.

Control of Genital Growth and Mating Behavior in Male Rats

POSTNATAL GROWTH OF THE PENIS

Since the effects of androgen on development of the sex organs and of central neural mechanisms controlling behavior have been described as analogous, it is instructive to examine the ways in which testis hormone affects the penis. At the time of birth the genital tubercle of male rats is quite small and bears no external resemblance to a penis. Nevertheless, even if a male is castrated within a few hours after birth the tubercle eventually develops into a recognizable penis which is very small but complete in all of its parts and in their physical interrelations. In other words postnatally secreted gonadal hormone is not needed for the differentiation or "organization" of this structure. Of course at an earlier point in development prenatal testosterone may exert effects which in turn influence the nature of postnatal genital growth (Nadler, 1969).

Although it differentiates normally in the absence of postnatal testosterone, the penis of neonatally castrated rats does not possess normal capacities for growth. Beach and Holz (1946) castrated males at 1, 21, 50, 100, 150, and 350 days of age. Approximately 100 days after operation all castrates were given a series of testosterone injections after which different parts of the penis were measured. Some of the results are shown in Fig. 1. It is apparent that when they were given testosterone starting at 100 days of age neonatal castrates failed to exhibit penile growth comparable to that exhibited by males which had been gonadectomized at 3 weeks of age. The latter group was nearly as responsive as 50-day castrates, although there may have been some slight impairment of growth in males deprived of the testes at 21 days of age.

More recently, the effects of early castration and androgen treatment on the rat penis have been reexamined in the author's laboratory with a different approach (Beach *et al.*, 1969). Separate groups of males castrated on the day of birth were treated with testosterone propionate (TP) at different times during the first 2 weeks of life. Then, beginning at approximately 300 days of age, several animals from each group were subjected to a prolonged series of daily injections of the same androgen. At the conclusion of treatment comparisons of penis size were made between the various injected groups and between groups that had received

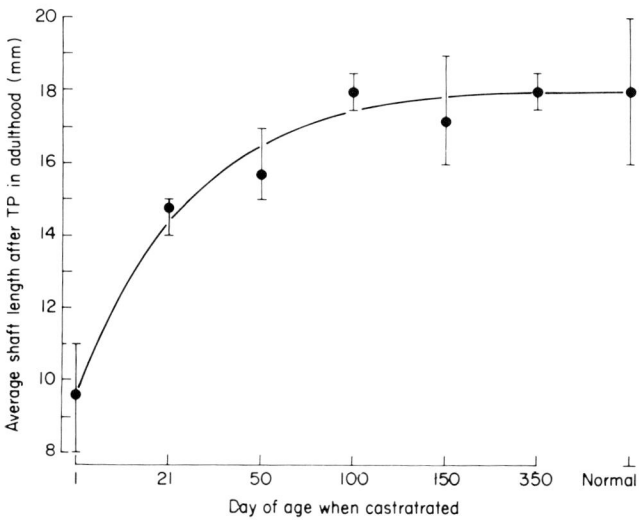

FIG. 1. The effect of age at castration on penis growth in response to TP treatment in adulthood.

androgen at different times in infancy but no follow-up treatment in adulthood.

The results as summarized in Table 1 were clear and convincing. Among neonatal castrates which had received no androgen treatment in adulthood there were no systematic intergroup differences in penis

TABLE 1
Effects of Androgen Treatment in Adulthood on the Penis of Neonatally Castrated Rats[a]

Days after birth when androgen was given	Androgen given in adulthood				No androgen in adulthood			
	N	Shaft length (cm)	Glans diameter (cm)	Penis weight/ body weight	N	Shaft length (cm)	Glans diameter (cm)	Penis weight/ body weight
No androgen	4	1.30	2.35	0.030				
1 and 2	4	1.70	2.90	0.063	6	1.30	2.18	0.020
3 and 4	4	1.90	2.86	0.053	5	1.17	1.93	0.017
5 and 6	5	1.60	2.83	0.047	4	1.17	2.12	0.022
9 and 10	4	1.45	2.81	0.037	4	1.30	2.10	0.021
13 and 14	4	1.42	2.47	0.034	1	1.40	1.73	0.011
Intact males					4	2.30	3.25	0.066

[a] Beach et al., 1969.

size. There were, in other words, no obvious effects of the testosterone which had been injected on two consecutive days between the first and fourteenth day of life. Nevertheless, very important intergroup differences existed, and these were differences in sensitivity or potential for growth in response to androgen treatment in adulthood.

When testosterone injections were instituted while the animals were approximately 300 days old, those males which had been given exogenous androgen on the first and second or third and fourth days of life showed the most marked penile growth, and those given no treatment in infancy showed the least. Rats in whom perinatal treatment had been delayed until 2 weeks of age were only slightly more responsive than untreated controls to testosterone treatment in adulthood. Penis size in the remaining groups fell between these two extremes, and there was a strong indication that capacity for phallic growth under the influence of exogenous androgen supplied in adulthood was systematically related to the time after birth at which the "priming" treatment with testosterone had been administered.

MOUNTING, INTROMISSION, AND EJACULATION RESPONSES

In the normal male ramstergig development of the neural mechanisms responsible for mediation of "masculine" copulatory responses is totally dependent upon the presence of endogenous testicular androgen during the period of high neural sensitivity. If androgen is lacking at this time, the mechanisms will not develop, and in adulthood the affected individuals cannot be induced to show any elements of the male copulatory pattern. The situation is less clear-cut in the case of the male rat.

Males Castrated in Infancy

Some investigators believe that the neural basis for masculine copulatory performance never becomes completely organized in male rats that have been castrated within the first 4 days of life, but other workers have questioned this conclusion. In our 1946 study on the effects of castrating male rats at different ages Holz and I set forth the following conclusion (p. 138).

> It may be concluded that, with the important exception of its effects upon the initial stages of penis growth, postnatally secreted testis hormone is not essential to the development and functional organization of mechanisms for sexual behavior in the male rat.

This conclusion was based upon several considerations.

1. The responses of all males to receptive females were tested in adulthood before androgen therapy began. The scale employed ranged from 0 ("no response to female or only brief, initial investigation") to 5 ("mounting at least once with complete copulatory pattern"). The pattern referred to is described nowadays as "mounting with intromission." Application of this scale to the results of three preinjection tests showed that the average score for males castrated at birth was 2.78, whereas averages for all other groups of untreated castrates ranged from 1.26 to 2.00. In other words, without any androgen treatment day-1 castrates actually were more responsive to estrous females than castrates in any of the other five groups.

2. When injections of testosterone propionate began, the neonatal castrates responded more rapidly than any other group in terms of first showing mounting without and mounting with the intromission pattern. The average amount of TP injected before the first display of the intromission response was 2.3 mg in the case of the day-1 castrates, and for the remaining five groups (castrated from day 21 to day 350), corresponding averages ranged from 2.7 mg (day 350) to 3.7 mg (day 150). Judged on this basis, the responsiveness or sensitivity of neonatal castrates to exogenous androgen administered in adulthood exceeded the responsiveness of males which had been castrated at later ages.

3. No matter how much androgen they received in adulthood, neonatal castrates showed the insertion pattern much less frequently than members of any other group. Although this response was shown by 100% of all groups, the average frequency per test in which it occurred at least once was 4.1 for day-1 castrates versus 7.3 to 18.0 per test for the other groups. Almost certainly, it was this infrequency of intromission and the consequent limitation of penile stimulation which accounted for the fact that only one of the neonatal castrates ever reached the point of ejaculation; and he did so only once.

Although the frequency of apparent intromission was limited by the possession of a very small penis, the overall response of day-1 castrates to receptive females clearly revealed marked and continuing sensitivity to the exogenous androgen treatment. During tests in which mount-without-intromission responses occurred they were shown an average of 3.8–7.3 times per test by rats which had been castrated between the ages of 21 and 350 days, but the average for day-1 castrates was 26.0 times per test. The average frequency in the first 15 tests while testosterone was being administered rose steadily from 10.2 to 42.0 per test. There seems to be no reason for doubting that the responsiveness of day-1 castrates to exogenous androgen was at least as great as that of males gonadectomized later in life.

TABLE 2

Copulatory Responses Shown by Male Rats before and after Removal of Part of the Os Penis[a]

Male	Mean frequency per test in 3 tests before operation			Mean frequency per test in 3 tests after operation		
	Mount without insertion	Mount with insertion	Ejaculation	Mount without insertion	Mount with insertion	Ejaculation
1	3.7	11.7	1.0	13.0	3.0	0
2	1.3	9.7	1.0	12.7	1.7	0
3	0.3	11.7	0.7	20.7	3.0	0

[a] Beach and Holz, 1946.

4. Because of our belief that the behavior of neonatal castrates differed from that of other groups solely because intromission ability was impaired by lack of penis development, Holz and I prepared an additional group of males to test the effects of intromission failure. Three rats which had demonstrated normal copulatory behavior in three preoperative tests were subjected to an operation in which approximately 5 mm of the *os penis* were removed. In a fourth male the bone was cut but not removed. The results are shown in Table 2.

The control rat with the sham operation showed an average per test of 0.7 mounts without insertion, 9.0 mounts with insertion, and 1.0 ejaculation. In contrast, the three animals deprived of a segment of the baculum exhibited a copulatory pattern identical with that displayed by day-1 castrates under the influence of exogenous androgen. This behavior was characterized by a high frequency of mounts without insertion, low frequency of mounts with insertion, and absence of ejaculation. Inasmuch as the three males in this supplementary experiment were endocrinologically normal, it seems reasonable to refer the postoperative change in behavior exclusively to mechanical difficulty which reduced the frequency of insertion and thus deprived the animals of sufficient genital stimulation to elicit ejaculation. Precisely the same explanation can be applied to the mating performance of neonatally castrated males without any additional assumption of deficiencies in hypothetical mechanisms within the central nervous system.

Behavioral results obtained in the study by Beach and co-workers (1969) revealed a relationship between the time of androgen treatment in infancy and the coital performance of neonatal castrates under the influence of exogenous testosterone in adulthood. Mounting and thrusting without intromission occurred at about the same rate in all groups, demonstrating that androgen treatment in adulthood was equally stimu-

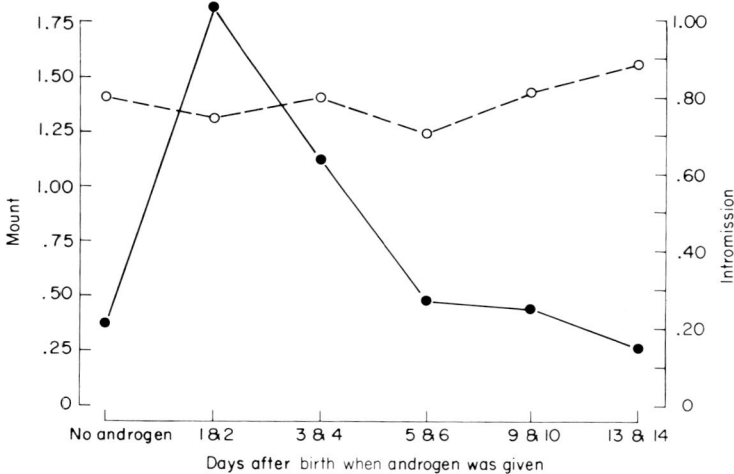

FIG. 2. Two types of mounting by adult male rats castrated at birth and given TP at different times after birth. ○----○, mount with thrust; ●——●, intromission pattern; responses are per minute. (From Beach et al., 1969.)

lating regardless of the occurrence and timing of testosterone therapy in infancy (Fig. 2). In contrast, the rate at which mounts with intromission were achieved was plainly influenced by the age at which androgen had been given during the first 2 weeks of life.

We believe that intromission frequency was controlled by penis size, and this conclusion is supported by the relationship shown in Fig. 3.

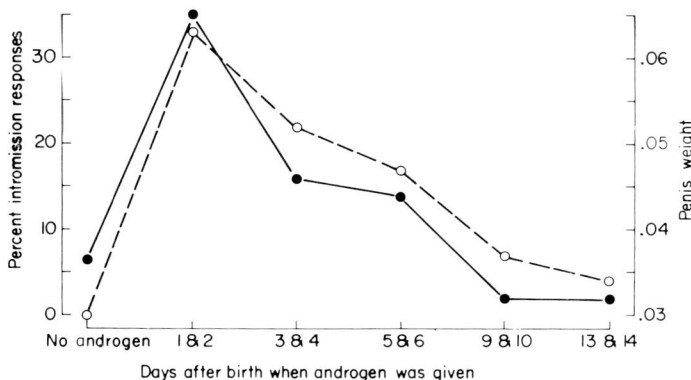

FIG. 3. Relative frequency of intromission (percent) compared with penis weight ratio in male rats castrated at birth and given TP on different days postpartum. ○----○, penis weight ratio; ●——●, percent intromission responses. (From Beach et al., 1969.)

Behavior is represented by the percentage of all mounts that involved intromission, and penis size is reflected in the ratio penis weight/body weight. It can be seen that the two measures show high covariance as a function of the age that testosterone was given during infancy.

Gerall *et al.* (1967) also found that male rats castrated at birth and treated with testosterone in adulthood exhibited a high frequency of mounting but never ejaculated. Furthermore, of 12 males castrated by day 5 postpartum, only one ejaculated. These workers reached the following conclusion with respect to the effects of postnatally secreted or injected androgen (p. 212).

> The male pattern ... probably is related to development of a penile organ. Penile weights ... are inversely related to the age of castration. In the present study ... there is a correspondence between some aspect of the structure of the penis and the presence of the ejaculatory response in the male. Therefore, early androgen appears to permanently affect metabolic processes in the somatic organs and may determine their capacity to provide adequate feedback necessary to exceed thresholds for evoking various response systems and consummatory reflex mechanisms.

A recent study by Stern (1969) reveals that neonatally castrated male rats injected daily with 25 μg of androstenedione for 20 days postpartum respond to ovarian hormones in adulthood by exhibiting lordosis as frequently as either neonatal castrates given no treatment in infancy or normal females. By this criterion the androstenedione did not interfere with "organization" of the female pattern in the genetic males. However, when the same rats were treated with TP in adulthood, all of them copulated and ejaculated, which proves that central nervous system mechanisms for masculine coital performance were functional. Neonatally castrated males given no treatment in infancy mounted quite frequently after TP administration in adulthood but achieved intromission very rarely and never ejaculated. The key difference between the two groups was in penis length, which was 19.5 mm in androstenedione-treated males and only 16.1 mm in the control castrates.

Goldfoot *et al.* (1969), in a very similar investigation which antedated that of Stern, obtained almost identical results. Although only 33% of their androstenedione-treated subjects ejaculated as compared with 100% of Stern's rats, in both groups some neonatally castrated males showed both lordosis and the full male pattern after receiving androstenedione in infancy.

Males Treated with Antiandrogen or Estrogen Early in Development

We have already noted that when pregnant rats are treated with the antiandrogen cyproterone and their male offspring are also given cyproterone in infancy, the males do not exhibit normal masculine copulatory responses in adulthood with TP treatment (Neumann and Elger, 1965). The original report included no quantitative description of behavior shown by the "feminized" males, but more recently, Nadler (1969) has provided the necessary details. Male rats exposed to cyproterone in fetal life and given TP as adults mount receptive females very frequently but rarely achieve intromission and never ejaculate. Nadler believes that the behavioral deficiency is due chiefly to the very small phallus possessed by cyproterone-treated males.

Estrogen administered to neonatally castrated male rats within 4 days postpartum increases the frequency of mounting behavior when the subjects are treated with androgen in adulthood (Whalen and Edwards, 1967; Levine and Mullins, 1964). However, males subjected to such treatment do not execute normal coital responses (Levine and Mullins, 1964; Whalen, 1964; Harris and Levine, 1965). Although mounting may occur frequently, it often is misdirected with the result that intromission and ejaculation are not achieved (Levine and Mullins, 1964; Whalen, 1964).

Feder (1967) administered estrogen to intact male rats 2 to 5 days after birth and to other males 20 days postpartum. In the first groups masculine coital responses shown in adulthood were incomplete, but in the group treated later the pattern was normal. It is relevant to observe that administration of estrogen to male rats shortly after birth permanently reduces penile growth (Arai, 1964).

LORDOSIS, DARTING AND CROUCHING, AND EAR WIGGLING

Since they do not possess neural mechanisms capable of mediating feminine copulatory behavior, male ramstergigs never show lordosis or any ancillary receptive responses. Administration of ovarian hormones has no effect upon their behavior. In the male rat the situation is quite different.

Normal Male Rats without Experimental Treatment

Observations by Stone (1924) and Beach (1938) of the display of lordosis by untreated male rats which also exhibited normal masculine copulation show that neural mechanisms for both patterns can develop and function in the same individual. The most extensive study of bisexual behavior in a male rat was reported by the present writer (Beach, 1945). The male involved was exceptionally responsive to receptive females. Most male rats placed with an estrous female reach the point of ejaculation after achieving 8 to 10 intromissions. Following a post-ejaculatory rest of approximately 5 minutes, copulation is resumed, and the second ejaculation usually occurs after approximately 5 to 6 intromissions. The male which showed receptive behavior was observed in three tests with estrous females. In the first test his score was 5 intromissions and 2 ejaculations. In the second it was 9 intromissions and 3 ejaculations, and in the third it was 13 intromissions and 4 ejaculations. Anyone who has conducted mating tests on rats will recognize this as a unique demonstration of masculine copulatory performance.

In the course of three tests with male partners the experimental male was mounted 13, 13, and 19 times and showed lordosis 11, 12, and 12 times. The resulting average Lordosis Quotient of 83 falls well within the range shown by intact estrous females. In the same three tests the experimental male exhibited the darting and crouching response 17, 7, and 10 times, and displayed ear wiggling 9, 2, and 7 times. This combination of lordosis and ancillary feminine responses rendered the male's behavior qualitatively and quantitatively comparable to that of a normal female in full behavioral estrus. Histological examination of the testes and seminal vesicles revealed normal spermatogenesis and testosterone secretion. Here again is evidence to prove that mechanisms for both feminine and masculine coital patterns can differentiate and function side by side in the same brain, so to speak.

Despite the existence of a few behaviorally bisexual males, there is a good deal of evidence to prove that in most male rats the frequency and completeness of receptive behavior can be markedly increased by appropriate manipulation of the endocrine condition early in development.

Males Exposed to Antiandrogen Pre- and Postnatally

Neumann and Elger (1965) treated pregnant rats with cyproterone and continued the same treatment of male offspring postnatally. It is reported that these males exhibited female behavior when given ovarian hormone in adulthood. This report did not include the quantitative measures necessary to evaluate the degree of "behavioral feminization" that had occurred, but a subsequent study of Nadler (1969) provides the essential data. The percentage of Nadler's cyproterone-treated males displaying lordosis after estrogen and progesterone treatment in adulthood was nearly equal to the percentage of normal females so responding, and the average Lordosis Quotients of the two groups were essentially the same.

Males Castrated in Infancy

Numerous experiments have shown that if male rats are castrated at birth and treated with estrogen and progesterone in adulthood, they will display receptive behavior comparable in quantity and quality to that exhibited by estrous females (Harris, 1964; Grady et al., 1965; Feder and Whalen, 1965; Walen and Edwards, 1966; Beach et al., 1969). Grady and co-workers (1965) castrated male rats at 10 days of age and reported that such animals "failed to give typical female responses when injected with ovarian hormones." It is added, "[these findings] supported our hypothesis that it is the presence of testicular hormone during the period of differentiation that masculinizes the individual."

Treatment of Neonatal Castrates with Gonadal Hormones

If neonatally castrated male rats are injected with TP within the first 5 days postpartum, they display very little if any receptive behavior in adulthood (Harris and Levine, 1962; Grady et al., 1965; Whalen and Edwards, 1967). The effects of androgen treatment of neonatal castrates are reduced if the hormone is given at 9 and 10 days of age; and androgen administered when the castrates are 13 and 14 days old has no inhibiting influence on the response to estrogen and progesterone in adulthood (Beach et al., 1969).

The results of castration at birth and of treating infant castrates with testosterone are clearly in accord with the theory that the neural basis for receptive behavior in male rats is organized provided androgen is absent and that the organizational process is inhibited or disrupted if androgen is present during the first 5 or 6 days of life. However, evidence based upon the behavior of neonatal castrates does not compel acceptance of this particular interpretation for all species. For example, a study of receptive behavior shown by male guinea pigs castrated in infancy led to the following conclusion (Gerall et al., 1967, p. 211).

> It is improbable that the presence of the lordosis response in the neonatally castrated male is due to experimentally induced differentiation of a female neural system. This response can be induced in normal male guinea pigs for a short period after birth . . . Therefore, formation of the neural mechanism necessary for lordosis is probably independent of hormones in both sexes.

There are other lines of evidence to suggest that even in the rat, interference with receptive responses in adulthood does not demand the presence of testicular hormone during development. It is not necessary to treat neonatally castrated rats with androgen in order to depress or eliminate their subsequent display of receptive behavior following administration of estrogen and progesterone. Precisely the same result can be achieved if infant castrates are injected with estradiol benzoate during the sensitive period (Feder and Whalen, 1965; Levine and Mullins, 1964; Whalen and Edwards, 1967). This shows that a nonandrogenic gonadal steroid can interfere with development of the neural organization for feminine responses, but it does not disprove the theory that such inhibition normally is controlled by endogenous testosterone. There is, however, still other evidence that necessitates reexamination of this tenet.

Male Rats Castrated as Juveniles or as Adults

Mention has been made of male rats that display the complete mating patterns of both sexes without receiving any experimental treatment. The execution of mounting, intromission, and ejaculation indicates that these individuals developed under the influence of endogenous androgen, but their display of lordosis and ancillary receptive responses shows that androgen failed to inhibit organization of the brain mechanisms mediating feminine behavior. It can now be added that even in "normal" male rats the basis for receptive behavior *does* differentiate despite the presence of testis hormone in infancy.

Grady and co-workers (1965) were unable to elicit appreciable degrees of receptive behavior in male rats that had been castrated 10 days postpartum, but later studies show that this can be achieved provided the appropriate schedule of estrogen treatment is followed. In all of the experiments mentioned thus far male rats have been tested for receptive behavior under the influence of hormonal treatment which is known to elicit receptivity in spayed females. This customarily consists of one or two injections of estradiol benzoate followed 2 days later by one injection of progesterone.

Davidson (1969) castrated male rats in adulthood and studied their behavior after administration of estradiol benzoate. Amounts of estrogen adequate to elicit the complete feminine mating pattern in spayed females were ineffective when given to castrated males, but a series of eight daily injections beginning 6 weeks postoperatively evoked lordosis behavior at "a level approaching that seen in females at the height of behavioral receptivity." The addition of progesterone had no effect on this behavior.

Other investigators have reported confirmatory results. Male rats castrated at 30 days of age have been induced to exhibit the lordosis response after 26 daily injections of estradiol benzoate starting on the 73rd day (Aren-Engelbrektsson *et al.*, 1970). In this experiment the receptive behavior evokable in males castrated at 30 days was inferior to that shown by estrous females or by males castrated at birth and given ovarian hormones in adulthood. It consisted of sluggishly performed lordosis responses to strong mounts by stimulus males. There was none of the ancillary behavior (darting and crouching, ear wiggling, etc.) which marks the behavior of fully receptive females and of at least some neonatally castrated male rats. Nevertheless, the lordosis response was shown by 73 to 90% of the males in different treatment groups. Furthermore, the reaction occurred with an average frequency of 13.0 per test for males receiving 106 μg/day and 5.0 per test for rats receiving 10 μg/day. This is sufficient evidence to show (i) that the neural substrate for the lordosis response is functionally organized, and (ii) that the response to exogenous estrogen is to some degree dose dependent, a fact which had earlier been demonstrated by Davidson (1969).

It becomes increasingly apparent that neural mechanisms capable of mediating lordosis and possibly ancillary receptive responses as well are organized in the central nervous system of male rats despite the presence of testis hormone during prenatal and early postnatal periods. Furthermore it seems that in males, as in females, the responsiveness of these mechanisms to external stimulation is temporarily increased under the immediate influence of estrogen. Finally, the existence of functional mechanisms for receptive responses in males is in no way incompatible with the simultaneous existence of mechanisms for mediation of mounting, intromitting, and ejaculating.

Control of Mating Behavior in Female Rats

LORDOSIS, DARTING AND CROUCHING, AND EAR WIGGLING

In the female ramstergig the neural basis for receptive behavior differentiates in the absence of androgen but cannot do so if androgen is present during developmental periods of high sensitivity. This may also occur in the case of the female rat, but the evidence is equivocal.

Females Treated with Androgen Early in Development

Confidence in the validity of the "organizational theory" as applied to females has been encouraged by the demonstration that female rats exposed to androgen during the appropriate period of development do not show normal receptive behavior in adulthood under the influence of endogenous or exogenous ovarian hormones (Harris and Levine, 1962; Barraclough and Gorski, 1962; Grady et al., 1965; Ward, 1969). However, the primary receptive response rarely is completely suppressed. In all experiments some androgenized females have been observed which exhibited at least occasional lordosis when mounted vigorously by stimulus males.

Gerall and Ward (1966) treated pregnant rats with TP and studied the coital behavior of the female offspring. They found that 37% of 30 females masculinized by prenatal exposure to androgen exhibited spontaneous estrous behavior, and when exogenous estrogen and progesterone were administered, this proportion rose to 52%. Nadler (1969) administered a single injection of TP to pregnant rats and examined the female offspring after ovariectomy in adulthood. Under the influence of exogenous ovarian hormones 90% of the masculinized females showed lordosis, but the average lordosis quotient was lower than that of control females.

Clemens *et al.* (1969) treated infant female rats with TP and tested for lordosis responses in adulthood. They concluded that reactivity to estrogen was unaffected, but early androgen administration reduced the behavioral responsiveness to progesterone. This is particularly interesting in conjunction with Davidson's report (1969) that, although males castrated in adulthood will display lordosis after a series of estrogen injections, the addition of progesterone does not enhance the response.

Females Treated with Estrogen Early in Development

Another finding of relevance to the interpretation of effects of early androgen treatment on the female rat's nervous system is the demonstration that receptive behavior in adulthood is as greatly depressed by estrogen injections during the first few days of life as it is by the administration of androgen at that time. This effect has been demonstrated by many investigators (Koster, 1943; Harris and Levine, 1962; Whalen and Nadler, 1963; Levine and Mullins, 1964; Feder and Whalen, 1965; Whalen and Edwards, 1967). It appears that it is not necessarily the presence of androgen which produces changes in adult behavior, but perhaps the critical feature is a disturbance of the normal neonatal endocrine balance—a disturbance which can be initiated by more than one type of gonadal steroid.

MOUNTING, INTROMISSION, AND EJACULATION RESPONSES

Female ramstergigs which have not been treated with androgen in infancy never display any masculine copulatory responses because the neurophysiological basis for such behavior is not organized in normal females. The "organizational theory" in its pristine form does not apply quite so perfectly to female rats. A substantial proportion of untreated female rats from certain strains whose nervous systems have never been exposed to testicular androgen execute mounting and thrusting responses when tested with other females that are in estrus.

Females Subjected to No Experimental Treatment During Development

The results of two experiments dealing with mounting are summarized in Tables 3 and 4. Table 3 shows the frequency with which one

TABLE 3
Mounting Responses Shown by 15 Female Rats in 390 Tests with Estrous Females[a]

	Type of mounting response		
	Mount with clasp only	Mount with palpation and thrusting	Mount with thrusting and intromission pattern
Percent of tests with mounting	76.1	34.2	5.4
Mean frequency per positive test	4.2	3.0	1.6

[a] Beach and Rasquin, 1942.

group of intact females displayed mounting when tested repeatedly with receptive females as stimulus partners (Beach and Rasquin, 1942). The average number of tests involved was 26 ($R = 17–40$), and it was found that the frequency of mounting tends to increase with repeated testing. Mounting frequency did not vary in different stages of the estrous cycle. It was not affected by endogenous ovarian hormones.

Table 4 reveals the effects of TP treatment in adulthood on the mounting behavior of females which were gonadectomized at 21 to 23 days of age (Beach, 1942). Exogenous androgen more than doubled the number of mounts per test and produced a threefold increase in the proportion of those mounts which involved palpation and thrusting. For purposes of comparison an analysis was made of 742 mounting responses by 12 normal male rats. The percentage of distribution was as follows: mount the clasp only, 2%; mount with palpation and thrusting, 28%; mount with thrusting and intromission pattern, 63%; and mount with

TABLE 4
Mounting Behavior Shown by Ten Prepuberally Spayed Female Rats before and after Treatment with Testosterone Propionate[a]

			Percent of all mounts falling in each category		
Tests (No.)	Total TP (mg)	Mounting responses	Mount with clasp only	Mount with palpation and thrusting	Mount with thrusting and intromission pattern
100	Pretreatment	539	71	28	1
50	2–10	471	36	58	6
50	12–24	581	13	78	9

[a] Beach, 1942.

ejaculation pattern (never seen in females), 7%. Clearly, the mounting by females fell far short of the male's copulatory performance, but it was sufficient to indicate that without androgenic stimulation during development the female rat's nervous system is capable of mediating all of the masculine responses with the noteworthy exception of the ejaculatory pattern. The absence of this final response may or may not be due to a central nervous system deficiency. As we shall see, alternative interpretations are available.

Females Treated with Androgen Early in Development

Several experiments have shown that prenatal or early postnatal androgen treatment increases mounting behavior shown by female rats after administration of TP in adulthood (Koster, 1943; Harris and Levine, 1965; Nadler, 1965). Gerall and Ward (1966) noted that administration of testosterone to pregnant rats resulted in female offspring which, when given androgen in adulthood, showed less mounting than normal males but considerably more than control females which were treated with androgen as adults but not during development. The investigators (Gerall and Ward, 1966, pp. 374–375) interpreted their findings as follows.

> . . . if sufficient androgen is circulating in the fetal rat at a given period, mechanisms or tissues which participate in reproductive behavior of the female rat can be permanently altered. . . . The relatively large prenatal amounts of TP utilized in this study probably permitted sufficient androgen to be present during the developmental period of the female behavior center to alter its natural scheme of growth. . . . The results of this experiment are consistent with the hypothesis proposed by Young and his colleagues . . . that androgen circulating during critical periods of fetal development organizes neural tissue mediating reproductive behavior into structures possessing male behavior integrative capacities.

The most extreme effects of androgen treatment on behavior of female rats were obtained by Ward (1969), who combined prenatal and early postnatal administration of TP. When they were given testosterone as adults, 70% of Ward's subjects exhibited the ejaculatory pattern at least once. In spite of this performance, the average frequency of intromission responses in all tests combined was only 2.8 per test, as compared with 11.5 per test for a normal male control group. This should be compared with Beach and Rasquin's report (1942) of 1.3 such responses per test shown by normal, untreated female rats (Table 3). Ward's females possessed genital organs "indistinguishable from the penis of the normal male." The possibility is obvious that possession of a well-developed copulatory organ permitted more frequent occurrence of vaginal penetration in at least some tests and that the appearance of the ejaculatory response could have been due to the resultant genital stimulation rather than to a more complete stage of organization in crucial central neural circuits.

Ward's finding that female rats exposed to testosterone both prenatally and immediately postnatally are capable of ejaculatory responses if given androgen in adulthood confirms an earlier report based on a comparable experiment by Whalen and Robertson (1968).

Females Treated with Estrogen Early in Development

The tendency for female rats to display mounting, intromission, and ejaculation responses when treated with androgen in adulthood can be increased if the females are injected with estrogen very soon after birth. In other words, the presumed "masculinization" does not demand the presence of androgen during the sensitive period of development. Levine and Mullins (1964) injected 4-day-old female rats with estradiol benzoate and then gave these same animals TP in adulthood. The frequencies of mounting and intromission patterns exceeded those of females not treated in infancy, and a few of the experimental females displayed the ejaculatory pattern.

Control of Mating Behavior in Guinea Pigs

BEHAVIOR OF FEMALES

Lordosis in Normal and Spayed Animals

In adult female guinea pigs the tendency to display lordosis is strongly influenced by ovarian hormones and closely correlated with the development of ovarian follicles (Young *et al.*, 1938). Spayed females exhibit normal receptivity after administration of estrogen and progesterone (Hertz *et al.*, 1937). Gonadectomized adult females do not exhibit lordosis in the absence of ovarian hormones, but this response is readily evoked by mechanical stimulation of newborn infants for the first 2 to 5 hours postpartum (Boling *et al.*, 1939). The same reflex has been demonstrated in fetal guinea pigs removed from the uterus approximately 4 days before term (Beach, 1966). No hormone treatment of fetal or neonatal animals is required, and the response has been shown to be independent of maternal ovarian hormone. Furthermore, if females 2 or 3 days old are injected with estrogen and progesterone, they do not reliably exhibit lordosis. When they first described lordosis in neonatal guinea pigs, Boling *et al.* were reluctant to equate it with "the true heat response." Their hesitancy was not based upon any obvious difference between the behavior shown by newborn animals and adult females in estrus but rather upon the facts that (i) the neonatal female's response is independent of estrogen and progesterone, and (ii) the same reaction is evokable in infant males as readily as in females. Regardless of whether the lordosis of 2-hour-old females is labeled "receptive behavior" or not [and an alternative interpretation has been proposed by Beach (1966)], it is clear that the neuromuscular basis for lordosis is fully organized prior to birth and can function in very young animals without the support of ovarian hormone.

Mounting in Normal and Spayed Females

Neural mechanisms capable of mediating mounting and thrusting behavior are well developed in female guinea pigs. This behavior normally is associated with estrus, and in its execution "few if any males are as vigorous as the most active females" (Young et al., 1935). It appears that responses normally associated with intromission and ejaculation in the male are not shown by mounting females (Young and Rundlett, 1939). Spayed female guinea pigs can be induced to mount as frequently as intact females in estrus by injection of estrogen followed by progesterone (Young and Rundlett, 1939).

Diamond (1965) injected spayed females with TP or with estrogen and progesterone in an attempt to induce mounting. Uninjected females did not mount. In response to androgen treatment the subjects mounted an average of 4.2 times per test, but after administration of estrogen and progesterone the average frequency was 20.5 mounts per test.

Effects of Prenatal Androgen Treatment on Lordosis

From the historical point of view the most important experiment bearing on this problem was the one reported in 1959 by Phoenix and co-workers. They found that female offspring whose mothers were treated with TP at the appropriate time during pregnancy were born with genitalia masculinized to such an extent that the genetic sex of the individual could only be identified by laparotomy. Behavior also was modified. In adulthood the pseudohermaphroditic females were ovariectomized, injected with estrogen and progesterone and compared with spayed control females that had never received androgen. The control group showed lordosis in 89% of their tests as compared with 22% for experimental females. The average duration of heat was 5.7 and 2.5 hours, respectively, for the two groups. Mean duration of lordosis in control females was 11.5 seconds and for masculinized females it was 2.0 seconds. The effects of prenatal TP obviously was "probabilistic" or relative rather than absolute, but the effects were unchanged when the females were retested 1 year later. The same effects could not be produced by TP injection which began at birth and continued for 80 days. This treatment induced only temporary suppression of lordosis.

In a follow-up study, Goy et al., (1964) determined that the period of maximal sensitivity to the inhibiting effects of androgen on lordosis in adulthood occurs in the second trimester between 30 to 55 days gestational age. As in the earlier experiment, exposure to TP during the period of maximal sensitivity greatly reduced the proportion of tests in which lordosis occurred and attenuated the average duration of the length of heat and of the lordosis response.

In connection with the two investigations just described it is significant that Meidinger (1962) tested females for the lordosis response during the first few hours postpartum and found that is was not impaired in individuals which had been exposed to androgen at any stage of fetal life. This result indicates that although responsiveness to ovarian hormones in adulthood may be drastically reduced, neuromuscular connections essential for the execution of lordosis are functional in pseudohermaphroditic females prior to parturition, and this finding is exceedingly difficult to reconcile with the concept of disorganization within the central nervous system.

Effects of Prenatal Androgen Treatment upon Mounting

Phoenix and co-workers (1959) examined the mounting behavior of prenatally masculinized females and control females after both groups had been ovariectomized in adulthood. The behavior of both types of females was compared with that of neonatally castrated males before any of the animals had received hormonal treatment, again when they had been injected with estrogen and progesterone, and finally after all three groups had been injected with 2.5 mg of TP daily for 16 days.

Prior to any hormone therapy the spayed control females did not mount. Hermaphroditic females did so in only 4.4% of their tests, and neonatally castrated males mounted in 11.8% of their tests. Injections of estrogen and progesterone induced control females to mount in 10.7% of the tests, and comparable scores for the masculinized females and castrated males were 5.6 and 16.7%, respectively. Administration of 40 mg of TP (16 daily injections) produced less mounting in control females than they had shown under the influence of ovarian hormones (5.8% of tests positive), but androgen was more effective than estrogen and progesterone in pseudohermaphrodites (15.4% tests positive) and in male castrates (20.5%).

Goy and co-workers (1964) found that the tendency of pseudohermaphroditic females to exhibit mounting when injected with ovarian hormones in adulthood varied according to the stage of fetal life during which androgen was administered. The highest frequency of response was shown by females which had been exposed to androgen between the gestational ages of 30 to 55 days. This is the same interval in which TP most effectively inhibits the lordosis response in adulthood.

Gerall (1966) compared the effects of TP treatment on the mounting behavior of prenatally masculinized females with that of intact and castrated males and of females spayed in adulthood. Prior to any hormone administration intact males mounted frequently, but the other three groups rarely showed such behavior. Daily injections of TP produced a distinct increase in mounting by spayed control females, pseudohermaphrodites, and castrated males. The latter two groups mounted much more often than the female controls. The masculinized females also exhibited a response never seen in normal females (Gerall, 1966, pp. 367–368).

> It should be noted that after androgen treatment some of the pseudohermaphrodites exhibited an ejaculatory response during mating tests. Thus, it can be concluded that the pseudohermaphrodite has complete response potentiality to perform as a male.

BEHAVIOR OF MALES

Mounting, Intromission, and Ejaculation in Normal and Castrated Adults

Intromission and ejaculation depend upon the presence of androgen. Grunt and Young (1953) found that males castrated in adulthood ceased showing the ejaculatory pattern within 5 weeks postoperatively. When TP was administered, the response was restored, and, most importantly, individual differences in the intensity and frequency of coital performance noted before gonadectomy reappeared when castrates were treated with equal amounts of androgen. Gonadectomy reduced but did not eliminate mounting, and subsequent TP therapy returned the frequency of this response to preoperative levels.

Effects of Neonatal Castration on Mounting, Intromission, and Ejaculation

Goy et al. (1964) recorded the display of mounting responses by neonatally castrated males that had received no androgen treatment. The average frequency was 8.6 mounts per 10-minute test. Riss and his colleagues (1955) castrated males within 2 days postpartum. One group of such males was given no hormone treatment in infancy, while members of two other groups received daily injections of TP at dosages of 25 μg or 500 μg/100 gm body weight. Treatment began on the day of operation and continued throughout the experiment. Weekly mating tests with estrous females were conducted until an animal ejaculated or until he was 17 weeks old.

Neonatal castrates treated with 500 μg TP/100 gm body weight exhibited development of mating behavior equal to that of intact control males, but castrates receiving only 25 μg/100 gm body weight were inferior to both of the other groups, and untreated castrates were even less active. Some of the major findings are summarized in Table 5 which includes information concerning penile development. The table shows that the four groups differed very little with respect to the execution of the mounting response. Five of six neonatal castrates that had never

TABLE 5
Mating Behavior of Neonatally Castrated and Intact Male Guinea Pigs[a,b]

Group and measure	Mean weeks age at first appearance	Proportion of group displaying responses during experiment
Mounting response		
Untreated castrates	5.0	5/6
25-μg TP castrates[c]	6.9	6/6
500-μg TP castrates[c]	4.4	6/6
Intact controls	4.7	7/7
Intromission response		
Untreated castrates	—	0/6
25-μg TP castrates	13.1	2/6
500-μg TP castrates	6.1	6/6
Intact controls	7.3	7/7
Ejaculation response		
Untreated castrates	—	0/6
25-μg TP castrates	11.1	1/6
500-μg TP castrates	8.4	6/6
Intact controls	7.9	7/7

	Mean	SD	N
Penis length (cm)/100 gm body weight			
25-μg TP castrates	0.44	0.04	9
500-μg TP castrates	0.55	0.06	8
Intact controls	0.57	0.05	6

[a] Riss et al., 1955.

[b] Behavioral scores based exclusively on performance of socially reared males from the heterogeneous strain.

[c] Daily dose/100 gm body weight administered from operation to end of testing.

received TP began mounting as early as intact males. No data were presented to show the frequency of mounting.

With respect to the achievement of intromission the castrates receiving the 500 μg TP were equal to the intact controls, but 25 μg TP/100 gm body weight stimulated the intromission response in only two of six neonatal castrates. Untreated castrates never achieved insertion. The ejaculatory pattern was shown by only one castrate receiving the lower dose of TP but by all six castrates injected with 500 μg/100 gm body weight. The infrequent display of intromission and ejaculation by animals given 25 μg/100 gm body weight could be due to the fact, reflected in Table 5, that growth of the penis in these animals was significantly reduced. This possibility did not go unnoticed by Riss' group. The results of this investigation are quite comparable to those of similar studies on rats described earlier in this paper.

A finding of considerable importance has to do with the response of untreated neonatal castrates to androgen administered after the period represented in Table 5. Although they had been deprived of testis hormone from the second day of life and had received no exogenous androgen during development, five of the six males in this group copulated and ejaculated as adults after 4 to 6 weeks of daily injections containing 500 μg TP. Apparently the neural mechanisms for the complete masculine coital patterns are prenatally organized in the male guinea pig and are normally responsive to androgen when it is supplied in maturity. Interpretation of their findings by Riss and co-workers is reflected in the following quotation (Riss et al., 1955, pp. 144 and 146).

> The sexual behavior of animals castrated at birth and receiving no hormone therapy provided evidence that the presence of the testes is not necessary for the organization of sexual behavior. . . . The data suggest the role of t.p. to be that of an activator rather than a direct organizer of behavior.

Effects of Antiandrogen and of Estrogen on Mounting, Intromission, and Ejaculation

Goldfoot (cited in Phoenix et al., 1968) injected pregnant guinea pigs with cyproterone acetate (CA) and studied the morphology and behavior of the male offspring. The infant males showed "extensive feminization of the external genitalia" and never exhibited either ejaculation or intromission. Although they were treated with estrogen and progesterone the experimental males failed to display the typical female lordosis pattern. Zucker and Kuehn (cited in Phoenix et al., 1967) obtained different results. They also studied the adult behavior of male guinea pigs prenatally exposed to cyproterone acetate. Males whose dams received from 3 to 10 mg daily on days 27 through 57 of gestation ejaculated in approximately the same proportion of tests as normal controls. Males exposed to 15 mg CA during the same period never achieved intromission and of course did not ejaculate.

Phoenix *et al.* (1959) castrated males at 21 days of age and later examined them for mating responses. Prior to any hormone treatment these castrates showed an average of 11.8 mounts/test when placed with females in heat. In similar tests ovariectomized females never mounted estrous partners. When the male castrates were treated with estrogen and progesterone, their average mount frequency increased to 16.7 mounts/test. Spayed females under the same hormonal regime showed an average of 10.7 mounts/test. Administration of TP to castrated males (2.5 mg/day for 16 days) evoked display of 20.5 mounts/test. No mention is made of intromission or ejaculation patterns.

Lordosis

There are no published accounts to indicate that intact untreated adult male guinea pigs ever display receptive behavior comparable in intensity and frequency to the estrous responses which have been observed in a small number of male rats without any experimental treatment (Stone, 1924; Beach, 1938, 1945). Nevertheless, it is clear that from birth and even in late fetal life all genetic male guinea pigs possess a neuromuscular organization capable of mediating the lordosis response. This is proven by the display of this reaction by males which have just been born (Boling *et al.,* 1939; Meidinger, 1962) or removed from the uterus 4 days prepartum (Beach, 1966). It must be emphasized that in males (and females) of these ages the execution of lordosis is independent of ovarian hormones. Furthermore the response is the same in both sexes with respect to frequency of occurrence, ease of elicitation, and duration.

Phoenix and co-workers (1959) castrated male guinea pigs before they were 21 days old and compared their behavioral response to estradiol and progesterone with that of spayed females. The proportion of tests in which lordosis occurred was 38% for the males and 89% for females. Mean latencies to the beginning of heat were 6.0 (males) and 5.7 (females) hours. Average duration of heat was 1.2 hours for males and 5.7 hours for females. The median duration of the longest lordosis was 2.0 seconds for males and 11.5 seconds for females.

The inferior performance of male castrates might be interpreted as a result of preoperative androgenic stimulation of the masculine nervous system, particularly stimulation occurring during fetal development. An attempt to evaluate this possibility was made in the previously described study by Goldfoot, who injected pregnant females with the antiandrogen cyproterone acetate and studied the behavior of the male offspring. Although these males exhibited extensive feminization of the genitalia, none of them could be induced to exhibit lordosis when treated with estrogen and progesterone.

Control of Mating Behavior in Golden Hamsters

BEHAVIOR OF FEMALES

Lordosis

Normal females show lordosis only during estrus, and the same response of equal intensity and duration is reliably induced in spayed individuals by the injection of estrogen followed by progesterone (Beach and Kislak, 1955; Tiefer, 1970). Swanson and Crossley (1970) injected different groups of 2-day-old females with 10 μg TP, 300 μg TP, or the inert vehicle. Members of each group were spayed in adulthood, and their reactions to exogenous gonadal hormones were tested. Females of both treated groups exhibited clitoral enlargement, and the effect was most pronounced in the group which had received the higher dosage of TP in infancy. Despite this evidence of masculinization the vagina remained patent in all cases, and prior to ovariectomy in adulthood four females from the two treatment groups displayed regular 4-day vaginal cycles and were fully receptive when in vaginal estrus, proving that central nervous system mechanisms mediating female behavior were organized and functional. Three of the four were impregnated and delivered and reared litters. Most of the remaining 21 females given androgen in infancy displayed irregular vaginal cycles and showed lordosis only when mounted quite vigorously during estrus. When these animals were spayed and given estrogen and progesterone, their receptive behavior was of the same degree as it had been preoperatively during natural estrus.

Nucci and Beach (1971) injected pregnant hamsters with 2.0 mg TP on days 11–13, 12–14, or 13–15 of the 16-day gestation period. When they were adult, ovariectomized female offspring were injected with estrogen and progesterone and tested for sexual receptivity. Despite anatomical masculinization, as indicated by the absence of an external vagina, all 18 experimental females exhibited mating responses indistinguishable from those of normal females.

Mounting

According to Tiefer (1970), normal female hamsters rarely mount conspecifics. In this respect the hamster is like the ramstergig but dissimilar to the rat and guinea pig, for which frequent mounting behavior has been described earlier. Tiefer tested nine females for the display of mounting responses to receptive stimulus partners and observed that six never mounted, two showed one mount each, and the remaining female, mounted in four tests, showing the intromission pattern a total of seven times. These same females were given daily injections of 200 μg TP for 1 month, but this treatment produced no increase in mounting behavior. It will be recalled that comparable treatment evoked marked increases in mount frequency shown by female rats and guinea pigs.

Swanson and Crossley (1970) injected spayed hamsters with 500 μg TP daily for 4 weeks and tested for mounting responses to receptive females. Only two of eleven androgen-treated females ever mounted a stimulus female, and only one individual showed the intromission response during one test. The ejaculation pattern never occurred. In contrast to these spayed control females, other females masculinized by prolonged TP treatment from the second day of life (10 μg or 300 μg TP daily) reacted to androgen therapy in adulthood by frequently mounting other females that were in estrus. Fourteen of sixteen individuals in the two infant-treatment groups showed mounting, although at a level significantly below that characteristic of castrated males given the same amount of TP. Many of the mounts by females were incorrectly oriented, but an appreciable number ended in an intromission pattern. The ejaculatory response was never seen.

Nucci and Beach (1971) examined mating behavior of 18 female hamsters that had been exposed to TP stimulation in utero. In a total of 126 tests, preceded by 28 daily injections of 200 μg TP, only one female showed mounting responses and this occurred only two times in a single test.

BEHAVIOR OF MALES

Mounting, Intromission, and Ejaculation

Male hamsters castrated in adulthood cease showing intromission and ejaculation responses within 1 month after operation, but mounting behavior survives for much longer. The normal coital pattern can be reinstated by treating castrates with sufficient amounts of TP (Beach and Pauker, 1949). Tiefer (1970) has also reported that males castrated as adults and then given TP achieved intromission and ejaculation as often as intact males.

Eaton (1970) castrated male hamsters at birth and divided them into three groups. One group received a single injection of TP on day 1 and a second group was given the same treatment on day 15. A third group of neonatal castrates was injected on day 1 with the inert vehicle.

Control groups consisted of males and females gonadectomized in adulthood. When they became mature all neonatal castrates were given a series of TP injections and tested with receptive females. At the same time the control male group received identical androgen therapy. Neonatal castrates that had been injected with oil at birth or with TP at 15 days postpartum mounted stimulus females at frequencies considerably below those shown by control males. None of the experimental males that had received injections of oil on day 1 or of TP on day 15 achieved intromission and of course none ejaculated. Of the nine neonatal castrates given TP on day 1 only five achieved ejaculation and this performance demanded extension of the test period beyond the standard length of 5 minutes. All control males castrated in adulthood ejaculated within 5 minutes of testing. The average penis lengths for neonatal castrates receiving oil on day 1 or TP on day 15 were considerably shorter than the same measurements for controls castrated in adulthood. Experimental subjects given TP on day 1 had an average penis length equal to that of control males, but the overall size of the organ was considerably reduced as indicated by an average weight of 0.163 gm for controls in contrast to 0.133 gm for experimental cases.

Lordosis

Swanson and Crossley (1970) castrated adult male hamsters and tested for receptive responses after administration of estrogen and progesterone. When mounted by normal stimulus males, the experimental animals ". . . showed prompt receptivity. They adopted the lordosis posture and held it for a prolonged period." Tiefer (1970) has examined this behavior in greater detail and finds that in some respects castrated males treated with ovarian hormones behave differently than receptive females.

Males castrated as adults were injected with estrogen or with estrogen and progesterone. The combined treatment was more effective in inducing lordosis. Under its influence 100% of the males exhibited the lordosis response, and it occurred in 97% of their tests, as compared with 96% of the tests given to spayed females receiving the same hormonal treatment. Male castrates did not maintain lordosis as long as the control females. The mean time per 5-minute test spent in lordosis was 267 seconds for females and 116 seconds for males. The average duration of the longest lordosis per animal was 285 seconds for females and 94 seconds for males. Males usually maintained the lordosis posture only while they were mounted, whereas females tended to remain in lordosis while the stimulus male mounted and dismounted several times in succession.

Although she never observed normal males exhibiting lordosis, Tiefer did record this behavior shown by adult castrates while they were receiving daily injections of TP. Two-thirds of her subjects exhibited brief lordosis responses in 44% of their tests. Exogenous androgen did not have this effect on spayed females.

Swanson and Crossley (1970) studied the execution of lordosis responses in males that had been treated with TP at 2 days of age and castrated in adulthood. When they were subsequently injected with estrogen and progesterone, the TP males showed less receptive behavior than control male castrates given the same ovarian hormones in adulthood. Experimental animals that had received 10 μg TP in infancy exhibited lordosis only when they were mounted quite vigorously by stimulus males, and members of the group given 300 μg TP on day 2 never showed lordosis. No quantitative measures of behavior were included in this report.

Eaton (1970) castrated male hamsters on the day of birth and immediately injected two groups with either 500 μg of TP or the inert vehicle. A third group of neonatal castrates was given 500 μg TP on day 15. When they were treated with estrogen and progesterone and tested with stimulus males during adulthood, the control males and those receiving TP on day 15 showed lordosis behavior which was equal in most respects to that of spayed females given the same ovarian treatment. The females and the two male groups did not differ significantly with respect to average latency, frequency, or duration of the response. In contrast, only 30% of the neonatal castrates injected with TP on day 1 and given estrogen and progesterone as adults ever showed lordosis. In the animals that responded at least once the behavior was manifestly inferior to that of control females. Latency from treatment to the first occurrence of lordosis was protracted, average frequency per test was very low, and average duration was greatly attenuated.

Alternative Types of Interpretation

As a psychologist, my interest in the behavior of organisms supersedes my concern with the activity of the nervous system, which is, after all, the primary concern of the neurologist. Only those neuroanatomical or neurophysiological facts possessing demonstrable relevance to behavior are of immediate usefulness in the search for explanations of behavior. Theories or interpretations formulated in terms of hypothetical neurological or biochemical mechanisms are no more "scientific," "fundamental," or "valid" than theories stated exclusively in S–R terms without even a passing reference to neurons or hormones. This is not to deny the contributions which information about the nervous system can make and has made to our understanding of behavior. It is merely a declaration that facts and laws pertaining to behavior stand in no need of "validation" by correlating behavioral and neurophysiological phenomena.

HYPOTHETICAL CONSTRUCTS

In spite of the obvious truth of the foregoing generalization, most students of behavior always have and always will derive a feeling of security and superiority from theories that purport to "explain" behavior in terms of known or imagined "circuits," "centers," or "mechanisms" having a permanent address somewhere in the central nervous system. Actually, nearly all such "mechanisms" consist of hypothetical constructs which are defined as follows (English and English, 1958).

> . . . an entity or process that is inferred as actually existing (though not at present fully observable) and giving rise to measurable phenomena, including phenomena other than observables that led to hypothesizing the construct.

Now if any reader doubts that proponents of the theory mean exactly and specifically that androgen "organizes" or "disorganizes" brain mechanisms responsible for copulatory behavior in rats, guinea pigs, and some other mammals, any such doubt should be dispelled by the following quotations which were presented *in extenso* earlier in this paper. According to Goy and his colleagues (1968, p. 36),

> . . . androgen, or some particular androgens [are] responsible for determining the organization of the neural tissues that mediated sexual behavior.

Or, according to Gerall (1966, p. 367),

> . . . an androgenic substance . . . "organizes" or induces the undifferentiated sexual neural areas to develop into a center regulating male behavior. In the absence of such a substance, the intrinsic tendency in mammals is for the relevant neural tissue to be organized into female behavior controlling regions.

With a single exception I am aware of absolutely no evidence based upon direct examination of the nervous system that would substantiate the foregoing claims. The exception is provided by experiments on the ramstergig, and the crucial evidence is illustrated in Fig. 4. This is a photomicrograph of a nerve tract which very closely resembles an extremely important tract situated in the anterior hypothalamus of the female ramstergig. The function of the analogous tract in the ramstergig is essential to the display of sexually receptive behavior. Figure 4B shows how the tract would appear in a normal female ramstergig. Obviously, it is quite well organized and in excellent condition to transmit informa-

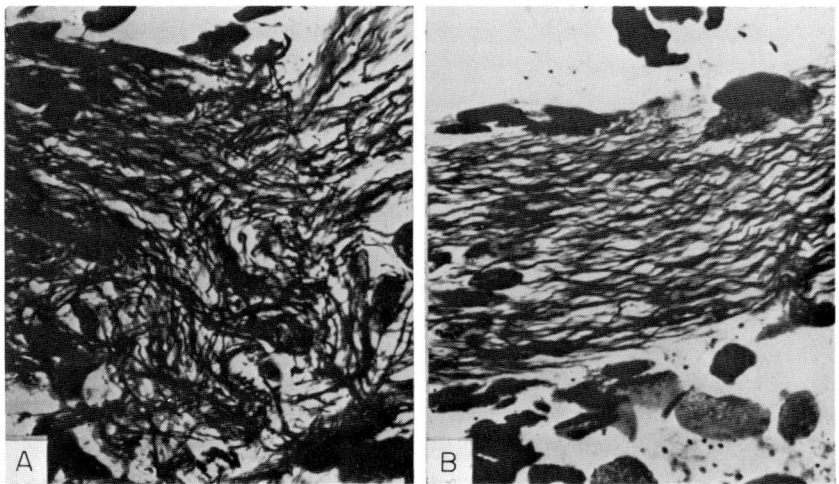

FIG. 4. Simulation of a brain mechanism for receptive behavior in a normal female ramstergig (B) and a female treated with TP prenatally (A). Androgen-induced disorganization in A is obvious.

tion rapidly and without distortion from one part of the hypothalamus to another. Figure 4A shows how the analogous tract would appear in the brain of a female ramstergig which had been treated with TP during the fetal and neonatal periods. No one could deny that *this* tract is horribly disorganized, just as the theory would predict. Obviously any information or message trying to find its way from one end to the other would be irretrievably lost in the tangled and thoroughly disorganized neural mechanism.[2]

SLASH-AND-BURN

In many parts of the world untended land that has been overgrown by trees, bushes, and weeds is cleared for agricultural use by felling or girdling the smaller trees, slashing away the brushy growth, and setting fire to the entire area. This slash-and-burn method is crude but effective because it quickly removes impediments to planting useful crops and simultaneously adds organic fertilizer to the soil which will stimulate and support the new growth of desired species. At the same time the

[2] The only existing photomicrograph of a ramstergig brain was lost, but the picture shown here is just as accurate and reliable as the original. It is published with the generous permission of R. W. Sperry and shows sections of the optic tract of an amphibian. Figure 4B shows a normal tract, while A shows a tract regenerated after experimental transection (Sperry, 1943).

method spares mature, well-established trees while clearing away the trash.

Metaphorically speaking, the area of speculation or phantasy wherein flourishes the organizational theory of hormonal action is long overdue for slash-and-burn treatment. When the smoke clears away and the ashes settle, we will note the elimination of many stunted trees and thick coppices which have been dominating fertile terrain and preventing the growth of species capable of bearing valuable fruit. At the same time a number of healthy, mature trees will have survived the treatment by fire.

One of the first victims of the clearing away project should be certain unwarranted generalizations about behavior which depend upon highly questionable extrapolations from perfectly sound evidence relating to hypothalamic control of hypophyseal function. There seems to be no reason to question that the gonadotropic function of the pituitary is cyclic in female rats and acyclic in males. It is also well recognized that this sex difference is related to functional differences in the hypothalamus. Finally, few, if any, experts deny that when male rats are deprived of endogenous testosterone from birth, their pituitaries are capable of cyclic function in adulthood; and if female rats are injected with TP very soon after birth, their pituitaries are functionally acyclic in adulthood. Appropriate pituitary transplantation experiments have established the fact that the "developmental" effects of endogenous or exogenous androgen are exerted upon the brain and not upon the hypophysis. Returning to our metaphor, these facts are healthy trees which will not be permanently injured by the slash-and-burn treatment.

The aforementioned effects of androgen upon the brain's control of hypophyseal function and consequent ovulatory cycles are not at issue here, but what can be most seriously challenged is the derived assumption that during the same period of development androgen stimulates differentiation and functional organization of imaginary brain centers that eventually will control masculine mating behavior. Equally unsupported is the complementary belief that in very early development androgen actively inhibits "organization" of a central nervous system mechanism destined for eventual mediation of feminine copulatory responses.

There are at least two reasons for applying our slash-and-burn tactic to this particular theoretical underbrush. First, the basic assumptions are contradicted by the results of many experiments that were summarized in the first part of this paper. Second, the analogy which originally gave rise to the theory is completely untenable. This has been trenchantly pointed out by Whalen (1968, p. 315).

Mating behavior differs strikingly from ovulation along several dimensions. Ovulation is a discrete event—it can either occur or not occur under a particular hormonal condition. It does not occur to a greater or lesser degree. Mating on the other hand, can occur in varying degrees. It can be more or less intense. In a given animal, ovulation cannot occur in both the male pattern and in the female pattern simultaneously or closely linked in time. Mating in a given animal, however, can occur in both the male and female pattern within a single relatively limited observation period. The genetic and hormonal female can exhibit female and male behavior alternatively.

Another well-established body of evidence is derived from numerous experiments demonstrating that if sufficient amounts of androgen are present during the appropriate stages of ontogeny, tissues derived from the primitive urogenital sinus may develop into a penis, seminal vesicles, and a prostate gland. This result occurs naturally in male mammals and can be induced artificially in females of some species by treatment with TP at the appropriate stage of development. Contrariwise, in the absence of testosterone, urogenital sinus tissue in males and in females gives rise to an external vagina and associated feminine accessory structures. Here is another healthy tree that will survive any slash-and-burn attack. However, the undisputed effects of testosterone upon differentiation of various sex accessories has sometimes been mistakenly taken as an omen pointing to the nature of developmental processes in the brain. This conclusion is reflected in the following quotations. As discussed by Phoenix and his colleagues (1968, p. 35),

> We viewed the action of the gonadal hormones on central nervous tissue in the developing fetus as analogous to their action on genital tract tissue, including those tissues constituting the external genitalia.

While Diamond (1968, p. 426) observed that

> ... the same hormonal processes involved in genital differentiation are also active in differentiation of the neural tissues which mediate behavioral activities.

In view of the faithful reliance which seems to be placed on this analogy at least two questions must be raised concerning the legitimacy of the underlying extrapolation. The first has to do with the propriety of generalizing from the effects on genital structures to effects on nerve cells. The second, already mentioned in this paper, derives from the fact that although the undifferentiated genital tubercle in some species seems to have the capacity to develop into either masculine or feminine genitalia, *it cannot give rise to both types in the same individual*. One animal cannot possess a clitoris *and* a penis, or a scrotum *and* vaginal labia. Intermediate or anomalous conditions such as hypospadias or extreme clitorial hypertrophy have no bearing on this argument since they do not represent structural duplication of parts or simultaneous development of both masculine and feminine accessories.

Unlike the external genital apparatus, the neural bases for mounting, thrusting, inserting, and ejaculating can coexist in the same individual along with mechanisms capable of mediating hopping and darting, crouching, ear wiggling, and execution of lordosis. There is no obvious evolutionary reason why this should not be so. The capacity of an intact male to display lordosis does not detract from his ability to fertilize a female. Normal females that show mounting also show lordosis and thus are capable of reproduction. In contrast to this situation, which relates only to behavior, the development of normal male or female external genitals in mammals represents mutually exclusive alternatives. This constitutes a biological imperative. To effectively participate in sexual reproduction a testis-bearing mammal must be equipped with an intromittent organ and an appropriate associated duct system. Similarly, the ovum-producing mammal must possess not only a uterus but also a peripherally located vessel connected to the uterus and suited to the acceptance and conservation of sperm. Since the external vagina and scrotum develop from the same primordium, only one or the other can be produced.

If our slash-and-burn treatment leaves standing only those metaphorical trees that represent reasonably well-established facts concerning hormonal effects on development, and reduces to ashes the more fragile and flammable saplings, bushes, and ferns which stood for unproven and tenuous speculations regarding connections between neurontogeny and adult behavior, are we then reduced to dealing only with the neural control of ovulation or with hormonal influence upon genital differentiation? Not at all! There remain many stalwart, full-grown "trees" which are just as valuable and just as theoretically important as any of those which symbolize our knowledge of brain–pituitary relations or phallic epigenesis.

HORMONE–BEHAVIOR RELATIONSHIPS

These frequently ignored "trees" represent hard-earned knowledge regarding relationships between gonadal hormones and behavior. Many theorists are so sadly and seriously afflicted with neurophilia (which in its terminal phases inevitably develops into cerebromania) that they are able seriously to entertain only those interpretations of behavior which are couched in the vocabulary of the neurologist.

Speaking only for one observer I am impressed, not with ill-defined, idiosyncratic theories which attempt to explain the evidence in terms of vaguely identified brain mechanisms; rather, am I powerfully convinced by the behavioral evidence itself. When we separate the seed of data from the chaff of neurophysiological speculation what is our harvest? It is a collection of solidly established facts pertaining to relationships between certain hormones and certain patterns of behavior. The following "sample" experiments will stand as representative of the entire body of relevant evidence.

1. Spayed adult guinea pigs were injected with 3.32 μg of estradiol benzoate followed 36 hours later by 0.2 mg of progesterone. Several hours after the administration of progesterone 90 to 95% of the females began to display the lordosis response. This response occurred in 89% of the tests. The most commonly used form of stimulation involved "fingering" by the experimenter, which included stroking the female's rump and anogenital region. Tested in this manner the average female continued to show the lordosis response for 5.7 hours. The mean duration of lordosis was 11.5 seconds.

2. A second group of female guinea pigs was exposed to TP during prenatal development. When they were born these females showed pronounced masculinization of the external genitalia. Furthermore when they were spayed and treated in adulthood with the same combination of ovarian hormones that had been given to the original groups of control females, the responses of the TP-treated group was not the same as that of the control group. The experimental (TP) group showed lordosis in only 22% of their tests. They retained the ability to exhibit lordosis for only 2.5 hours, and the average duration of the lordosis response in TP-treated females was only 2.0 seconds.

Later on the adult spayed females in these two groups were treated with equal amounts of TP and then placed with other females that were sexually receptive. The group which had been exposed to TP prenatally mounted stimulus females much more frequently than did the control females never given TP before adulthood.

Here endeth the hard-core evidence pertaining to the effects of prenatal TP treatment on sexual behavior of adult female guinea pigs. It can be summarized as follows: (i) The external genitalia are masculinized; (ii) the tendency to show lordosis when given estrogen and progesterone in adulthood is reduced; and (iii) the tendency to mount other guinea pigs when given TP in adulthood is increased. With the exception of changes in genital anatomy, the effects of androgen stimulation in fetal life consist of changes in behavioral responsiveness to gonadal hormones in adulthood.

This same simple formula applies to data gathered in numerous experiments on other species. The only proven behavioral effect of administering TP to newborn or fetal female rats is a markedly reduced tendency to display lordosis and other receptive responses when given estrogen and progesterone in adulthood. I seriously doubt the claim that there is an increased tendency to mount other rats when treated with TP in adulthood (Beach and Rasquin, 1942; Beach, 1942; Whalen et al., 1969).

As far as the opposite sex is concerned, castrating a male rat at birth has only one consistent direct effect upon mating behavior. As an adult such a male will be more likely than normal members of his sex to exhibit lordosis if he is injected with ovarian hormones. As already explained, the incomplete masculine coital performance characteristic of neonatal castrates when they are given TP in adulthood is an indirect effect reflecting underdevelopment of the copulatory organ.

PERMANENT MODIFICATION OF BEHAVIORAL CONTINGENCIES

It should be entirely clear that the experiments so far reported involving effects upon adult behavior of changing the hormonal conditions during selected periods of development have not involved study of the effects of such treatment upon the central nervous system. In all such investigations the dependent variable has been adult behavior. More specifically it has been a few patterns of behavior the occurrence of which normally is dependent upon or facilitated by concurrent support by gonadal hormones. In other words, what has been investigated in all of these studies are the effects of presence or absence of testosterone during early development on the behavior that occurs in adulthood when different gonadal hormones are present.[3]

In a sense we (the present author included) have been investigating different sets of behavior contingencies in which the independent variable is hormonal state during development and the dependent variable

---

[3] It is to be explicitly noted that this paper deals exclusively with copulatory behavior in rodents. Evidence is currently accumulating to show that there are other kinds of behavior which can be modified by testosterone treatment of females at appropriate developmental stages. Thus social behavior is partially masculinized in female rhesus monkeys whose mothers were injected with TP during pregnancy (Phoenix et al., 1968). In the author's laboratory female dogs are being treated with TP before birth and during infancy. When they reach adulthood, some of these females consistently assume the masculine posture for urination. In neither the monkeys nor the dogs does the occurrence of masculine behavior depend upon androgen administration after early development is completed. In other words, no "activational effects" are involved.

is behavioral responsiveness to gonadal hormones in adulthood. The effect of a given independent variable, e.g., a certain amount of TP administered during a definite period in development, is definable as a quantitatively expressible reduction in the probability that administration of a given amount of ovarian hormone in adulthood will be followed by the appearance of a measurable degree of feminine mating reactions in response to particular forms of external stimulation.

The probability ("response probability") that a particular response will occur under a given set of physiological conditions combined with a predetermined pattern of environmental stimulation can be abbreviated as RP. Thus one effect of absence of testosterone during the first 10 days of a male rat's life is to increase the RP for lordosis when that male is given estrogen and progesterone in adulthood and at that time is stimulated by being mounted by another male.

The RP concept resembles an intervening variable and bears no relation to a hypothetical construct. Whereas the latter refers to an entity or process that actually exists (such as an as-yet-unidentified brain mechanism), an intervening variable has no properties except those of the empirical data of which it is an abstraction. It is not an entity and not a cause, but simply a statement of a series of quantitative relationships. Conceptualizing the effects of hormone action on development in terms of permanently modifying the RP for certain behavioral responses in adulthood could have several salutary effects. It could concentrate attention on organismic patterns of behavior and their control by environmental stimuli. At the same time the RP concept compels the inclusion of physiological variables in the interpretation of S–R relationships, and, therefore, study of the so-called activational effects of hormones could not be neglected.

Viewing the purported organizational effects of androgen in the context of the RP concept rather than focusing exclusively upon development of central nervous system mechanisms may quite possibly provide new perspective for future experiments. For example, granted that exposure to androgenic stimulation early in development will permanently lower the RP for lordosis in adulthood, it is also true that several other variables simultaneously affect the same RP, and systematic manipulation of these other variables might ultimately increase our understanding of how hormone treatment in infancy alters behavior in adulthood.

For example, one variable affecting the lordosis RP is the current hormonal state of the individual. Unless she is under the influence of estrogen and progesterone, the normal female rat's lordosis RP is virtually zero. Now, a male rat castrated in adulthood and given the same quantities of estrogen and progesterone that are effective in the spayed female will show a lordosis RP of zero. According to one theory, this male's failure to exhibit lordosis is due to lack of organization of the brain mechanisms that normally mediate this response. When the same apparent behavioral deficit is considered in terms of the RP concept, the question arises as to what other variables might be manipulated to change the RP. A very obvious one is hormonal treatment given just before behavioral test, and as reported earlier in this paper when the same castrated male rat is given a series of daily estrogen injections, his RP for lordosis eventually approximates that of an intact female in estrus (Davidson, 1969). In other words, the original RP of zero was due not to some structural or organizational deficiency in the brain but to the fact that a male castrated in adulthood is less sensitive than a spayed female to exogenous ovarian hormone.[4]

Another independent variable mentioned in connection with the definition of the RP concept is the external stimulus. Investigating the effects of this variable in combination with variations in early hormone treatment could enlarge our comprehension of the ways in which hormones acting during development affect behavior occurring in adulthood. The importance of this source of variability on the ultimate effects of early hormone manipulations has been overlooked or ignored in the majority of relevant experiments. There seems to have been an implicit assumption that whatever the effect of the presence or absence of androgen during development might be, it will be restricted to the motor or executive elements in the hypothesized mechanisms for coital behavior. Little attention has been given to alternative possibilities. For example, perceptual functions might have been interfered with, or there may have been a reduction of sensitivity to stimulation within cells which normally respond to the hormone or hormones involved.

One very peculiar outcome of this cavalier disregard for the importance of differences in stimulus properties as determinants of the RP for behavior has been the widespread practice of testing a female for sexual receptivity without ever observing her reactions to a male. Many

[4] It is of course quite obvious that such differences in sensitivity could very well have a neural basis, and this certainly demands investigation. However, the heuristic thrust of this paper is a plea for primary emphasis upon analysis of relationships between observable behavior and controllable environmental stimuli, with physiological explanations being given no special priority. Neurological concepts are essential, but they are also seductive; when allowed to get out of hand, they can blind the student to his primary responsibility which is to describe and define behavioral phenomena in stimulus and response terms and to hold clearly in mind that the behavior of an organism—rat or man—is more than the summed behavior of its component organs or organ systems.

experiments on guinea pigs and rats have used as the only behavioral measure for immediate hormonal effects the female's reaction to "fingering" by the experimenter. This may suffice to indicate sensitivity of the lordosis reflex, but it does not qualify as a valid index to the female's receptivity or readiness to copulate with a male (Adler and Bell, 1969; Michael, 1961).

A very sensitive measure of the lordosis RP in male and female rats, and thus an indirect sign of the degree to which early hormone conditions have increased or decreased tendencies toward feminine mating behavior, is the quality and quantity of stimulation necessary and sufficient to evoke a standard degree of lordosis (Ball, 1937). When the RP is very high, an animal may show lordosis if the partner merely sniffs the experimental rat's anogenital region. At the opposite extreme an exceedingly low RP is indicated when lordosis can only be evoked by repeated mounts executed with pronounced vigor by a very heavy male. Interpretations or hypotheses based on the RP concept should remind and encourage the theorist to take account of all major variables which affect the probability that the selected response will occur. This in turn forces the experimentalist to include in his investigations the study of not just one but of several sets of behavioral contingencies, and in the present context this would include examination of possible effects of hormone treatment during development upon the RP for mounting, and for other adult coital reactions under different conditions of controlled external stimulation.

A Final Word and Apologia

No one is more fully aware than I that many readers will feel that I am tilting windmills or battling with straw men. It is true that many writers who have almost casually invoked the organizational concept of early hormone action have been using it as a figure of speech rather than a definite and precise explanatory concept. In fact most of those authors who use the term most frequently have been too careful or too careless to define specifically just what they mean by the term "organization."

Furthermore, the same writers may use one concept in one article and a different concept at another time. For example, at one point in an article written by Phoenix et al. (1968, p. 35) the authors stated that they

> . . . viewed the action of the gonadal hormones on central neural tissue in the developing fetus as analogous to their action on genital tract tissue, including those tissues constituting the external genitalia.

Twelve pages later in the same article (1968, p. 47) the following definition appears.

> The term "organizing action of testosterone" is used in the sense of setting a bias on a system such that differential sensitivity and responsiveness are built into the mechanism.

More recently, Diamond (1968) has stressed several of the points that have been made in the present article. He notes that there is no evidence to support the belief that there exists "a simple male versus female mechanism for setting sexual thresholds within the nervous system." He adds that the sexual behavior repertoires of male and female may be parallel and discontinuous rather than unidimensional and continuous with "male" at one end and "female" at the other.

Finally, W. C. Young, who more than any other single worker was responsible for introducing the concept of "organizational" versus "activational" effects of gonadal hormones on mating behavior, wrote as follows (1961, p. 1199):

> It has long been recognized that [hormones] might organize patterns of behavior . . . in the opinion of this writer, this would be in the sense of producing changes in the responses to hormones different from those normally associated with an individual, giving due regard to age, sex, strain and species.

At an earlier date Phoenix and co-workers had written in a somewhat similar vein (1959, p. 369):

> The data are uniform in demonstrating that an androgen administered prenatally has an organizing action on the tissues mediating mating behavior in the sense of producing a responsiveness to exogenous hormones which differs from that of normal adult females.

So far so good, except for the rather idiosyncratic use of the term "organizing action." However, on the same page appears the following paragraph.

> Attention is directed to the parallel nature of the relationship, on the one hand, between androgens and the differentiation of the genital tracts, and on the other, between androgens and the organization of the neural tissue destined to mediate mating behavior in the adult.

It is difficult to reconcile these two statements.

In the light of all this sweet reasonableness including the several points of agreement between authors just cited and the theoretical position recommended in the present paper, what possible justification can be offered in defense of this lengthy diatribe directed against the organizational concept of hormone action during fetal and neonatal life stages?

My justification rests upon the fact that the organizational theory was originally expressed and continues to be stated in such ambiguous and even contradictory terms that it is rapidly leading to a state of utter confusion and futile disputation. As is so often the case, it is not the initial, tentative, provisional interpretations proposed by the original investigators that cause the mischief. Rather it is the subsequent, second-order writings formulated by others, who read selectively only the positive sections of published experimental reports and who lack any first-hand knowledge of the qualifications and restrictions which formed essential components of the original conclusions.

It is the purpose of this presentation to expose the weaknesses and contradictions that tend to weaken the theory that testosterone controls the organization of mechanisms in the brain which are destined to mediate copulatory behavior in adult males and females. At the same time I have attempted to review the reliable evidence demonstrating important relationships between hormonal conditions during development and mating responses shown during adulthood. It is suggested that at the present state of knowledge formal and quantitative statements of such relationships can better be made in terms of intervening variables based upon directly observable S–R relationships than in terms of hypothetical constructs such as imaginary brain mechanisms.

REFERENCES

Adler, N. T., and Bell, D. (1969). Constant estrus in rats: Vaginal, reflexive and behavioral changes. *Physiol. Behav.* Vol. 4, 151–153.

Aria, Y. (1964). Long-lasting effects of early postnatal treatment with estrogen on pituitary-gonadal system in male rats. *Endocrinol. Jap.* Vol. 11, 153–158.

Aren-Engelbrektsson, B., Larsson, K., Sodersten, P., and Wilhelmsson, M. (1970). The female lordosis pattern induced in male rats by estrogen. *Horm. Behav.* Vol. 1, 181–202.

Ball, J. (1937). A test for measuring sexual excitability in the female rat. *Comp. Psychol. Monog.* Vol. 14, 1–37.

Barraclough, C. H., and Gorski, R. A. (1962). Studies on mating behaviour in the androgen-sterilized female rat in relation to the hypothalamic regulation of sexual behaviour. *J. Endocrinol.* Vol. 25, 175–182.

Beach, F. A. (1938). Sex reversals in the mating pattern of the rat. *J. Genet. Psychol.* Vol. 53, 329–334.

Beach, F. A. (1942). Male and female mating behavior in prepuberally castrated female rats treated with androgens. *Endocrinology* Vol. 31, 673–678.

Beach, F. A. (1945). Bisexual mating behavior in the male rat: Effects of castration and hormone administration. *Physiol. Zool.* Vol. 18, 390–402.

Beach, F. A. (1966). Ontogeny of "coitus-related" reflexes in the female guinea pig. *Proc. Nat. Acad. Sci. U. S.* Vol. 56, 526–532.

Beach, F. A., and Holz, A. M. (1946). Mating behavior in male rats castrated at various ages and injected with androgen. *J. Exp. Zool.* Vol. 101, 91–142.

Beach, F. A., and Kislak, J. M. (1955). Inhibition of aggressiveness by ovarian hormones. *Endocrinology* Vol. 56, 684–693.

Beach, F. A., and Pauker, R. S. (1949). Effects of castration upon mating behavior in the male hamster (*Cricetus auratus*). *Endocrinology* Vol. 45, 211–221.

Beach, F. A., and Rasquin, P. (1942). Masculine copulatory behavior in intact and castrated female rats. *Endocrinology* Vol. 31, 393–409.

Beach, F. A., Noble, R. G., and Orndoff, R. K. (1969). Effects of perinatal androgen treatment on responses of male rats to gonadal hormones in adulthood. *J. Comp. Physiol. Psychol.* Vol. 68, 490–497.

Boling, J. L., Blandau, R. J., Wilson, R. G., and Young, W. C. (1939). Post-parturitional heat responses of newborn and adult guinea pigs. Data on parturition. *Proc. Soc. Exp. Biol. Med.* Vol. 42, 128–132.

Clemens, L. G., Hiroi, M., and Gorski, R. A. (1969). Induction and facilitation of female mating behavior in rats treated neonatally with low doses of testosterone propionate. *Endocrinology* Vol. 84, 1430–1438.

Davidson, J. M. (1969). Effects of estrogen on the sexual behavior of male rats. *Endocrinology* Vol. 84, 1365–1372.

Diamond, M. (1965). The antagonistic actions of testosterone propionate and estrogens and progesterone on copulatory patterns of the female guinea pig. *Anat. Rec.* Vol. 151, 449. Abst.

Diamond, M. (1968). Genetic-endocrine interactions and human psychosexuality. *In* "Perspectives in Reproduction and Behavior" (M. Diamond, ed.), pp. 417–443. Indiana Univ. Press, Bloomington, Indiana.

Eaton, G. (1970). Effect of a single prepubertal injection of testosterone propionate on adult bisexual behavior of male hamsters castrated at birth. *Endocrinology*. Vol. 87, 934–940.

English, H. B., and English, A. C. (1958). "A Comprehensive Dictionary of Psychological and Psychoanalytical Terms." David McKay, Inc., New York.

Feder, H. H. (1967). Specificity of testosterone and estradiol in the differentiating neonatal rat. *Anat. Rec.* Vol. 157, 79–86.

Feder, H. H., and Whalen, R. E. (1965). Feminine behavior in neonatally castrated and estrogen-treated male rats. *Science* Vol. 147, 306–307.

Gerall, A. A. (1966). Hormonal factors influencing masculine behavior of female guinea pigs. *J. Comp. Physiol. Psychol.* Vol. 62, 365–369.

Gerall, A. A., and Ward, I. L. (1966). Effects of prenatal exogenous androgen on the sexual behavior of the female albino rat. *J. Comp. Physiol. Psychol.* Vol. 62, 370–375.

Gerall, A. A., Hendricks, S. E., Johnson, L. L., and Bounds, T. W. (1967). Effects of early castration in male rats on adult sexual behavior. *J. Comp. Physiol. Psychol.* Vol. 64, 206–212.

Goldfoot, D. A., Feder, H. H., and Goy, R. W. (1969). Development of bisexuality in the male rat treated neonatally with androstenedione. *J. Comp. Physiol. Psychol.* Vol. 67, 41–45.

Goy, R. W., Bridson, W. E., and Young, W. C. (1964). Period of maximal susceptibility of the prenatal female guinea pig to masculinizing actions of testosterone propionate. *J. Comp. Physiol. Psychol.* Vol. 57, 166–174.

Grady, K. L., Phoenix, C. H., and Young, W. C. (1965). Role of the developing rat testis in differentiation of the neural tissues mediating mating behavior. *J. Comp. Physiol. Psychol.* Vol. 59, 176–182.

Grunt, J. A., and Young, W. C. (1953). Differential reactivity of individuals and the response of the male guinea pig to testosterone propionate. *Endocrinology* Vol. 51, 237-248.

Harris, G. W. (1955). "Neural Control of the Pituitary Gland." Arnold, London.

Harris, G. W. (1964). Sex hormones, brain development and brain function. *Endocrinology* Vol. 75, 627-648.

Harris, G. W., and Levine, S. (1962). Sexual differentiation of the brain and its experimental control. *J. Physiol. (London)* Vol. 163, 42P-43P.

Harris, G. W., and Levine, S. (1965). Sexual differentiation of the brain and its experimental control. *J. Physiol. (London)* Vol. 181, 379-400.

Hertz, R., Meyer, R. K., and Spielman, M. A. (1937). The specificity of progesterone in inducing receptivity in the ovariectomized guinea pig. *Endocrinology* Vol. 21, 533.

Koster, R. (1943). Hormone factors in male behavior of the female rat. *Endocrinology* Vol. 33, 337-348.

Levine, S., and Mullins, R. F., Jr. (1964). Estrogen administered neonatally affects adult sexual behavior in male and female rats. *Science* Vol. 144, 185-187.

Lillie, F. R. (1917). The free-martin; a study of the action of sex hormones in the foetal life of cattle. *J. Exp. Zool.* Vol. 23, 371-385.

Meidinger, R. (1962). Differential effect of testosterone propionate given prenatally on sexually dimorphic and sexually isomorphic measures of behavior in the guinea pig. *Amer. Zool.* Vol. 2, 540.

Michael, R. P. (1961). Observations upon the sexual behaviour of the domestic cat (*Felis catus* L.) under laboratory conditions. *Behaviour* Vol. 28, 1-24.

Moore, C. S. (1919). On the physiological properties of the gonads as controllers of somatic and psychical characteristics. I. The rat. *J. Exp. Zool.* Vol. 28, 137-160.

Nadler, R. D. (1965). Masculinization of the female rat by intracranial implantation of androgen in infancy. Unpublished Doctoral Dissertation, University of California, Los Angeles, California.

Nadler, R. D. (1969). Differentiation of the capacity for male sexual behavior in the rat. *Horm. Behav.* Vol. 1, 53-63.

Neumann, F., and Elger, W. (1965). Physiological and psychical intersexuality of male rats by early treatment with an antiandrogenic agent (1, 2 a-methylene-6-chloro-Δ^6-hydroxyprogesterone acetate). *Acta Endocrinol.* Vol. 100, Suppl. 174.

Nucci, L. P., and Beach, F. A. (1971). Effects of prenatal androgen treatment on mating behavior in female hamsters. *Endocrinology* (in press).

Pfeiffer, C. A. (1936). Sexual differences of the hypophyses and their determination by the gonads. *Amer. J. Anat.* Vol. 58, 195-225.

Phoenix, C. H., Goy, R. W., Gerall, A. A., and Young, W. C. (1959). Organizing action of prenatally administered testosterone propionate on the tissues mediating mating behavior in the female guinea pig. *Endocrinology* Vol. 65, 369-382.

Phoenix, C. H., Goy, R. W., and Resko, J. A. (1968). Psychosexual differentiation as a function of androgenic stimulation. *In* "Perspectives in Reproduction and Sexual Behavior" (M. Diamond, ed.), pp. 33-49. Indiana Univ. Press, Bloomington, Indiana.

Phoenix, C. H., Goy, R. W., and Young, W. C. (1967). Sexual behavior: general aspects. *In* "Neuroendocrinology" (L. Martini and W. F. Ganong, eds.), pp. 163-196. Academic Press, New York.

Riss, W., Valenstein, E. S., Sinks, J., and Young, W. C. (1955). Development of sexual behavior in male guinea pigs from genetically different stocks under controlled conditions of androgen treatment and caging. *Endocrinology* Vol. 57, 139-146.

Spemann, H. (1938). "Embryonic Development and Induction." Yale Univ. Press, New Haven, Connecticut.

Sperry, R. W. (1943). Visuomotor coordination in the newt (*Triturus viridescens*) after regeneration of the optic nerve. *J. Comp. Neur.* Vol. 79, 33–55.

Steinach, E. (1912). Willkurliche Umwandlung von Saregetiermannchen in Tiere mit ausgepragt weiblichen Geschlechtskaracteren und Weiblicher Psyche. *Pfluegers Arch. Gesamte Physiol. Menschen Tiere* Vol. 144, 71–108.

Stern, J. J. (1969). The neonatal castration, androstenedione, and mating behavior of the male rat. *J. Comp. Physiol. Psychol.* Vol. 69, 608–612.

Stone, C. P. (1924). A note on "feminine" behavior in adult male rats. *Amer. J. Physiol.* Vol. 68, 39–41.

Swanson, H. H., and Crossley, D. A. (1970). Sexual behaviour in the golden hamster and its modification by neonatal administration of testosterone propionate. *In* "Proceedings of the International Conference on Hormones in Development" (M. Hamburgh and E. J. W. Berrington, eds.). Nat. Found., New York (in press).

Tiefer, L. (1970). Gonadal hormones and mating behavior in the adult golden hamster. *Horm. Behav.* Vol. 1, 189–202.

Ward, I. L. (1969). Differential effect of pre- and postnatal androgen on the sexual behavior of intact and spayed female rats. *Horm. Behav.* Vol. 1, 25–36.

Whalen, R. E. (1964). Hormone-induced changes in the organization of sexual behavior in the male rat. *J. Comp. Physiol. Psychol.* Vol. 57, 175–182.

Whalen, R. E. (1968). Differentiation of the neural mechanisms which control gonadotrophin secretion and sexual behavior. *In* "Perspectives in Reproduction and Sexual Behavior" (M. Diamond, ed.), pp. 303–340. Indiana Univ. Press, Bloomington, Indiana.

Whalen, R. E., and Edwards, D. A. (1966). Sexual reversibility in neonatally castrated male rats. *J. Comp. Physiol. Psychol.* Vol. 62, 307–310.

Whalen, R. E., and Edwards, D. A. (1967). Hormonal determinants of the development of masculine and feminine behavior in male and female rats. *Anat. Rec.* Vol. 157, 173–180.

Whalen, R. E., and Nadler, R. D. (1963). Suppression of the development of female mating behavior by estrogen administered in infancy. *Science* Vol. 141, 273–274.

Whalen, R. M., and Robertson, R. T. (1968). Sexual exhaustion and recovery of masculine copulatory behavior in virilized female rats. *Psychon. Sci.* Vol. 11, 319–320.

Whalen, R. E., Edwards, D. A., Luttge, W. G., and Robertson, R. T. (1969). Early androgen treatment and male sexual behavior in female rats. *Physiol. Behav.* Vol. 4, 33–39.

Young, W. C. (1961). The hormones and mating behavior. *In* "Sex and Internal Secretions" (W. C. Young, ed.), 3rd ed., Vol. 2, pp. 1173–1239. Williams & Wilkins, Baltimore, Maryland.

Young, W. C., and Rundlett, B. (1939). The hormonal induction of homosexual behavior in the spayed female guinea pig. *Psychosom. Med.* Vol. 1, 449–460.

Young, W. C., Dempsey, E. W., and Myers, H. I. (1935). Cyclic reproductive behavior in the female guinea pig. *J. Comp. Physiol. Psychol.* Vol. 19, 313–335.

Young, W. C., Dempsey, E. W., Myers, H. I., and Hagquist, C. W. (1938). The ovarian condition and sexual behavior in the female guinea pig. *Amer. J. Anat.* Vol. 63, 457–487.

Young, W. C., Goy, R. W., and Phoenix, C. H. (1964). The hormones and sexual behavior. Broad relationships exist between the gonadal hormones and behavior. *Science* Vol. 143, 212–218.

EXPERIENTIAL BACKGROUND FOR THE INDUCTION OF REPRODUCTIVE BEHAVIOR PATTERNS BY HORMONES

DANIEL S. LEHRMAN

There are a variety of events that take place after birth that have an effect upon the type of reproductive behavior an animal will show, that is, upon the probability that it will show different sorts of reproductive behavior and different kinds of orientation toward different objects.

Reproductive behavior is species-typical, that is, we can say that the behavior pattern is characteristic of the species. Animals of different species differ in characteristic ways with respect to these patterns. All animals reared in a normal environment show the behavior without any opportunity for having observed other animals, and the behavior appears in recognizable form without any apparent need for practice. It meets all the criteria for the sort of species-specific behavior that is ordinarily thought of as developing independently of experience.

It can be demonstrated that the experience the animal had before it became sexually mature contributes to the way in which hormones acting on the brain or on peripheral structures elicit the behavior patterns that we think of as being characteristic of the species. For example, very early experience, even experience pre-weaning, can have an effect upon the sort of sexual behavior that a male rat can show. If male rats are reared by hand and removed from their parents very, very early—this is very difficult to do, but a technique has been developed by which it can be done—then, when they are mature, they show drastically reduced ability to perform normal sexual behavior (Thoman and Arnold, 1968). In addition, Dr. Larsson recently found that if, instead of rearing them by hand, one male rat is reared alone with its mother, approximately the same effect is obtained (Hard and Larsson, 1968). Being reared apart from a litter, or without the stimulation afforded by a litter very early in pre-weaning life, has the effect of reducing the intensity and frequency of male sexual behavior.

Behavioral experience that takes place after weaning, but substantially before puberty, also has an effect on the organization of sexual behavior. For example, the late William C. Young and his colleagues showed that the amount of social experience that the guinea pig has between the ages of 10 and 25 days of age with other guinea pigs of the same age, noticeably affects the level of sexual behavior that they show when mature and the amount of sexual behavior they show if they are castrated and then given a dose of male hormone. This early experience, which occurs after weaning but before puberty, has an effect on the way in which the tissues respond to the male hormone so as to give rise to the sexual behavior. These are experiential effects that do not constitute practicing the behavior, and they do not constitute observing other animals doing the behavior, but they are experiential effects nevertheless (Young, 1961).

It is also possible to show that actual reproductive experience, the initial level of which is partly determined by prepubertal social experience and by pre-weaning experience with the mother and with littermates, in turn has an effect upon the developing efficiency of reproductive behavior. For example, birds and mammals that have previously bred are more efficient in producing young than animals that have not previously bred. These differences are easily demonstrated. Rochelle Wortis and I (Lehrman and Wortis, 1967) compared the reproductive efficiency of ringdoves that were breeding for the first time, with ringdoves of the same age that had had previous breeding experience. We found that the birds with previous breeding experience laid eggs sooner, they incubated more efficiently, they raised their young more efficiently and reared more young to maturity. In all the respects in which you can measure the efficiency of behavior, the experienced birds were superior. It is a well-known phenomenon that the first breeding experience is rather inefficient. Observations of rhesus monkeys breeding for the first time have proved them to be inefficient in rearing young, that is, in reacting appropriately to the different parts of the body of the young and in keeping the young appropriately oriented to the nipple.

The effects of injected hormones on animals that have had previous experience are strikingly different from the effects of such injections upon animals that have not had previous experience. Male cats that have had sexual experience before they were castrated show sexual behavior persisting after castration for substantially longer than do male cats that have not had sexual experience before being castrated at the same age (Rosenblatt and Aronson, 1958). An interesting point is that this phenomenon is not found in dogs. In experiments done recently by Frank Beach (1970) inexperienced dogs did not differ substantially from experienced dogs.

It is clear that there are striking species differences with respect to the role that experience plays. If you inject progesterone into ringdoves that have had previous breeding experience and into ringdoves that have not had previous breeding experience, there are striking differences in the frequency with which the progesterone will induce the birds to sit on eggs. The median time that it takes before experienced birds injected with progesterone stand on the nest—in one experimental setup—after they are put in the cage, is under a minute. The median time with inexperienced birds would be on the order of an hour or so. The median time until the experienced bird is actually sitting, is on the order of 25 minutes, the median time with inexperienced birds is on the order of 25 or 26 *hours*. Also, the number of birds that eventually find the eggs in these circumstances is substantially higher among experienced birds than among inexperienced birds.

George Michel in our laboratory is now trying to find out what part of the breeding cycle an adult has to experience so that later on it will act as an experienced bird rather than as an inexperienced bird when it is injected with progesterone. He finds that if the birds experience nest building but not the laying of eggs or the sitting on eggs, there is a substantial improvement in the readiness with which they will sit on the eggs later on, after they have been injected with progesterone and after a period during which they have not been in the breeding situation. That is not terribly surprising when you consider the fact that although there are very striking differences between the frequency with which experienced and inexperienced birds will sit on eggs as a consequence of progesterone injections, inexperienced birds who are breeding for the first time always, or almost always, sit on the eggs.

That is an extraordinary thing and worth thinking about. If you were to use an animal's ability to sit on the egg appropriately the first time it ever bred as a criterion for the role of experience, you would not be able to demonstrate a learning curve between the first, second, third, and fourth breeding experience nor could you say that the animal is somehow learning to sit on the eggs. If you wanted to compare birds breeding for the first time and for the second time, with respect to their reaction to the eggs, you would not be able to detect any difference in the frequency with which they would sit on the eggs after having laid them. They all sit on the eggs. You would have to say that experience does not play any significant role in determining whether the birds could sit on the eggs. However, if you take birds that are not in a breeding situation, and inject them with a hormone capable of inducing them to sit on eggs, you find striking differences between experienced and inexperienced birds: 75% of the experienced birds sit on the eggs, while only 20% of the inexperienced birds sit on the eggs.

In order to understand the role of experience you have to think not only of the repeated cycles or repeated breeding experiences that may lead to an improvement in the behavior of the animals—in the sense of the animal's learning how to do it better as it breeds over and over again—but that the experience of an animal during the first part of its breeding cycle is actually playing a role in orienting it appropriately to the environment during the later parts of the same breeding cycle.

All of these effects showing the role of pre-weaning experience, of post-weaning experience during prepubertal life, of actual breeding experience, of the experience during the early parts of the cycle and during the later parts of the cycle, and the striking differences in the way the animal responds to hormones are the effects of experience that the individual animal has had during its life. These are effects on the kind of behavior that leaps to mind when one thinks of complex "innate" behavior patterns.

There are different approaches to discussing these behavior patterns and analyzing their development. If I concentrate on attempts to elucidate the role of individual experience in organizing the behavior and determining its various characteristics, and if Dr. Sperry (see p. 27) devotes the bulk of his efforts to showing that fixed patterns in the central nervous system are the rule in many of the behavior patterns that were previously assumed to be determined by experience, this does not necessarily mean that Dr. Sperry and I disagree with each other about the interpretation of his data or of ours. I believe that Dr. Sperry, in a sense, stopped at a certain point, a point from which I started.

If a bird that has had previous breeding experience sits on eggs or responds to hormone injections much more efficiently by finding the eggs than a bird that has not had such experience, this does not imply that the basic mechanisms in the central nervous system that respond to the hormones and are responsible for the organization of the behavior are themselves organized through the kind of experience that was described. It implies that we have to have a different way of conceiving of the relationship between the patterns that Dr. Sperry studies and the behavior that I am describing. Dr. Sperry has demonstrated that the retina of an amphibian has a complex reliable topographical relationship with visual centers in the brain, and that outgoing nerve fibers find those relationships when they grow, in spite of the most drastic attempts to interfere with them. This implies that the visual input while the connections are growing is not playing a role in determining how the connections will be made.

It is obvious from work done by others (Hubel and Wiesel, 1959) that in the eye of the cat equally precise connections are made which have equally elaborate geographical correspondences between central surfaces and retinal surfaces. The sort of physiological connection that was the basis of what happened in the frog is equally rigid in the cat. The dominant visual response of the cat is to move its paw in such a way as to reach at a moving object. This ability, however, depends to some extent upon the cat's experience with paw–eye coordination (Held and Hein, 1963).

It has been shown that the topographical organization of the orientation of visual fields in the cat cortex is present at birth, or at the time the eye opens, but that it deteriorates if the eyes are kept closed (Hubel and Wiesel, 1959).

There are a number of things you can say about that. Finding that the organization exists when the eye first opens, you can say it develops without experience, and that would be true. You can say that the organization of the visual cortex is not as fine or as precise and detailed as it is going to be later on, because the cat has not yet had any visual experience and that would be true too. Depending upon your orientation toward these problems, you can interpret the way a light-deprived 6-week-old cat reacts visually to the world by saying there was an innate mechanism which developed and then deteriorated through nonuse. In that way, you can imply that experience plays no role in determining the behavior of the adult animal. *Or*, you can say that the organization that you see in the normal 6-week-old cat depends to some extent upon experience. Either of those two formulations is perfectly correct, provided it is clearly understood who is saying what.

It is not necessary to conceive of the relationship between growth processes and experience in dichotomous either/or terms, by assuming that the behavior of an adult animal is divisible by an observer of behavior into units, each of which can be described as dependent or not upon experience, or as innate or acquired. It might be correct to say that you can divide the adult behavioral pattern of an animal into units, but it is not possible to say each unit can be described as totally dependent on experience or totally independent of experience.

When I study reproductive behavior patterns in terms of the kind of experiences that played a role in determining the development of these hormone-induced behavior patterns, I am choosing for analysis one sort of influence that operates during development. This is by no means the same thing as saying that all these behavior patterns are learned, because, if we were to say that all these behavior patterns are learned, that would be implying that a bird of one species could learn to perform the courtship pattern of a bird of another species, or that a bird that normally sits on its eggs could learn to incubate its eggs by building a pile of rotting vegetation and letting the heat of the rotting vegetation incubate the eggs, which some birds do. By studying the role of experience in the development of these behavior patterns one does not imply that they are "learned," in any conventional sense.

I think it is not correct to refer to this sort of developmental research as expressing an "environmental" orientation in the sense that it denies the sort of growth processes and the sort of neural organization that Dr. Sperry describes. The problems posed by Dr. Sperry about neural organization are rather similar to those dealing with complex reproductive behavior patterns. Both have physiological responses underlying them, mechanisms that you could no doubt show develop independently of traditional forms of experience and form a part of the neurophysiological basis for the behavior patterns. However, you cannot extrapolate from that fact the assertion that experience is not relevant to the behavior patterns or to the neural organization. The formulation I have suggested does not require that people who study one aspect of development are "environmentalists" and people who study another aspect of development are "hereditarians."

REFERENCES

Beach, F. A. (1970). Coital behavior in dogs: VI. Long-term effects of castration upon mating in the male. *J. Comp. Physiol. Psychol. Mon.* Vol. 70, Part 2, 1–32.

Held, R., and Hein, A. (1963). Movement-produced stimulation in the development of usually guided behavior. *J. Comp. Physiol. Psychol.* Vol. 56, 872–876.

Hubel, D. H., and Wiesel, T. N. (1959). Receptive fields of single neurones in the cat's striate cortex. *J. Physiol.* Vol. 148, 574–591.

Hard, E., and Larsson, K. (1968). Dependence of adult mating behavior in male rats on the presence of littermates in infancy. *Brain, Behavior & Evolution* Vol. 1, 405–419.

Lehrman, D. S., and Wortis, R. P. (1967). Breeding experience and breeding efficiency in the ringdove. *Anim. Behav.* Vol. 15, 223–228.

Rosenblatt, J. S., and Aronson, L. R. (1958). The influence of experience on the behavioral effects of androgen in pre-puberally castrated male cats. *Anim. Behav.* Vol. 6, 171–182.

Thoman, E. B., and Arnold, W. J. (1968). Effects of early social deprivation on maternal behavior in the rat. *J. Comp. Physiol. Psych.* Vol. 65, 55–59.

Young, W. C. (1961). The hormones and mating behavior. *In* "Sex and Internal Secretions," Williams and Wilkins, Baltimore.

EFFECTS OF ENVIRONMENT ON DEVELOPMENT OF BRAIN AND OF BEHAVIOR

MARK R. ROSENZWEIG

This paper is concerned with post-weaning development of brain and of behavior in animal subjects, largely rodents. Specifically, it considers both ways in which differential environments may affect development and how such effects may be interpreted. In the successive sections of this chapter, I will take up the five main questions listed below, surveying both empirical evidence and methodological problems that have come out of attempts to answer them:

I. How does the post-weaning environment affect the brain—anatomically, chemically, and electrophysiologically? In other words, what measurable alterations are produced in the brain by modifications of such aspects of the environment as social grouping, cage size, and stimulus objects?

II. Are the observed cerebral changes all due to different degrees of impoverishment of environment, or are some due to enrichment of environment above the "normal" baseline? This requires us to consider how a "normal" baseline can be defined.

III. How does previous post-weaning environment affect problem-solving behavior, and can some of the effects be attributed to enrichment of the environment?

IV. Can some of the behavioral consequences of previous environmental treatment be shown to depend upon some of the cerebral effects?

V. Can some of the cerebral effects of previous environmental conditions be demonstrated to be due to learning that took place in that environment? This requires us to consider what experimental designs and outcomes would permit a positive answer to this question.

The unexpected finding that experience engenders anatomical as well as chemical changes in the brain poses problems of interpretation. The meaning of the changes is not yet known, but, on the general assumption that brain processes and behavior are closely correlated, we believe that seeking to interpret them will increase our understanding of both brain and behavior.

Before taking up the first question, I wish to state explicitly that the terms "enriched environment" and "impoverished environment," which will be encountered at several points, are employed in this chapter only as convenient designations for experimental conditions that have been described in detail elsewhere. The terms are not used here in an evaluative sense. Furthermore, it is not implied that other conditions that might also be described as "enriched" or "impoverished" would necessarily have similar cerebral or behavioral effects. As will be discussed later in this paper, it is an empirical matter to determine what conditions are effective, and at what ages, for what kinds of subjects, and on what measures.

Effects of Post-Weaning Environment on Brain

The brains of most mammals are far from mature at weaning, even though the animal is then able to fend for itself. The brain of the 25-day-old rat, for example, weighs only about two-thirds of its adult value. The considerable growth that occurs after weaning can be altered by environmental influences. Furthermore, even the adult brain can be modified by experience, as we shall see.

Whether modifications due to experience include changes in neural circuits, and, if so, what types of circuit modification can be accomplished in this way, are subjects of current research and debate. Those whose research has been largely in the field of embryonic development are impressed by the intricate circuits that develop without any specific environmental influences; only nutritive support seems to be required. Those who study learning, the prolonged growth of learning capacity with age in mammals and the different paths that this may take, frequently suppose that new neural connections are developed to make these behavioral modifications possible.

Sperry (1965) has discussed several possible effects of use on neural elements:

> One can arbitrarily distinguish use effects that consist of stamping in and preserving neural organization developed in growth, from use effects that add new organization, anatomical or physiological, to the developed system. Despite common impressions to the contrary (especially in psychology) it appears to be mainly the former that has been involved in most of the sensory deprivation studies to date (Sperry, 1951). The above distinction tends to break

down, however, in the central association areas, where the growth pressures are more diffuse. It is not clear at present to what extent fractional parts of a neuron, like synaptic endings, and separate dendritic branches, spines, or other elements may undergo disuse atrophy, leaving other parts of the same neuron normally functional. . . .

Furthermore, it remains an open question whether the effects of function— that is, learning and memory—add or subtract any actual fiber structures or synaptic connections to the established morphology. It is possible, though not particularly indicated, that the neural changes implanted by learning and memory are essentially physiological in nature; membrane or other micro or molecular changes could affect excitatory threshold conductance, and resistance to impulse transmission, or endogenous discharge properties all within the already established morphological networks. Between the strictly inherited organization of the behavioral networks and the strictly acquired, we recognize an important intermediate realm of nervous development in which function and growth go on simultaneously with mutual interactions. The anatomical effects of functional influence during these stages may not be large or even visible under the light microscope, but the minute differences may be critical in terms of behavior, especially with reference to human childhood.

Székely (1966), who has also investigated embryonic determinants of neural circuits, stresses the need for new connections to ensure plasticity. He points out that a system of specific connections, secured once and for all by attraction or repulsion of specific biochemical or antigen–antibody character, leaves no room for phenomena of conditioning and learning. He maintains that to hold a neuronal specificity theory would be to attribute a switchboard-like character to the nervous system in general.

With such considerations in mind, let us look at some cerebral effects produced by differential environmental treatments. First, however, let us note briefly some historical background of such research.

INCONCLUSIVE EARLY RESEARCH

The idea that training or experience might alter brain measures goes back at least to the 18th century. The Piedmontese anatomist M. V. Malacarne gave training to one member of several pairs of animals and no training to the other. Effects of training could, he concluded, be seen in changes in the cerebellum. It was doubtless with this experiment in mind that the German physician S. T. von Soemmering wrote as follows in his major book on human anatomy (1791):

Does use change the structure of the brain?
Does use and exertion of mental power gradually change the material structure of the brain, just as we see, for example, that much used muscles become stronger and that hard labor thickens the epidermis considerably? It is not improbable, although the scalpel cannot easily demonstrate this.

During the 19th century, speculation and some observations were brought to this question by varied contributors such as Spurzheim, Darwin, Broca, and Galton. Lack of adequate experimental and statistical techniques, however, precluded a clear demonstration of effects of experience on the brain. Furthermore, during this period data were accumulating on the relative stability of the brain as compared with other organs. Thus there arose the conclusion that the brain could not be altered measurably by experience, and this had assumed the force of dogma by the beginning of the 20th century. Sperry (p. 27) has pointed out that many investigators 30 years ago believed neural circuits to be highly plastic, but this does not contradict the fact that they did not expect or look for measurable changes in brain anatomy or chemistry.

Only in the 1950's and 1960's have investigators convinced themselves that they could alter the brain anatomically and chemically through differential experience. As we have stated previously (E. L. Bennett *et al.*, 1964), we did not at the outset of our research intend to look for changes in the size or weight of the brain, because the hypothesis that "cerebral exercise" can increase the size of the brain had been pretty generally abandoned by the start of the 20th century. Indeed, we had completed several experiments and had published two papers on effects of experience on brain chemistry (Krech *et al.*, 1960; Rosenzweig *et al.*, 1961) before further examination of the data suggested that there were anatomical changes as well (Rosenzweig *et al.*, 1962).

IMPOVERISHED ENVIRONMENT

By now it is well known that deprivation of vision early in life modifies both the retina and the brain. Riesen (1966) had reviewed in detail effects on the nervous system and on behavior of deafferentation or of occlusion of an intact sensory system. Among the cerebral effects of dark-rearing or occlusion of the eyes are reduced diameters of cell nuclei in the visual cortex (Gyllensten *et al.*, 1965), decreased cortical vascularity (Gyllensten, 1959), and continued immaturity of form of cortical evoked potentials (Scherrer and Fourment, 1964). Baxter (1966) reported that dark-raised kittens showed no differences in spontaneous EEG, but that their responses to flicker were significantly below normal. After 10 months in the dark, recovery of behavioral capacities was poor in cats kept in laboratory cages but was clearly better in the complex environment of the experimenter's home. Coleman and Riesen (1968) have reported that cats kept in the dark develop fewer higher order branches in the dendrites of neurons in the visual cortex than do visually experienced littermates. Actually, only three pairs of animals were used, and no effect was found in one pair. Clearly, a larger sample will be required before one can reach any conclusion about effects of visual experience on the branching of dendrites in the visual cortex.

Hubel (1957) and Wiesel and Hubel (1966) have reported an interesting series of studies indicating that the connections necessary for binocular interaction develop even without visual experience but that they can be disrupted by independent activation of the eyes. Thus this effect results, not from active competition, but from failure of cooperation of the eyes (Hubel, 1967).

Globus and Scheibel (1967) found a significant reduction in the number of dendritic spines on the apical shafts of pyramidal cells in the striate cortex of young rabbits following unilateral enucleation or lesion of the lateral geniculate. There were no clear changes in the cell bodies or in the dendritic arbors (also see Fifková, 1967). Rats allowed vision but kept in an impoverished environment also show differences in brain chemistry and anatomy when compared with colony controls (E. L. Bennett *et al.*, 1964). In the impoverished condition (IC) rats live singly in small bare cages, but other features of the environment are the same as for colony animals. The IC rats show, in comparison with standard colony (SC) littermates, lesser weight of cortical tissue, lesser thickness of cerebral cortex, and differences in the activities of cortical acetylcholinesterase (AChE) and cholinesterase (ChE).

Compensatory Changes?

Krech *et al.* (1963) found that rats blinded at weaning showed, 80 days later, lesser cortical mass than sighted littermates in every cortical region measured except the somesthetic region. The somesthetic region actually weighed somewhat more in blinded than in sighted rats. Dark-reared versus normally reared rats showed a similar trend (E. L. Bennett *et al.*, 1964). We hypothesized that the animals deprived of sight might be relying more on tactile sensitivity and kinesthesis, and that this might produce "compensatory" development of the somesthetic area. MacNeill and Zubek (1967) failed to find increased weight of somesthetic cortex among dark-reared rats, but they suggested that this may have occurred because they had not used as complex a somesthetic environment as did the Berkeley group. Auditory cortex was not measured in the previous studies, but Gyllensten *et al.* (1966) have reported that rearing mice in the dark leads to hypertrophy of the auditory area.

ENRICHED ENVIRONMENT

Adding stimulation to the baseline environment may also alter the nervous system. Heron and Anchel (1964) raised experimental rats in an environment containing continuous flashes and clicks given at a 5-per-second rate. These animals showed more spontaneous electrocortical spindling than did control rats, and their spindles showed a 5-cycle rhythm rather than the 7-cycle rhythm of controls.

We have previously shown that rats put in an enriched environment at weaning develop differences in brain weights and brain chemistry (E. L. Bennett *et al.,* 1964) and in brain anatomy (Diamond, 1967) when compared with littermates kept under either colony or isolated conditions. The enriched environment in this case consists of being housed in a group of 10 to 12 animals in a large cage which contains varied stimulus objects; other aspects of the environment are the same as for colony animals. In the enriched condition (EC) rats develop greater weight of cerebral cortex, greater depth of cortex, and greater total activities of acetylcholinesterase (AChE), cholinesterase (ChE), and hexokinase in cortex than do their colony or isolated littermates. We have replicated these effects in a large number of experiments (Rosenzweig *et al.,* 1969; E. L. Bennett and Rosenzweig, 1970). The greater thickness of cortex in EC than in IC rats has also been replicated recently by Walsh *et al.* (1969). These EC–IC differences, and certain others that are based on smaller members of observations, are shown in Table 1 for a standard sample of the occipital region of the cortex. The table shows results only for experiments of 80-day duration conducted with the Berkeley S_1 strain of rats. Corroborating results have also been obtained in experiments with other strains and with other experimental durations. There is not space here to present detailed descriptions of the

TABLE 1

Effects of Differential Experience on Occipital Cortex of S_1 Rats Kept in Enriched or Impoverished Conditions from 25 to 105 Days of Age

Measure	Percentage differences (EC-IC)	P	EC > IC (No.)
Weight	6.2	<0.001	114/151
Total protein	7.8[a]	<0.001	25/32
Thickness	6.3	<0.001	47/52
Total AChE	2.6	<0.01	90/150
Total ChE	10.2	<0.001	86.5/108
Total hexokinase	6.9[b]	<0.01	17/21
Neurons (No.)	−3.1	NS	7/17
Glia (No.)	14.0	<0.01	12/17
Perikaryon cross section	13.4	<0.001	11.5/13

[a] Weight difference 7.0% in these experiments.
[b] Weight difference 5.5% in these experiments.

TABLE 2
Comparisons of Percentage Differences between EC and IC Brain Weights from Experiments of Various Durations[a,b]

Duration (days)	80	30	30
Hours per day in EC	24	24	2
Experiments (No.)	14	10	3
Pairs (No.)	151	111	28
Percentage differences			
Occipital cortex	6.2†	10.4†	15.0†
Total cortex	4.1†	6.5†	4.1†
Rest of brain	−1.0*	1.0*	−0.4
Cortex/rest	5.2†	5.4†	4.6†

[a] Male S_1 rats; experiments started at about 25 days of age.
[b] Key: (*) $P < 0.01$; (†) $P < 0.001$.

behavioral conditions, the standardized methods for taking brain samples, or the chemical methods; the reader is referred to our original reports for these matters.[1]

It is easier to produce the cerebral changes than we originally supposed. As Table 2 shows, lessening the duration of EC–IC treatment from 80 to 30 days does not decrease the percentage differences between EC and IC in brain weights. In fact, for the occipital cortex the difference is larger after 30 days than after 80 days. The exposure to the complex environment can even be reduced to 2 hours per day over a 30-day period without lessening the EC–IC difference, as will be seen in the right-hand column. The ratio of cortical weight to that of the rest of the brain is a particularly stable measure and is virtually identical for all three conditions of Table 2.

Questions about Basic EC–IC Effects

Five of the main questions which arise in regard to our experimental results will be considered next.

How Can the Brain Samples Be Dissected Accurately and Without Contamination of Cortex by White Matter? We have described in detail how we employ a small calibrated plastic T-square to locate standard samples of the occipital, somesthetic, and motor regions of the cortex (Rosenzweig et al., 1962; Krech et al., 1963). A step-by-step procedural description has been made available in dittoed form to any investigator

---

[1] Note added in proof: Our most recent and fullest description of methods and report of results is the following chapter: Rosenzweig, M. R., Bennett, E. L., and Diamond, M. C. (1971). Chemical and anatomical plasticity of brain: replications and extensions. In "Macromolecules and Behavior" (J. Gaito, ed.), 2nd ed. Plenum Press, New York.

requesting it. A few of the points should be emphasized here. When a cortical sample has been circumscribed with a scalpel, it can readily be peeled from the white matter, because in rodents the cortex is quite soft and can easily be separated from the rather firm white matter; this mechanical difference is not as great in carnivores or primates. The animals are sacrificed by code numbers so that matched animals from different conditions are taken in immediate succession, but the person doing the dissection does not know from what condition any particular animal came. Fortunately, one skilled collaborator, Mrs. Marie Hebert, has done all our dissections since 1959; therefore, we have not had to test how reliably another person could perform this task. Our own results have been extremely reproducible over many years and many experiments (e.g., see Fig. 4-4 in E. L. Bennett and Rosenzweig, 1968). As has been noted above, we did not originally expect to find brain weight differences, and we overlooked these effects in several experiments, but they were there to be found. As a last point, we may note that the measures of cortical thickness, which do not involve removal of cortex from white matter, corroborate the measures of tissue weight.

May the EC–IC Differences in Tissue Weight Arise from Differences in Fluid Content? For reasons that we had given in 1964 (E. L. Bennett et al., 1964) we were sure that changes in fluid content could not account for the EC–IC weight differences. Nevertheless, the question continued to be asked, so we decided to seek a direct answer. Tissues from a 30-day EC–IC experiment were dissected, and fresh weights were taken in the usual manner. Then the tissues were lyophilized, losing more than three-quarters of their original weight. The dried tissues were reweighed, and the percentage EC–IC differences were virtually identical with those previously found for the fresh tissue (E. L. Bennett *et al.*, 1968).

Since Some EC–IC Percentage Differences Diminish with Longer Periods in the Experimental Environments, Does This Mean That the EC Brain Values Actually Decrease? No, the fact that some differences between EC and IC are larger after 30 than after 80 days does not mean that the EC values reach a peak and then decrease. Both EC and IC brain weights are increasing rapidly at 25 days of age, when the rats are put into the experimental environments. The EC gains more rapidly at first, and then its rate of increase slows down; the IC gains more slowly at first, but then does not show as much of a change in rate as does the EC, so the gap between the two diminishes.

Do Nutrition and Body Weights Play Roles in Determining the Differences in Brain Weights? All animals—whether in the enriched, colony, or improvished conditions—have food and water available at all times. Standard laboratory chow pellets are used. We have not measured food intake. As we have reported, at the end of differential treatment started at 25 days of age and terminated at 105 days, the EC rats weigh about 10% less than their IC littermates. Thus the heavier brain weights of EC animals are achieved despite lower body weights. It would not be correct to take the ratio of brain weight to body weight because the brain, unlike most organs, does not grow as a direct function of body weight. One can properly, within an experiment, correct brain weight for its covariance on body weight; doing this increases somewhat the percentage EC–IC differences that we have reported above.

In our experiments the different treatment groups are equivalent in weight at the outset. Some investigators have matched animals for body weight at the end of the experiment, but this can distort the results by selecting only the heaviest animals from one group and the lightest from another.

Are There Seasonal Effects in the Size of EC–IC Differences, Perhaps Reflecting Hormonal Changes? We have looked for possible seasonal effects in our results but have not found any evidence for their existence. Perhaps the laboratory rat has had seasonal cycles bred out of it, and the uniform laboratory environment would also tend to obscure seasonal effects. Feral animals with which we have begun to work (see below) may reveal seasonal differences in brain responses to environment, but perhaps they will appear only where climatic changes are more pronounced than in Berkeley, California.

Further Effects of Enrichment

In order to test whether neuronal connectivity might be affected by differential environments, we have undertaken, in collaboration with Dr. Albert Globus, to count dendritic spines of pyramidal cells in the occipital area. This was done in littermates assigned to EC or IC for the period 25 to 55 days of age. Preliminary results indicate that the number of spines per unit of dendritic length is somewhat greater in EC than in IC. Furthermore, since cortex is significantly thicker in EC animals, dendritic length is probably greater in EC animals and, as a consequence, the total number of spines is probably greater in EC than in IC. The greater number of total spines in EC, as compared to IC animals, appears to be related principally to greater length of dendrites rather than to closer spacing of spines along the dendrites.

Altman *et al.* (1968) have reported that either living in an enriched environment or 2 months of formal training increase hemispheric length of rats by about 5% over that of colony controls. We have found enriched-environment rats to show only a 1% increase in length of the cerebral hemispheres over that of colony littermates; a difference of this magnitude is commensurate with the 3% increase observed in brain weight (Rosenzweig and Bennett, 1970).

Because of indications that the hippocampus may be importantly involved in learning and memory storage, we undertook measures of hippocampal thickness in S_1 littermate pairs kept in EC or IC from 25 to 105 days of age (Diamond et al., 1970). Hippocampal thickness was measured on the same slides that were used for cortical thickness, and this was done for all six experiments for which we have reported cortical thickness (Diamond et al., 1966, 1967). We considered data for only those pairs in which the hippocampus of both littermates could be measured. For 51 pairs the mean EC hippocampal thickness was 2.4% greater than that of IC ($P < 0.05$); in 30 of the 51 pairs the EC rat showed greater thickness than the IC rat. This difference in hippocampal thickness is smaller and less reliable than the EC–IC difference in cortical thickness, as can be seen by comparison with the cortical thickness results of Table 1 (6.3%, $P < 0.001$); the hippocampal and cortical thickness data are based largely, but not entirely, on the same pairs. Whereas each of the experiments showed a cortical difference in favor of the enriched condition, the hippocampal results were highly variable, with only four of the six experiments yielding differences in favor of the EC. Walsh et al. (1969) have recently presented measures of both cortical and hippocampal thickness from a single experiment with nine EC and eight IC rats. They report EC–IC differences of 4.9% ($P < 0.01$) for cortical thickness and of 5.7% ($P < 0.05$) for hippocampal thickness. It should be noted that their hippocampal results also show greater variability than the cortical results, since the statistical significance of the hippocampal effect is lower even though the percentage difference is larger than the cortical effect. It appears, then, that there probably is an EC–IC difference in hippocampal thickness but that it is less consistent and reliable than the cortical thickness effect. Walsh et al. (1970) also state that they have confirmed our report (Diamond et al., 1966) of an increased glial/neuronal ratio in the cortex of EC as compared to IC rats. They also present cell counts for the hippocampus, indicating large and highly significant EC–IC differences for various types of glial cells.

Species generality of the main effects has been tested by subjecting other species of rodents to differential environments. La Torre (1968) found significant differences in brain weights and brain enzymes between EC and IC mice. We have recently run Mongolian gerbils (*Meriones unguiculatus*) in our enriched, colony, and impoverished situations for a month, starting at 30 days of age (Rosenzweig and Bennett, 1970). In the two gerbil experiments, the EC differed significantly from the SC on several measures of brain weights and enzyme activities; on most measures IC animals differed in the opposite direction. Thus these results are not restricted to rats.

The Problem of Baseline for Experimental Environments

In trying to measure effects of an enriched environment on development of brain and behavior, the problem of an appropriate baseline assumes major importance. It is assumed that enrichment is in reference to "normal" living conditions for the animal in question, but what is "normal," especially in the case of animals that have been domesticated or animals that have been bred for laboratory life?

From our first experiments (Krech *et al.*, 1960) we employed a standard colony (SC) group as a baseline. Although this condition does not represent the life of feral rats, it is the baseline for most animal experiments in psychology, anatomy, physiology, and brain biochemistry and thus provides a common point of reference. Nevertheless, we have noted (Krech *et al.*, 1966, p. 103) that "The SC animals are somewhat impoverished, since they spend all their time in small cages with only two cagemates and have no opportunity to explore new territory . . . ." The fact that the reference group may be somewhat impoverished may not be too serious if one is studying effects of further impoverishment, unless the baseline condition already produces all of the effects of impoverishment, leaving no apparent effect for the more restricted condition labeled "impoverished." Lessac and Solomon (1969, p. 15) commented on this problem in the following way when describing their experiment on learning in "normally" reared and isolated beagles:

> The definition of "normal" rearing is a difficult one. In a laboratory there is no "wild" environment, and so the ethologists stress how "abnormal" the laboratory is. But in the "wild" there are no psychologists teaching animals complex, abstract concepts! There seems to be no alternative, at the moment, to the purely arbitrary definition of normal rearing for each experiment. . . . In the case of the experiment the authors describe, normal rearing consisted of kennel-like treatment of beagles. . . .

When possible effects of enrichment, rather than impoverishment, are to be studied, the problem of baseline becomes even more critical. If the reference group is itself impoverished, then a condition that is enriched above the baseline may, nevertheless, be impoverished on an absolute scale (if such a scale exists). This possibility is presented diagrammatically in Table 3, hypothesis A. In this case effects attributed to enrichment would represent only the results of lessened impoverish-

TABLE 3
Hypothesis Relating Laboratory Conditions to "Natural" Baseline

Scale of environmental stimulation for learning	Hypothesis A	Hypothesis B
High		Enriched laboratory condition
	---------------"Natural" baseline---------------	
	Enriched laboratory condition	
		Standard colony condition
Low	Standard colony condition Impoverished laboratory condition	Impoverished laboratory condition

ment. However, even if the colony condition is somewhat poorer than the natural baseline, it is nevertheless possible that the enriched laboratory condition is more stimulating and presents more opportunities for learning than occur for the species in nature. This is hypothesis B in Table 3. Our difficulty is that we have not been able to find a sure way to determine, for domesticated animals, whether our experimental conditions resemble case A or case B.[2]

In the case of man, who has domesticated himself, it is also difficult if not impossible to determine or define a natural baseline of environmental conditions. Thus Mussen (1967, p. 68), in reviewing studies of effects of maternal care on emotional and intellectual development in children, concluded that ". . . dramatic difficulties and maladjustments characterize children who encountered exceptional deprivation of intimate, personal, or warm maternal care in earliest years." He went on to comment, "Apparently a minimum amount of such care is required for adequate development and adjustment . . ." but he noted that ". . . it is not possible to define this minimum precisely." With man it is, of course, a problem of intense interest, both theoretical and practical, whether enrichment beyond any particular environment that is the norm for a given time and place will alter brain, emotion, and intelligence. Vandenberg (1968) has used a botanical analogy, asking if there is only an effect of *stunting* from lack of early stimulation or if, on the contrary, enriched experience can act like a *hothouse,* forcing an early bloom

---

[2] Note added in proof. Experiments conducted in 1970 and 1971 support hypothesis A. In these experiments laboratory rats put for 30 days in a large outdoor enclosure developed brain measures further in the enrichment direction than did littermates kept in the laboratory-enriched condition.

which is nevertheless no different from a normal bloom, or if it acts like a *fertilizer,* producing bigger and better yields.

RESEARCH WITH FERAL ANIMALS AS A POSSIBLE SOLUTION

In the face of difficulties of solving the problem of the baseline with domesticated animals, it may be possible to make headway by working with feral animals. In their case, a natural baseline can be determined. An example of such research, with forest and urban monkeys, will be discussed later in this paper.

In order to attempt to relate results of environmental enrichment and impoverishment to a feral baseline, our research group is therefore undertaking work with a species of deermouse, *Peromyscus maniculatus*. These animals can be trapped wild near our laboratories, and wild-trapped individuals adjust readily to laboratory conditions (Kavanau, 1967). In the Field Station for Animal Behavior above the Berkeley campus, we can raise *Peromyscus* under seminatural conditions, adding enrichment or restricting the stimulation available. Thus we hope to be able to compare brain and behavior of deermice taken directly from the wild with those subjected to a variety of artificial conditions. When results have been obtained from these experiments, they should be helpful in interpreting the findings already made on laboratory rodents—rats, mice, and gerbils.

Effects of Previous Post-Weaning Environments on Problem-Solving Behavior

Since Hebb (1949) presented evidence that enriched experience could improve problem-solving ability in the rat, there has been a moderate amount of research on effects of both enrichment and impoverishment, using several species—rats, mice, dogs, and monkeys—and a variety of behavioral tests. By and large, enrichment has been reported to produce improved performance and impoverishment to impair performance. Before we accept this generalization as our conclusion, however, we should look a little deeper into the reports. Fifteen years ago Beach and Jaynes (1954, pp. 256–257) cautioned that ". . . much if not most of the presently available evidence bearing upon this problem is equivocal and of undetermined reliability." Although considerable work has been done since that time, it is still true that the reproducibility of findings is not yet well established, even for many of the most often-cited reports. Our own experience has been that even "statistically significant" results from a single experiment may not withstand the test of replication. The requirement of successful replication (which seems to our group to be essential) has unfortunately not been attempted in most of the studies whose descriptions follow. Examining representative studies will bring out three lines of evidence that at least qualify, if they do not in fact contravert, any generalization:

a. The findings are highly specific to species and even to strain of animal, to the ages at which differential experience is given, and to the particular test used. In many cases changing one of these factors can wipe out effects. This makes it both difficult and dangerous to attempt to generalize from the results or to try to extrapolate results obtained on infrahuman animals to human subjects.

b. Some of the reported effects are subject to different interpretations than those originally proposed and accepted, as further research now shows.

c. There are some striking exceptions that require attention.

Perhaps some of these difficulties and discrepancies will disappear with further and better research. Given the importance of this field and the frequency with which it is cited in regard to educational and social policy, there is a clear need for extensive parametric research involving a variety of experimental conditions, behavioral tests, and species of subjects.

SPECIFICITY OF EFFECTS

Let us now consider a few examples that illustrate the difficulty of generalizing on the as yet spotty and incomplete studies in this field.

Strain Differences

Cooper and Zubek (1958) tested McGill bright and dull strains of rats in the Hebb–Williams apparatus. Some animals of each strain were raised in colony conditions, some in enriched conditions, and some in isolation in a restricted environment. Cooper and Zubek reported that the scores of the bright strain were not improved by environmental enrichment but were impaired by environmental restriction. Conversely, their dulls were benefited by enrichment but were not harmed by restriction. Only when coming from the usual colony condition did their two strains differ; coming from the enriched environment, the dulls caught up with the brights, and coming from the restricted environment, the brights sank to the level of the dulls.

Age at Which Differential Experience Is Given

Following a preliminary finding of Hymovitch (1952) that enriched experience must occur before maturity if it is to improve problem performance, Forgays and Read (1962) examined this question in greater detail. They used a 21-day period of differential experience, starting either at birth, at day 22 (weaning), or at days 44, 66, or 88. The restricted-experience animals lived in small cages. Testing of all groups began at 114 days of age. No differential effects were found in errors in a Y-maze, but there were significant differences in errors on the Hebb–Williams test. The 21 days immediately following weaning were found to be more effective in reducing error scores than were either earlier or later periods. The results of Nyman (1967) differ from those of Forgays and Read, since Nyman found that benefits for later spatial discrimination learning were most marked when exposure to the free environment was given from 50 to 60 days of age rather than either from 30 to 40 or 70 to 80 days. Significant effects of enriched environment were found both on an alternation maze and on the Hebb–Williams test; no effects were found in a visual discrimination task in a T-maze.

We have studied behavior of enriched-environment and isolated rats on both a visual reversal discrimination task in the Krech apparatus and in the Lashley III maze. Separate groups were tested after 30 days of EC–IC experience starting at different ages, and only one test was used with any group. In the visual reversal discrimination task, animals learn first to go to all the lighted alleys in the apparatus, regardless of the side. When an animal has learned this task to criterion, it is then reversed to the dark-correct task; reversals are continued over 9 days of testing. When EC–IC experience was started at 25 days of age, the EC rats solved significantly more reversal problems than their IC littermates, and the EC's made significantly fewer errors per reversal problem; this is shown in the upper section of Table 4. But results were quite different when the EC–IC experience was given later in rats' lives—either from 60 to 90 or from 90 to 120 days of age. Now the EC animals actually solved somewhat fewer problems and made somewhat more errors per problem than did the IC's. These differences in favor of the IC groups are not significant in most cases, but it is clear that the differences produced by 25- to 55-day exposure are not produced by the later periods. It might be asked whether age at testing, rather than age of exposure, might account for the altered effect. We believe not, because of results with other groups put into the EC or IC at 25 days and kept there until testing at 85, 105, or 185 days of age (E. L. Bennett and Rosenzweig, 1971). These groups continued to show differences in favor of the EC animals.

TABLE 4

Relative Performance of Rats on Visual Reversal Discrimination after 30 Days of Enriched (EC) or Impoverished (IC) Experience Starting at Various Ages

EC–IC period (days)	N (litters)	EC/IC (mean number of problems solved)	P	EC/IC (mean errors per reversal)	P
25–55	10	1.45	<0.01	0.64	<0.01
	7	1.30	<0.10	0.66	<0.05
	10	1.69	<0.001	0.52	<0.001
	27	1.49	<0.001	0.60	<0.001
60–90	10	0.63	<0.01	1.60	<0.05
	10	0.88	NS	1.31	<0.10
	10	1.07	NS	1.03	NS
	30	0.92	NS	1.17	NS
90–120	10	0.86	NS	0.93	NS
	10	0.89	NS	1.15	NS
	10	0.92	NS	1.03	NS
	30	0.89	<0.10	1.03	NS

The Lashley maze yields rather different results. The 25- to 55-day exposure to EC or IC does give significantly better performance of the EC animals, as is shown in the left half of Table 5. But differential experience during the 60- to 90-day period also shows superiority of the EC groups. Inspection of the data on successive experiments shows that the 60- to 90-day Lashley results were as strong as the 25- to 55-day results on experiments 1, 2, and 4. We cannot tell why the third 60- to 90-day experiment was out of line with the other results. It is clear that

TABLE 5

Relative Performance of Rats on Lashley III Maze after 30 Days of Enriched (EC) or Impoverished (IC) Experience Starting at 25 or 60 Days of Age[a]

	Period of EC–IC experience								
	25–55 days				60–90 days				
Experiments	1	2	3	1–3	1	2	3	4	1–4
Trials 2–5	0.59	0.81	0.68	0.69	0.58	0.77	1.12	0.66	0.78
P	<0.05	NS	<0.10	<0.01	<0.05	NS	NS	<0.05	<0.05
Trials 2–15	0.64	0.85	0.74	0.74	0.67	0.84	1.00	0.76	0.82
P	<0.10	NS	NS	<0.05	<0.10	NS	NS	0.10	0.05

[a] Ratio of errors: EC/IC.

60- to 90-day Lashley results are closely similar to the result of 25- to 55-day exposure; certainly they do not show the inversion found for the later period when the test was Visual Reversal Discrimination. An interpretation of the difference between effects on the Visual Reversal Test and the Lashley III maze will be offered in the next section.

Behavioral Test Employed

Most investigators have reported finding differences between enriched and impoverished animals with one test but not with another. One of the first of these reports was that of Bingham and Griffiths (1952), who found no differences in behavior of the groups of rats in visual discrimination with the Lashley jumping-stand apparatus, but who found significant effects in two mazes. Hymovitch (1952) found significant effects when he used the Hebb–Williams test, but did not find group differences on a multiple T-maze. As was mentioned above, Forgays and Read (1962) did not find differences on a Y-maze, but they found differences with the Hebb–Williams test, which presents a series of problems successively within the same enclosure. In the case of our visual discrimination reversal problem, the first light-correct problem can be considered as a simple dark–light visual discrimination task. On this task the enriched and impoverished animals did not differ significantly, although they did on the succeeding reversal problems, at least when the differential experience had been given immediately after weaning.

Wilson *et al.* (1965) have pointed out that it is paradoxical that several investigators have found significant effects of experience on performance in the Hebb–Williams test since performance on this test does not improve with age or with phyletic status (Warren, 1965). They suggest that performance on the Hebb–Williams test may benefit specifically from experience in exploring open fields, which is characteristic of most "free environment" conditions.

The Visual Reversal Discrimination task differentiates between EC and IC rats only when differential experience is given immediately after weaning, whereas the Lashley III maze shows EC to be superior whether the EC period extended from 25 to 55 days or from 60 to 90 days of age. These results were presented above in conjunction with Tables 4 and 5. This rather puzzling difference between the two tests finds an explanation when we consider results for SC animals, which were included in several of these behavioral experiments. On the Visual Reversal Task, run after 25- to 55-day differential experience, EC and SC made similar numbers of errors, and IC was inferior to both. Thus this test appears to be sensitive to restriction of experience from the colony level and not to enrichment. When IC is begun only at 60 days of age, it is not effective because the rats have already had colony experience and this cannot be effaced. On the Lashley III maze, SC and IC rats make similar numbers of errors, and EC rats make significantly less. This test is thus sensitive to enrichment of experience above the colony level. Furthermore, enrichment can be given and have effect not only immediately after weaning but also at 60 days of age and quite possibly even later.

Is Reactivity of the Restricted Animal the Main Factor?

Woods et al. (1960) believed that the restricted-experience animals have a greater tendency to explore than enriched-experience animals and that on many tests exploratory activities will be counted as errors against the previously isolated rats. Actually, whether enriched or restricted animals explore more is a function of the testing situation (Forgus, 1954; Lore and Levowitz, 1966).

Myers and Fox (1963) have cited an increase in fearlike responses as a cause of poor maze performance of their isolated rats. Such responses have not been noticed with our extremely tame strains. It will clearly be important to determine whether differences in problem solving after differential experience should be ascribed to motivational or emotional changes, on the one hand, or to perceptual or intellectual changes, on the other hand. This question will be considered again later under interpretation of the isolation effect.

Are the Differences Induced by Differential Experience Transitory or Enduring?

Most investigators using rats as subjects have not continued to test them long enough to determine whether differences in problem-solving ability following exposure to differential environments are transitory or enduring, that is, whether or not they persist during prolonged testing. (We are not here considering the durability of effects during the interval between the end of differential experience and the onset of testing, because that has already been demonstrated.) Hebb (1949, pp. 298–299), in the initial report on this question, stated that the rats reared as pets improved more during testing than the cage-reared animals. He concluded that there was a permanent effect of early experience on problem solving at maturity: "The . . . richer experience of the pet group during development made them better able to profit by new experiences at maturity—one of the characteristics of the 'intelligent' human being." Forgays and Forgays (1952) gave their animals two successive tests on the standard series of Hebb–Williams problems. Both enriched and restricted animals improved to the same extent, keeping the difference constant, and these authors concluded, on the basis of a rather short period of testing, that the differences were enduring. In our own studies, the behavioral differences between previously enriched and impoverished animals have tended to disappear during testing. This was found with all three tests that we have used—visual reversal discrimination problems in the Krech hypothesis apparatus, the Lashley III maze, and the Hebb–Williams test. Note in Table 5 that EC–IC error ratios departed further from 1.0 on trials 2–5 than on trials 2–15; that is, adding more trials tended to wash out the differences quite early in the program of testing.

Fuller (1966) found restricted beagles to be inferior to controls in reversal learning, but only on the first five reversals. Thereafter there was no significant difference between restricted-experience animals and pets.

Research with monkeys, to be described below, also has failed to demonstrate any lasting effects of either enrichment or impoverishment on intellectual ability. Animal studies, therefore, provide little support for supposing that even prolonged differential experience leads to long-lasting changes in ability.

INTERPRETATIONS OF THE BEHAVIORAL EFFECTS

Several investigators have interpreted results of early deprivation studies as showing that withholding various types of stimulation delays the learning of associations important to organized adult behavior. This has been attacked from two directions:

a. Fuller and Clark (1966) have suggested that the effects are not entirely due to isolation but to the changes between the two environments. Under especially favorable circumstances, including forced contact with the handler, a suitable dose of chlorpromazine during the transition period, and a robust genotype, the postisolation syndrome can be totally eliminated. Thus much perceptual organization can take place with minimal stimulation, and this can be shown if interfering behavior is controlled.

b. Lessac and Solomon (1969), using a pretest, posttest design, studied effects of one year of isolation as compared with kennel life in beagles. Learning abilities found at 12 weeks of age remained little changed after one year of kennel treatment, but several tests showed impairment and disturbance after one year of isolation. Thus, isolation was considered not to retard development but to lead to a destructive or atrophic process. It might well be objected that little further development could have been expected on tasks that the dogs were already performing well at 12 weeks of age; perhaps more difficult tests should also have been included in the battery. This objection appears to be met by work with monkeys, to be discussed in the next section.

A STRIKING EXCEPTION—RESULTS WITH MONKEYS

Recent work with monkeys indicates that differential environmental experience may not produce lasting effects on intellectual ability. The manipulations have included both deprivation in comparison with colony experience and enrichment in comparison with the natural forest environment.

Harlow and his associates, who have carried out well-known studies on effects of isolation on social behavior of monkeys (Harlow and Harlow, 1965), began to test in the 1960's for effects of isolation on learning ability. An initial report from the Wisconsin laboratory by Mason and Fitz-Gerald (1962) indicated that a single monkey isolated for its first 90 days performed rather normally in both formation of learning sets and form discrimination. Rowland (1964) reported no significant difference in development of learning sets between monkeys severely isolated for their first 6 months and partially restricted controls. The isolated animals did show more performance problems than the controls, and the isolated animals were inferior to the controls over the first 200 problems—a far longer series than has been used in testing other species of animals. Griffin and Harlow (1966) reported that monkeys isolated for their first 3 months showed severe withdrawal and behavioral peculiarities when removed from the isolation chambers. Although the animals isolated for 6 months in Rowland's study were crippled in social behavior, the 3-month isolates showed no social abnormalities, nor were they deficient in learning performance. Commenting on their failure to find effects on learning ability, Griffin and Harlow (p. 546) point out, "The apparent contradiction between rhesus monkeys and other species on learning after isolation may be an artifact of the types of tasks employed. Tasks that do not extensively adapt Ss or do not discard data indicating problems in adaptation will probably show performance deficits."

Further unpublished results (Harlow, 1968) replicate the lack of deficits in learning ability in isolated monkeys. These results certainly suggest that we must be careful in accepting or generalizing on reports of intellectual deficits following environmental deprivation.

Work by Singh (1966, 1969) on effects of environmental enrichment on behavior of monkeys also indicates that intellectual ability remains unaltered. Singh studied both forest and urban rhesus monkeys in India.

The urban monkeys, when compared with forest dwellers, were more aggressive in relation to both man and other monkeys, more communal in their within-group relations, and more responsive to novel objects and situations, and they had come to prefer cooked food to raw fruits and vegetables. Six urban adults and six forest adults were given a battery of tests of intellectual ability in the Wisconsin General Test Apparatus. The forest animals performed poorly in the initial tests that called for visual discriminations, but this was attributed to their shyness or fearfulness. According to Singh (1969, p. 114), "Once they became used to the test situation they learned the solutions to all the test problems, simple or complex, as efficiently as the urban monkeys." Singh raises questions of definition and interpretation when he concludes that the urban way of life ". . . in general enhances their psychological complexity, but it does not advance their intelligence, although their behavior may appear to exhibit a high degree of shrewdness." At least it appears that formal tests of ability given to monkeys show no long-run effects of enriched experience above a natural baseline, just as the restricted environment described above did not affect problem-solving, once the monkeys were adapted to the test situation. Thus the infrahuman subjects closest phylogenetically to man, among those tested so far, show no permanent intellectual effects of prolonged differential experience.

Can Behavioral Effects of Environment Be Related to Cerebral Effects?

If enrichment of the environment increases certain brain measures and enhances problem-solving ability on certain tests, and if improverishment produces opposite effects on brain and behavior, can we conclude that the cerebral and behavioral measures are related to each other functionally? Can some of the behavioral effects be shown to depend upon some of the cerebral effects?

CORRELATING NORMAL DEVELOPMENT OF BRAIN AND BEHAVIOR

The question just stated is a special form of the more general question of relating development of brain to development of behavior. Since this is a question of interest to many participants in the symposium, it may not be amiss to make a few remarks at this point about complexities of this field that have prevented rapid progress.

First of all, many indices of brain maturation develop at different rates; obviously, not each of these can be correlated in the same way with overall behavioral maturation, yet one sometimes hears an investigator use his favorite measure as *the* index of maturation.

Second, on the behavioral side too, different measures mature at different rates. Thus Campbell (1967) has shown that the 20-day-old rat can be conditioned to avoid shock as readily as can the adult, but only by 50 days of age does retention reach the adult level. Apparently, the brain correlates of conditionability and of retention must be somewhat different. It will be important to determine whether improvement in memory with age will be found in other species as it has in the rat (and the guinea pig). If so, this may help to explain what is known as "childhood amnesia." Harlow (1959) has shown that while rhesus monkeys can be conditioned and can learn a Y-maze efficiently in their first few weeks, the ability to solve difficult problems is reached only at 4 or 5 years of age. What slowly maturing brain systems can account for this?

Third, a type of correlation that appears to work well for one species may not hold up for another. As an example for this, we may note that the Scheibels (1964) have shown rather persuasive correlations among development of neuroanatomy, electroencephalography, and behavior in kittens during their first 2 or 3 months. However, for the rat we have been told by two other investigators (Crain, 1952; Schadé, 1957) that the EEG is mature by 7 to 14 days of age! This is before the rat pup has opened its eyes and when it can scarcely locomote. (Crain at this Conference has stated that when he wrote that the EEG "patterns observed at 10 to 14 days were basically similar to those of the adult rat," he meant only that the adult pattern was beginning to emerge. He added that maturational changes in the EEG of the rat go on for weeks.) Gottlieb has shown in his paper (p. 67) that in a number of cases a behavioral response to stimulation may occur when histological evidence reveals that neural circuits for the response have not yet been completed. Clearly there is much still to be done in correlating normal development of brain and of behavior. Introducing further complications by varying the environment may help to test still more stringently proposed formulations that seek to relate development of brain and of behavior.

DIRECT MODIFICATION OF BRAIN

A few investigators in recent years have attempted to modify growth of the brain by physiological intervention, usually by hormonal or chemical means, and have searched for resultant effects on behavior. Some examples of effects of impairment will be followed by examples of cases of enhanced development.

Eayrs (1964) found that early interference with thyroid function in the rat decreased dendritic ramification in the cerebral cortex, and Eayrs and Lishman (1955) found that the same treatment impaired performance on the Hebb–Williams test. Waisman and Harlow (1965) produced experimental phenylketonuria in infant monkeys by feeding them excessive quantities of phenylalanine. The animals, like human phenylketonuric patients, showed elevated plasma levels of phenylalanine and had grand mal convulsions; presumably, they also suffered brain damage. On tests of problem-solving ability the experimental monkeys were slow to adapt and performed inadequately, suggesting the presence of an intellectual deficit. Haddad et al. (1969) reported that injection of a drug into pregnant female rats resulted in considerable reduction in size of the cerebral hemispheres of the young, without other signs of abnormality. As adults, these microcephalic rats made significantly more errors on the Hebb–Williams maze than did controls. Malnutrition during the fetal or lactating period has been shown by many investigators to impair growth of brain and to result in inferior behavioral performance. This is a major field of investigation and too large to attempt to treat here, but a few recent reviews can be noted—Scrimshaw and Gordon (1968), Cravioto (1968), and Eichenwald and Fry (1969).

Supernormal growth of brain can also be induced by various means. Thus Zamenhof (1942) reported that growth hormone increased growth of brain in rat fetuses. Clendinnen and Eayrs (1961) were unable to replicate these effects, but they did observe increased dendritic growth. Zamenhof et al. (1966) later reported findings in the same direction as the original effects, but smaller in magnitude. Block and Essman (1965) found enhanced learning ability in rats given the growth hormone treatment during fetal life. Ray and Hochhauser (1969) reported that growth hormone given during the fetal period enhanced learning of rats subsequently raised in isolation but had no consistent effect on performance of rats raised in an enriched environment. Bresler and Bitterman (1969) have recently reported, on the basis of a rather small number of cases, that fish whose brain size was increased by implantation of additional tissue were also superior in problem-solving behavior. Zamenhof and van Marthens (1970) have reported that reducing the number of fetuses in the rats increases the brain size and cerebral DNA of those born, and learning ability of these rats and of controls is being compared. Wimer and Prater (1966) bred mice selectively for high or low total brain weight. They state, "The high selection lines scored significantly higher than the low lines in locomotor activity in the open field and discrimination learning performance in a water maze. These findings were supported by correlations between brain weight and behavioral scores within unselected control lines."

The evidence available on both impaired and supernormal brains is consonant with the hypothesis that modifying brain can thereby modify ability. What does evidence on environmental effects add to this picture?

DIFFICULTIES IN RELATING BEHAVIORAL TO CEREBRAL EFFECTS

By 1966 many replicated experiments in our laboratories had demonstrated that (a) the ratio of cortical to subcortical weight in the rat correlated positively with problem-solving ability (Rosenzweig *et al.*, 1967; E. L. Bennett and Rosenzweig, 1968), (b) enriched experience increased significantly the cortical–subcortical weight ratio, and (c) 30 days of differential experience following weaning led to significantly better problem-solving scores in EC than in IC littermates (Krech *et al.*, 1962; Bennett and Rosenzweig, 1970). It would have been tempting to suppose that the behavioral differences between EC and IC animals reflected the brain changes induced by the differential environments. We set about to test this hypothesis by determining whether it would hold over a wider range of conditions that produce the cerebral effects. These included varying the length of the EC–IC treatments, adding SC groups for baseline comparisons, starting the treatments at later ages than weaning, and using EC exposure of only 2 hours/day.

The results indicated that there is no overall relation between problem-solving scores and the cortical/subcortical weight ratio (or other brain measures that we have tested). For example, as we showed in Tables 4 and 5, if 30 days of EC–SC–IC treatment is given between 60 and 90 days of age instead of between 25 and 55 days, then EC rats are not superior to IC on the visual reversal discrimination test. At the later age there is still a difference in favor of the EC on the Lashley III maze, but it is not as consistent as when differential environment was introduced at the earlier age. This is not a matter of age at testing but of age at onset of EC–IC treatment, because if rats are kept in EC or IC from 25 to 105 days of age, the EC animals are still superior on the visual reversal problem.

The results of giving EC for 2 hours/day over a 30-day period also show complex relations between cerebral and behavioral effects. Whereas the EC–IC brain differences are about as great as when EC is maintained for 24 hours/day, the 2-hour EC rats are not superior to IC in the visual reversal discrimination test, but the EC do perform better than IC on the Lashley III maze. Thus, in this regard, the relatively simple Lashley III maze appears more sensitive to prior experience than does the reversal discrimination test.

It is evident that while we have been able to demonstrate both significant cerebral effects and significant behavioral effects of prior environmental manipulations, we have not found any simple way of relating these two sets of observations.

Part of the difficulty may be that we have been attempting to measure transfer effects from our environments to quite different test situations. It might be more fruitful instead to attempt to relate the brain changes to the learning that takes place in the differential environments. We have therefore begun to measure learning with regard to the features of the various environments to which different groups are exposed. Such measures of learning may correlate with the cerebral effects produced by the same environments.

Although we have not yet measured what learning occurs in the enriched environment, experiments of others convince us that we will be able to find evidence of such learning. We note, for example, a series of experiments performed at Cornell by Gibson, Walk, and Tighe (e.g., Gibson and Walk, 1956; Gibson et al., 1959) in which rats exposed to visual forms in their cages over a period of weeks later discriminated these forms more rapidly than did nonexposed controls. Recently Kerpelman (1965) and T. L. Bennett and Ellis (1968) have confirmed these results but have suggested that reinforced experience (presence of food and water during exposure) may be important for the facilitation of discrimination. If this requirement proves to be true, our conditions meet it, since food and water are available in the EC. Kerpelman also pointed out that certain results indicated that novelty and perceptual change may themselves reinforce learning about the stimuli. Again, our EC includes this factor.

Are Some Cerebral Effects of Enriched Environment Due to Learning?

A number of investigators have been attempting to find cerebral changes induced by learning or enriched experience. Experiments with formal training have mostly involved rather brief sessions, usually less than an hour in length, although some have included sessions distributed over a few days. A number of papers have reported that trained animals show, as compared with controls, changes such as increased brain RNA, altered base ratios of RNA, increased incorporation of radioactive precursors into RNA or protein, and so on. Among recent reviews of this type of research are those of Glassman (1969) and E. L. Bennett and Rosenzweig (1971). Both conclude that the changes found during training have not yet been unequivocally related to learning, that is, it is possible that the changes observed may be due to other variables present in the experimental situation, such as sensory stimulation, changes in attention, and restoratory processes in activated tissue. Since several reviews of work with formal training are available, I will not carry this further here but will instead concentrate on cerebral changes with relatively prolonged differential experience. This will indicate the current status and concepts of work of our group in Berkeley and will include some unpublished studies.

Two broad strategies are available for investigating whether the cerebral effects of environmental experience are due to learning—a direct frontal approach and the elimination of alternative hypotheses. Following the direct strategy, one attempts to demonstrate that the cerebral effects of an enriched environment can be duplicated by giving prolonged training to the experimental subjects. Appropriate controls are required to show that the effects are produced by training as such and cannot be attributed to related variables such as stimulation, locomotion, state of attention, and so on.

Following the second strategy, one considers all the alternative explanations that he and his colleagues and critics can think up to account for the observed effects and tests them. While this strategy may never succeed fully, it may, in a sense, fail and yet succeed. It may never succeed fully because as many alternative explanations as can be lopped off, others spring up to be tested; furthermore, the true hypotheses may remain invisible and so untestable. The attempt to eliminate all alternatives may fail in the sense that one of the alternatives may, in fact, turn out to be correct. The failure then turns into success because, although the original hypothesis was wrong, the correct explanation has now been discovered. Our group has been attempting to follow both approaches, and no one will be surprised to hear that, although we have learned quite a bit along the way, we are still far from a definitive solution to the problem.

We first became ensnared by problems of brain responses to training and environment because of research that we were conducting during the 1950's on relations between brain measures and learning ability. Some results of that work suggested that rats tested on more difficult problems developed values on certain brain measures different from rats tested on easier problems or not tested at all (Rosenzweig *et al.*, 1961). In order to try to maximize the suspected brain effects, we decided to subject animals to an enriched environment where opportunities for learning would be present 24 hours a day and where the situation would change each day. This drew us into studying how a number of chemical and anatomical measures varied according to environmental treatment and to trying to determine the important dimensions of the differential environments. Since 1966 we have also been testing whether cerebral effects could be induced by formal training alone. Let us consider first certain tests of alternative hypotheses and then return to the frontal approach. For brevity, we will confine ourselves here chiefly to measures of brain weights. The tests of alternative hypotheses will be summarized here and will be given more fully elsewhere.

TESTS OF ALTERNATIVE HYPOTHESES

Acceleration of Brain Maturation

Since there have been some reports that early handling accelerates eye-opening and the appearance of certain reflexes, it might be hypothesized that the greater cortical growth in EC, as compared to IC, represents earlier development of the EC brain. Two lines of evidence oppose this hypothesis. (a) In some respects, the pattern of EC–IC differences runs contrary to changes with age. For example, the ratio of cortical to subcortical weight decreases with age in the rat, but EC leads to a greater ratio than in SC or IC. (b) EC–IC differences can be induced in adult rats, in which the brain is mature, as readily as in young animals whose brains are still growing rapidly.

Differential Handling

In our original experiments, EC rats were handled several times a day, while IC animals were handled only weekly, for weighing. Since handling has been shown to affect certain physiological variables, it might be important in our experiments. Control experiments demonstrated that handled versus nonhandled rats did not differ in the brain measures we employ (Rosenzweig et al., 1968a). In recent drug experiments, both EC and IC rats are handled daily for injections, and the usual EC–IC differences develop. In other recent experiments, some rats have been given 20 runway trials per day for a month, each trial involving handling, and little or no cerebral difference developed between runway rats and their IC controls.

Dr. Schapiro has informed me of a study demonstrating that preweaning handling plus varied sensory stimulation affected dendritic spines of rats (Schapiro and Vukovich, 1970). The manipulations included changes of body temperature and administration of electric shock, so that the results might better be considered in relation to stress than to sensory stimulation. Rats stimulated (or stressed) during the first 2 weeks of life showed increased numbers of dendritic spines per unit of dendrite length and also had increased numbers of neurons stained. It will be recalled that our post-weaning EC treatment appeared to produce a greater total number of spines but not much of an increase per unit of dendrite length.

Differential Locomotion

Since EC rats are more active than IC rats, differential locomotion might be a factor in producing the cerebral effects. Control experiments, in which some rats had free access to an activity wheel and others did not, failed to show any cerebral differences between the two groups (Rosenzweig et al., 1968a). In recent maze experiments, groups given extensive daily runway activity failed to show differences from a group simply placed in a food box.

Stress

It has been suggested that our IC rats might suffer from "isolation stress" or, conversely, that the EC rats might be stressed by overstimulation. Dr. Williamina Himwich (1969) has pointed out that there may be nonspecific effects of stress on the brain as on the rest of the body. We began to take up in the 1950's the question of whether stress might be responsible for the EC–IC differences in brain measures. Neither the EC nor the IC group was found to differ from colony controls in adrenal

TABLE 6

Comparisons of Environmental and Stress Effects on Rats: Percentage Differences in Weights of Tissue Samples[a,b,c]

	EC vs IC among		Stressed vs nonstressed among	
	Nonstressed	Stressed	EC	IC
Cortex				
Occipital	13.8†	12.2†	1.1	2.5
Somesthetic	6.4	4.4	−0.7	0.7
Remaining dorsal	5.4	3.3	−2.9	−1.0
Ventral	4.6	6.6*	−1.4	−3.4
Total	6.0†	5.6†	−1.8	−1.3
Rest of brain	1.8	−1.1	−2.1	−1.5
Total brain	3.6	3.1	−2.0	−1.4
Cortex/rest	4.1†	4.4†	0.0	0.0
Body weight	−8.8†	−3.5	−7.0	−12.1
Adrenal weight	−1.5	−8.1	5.0*	12.8†
Adrenal/body	2.7	−2.7	17.6†	24.3†

[a] From Riege and Morimoto, 1970, Table 5.
[b] $N = 32$ for each of the four groups: EC and IC, stressed and nonstressed.
[c] Key: (*) $P < 0.05$; (†) $P < 0.01$.

weights per unit of body weight. In stress experiments, daily sessions of electric shock over a 30-day period did not alter the brain measures we took (Rosenzweig, 1966, 1970).

Riege and Morimoto (1970) have recently done experiments in which EC and IC rats were either stressed by tumbling or kept under the usual EC and IC; one of the three experiments also included SC and SC-stress groups. Table 6 summarizes the EC–IC and stress–nonstress effects for the data of all three experiments combined. The usual significant EC–IC brain differences occurred among both stressed and nonstressed rats, but there was not a significant effect of EC–IC on adrenal weight. Stress did not affect any brain weight measure significantly, but it did cause a significant increase in adrenal weights, which EC–IC treatment did not affect. Comparison of EC and IC with SC demonstrated that the effects of explicit stress did not follow either the EC or the IC pattern.

Hormonal Mediation

Perhaps the effects measured in the nervous system might be mediated by a hormonal route, since hormones influence brain development, at least early in life (Eayrs, 1964; Balázs *et al.*, 1969). That is, the differential environments might stimulate differential activity on the part of various endocrine glands, and this in turn might alter brain growth. For a partial test of this hypothesis we decided to hypophysectomize rats, thus eliminating pituitary hormones and reducing function in all endocrines that receive tropic secretions from the pituitary. If the EC–IC effect occurred in spite of hypophysectomy, then the possibility of hormonal mediation of the effect could be eliminated for those glands controlled by the pituitary and for the pituitary itself.

Three successive experiments were performed, the first two with male rats of the inbred Fischer strain and the third with male Long–Evans rats. Each experiment included several sets of foursomes, each consisting of hypophysectomized EC and IC and control EC and IC. In each case the rats were hypophysectomized a few days after weaning, maintained for about 10 days under colony conditions, and then placed in EC or IC where they were kept for 30 days. The data include only those hypophysectomized rats that had complete operations, as verified by weights of target organs and inspection of the sella turcica.

The experiments with Fischer rats showed diminished but statistically significant EC–IC cerebral differences among the hypophysectomized rats. The Long–Evans experiment—the largest and the one with least mortality—yielded EC–IC effects among the hypophysectomized rats that were quite comparable, on several measures, to those found among the controls. As Table 7 shows, the pattern of distribution of weight effects among brain regions was also similar between operated

TABLE 7
Effects of Differential Environments and Hypophysectomy on Brain Weights[a,b]

	% Environmental effects among[c]		% Hypophysectomy effects in[d]	
	Hypophysectomized	Controls	EC	IC
Occipital cortex	8.9‡	12.5‡	−6.4‡	−3.3
Total cortex	5.6†	3.6*	−3.7*	−5.5†
Rest of brain	0.2	−1.1	−7.8‡	−9.0‡
Total brain	2.6	1.0	−5.9‡	−7.5‡
Cortex/rest	5.3‡	4.8‡	4.4‡	3.9‡
Body weight	−1.3	−9.1‡	−65.3‡	−68.0‡

[a] Long–Evans strain; $N = 15$ per condition.
[b] Key: (*) $P < 0.05$; (†) $P < 0.01$; (‡) $P < 0.001$.
[c] $100 \times$ (EC minus IC)/IC.
[d] $100 \times$ (hypophysectomized minus control)/control.

and control rats. These rather normal brain effects occurred despite the fact that the operation virtually halted body growth, as the table also reveals. We conclude that the EC–IC brain effects can occur despite the absence of differential response in endocrines controlled by the pituitary and despite the total absence of pituitary hormones.

Visual Stimulation

Since in the rat the largest effects are found in the occipital region of the cortex, and this contains the primary visual projection area, we wondered whether the visual features of the enriched condition might be particularly important in inducing the EC–IC differences. This was found not to be the case, since blinded or dark-raised rats also developed significant EC–IC differences (see Tables IV and VI in Rosenzweig et al., 1969). Presence or absence of visual stimulation does affect brain values, but substantial EC–IC effects can occur in the absence of vision. It should be noted that in the rat the occipital cortex is not exclusively visual but responds as well to stimulation of other modalities, including audition and tactile sensitivity.

Stimulation from Other Animals and from Inanimate Objects

The two features that characterize the impoverished condition in all these experiments are that the cage contains a single rat and that there are no manipulanda except for food pellets (and, in some cases, shavings). The enriched condition, however, includes a group of 10 to 12 rats and a variety of objects.

In order to study the relative importance of these factors and their possible interaction, both social and stimulus conditions were varied in two experiments carried out during 1969 with rats of the inbred Fischer strain. The first experiment included 12 rats per group and the second experiment, 11 per group. All groups were put in the experiment at 60 days of age and kept there for 30 days. The following seven conditions were in common for the two experiments, and these are indicated in the designations at the bottom of Fig. 2. Rats of one group in each experiment remained isolated in individual colony cages (IC) for 24 hours/day. Two groups were removed from their individual cages for 2 hours/day and put singly in either a large cage with stimulus objects (EC) or in an empty large cage (LC). Two further groups were also removed from their individual cages for 2 hours daily and put in groups of 11 or 12 into EC or LC. The final two groups lived for 24 hours/day in EC or LC.

Figure 1 is based on behavioral observations made in the large cages when animals were placed there for 2 hours/day. This figure is based on experiment 1, which included groups of three in EC and LC, as well as single animals and groups of twelve. The figure shows that activity increased regularly with group size, and the presence of objects reliably

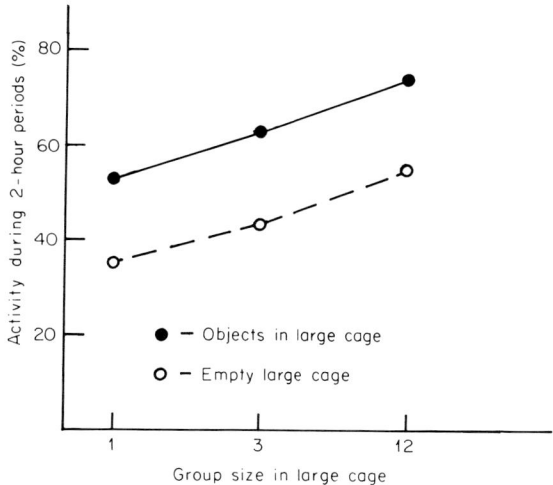

FIG. 1. The percentage of time spent in some type of activity during a 2-hour period in LC (large empty cage) or EC (large cage with stimulus objects). For this presentation, all types of observable activity have been lumped together; animals not counted as active appeared to be completely inactive or asleep. Percentage of activity is seen to increase progressively with the number of rats in the cage together; for a given number, the EC condition evoked more activity than did the LC. Subjects were male rats of Fischer inbred strain, run from 60 to 90 days of age; each point is based on 12 rats.

increased activity in groups of each size. There was no indication of interaction between effects of group size and stimulus objects on the amount of activity displayed.

Figure 2 presents results for the cortical/subcortical brain weight ratio for the two experiments combined. Note that putting single rats into a large cage for 2 hours a day had no effect on this brain measure (nor did it affect any of our other measures). This sort of result (obtained in other experiments as well) refutes the comment that simply handling a rat and transferring it to another cage for 15 minutes a day could produce the effects we observe. In fact, we see in the experiments shown in Fig. 2 that even placing rats in a group in a large empty cage for 2 hours a day did not yield a significant effect. Only when rats had both social stimulation and stimulation from varied objects did the brain measures change significantly. Apparently, both types of stimulation are necessary, perhaps because the social condition makes the rats more active and thus increases their commerce with the cage objects.[3]

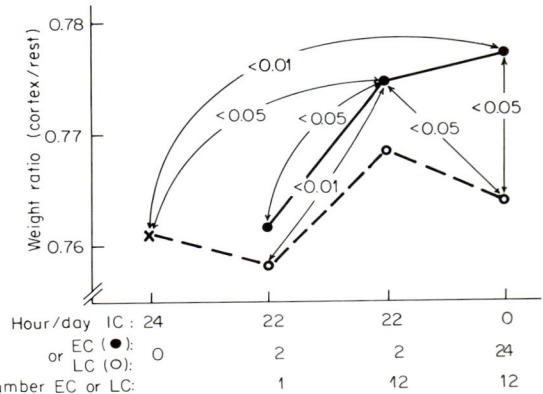

FIG. 2. Ratio of weight of cerebral cortex to that of the rest of the brain for groups given various environmental conditions. The results of two experiments are combined; N = 23 per point. Subjects were male rats of inbred Fischer strain, run from 60 to 90 days of age. Animals put into large empty cages (LC), whether singly or in groups and whether for 2 or 24 hours, did not differ significantly from rats kept in isolation in the home cage throughout the day (IC). Rats put singly into EC also did not differ from IC, but those in EC groups did differ significantly from IC, whether the group EC experience lasted for 2 or 24 hours a day.

[3] The hypothesis that social stimulation might be needed only to facilitate interaction of the rats with the stimulus objects was borne out by subsequent experiments. In these, single rats in EC for 2 hours/day showed the cerebral effects, provided they were put in EC under circumstances that favored their interaction with the complex environment.

Drug Experiments

It might be asked whether social and inanimate stimuli produce some direct effect upon the brain or whether the cerebral effects require some active process of response on the part of the subjects. Experiments employing excitant or depressant drugs suggest an answer to this question. Animals were given an injection of a drug or of saline shortly before a 2-hour daily EC session, and this was continued over a 30-day period. The other 22 hours/day were spent in single cages. Other animals spent 24 hours/day in single cages, and these also received daily injections. The excitant drug significantly increased brain weight effects of EC, whereas the depressant decreased them. In the isolation condition the drugs had little or no effect. In the enriched condition, all three groups—excitant, saline, and depressant—explored the new situation actively at the start. The excitant-injected rats kept up their activity, while the saline group soon began to habituate, and the depressed rats showed a more rapid decline of activity, some even going to sleep during the 2-hour period. It appears then that active commerce with the stimuli is required to develop the cerebral effects characteristic of the EC. The locomotion itself is unlikely to cause the effects, as we have already seen.

Another way of interpreting these results is that activation of the brain will not by itself produce the cerebral effects; this is seen in the lack of effect of the excitant IC groups. However, activation seems to prepare the rats to be affected by the enriched environment.

TESTS OF THE LEARNING HYPOTHESIS

Now let us come to attempts to test directly the hypothesis that at least some of the EC effects are produced by prolonged learning and therefore reflect the operation of mechanisms of learning or of memory storage. The findings that we have just reviewed are consistent with this hypothesis, i.e., the observations that 2 hours a day of exposure to a complex environment bring about cerebral changes and that these require active commerce with the stimuli. Even before making these recent findings, we had begun to test whether variation in formal training alone might produce measurable cerebral effects. Several experiments were done with operant conditioning devices. In these experiments one animal of each pair mastered a succession of problems, mostly to visual stimuli in a Skinner box, while its yoked-control littermate received a pellet whenever the first rat earned one. No significant differences in cerebral weights were obtained, but some significant effects were found in chemical measures when data from three experiments were combined.

The effects obtained were relatively small, and their pattern did not resemble that obtained in the EC–IC case. Further experiments were run with various automatic mazes, at least 50 trials being given per day over a 30-day period. When maze rats were compared with runway-control and with food-control rats, only small and nonsignificant differences were found. Work in this direction is continuing, using more challenging learning tasks.

If the more demanding learning tasks appear to produce cerebral effects, then we will be faced with the problem of devising fully adequate controls. Our yoked-control and runway-control rats have not had as varied a stimulus situation as have their trained brothers. Although this can be provided, can we assure that the control animals attend as well and respond as actively to the stimuli as do the animals whose food depends on this? On the other hand, it is probable that the rat is doing some learning in any situation, no matter how impoverished it is. This need not cause us concern, since we know that even with considerable learning occurring, no cerebral effects could be detected on the measures we use. Perhaps the best we can hope to find is that when training programs of progressive degrees of difficulty are established, employing the same stimulus materials, then brain changes of progressive magnitude will occur (at least as long as the subjects are able to master the problems). If relatively simple research designs of this sort appear to yield results, undoubtedly tighter and tighter controls will be brought to bear.

Summary

Many investigators have demonstrated cerebral effects of differential environmental treatments. Deprivation of visual stimulation causes a variety of changes in occipital cortex, including reduced diameters of cells, altered electrical responses, decreased numbers of dendritic spines, lesser weight and thickness, and differences in enzymatic activities. Other cortical regions may show "compensatory" changes. Differential experience with cagemates and with stimulus objects also leads to a variety of modifications in the rodent brain and especially in the cerebral cortex. These include changes in cerebral cortex in weight (both wet and dry) and in thickness; in total activities of acetylcholinesterase, cholinesterase, and hexokinase; and in number of glial cells and in size of perikarya. On several brain measures, enrichment of experience above the colony level leads to changes that are opposed in direction to those caused by impoverishment of experience. Mice and gerbils show cerebral effects of differential environments rather similar to those seen in rats.

Whether some of these results are truly due to enrichment or only to lessened impoverishment cannot be determined until experiments include a baseline of feral animals living under natural conditions. For this reason we have begun such experiments with native deermice (*Peromyscus*).

Post-weaning enrichment of environment has often been reported to improve problem-solving ability and impoverishment to impair such ability. Examination of the studies shows that findings are highly specific to the species and even strain of subjects used, to the ages at which differential experience is given, and to the particular behavioral test employed. There is little evidence to show that behavioral differences induced by prior environmental experience are enduring. Work with monkeys indicates no permanent intellectual effects of prolonged differential experience. Given the present spotty state of the field, it is difficult to generalize on the results and risky to try to extrapolate findings obtained on infrahuman animals to human beings.

Establishing functional relationships between the cerebral and the behavioral effects of differential experience has not yet proved possible. More work has been done to attempt to correlate normal development of brain and of behavior, yet there are also pitfalls in this area, some of which were discussed. A further approach was suggested.

Several investigators have reported changes in brain RNA and proteins following formal training, but it is not yet possible to attribute these unequivocally to learning as distinguished from certain tied variables. Similarly, it has not yet been possible to determine whether some of the cerebral effects of differential environments can be attributed to the differential learning that takes place in them. A number of alternative hypotheses to account for the cerebral effects have been shown to be untenable or unlikely on the basis of experimental results; these include hypotheses related to acceleration of brain maturation, differential handling, differential locomotion, stress, visual stimulation, differential endocrine response, and cerebral activation. However, when attempts have been made to see whether giving or withholding formal training would produce brain differences like those resulting from enriched or impoverished experience, our cerebral measures have shown only negligible effects. More challenging learning tasks are now being employed for this research. Problems of controls to separate effects of learning from those of tied variables were mentioned.

ACKNOWLEDGMENTS

Most of the research of the author described in this paper was done in collaboration with Dr. Marian C. Diamond and Dr. Edward L. Bennett. It is currently supported by NSF Grant GB-8011 and by the U. S. Atomic Energy Commission. The drug studies are being done in collaboration with Dr. Bennett and are supported by Office of Education Grant 0-9-140398-4512 (057). I wish to acknowledge the aid of chemists Marie Hebert and Hiromi Morimoto, anatomists Bernice Lindner and Alma Raymond, animal technicians Don Gassie, Phillip Low, Todd Grant, and Karl Churchill, and secretary Jessie Langford.

REFERENCES

Altman, J., Wallace, R. B., Anderson, W. J., and Das, G. D. (1968). Behaviorally induced changes in length of cerebrum in rats. *Develop. Psychobiol.* Vol. 1, 112–117.

Balázs, R., Brooksbank, B. W. L., Davison, A. N., Eayrs, J. T., and Wilson, D. A. (1969). The effect of neonatal thyroidectomy on myelination in the rat brain. *Brain Res.* Vol. 15, 219–232.

Baxter, B. L. (1966). Effect of visual deprivation during postnatal maturation on the electroencephalogram of the cat. *Exp. Neurol.* Vol. 14, 224–238.

Beach, F. A., and Jaynes, J. (1954). Effects of early experience on the behavior of animals. *Psychol. Bull.* Vol. 51, 239–263.

Bennett, E. L., and Rosenzweig, M. R. (1968). Brain chemistry and anatomy: Implications for theories of learning and memory. *In* "Mind as a Tissue" (C. Rupp, ed.), pp. 63–86. Harper (Hoeber), New York.

Bennett, E. L., and Rosenzweig, M. R. (1971). Potentials of an intellectually enriched environment. *In* "Dysnutrition in the Seven Ages of Man." Univ. of Calif. Med. School, San Francisco, California (in press).

Bennett, E. L., Diamond, M. C., Krech, D., and Rosenzweig, M. R. (1964). Chemical and anatomical plasticity of brain. *Science* Vol. 146, 610–619.

Bennett, E. L., and Rosenzweig, M. R. (1971). Chemical alterations produced in brain by environment and training. *In* "Handbook of Neurochemistry" (A. Lajtha, ed.), Vol. 6, pp. 173–201. Plenum Press, New York.

Bennett, E. L., Rosenzweig, M. R., and Diamond, M. C. (1968). Rat brain: Effects of environmental enrichment on wet and dry weights. *Science* Vol. 163, 825–826.

Bennett, T. L., and Ellis, H. C. (1968). Tactual-kinesthetic feedback from manipulation of visual forms and nondifferential reinforcement in transfer of perceptual learning. *J. Exp. Psychol.* Vol. 77, 495–500.

Bingham, W. E., and Griffiths, W. J. (1952). The effect of differential environments during infancy on adult behavior in the rat. *J. Comp. Physiol. Psychol.* Vol. 45, 307–312.

Block, J. R., and Essman, W. B. (1965). Growth hormone administration during pregnancy: A behavioral difference in offspring rats. *Nature (London)* Vol. 205, 1136–1137.

Bresler, D. E., and Bitterman, M. E. (1969). Learning in fish with transplanted brain tissue. *Science* Vol. 163, 590–592.

Campbell, B. A. (1967). Development studies of learning and motivation in infraprimate mammals. *In* "Early Behavior" (H. W. Stevenson, E. H. Hess, and H. L. Rheingold, eds.), pp. 43–71. Wiley, New York.

Clendinnen, B. G., and Eayrs, J. T. (1961). The anatomical and physiological effects of prenatally administered somatotrophin on cerebral development in rats. *J. Endocrinol.* Vol. 22, 183–193.

Coleman, P. D., and Riesen, A. H. (1968). Environmental effects on cortical dendritic fields. I. Rearing in the dark. *J. Anat.* Vol. 102, 363–374.

Cooper, R. M., and Zubek, J. P. (1958). Effects of enriched and restricted early environments on the learning ability of bright and dull rats. *Can. J. Psychol.* Vol. 12, 159–164.

Crain, W. M. (1952). Development of electrical activity in the cerebral cortex of the albino rat. *Proc. Soc. Exp. Biol. Med.* Vol. 81, 49–51.

Cravioto, J. (1968). Nutritional deficiencies and mental performance in childhood. *In* "Environmental Influences" (D. C. Glass, ed.), pp. 3–51. Rockefeller Univ. Press, New York.

Diamond, M. C. (1967). Extensive cortical depth measurements and neuron size increases in the cortex of environmentally enriched rats. *J. Comp. Neurol.* 1967, Vol. 131, 357–364.

Diamond, M. C., Rosenzweig, M. R., and Bennett, E. L. (1970). Unpublished data.

Diamond, M. C., Law, F., Rhodes, H., Lindner, B., Rosenzweig, M. R., Krech, D., and Bennett, E. L. (1966). Increases in cortical depth and glia numbers in rats subjected to enriched environment. *J. Comp. Neurol.* Vol. 128, 117–125.

Eayrs, J. T. (1964). Endocrine influence on cerebral development. *Arch. Biol.* Vol. 75, 529–565.

Eayrs, J. T., and Lishman, W. A. (1955). The maturation of behaviour in hypothyroidism and starvation. *Brit. J. Anim. Behav.* Vol. 3, 17–24.

Eichenwald, H. F., and Fry, P. C. (1969). Nutrition and learning. Inadequate nutrition in infancy may result in permanent impairment of mental function. *Science* Vol. 163, 644–648.

Fifková, E. (1967). The influence of unilateral visual deprivation on optic centers. *Brain Res.* Vol. 6, 763–766.

Forgays, D. G., and Forgays, J. W. (1952). The nature of the effect of free-environmental experience on the rat. *J. Comp. Physiol. Psychol.* Vol. 45, 322–328.

Forgays, D. G., and Read, J. M. (1962). Crucial periods for free-environmental experience in the rat. *J. Comp. Physiol. Psychol.* Vol. 55, 816–818.

Forgus, R. H. (1954). The effect of early perceptual learning on the behavioral organization of adult rats. *J. Comp. Physiol. Psychol.* Vol. 47, 331–336.

Fuller, J. L. (1966). Transitory effects of experiential deprivation upon reversal learning in dogs. *Psychonom. Sci.* Vol. 4, 273–274.

Fuller, J. L., and Clark, L. D. (1966). Genetic and treatment factors modifying the post-isolation syndrome in dogs. *J. Comp. Physiol. Psychol.* Vol. 61, 251–257.

Gibson, E. J., and Walk, R. D. (1956). The effect of prolonged exposure to visually presented patterns on learning to discriminate them. *J. Comp. Physiol. Psychol.* Vol. 49, 239–242.

Gibson, E. J., Walk, R. D., and Tighe, T. J. (1959). Enhancement and deprivation of visual stimulation during rearing as factors in visual discrimination learning. *J. Comp. Physiol. Psychol.* Vol. 52, 74–81.

Glassman, E. (1969). The biochemistry of learning: An evaluation of the role of RNA and protein. *Annu. Rev. Biochem.* Vol. 38, 605–646.

Globus, A., and Scheibel, A. B. (1967). Synaptic loci on visual cortical neurons of the rabbit: The specific afferent radiation. *Exp. Neurol.* Vol. 18, 116–131.

Griffin, G. A., and Harlow, H. F. (1966). Effects of three months of total social deprivation on social adjustment and learning in the Rhesus monkey. *Child Develop.* Vol. 37, 533–548.

Gyllensten, L. (1959). Postnatal development of the visual cortex in darkness (mice). *Acta Morphol. Neer.-Scand.* Vol. 2, 331–345.

Gyllensten, L., Malmfors, T., and Norrlin, M. L. (1965). Effect of visual deprivation on the optic centers of growing and adult mice. *J. Comp. Neurol.* Vol. 124, 149–160.

Gyllensten, L., Malmfors, T., and Norrlin, M. L. (1966). Growth alteration in the auditory cortex of visually deprived mice. *J. Comp. Neurol.* Vol. 126, 463–470.

Haddad, R. K., Rabe, A., Laqueur, G. L., Spatz, M., and Valsamis, M. P. (1969). Intellectual deficit associated with transplacentally induced microcephaly in the rat. *Science* Vol. 163, 88–90.

Harlow, H. F. (1968). Personal communication.

Harlow, H. F. (1959). The development of learning in the rhesus monkey. *Amer. Sci.* Vol. 47, 459–479.

Harlow, H. F., and Harlow, M. K. (1965). The affectional systems. In "Behavior of Non-human Primates" (A. M. Schrier *et al.*, eds.), Vol. 2, pp. 287–334. Academic Press, New York.

Hebb, D. O. (1949). "The Organization of Behavior." Wiley, New York.

Heron, W., and Anchel, H. (1964). Synchronous sensory bombardment of young rats: Effects on the electroencephalogram. *Science* Vol. 145, 946–947.

Himwich, W. A. (1969). The effect of environment upon the developing brain. In "The Future of the Brain Sciences" (S. Bogoch, ed.), pp. 237–252. Plenum Press, New York.

Hubel, D. H. (1967). Effects of distortion of sensory input on the visual system of kittens. *Physiologist* Vol. 10, 17–45.

Hymovitch, B. (1952). The effects of experimental variations on problem-solving in the rat. *J. Comp. Physiol. Phychol.* Vol. 45, 313–321.

Kavanau, J. L. (1967). Behavior of captive white footed mice. *Science* Vol. 155, 1623–1639.

Kerpelman, L. C. (1965). Preexposure to visually presented forms and nondifferential reinforcement in perceptual learning. *J. Exp. Psychol.* Vol. 69, 257–262.

Krech, D., Rosenzweig, M. R., and Bennett, E. L. (1960). Effects of environmental complexity and training on brain chemistry. *J. Comp. Physiol. Psychol.* Vol. 53, 509–519.

Krech, D., Rosenzweig, M. R., and Bennett, E. L. (1962). Relations between brain chemistry and problem-solving among rats raised in enriched and impoverished environments. *J. Comp. Physiol. Psychol.* Vol. 55, 801–807.

Krech, D., Rosenzweig, M. R., and Bennett, E. L. (1963). Effects of complex environment and blindness on rat brain. *Arch. Neurol.* Vol. 8, 403–412.

Krech, D., Rosenzweig, M. R., and Bennett, E. L. (1966). Environmental impoverishment, social isolation and changes in brain chemistry and anatomy. *Physiol. Behav.* Vol. 1, 99–104.

La Torre, J. C. (1968). Effect of differential environmental enrichment on brain weight and on acetylcholinesterase and cholinesterase activities in mice. *Exp. Neurol.* Vol. 22, 493–503.

Lessac, M. S., and Solomon, R. L. (1969). Effects of early isolation on the later adaptive behavior of beagles: A methodological demonstration. *Develop. Psychol.* Vol. 1, 14–25.

Lore, R. K., and Levowitz, A. (1966). Differential rearing and free versus forced exploration. *Psychonom. Sci.* Vol. 5, 421–422.

MacNeill, M., and Zubek, J. P. (1967). Effects of prolonged visual deprivation (dark-

rearing) on the weight of the sensory cortex of the rat. *Can. J. Psychol.* Vol. 21, 177–183.
Mason, W. A., and Fitz-Gerald, F. C. (1962). Intellectual performance of an isolation reared monkey. *Percept. Mot. Skills* Vol. 15, 594.
Mussen, P. (1967). Early socialization: Learning and identification. "New Directions in Psychology," Vol. 3, pp. 51–110. Holt, New York.
Myers, R. D., and Fox, J. (1963). Differences in maze performance of group-vs isolation-reared rats. *Psychol. Rep.* Vol. 12, 199–202.
Nyman, A. J. (1967). Problem solving in rats as a function of experience at different ages. *J. Genet. Psychol.* Vol. 110, 31–39.
Ray, O. S., and Hochhauser, S. (1969). Growth hormone and environmental complexity effects on behavior in the rat. *Develop. Psychol.* Vol. 1, 311–317.
Riege, W. H., and Morimoto, H. (1970). Effects of chronic stress and differential environments upon brain weights and biogenic amine levels in rats. *J. Comp. Physiol. Psychol.*, Vol. 71, 396–404.
Riesen, A. H. (1966). Sensory deprivation. *In* "Progress in Physiological Psychology" (E. Stellar and J. M. Sprague, eds.), Vol. 1, pp. 117–147. Academic Press, New York.
Rosenzweig, M. R. (1966). Environmental complexity, cerebral change, and behavior. *Amer. Psychol.* Vol. 21, 321–332.
Rosenzweig, M. R., and Bennett, E. L. (1970). Effects of differential environments on brain weights and enzyme activities in gerbils, rats and mice. *Develop. Psychobiol.* Vol. 2, 87–95.
Rosenzweig, M. R., Krech, D., and Bennett, E. L. (1961). Heredity, environment, brain biochemistry and learning. *In* "Current Trends in Psychological Theory," Pittsburgh Symposium [no editor], pp. 87–110. Univ. of Pittsburgh Press, Pittsburgh, Pennsylvania.
Rosenzweig, M. R., Krech, D., Bennett, E. L., and Diamond, M. C. (1962). Effects of environmental complexity and training on brain chemistry and anatomy: A replication and extension. *J. Comp. Physiol. Psychol.* Vol. 55, 429–437.
Rosenzweig, M. R., Bennett, E. L., and Diamond, M. C. (1967). Effects of differential environments on brain anatomy and brain chemistry. *In* "Psychopathology of Mental Development" (J. Zubin and G. Jervis, eds.), pp. 45–56. Grune and Stratton, New York.
Rosenzweig, M. R., Krech, D., Bennett, E. L., and Diamond, M. C. (1968a). Modifying brain chemistry and anatomy by enrichment or impoverishment of experience. *In* "Early Experience and Behavior" (G. Newton and S. Levine, eds.), pp. 258–298. Thomas, Springfield, Illinois.
Rosenzweig, M. R., Love, W., and Bennett, E. L. (1968b). Effects of a few hours a day of enriched experience on brain chemistry and brain weights. *Physiol. Behav.* Vol. 3, 819–825.
Rosenzweig, M. R., Bennett, E. L., Diamond, M. C., Wu, S-Y., Slagle, R. W., and Saffran, E. (1969). Influences of environmental complexity and visual stimulation on development of occipital cortex in rat. *Brain Res.* Vol. 14, 427–445.
Rosenzweig, M. R., Bennett, E. L., and Diamond, M. C. (1971). Cerebral effects of differential environments occur in hypophysectomized rats (in preparation).
Rowland, G. L. (1964). The effects of total social isolation upon learning and social behavior in rhesus monkeys. Doctoral Dissertation, University of Wisconsin.
Schadé, J. P. (1957). "Electro-area-grafie van de Cortex Cerebri." F. von Rossem.

Schapiro, S., and Vukovich, K. R. (1970). Early experience effects upon cortical dendrites: A proposed model for development. *Science* Vol. 167, 292–294.

Scheibel, M. E., and Scheibel, A. B. (1964). Some neural substrates of postnatal development. *In* "Review of Child Development Research" (M. L. Hoffman and L. W. Hoffman, eds.), pp. 481–519. Russell Sage Found., New York.

Scherrer, J., and Fourment, A. (1964). Electrocortical effects of sensory deprivation during development. *In* "Progress in Brain Research" Vol. 9, pp. 103–112. Am. Elsevier, New York.

Scrimshaw, N. S., and Gordon, J. E., eds. (1968). "Malnutrition, Learning and Behavior." MIT Press, Cambridge, Massachusetts.

Singh, S. D. (1966). Effect of human environment on cognitive behavior in the rhesus monkey. *J. Comp. Physiol. Psychol.* Vol. 61, 280–283.

Singh, S. D. (1969). Urban monkeys. *Sci. Amer.* Vol. 221, 108–115.

Sperry, R. W. (1951). Mechanisms of neural maturation. *In* "Handbook of Experimental Psychology" (S. S. Stevens, ed.), pp. 236–280. Wiley, New York.

Sperry, R. W. (1965). Embryogenesis of behavioral nerve nets. *In* "Organogenesis" (R. L. DeHaan and H. Ursprung, eds.), pp. 161–186. Holt, New York.

Székely, G. (1966). Embryonic determination of neural connections. *Advan. Morphog.* Vol. 5, 181–219.

Vandenberg, S. G. (1968). The nature and nurture of intelligence. *In* "Genetics" (D. C. Glass, ed.), pp. 3–58. Rockefeller Univ. Press, New York.

Von Soemmering, S. T. (1791). "Von Baue des menschlichen Koerpers," Vol. 5, Part 1, p. 91. Barrentrapp & Wenner, Frankfurt am Main.

Waisman, H. A., and Harlow, H. F. (1965). Experimental phenylketonuria in infant monkeys. *Science* Vol. 147, 685–695.

Walsh, R. N., Budtz-Olsen, O. E., Penny, J. E., and Cummins, R. A. (1969). The effects of environmental complexity on the histology of the rat hippocampus. *J. Comp. Neurol.* Vol. 137, 261–266.

Walsh, R. N., Budtz-Olsen, O. E., and Torok, A. (1970). *Developmental Psychobiol.* In press.

Warren, J. M. (1965). Comparative psychology of learning. *Annu. Rev. Psychol.* Vol. 16, 95–118.

Wiesel, T. N., and Hubel, D. H. (1966). Spatial and chromatic interactions in the lateral geniculate body of the rhesus monkey. *J. Neurophysiol.* Vol. 29, 1115–1156.

Wilson, M., Warren, J. M., and Abbott, L. (1965). Infantile stimulation, activity, and learning by cats. *Child Develop.* Vol. 36, 843–853.

Wimer, C., and Prater, L. (1966). Some behavioral differences in mice genetically selected for high and low brain weight. *Psychol. Rep.* Vol. 19, 675–681.

Woods, P. J., Ruckelshaus, S. I., and Bowling, D. M. (1960). Some effects of "free" and "restricted" environment rearing conditions upon adult behavior in the rat. *Psychol. Rep.* Vol. 6, 191–200.

Zamenhof, S. (1942). Stimulation of cortical cell proliferation by the growth hormone. III. *Physiol. Zool.* Vol. 15, 281–292.

Zamenhof, S., and van Marthens, E. (1970). Studies on some factors influencing cell number in prenatal brain. *In* "Problems of Nutrition in the Perinatal Period." *60th Ross Conf. Pediat. Res.*, Verbatim transcript, 137–149. Columbus, Ohio.

Zamenhof, S., Mosley, J., and Schuller, E. (1966). Stimulation of the proliferation of cortical neurons by prenatal treatment with growth hormone. *Science* Vol. 152, 1396–1397.

IV. COMPARATIVE CONSIDERATIONS OF THE DEVELOPMENT OF SOCIALIZATION

SUCKLING AND HOME ORIENTATION IN THE KITTEN: A COMPARATIVE DEVELOPMENTAL STUDY[1]

JAY S. ROSENBLATT

The comparative study of behavioral development has received little attention in recent years, the current emphasis being mainly on intensive analysis of specific behavior patterns and their physiological basis. Schneirla's writings (1957, 1959, 1965) exemplify the value which the comparative approach to problems in the evolution and the development of behavior can have in formulating basic concepts for the understanding of animal behavior. The research on which this presentation is based was done under the supervision of and in collaboration with Dr. T. C. Schneirla and the concepts advanced are strongly influenced by his approach to the study of behavioral development.

The aim of this paper is to explore the possibilities of the comparative approach to behavioral development through an examination of suckling and home orientation in newly born kittens. Suckling is initiated within a few minutes after birth and home orientation first appears around 5 days after birth. There are important changes in both of these behaviors from their first appearance onward. Our discussion will deal with the way in which learning is involved in the behavioral processes of the newly born kitten as revealed by developmental analysis of these distinct but related early behavioral adjustments.

---

[1] This presentation is dedicated to Dr. T. C. Schneirla whose death, the summer of 1968, was a great loss both as a person and a teacher. The research reported in this article was supported by grants from the National Science Foundation and the Rockefeller Foundation to Dr. T. C. Schneirla and from the United States Public Health Service MH-16744 and MH-08604 to Dr. J. S. Rosenblatt. I wish to acknowledge Dr. Gerald Turkewitz's contribution to the research and to thank Mr. Robert J. Woll for allowing me to use the results of his study. Contribution number 91 from the Institute of Animal Behavior, The State University, Newark, New Jersey.

Introduction

Scott (1958, 1968) has proposed that early behavioral development among many altricial young, and particularly the puppy, is based upon the maturation of sensory and motor processes and that learning does not make an important contribution to development until some time after birth. This hypothesis, which has come to be called the "critical period" theory, is in large part based upon several studies indicating that conditioned responses could not be established in puppies before the third week. Fuller *et al.* (1950), James and Cannon (1952), and, more recently, Cornwell and Fuller (1961) were unable to condition tactile, olfactory, visual, or auditory stimuli to the shock-induced, leg-withdrawal response of the puppy until 3 or 4 weeks of age (Volokhov, 1959).

Subsequent studies have shown however that puppies, kittens, and young of several mammalian species, soon after birth, can be conditioned to stimuli associated with suckling responses and that suckling and related responses can be selectively modified through reinforcement. Kittens develop individual nipple position preferences shortly after birth (Wodinsky *et al.*, 1955; Ewer, 1959, 1961) and distinguish the home region from other regions of the home cage before the end of the first week (Rosenblatt *et al.*, 1969). Puppies can be trained, before the end of the first week, to increase their sucking from a milk-filled nipple and to decrease it when fed an aversive tasting fluid. In addition to the selective increase and decrease of sucking in feeding situations, conditioned responses to handling cues have been established: struggling efforts decrease or increase in advance of contact with the milk-filled nipple (Stanley *et al.*, 1963). Stanley *et al.* (1970) have shown even earlier learning in 2- to 3-day-old puppies that were reinforced by feeding for their selection of either a soft-textured or wire-textured approach to the nipple (Toropova, 1961).

Rat pups fed by stomach tube for the first 3 days develop a different pattern of responses to the handling and tube-feeding procedure than similarly aged pups that have suckled from the mother (Thoman *et al.*, 1968). Suckling patterns can also be modified in the human infant by selectively reinforcing one or another feature, as was originally noted clinically by Gunther (1961). Lipsitt (1967), and Lipsitt and Kaye (1964), and Siqueland and Lipsitt (1966) have used nipple-elicited sucking or dextrose solution to condition or selectively reinforce sucking and head turning in relation to feeding, and Kessen (1967) has also altered certain features of sucking. Both monkey infants and rabbit pups have been conditioned to respond to stimuli associated with feeding at very early ages (Harlow, 1959; Mason and Harlow, 1958; Ivanitskii).

If the studies which were successful and those which failed to demonstrate early learning in mammalian newborn are compared, it becomes clear that stimuli can be substituted and responses selectively reinforced with respect to early suckling but not in relation to shock-induced leg withdrawal. Learning in the neonate is therefore closely related to behavioral processes that have already developed in the neonate and cannot function in relation to those which are not yet in the repertoire of the newborn. Leg withdrawal is apparently not yet sufficiently developed in the very young puppy (i.e., less than 3 weeks of age) to provide a basis for learning and the perceptual capacities available to the puppy are very likely too limited for the kind of learning that was required in these studies.

Learning is therefore closely related to the developmental status of the newborn and cannot be studied independently or arbitrarily. The relationship between learning as based upon experience, and innate behavior, based upon maturation, varies according to many circumstances that are operative in the life situation of the neonate. Processes arising from these two sources (i.e., experience and maturation) are fused in different ways in functionally different behavior patterns arising under different environmental conditions. It is the aim of this paper to analyze certain features of early behavioral development in kittens in terms of the fusion of experience and maturation-based processes (Schneirla, 1957, 1959, 1965; Schneirla and Rosenblatt, 1961, 1963).

Contrasting Views on Suckling Development of Kittens

The views of Kovach and Kling (1967) and Ewer (1959, 1961) on suckling development contrast sharply with those we have proposed (Rosenblatt *et al.*, 1961; Schneirla and Rosenblatt, 1961) on many points and lead to a different interpretation of available data. For example, Ewer (1961) observed, as we have (Schneirla *et al.*, 1963), that suckling is rarely initiated by kittens during parturition but appears only after parturition has been completed. On the few occasions during parturition when newborn locate a nipple they may attach to it and appear to suckle (shown in Fig. 1, p. 132 of Schneirla *et al.* 1963 reference), but shortly thereafter they are detached from the nipple by the activity of the mother during the delivery of the next fetus.

Ewer (1961) has suggested that failure of kittens to initiate suckling during parturition rests on the absence of the proper releasing stimulus from the nipple to elicit the innate act of nipple grasping. She argues, from the fact that there is a short interval after parturition in which suckling is initiated by all members of a litter, that the nipple grasping stimulus becomes available only at this time.

Our observations suggest that the many activities in which the mother engages during parturition prevent the kittens from suckling at this time. The mother shifts frequently from one parturitive activity to another, requiring that she change her posture from sitting at one time, to rising and then lying down shortly afterward, and her activities such as licking herself, the fetuses, placentas, and the cage floor, make it extremely unlikely that the newly born kittens will have the opportunity and the guidance required for them to locate and attach to her nipples before parturition has been completed. Moreover there are many stimuli to distract the newborn during parturition and these increase as it continues. Kittens crawl and nuzzle in contact with one another, or nuzzle the mother's legs or tail, the uneaten placentas, the many objects covered with birth fluids, etc. This prevents them from reaching the mother's mammary region which in any event is not within their reach during most of parturition.

Not until parturition has been completed, the birth fluids have been cleaned by the mother, placentas have been consumed, and the mother has become inactive during what we have described as the postpartum resting interval, are kittens likely to be able to locate the mother's nipples and attach to them. We do not believe, as Ewer suggests, that orientation to the nipples is based upon an innately organized appetitive behavior nor that nipple grasping can be understood simply as an innate act in response to a specific releasing stimulus. We feel, rather, that the early crawling and nuzzling movements of the newborn are guided by features of the mother's body as well as her actions (e.g., licking which orients the kitten to the mother's body) leading the kitten to nuzzle in her fur. Once this has begun, forward movement is maintained by contact with the fur until the kitten reaches the region surrounding the nipple. There, nuzzling changes to gentle nose tapping and this in turn results in accidental contact with the protruding nipple which elicits mouthing movements, during which the kitten may grasp a nipple and initiate sucking. In contrast to the situation during parturition the stable situation provided for the newly born kittens by the mother, resting on her side after parturition, makes it more likely that the general approach of the kitten will be guided by steps toward the nipple region; there the more specific head and mouth movements (i.e., nose tapping, nipple grasping) will be elicited, and suckling will be initiated.

Our view of suckling development in kittens also differs from that of Kovach and Kling (1967) who believe that suckling development is based upon the maturation of the sucking reflex. These investigators

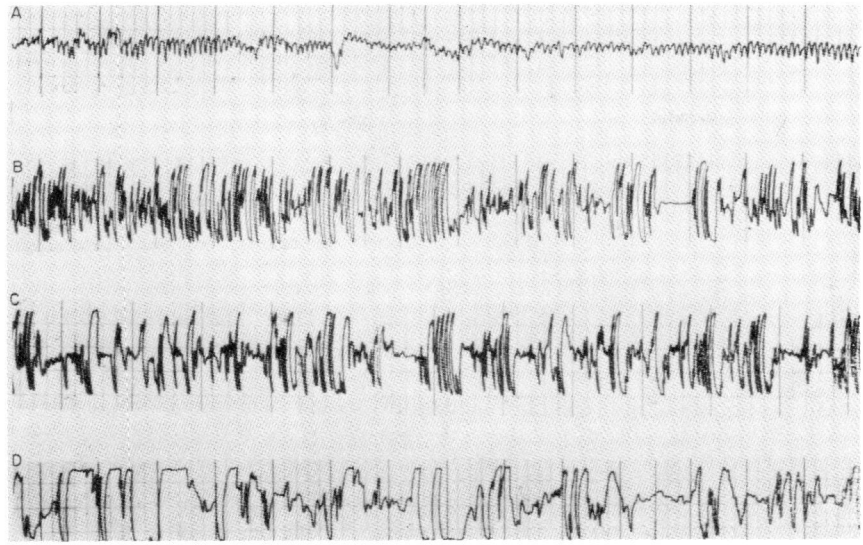

FIG. 1. Records of initial sucking responses with rubber nipple of kittens, at birth (A), after 4 days suckling from mother (B), after 10 days suckling from mother (C), and after 20 days suckling from mother (D). (Taken from Kovach and Kling, 1967.)

propose that during its maturation the sucking reflex is at first easily elicited by nipple stimulation, but that it then becomes more difficult to elicit. From this, they suggest it is more difficult for suckling to be initiated or to be transferred from one suckling object to another (e.g., mother's nipple to an artificial rubber nipple) as the kittens become older.

Records are presented of sucking elicited by placing kittens on a rubber nipple at birth, 4, 10, and 20 days of age (Fig. 1). While sucking was readily elicited in the newborn kitten, at 4 days of age, there was already some indication of nipple rejection and by the 10th day nipple rejection predominated as it did on the 20th day. That this was not a transient response to the nipple was shown by the continued rejection of the nipple by a kitten made to feed entirely from the artificial rubber nipple in place of the mother's nipple from which it had fed until the 9th day (Fig. 2). The kitten continued to reject the nipple for 2 days after removal from the mother before showing some sucking; eventually it sucked from the nipple voluntarily, locating it and grasping it alone. The nipple therefore was not by its very nature an aversive stimulus.

Essentially what Kovach and Kling (1967) propose is that the suck-

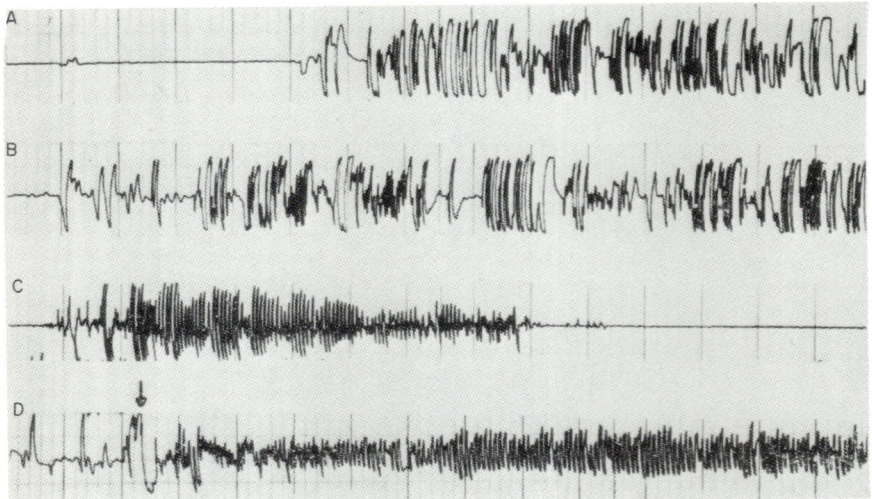

FIG. 2. Records of sucking responses with rubber nipple of a kitten that suckled from the mother for the first 9 days. Daily records from the 10th to 14th day shown in lines A to D; arrow over line D shows first independent suckling. (Taken from Kovach and Kling, 1967.)

ing reflex, as an innate component of suckling, can be traced separately throughout the suckling period. Their view is that experience only plays a role in the development of behavior for locating the nipple. This normally involves some features of responsiveness to the mother and, hence, may be considered in part social behavior. This component of suckling also, they believe, can be analyzed separately from the sucking reflex.

They state (Kovach and Kling, 1967, p. 100):

> Our data show specific sensory motor mechanisms associated with the initiation and development of neonate sucking behavior and we feel that the critical period concept, not as a period for early socialization, but as a period for the availability of neonate reflexes on which the establishment of persistent behavior patterns may be based is useful, if not necessary, for identifying the separate maturational and experiential factors in the development of neonate sucking behavior.

At birth, movements that are employed in locating the nipple and grasping it are the product of prenatal maturational processes and stimulational effects *in utero*. Fetal movement of the forelimbs and head provides a good deal of anterior end stimulation (Coronios, 1933; Carmichael, 1946; Schneirla, 1965) upon which could be based the early appearance of head turning and mouth opening in the newly born kitten. Notwithstanding this earlier development, the initial efforts of the newborn to suckle are undoubtedly largely successful because of the sequence of highly differentiated stimuli (i.e., mother's body, fur, bare region surrounding the nipple, protrusion of the nipple, and the variety of graded tactile, thermal, and olfactory stimuli) which guide the kitten to the nipple (McBride, 1963). However, from the first sucklings on, the

TABLE 1
Nipple Position Preferences of Kittens from Various-Sized Litters[a]

Litter size	Kittens	Days postpartum	Nipple position[b] (anterior) 1	2	(posterior) 3	4
2	Tiger	7	0	1	<u>58</u>	5
	Yellow	7	0	9	7	<u>52</u>
2	Mot	7	52	<u>157</u>	14	22
	Black	7	3	3	<u>91</u>	35
3	Tiger	8	1	7	<u>28</u>	<u>123</u>
	Green	8	0	38	<u>93</u>	52
	Bl–Wh	8	0	40	<u>178</u>	28
3	GW	14	0	11	<u>179</u>	9
	Mot	14	1	58	73	<u>160</u>
	NT	14	6	67	<u>109</u>	34
4	Green	14	2	49	<u>147</u>	56
	Yellow	14	1	91	<u>151</u>	79
	Mot	14	1	28	<u>108</u>	<u>135</u>
	Red	14	1	53	<u>44</u>	<u>144</u>
5	Red	6	0	<u>63</u>	24	12
	BW	6	0	7	<u>74</u>	9
	GW	6	0	<u>85</u>	12	3
	Mot	6	0	8	<u>71</u>	9
	Black	6	0	8	11	<u>99</u>
7	Yellow	3	15	11	10	5
	Red	3	1	5	<u>24</u>	8
	Blue	3	6	9	8	<u>34</u>
	White	3	1	3	9	<u>28</u>
	NT	3	1	<u>16</u>	10	8
	BY	3	9	<u>22</u>	7	1
	RY	3	2	3	7	<u>27</u>

[a] The frequency of sucklings on the four different nipple positions over the number of days indicated is given in the table.

[b] Each kitten's preferred nipple position is underlined. Several kittens showed preferences for two nipple positions and an occasional kitten showed no clear preferences.

pathway to the nipple, the base of the nipple, and stimuli from the nipple itself are used by the kittens as the basis for the development of individually specialized nipple position preferences (Wodinsky *et al.,* 1955; Ewer, 1959, 1961).

The rapid formation of these suckling patterns in newborn kittens is exemplified in the records of several litters shown in Table 1. Nipple locations on the mother are numbered anterior to posterior, 1 to 4, each position referring to the pair of nipples at that location. Position preferences were established as early as the first day in kittens of several litters and were maintained from then on; by the end of the third day more than 80% of the kittens suckled from a single nipple position at each feeding. The rate at which the preferences were established was independent of litter size (Table 2). Ewer (1959, 1961) has reported substantially the same findings with clear evidence in her observations that preferences may be established for individual nipples rather than pairs of nipples.

There are no indications that kittens which prefer one or another nipple region differ in weight, or that their rates of growth or levels of activity are different. Kittens tend to develop preferences for those nipples on which they have suckled during the first and second days. They show a rapid improvement in the speed with which they find their preferred nipple and attach to it during this period. Improvement during

TABLE 2
Distribution of Ages by Litter Size at Which Nipple Position Preferences Were Established[a]

Day	Age							
	1	2	3	4	5	6	7	8
	2	2	2	3				3
	4	2	2	4				3
	5	2	4					
	5	3	4					
		3	4					
		3	4					
		5	7					
		5	7					
		5	7					
		7						
Total	4	10	9	2				2

[a] Criteria for establishment of nipple position preference was 70% frequency of suckling at a nipple position and day-to-day consistency. Five kittens did not meet these criteria but three were observed for only 3 days. Numbers indicate litter size.

the first week is based upon maturation of sensory and motor functions (Langworthy, 1929; Windle, 1930; Tilney and Casamajor, 1924) and their early experience with particular sensory cues.

The various nipple regions appear quite similar and the nipples are hardly different, yet to the kittens of a litter each nipple region differs from the others. The differences may be chiefly in their olfactory characteristics as Ewer (1961) suggests. Movement toward the mother for feeding becomes more efficient as the kitten's nuzzling in the fur is guided to the nipple region more effectively by specific sensory stimuli, and nipple grasping is performed with greater accuracy. The same improvements are displayed by each of the kittens of a litter, at slightly different times, perhaps, but more importantly, in relation to slightly different sensory cues which distinguish the different nipple regions.

These developmental changes cannot be divided into components as Kovach and Kling (1967) indicate, nor do their maturational and learning tests with the rubber nipples support such an interpretation. In their study, the 4-, 10-, and 20-day-old kittens were removed from their mothers, with whom they had been suckling, and were placed on the rubber nipple. It is highly likely, in view of the evidence for rapid learning of nipple position preferences, that the kittens distinguished the difference between their accustomed nipple and the new one and refused to suckle from the latter. Since from the age of 2 or 3 days, kittens regularly distinguish between two neighboring nipples on the mother and suckle from one and not the other it is not surprising to find that they do not grasp a nipple when offered one that differs so greatly from their own. While kittens do not always reject a nonpreferred nipple on the mother, as, for example, when they mistakenly take a wrong "nipple," they readily abandon it when the rightful owner nuzzles at it. However, when they are sucking from their preferred nipple they hold on tenaciously when an intruder attempts to take it from them.

Kovach and Kling (1967) contend that the sucking reflex is based upon a different mechanism than the nipple searching pattern and that the course of each can be studied separately throughout the suckling period. They cite the study discussed above to support this view. As we have indicated, because of the degree of discrimination even very young kittens exercise in grasping the mother's nipples, this study lends itself to a different interpretation. It suggests that the mechanism of nipple grasping is inseparable from the mechanism of nipple searching under normal circumstances and that the two form parts of a single suckling pattern. For the experienced kitten the nipple is located at the end of a pathway which it has learned to follow. The path is defined by tactile–olfactory stimuli (as we shall show later) and perhaps thermal stimuli as well which the kitten follows in sequence until it reaches the base of the nipple. Our observations indicate that the kitten is quite selective in responding to the stimuli it encounters as it crawls toward the nipple. Each prominent object is sampled then passed by if it does not form part of the pathway to the preferred nipple. Encountering a familiar stimulus in the course of its nuzzling excites the kitten to explore it further while an unfamiliar stimulus leads to rapid withdrawal of interest and turning away. Responses between these two extremes are observed when kittens make contact with a nonpreferred nipple: they explore it for a short period then veer away toward the preferred nipple.

In our studies on brooder-fed kittens (see below) and those raised by their mothers we have observed that the preferred nipple is "identified" not only by stimuli from the nipple and its surroundings, but also by the path which the kitten takes to reach it. This was indicated in a study with brooder-fed kittens in which it was known that the kittens were using an olfactory path to the nipple and the same olfactory stimulus on the nipple and nipple base to identify and suckle from the one nipple of a pair that supplied milk (see Fig. 5). Normally when the odor was present on the brooder cover, nipple, and base, the kitten rapidly crawled to the nipple, nuzzling as it moved, made contact with the base, then the nipple, and soon grasped it and sucked. As a test, the nipple and its base were washed clean of the odor but the brooder cover with the odor path was left in place. The kittens crawled along the path to the nipple and, ignoring the absence of the familiar odor on the nipple and its base, grasped the nipple and sucked.

Further tests were made but in these tests the brooder cover was removed and a fresh one put in its place, with the familiar odor path absent. On an occasion when the kitten crawled slowly, and by a less definite path, toward the nipple and reached the base of the nipple it nuzzled it for a period but then turned away and did not grasp the nipple. In the previous test, the following of the path leading to the nipple prepared the kitten to grasp the nipple even though the nipple itself no longer had the familiar odor. When the kitten was unable to follow a path to the nipple because the familiar path was absent, the nipple and its base were explored more closely and finally rejected. Another test showed that if the odor path is absent but the kitten comes upon the nipple and its base containing the familiar odor it explores them and then grasps the nipple and sucks.

Path-taking to the nipple and nipple grasping and sucking are a single suckling pattern in experienced kittens. Terminal elements of the pattern (i.e., nipple grasping and sucking) are "aroused" by introductory elements (i.e., crawling along the path toward nipple). The sensory stimuli which guide the kitten toward the nipple and those which enable it to distinguish the preferred nipple need not be the same (i.e., olfactory) as in the test situations described above. We have also tested kittens in brooders in which the path to the nipple was indicated by odor stimuli, and the preferred nipple was distinguished from the nonpreferred one by the surface texture of the nipple base with the same results as described above.

In an interesting study with rabbit pups Ivanitskii (Table 3) has found that the suckling of 10- to 12-day-old young may be considered a pattern with elements that are similar to those described in somewhat older kittens. She conditioned the head-lifting response used to search for the mother's nipple in 1- to 5-day-old pups using an odor as the conditioned stimulus. To the odor presented on the experimenter's palm the pups raised their heads as they do when the mother approaches them to nurse. After the fifth day she stopped presenting the odor and waited until the tenth day before reintroducing it on her palm. At that age the young typically run to the entrance of the pen to nurse from the mother when she enters once a day. What Ivanitskii found was that the pups, in response to the conditioned odor, exhibited not the earlier suckling pattern with which it had been associated but the

TABLE 3
Conditional Feeding Response in Newly Born Rabbits During the First Two Weeks[a]

Age: Day 1 through 9	Day 10 onward
1. Feeding pattern: "search for nipple" arousal by mother raises head crawls under mother's body, turns on back, sucking sounds, licks	"search for mother" rapid running around nest runs to mother's compartment runs to mother and suckles (eyes open day 10)
2. Unconditioned stimulus: mother in contact with young, nurses them	mother entering young's compartment (i.e., visual, auditory, and perhaps, tactile stimulation)
3. Conditional stimulus: odor (oil of camphor) on mother's mammary region presented days 1 to 5 No presentation of conditional stimulus between days 6 and 9 No test between days 6 and 9	
4. Test conditional stimulus: (odor) presented on palm of hand	test on day 10 and thereafter
5. Response obtained in test: "search for nipple"	"search for mother"

[a] Ivanitskii.

FIG. 3. Brooder and nipple, used by Kovach and Kling, shown inside incubator. (Taken from Kovach and Kling, 1967.)

more mature pattern of suckling, although the odor had not been present during the development of this later suckling pattern.

The view that, in early development, progress in suckling is based upon maturation and experience acting together may also clarify some of the difficulties which Kovach and Kling (1967) report in their attempt to establish brooder feeding in newly born kittens and older kittens of various ages. The brooder which Kovach and Kling used is shown in Fig. 3 and, for comparison, the brooder which we used in an earlier study (Rosenblatt et al., 1961) is shown in Fig. 4. The two brooders differ mainly with respect to the ease with which kittens can locate the nipple and grasp it, given their mode of exploration by crawling with the head lowered in contact with the floor or brooder surface and oscillated from side-to-side. Notable in the Kovach and Kling brooder is the absence of any continuous smooth surfaces on which the kitten can crawl, nose against the floor, that would lead it to the base of the nipple. A kitten nuzzling over the brooder surface would be diverted into corners, crevices, and sections of the brooder far from the nipple. Our brooder, however, was designed to minimize distraction by providing a continuous surface with smoothly rounded edges and corners. The nipple protrudes from the surface, as it does from the mother. The round belly of the brooder stimulated kittens to crawl upward on its surface and the short narrow nipple, which was located centrally where the kittens were most likely to make contact with it, could be easily grasped (Stavsky, 1932).

Using their brooder, Kovach and Kling (1967) found that newborn

FIG. 4. A week-old kitten in suckling position at the brooder. (Taken from Schneirla and Rosenblatt, 1961.)

kittens were unable to learn to locate the nipple and suck from it during 10 days of training (Table 4) and 2- and 4-day-old kittens required 7 and 5 days, respectively, to begin to take milk by themselves. Using our brooder, kittens started at birth and 2 or 3 days of age were fed by syringe and nipple during the first day; they explored the brooder and were placed on the nipple several times on the second day; and, by the third day they began to take milk by themselves.

With the Kovach and Kling brooder, to locate the nipple successfully, the kittens had to avoid nuzzling and approach the nipple directly head-on. Not until the kittens were 7 days of age could they begin to accomplish this, and from then on brooder feeding was initiated regularly after 3 days of training. Older kittens (i.e., 20- and 26-day-old kittens) were no faster in establishing nipple feeding than young kittens (7-, 8-, and 12-day-old kittens).

From their results, however, Kovach and Kling (1967) propose that

TABLE 4
Initiation of Suckling in Kittens Reared in the Kovach and Kling Brooder[a]

Age interval when started in brooder (days)	N	Latencies of first independent feeding (hours)	
		(Average)	(Range)
0	2	No independent feeding in 240 hours	
2–4	5	135	111–157
7–8	13	82	56–94
12	4	81	68–92
20–26	5	73	62–92
31–40	7	11	2–32

[a] Adapted from Kovach and Kling (1967).

there is a critical period from the 7th to the 26th day during which the kitten's ability to learn brooder feeding matures. They leave no doubt that they believe the critical period is determined by the maturation of learning ability in the kitten, aided by the onset of vision, rather then that the nature of the brooder and the difficulty of locating the nipple because of its inaccessibility to a newly born kitten may have determined the period during which kittens could gain the experience necessary to learn brooder feeding.

According to our view of the situation, older kittens that were able to walk up to the brooder directly and did not have to nuzzle, being less dependent upon tactile and olfactory stimuli to locate the nipple, should show even more rapid learning than 1- to 4-week-old young. This, in fact, was found: after the 31st day brooder feeding was learned in one-third the time required by the younger kittens. But here again Kovach and Kling (1967) propose that there is a second critical period for learning to feed from the brooder.

Since we have already found that kittens can learn to feed from our brooder on the third day, when they have been placed with it at birth, one would have to propose a critical period occurring at this age, also, in addition to the two periods that have already been proposed by Kovach and Kling. It would seem more fruitful, rather than multiplying the number of critical periods necessary to account for the fact that kittens learn to feed from different brooders at different ages, and that they learn more rapidly at a later age than an earlier one with the same brooder, to try to understand the relationship between behavioral capacities of kittens at different ages and the characteristics of the brooder. From this point of view the use of different brooders, each varied systematically in relation to one or another feature (e.g., surface texture, location of nipple, shape, etc.) might be a useful procedure for studying the relationship between the kitten's behavioral capacities at various ages and its learning (Schneirla and Rosenblatt, 1963).

Studies of this sort have been started at the Institute of Animal Behavior, by Mr. Robert Woll, a graduate student who is working with me. He has simplified even further the brooder with which I had worked some years ago, eliminating the side arms and center alley of the earlier brooder, and, in addition, he has added a second nipple alongside and 4 inches from the original nipple (Fig. 5). Molded rubber discs, 2 inches in diameter, are used as bases surrounding the nipples (i.e., flanges). Mr. Woll has been studying the ability of newly born kittens to use either tactile or olfactory stimuli from the flanges as the basis for learning the location of a nipple that provides milk. Two flange textures have been used, one consisting of a raised pattern of concentric circles and the other a raised dot pattern; smooth-surfaced flanges are used when olfactory stimuli are studied by placing different odors (i.e., men's cologne, oil of wintergreen) on the surface of each flange (Fig. 5).

Although Mr. Woll has not yet completed his studies he already has some results that are relevant to the present discussion. His procedure for training kittens to suckle from the brooder nipple involves feeding them by hand during the first day after birth with a syringe at the tip of which is the nipple that is later used with the brooder. When the kittens are later placed on the brooder they are required to locate and attach to only one of the two nipples that are present, since only one nipple is open at the tip and provides them with milk. The milk-

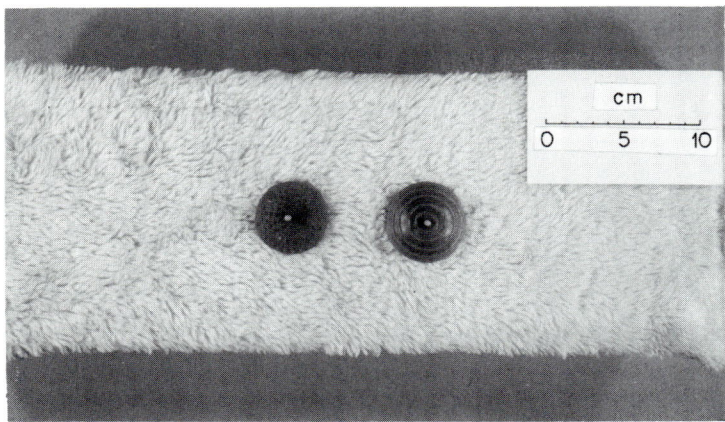

FIG. 5. Woll brooder with two nipples and textured flanges at the base of each nipple. Brooder is mounted at a 45° angle to the floor.

filled nipple can be identified by one of the two textures in one study, and by one of the two odors in another study. To facilitate their learning, during the first day's hand feeding, Mr. Woll surrounds the syringe nipple with the positive flange the kittens will later have to locate in the brooder. Thus kittens begin to experience the positive flange in association with receiving milk from a nipple from their first feeding on, during the first day. When kittens are placed with the brooder at the beginning of the second day, their nuzzling on the two flanges is recorded using a phonograph cartridge to pick up slight pressure applied to the flange, and nipple sucking (i.e., on both the open and blind nipples separately) is also recorded using a pressure transducer located between the milk supply and the nipple.

Identification of the positive flange texture or odor was learned first by kittens as a result of the procedure used, and this formed the basis for path-taking to the nipple and nipple grasping. Using its experience with the positive flange during the first day in the brooder, the

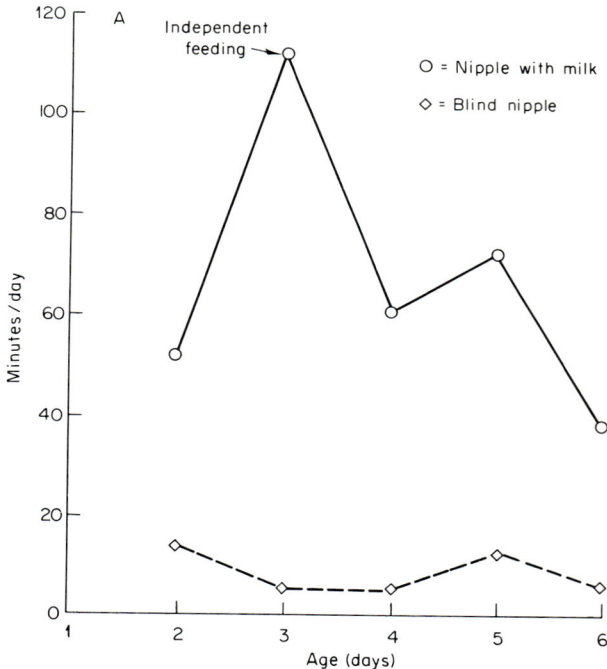

FIG. 6. Tactile discrimination learning of positive flange texture by newly born kittens reared in a brooder: total time spent nuzzling the two flanges (A), mean duration of nuzzling bouts at each flange (B).

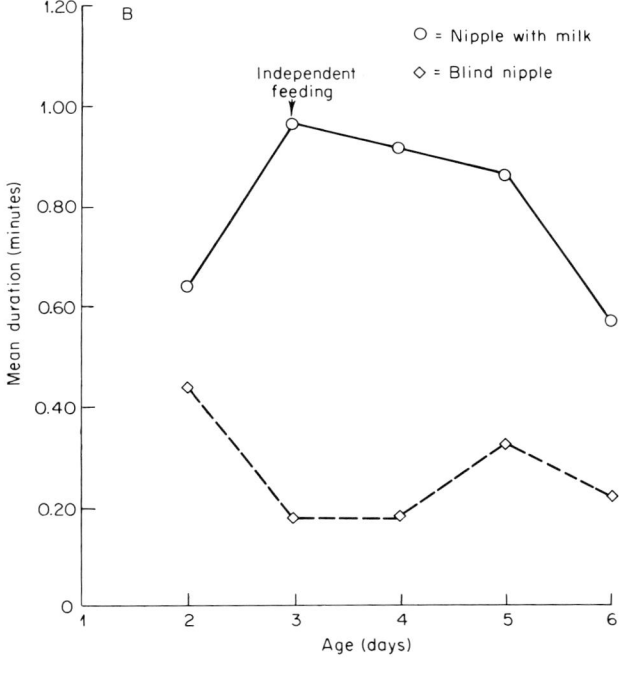

FIG. 6. (*continued*)

kitten nuzzled the flange with the positive *texture* for a longer total time over the first 24 hours, and thereafter, as well as at each feeding effort (Fig. 6). Though odors are more difficult for the experimenter to control, nevertheless, by the third day, the positive flange with an odor was also given more attention than the negative flange (Fig. 7). Our brooder nipples, like those of other brooders with artificial nipples (Toropova, 1961; Stanley *et al.*, 1970), are not as easily grasped, initially, as the mother's nipples; nevertheless the kitten made greater efforts to grasp the nipple associated with the positive flange than the negative flange. This, we believe, was a consequence of the greater amount of time the kitten spent nuzzling over the entire surface of the positive flange. The negative flange was nuzzled for only a short period before the kitten turned away from it, but the positive flange elicited a great deal of excitement from the kitten and it nuzzled it, as we have indicated, for long periods.

The path to the positive nipple appeared to be formed as a consequence of the kitten's initial preference for the positive flange. In the course of its continued attention to this flange the kitten's body rested

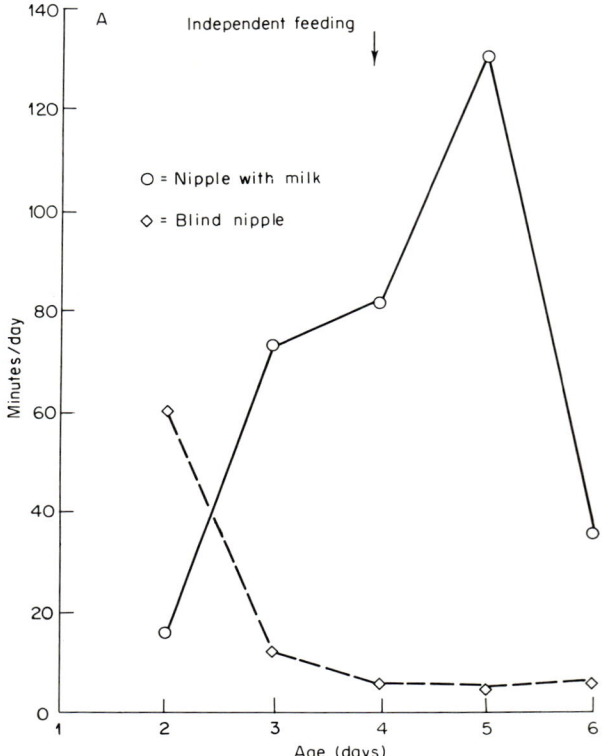

FIG. 7. Olfactory discrimination learning of positive flange odor by newly born kittens reared in a brooder: total time spent nuzzling the two flanges (A), mean duration of nuzzling bouts at each flange (B).

against the brooder and the floor area in front, and its nuzzling circled the outer edge of the flange. We believe, therefore, that odors from the kitten and milk were deposited in the form of a path from the floor and base of the brooder to the flange and a short distance into an area around the flange.

The odor path, supplemented by a matted down tactile region, leading to the positive flange and nipple, provided the kitten with a continuous stimulus trail from the floor in front of the brooder, on the brooder cover, and on the surface of the flange and the surrounding area until the nipple itself was reached. The kitten soon began to use this trail to reach the nipple and in the course of learning to follow the trail, the components of suckling were formed into a pattern.

Last to be developed was the nipple grasping component of the pat-

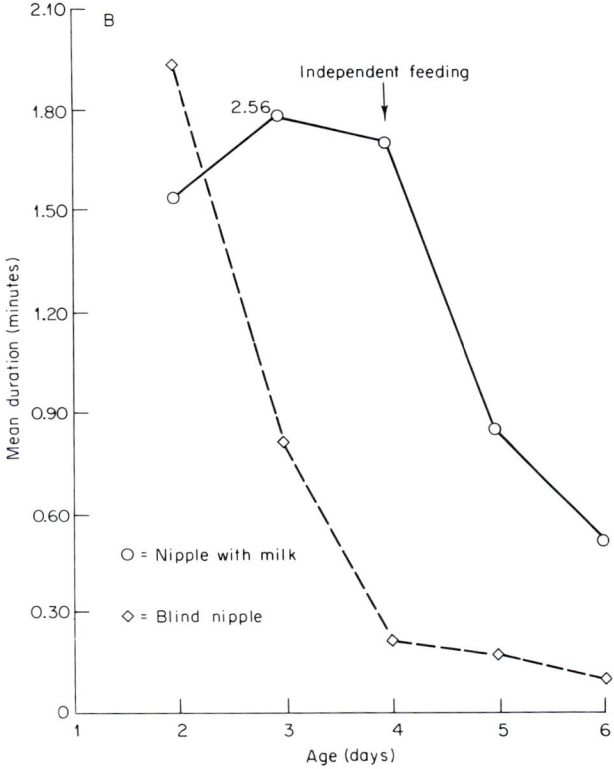

FIG. 7. (*continued*)

tern. The difficulty lay in the fact that, short as it was, the nipple was still too long for the kittens. Typically a kitten after making contact with the nipple during nuzzling of the flange, draws back its head, opens its mouth, and lunges forward. With the nipple as long as it was, the kitten could not accurately direct itself at the nipple and at the same time grasp it in its mouth. The kitten therefore adopted the behavior of remaining in mouth contact with the nipple, moving its head sideways to bend the nipple, and then allowing the nipple to spring back into its mouth and grasping it or some variation of this action. This rather skilled behavior on the part of the kitten required considerable practice, and, in addition, was based upon the prior establishment of the suckling pattern we have described above. Mr. Woll, in his recent work, has found some kittens that are able to grasp the nipple by themselves and suck at 12 to 24 hours of age although they are not yet able to locate the nipple reliably.

When nipple grasping appears, on the third and fourth days in the kittens for which records are shown in Figs. 6 and 7, the total duration of nuzzling and the duration of each nuzzling session before nipple grasping become shorter as the kittens become more efficient in suckling. Further improvements occur as the kittens gain greater control over their movements, particularly their head movements since the head functions as a probe determining the direction of their locomotion. They do not lunge forward to one or another side as readily while nuzzling the path to the flange, thereby losing the path and having to regain it. When they reach the flange they do not lunge past it as often as before, but instead they reduce the amplitude of their nuzzling movements, begin to make fine nose tapping movements, and more carefully search the flange until they make contact with the nipple. The nipple is grasped more rapidly also.

The rate at which kittens learn to feed alone from the brooder is therefore subject to considerable variation depending upon many factors. By using a less well-defined nipple flange in our earlier studies we found that kittens were delayed by one day in learning a path to the nipple. Brooder-reared puppies (Stanley *et al.*, 1970) learned to approach the nipple almost from the beginning of their training by crawling over a soft cloth brooder cover, but they were delayed nearly 4 days (i.e., 5 trials/day) when a hard wire cloth covered the brooder. Therefore, another factor which may influence the difficulty of the brooder is its surface texture: the soft cloth and hard wire surfaces each covered different halves of the brooder with nipples at the far end of each half. Since all puppies initially favored the soft cloth surface, those puppies that learned to locate the nipple at the far end of the soft brooder surface learned which side to turn to and also how to grasp the nipple much more rapidly than those puppies that had to restrain their tendency to enter the half of the brooder with the soft cover in order to obtain milk at the far end of the hard wire brooder surface.

Features of the brooder which facilitate learning to feed independently by the newborn may be irrelevant to an older kitten (e.g., 20 days) that does not depend upon nuzzling in order to find the nipple but is able to approach the nipple directly without contact with surrounding regions of the brooder. A nipple protruding in the manner of the Kovach and Kling brooder might in fact facilitate learning by older kittens since the nipple can be reached directly without the kittens having to crawl over the surface of the brooder.

The point, of course, is that knowing the relationship between the nature of the kitten's activity and the demands of the task required for locating and attaching to the nipple would enable one to assess the relative difficulty of a brooder for self-feeding. More difficult brooders are likely to be learned more rapidly by older kittens, the difficulty being considered in relation to the kitten. Before one can say that the kitten's ability to learn to feed independently has improved with age, and certainly before this can be accounted for by the concept of "critical period," the brooders themselves must be studied in relation to kitten behavior.

In pursuit of factors determining the maturation of the sucking reflex in relation to suckling, Kovach and Kling (1967) reared a group of kittens individually, in isolation from the mother. The kittens were prevented from sucking and were fed by inserting a tube into the stomach and injecting an adequate amount of milk into it. At various ages after birth individual isolated kittens were returned to mothers that were nursing their own young and the suckling behavior of the isolates were observed. The results, shown in Table 5, indicated that kittens returned to mothers after the 19th day did not initiate suckling with the mother.

TABLE 5
Effects of Isolated Rearing and Tube- or Brooder-Feeding on Suckling and Social Behavior upon Return to the Mother

Kovach and Kling (1967)					Schneirla and Rosenblatt (1963)	
Period of isolation + tube-feeding	N	Average latency to suckle (minutes)	Latency of sustained contact (minutes)	Latency to suckling (minutes)	Period of isolation + feeding from brooder with nipple (days)	N
4 hours–6 days	1	30	4	85	0–7	3
			10	335		
4 hours–9 days	2	30	138	273		
		Average =	51	191		
4 hours–16 days	1	300	22	45	6–23	5
			35	317		
4 hours–19 days	2	180	48	1514		
			64	1755		
			143	2280		
		Average =	62	1182		
4 hours–23 days	1	No suckling	60	No suckling	2–44	4
			1480	No suckling		
4 hours–24 days	2	No suckling	2687	No suckling		
			4200	No suckling		
4 hours–35 days	1	No suckling				
		Average =	2107			

Characteristically, Kovach and Kling (1967) tend to minimize the psychological context within which sucking occurs, and in this case they attach little importance to social factors in the initiation or the failure of initiation of suckling with the mother. This is particularly important when one begins to study suckling in kittens beyond the age of 3 weeks but is also of great importance in younger kittens.

We have shown that there is a steady development of suckling in the direction of increasing participation of kittens in the initiation of suckling between the young and the mother (Fig. 8; Rosenblatt et al., 1961). With the onset of visual regulation of suckling approaches to the

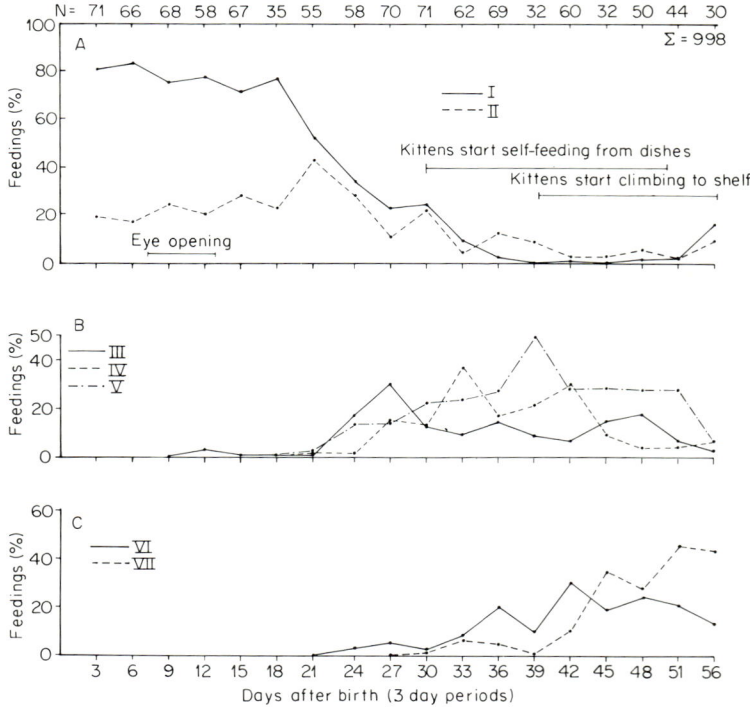

FIG. 8. Mother–kitten feeding relationships from birth to 2 months. The graphs represent different ways in which nursing and suckling are initiated and the frequency of each type of feeding; analysis of three litters. (A) I. Mother approaches kittens in home corner. II. Kittens crawl to mother nearby in home corner. (B) III. Kitten crawls to mother, lying, sitting, out of home. IV. Kitten approaches mother, sitting, standing, at food dishes. V. Mother wandering, kitten approaches her when she comes to rest. (C) VI. Mother wandering, kitten approaches her while she moves around cage. VII. Kitten approaches mother coming down from shelf, kitten "begs" toward mother on shelf, kitten climbs to mother on shelf.

mother, around the third week, and based upon earlier nonvisual approaches to her, social processes become increasingly important in the suckling behavior of kittens. The effects of isolation on suckling development cannot be understood without reference to these social changes in the kittens and in the mother. We wish therefore to compare our results in which this factor was considered with those of Kovach and Kling (1967).

Our own study (Schneirla and Rosenblatt, 1963) is relevant here since kittens were also reared in social isolation but allowed to suckle, albeit on a brooder with artificial nipple, and then they were returned to their mothers. The isolated kittens in our study, in contrast to those reared by Kovach and Kling, developed an effective pattern of suckling at the brooder nipple and they treated the brooder in many respects as equivalent to the mother. They slept in the saddle of the brooder, crawled over its surface, and, if placed at a distance, they vocalized until they had found their way back and then came to rest on it.

In Table 5 we compare the suckling of isolates that were tube-fed with isolates that suckled from a brooder for roughly equivalent periods of early development, insofar as this can be done with the data from the two studies. What emerges from the comparison is that until an age was reached at which kittens no longer initiated suckling with the mother, which was after the 19th day in the tube-fed and after the 23rd day in this sample of brooder-fed isolates, the tube-fed kittens initiated suckling with a shorter latency than the brooder-fed kittens. All three brooder-fed kittens that were isolated from birth to the seventh day required a longer period to initiate suckling than the nearest age groups of tube-fed kittens. Tube-feeding appears, strangely enough, to have facilitated the initiation of feeding from the mother compared to brooder feeding which was, of course, much more similar to feeding from the mother. This suggests that the alternative suckling pattern with the brooder interfered with the initiation of suckling with the mother rather than facilitated it.

That the difficulty for the brooder-fed kittens 23 days of age and younger was the initiation of suckling and not responding positively to the mother is shown by their relatively short latencies for the first sustained contact with her. In the 7-day-old kittens two of the latencies are short enough for suckling to have appeared as early as it did in the tube-fed isolates but suckling was delayed after this initial contact and did not appear until 1 to 5 hours later. In the 23-day-old, brooder-fed isolates all of the contact latencies were shorter than the suckling latencies of the tube-fed isolates, but suckling did not appear until nearly 5 to 36 hours later in four of the five kittens.

The difficulty encountered by the older kittens of the Kovach and Kling (1967) study, and ours—those that were socially isolated and either tube-fed or brooder-fed—that resulted in their failure to initiate a suckling relationship with the mother can be traced to their reactions to the mother. Compared to 23-day-old kittens, the brooder-fed isolates, at the older age of 44 days, showed a marked increase in the time required to make the first sustained contact with the mother (Table 5). Except for one of the older kittens, all required more than a day, and one kitten required close to 3 days before it would initiate contact and remain in contact with the mother. Failure to suckle from the mother was due, therefore, in large part to the kitten's inability to achieve an adequate social adjustment to her.

At the ages when they were returned to their mothers, the older tube-fed isolates were apparently still capable of partially adjusting to the mother socially, but the 35-day-old kitten of this group was less able than the 23- or 24-day-old kittens. Unfortunately we do not have a group of brooder-fed isolates (i.e., isolated from birth) to compare with the 23- and 24-day-old, tube-fed kittens in order to determine the social responses (i.e., other than suckling) of these kittens in the presence of the mother and littermates.

The analysis of tube-fed and brooder-fed isolates makes it clear, thus far, that the failure to initiate suckling from the mother in the older tube-fed kittens was not a function simply of the waning of a sucking reflex (i.e., greater difficulty of initially eliciting sucking) after the third week. Nor was the appearance of suckling in the younger tube-fed isolates evidence of the retention of the sucking reflex in the absence of the experience of sucking from either the mother or a brooder.

The absence of suckling in the tube-fed kittens during their isolation served mainly to *prevent the development of a suckling pattern* and this, in turn, left them freer to establish such a pattern when they were returned to the mother. If a recent study on tube-fed rats reared in isolation (Thoman *et al.*, 1968) has any bearing on the tube-fed kittens of this study, then the kittens were not without sucking experience. Moreover there is a good likelihood that the tube-fed kittens had formed a feeding pattern in relation to the tube-feeding.

Tube-fed rats after 3 days react to the procedures used in tube-feeding quite differently than rat pups that have suckled from the mother. When they are held in the hand, as in tube-feeding, more of them become active generally (i.e., body wriggling) and show mouth movements than do pups that have not been tube-fed even if they have been handled without tube-insertion or have had an empty tube inserted into their stomachs (Table 6). A greater percentage of the tube-fed pups show mouth opening and suckling responses when a clean

TABLE 6
Three-Day-Old Mother-Reared (Suckled) and Incubator-Reared (Tube-Fed) Rat Pups Tested by (1) Holding in Hand, and (2) Tube Insertion into Mouth and Esophagus[a]

| | | Held in hand | | Insertion of clean tube into: | | | |
| | | | | Mouth | | Esophagus | |
Group treatment	N	Body wriggle (%)	Mouth movements (%)	Suck (%)	Mouth tightly shut (%)	Suck (%)	Eject (%)
Mother-reared							
Suckle only	12	17	0	17	33	0	75
Suckle + tube	12	0	0	17	42	0	92
Suckle + handle	11	18	9	27	27	0	55
Incubator-reared							
Tube fed	10	80	40	70	0	40	20

[a] Data taken from Thoman et al. (1968).

empty tube is inserted down the esophagus and a considerable percentage of these pups react by making suckling movements. None of the mother-fed pups react in this way; instead the large majority of them attempt to eject the tube.

Social responses to the mother are involved in the earliest suckling of the kitten since suckling itself is a social response. During the first 3 weeks, however, the initiative in the social relationship between the mother and the young during suckling is taken more often by the mother than the young (see Fig. 8). After the third week, the young increasingly take the initiative in feeding and in many other aspects of social behavior between mother and young (e.g., play directed at mother, sleeping in contact with the mother). These social responses of the kitten to the mother now play an increasingly greater role in determining the nature of suckling approaches. Thus the effects of social isolation upon the development of suckling are more likely to manifest themselves during this period than during earlier ones. Kittens isolated from the litter during the period of rapid broadening of social relationships with the mother, that is from the 23rd to 44th day, are unable to resume a suckling relationship with the mother upon their return to the litter, and, in all instances, the difficulty lies in their failure to initiate sustained contact with her for an average of nearly 2 days (Schneirla and Rosenblatt, 1961).

It is difficult to escape the conclusion that among the older, tube-fed isolates the failure to initiate suckling was based upon their inadequate social response to the mother rather than specifically to the waning of sucking. We have observed 33-day-old kittens resume suckling from the mother after 15 days in isolation with brooder feeding. They required an average of 15 hours to begin suckling on the mother but, significantly, again the greater part of this time was spent in adjusting to the new feeding situation; this, in part, required that they overcome the competing pattern of brooder feeding, not that they make an adequate social readjustment to the mother, a process that was begun after an average of only 46 minutes (Schneirla and Rosenblatt, 1963). Undoubtedly, for these kittens, the rapid social readjustment to the mother after the period of isolation was facilitated by their first $2\frac{1}{2}$ weeks spent in the litter.

Our comments on the study by Kovach and Kling (1967) suggest that there is an alternative way of viewing the development of suckling in newly born kittens that does not depend upon dichotomizing developmental processes in terms of the concepts of *innate* and *learned* behavior. We shall attempt to trace the development of suckling through the various phases from birth through weaning with the aim of providing a basis for comparing this early behavior pattern with the pattern of home orientation which appears in kittens during the same early period.

Undoubtedly circumstances in the early environment of the kitten and features of the kitten's behavior favor the initiation of suckling at the earliest opportunity, and this arises shortly after birth in the mother's postpartum resting period. However, an argument for the early appearance of suckling in ontogeny that is based upon its functional significance does not contribute to our understanding of the factors that govern its appearance. One can acknowledge the role of natural selection acting to assure the adaptive embryonic growth of trigeminal nerve fibers to the mouth region to produce early sucking, as Anokhin (1964) has shown, and of a relatively stereotyped sucking response as Ewer (1961) has suggested, yet feel that there still remains the problem of analyzing how early suckling is initiated. Behavioral capacities of the newborn revealed by an analysis of early suckling are likely to play a role in its later development either by an elaboration of these capacities or by their gradual modification through postnatal changes.

Early suckling in kittens is initiated with the mother at close range. Typically she lies down in front of the kittens, encloses them between her outstretched fore- and hindlegs, thereby confining their activity to the vicinity of her mammary region. In this situation, when the kitten is aroused, its behavior is channeled toward the mother's nipple region by stimulation it receives from several sources: the mother, neighboring kittens, and features of the mother's body that it encounters while nuzzling (McBride, 1963). The mother's licking is of necessity directional and the newborn, pushing itself toward her head when she licks it, finds itself against her body when she lifts her head away and stops licking (Alexander and Williams, 1964). Littermate arousal may at first offer no directionalization but as soon as one, or several, kitten(s) begins to crawl toward the mother's mammary region, body contact with littermates stimulates a similar direction of crawling in neighboring kittens.

Kittens probe their environment by means of an advancing movement of the head which at the same time oscillates in a side-to-side motion (i.e., nuzzling) (Tilney and Casamajor, 1924; Langworthy, 1929; Prechtl, 1952; Moulton, 1967). With the mother lying on her side, nuzzling usually proceeds along the round surface of her body toward the upper line of nipples, but, on occasion, kittens nuzzle downward and are trapped for a period between the mother's body and the floor surface, the nipples on the lower side of her body usually being unavailable to the kittens. As the kitten advances, its broad nuzzling movements sweep over the fur surface until the short fur surrounding the areola is encountered. Then nuzzling stops and detailed nose nose tapping begins, accompanied by slowing of forward movement; the kitten arches its neck and directs its nose downward. Advancing slowly from the border of the areola to the bare surface surrounding the nipple, the kitten continues its detailed nose tapping. Should it begin to nuzzle the areas surrounding the nipple it encounters the fur border region again and after brief nuzzling it turns back to the nipple base. Eventually contact with the nipple elicits slight head withdrawal accompanied by mouth opening and closing. These movements may occur several times before the kitten lunges forward during one mouth-opening movement, grasps the nipple in its mouth, and begins sucking (McBride, 1963).

In its initial efforts, therefore, the kitten is led by stages to the nipple region and there, its forward movement having been slowed, its nuzzling narrowed, and its attention focused, the kitten encounters the nipple which elicits a specialized mouth grasping response. During nuzzling the kitten's entire frontal facial area is stimulated tactually, eliciting forward locomotion. Upon contact with the areola, and later the nipple, only the kitten's nose and mouth areas are stimulated slowing locomotion and eliciting specific mouth movements, head lunging, and nipple grasping.

The early pattern of suckling predominates only for a short time. Kittens begin to adopt particular nipple positions for suckling, which they make efforts to locate at each feeding, and ignore the remaining nipples while en route to their own nipple position. The development of individual nipple position preferences represents a departure from the earlier mode of suckling and provides evidence that the newborn pattern of suckling, which was based initially upon canalization has given way to a pattern in which an active selection by the kitten of one among several nipples, whose position the kitten is now able to identify, has been established.

Although the development of nipple position preferences tends to reduce the competition for particular nipples among the kittens of a litter, reducing even the small amount of fighting that can sometimes be seen at the mammary region, nevertheless this may simply be the byproduct of a learning process that has a more important function in the behavioral development of the kitten. Nipple position preferences develop among single-kitten litters where the question of competition for nipples is precluded, and Deets and Harlow (1970) have found that monkey infants that face no competition for nipples also develop nipple preferences (see also Ewbank, 1964, 1967; Salk, 1960; Van Lawick-Goodall, 1967).

Nipple positions on the mother's mammary surface may be identified, initially, as in our brooder-reared kittens, by odor or tactile stimuli which distinguish one nipple position from the others. The stimulus basis of nipple position preferences with the mother has not yet been determined, but once the preference is established kittens can begin to develop a route to the preferred nipple as they do in the brooder once they have identified the flange at the base of the milk-filled nipple.

Toward the end of the first week, with nipple positions established and routes leading to the nipple gradually being formed, kittens appear to be more easily aroused to initiate suckling than earlier. In part they appear more sensitive to stimulation than newborn but even more striking is their increased readiness to initiate suckling almost exclusively whenever they are awakened. We have found that the same behavior occurs in brooder-reared kittens who immediately crawl to the brooder-nipple whenever they are awakened even though they may have just suckled. In the litter this change is most evident in the readiness with which kittens begin to crawl toward the mother after she has licked them but before she has lowered her body to the floor in the usual nursing position. Several kittens may locate and attach to the posterior nipples while the mother is still sitting in contact with the litter while others begin to orient to her nipple region only when she lowers her body within reach and they, in turn, rapidly attach to their nipples as she assumes the nursing position (Fig. 8). As the circumstances under which suckling is initiated become more varied kittens gain experience in locating their preferred nipple positions from different nearby starting points while in contact with the mother. By the end of the second week they are quite versatile in their approaches to the nipple and in the ease with which they grasp it; in the same way, kittens feeding on a brooder also become versatile in approaching the nipple from various directions, along different paths, each time distinguishing the milk-filled nipple by nuzzling at the identifying flange.

Occasions arise from birth onward, and increase after the second week, when the mother is resting in the home region, out of contact with the litter, and individual kittens initiate suckling approaches to her that terminate in feeding (Fig. 8). Initially, when the eyes are still sealed, kittens that have become separated from the litter may come upon the mother incidentally during their wandering in the home region and they eventually locate their nipples and suckle. After the eyes have opened during the period from the seventh to the ninth day, a week intervenes before there is a marked increase in feedings that are initiated by the approach of kittens to the mother. By the 21st day, 40% of feedings are initiated in this manner and from then on there is a steady increase in kitten-initiated feedings, with the help of the mother, as the mother's own tendency to initiate feedings by approaching the kittens in the home declines (Fig. 8).

There is evidence of the growing ability of kittens to orient to their environment on a visual basis during this period, a development which leads eventually to the decline in their dependence upon the home region as an orientation center allowing them, therefore, to leave the home and approach the mother even when she is no longer within the home itself (Warkentin and Smith, 1937; Ellingson and Wilcott, 1960; Rosenblatt *et al.*, 1969; Rose and Lindsley, 1965; Karmel *et al.*, 1970).

Initially visually aroused and guided crawling approaches to the mother bring the kittens to various body regions (e.g., her tail, hindleg, or back) which may be remote from the region around the preferred nipple that has become familiar to the kitten during its earlier feedings. At these unfamiliar body regions the kitten responds to contact with the mother's body much as it did as a newborn, nuzzling in the fur along contours of her body, into crevices etc. until it moves within range of the familiar regions that are part of the route to its own nipple position. With the mother, as well as the brooder, kittens become highly excited when they have picked up the trail of the nipple and they move rapidly from this point directly to the nipple.

Although the behavior of kittens that suckle from the mother and from the brooder is similar at equal ages, and suckling development with the brooder parallels its development with the mother up to around

4 weeks of age, the two patterns must be organized on somewhat different bases. When brooder-reared kittens of 1 week or 3½ weeks of age were returned to their mothers, as we have seen, they had relatively little difficulty approaching and remaining in contact with the mother (see Table 5), but they were unable for the most part to initiate suckling. The week-old kittens nuzzled continuously, much as newborns do, following the contours of the mother's body, pausing at the nipple base, and making contact with the nipples. Nevertheless an average of more than 3 hours was required, by which time the kittens were quite hungry, before suckling was initiated. The 3-week-old kittens also nuzzled the mother's body for long periods but their nuzzling resembled less the canalized nuzzling of younger kittens and more the sampling of a variety of body regions. The nipple region did attract their nuzzling efforts more than other regions but it was many hours (i.e., an average of nearly 20 hours) before suckling was initiated by these kittens. The facility with which mother-reared kittens locate the nipples even from points of initial contact with the mother that are remote from their nipples, and do so increasingly more rapidly as they gain experience in approaching the mother from a distance, is based upon their previously established suckling pattern, a pattern that is lacking in the brooder-reared kittens.

The progress in suckling made by kittens in the period that follows, in which visually guided approaches to the mother increasingly predominate, is based upon the development of the kitten's ability to initiate a more direct approach to the mother's mammary region, a process that can be traced through stages in which visual approaches are initially directed to the mother's head and tail than to the nipples and only gradually oriented directly to her nipples (Fox and Weisman, 1970). With the perception of the mother provided by seeing her at a distance, features of the mother's behavior which could have no significance for the kitten when it was limited by its perceptual capacities to proximal sensory systems, becomes increasingly important in the kitten's suckling approach. In this development we see the increasing role that the kittens' general social behavior plays in suckling and can understand the difficulty which socially isolated kittens have in initiating suckling when they are returned to the litter at later ages (Walters and Parke, 1965).

Suckling approaches become increasingly adjusted to the waning maternal responsiveness of the mother during the last weeks of the lactation period. First there is a period from the third to the fifth and sixth week during which kittens learn to approach the mother only when she is sitting or lying, or when she is feeding (Fig. 8). Then the kittens begin to solicit feeding from the mother when she is moving about the cage or is out of reach on a shelf mounted high on the side wall of the cage; they follow her as she wanders and make efforts to grasp a nipple when she pauses for a moment. Their suckling approaches at this time (fifth to eighth week, Fig. 8) are based upon their ability to detect the significance of her behavior: they respond to the subtle actions indicating that she is prepared to allow them to suckle and to the evasive and escape or cuffing actions she uses to prevent them from suckling.

Development of Home Orientation in Kittens

Scott and Bronson (1964) have suggested that until a puppy reaches the age of 3 weeks, it is not distressed by removal from the familiar nest or by separation from the mother and litter unless the removal is accompanied by cooling, hunger, or injury. Perhaps the altricial young of several other mammalian species develop more rapidly, but studies indicate that familiarity of the nest is comforting to them and removal causes distress. Gregory and Pfaff (1970) found that young rats begin to aggregate in nest sawdust in preference to sawdust without nest odors around the 9th to 12th day, and Turkewitz (1966) found a sharp increase around the 12th day in returns to the nest when young were placed at a distance from it. Odor-based preference for the nest pan and nest material has been reported as early as the first day in rat pups (Rouger et al., 1967). There are scattered reports of home orientation in rabbits and squirrels at various ages, but generally this feature of early development has received little systematic study. The following report on the kitten, taken from our recent paper (Rosenblatt et al., 1969) is perhaps the fullest study to date.

Beginning around the fifth day, when kittens were placed in the corner adjacent to the home region about 18 inches from the border of the home quadrant and facing into the center of the cage, they vocalized for a brief period, at medium to low intensity, and then they crawled forward, turned, and headed toward the home. When they reached the home they crawled into it and soon came to rest (Fig. 9). When placed directly in the home region, facing toward the center of the cage, they crawled forward for a short distance, vocalized less than in the adjacent quadrant, turned back toward the corner, and eventually came to rest, usually in the center of the home region. Kittens placed in the corner diagonally opposite from the home, about 28 inches from the home, vocalized for longer periods and at higher intensity than in the home or adjacent quadrants and crawled in a circuitous path that did not carry them any great distance from the starting point.

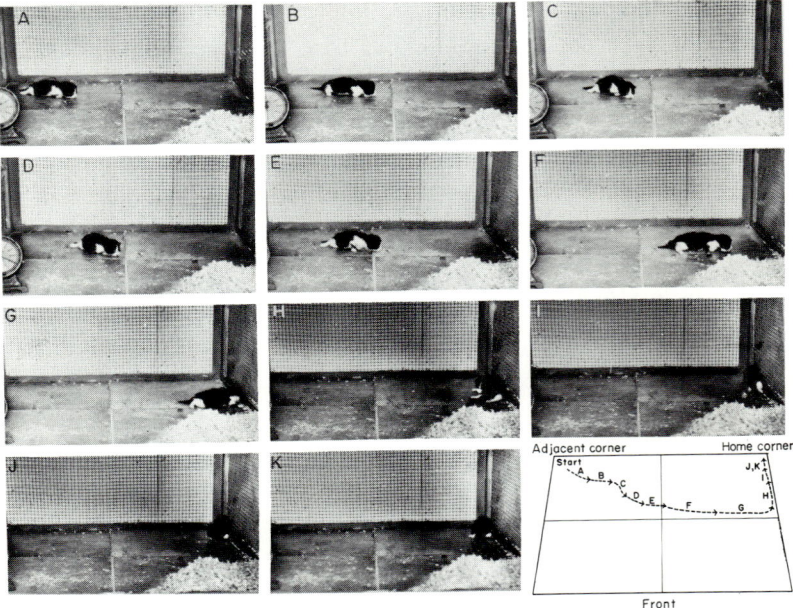

FIG. 9. Home orientation in a 5-day-old kitten with eyes still closed. Drawing shows the path taken from the starting point in the adjacent corner to the home corner, where the kitten comes to rest.

Home orientation was indicated among kittens by their behavior in each of the corners of the home cage: in the adjacent corner they crawled to the home, but they remained in the home when placed there, and in the diagonal corner they wandered near the starting point. Their vocalization in each of the corners differed also: as Fig. 11 shows, the intensity of vocalization declined gradually in each of the corners, but it remained higher in the diagonal corner than in the adjacent corner, and in the adjacent corner it remained higher than in the home region.

In our study kittens were tested also in an entirely strange cage (i.e., field) which contained none of the familiar cage odors and was, in fact, washed between daily tests. Observing the contrast between their behavior in the field and in the home cage was extremely important. In the field vocalization did not decline, but rose to the highest intensity and kittens did not wander as they did in the diagonal corner. They remained immobile except for slow head oscillations, their forelegs drawn up against the body, vocalizing loudly (Fig. 10).

The development of home orientation proceeded in stages, the first of which was marked by the accomplishment of the trip from the ad-

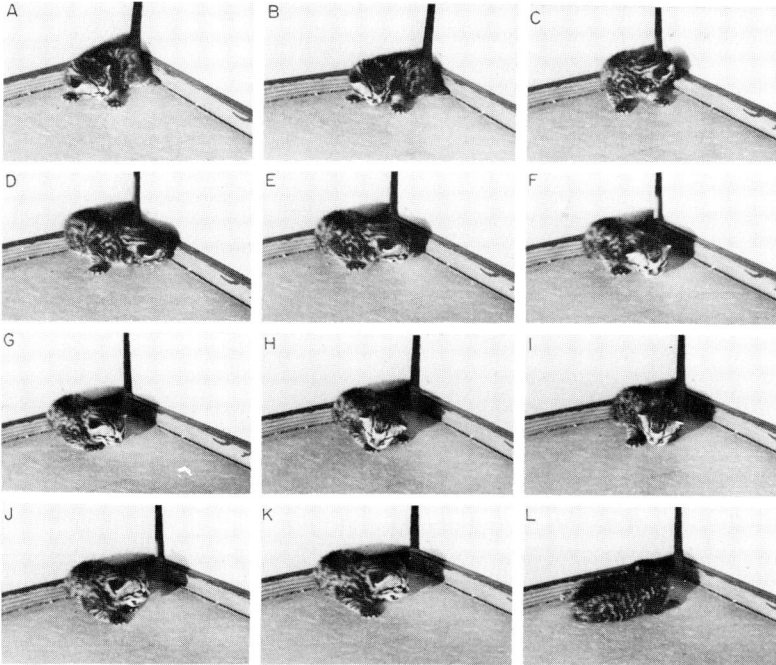

FIG. 10. (A-L). A 12-day-old kitten tested in the field showing disturbance as indicated by forelegs drawn up against body, restricted head movement, no locomotion, vocalizing, piloerection, and ears drawn forward.

jacent corner to the home (Table 7). The second stage occurred a week later when the trip from the diagonal corner to the home was successfully accomplished by an increasing number of kittens. The behavior of kittens that made successful trips to the home from the adjacent corner, and later from the diagonal corner, was characterized by three features: the first was their *arousal to activity* when placed on the floor surface outside the home, which consisted of almost immediate initiation of locomotion accompanied by vocalization of medium or low intensity; second, after a few moments, they appeared to *adopt a path*, and they maintained locomotion along this path; third, if the path they had adopted led them to the home, they entered the home site and began the process of the *settling* (i.e., settling reaction).

When they entered the diagonal or adjacent quadrants of the cage (when started in either the adjacent or diagonal corners, respectively) they did not come to rest but remained active and soon left that quadrant, headed generally in the direction of the home. The small percent-

TABLE 7

Terminations and Departures of Kittens in Home Orientation Tests from the Second to the Twenty-Second Day

Age period (days)	Terminations (%) in home quadrant when started in:			Depart from: Started in:	Departures (%)				
	Home	Adj.	Diag.		Home	Home Adj.	Diag.	Adj.	Adj. Diag.
2–4	88	34	8		12	20	33	46	33
5–7	89	73	22		12	9	14	63	50
8–10	92	73	21		13	7	0	72	33
11–13	90	72	24		12	2	0	74	76
14–16	83	78	42		19	6	14	72	61
17–19	73	76	42		45	8	23	79	50
20–22	40	84	53		73	12	18	89	71
Number of tests	296	307	282	Total entries and placements	296	222	87	307	101

age of departures from the home quadrant (Table 7) by kittens that had either been placed there at the start of tests or had entered on their own during a test started in the other quadrants indicated the special significance of this region in the orientation behavior of the kitten. No other region of the cage normally functioned in the same way: departures from the adjacent and diagonal quadrants increased as orientation to the home developed (Table 7).

The development of the home as an orientation center was based upon the special conditions which arise in this area as a result of its use during parturition and during postparturitional care and huddling of the young. The home was usually situated to the rear and near one corner of the living cage and occupied an 18-inch-square quadrant of floor space out of a total 36-inch-square.

There was little difficulty in determining the home site of a litter since the kittens remained there when alone and the mother nursed them at this site. During the tests, however, the mother and litter were removed and what remained in the home cage as a basis for orienting to the home, adjacent, and diagonal quadrants must have been deposited there by the mother and litter. Since the field was in all respects similar to the home cage, except that the home cage was occupied by the mother and litter this must have provided the basis for the kittens' ability to differentiate the floor of the home cage from that of the field. Few stimuli could be operative in view of the fact that home orientation from the adjacent corner developed prior to the age at which the kittens opened their eyes (i.e., seventh to ninth day), and we took precautions to place the field in the same relationship to the prevailing window and room light as the home cage. Wall-hugging, not a prominent feature of home orientation, in itself would not enable kittens to differentiate among the corners.

We have assumed, therefore, that olfactory cues were used by kittens both in differentiating among the cage regions and in finding their way to the home. To test this assumption, and to determine whether the olfactory cues were airborne or floor surface deposits, we removed the soiled home quadrant floor panel and replaced it with a freshly washed panel. We then tested a litter of 4- to 18-day-old kittens that were successfully reaching the home from the adjacent corner. After the test the floor panel was left in place overnight to accumulate olfactory deposits from the mother and litter and the next day the kittens were tested with this panel at the home site. This procedure was repeated each day.

The results of these tests clearly implicated floor deposits from the mother and litter both in the arousal of kittens to activity and in their orientation to the home. With regard to orientation, kittens crawling from the adjacent corner to the home abruptly halted their crawling at the border between the adjacent and home quadrant as they began to enter the freshly washed home quadrant. They backed away from the home quadrant, pivoted, and came to rest in the adjacent quadrant near the border of the home. This was the cage region in which floor deposits were most heavily concentrated after the regular home quadrant was removed. When kittens were placed directly in the freshly washed home quadrant, they began to crawl and vocalize and gradually found their way to the adjacent quadrant. This contrasted sharply with the usual effect of the home in quieting the kittens and inducing them to come to rest.

After the freshly washed home quadrant had been in place for 24 hours it acquired a significant amount of olfactory deposits from the mother and litter and as a result it partially regained the capacity to serve as an orientation center. The accumulation of olfactory-stimulating material was not sufficient however to reinstate the home quadrant to its normal position as the principal orientation center. In a number of tests, kittens still came to rest in the region of the adjacent quadrant indicated above, but the quadrant left in place overnight was far more acceptable to kittens than the freshly washed home quadrant had been.

The results of these tests also confirmed our belief that kittens used floor deposits rather than airborne odors to find their way to the home. Removal of the home quadrant did not prevent kittens that were placed in the adjacent corner from crawling in their normal manner in a path toward the home quadrant; when, having crossed the border, they sniffed the floor of the home quadrant they were disturbed and withdrew from the home.

One must, therefore, assume that in the region between the adjacent corner and the border of the home the olfactory floor deposits provide a basis for kittens to determine the direction in which the home lies. Cues must be frequent and closely spaced since the absence of cues over a small floor area at the entrance of the freshly washed home quadrant was sufficient for kittens to halt their movement and withdraw.

The distribution of floor deposits to which kittens are reacting in orienting to the home may be indicated by the pattern of discoloration on the cage floor which gradually appears as the mother and litter occupy the home. The floor of the home region initially stands out from the rest of the cage floor because of the dark stain which is located there. Since the home serves as the parturition site, these stains are the dried birth fluids, mixed with blood, which have been absorbed by the slightly porous asbestos floor panel. When kittens enter the home region during adjacent corner tests they generally crawl through this region, move to its edge, then turn and return to it, and then they come to rest. Radiating out from this darkly stained region are lighter colored stains in irregular patches. Close to the home region these patches are brownish in appearance and further from the home they are light brown, gradually merging in appearance with the original grey color of the asbestos floor panel.

Since freshly washed panels placed in the home for 24 hours accumulate floor deposits in sufficient quantity to reduce the kittens' withdrawal it is clear that these floor substances continue to be deposited by the mother and litter after parturition. We believe that the heaviest deposit occurs in the home and that regions outside the home receive less of the deposit. Deposits are spread thoughout the cage floor from the home through the activity of the mother, since the kittens, at this early age, are rarely out of the home.

The olfactory basis of home orientation therefore arises and changes concurrently with the development of home orientation in the kittens. We believe that the gradual change in the distribution of olfactory material on the cage floor plays an important role in the kittens' development of home orientation, but that it is also important that kittens have experience with these odors.

Several kittens were tested in this regard: they were taken from the mother at birth and raised in isolation with a brooder and nipple supplied with milk. When their littermates were successfully finding their way to the home site from the adjacent corner and acting appropriately in the home quadrant, around the sixth and seventh day (or even later with one kitten, i.e., the fourteenth day), these kittens were tested in their "home" cages. Although the olfactory basis for home orientation existed in each of the cages, these kittens, lacking experience with the odors of the home cage, were unable to orient to the home nor did they give any but the slightest indication that the home cage was other than a strange place for them. In their isolation chamber these kittens were quite able to orient to the brooder as a home site. It is apparent, therefore, that kittens require experience with the olfactory substrate before they respond to its distribution on the cage floor and orient to the home.

The nature of this experience cannot be specified by our study. This experience however can be gained during routine activities within the confines of the home region. Our normative observations indicate that kittens rarely are found outside the home region until the end of the third week. Occasionally they are found in the adjacent quadrant, for example, when the mother's body extends into this quadrant and kittens, resting against her body, are left there when she rises and leaves them. Then they either crawl back to the home on their own or are retrieved there by the mother. In the course of our study several kittens from each of a number of litters that were being tested for home orientation were deliberately not tested until their littermates were successfully reaching the home from the adjacent corner (i.e., fifth and seventh days) or from both the adjacent and diagonal corners (i.e., thirteenth to sixteenth day). These kittens therefore were tested for the first time when there were well-defined pathways to the home. Their home orientation performances matched those of their more test-experienced littermates with respect to successful orientation from the adjacent corner, by the younger kittens, and from the diagonal corner, by the older kitten. Moreover, they remained in the home when placed there. Experience gained almost exclusively while they were living in the home region provided the basis for the kittens' ability to use these cagewide cues for home orientation.

An essential feature of this experience was, undoubtedly, the olfactory stimulation provided by the litter which serves in general as a background stimulus–condition setting the affective tone of the kitten in the performance of a variety of specific activities. Basic to the development of home orientation was the kittens' response to the odors present in the home and in the adjacent and diagonal corners. In the earliest period, at birth and for a short time afterward, kittens were disturbed when they were placed alone on any floor surface and their disturbance was relieved

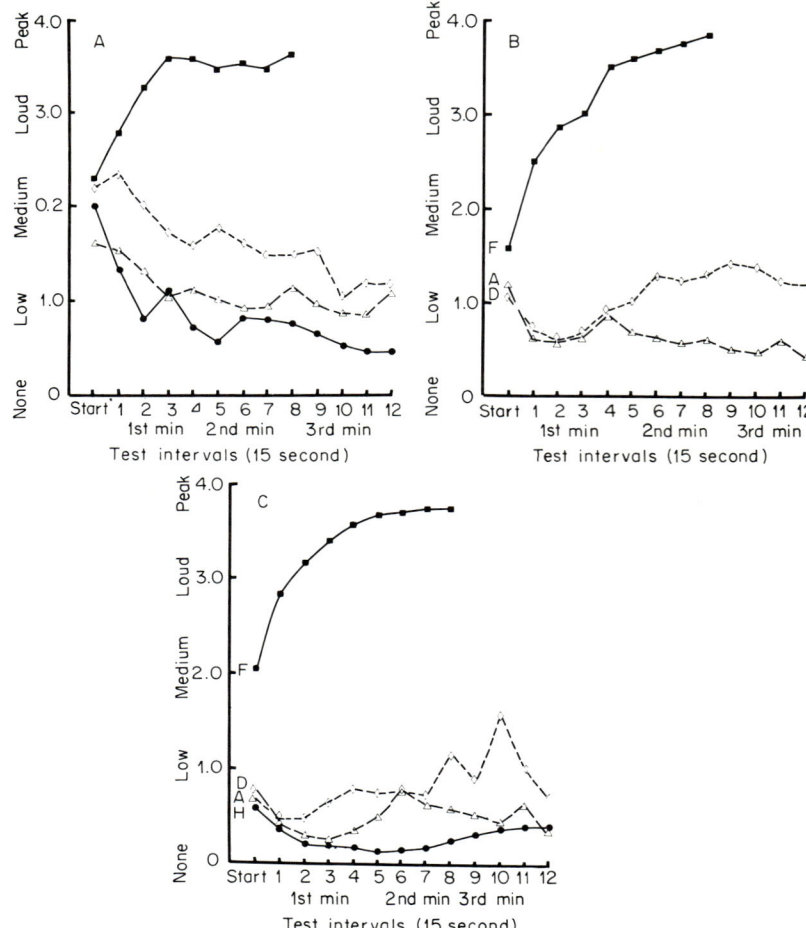

FIG. 11. (A–C). Average intensity of vocalization in a group of eight kittens during successive 3-minute orientation tests in the home, adjacent, and diagonal corners of the home cage and during 2-minute tests in a corner of the field. Vocalization at the start and during successive 15-second periods of tests are presented for age periods of (A) 1–4 days, (B) 5–7 days (except home corner), and (C) 8–10 days. Solid circles, home corner; open triangles, adjacent corner; open diamonds, diagonal corner; solid square, field corner.

only when they regained contact with the mother. Within a few days, however, while the floor of the field continued to produce strong disturbance, the corners of the home cage, even in the absence of the mother and littermates, gradually reduced the kittens' disturbance (Fig. 11).

As early as the first to the fourth day, kittens were capable of distinguishing their general location, whether in the field or in the home cage. Their vocalization in each of these locations differed markedly: their disturbance mounted in the field and was gradually relieved in the home cage (Fig. 11). The first indication of orientation was to be found, therefore, in the kittens' emotional responses to olfactory stimuli which differed in the home cage and field because of their spatial separation. These two different regions did not share even to a small degree the crucial olfactory stimuli to which kittens had become adapted soon after birth.

All regions of the home cage however shared a common odor. As a consequence there was a uniform reduction in the kittens' vocalization when they were placed in either the home, or in adjacent or diagonal corners (Fig. 11). Very early, however, the home corner of the home cage emerged as a special site: kittens placed in the home were more rapidly calmed, and their vocalization was maintained at a lower intensity, than when they were placed in either the adjacent or diagonal corners. In reality the three corners of the cage formed a graded series in which the kittens' responses in each of the corners corresponded to the spatial distance of the corner from the home site. This in turn was related to the accumulation of litter odor in each of the corners and therefore to the amount of olfactory stimulation the kittens received.

The kittens' ability to distinguish among the different regions of the home cage, what we have termed "regional differentiation" (Rosenblatt et al., 1969), preceded their ability to crawl from the adjacent corner to the home by several days and their ability to orient to the home from the diagonal corner by more than a week. It is likely that olfactory differences among the three widely separated corners arose earlier than did odor gradients that were sufficiently detailed to enable kittens to detect differences in floor odors over the short distances (i.e., 3 or 4 inches) which their noses moved during nuzzling of the floor while crawling (Moulton, 1967). However, it could be that an odor gradient existed at this time (i.e., day 1 to 4) but that the kittens could not yet detect it with the olfactory acuity available to them.

In each of the cage corners movements during an early period of testing were essentially the same and this was true with regard to the field corner as well. Kittens crawled a short distance in one direction then pivoted and crawled again for a short distance before pivoting once again, and so on. This resulted in circuitous paths that did not carry the kittens more than a few inches from the starting point, and often kittens ended the 2- or 3-minute test near the corner in which they had been placed.

This early phase of crawling in a circuitous path near the starting points gave way to different patterns of locomotion in each of the cage corners and in the field corners at the same time that kittens indicated by their vocalizations that they were able to differentiate among these regions (Fig. 12).

The situation in the adjacent corner will be analyzed first since vocalizations indicated that only a moderate level of emotional disturbance persisted in this corner. Shortly after they were placed on the floor of the adjacent corner, kittens thrust forward out of the corner in one or another direction then slowed and began to pivot and crawl, alternately, while nuzzling the cage floor (Fig. 12A). Gradually, on the fourth and fifth days, movements toward the home site predominated, though the kittens did not yet reach the home and often pivoted and crawled back and forth along the corridor between the adjacent and home corners. After the fifth day, the initial thrust was oriented toward the home corner through the central area of the adjacent quadrant and forward crawling was maintained longer than it had been earlier. The path therefore extended into the home quadrant and the kittens now kept crawling further into the home, often with guidance provided by contact with the side wall of the cage. In the home quadrant a series of turns were made as the kitten first crawled through the home site, turned at its border and crawled back into the home site, until finally it came to rest at this site. In tests on the eighth and ninth days any movement in a direction away from the home site was quickly corrected and the path toward the home was rapidly traversed; in less than 90 seconds after the start of the tests most kittens had reached the home and come to rest, asleep, in this region.

Vocalization in the course of this development (Fig. 11) shows that throughout the period when kittens were in the adjacent quadrant and had not yet reached the home (i.e., days 1 to 4) there was continual and steady low level disturbance. When the kittens began to reach the home region (i.e., days 5 to 7) their disturbance gradually subsided during the first minute of the tests. After the first minute, those kittens that remained outside the home continued to vocalize and this remained fairly steady for the remainder of the test until these kittens subsequently found their way to the home.

The disturbance induced by being outside the home site prodded the kittens to move out of the adjacent corner but until they could find their way to the home their disturbance was not relieved (beyond the initial relief afforded by their placement in the home cage itself). This characterized their behavior during the phase of regional differentiation.

The process of following an olfactory path to the home developed slowly in kittens. The floor scanning movement of the head enabled

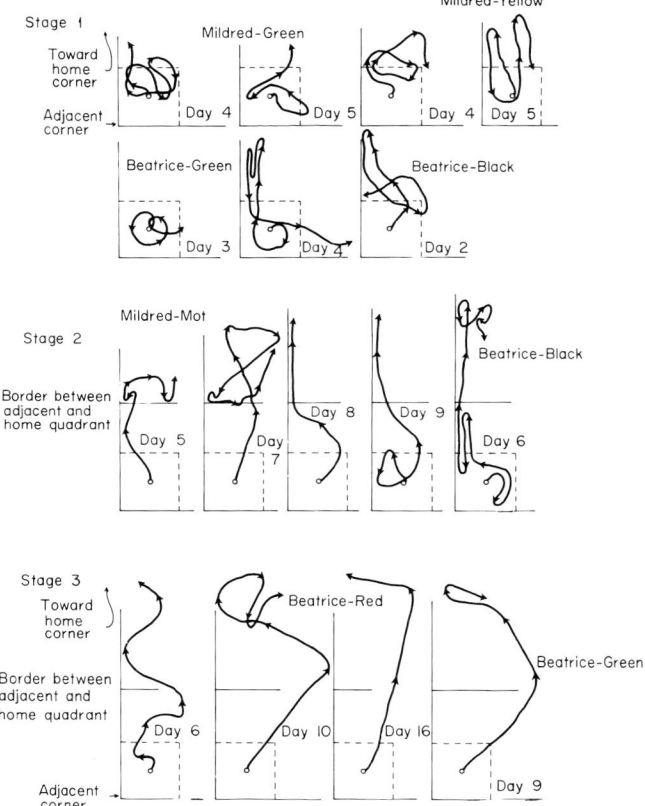

FIG. 12A. Typical paths taken by kittens started in the adjacent corner of the home cage from the first to the 22nd day. Paths were traced from the original records. The arrows show the distance and direction crawled during successive 15-second periods. Stage 1. Crawling for short distances, interrupted by pivoting, followed by resumption of crawling. Note tendency to maintain contact with wall, in most cases, that common to the adjacent and home corners. Stage 2. Extended movement into the home quadrant and soon afterward into the home corner. Crawling more continuous, less frequently broken by pauses with pivoting and head oscillations. Wall-hugging still present but confined almost entirely to the wall common to the adjacent and home corner. Stage 3. Kittens move from the adjacent corner to the home corner without contact with the wall until they have entered the home corner. Crawling is extended and continuous without interruption by pivoting until the home corner is reached.

kittens to pick up the olfactory gradient only with difficulty. It required that the head in its side-to-side motion move over a region that was sufficiently different at the center and at the termination of the motion to enable kittens to detect the direction of change in olfactory stimulation. The path to the home was finally formed by movements away from regions of lesser concentration of olfactory material and veering toward regions of greater concentration of this material.

When a gradient of stimulation leading to the home gradually became available or was detected by the kittens, they adopted it at first for short intervals of crawling, later for extended periods of crawling, and still later almost continuously. As they moved along the gradient to the home and especially when they entered the home, their disturbance gradually subsided and after they had been in the home site for a short time, crawling to its outer borders and turning back into it, the kittens were sufficiently calmed to fall asleep.

Coming to rest in the home site was not an automatic reaction in the kittens: upon reaching the home region kittens continued the crawling which had carried them into the home site and began to leave this site. At some point, however, they halted, turned, and crawled back toward the center of the home site. This action was repeated several times at each entry into the home, before the kittens came to rest, and a similar pattern was observed in kittens that were placed directly in the home corner at the start of tests.

While placement in the adjacent corner elicited path-taking to the home under the impetus provided by the low level of disturbance that was maintained in the kittens outside the home, placement in the home corner itself emphasized a different aspect of the orientation pattern. Near the home site disturbance was reduced to a minimum within the first minute of the test. When placed at the high point of the olfactory gradient, kittens could only move a short distance away from this region before the reduction in olfactory stimulation would disturb them. In this situation, therefore, kittens crawled for a short time in a circuitous path around the starting point then soon came to rest and fell asleep (Fig. 12B). The home site had to be located and its location was determined by passing through it, reaching its outer boundary, veering away from the reduced concentration of the material encountered there, and crawling for a period before settling within the area of optimal concentration of olfactory deposits. At times, when the home site included the side wall of the home quadrant, kittens settled in contact with this wall and this facilitated the reaction of coming to rest in the home.

At the end of the first week the absence of disturbance in the home corner left kittens free to crawl within the confines of the home quadrant, without leaving it, and their paths at this time nicely traced for us the location of the boundaries of the home site for the kittens themselves. While the movement of the kittens when they were placed outside the home region (i.e., adjacent and diagonal corners) was toward the home

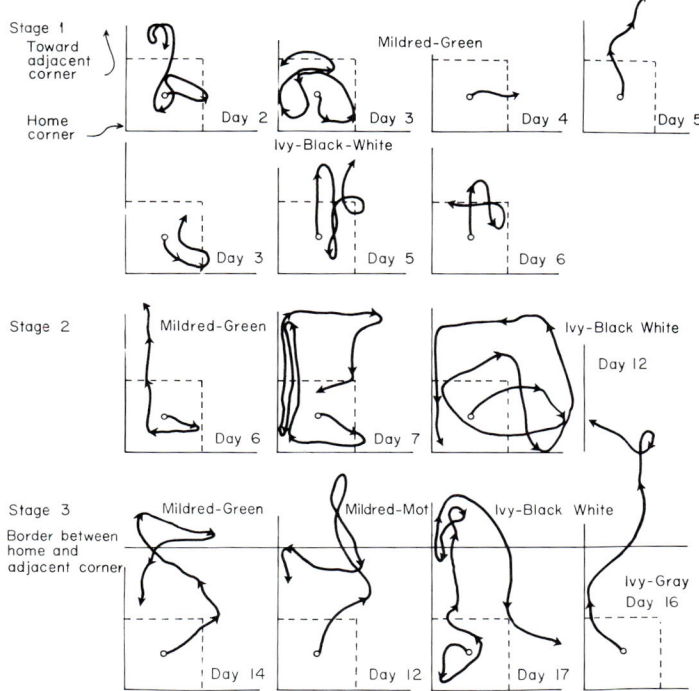

FIG. 12B. Typical paths taken by kittens started in the home corner of the home cage from the first to the 22nd day. Paths were traced from the original records. The arrows show the distance and direction crawled during successive 15-second periods. Stage 1. Pivoting movements and crawling for short distances within the home corner or the home quadrant. Stage 2. Crawling along border of the home quadrant and turning back into the home corner. Stage 3. Extended movement out of the home quadrant followed by return to the home quadrant, later often by continued movement at a distance from the home quadrant.

site, propelled by their disturbance and guided by the gradient of odors leading to the home region, their movement in the home corner, where they were quiet throughout most of the test, was outward from the home site. At first their movements did not carry them outside the home quadrant: they sketched its border by crawling around the edge of the home region. Gradually, however, they made short excursions into the adjacent quadrant but returned to the home. This development reached its culmination after the 16th day when kittens that were placed in the home corner began to leave the home quadrant (Table 7 and Fig. 12B) while kittens that were placed in the adjacent and diagonal corners continued to crawl to the home, and, once there, came to rest.

During the first week the diagonal corner presented the kittens with

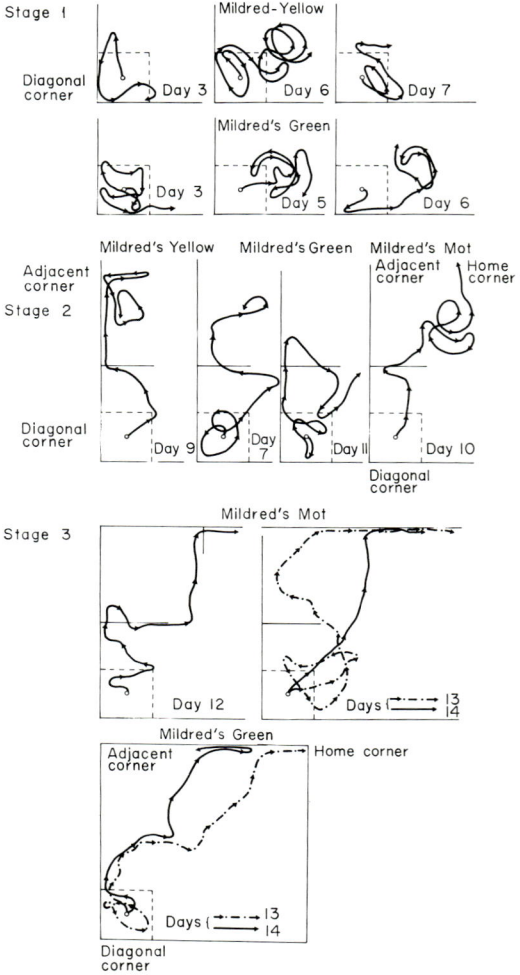

FIG. 12C. Typical paths taken by kittens started in the diagonal corner of the home cage from the first to the 22nd day. Paths were traced from the original records. The arrows show the distance and direction crawled during successive 15-second periods. Stage 1. Kittens perform a series of circuitous paths and short crawls that are mainly random. They remain in the diagonal quadrant. Stage 2. Extension of movement into the quadrant adjoining by means of increased crawling over straight paths. Pivoting movements decrease in frequency and duration. Stage 3. Early in this stage kittens often reach the home corner by first entering the adjacent corner and then after a sharp turn, crawling or walking into the home. Later, they crawl or walk to the home corner directly on a diagonal through the open central area of the cage.

a situation in which their disturbance was higher than in the adjacent corner and in fact rose during the tests (Fig 12C), while the olfactory gradient was not sufficiently well-defined between the diagonal and home corners, until the end of the second week, to enable the kittens to find their way to the home. As in the adjacent corner kittens began to extend the range of their movements away from the starting point but now the direction was toward the adjacent quadrant rather than the home site. For the kittens placed in the diagonal corner, the adjacent quadrant functioned in some respects as the home but this path developed several days after the path from the adjacent corner to the home corner had appeared. It is likely that a gradient of olfactory stimulation between the diagonal and adjacent corners was formed before the gradient leading directly from the diagonal corner to the home. While arrival in the adjacent corner served to quiet the kittens somewhat, it did not cause them to settle down to rest. The kittens remained active in the adjacent quadrant and many of them resumed their movement toward the home site, adopting the path which they had already taken in tests started directly in the adjacent corner.

Shortly thereafter kittens were able to pick up the trail directly to the home while still in the diagonal quadrant: they crawled toward the adjacent quadrant but shortly before they entered it they turned toward the home and entered it.

In the field kittens were faced with the most extreme conditions in relation to the processes underlying home orientation. Devoid of cage odors, the field produced such a high degree of disturbance that nearly all locomotion was inhibited. After the first day kittens "froze" in place, or backed into the field corner and vocalized at peak intensity throughout the test (Fig. 12D). While their emotional disturbance was clearly the factor which prevented them from moving, an added factor was the absence of any olfactory gradient, such as was present in the adjacent and diagonal corners, which the kittens could follow and thus move out of the field corner.

There were gradual changes in the kittens' behavior while orienting to the home region from the adjacent and diagonal corners. As crawling gradually changed, kittens lifted their heads from the floor and the earlier pattern of continuously nosing the floor surface in front of them gave way to a pattern in which kittens only periodically nosed the path in front. As walking developed, a nose tapping of the floor appeared as the method of sampling the cage floor. Presumably kittens were able to make use of periodic samples of the odor gradient to guide them to the home. At about the age of 14 to 18 days, when nose tapping began, there was evidence that kittens were beginning to make use of visual cues to

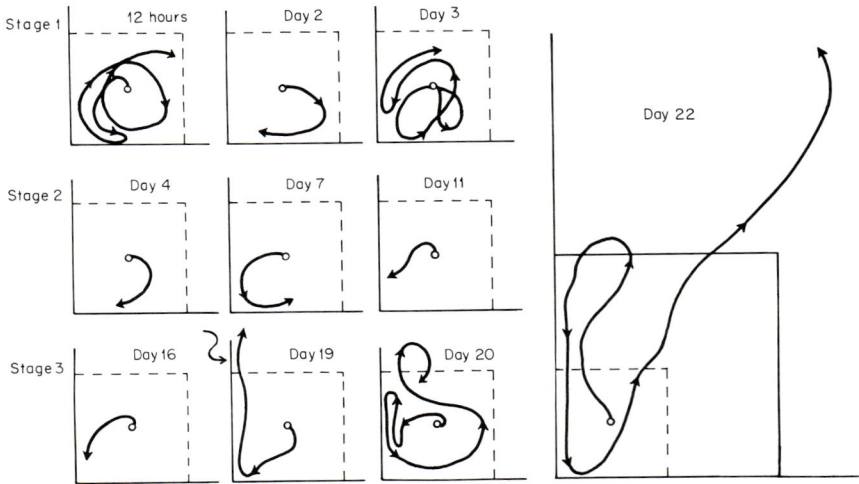

FIG. 12D. Orientation performance of a single kitten (Mildred-Mot) in the test field during the period from 12 hours after birth to the 22nd day. Performance is typical of the majority of kittens tested in the field. Stage 1. 12 hours to 2 days. Stage 2. Day 3 to day 16. Stage 3. Day 19 to day 22.

orient to the home. At this age, for the first time, a reduction of the kittens' ability to see the inside of the cage and the cage surroundings reduced the success of orientation to the home (Rosenblatt et al., 1969). There were indications therefore that the kittens passed through a period in which they made use of olfactory and visual cues, jointly, in orienting to the home, before the use of vision predominated and further changes took place in the pattern of home orientation. In the home corner, movement out of the home quadrant, already begun during olfactory-based orientation, was aided by the use of visual cues. At first kittens placed in the home began to approach the front of the cage where the observer could be seen; then they turned and wandered throughout the cage. Sometime later (i.e., the 18th to the 21st day) kittens placed in the adjacent and diagonal corners also viewed the observer from the home quadrant after they had gone to it and with tests of longer duration they might have wandered out of the home to approach him.

Orientation to the home gradually waned after the 21st day. In the field kittens began to leave the corner in which they had been placed and wandered cautiously throughout the field vocalizing loudly and frequently sampling the floor surface with nose tapping.

Normally kittens begin to orient to the mother at this age and they remain near her, approaching her for feeding, and leaving the home to do so. Developments in suckling and home orientation coalesce at this stage of kitten development as the mother becomes not only the center of orientation for kittens but more and more, on their own initiative, they approach her to initiate suckling.

When the pattern of home orientation based upon olfactory deposits declines there arises in certain situations, an orientation to the home which is based upon the kittens' attachment to visually prominent objects that are familiar. A box or a furry skin serving as the home in a larger pen than the laboratory cage we have used, may be used as a home site where kittens sleep and to which they return whenever they are disturbed. Thus kittens 3 weeks of age and older may be seen alternately congregating around the mother or at the home site, or the litter may be divided between these two localities. A young high-school student (Smith, 1965) was the one who called my attention to this latter phase of visual orientation to the home which she discovered by testing kittens with a fur coat at the home site, and we have confirmed these observations in kittens reared in large outdoor pens with a box on its side serving as the home.

The latter phase of orientation to a home region in kittens may be the basis for the attachment to a familiar locality which has been noted in adult cats. Several investigators have noted that male cats will exhibit sexual behavior only in an arena in which they have previously deposited their own distinctive odor (Rosenblatt, 1953; Green *et al.*, 1957; Michael, 1961). Though visual stimuli undoubtedly play the major role in defining the adult cats territorial routes (Leyhausen, 1965; Leyhausen and Wolff, 1959), odors may play the role of establishing a general background within which the animal is comfortable.

Discussion

Our analysis of early behavior in the kitten has shown that its earliest adjustments are developed in relation to two main features of its environment, the mother and the home site. These patterns of adjustment, suckling and orientation to the home, were traced in their development from birth onward but no attempt was made to compare the courses of their development in any detail. In this section we shall compare the development of these patterns of behavior. Are there any similarities in the phases of development of these two patterns of behavior? On what bases are they differentiated into two separate behavior patterns? In what ways can the processes underlying behavioral development in kittens be uncovered by the study of suckling and home orientation?

There is some validity, based upon the newly born kitten's behavior and development, for distinguishing between suckling and orientation to the home site on a functional basis. There are, of course, dangers in pursuing an analysis of behavioral development from the starting point of functional distinctions between behavior patterns. The dangers are of two sorts: on the one hand, the functions of the behaviors may be viewed as causal factors in the organization of these patterns without evidence that this is the case, and, on the other hand, after distinctions between behavior patterns have been made on the basis of functional differences, the causal factors may also be viewed as necessarily distinct when in fact some causal factors may be shared by both behavior patterns while others may contribute to one or the other behavior only.

The functional distinction between suckling and home orientation is supported, in part, by the fact that each of these patterns is directed toward different aspects of the kitten's environment. Suckling is directed toward the mother, and, as such, it is from the beginning a social behavior; this despite the claim of Kovach and Kling (1967), based upon a narrow definition of social behavior, that the social aspects of suckling can be separated from the sensory–motor aspects. Orientative responses to the home site, however, are directed to features of the kitten's physical environment. Suckling responses function to bring the kitten into contact with the mother for feeding, while responses to the home site enable the kitten to remain in the home and therefore to engage in the various activities with its littermates (e.g., huddling, sleeping, and feeding from the mother).

The distinction between a kitten's responses to the mother and to the home site, the former being social and the latter nonsocial, is a relative one. It cannot be too sharp, since the significance of the home site in the development of home orientation is itself based upon the use of the home as a social habitat by the mother and kittens. Nevertheless, as sources of stimulation during the kitten's early development, the mother, initially, and the littermates, somewhat later, provide the basis for the continuous expansion of motivational, perceptual, and response processes underlying socialization.

Developments in orientation to the home site, however, are based upon the kitten's capacities for spatial orientation to significant features of its environment. Features of the environment are significant in relation to the kitten's developmental stage: early in the litter period (i.e., the first 3 weeks) the home site is significant because of the kitten's response to the litter odors that are deposited there, and other areas of the surrounding cage floor are significant only in relation to the home site.

As development proceeds, the behavior repertoire of the kitten increases and becomes more varied; new features of the environment take on specialized significance and the spatial orientation capacities of the kitten develop to keep pace. At 45 days of age the home site is only one of several cage regions that is used by the kitten; different regions may be used for resting and sleeping, for feeding, and for play among the kittens and still another cage locality is used for elimination.

The spatial orientation capacities of adult cats living under semi-field conditions on farms and city surroundings are highly developed in close relation to the use of many functionally specialized localities and to the maintenance of stable social relations among neighboring individuals. Leyhausen and Wolff (1959) and Leyhausen (1965) have shown that individual cats occupy a home site (i.e., first-order home, Hediger, 1950) which has trails radiating outward to a specialized hunting area, and localities for resting, sunbathing, rubbing, and other activities such as communal grouping (Wilson and Weston, 1947).

The interaction of spatial orientation capacities with other areas of behavioral functioning in the cat and their mutual dependence is evident in the sexual behavior of males (Green et al., 1957; Rosenblatt, 1953; Michael, 1961) and in maternal behavior, where spatial dislocation seriously interferes with the mother's behavior toward her young.

There is therefore justification for considering the elaboration of psychological capacities for spatial orientation, based upon responses to the behaviorally conditioned physical environment as the counterpart to the elaboration of social responses to species mates in the early development of kittens.

Turning now to a comparison of suckling and home orientation, there are basic similarities in the phases of development of these two behavior patterns during all age periods. They are found amid differences that are apparent and are themselves important features of the development of these behavior patterns (see Table 8 for a summary).

Suckling and home orientation have their origins in the newly born kitten's initial reactions to the predominantly low intensity stimuli that prevail in its interaction with the mother (Table 8). Interactions with littermates are significant during huddling but in the early phases of suckling while they may facilitate arousal and orientation to the mother they also distract the kitten from the mother's nipple region, eliciting nuzzling of their fur in competition with the mother's.

Kittens are highly aroused soon after parturition: the initiation of respiration, licking by the mother, contact with littermates, and drying of their wet fur combine to stimulate the kitten to crawl in the vicinity of the mother. Under these circumstances, the actions of the mother in lying down, encircling the litter, and presenting her mammary region, begins the process of the channeling of the newborn's activity to her nipples.

Responses to the home site are absent at birth and for a period

TABLE 8
Corresponding Developments in Suckling and Home Orientation during Phases of Early Development in the Kitten

Suckling development		Phases of development	Development of home orientation
Initiation of suckling: Newborn, aroused by stimuli from delivery and early contact with mother, littermates, and features of environment, is channeled by low intensity tactile, olfactory, and thermal stimuli from mother's body to approach nipples. Nipple-grasping elicited by nipples and suckling initiated. Arousal subsides during suckling.	*Phase I* birthday 1	Newborn responds to low intensity tactile, thermal, and olfactory stimuli with general or specific approach responses and associated affective reaction. Activity initiated by arousal of varying intensity produced by stimuli from both external and internal sources (e.g., vestibular-proprioceptive stimuli).	*Appearance of settling reaction:* During first day kittens react to separation from mother by becoming mildly aroused. By means of a simple movement over a short distance they regain contact, become calm, then fall asleep (i.e., settling reaction).
Establishment of nipple position preferences: More readily aroused to suckle by channeling of arousal processes but kitten no longer grasps any nipple it contacts. Nipple-grasping elicited mainly by tactile and olfactory stimuli from specific nipple positions. Beginning formation of path to nipple position on basis of discriminated stimuli at preferred nipple position.	*Phase II* day 1–4	Conditioned responses formed to specific tactile, thermal, and olfactory stimuli. Stimulus-intensity effects on kitten begin to weaken but remain operative in many responses.	*Regional differentiation in home cage:* Settling reaction becomes conditioned to olfactory stimuli from litter odors deposited on cage floor. Kitten now becomes mildly disturbed by removal from the home site, where the odors are optimally concentrated. Kitten differentiates home, adjacent, and diagonal corners showing greater disturbance at more distant regions in relation to the home. Kitten maximally disturbed, to point of "withdrawal reaction," in field. Spatial aspect of settling reaction established by shift to olfactory stimuli distributed spatially on the cage floor.

Beginning of approaches to mother at a distance in the home: Path to nipple extended from starting point at a distance from mother. Arousal processes underlying motivation now specific to suckling. Paths to nipple region extended to remote regions of mother's body. Reduced dependence upon low intensity stimuli in finding the nipple.	Phase III day 5–14	Conditioning extended to stimuli appearing earlier in behavioral sequences. Arousal, which initiates activity, becomes increasingly specific and takes on properties deriving from perceptual and motor activities of the behavior pattern. Behavior sequences are increasingly integrated as extended actions with component parts.	Oriented movements to the home site: Kittens begin to develop paths to the home first from the adjacent corner of the cage. Continuing accumulation of odor gradient which kittens follow in finding their way to the home. Mild arousal increasingly channeled into path-taking to home, representing the development of a movement component added to the primary affective basis of the settling reaction underlying home orientation.
Further development of distance approaches for suckling based on visually-aroused processes: Suckling approaches begin to be initiated at greater distances and in relation to broader aspects of mother's behavior. Nipple localization processes become increasingly based upon vision but still dependent upon tactile-olfactory stimuli. Motivational processes increasingly influenced by social experience.	Phase IV day 15–21	Onset of visually aroused orientation processes; conditioning now includes visual aspects of situations. Advances in motivational, perceptual, and locomotor processes based upon widening scope of kitten's activity in relation to social and physical environment.	Shift in basis of home orientation: The onset of visually guided orientation at first leads to improvements in home orientation based jointly on olfaction and vision, then leads to decline of olfactory-based home site. Kittens shift to mother as center of orientation but if visually prominent home present, visually based home orientation may develop. Disturbance-based orientation of the early periods undergoes change in motivational basis, merging with social and other more advanced motivational systems.

TABLE 8 (*Continued*)

Suckling development	Phases of development	Development of home orientation
Predominance of kitten-initiated feeding approaches: As maternal behavior declines, kitten-initiated suckling approaches predominate. Kittens make subtle behavioral adjustments to mother's perceived readiness to nurse and follow or solicit from mother as means of influencing her behavior. Nonsuckling social behavior toward mother and with littermates increases. Suckling eventually recedes as the primary relationship between kittens and mother as the kittens initiate independent feeding, often with mother's help.	*Phase V after day 21* Further advances in motivational, perceptual, and locomotor processes underlying orientative adjustments grounded in visually dominated processes. Social repertoire broadened and more varied than earlier. Increasing complexity of orientation to physical environment.	*Spatial orientation based on various functional patterns of behavior*: Orientation in the physical environment increasingly conditioned by a variety of functional patterns including feeding, sleeping, play, resting, elimination etc.

afterward; however, the kittens respond to the mother shortly after birth in a manner that strongly resembles their later response to the home site (Coronios, 1933). Normally kittens remain with the mother after feeding, resting in contact with her body. If they are removed, experimentally, and placed on a hard cool surface, they begin to vocalize and crawl, usually pivoting in place (Hofer, 1970). If during their disturbance they are placed near the mother once again, they react by crawling into contact, burying their head in her fur, and becoming quiet. Shortly afterward they fall asleep. This reaction is referred to as the "settling reaction."

The same quieting effect on kittens can be produced by placing them on a soft warm surface, inclined 30° to stimulate crawling, and fitted with a canopy at the upper end. Kittens react by crawling upward and when they reach the canopy they crawl under it, bringing their head into contact with the soft surface, and fall asleep (Turkewitz, 1957). Thus, contact and thermal stimuli elicit the settling reaction; odors need not be present.

There is characteristically a difference in the level of arousal of kittens at the initiation of suckling and the occurrence of a settling reaction. It forms, in part, the basis for further differences which arise during the development of these two patterns of behavior. Suckling is generally initiated at a higher level of arousal than that which initiates the settling reaction.

In the course of an approach for suckling, kittens are exposed to a variety of stimuli from the mother and these elicit responses of the sort we have described, enabling the kitten to locate a nipple and to suckle. The high level of arousal which initiates suckling is not reduced until the kittens have gained nipples and suckled for a period. Slowly their arousal subsides and at the termination of a suckling session nearly all the kittens are asleep.

The flow of milk undoubtedly plays a role in reducing the kittens' arousal. Kittens suckling from a blind-ended nipple (i.e., in the brooder) or one which does not provide milk (including a mother that is dry) release the nipple after a short period and resume nuzzling (Woll and Rosenblatt, 1970; Koepke and Pribram, 1970). Milk flow therefore stimulates kittens to remain attached and suckling. In addition the kittens' arousal must be reduced by the ingestion of milk and the accompanying stomach distention and metabolic effects.

The settling reaction typically follows a relatively low level of arousal induced by separation from the mother. Usually kittens need make only a small shift in their position involving crawling—a nonspecific movement is sufficient in most instances—in order for them to reduce their disturbance by regaining contact with the mother (Coronios, 1933).

One can observe the way in which level of arousal in a litter of kittens is related to their behavior on making contact with the mother. Soon after a feeding, kittens that have become separated from the mother will crawl back into contact and immediately fall asleep. As the time since the last feeding grows longer, one or another kitten will become aroused by being separated from the mother and upon making contact with the mother it will begin to nuzzle and eventually locate and grasp a nipple. The remaining kittens of the litter will soon be aroused and they too will begin to suckle.

From the beginning, the suckling pattern of newly born kittens is more complex than the settling reaction. While the settling reaction involves only a single movement or at best a short period of crawling and pressing into the mother's body, suckling involves a succession of behavioral adjustments by the kitten to many specific aspects of the mother in the course of its approach to the nipple region and nipple grasping. Each component of suckling may be simple in its organization consisting mainly of responses such as forward progression of the anterior end, halting, turning, mouth opening, head lunge, etc. (Tilney and Casamajor, 1924; Langworthy, 1929; Windle, 1930). But there are a greater number of these components in the initial suckling pattern than in the settling reaction of the kitten. Since these are basic responses of the newborn to low intensity stimulation they are reliable responses, and, given the guidance of the mother's body, all kittens achieve suckling shortly after birth.

The second phase of the development of suckling and home orientation (i.e., day 1 to 4) is introduced by the formation of nipple position preferences and the appearance of regional differentiation among cage localities and between the home cage and the field (Table 8). These developments are based upon experience gained during the first day and indicate the early entry of learning into developmental processes.

Evidence of home orientation first appears during this phase of early development. After the kitten has been in the litter for a day removal from the home site (which has been cleared of the mother and litter) has a disturbing effect upon the kitten much as removal from the mother did earlier. The effect is a graded one, as we have shown, the degree of disturbance depending upon the distance from the home site (within the home cage) that the kitten is placed. Simple conditioning of the settling reaction to odor stimuli in the home and generalization according to the intensity of odors would account for the kitten's reactions in each of the cage corners. Olfactory stimulation in the field lies outside the range of the odor gradient in the home cage. The distinction between home cage and field is therefore established rapidly and the kittens react very differently in these two localities. In the home cage the different corners stimulate mild arousal that activates locomotion but in the field, after an initial period, prior to differentiation of the field from the home cage, when kittens are somewhat active, all activity in the field ceases, except for vocalizing and minimal movement of the head, and kittens react with virtual "withdrawal."

The conditioning of litter odors to the earlier tactile and thermal stimulus effects (from the mother) initially carries with it little in the way of specific movement responses. Simple movements were involved in reaching the stimulus (i.e., the mother) which evoked the settling reaction. The main effect of conditioning is to transfer the emotional component of the settling reaction to the new olfactory stimulus. The kitten reacts now to reduction in the olfactory stimulus as it did to the earlier reduction in tactile and thermal stimuli, becoming mildly or strongly aroused depending upon the magnitude of the change in olfactory stimulation.

The transfer of the settling response to litter odors introduces a spatial orientation aspect to the settling reaction that was not present when reactions were to tactile and thermal stimuli from the mother. Since the odor is deposited in a gradient on the floor of the home cage, in order to maintain contact with it, and to reach the optimal level of the odor, the kitten must develop the motor components of the pattern to keep pace with the development of its perceptual capacities.

The establishment of nipple position preferences is based upon conditioning of nipple grasping and suckling to tactile and olfactory characteristics of specific nipples. As such it represents a departure from the kitten's earlier dependence upon the channeling effect of the low intensity stimuli it encountered during suckling. Now specific stimuli within the array presented by the mother during suckling take on significance and for each kitten the significant stimuli are slightly different.

The identification of specific nipple positions enables kittens to begin the process of establishing paths on the mother's body which lead them to their preferred nipple positions. These paths are formed first in the vicinity of the nipple base and later from more distant regions still in the vicinity of the preferred nipples. The general suckling approach is continually made more specific in this process and the separate movements are organized into a more integrated pattern than was the case earlier. What was a complex pattern based upon a succession of simply organized response to the appearance, in succession, of channeling stimuli, becomes a more smoothly organized pattern in which earlier movements in the approach prepare the kitten to adjust to the stimuli, which appear later in the sequence.

The transition from suckling based upon the channeling effects of stimuli to effects based upon experience is a gradual one and occurs unevenly, no doubt, with respect to different aspects of the suckling pattern. The channeling effects of certain aspects of the mother are present even as late as 3 or 4 weeks of age, but in the 6-day-old kitten the channeling and experienced-based effects of stimuli are present, side-by-side. Brooder-reared kittens returned to the mother at 6 days of age crawl into contact with her and nuzzle soon after they are placed in the litter, but contact with nipples does not elicit nipple grasping for some time. This aspect of suckling in the isolates has become specifically related to brooder-nipple stimuli and is no longer easily aroused by the previously effective nipple stimuli from the mother.

Although there is considerable correspondence between developments in suckling and home orientation during this second phase, based upon the entry of learning into developmental processes, there are important differences as well (Table 8). Since learning necessarily arises in the course of specific activities in which the kittens are engaged, its character and the effects which it has upon behavioral development must be specifically in relation to these activities. Learning introduced into the complex pattern of suckling affects one aspect of the pattern first then gradually widens its influence upon the pattern. However, in the relatively simple pattern of settling, learning produces a marked change, shifting the reaction to a new stimulus basis, almost as a whole.

A phase of steady advances in suckling and home orientation occurs in the period from the fifth to the fourteenth day based upon changes that were begun in the previous phase (Table 8). In suckling, approaches initiated at a distance from the mother begin to appear although feedings are still initiated predominantly by the mother (Fig. 9). The significance of this development lies in the motivational changes that are implied and in the (nonvisual) perceptual adjustment required to find the nipples from various starting points that are increasingly more remote. In the development of home orientation, the gradual formation of paths to the home from the adjacent corner, early in this phase, and from the diagonal corner, toward the end of it, are the main achievements.

Suckling approaches initiated at a distance from the mother signal a change in the motivational basis of suckling. Earlier suckling approaches were based on heightened arousal (e.g., hunger) which was rapidly channeled to feeding by the proximity of the mother and the drawing effect of the stimuli she presented. In brooder-reared kittens also we have seen that any kind of stimulation (e.g., genital stimulation with cotton to force urination and defecation) is channeled into feeding from the brooder. With the appearance of self-initiated feeding approaches, it is clear that heightened arousal has become specific for the kitten in terms of the feeding situation. The process of outgrowing the initial basis of the suckling response to the mother in terms of low intensity stimulus effects and of grounding it on experienced-based processes advances considerably during this period and lays the basis for further advances in the period which follows.

In home orientation during the period from the fifth to the fourteenth day there is the development of paths to the home from the adjacent corner and later from the diagonal corner of the home cage. Further accumulation of litter odors deposited in the regions between the home site and outer corners to form an odor gradient leading to the home is an important factor in the development of paths to the home during this phase. As the disturbance created by displacing kittens from the home is not easily relieved by a simple movement, as it had been earlier, kittens begin to extend the range of their activity, at first in a circuitous path, then, increasingly in a path which is directed toward the home site. They respond to the gradient of litter odors deposited on the cage floor by extending their forward movement in the direction of the gradient and inhibiting movement that takes them in other directions. Movement is maintained by their continuing disturbance and by the fact that the litter odors which they follow to the home gradually reduce their disturbance. Not until they reach the home site, however, are they in the zone in which the odors are at their optimal concentration and only then does the settling reaction appear followed by sleep.

Path-taking to the home from the adjacent corner appears early and during the remainder of this period it undergoes improvements. It appears earlier as testing continues indicating that the adoption of the path to the home has become an integral part of the disturbance produced by displacement from the home. Accompanying this change is a gradual change in the kitten's path-taking behavior. The path is sampled at intervals rather than, as earlier, followed in detail almost continuously. *The odor gradient is now used by the kitten to find the way to the home whereas earlier, following the gradient led the kitten into the home.*

As suckling and home orientation diverge the differences between them appear to be greater than the similarities. The major differences between these patterns are the following: home orientation is grounded on motivational processes which arise from the disturbance produced by reduction in principally one sensory stimulus, namely odors from the litter, and path-taking to the home is based upon variations in its concentration in the form of gradients between cage regions. The motor pattern involved in orienting to the home is a nonspecific one and at the termination of the orientation process no distinctive response occurs except that which we have termed the settling reaction: the kitten simply comes to rest and often falls asleep.

Suckling, however, is governed by multisensory stimuli; it involves a succession of different movement patterns and is terminated by a specific local response, nipple grasping and sucking. The motivational basis of suckling is broad, consisting of internal processes related to feeding and social processes related to the kitten's social relationship with the mother. It contrasts with the rather narrow basis upon which home orientation develops at this time.

Common to the development of both patterns, in the phase we have been discussing, are the advances in motivational processes underlying these two patterns, involving increasing specificity of arousal and greater integration of motivational processes with perceptual and motor processes; there is above all a growing importance of experience in determining the kitten's response to sensory stimuli (Table 8).

The beginning of visual functioning during the fourth phase, from the 15th to 21st day, has effects upon suckling that are quite different from its effects on home orientation. Early in this phase, from about the 15th to the 18th day, visions adds to trends already evident in both behavior patterns during the earlier phase; as this phase continues, suckling development advances while home orientation, in the form which we have been discussing, begins to decline.

Suckling approaches are now initiated by the kittens from a distance, increasingly, and the kittens begin to attend to the mother's behavior before initiating an approach to her. According to her activity, the kitten may approach her directly to suckle, or it may simply remain in her vicinity until she lies down. Then the kitten will initiate a suckling approach to her. There are therefore many new influences upon the kitten's motivational and perceptual processes in relation to feeding and these are largely social in nature. Nipple position preferences are still largely maintained but now these positions are located while the mother is standing or sitting and kittens depend upon a visual approach to the nipples rather than upon their previous behavior of prolonged nuzzling exclusively.

With the onset of vision, there is an initial improvement in home orientation: kittens placed in the adjacent corner use odors and visual cues in returning to the home while kittens placed in the diagonal corner simply walk across the cage directly to the home using both vision and olfaction. The kittens' behavior in the home, however, points to the principal change that occurs during this phase: they no longer remain in the home but instead wander around the cage and eventually approach the experimenter. In a short time, kittens no longer return to the home from the adjacent and diagonal corners but they wander around the cage and stand near the experimenter. In the litter situation kittens can be seen congregating in the vicinity of the mother at this age and when they rest it may be in any corner of the cage. Even in the field kittens no longer "freeze" in one corner: they wander around the field, cautiously, still vocalizing somewhat, and nose tapping on the floor, and eventually they approach the experimenter and gaze at him.

Since home orientation develops on the basis of the kitten's disturbance when removed from the odors of the home site, and movements to the home are based upon the kitten's response to the odor gradient on the floor of the home cage, then home orientation declines with the onset of vision, as the kitten's dependence upon olfactory stimuli is reduced. As we have indicated, in place of orientation to the home, there develops an orientation to the mother and since she moves about the cage, no particular cage locality acquires the significance that the home site had on the basis of odor deposits. The kittens remain dependent upon the general cage odor and they are somewhat disturbed if this is altered or if they are removed from it.

Where the home site has been made visually prominent kittens begin to orient to the home on the basis of vision alone starting on the 16th day with a minimum of wall-hugging to aid them. By the 18th day all of the kittens of a litter of five that were tested under these conditions were able to reach the home from a distance of 28 inches. Their time for the trip improved from a maximum of 3 minutes on the 22nd day to 1 minute on the 29th day and 40 seconds on the 41st day, the last day on which they were tested.

Visually determined orientation to the home may develop initially on the basis provided by the earlier olfactory determined home orientation, and the absence of familiar visual stimuli may produce disturbance in kittens similar to that produced by the absence of home site odors. There is some evidence that this is so since placing a kitten in a new environment elicits visual searching activity, involving visually guided movement to all parts of the environment; there is, no doubt, an olfactory basis for the heightened activity of the kitten in the new environment, but it is doubtful that this is the only basis for the exploratory activity. Similarly, it would be difficult for a kitten to establish visual familiarity with an environment without simultaneously adapting to the odors.

After the 21st day there is a gradual increase in the variety of activities which kittens engage in as their perceptual abilities open avenues of stimulation previously unavailable to them and their motor activity matures, enabling them to engage in various types of play with their littermates, the mother, and inanimate objects. The fifth phase of development (Table 8) extends, in our scheme, through the remainder of the suckling period, though it could readily be divided into several developmental phases (see Fig. 9). Maternal behavior begins to decline toward the middle of this phase and kittens are forced to adjust their suckling approaches to the gradual withdrawal of the mother's care: as she begins to draw away from the kittens, avoiding and evading their suckling approaches they become more persistent and ingenious in following her and soliciting until they find an opportunity to suckle. Subtle interactions between the kittens and the mother in suckling and a broadening of their relationship to include nonfeeding social behavior lays the basis for the transition to weaning as the mother aids in the kittens' development of independent feeding (Wilson and Weston, 1947).

During this period there occurs the initial stages of the incorporation of orientation to the home site into a broader pattern of spatial orientation to relevant features of the environment (Table 8). Spatial orientation capacities are interwoven with social behavior, feeding, sleeping, play activity, and elimination patterns. As new functions arise (e.g., sexual behavior) spatial orientation develops to keep pace and the basis of orientation processes becomes increasingly complex (Hediger, 1950) compared to its beginning in the simple disturbance reaction of the newborn to separation from the mother.

Concluding Remarks

There are corresponding phases in the development of suckling and home orientation in kittens at various ages (Table 8) which we have attempted to delineate through an analysis of the processes underlying the behavioral organization of these behavior patterns. At each stage of development we have suggested the behavioral capacities which form the basis for these distinct behavior patterns. Progressive development from one phase to the next has been traced in relation to the kitten's underlying behavioral capacities at a given stage of development, the specific features of the environment to which it is responsive, and its behavioral attainments to that age. The analysis has been *cross-sectional* with respect to the comparison of suckling and home orientation at similar ages, *longitudinal,* with respect to the development of each of these behavior patterns through several developmental phases, and with respect to the development of underlying behavioral capacities, and we have attempted to combine these two types of analysis throughout. What has emerged from this analysis, we believe, is an appreciation of the similarities of basic processes underlying various aspects of behavioral development as well as some understanding of how specialized functional patterns arise in development.

Emphasis on the basic capacities underlying functionally distinct behavior patterns may obscure the equally important and interesting processes which give rise in development to different behavior patterns contemporaneously within the same individual. Some examples of the way in which basic capacities and special features are interwoven in development can be given now from the studies we have presented.

Although suckling and the settling reaction to the mother share the neonate's basic capacity of approaching low intensity tactile, thermal, and olfactory stimuli, they differ because of the kitten's level of arousal at the different times. Under conditions of heightened arousal contact further excites the kitten (Coronios, 1933) and its activity is maintained until it eventually reaches the nipple. Contact with the mother under conditions of mild or low level arousal calms the kitten and no further activity occurs. One consequence in the kitten's development of the initial differentiation between arousal levels and the reinforcing or dampening effect on motor activity of stimuli from the mother, appears to be, that in suckling, from the beginning, the affective component of behavior is interwoven into a somewhat complex action-pattern having both general and specific components. By contrast, in the settling reaction there is an emphasis upon the affective reaction and only minimal interweaving, at the beginning, with any specific action pattern. This difference is maintained when, in the second developmental phase, nipple positions are established and regional orientation appears. The establishment of nipple positions emphasizes conditioning of the action of nipple grasping to specific stimuli; regional differentiation, by contrast, is based mainly upon the kitten's affective response to perceived differences in its olfactory environment. Motor aspects are nonspecific though expressive of the kitten's affective state.

There are varied relationships between environmental stimuli and developmental processes that are not easily encompassed by broad formulations about the organism and its environment during development. During early phases of suckling development (e.g., day 2 to 14) the mother presents a relatively constant stimulus array to the kitten at each suckling episode. Therefore changes in suckling during this period are based mainly on changes in the kitten's responses to these stimuli—a process which is focused by the adoption of individual nipple position preference. However, in the development of home orientation during this same period, the environment is changing (i.e., odors are being deposited) at the same time that the kitten's ability to respond to olfactory stimuli and to locomote are undergoing development. Path-taking to the home, therefore, cannot be viewed in precisely the same terms as the formation of paths to the nipples: in the development of the one, the kitten may largely be keeping pace with the changing floor stimulation, while in the other, it is forming and reorganizing its own behavioral processes. In this respect there are many parallels in the suckling development of kittens with the mother and with a brooder during the first 3 weeks but the suckling patterns which develop in these two different situations after this age begin to diverge. It is precisely because the mother's behavior begins to change after the third week, as a consequence of alterations in her maternal condition, that kittens, keeping pace with these changes, develop a different suckling pattern than brooder-reared kittens that need not adjust to any changes in the brooder other than those which arise from their own responses to it. The conclusion reached by Koepke and Pribram (1970) that the suckling development of kittens given daily periods of contact with an inactive mother (i.e., anesthetized during nursing) was typical is based upon incomplete data: the full range of behavioral adjustments to the mother could not be observed under these experimental circumstances since the mother herself could not contribute in a continuous manner to the development of these adjustments. What was observed, however, more closely parallels kittens' behavior in the brooder and this we have noted is not typical compared to the behavior of mother-reared young.

Finally, the maturation of visual function has different effects upon the development of suckling and home orientation, raising questions, therefore, about any blanket formulation that can be made about maturational processes in relation to behavioral development. The development of suckling is extended by vision along lines continuous with previous developments and in dependence upon them. With the development of vision, home orientation gradually wanes in relation to its olfactory basis, after some initial improvements. It then develops on an entirely new basis, influenced by functional patterns, that are quite different from its origins in the kitten's settling reaction and responsiveness to cage odors.

The present study represents an extension of the theoretical statements which Dr. Schneirla and I (Schneirla and Rosenblatt, 1963) made some years ago in replying to an article on critical periods in behavioral development by Scott (1962). It is appropriate in concluding, therefore, to restate our position, though at that time our concern was focused on processes of social development.

> "In the social development of the cat, we are led to the idea that striking changes in the essential progression are grounded not only in the growth-dependent processes of maturation but also, at the same time, in opportunities for experience and learning arising in the standard female–litter situation. This conception of social ontogeny encourages stressing not just one or a few chronologically marked changes in behavior patterns, but rather indicates that normally each age period is crucial for the development of particular aspects in a complex progressive pattern of adjustment.

REFERENCES

Alexander, G., and Williams, D. (1964). Maternal facilitation of sucking drive in newborn lambs. *Science* Vol. 146, 665–666.

Anokhin, P. K. (1964). Systemogenesis as a general regulator of brain development. *Progr. Brain Res.* Vol. 9, 54–86.

Carmichael, L. (1946). The onset and early development of behavior. *In* "Manual of Child Psychology" (L. Carmichael, ed.), pp. 60–185. Wiley, New York.

Cornwell, A. C., and Fuller, J. L. (1961). Conditioned responses in young puppies. *J. Comp. Physiol. Psychol.* Vol. 54, 13–15.

Coronios, J. D. (1933). The development of behavior in the fetal cat. *Genet. Psychol. Monogr.* Vol. 14, 283–386.

Deets, A. C., and Harlow, H. F. (1970). Nipple preferences in nursing singleton- and twin-reared rhesus monkey infants. *Develop. Psychol.* Vol. 2, 159–162.

Ellingson, R. J., and Wilcott, R. C. (1960). Development of evoked responses in visual and auditory cortices of kittens. *J. Neurophysiol.* Vol. 23, 363–375.

Ewbank, R. (1964). Observations on the suckling habits of twin lambs. *Anim. Behav.* Vol. 12, 34–37.

Ewbank, R. (1967). Nursing and suckling behaviour amongst Clum Forest ewes and lambs. *Anim. Behav.* Vol. 15, 251–258.

Ewer, R. F. (1959). Sucking behavior in kittens. *Behaviour* Vol. 15, 146–162.

Ewer, R. F. (1961). Further observations on suckling behaviour in kittens together with some general consideration of the interrelations of innate and acquired responses. *Behaviour* Vol. 17, 247–260.

Fox, M. W., and Weisman, R. (1970). Development of responsiveness to a social releaser in the dog: Effects of age and hunger. *Develop. Psychobiol.* Vol. 2, 277–280.

Fuller, J. L., Easler, C. A., and Banks, E. M. (1950). Formation of conditioned avoidance responses in young puppies. *Amer. J. Physiol.* Vol. 160, 462–466.

Green, J. D., Clemente, C. D., and De Groot, J. (1957). Rhinencephalic lesions and behavior in cats. *J. Comp. Neurol.* Vol. 108, 505–545.

Gregory, E., and Pfaff, D. (1970). Development of olfactory-guided behavior in infant rats. Submitted for publication.

Gunther, M. (1961). Infant behaviour of the breast. *In* "Determinants of Infant Behaviour" (B. M. Foss, ed.), pp. 37–39. Methuen, London.

Harlow, H. F. (1959). The development of learning in the rhesus monkey. *Amer. Sci.* Vol. 47, 459–479.

Hediger, H. (1950). "Wild Animals in Captivity." Butterworth, London and Washington, D. C.

Hofer, M. A. (1970). Physiological responses of infant rats to separation from their mothers. *Science* Vol. 168, 871–873.

Ivanitskii, A. M. The morphophysiological investigation of development of conditioned alimentary reaction in rabbits during ontogenesis. *Works Higher Nerv. Activ., Physiol. Ser.* Vol. 4, 126–141.

James, W. T., and Cannon, D. J. (1952). Conditioned avoiding response in puppies. *Amer. J. Physiol.* Vol. 168, 251–253.

Karmel, B. Z., Miller, P. H., Dettweiler, L., and Anderson, G. (1970). Texture density and normal development of visual depth avoidance. *Develop. Psychobiol.* Vol. 3, 73–90.

Kessen, W. (1967). Sucking and looking: Two organized congenital patterns of behavior in the human infant. *In* "Early Behavior and Developmental Approaches" (H. W. Stevenson, E. H. Hess, and H. L. Rheingold, eds.), pp. 147–179. Wiley, New York.

Koepke, J. E., and Pribram, K. H. (1970). Effect of milk on the maintenance of sucking kittens from birth to six months. *J. Comp. Physiol. Psychol.* (in press).

Kovach, J. A., and Kling, A. (1967). Mechanisms of neonate sucking behavior in the kitten. *Anim. Behav.* Vol. 15, 91–101.

Langworthy, O. R. (1929). A correlated study of the development of reflex activity in foetal and young kittens and the myelinization of tracts of the nervous system. *Contrib. Embryol., Carnegie Inst. Wash.* Vol. 20, No. 114, 127–171.

Leyhausen, P. (1965). The communal organization of solitary mammals. *Symp. Zool. Soc. London* No. 14, 249–263.

Leyhausen, P. and Wolff, R. (1959). Das Revier einer Hauskatz. *Z. Tierpsychol.* Vol. 16, 666–670.

Lipsitt, L. P. (1967). Learning in the human infant. *In* "Early Behavior and Developmental Approaches" (H. W. Stevenson, E. H. Hess, and H. L. Rheingold, eds.), pp. 255–257. Wiley, New York.

Lipsitt, L. P., and Kaye, H. (1964). Conditioned sucking in the human newborn. *Psychon. Sci.* Vol. 1, 29–30.

McBride, G. (1963). The "teat order" and communication in young pigs. *Anim. Behav.* Vol. 11, 53–56.

Mason, W. A., and Harlow, H. F. (1958). Formation of conditioned responses in infant monkeys. *J. Comp. Physiol. Psychol.* Vol. 51, 68–70.

Michael, R. P. (1961). Observations upon the sexual behavior of the domestic cat (Felis catus L.) under laboratory conditions. *Behaviour* Vol. 18, 1–24.

Moulton, D. G. (1967). Olfaction in mammals. *Amer. Zool.* Vol. 7, 421–429.

Prechtl, H. F. R. (1952). Angeborenen Bewegungsweisen junger Katzen. *Experientia* Vol. 8, 220–221.

Rose, G. H., and Lindsley, D. B. (1965). Visually evoked electrocortical responses in kittens: Development of specific and nonspecific systems. *Science* Vol. 148, 1244–1246.

Rosenblatt, J. S. (1953). Mating behavior of the male cat. The role of sexual experience and social adjustments. Ph.D. Thesis, New York University.

Rosenblatt, J. S., Turkewitz, G., and Schneirla, T. C. (1961). Early socialization in the domestic cat as based on feeding and other relationships between female and young. *In* "Determinants of Infant Behaviour" (B. F. Foss, ed.), pp. 51-74. Methuen, London.

Rosenblatt, J. S., Turkewitz, G., and Schneirla, T. C. (1969). Development of home orientation in newly born kittens. *Trans. N. Y. Acad. Sci.* Vol. 31, 231-250.

Tobach, E., Rouger, Y., and Schneirla, T. C. (1967). Development of olfactory function in the rat pup. *Amer. Zool.* Vol. 7, 792-793.

Salk, L. (1960). Effects of normal heartbeat sound on the behavior of the new-born infant: Implications for mental health. *World Ment. Health* Vol. 12, 168-175.

Schneirla, T. C. (1957). The concept of development in comparative psychology. *In* "The Concept of Development" (D. B. Harris, ed.), pp. 78-108. Univ. of Minnesota Press, Minneapolis, Minnesota.

Schneirla, T. C. (1959). An evolutionary and developmental theory of biphasic processes underlying approach and withdrawal. *In* "Nebraska Symposium Motivation" (M. R. Jones, ed.), pp. 1-42. Univ. of Nebraska Press, Lincoln, Nebraska.

Schneirla, T. C. (1965). Aspects of stimulation and organization in approach/withdrawal processes underlying vertebrate behavioral development. *In* "Advances in the Study of Behavior" (D. S. Lehrman, R. A. Hinde, and E. Shaw, eds.), Vol. 1, pp. 1-74. Academic Press, New York.

Schneirla, T. C., and Rosenblatt, J. S. (1961). Behavioral organization and genesis of the social bond in insects and mammals. *Amer. J. Orthopsychiat.* Vol. 31, 223-253.

Schneirla, T. C., and Rosenblatt, J. S. (1963). "Critical periods" in the development of behavior. *Science* Vol. 139, 1110-1115.

Schneirla, T. C., Rosenblatt, J. S., and Tobach, E. (1963). Maternal behavior in the cat. *In* "Maternal Behavior in Mammals" (H. L. Rheingold, ed.), pp. 122-168. Wiley, New York.

Scott, J. P. (1958). Critical periods in the development of social behavior in puppies. *Psychosom. Med.* Vol. 20, 42-54.

Scott, J. P. (1962). Critical periods in behavioral development. *Science* Vol. 138, 945-958.

Scott, J. P. (1968). "Early Experience and the Organization of Behavior." Wadsworth, Belmont, California.

Scott, J. P., and Bronson, F. H. (1964). Experimental exploration of the et-epimeletic or care-soliciting behavioral system. *In* "Psychobiological Approaches to Social Behavior" (P. H. Leiderman and D. Shapiro, eds.), pp. 174-193. Stanford Univ. Press, Stanford, California.

Siqueland, E. R., and Lipsitt, L. P. (1966). Conditioned head-turning in human newborns. *J. Exp. Child Psychol.* Vol. 3, 356-376.

Smith, W. (1965). Personal communication.

Stanley, W. C., Cornwell, A. C., Poggiani, C., and Trattner, A. (1963). Conditioning in the neonate puppy. *J. Comp. Physiol. Psychol.* Vol. 56, 211-214.

Stanley, W. C., Bacon, W. E., and Fehr, C. (1970). Discriminated instrumental learning in neonatal dogs. *J. Comp. Physiol. Psychol.* Vol. 70, 335-343.

Stavsky, W. H. (1932). The geotropic conduct of young kittens. *J. Genet. Psychol.* Vol. 6, 441-446.

Thoman, E., Wetzel, A., and Levine, S. (1968). Learning in the neonatal rat. *Anim. Behav.* Vol. 16, 54-57.

Tilney, F., and Casamajor, L. (1924). Myolenogeny as applied to the study of behaviour. *Arch. Neurol. Psychiat.* Vol. 12, 1-66.

Toropova, N. V. (1961). Technique of artificial feeding of puppies in the early postnatal period. *Pavlov J. Higher Nerv. Activ.* Vol. 11, 137–138.

Turkewitz, G. (1966). The development of spatial orientation in relation to the effective perceptual environment in neonate rats. Unpublished Ph.D. Dissertation, New York University.

Turkewitz, G. (1957). Unpublished observation.

Van Lawick-Goodall, J. (1967). Mother-offspring relationships in free-ranging chimpanzees. *In* "Primate Ethology" (D. Morris, ed.), pp. 287–346. Aldine, Chicago, Illinois.

Volokhov, A. A. (1959). Comparative-physiological investigation of conditioned and unconditioned reflexes during ontogeny. *Pavlov J. Higher Nerv. Activ.* Vol. 9, 49–60.

Walters, R. H., and Parke, R. D. (1965). The role of the distance receptors in the development of social responsiveness. *In* "Advances in Child Development and Behavior" (L. P. Lipsitt and C. C. Spiker, eds.), Vol. 2, pp. 59–96. Academic Press, New York.

Warkentin, J., and Smith, K. U. (1937). The development of visual acuity in the cat. *J. Genet. Psychol.* Vol. 50, 371–399.

Wilson, C., and Weston, E. (1947). "The Cats of Wildcat Hill." Duell, Sloan, & Pearce, New York.

Windle, W. F. (1930). Normal behavioral reactions of kittens correlated with postnatal development of nerve-fibre density in the spinal grey matter. *J. Comp. Neurol.* Vol. 50, 479–503.

Wodinsky, J., Rosenblatt, J. S., Turkewitz, G., and Schneirla, T. C. (1955). The development of individual nursing position habits in new born kittens. *Eastern Psychol. Assoc.*

Woll, R. J., and Rosenblatt, J. S. (1970). Unpublished observations.

SOME PROBLEMS IN THE STUDY OF THE DEVELOPMENT OF SOCIAL BEHAVIOR

R. A. HINDE

The Problem of Social Development

In species with maternal care, much of the behavior of the newborn to its parent can be described reasonably adequately in stimulus–response (S–R) terms. We now know, for instance, a fair amount about the mechanisms by which the infant primate clasps its mother (e.g., Hines, 1942; Prechtl, 1956) and by which it finds the nipple and sucks (e.g., Gunther, 1955; Prechtl, 1958), and about the nature of some of the stimuli which the mother provides (e.g., Harlow and Zimmermann, 1959). Somehow, in the course of development, this simple stimulus–response interaction gives rise to the complex social relations we see in the adult animal. We habitually describe these with a quite different sort of language, using concepts like dominance, leadership, or role-taking which are not easily translatable into S–R terms. In moving from one sort of language to the other, we covertly recognize an increase in complexity which is perhaps too seldom made explicit.

The extent to which we are able to keep this increase in complexity in mind will influence the strategy we use in studying the development of social behavior. If, on the one hand, we are primarily interested in the continuity of the developmental sequence, we tend to focus on those aspects of adult behavior most readily reducible to stimulus–response terms, and to neglect its complexities. If, on the other hand, we focus on the differences between infant and adult, we tend to forget their continuity. In the related problem of the relations between adult social behavior in different phyla, Schneirla and Rosenblatt (1961) distinguished "biosocial" from "psychosocial" organization. In the former, bonds are situationally determined and limited in scope, while in the latter, the bonds depend on an intimate cooperation of maturation, experience, and learning. Such a distinction is of great value in, for instance, pinpointing the differences between insect and mammalian social organization, but as a dichotomy it is useful only insofar as the continuity of evolution is not under study.

The problems arising in the study of the development of social behavior do not differ in kind from those arising in other aspects of development. Indeed the development of relations with social companions is closely related to that of relations with the physical environment. For example, social development depends on changes occurring through interaction with the physical environment and with the organism's own body, both pre- and postnatally, as well as through interaction with other individuals. The posture which the human fetus adopts *in utero* affects its postnatal reflex behavior, and thus perhaps its early social interactions (Prechtl, cited Hinde, 1966). The development of visuo-motor abilities depends on interactions with the mother, the subject's own body, and the physical environment, which mutually affect each other (e.g., Held and Bauer, 1967; White and Held, 1966; White, 1970). The complexity of the physical environment affects an infant primate's interactions with its mother (Jensen *et al.*, 1968) and the presence of its mother or mother substitute affects its responsiveness to the physical environment (Harlow and Harlow, 1965, 1969). The development of social behavior is thus closely interwoven with that of other types of behavior. Furthermore, and perhaps most important of all, the development of social behavior involves processes similar to those necessary for the development of any other type of behavior—such as the emergence of object permanence (Piaget and Inhelder, 1966).

In the following sections some problems in the study of social development have been selected for discussion. Because their social relationships tend to be more complex than those of other species, attention is concentrated mainly but not entirely on subhuman primates.

The Problem of Classification

The study of behavior places the investigator immediately in an inescapable predicament; it demands the use of classificatory categories, but these inevitably falsify reality. To study behavior, we have to name items of behavior, the external factors which influence it, and the processes which supposedly determine it. Naming involves classifying items together into categories, with the implication of discontinuities between the categories: we must therefore be constantly aware of the extent to which our categories really do represent discontinuities and the degree to which they are a matter of convenience. Furthermore, our categories must be defined in terms of specific criteria, and the nature of these will make them relevant to some problems and not to others (Hinde, 1966).

This problem arises with peculiar force in the study of the development of behavior, for the first phase must involve description of development. Except in the case of animals which undergo metamorphosis or moult, development is continuous; but to describe development, it is often useful to divide its continuous course into stages. These can be helpful in the early phases of the study of development, including that of social development. For instance, juvenile, adolescent, subadult, and adult animals may have quite different relations within a group, and specification of the outstanding characteristics of these stages facilitates analysis.

The recognition of stages, however, soon runs into difficulties as analysis proceeds. First, as already mentioned, it too easily implies discontinuities in development where none exist. Second, since the stages are arbitrary, there is often little agreement between the stages recognized by different workers on the same species (see, e.g., Hinde, 1971). Third, to be of most use in the early phases of an investigation, stages should be based on as many characters as possible; thus the stages used by field workers on subhuman primates are often based on characters of both physical and social development (e.g., degree of behavioral dependence on mother), as well as on (estimated) chronological age. However, these may become dissociated if the conditions of development are changed. For example, Jensen et al. (1968) have shown that mother–infant relations in pigtail macaques are affected by the richness of the physical environment; and in rhesus monkeys they may be markedly altered by the presence of social companions (e.g., Hinde and Spencer-Booth, 1967): these effects are not correlated with comparable effects on physical development. Here, therefore, is a dilemma. The value of recognizing stages in development for comparing individuals, species or experimental treatments is likely to increase, the more aspects of development the stages comprehend; but the more aspects are comprehended, the more likely it is that a change in circumstances will bring dissociation between them, and therefore the smaller the range of circumstances in which the stages as defined are useful. In addition, the relations between characters of various types differ between species; thus stages based on multiple characters may be of little value for comparisons between species.

The classification of the social influences on development also poses difficulties. For example, most primates develop within a social group. While they interact most with their mother, they interact also with a variety of other social companions. It is convenient to classify these in terms of age/sex classes into peers, adult males, adult females, and so on. These categories are useful in part because they are easily recognizable, and in part because they can be manipulated experimentally. Thus much fruitful research at the University of Wisconsin has been concerned with the effect on behavioral development of rearing with or without a mother, with or without peers, and so on (e.g., Harlow and Harlow, 1965, 1969). However this has led to some dispute as to the relative importance of the mother and of peers for normal behavioral development (e.g., Meier, 1965). That such a dispute can arise is in part a consequence of the artificial nature of the categories themselves. Each category of social companion interacts with the infant in many ways, and these overlap between the categories. For instance, peers normally elicit play behavior and may act as grooming companions. The mother also interacts with her infant in both these ways, so that either may substitute at least in some degree for the other. Indeed, peers may even provide some of the "contact comfort" normally provided by the mother (Harlow and Harlow, 1965, 1969). The fundamental questions, therefore, would seem to be: what sorts of interaction are necessary for the infant rhesus, and to what extent? Which types of social companion normally provide these? To what extent can the different categories of social companion substitute for each other? In other words, the classification of social influences according to the companions which provide them may be obscuring important issues. That the questions just mentioned may not be the only pertinent ones will become apparent later.

A slightly different type of problem arises when we try to categorize the members of a group according to their social properties, as with "dominant" animals, or "leaders." At the one extreme, dominance can be defined in terms of a single relatively clear-cut criterion, such as priority of access to a food source. But if the concept of dominance is to be useful, we must be able to assess it in more than one way; it provides economy in proportion to the number of dependent variables it represents. In a study of captive baboons, Rowell (1966) found that the rankings of individuals in terms of a variety of behavior patterns involving approach/retreat were correlated with each other, but not precisely so. Other types of social interaction (e.g., "friendly" interactions) could be predicted only very approximately from the rank order based on the approach/retreat ones. Thus in her view the dominance hierarchy is a "way of expressing the predictability of interaction patterns in the group," with a limited but definable range and extent of usefulness. Rowell also emphasizes that dominance hierarchies as assessed by approach/retreat scores are not necessarily related to leadership or to relative success in attaining desirable objects in the environment.

Yet another type of classificatory device which must be treated with caution is that which groups phenomena across different types of behavior or across species. An obvious example is the concept of "sensitive period." Used to refer to an age-span during which an environmental influence must exert its effect for development to proceed normally, the term is merely descriptive and can be useful. But as soon as its use starts to become explanatory, difficulties arise; for there must be no implication that the factors which limit sensitive periods have anything in common from one case to another. Another example is provided by imprinting: usually used to refer to the process which restricts the social responses of nidifugous birds to a particular class of objects, it is sometimes applied to such diverse responses as the establishment of diurnal rhythms in insects and song-learning in birds (Thorpe, 1963), which have only limited characteristics in common with this.

In summary, while the need for classification is ubiquitous, we must be constantly aware of the limits of usefulness of the categories we set up.

Analysis and Resynthesis

Just because an animal's interactions with its social companions involve some of the most complex aspects of its behavior, an understanding of their development requires fragmentation of the problems, and progressive understanding at successively finer levels of analysis. But understanding of component processes does not necessarily imply understanding of the whole. For one thing, progressive analysis of one aspect of the problem can lead to neglect of others. For another, analysis alone can rarely provide a complete understanding of biological organization, for processes akin to resynthesis are necessary both to assess the relations between the parts and to assess the adequacy of the initial analysis.

As an example, we may consider again the question of imprinting. The general problem originally arose from observations of mate selection in nidifugous birds. Simplifying somewhat, the subsequent course of research has been as follows. The choice of mate seemed to be related to the nature of the object to which the newly hatched bird directed its filial responses. The most conspicuous of these responses was the following response. Experimental studies showed that this could at first be elicited by a wide range of objects, but that the range of effective objects rapidly became narrowed: objects encountered for the first time after a limited "sensitive period" would not elicit the response. The learning process involved was referred to as "imprinting." It was held to be a special form of learning chiefly on the grounds of its apparent irreversibility and rapidity, and its limitation to a sensitive period, and also because of the way in which it affected a type of behavior (mating) which did not appear until later in development (Lorenz, 1935).

Attention was focused on the factors limiting this sensitive period. It became apparent first that the end of the sensitive period was set by the development of fear responses to new objects, and later that this depended on experience of a familiar environment against the background of which "strange" objects elicited withdrawal responses (e.g., Bateson, 1966; Sluckin, 1964). The limits of the sensitive period were therefore related to the development of perceptual abilities and experience of the environment.

At the same time the problem of the sensitive period was restated in terms of the age-range during which the bird could develop a preference for a novel stimulus, as indicated by an approach response (Bateson, 1966). As a consequence, the earlier assumption that imprinting must be *completed* within the sensitive period was questioned: although, once the sensitive period is over, strange objects elicit withdrawal rather than approach, the process of restriction of preferences may go on for some time. On this view, imprinting becomes not a sudden, irreversible, all-or-none process, but something much more flexible: this is in harmony with a number of experimental findings, such as that length of exposure to the stimulus object is an important variable, and that exposure to objects later in development can modify preferences.

From the postulation of a unique type of learning process, research has thus led to an understanding of these phenomena in terms of the development of perceptual abilities and of familiarity with the environment—that is, in terms of processes known in other contexts and susceptible to study at more refined analytical levels.

But at this point it is necessary to stand back, to resynthesize the products of the analysis, and to reexamine the original problem. Even in the analysis of the following response itself, such a basic problem as why the birds approach conspicuous objects remains unsolved. Schneirla's view (e.g., 1965) that mild stimulation elicits approach from young animals, and the hypothetical mechanisms which he suggested, are too general to help understanding in the specific case. Bateson's finding that young birds actively search for conspicuous stimuli, and Bateson and Reese's demonstration (1968) of their reinforcing properties, advance the problem one stage, but the source of this reinforcing effect is left as an intrinsic and unanalyzed property of the organism. Bateson (1964) found that naive chicks show behavior which can be described as searching for a conspicuous object, but the intensity of the searching behavior shown by imprinted birds temporarily separated from the imprinting object is as yet not fully explained.

Turning to the original problem of the source of sexual preferences in adulthood, it is clear that early experience can affect this, but it is also clear that many other factors, both genetic and later experiential ones, may also do so (e.g., Warriner et al., 1963; Klinghammer, 1967). As yet we are only just beginning to get a little understanding of the interacting processes involved, and our progress can only be assessed by resynthesizing the results of the analyses of the partial problems.

The question of the level of analysis is of importance also in another way. While "each type of species-standard behavioral system requires investigation as a distinctive problem in development" (Schneirla and Rosenblatt, 1961), the scientist's role is to make generalizations, and generalizations across species may be valid at one level but not at another. This is particularly the case with social behavior, for apparently similar social systems may rest on quite dissimilar bases, while slight differences in interindividual relations may give rise to apparently gross differences in social systems.

The Problem of Monotropy

We are concerned here with the manner in which the young of most species come to direct many of their filial responses primarily toward one particular individual (i.e., "monotropy"). Here it is necessary first to emphasize again the variety of interactions between a young animal and its social companions. For example, as we have already seen, a young primate interacts with several categories of social companion. Toward each it shows a number of types of behavior—clinging, grooming, play, sex, and so on—though the proportion of each type of behavior varies between the categories of social companion. Rhesus monkeys brought up in a markedly impoverished social environment, and thus denied the opportunity for displaying these types of behavior, may develop into neurotic and asocial adults (Harlow and Harlow, 1969; Sackett, 1968). If the social environment is only partially depleted, they may compensate in some degree for the absence of one type of social companion by directing toward others the types of interaction which would otherwise have occurred with the absent one. For instance, infant rhesus brought up in groups of two to four, but without mothers, spend much time clinging to each other, thereby providing mutually the "contact comfort" which each would normally have obtained from its mother. What is not clear, however, is whether the requirements for normal development merely involve the infant getting the proper total amount of each type of interaction, or if it may not also be important that a major part of the infant's social behavior be directed toward one particular individual.

In human infants there is some evidence that the establishment of a relationship with a particular mother figure may be important. Normally, a number of filial responses are directed especially toward one person. These include smiling, crying on that person's departure, being comforted by being held by that person, orienting toward, approaching and following, greeting, and climbing on that person, and being reassured by that person (Ainsworth, 1967). For instance, in her study of Ganda children, Ainsworth found that up to nine months of age they focused most of their attachment behavior on one special person, and it was to that person that they turned if hungry, tired, or ill. Other figures might, however, be sought in other contexts—for instance, as play companions; the frequency with which this occurred increased after the child was 9-10 months old. Normally, the principal figure is the natural mother, presumably because she interacts most with the child and is most responsive to him. Bowlby (1969) refers to this tendency for the child to attach itself especially to one figure as "monotropy."

Bowlby (1969) cites evidence from two studies of human children (Ainsworth, 1967; Schaffer and Emerson, 1964) that infants who show an intense attachment to one figure are likely also to show attachments to subsidiary figures, whereas an infant who is only weakly attached tends to confine all his attachment behavior to one. Several explanations are of course possible. One is that the latter children have less "intrinsic" tendency to form attachments. Another, favored by Bowlby, is that the child which does not establish a strong relationship with one figure is, as a result, less able to do so with others. This is in harmony with evidence that the children who are slow in forming attachments are ones which, for reasons not consequent upon their own behavior, have received relatively little mothering. If Bowlby is correct, then the early establishment of a strong relationship may affect the tendency to form attachments later, and thus the development of social behavior.

It is therefore important to consider the factors that promote attachment to a particular figure early on. Bowlby mentions a number of developmental issues. There is for instance an initial tendency to respond to certain classes of stimuli, including the visual and auditory stimuli provided by the human caretakers. The infant learns the attributes of the individuals caring for him, and has a bias to approach whatever is familiar. (By analogy with recent studies of imprinting in birds, this might be rephrased as a tendency to approach objects conspicuous to him and to avoid strange ones; conspicuousness, familiarity, and strangeness are interrelated properties.) In addition, reinforcement plays an essential role. The precise nature of the reinforcing stimuli is, however, not yet clear. There is little evidence to support the traditional view that food plays a vital role. "Contact comfort" probably plays some role at first— that it may continue to do so later on is demonstrated by the attachments children show to cuddly objects, such as blankets and teddy bears. [Studies of nidifugous birds (Bateson and Reese, 1968) suggest that mere proximity to a conspicuous object may be reinforcing, but this has not yet been studied in human young.] More important than any of these, in Bowlby's view, is responsiveness to the infant's behavior. For instance Schaffer and Emerson (1964), in a study of Scottish children, found that the intensity of attachment behavior was positively associated with the extent to which the mother initiated interaction with the baby, and her readiness to respond to his cries, but not with a number of other variables. There are, of course, difficulties here, since the mother's tendency to initiate will vary with the responsiveness of her infant. However, it is clear that the role of such properties of the mother as her readiness to initiate interaction requires more precise analysis. Also, while it is known that specific types of attachment behavior (e.g., smiling) can be reinforced by social responding by the caretaker (e.g., Brackbill, 1958), it is not yet known how widespread such effects are— that is, whether types of attachment behavior other than the one specifically reinforced are affected.

Returning to subhuman primates, we may ask whether similar principles apply there. In the artificial conditions of the laboratory, a young rhesus can learn to direct the different social responses which it normally directs to its mother toward different objects—sucking toward a nipple on one mother surrogate, clinging toward terry cloth on another, for example. However, normally a relationship with one particular individual is established. As in the human case, this probably depends on several types of interaction. Clinging is certainly important, since infants spend more time on a cloth mother surrogate than on a wire one, even when fed on the latter (Harlow and Zimmerman, 1959); and they may, like human children, become attached to objects which provide only contact comfort (e.g., Hayes, 1951). Rhesus infants also adapt more readily to a strange situation in the presence of a mother surrogate to which they have learned to cling than in the presence of one which does not elicit clinging. This also indicates that the presence of an object with which an attachment has been formed influences adjustment to a strange situation. Other aspects of mother–infant interaction which may be important in forming the bond have been discussed by Mason (1965, 1967).

With one exception, studies of the role of social companions in the development of rhesus macaques involve a reduction in the total amount of interaction and often the elimination of any possibility of forming a relationship with one particular individual; the importance of the latter therefore cannot be assessed. It is noteworthy, though, that rhesus infants raised in "subtotal" social isolation are usually indifferent or brutal to their firstborn offspring. This is at least in harmony with the view that the absence of an affectional bond in early life hinders the development of such bonds later, though some of these affectionless mothers were much more adequate with later offspring (Harlow and Harlow, 1965).

The one experiment that is relevant concerns a comparison between own-mother raised infant rhesus and four infants which were rotated between mothers once a fortnight for 8 months. Here, the total amount of "mothering" received was more or less the same, but in one case it came always from the same individual, and in the other case from a different animal every fortnight. On the whole there were no marked differences between the groups in the nature of peer–peer interactions, though the multiple-mother infants did show a higher frequency of "disturbance" behavior. There was, also, a slight difference at 8 months in that the single-mother infants preferred a strange infant to a strange adult in a choice test, but the multiple-mothered infants showed no preference. This experiment, therefore, is not decisive with regard to the importance of monotropy for monkeys.

Another experiment suggests that too strong an attachment in infancy could mitigate against the subsequent development of social bonds. Infants with overrestrictive or inadequately rejecting mothers may be retarded or abnormal in the development of peer–peer relationships (e.g., Hansen, 1966). The situation is thus by no means simple and, insofar as its intensity can be measured along a single dimension, the mother–infant bond can be either too strong or too weak.

Scarcity of hard data permits this inconclusive discussion to do no more than point to the importance of the issue. If monotropy is important for man and is not important for monkeys, this places another limit on the generalizations about the development of social behavior which can be made from the study of subhuman forms.

The Problem of Changes or Differences in Social Interactions

Any measure of a social interaction depends on the behavior of both participants. A dominant animal is dominant not only because of his own behavior but also because of that of the animals subordinate to him. A leader leads because he is followed. For this reason a change, developmental or otherwise, in any measure of social interactions may be due to a change in the behavior of either of the participants. In order to disentangle their separate roles, measures of their interaction looked at in isolation are therefore not sufficient. It is, however, possible to make some progress by looking at the correlations between such measures.

Such a method has proved useful in studies of mother–infant relations in rhesus monkeys. For example, as the infant gets older, it spends more time off its mother and a higher proportion of that time at a distance from her. These changes in mother–infant interaction could be due to changes in the behavior of the mother, infant, or both. It is also the case that the proportion of occasions on which the infant attempts to gain the nipple and is rejected by the mother, and the role of the infant in maintaining proximity to the mother when it is off her (indicated by the difference between the percentage of approaches and leavings due to the infant), increase with age of the infant. These changes also could be due to alterations in the behavior of either participant. If we look at the correlations between these measures, however, we can arrive at a hypothesis as to which partner is immediately responsible for precipitating the age changes observed. Table I shows the direction in which each of the four measures of mother–infant interaction might change with each of four simple types of change in mother–infant interaction. It will be seen that, if the changes are limited to those indicated, an increase in time off the mother is more likely to be due to a change in the infant's behavior if

TABLE 1
Predicted Direction of Changes in Various Measures of Mother–Infant Interaction Produced by Four Types of Change in the Behavior of One of Them

	Time off mother	Frequency of rejections	Time more than 2 feet from mother (% of time off)	Difference between percentage of approaches and percentage of leavings due to infant (% approaches − % leavings)
Infant leaves mother more	+	−	+	−
Infant seeks proximity more	−	+	−	+
Mother seeks proximity more	−	−	−	−
Mother leaves infant more	+	+	+	+

it is associated with a decrease in the frequency of rejections, and vice versa. Similarly a change in the proportion of time off the mother that the infant spends at a distance from her is more likely to be due to the mother if positively correlated with the infant's role in maintaining proximity, and vice versa. In practice examination of correlation coefficients between median scores at successive ages indicates that the mother plays a major part in the increasing independence of the infant, even at ages at which it is she who is primarily responsible for maintaining proximity between them.

Table 1 suggests that time off will always be correlated with time at a distance from the mother, and the frequency of rejections with the infant's role in maintaining proximity, whichever of the four changes indicated on the left of the table occurs. But of course the actual changes which occur in the behavior of mother and infant are likely to be much more complicated than those indicated. The extent to which this is so will be partly revealed by the extent to which these pairs of measures depart from absolute correlation. For example, if we are considering the age changes in mother–infant interaction, correlation coefficients between time off and time at a distance from the mother, and between the frequency of rejections and the infant's role in maintaining proximity at successive ages, suggest that changes in mother–infant interaction with age can be described reasonably well in terms of changes of the type shown in the table (Hinde, 1969). By contrast, when the behavior of two twins was being compared, one infant spent more time off and more time at a distance from the mother than the other, and was rejected more by the mother, but took a smaller role in maintaining proximity to the mother, than its twin (Spencer-Booth, 1968b). Thus the difference between the twins cannot be ascribed solely to changes affecting all measures in the manner indicated in Table 1; a probable hypothesis, supported by other measures, is that this infant, being rejected by the mother on a higher proportion of the occasions when it approached her, learned to approach her less often.

In practice, of course, many measures in addition to the four shown in Table 1 are used. This correlational method has proved useful for examining age changes in mother–infant interaction, differences between individual mother–infant pairs, differences between group-living and isolated mother–infant pairs, and changes in mother–infant relations occurring after a separation experience (Hinde, 1969).

The method is applicable also to the dominance hierarchy situation. Arguments of the same basic nature are used, for instance, by Rowell (1966) in her analysis of hierarchy in a caged baboon group; she produces considerable evidence that the hierarchy is maintained as much by the behavior of the subordinate animals as by that of dominant ones.

The Problem of Roles

We have seen that, within a primate troop, each animal may interact with an infant in a number of different ways. To some extent it is possible to group the animals according to the nature of their interactions with the infant, and these groups roughly correspond with those based on other criteria, such as age, sex, and parental status. One way of expressing this is to say that the several age/sex categories have different *roles* with respect to the infant. This is a particular aspect of the more general fact that the behavior of individual animals is to some extent predictable in terms of their age, sex, etc., which in turn has been expressed by saying that they perform different roles within the society (Bernstein and Sharpe, 1966). The recognition of roles in this way is a potentially useful tool for comparing different societies (Gartlan, 1968). Since each animal passes through a number of the usual age/sex categories as it grows up, they could also be useful in the study of development.

In practice, however, the study of roles in primate societies is in danger of running into difficulties which must be recognized and overcome before much progress can be made. In the first place, while there can be no dispute that animals in different age/sex categories do behave differently, quantitative description of the manner in which they do so is not so easy. For instance, Bernstein and Sharpe (1966) studied a captive group of two adult and one subadult male, three adult female, one young mature female, a juvenile male, and three juvenile female rhesus. They recorded status, as determined by priority of access to desired food, and the percentage of time units which each animal spent in certain activities. Many of the data were presented in a table, and it is clear that there was considerable overlap between the age/sex categories for most (though not all) activities. While it is claimed that "the results demonstrate several differentiated activity profiles . . . related to sex, age, and status variables," the low numbers in each category do not permit statistical analysis, and the data do not really justify much more than a series of generalizations of the type: "These adult males spent less time in proximity to other animals and more time resting than did members of other categories." Discussion of differences related to status refer mostly to peculiarities of the (one) dominant male; the generality of these could be assessed only by studying the adult males in other troops.

As another example, Gartlan (1968), while giving a stimulating and critical theoretical account of these and related problems, used statistical techniques which leave much to be desired. He studied a troop of 20 *Cercopithecus aethiops* (three adult males, six adult females, one juvenile male, four subadult females, and six infants). He divided social interactions (neglecting maternal behavior and play) into seven "role categories" which appear to be based partly on physical description of the behavior and partly on its consequences. Summing all the incidents in each of these "role categories," he calculated the percentage contribution of each animal. The sum of the percentage contributions of the animals in each age/sex category was then taken to represent the contribution of that category. These contributions of the age/sex categories were compared with those which would be expected on the assumption that all individuals were equally likely to contribute, by a chi-square test. This test was based on percentages rather than absolute frequencies, and each entry into a cell was not independent of each other entry into it. Because of this misuse of chi square (Lewis and Burke, 1949), invalid conclusions were drawn about differences between categories. For instance, the conclusion that the contribution of each age/sex category to "jumping about" is other than would be expected by chance is based on the fact that 66% of the jumping about comes from adult males and 33% from juvenile males. However, another figure shows that all the jumping about contributed by adult males came from one of three individuals, and there was in any case only one juvenile male. Thus the conclusion about the category "adult males" is based on only one individual, and, indeed, since no absolute frequencies are given, could be based on only two observations of that male.

In addition to such practical matters, trouble is being stored up for the future by the diverse ways in which the word "role" is being used. Thus it may be used for:

a. A quantitative description of all the behavior of one animal or of a sample of animals selected from a group defined by independent criteria. For instance the roles of different age/sex classes of monkeys may refer to all the types of behavior they are seen to show. It is usually in this sense that Bernstein and Sharpe use the term.

b. A quantitative description of all the behavior of one or more of a sample of animals selected from a group by criteria related to the behavior described. This occurs, for instance, when categories are characterized in terms of "dominance," which is itself defined in terms of behavior. Bernstein and Sharpe state that the dominant male had the most complex role in the group.

c. The behavior of one or more animals while occupied in a particular way. Thus Gartlan refers to the behavior of a pair of birds, one of which incubates while its mate feeds, as involving (temporarily) distinct roles.

In all these cases, the behavior is often characterized by its consequences. Thus Gartlan, studying a monkey troop, used such categories as "friendly approach" and "social vigilance." Sometimes the behavior involves a number of patterns with related consequences, as when the behavior of an animal showing various patterns of infant care is described as "taking a maternal role." (Often "role" as used in this way becomes an intervening variable used to explain correlations between behavioral items—for example, observations that an animal carries, protects, and grooms infants is "explained" by saying it has taken a maternal role.) In this last case, the consequence is one deemed to promote the survival or reproduction of the group. As another example, the adult males of a primate group may be said to have a "protective" role.

The implication of an adaptive consequence introduces an additional and quite distinct factor. Neither all the behavior of individuals or demographic categories, nor all the differences between them, need be adaptive for the individuals or for the society as a whole. Gartlan implies that the categories he used do refer to adaptive features, but whether he is referring to the individual or the society is not clear, and his evidence is not given. Bernstein and Sharpe, though often apparently applying "role" to a category of behavior adaptive to the group ("Male A also served to terminate intra group fighting by attacking any animals in a disturbance . . .") at other times use "role differentiation" merely to refer to differences between the behavior of age/sex classes.

In conclusion, while the task of specifying in quantitative terms the behavior of each individual and type of individual within a society is certainly a proper one—and an urgent one as far as primate societies are concerned—it is clear that inadequate attention to practical, semantic, and conceptual matters could readily retard progress in this field.

The Problem of the Social Nexus

In analyzing the social influences on a developing infant, the first step is to assess the ways in which it interacts with each of its social companions. As we have seen, we can, if we so wish, describe the behavior of each category of social companion in terms of its "role" (see above) in the social environment of the infant. We shall find, of course, that these "roles" change with the age of the infant, but even acknowledging this, the picture we obtain is a simplified and essentially static one. For the infant is not merely a center of social influences, or the focus of a number of independent interactions; it is part of a complex nexus of social interactions, change in any part of which is likely to have ramifying consequences. As yet there is very little detailed data on such effects, but their potential importance is indicated in a number of ways.

SUBSTITUTIONS

As we have seen, if a certain category of social companion is absent, some of the ways in which the infant would have interacted with it may be compensated by increased interaction with another. For instance, when infant rhesus are brought up without mothers in small cages, they develop a together–together clinging pattern in which each provides the other with some of the contact comfort it would have obtained from its mother (Harlow and Harlow, 1965). If the mother of a socially living infant rhesus is removed, it may obtain contact comfort from another adult female or an adult male (Spencer-Booth and Hinde, 1967). If mother–infant pairs are brought up in isolation from others, the mother grooms the infant and the infant grooms the mother more than is the case with group-living animals (Hinde and Spencer-Booth, 1967). This same principle applies in reverse to the social companions. Thus an adult female without an infant of her own is rather more likely to interact with the infants of other females than is a mother (Spencer-Booth, 1968a).

INFLUENCES OF INTERACTION BETWEEN INFANT AND ONE SOCIAL COMPANION ON INFANT'S INTERACTIONS WITH OTHERS

Since at any stage in the life of an infant primate a number of social companions interact with it, they may compete for it. Thus interaction with one social companion may affect the infant's interactions with others.

This issue arises particularly in the reciprocal influences which mother and other adult females have on each other's behavior. In many species females other than the infant's own mother interact with them in a number of ways—inspecting, touching, grooming, cuddling, carrying, playing with, and behaving aggressively toward them. In some species the mothers are permissive, allowing other females fairly free access to their infants [e.g., langurs (Jay, 1963)]. In others the mothers attempt to reduce such interactions, either by threatening off the other females or by protecting the infants from them. Thus the mother's permissiveness affects the extent to which infants interact with other adult females. Comparing rhesus mother–infant pairs living alone with those living in groups, Hinde and Spencer-Booth (1967) found that the former group of infants spent more time off and at a distance from their mothers, and that this was due to greater permissiveness by the mothers. Thus the presence of the group companions affected the nature of the mother–infant relationship. The mother's permissiveness also no doubt affects the amount the infant plays with its peers, and vice versa, but hard data on this subject have not yet been obtained.

RELATIONSHIPS INITIALLY INDEPENDENT OF THE INFANT AFFECT ITS INTERACTIONS

The response of the mother rhesus to the attempts by other females to touch, carry, or play with the infant vary with her relationships with them. Females who are subordinate to her she may threaten off, but with females who are dominant to her she protects the infant by restricting its movements. She is most likely to allow access to the infant to females with whom she had previously had a friendly relationship—for instance, an older female infant of her own.

Furthermore, the relationship of a mother with other mothers may affect the infant's interactions with its peers. Mothers of fairly young infants not infrequently interfere when their infants are playing with others, especially when the play becomes rough. Each mother may interfere on behalf of her own infant, and it is to be expected that she would be influenced by her relationship with the other's mother. Qualitative observation confirms this (Rowell et al., 1964).

INTERACTION BETWEEN THE SOCIAL COMPANION AND THE INFANT AFFECTS THE FORMER'S BEHAVIOR AND SOCIAL RELATIONS

In a number of species the possession of a baby confers a special status. Qualitative observations suggest that mothers with young infants gain a certain immunity from the attacks and threats of others.

This immunity may apply also to animals other than the mother in only temporary possession of an infant. Thus in the Gibraltar macaque (*M. sylvana*) where, unlike the rhesus, males often interact with infants, males sometimes seem to use babies as a "passport" for approaching another animal in tense situations. The approaching male is usually the subordinate of the two (Deag and Crook, 1968). Similarly in the baboon (*Papio anubis*) Ransom and Ransom (1968) found that a male's possession of an infant may temporarily enhance his dominance status. Similar behavior occurs in *P. hamadryas* (Kummer, 1968).

INTERACTION BETWEEN THE INFANT AND THE SOCIAL COMPANION AFFECTS SOCIAL RELATIONS OF OTHER TROOP MEMBERS

The presence of an infant may affect not only the interactions of its (temporary or permanent) possessor with others, but also the interrelations among those others. A simple case is the competition among other females for proximity to the mother: this is seen frequently in captive groups of rhesus and other species. A more complex one concerns the protective role of adult males. In baboon troops the mothers and infants are usually near the adult males, and if danger threatens the latter are interposed between the females and its source. This effect of the mother–infant pair on others may be specific to particular individuals; thus an individual male baboon may stay close to a female with a young baby, moving when she moves (Hamburg, 1969) and acting as though ready to protect her.

TRIPARTITE RELATIONS

In the cases cited so far, the relations between two animals have been affected by a third. Here we are concerned with cases in which these individuals interact simultaneously in essentially different ways, each aiming its behavior at both of its partners (Kummer, 1967). For instance an infant, nestling against its mother and threatening an aggressor; the mother, protecting the infant and threatening the aggressor; and the aggressor, threatening the mother and trying to seize the infant, form such a relationship. We shall return to this case shortly.

The ways in which one animal may affect the relations between others listed above refer only to cases in which infants are concerned; many other types of effect occur in primate troops—cooperative action by two individuals against a third, aggression redirected from one animal to another, leading of one animal by another by "consent" of a third (e.g., Kummer, 1968), and so on. But the focus here is on development, and it is clear that any of the effects mentioned above may affect, directly or indirectly, the infant's social development. Detailed evidence in support of this view is, however, likely to be difficult to obtain. While it has been shown that gross social deprivation may affect development (Harlow and Harlow, 1965; Sackett, 1968), and there is strong evidence that partial deprivation may also have long-term effects (see also Spencer-Booth, 1969), to demonstrate that the interaction of an infant with a social companion may be so influenced by another social companion that the infant's development is affected requires techniques more sophisticated than those in use at present.

In the absence of experimental evidence, Kummer's descriptive data (1968) on the manner in which the tripartite relationship between infant, mother, and aggressor may affect subsequent social behavior is of the greatest interest. In the hamadryas baboon a subadult male often forms the center of a play group; the juveniles run to him and clasp him if disturbed. Since the infant, by threatening the aggressor, can induce the male to do likewise, the male is playing the maternal role in the tripartite relationship described earlier. Later, when females form a consort relationship with a male, he again plays a maternal role and the female an infant one with respect to aggressors. Thus the mother–infant–aggressor tripartite relationship is repeated in the play groups and again in the one-male groups which form a basic unit in hamadryas society. It seems at least reasonable to suppose that each stage in this sequence has a causal influence on the next.

Summary

In development, continuous change may give rise to differences in kind.

Classification of development into stages, of the factors which affect development, and of the processes involved, is an essential tool, but the limits of the usefulness of the categories used must always be borne in mind.

The analysis of development must be accompanied by resynthesis to assess the relations between the parts and the adequacy of the initial analysis.

The formation of particular individual relationships may be important in development.

Measures of social behavior nearly always depend on the behavior of two or more individuals. It is necessary to tease apart the role of these individuals in bringing about changes or differences in the measures.

The concept of "role" is likely to be useful in the study of social groups if statistical and semantic difficulties can be overcome.

The relationships within a social group form an intricate nexus, change in any one part of which may have ramifying consequences.

ACKNOWLEDGMENTS

I am grateful to P. P. B. Bateson and Yvette Spencer-Booth for their comments on the manuscript. The work was supported by the Royal Society and the Medical Research Council.

REFERENCES

Ainsworth, M. D. S. (1967). "Infancy in Uganda: Infant Care and the Growth of Attachment." Johns Hopkins Press, Baltimore, Maryland.
Bateson, P. P. G. (1964). Changes in the activity of isolated chicks over the first week after hatching. *Anim. Behav.* Vol. 12, 490–492.
Bateson, P. P. G. (1966). The characteristics and context of imprinting. *Biol. Rev.* Vol. 41, 177–220.
Bateson, P. P. G., and Reese, E. P. (1968). Reinforcing properties of conspicuous objects before imprinting has occurred. *Psychon. Sci.* Vol. 10, 379–380.
Bernstein, I. S., and Sharpe, L. G. (1966). Social roles in a rhesus monkey group. *Behaviour* Vol. 26, 91–104.
Bowlby, J. (1969). "Attachment and Loss," Vol. I. Hogarth, London.
Brackbill, Y. (1958). Extinction of the smiling response in infants as a function of reinforcement schedule. *Child Develop.* Vol. 29, 115–124.
Deag, J., and Crook, J. (1968). Personal communication.
Gartlan, J. S. (1968). Structure and function in primate society. *Folia Primat.* Vol. 8, 89–120.
Gunther, M. (1955). Instinct and the nursing couple. *Lancet* 575–578.
Hamburg, D. A. (1969). Observations of mother-infant interactions in primate field studies. *In* "Determinants of Infant Behaviour" (B. M. Foss, ed.), Vol. 4, pp. 3–14. Methuen, London.
Hansen, E. W. (1966). The development of maternal and infant behaviour in the rhesus monkey. *Behaviour* Vol. 27, 107–149.
Harlow, H. F., and Harlow, M. K. (1965). The affectional systems. *In* "Behavior of Nonhuman Primates" (A. M. Schrier, H. F. Harlow, and F. Stollnitz, eds.) Vol. 2, pp. 287–334. Academic Press, New York.
Harlow, H. F., and Harlow, M. K. (1969). Effects of various mother-infant relationships on rhesus monkey behavior. *In* "Determinants of Infant Behaviour" (B. M. Foss, ed.), Vol. 4, pp. 15–36. Methuen, London.
Harlow, H. F., and Zimmermann, R. R. (1959). Affectional responses in the infant monkey. *Science* Vol. 130, 421–432.
Hayes, C. (1951). "The Ape in our House." Harper, New York.
Held, R., and Bauer, J. (1967). Visually guided reaching in infant monkeys after restricted rearing. *Science* Vol. 155, 718–720.
Hinde, R. A. (1966). "Animal Behavior: A Synthesis of Ethology and Comparative Psychology." McGraw-Hill, New York.
Hinde, R. A. (1969). Analysing the roles of the partners in a behavioural interaction–mother-infant relations in rhesus macaques. *Ann. N. Y. Acad.* Vol. 159, 651–667.
Hinde, R. A. (1971). The development of social behaviour. *In* "The Behavior of Nonhuman Primates" (A. M. Schrier, H. F. Harlow, and F. Stollnitz, eds.), Vol. 3. Academic Press, New York.
Hinde, R. A., and Spencer-Booth, Y. (1967). The effect of social companions on mother-infant relations in rhesus monkeys. *In* "Primate Ethology" (D. Morris, ed.), pp. 267–268. Aldine, Chicago, Illinois.
Hines, M. (1942). The development and regression of reflexes, postures and progression in the young macaque. *Contrib. Embryol. Carnegie Inst.* Vol. 30, 153–209.

Jay, P. (1963). Mother-infant relations in langurs. *In* "Maternal Behavior in Mammals" (H. L. Rheingold, ed.), pp. 282–304. Wiley, New York.
Jensen, G. D., Bobbitt, R. A., and Gordon, B. N. (1968). Effects of environment on the relationship between mother and infant pigtailed monkeys (*Macaca nemestrina*). *J. Comp. Physiol. Psychol.* Vol. 66, 259–263.
Klinghammer, E. (1967). Factors influencing choice of mate in altricial birds. *In* "Early Behavior: Comparative and Developmental Approaches" (H. W. Stevenson, E. H. Hess, and H. L. Rheingold, eds.), pp. 5–42. Wiley, New York.
Kummer, H. (1967). Tripartite relations in Hamadryas baboons. *In* "Social Communication among Primates" (S. A. Altmann, ed.), pp. 63–72. Univ. of Chicago Press, Chicago, Illinois.
Kummer, H. (1968). Two variations in the social organization of baboons. *In* "Primates" (P. C. Jay, ed.), pp. 293–312. Holt, New York.
Lewis, D., and Burke, C. J. (1949). The use and misuse of the Chi-square test. *Psychol. Bull.* Vol. 46, 433–489.
Lorenz, K. (1935). Der Kumpan in der Umwelt des Vogels. *J. Ornith.* Vol. 83, 137–213, and 289–413.
Mason, W. A. (1965). The social development of monkeys and apes. *In* "Primate Behavior" (I. DeVore, ed.), pp. 514–543. Holt, New York.
Mason, W. A. (1967). Motivational aspects of social responsiveness in young chimpanzees. *In* "Early Behavior: Comparative and Developmental Approaches" (H. W. Stevenson, E. H. Hess, and H. L. Rheingold, eds.), pp. 103–126. Wiley, New York.
Meier, G. W. (1965). Other data on the effects of social isolation during rearing upon adult reproductive behaviour in the rhesus monkey (*Macaca mulatta*). *Anim. Behav.* Vol. 13, 228.
Piaget, J., and Inhelder, B. (1966). "La psychologie de l'enfant." Presses Univ. de France, Paris.
Prechtl, H. F. R. (1956). Die Entwicklung und Eigenart fruhkindlicher Bewegungsweisen. *Klin. Wochenschr.* Vol. 34, 281–284.
Prechtl, H. F. R. (1958). The directed head turning response and allied movements of the human baby. *Behaviour* Vol. 13, 212–242.
Ransom, T., and Ransom, B. (1968). Personal communication.
Rowell, T. E. (1966). Hierarchy in the organization of a caged baboon troop. *Anim. Behav.* Vol. 14, 430–443.
Rowell, T. E., Hinde, R. A., and Spencer-Booth, Y. (1964). "Aunt"-infant interaction in captive rhesus monkeys. *Anim. Behav.* Vol. 12, 219–226.
Sackett, G. P. (1968). The persistence of abnormal behaviour in monkeys following isolation rearing. *In* "The Role of Learning in Psychotherapy" (R. Porter, ed.), pp. 3–25. Churchill, London.
Schaffer, H. R., and Emerson, P. E. (1964). The development of social attachments in infancy. *Monogr. Soc. Res. Child Develop.* Vol. 29, No. 3, 1–77.
Schneirla, T. C. (1965). Aspects of stimulation and organization in approach/withdrawal processes underlying vertebrate behavioral development. *In* "Advances in the Study of Behavior" (D. S. Lehrman, R. A. Hinde, and E. Shaw, eds.), Vol. 1, pp. 1–74. Academic Press, New York.
Schneirla, T. C., and Rosenblatt, J. S. (1961). Behavioral organisation and genesis of the social bond in insects and mammals. *Amer. J. Orthopsychiat.* Vol. 31, 223–253.
Sluckin, W. (1964). "Imprinting and Early Learning." Methuen, London.

Spencer-Booth, Y. (1968a). The behaviour of group companions towards rhesus monkey infants. *Anim. Behav.* Vol. 16, 541–557.

Spencer-Booth, Y. (1968b). The behaviour of twin rhesus monkeys and comparisons with the behaviour of single infants. *Primates* Vol. 9, 75–84.

Spencer-Booth, Y. (1969). The effects of rearing rhesus monkey infants in isolation with their mothers on their subsequent behaviour in a group situation. *Mammalia* Vol. 33, 80–86.

Spencer-Booth, Y., and Hinde, R. A. (1967). The effects of separating rhesus monkey infants from their mothers for six days. *J. Child Psychol. Psychiat.* Vol. 7, 179–197.

Thorpe, W. H. (1963). "Learning and Instinct in Animals." Methuen, London.

Warriner, C. C., Lemmon, W. S., and Ray, T. S. (1963). Early experience as a variable in mate selection. *Anim. Behav.* Vol. 11, 221–224.

White, B. L. (1970). Child development research: An edifice without a foundation. *Merrill-Palmer Quart.* (in press).

White, B. L., and Held, R. (1966). Plasticity of sensorimotor development in the human infant. *In* "The Causes of Behavior: Readings in Child Development and Educational Psychology" (J. F. Rosenblith and W. Allinsmith, eds.). Allyn & Bacon, Boston, Massachusetts.

DIVERSITY IN THE STUDY OF THE DEVELOPMENT OF SOCIAL BEHAVIOR

C. G. BEER

"Social," "social behavior," and "sociality" are terms which have been used to refer to a variety of phenomena. Hence they are difficult terms to define. Any proposed definitions will probably encompass both too much and too little to be consistent with all instances of scientific usage, let alone common usage. For example, we might define "social behavior" as any behavior by one individual that is directed at or elicited by at least one other individual of the same species. Then we should have to say that social behavior is to be found in all animal phyla, with the possible exception of the sponges, even though many of the instances are outside the range of what students of social behavior have concerned themselves with. However, we should have to regard as nonsocial such behavior as that which occurs between a cuckoo chick and its foster parent, the interspecific communication of alarm signals that occurs in some mixed groups of birds and mammals, and the vocal mimicry that crosses species lines, even though this behavior may have obvious affinities to behavior we do call social which are more relevant to the study of particular social phenomena than are the affinities selected in our definition.

This problem about definition may be dismissed as a trivial semantic matter. Yet it illustrates a point about the present state of the study of social behavior. The science in its present state is more a science of particulars than a science of universals. The diversity of social phenomena has so far defied the hope that its study can be unified by general laws. To be sure, there are questions, and even theories, that can be applied to all instances of social behavior, but these, like the definitions, turn out to be so narrow that they apply to only restricted aspects of the behavior and so broad that they apply to many other biological phenomena as well. Such is the case as far as the matter of evolution is concerned.

But evolution suggests one reason why the comparative study of social behavior has had only very limited success in finding other kinds of unifying principles for its subject. Evolution has generated both diversity and change. Consequently the earth is populated by an immense variety of forms of life which differ to varying degrees from one another in the patterns of organization. Now the evolution of an organism depends upon the selection pressures to which the organism is subjected and the kind of thing that organism happens to be. Even if the selection pressures acting on two different kinds of organism were the same, the evolutionary outcomes would probably be quite different because of the differences in what selection had to select from. To exemplify the point consider the arthropods and vertebrates. In structural organization and other characteristics these two phyla differ markedly from one another, and the origins of these differences occurred so far back in time that neither the fossil record nor comparative anatomy has been able to settle questions about them. But in both phyla we find similar evolutionary accomplishments: for example, pattern vision, terrestrial life, powered flight, and social organization complex enough to be called society. Comparison, however, shows that in the case of each of these accomplishments the means evolved were different in the arthropods and vertebrates in accordance with the differences between arthropod and vertebrate patterns of organization and intricate relationships between structure and function. For example insect and mammalian societies appear to be built upon profoundly different principles (see Schneirla and Rosenblatt, 1961), and these differences can probably be related to differences in the structure and physiology of insect and mammalian nervous systems consequent, at least in part, on the different limitations on body size imposed on the two kinds of animals by their skeletal, respiratory, and circulatory arrangements (see Vowles, 1961). In general, evolution has probably given rise to as much diversity in processes controlling behavior as in patterns of anatomical organization. Hence the search for universal laws of social behavior is liable to be frustrated in the way that the search for a single archetypal plan to which all animal forms could be related was frustrated for anatomists in the early 19th century (see Russell, 1916).

But diversity is apparent even when one contemplates the social behavior of a single species. Since our business is with developmental aspects of social behavior, consider the various aspects of the social behavior of a species that can be looked at from a developmental point of view. We can focus on the individual and observe the emergence of its ability to produce and to respond to social signals "appropriately" and examine the processes that effect the transitions from what is present earlier to what is present later. We can focus on the relationships between parents and offspring and observe the progressive changes which take place as the offspring increase in age, and we can attempt to sort out the determinants and consequences of these changes. We can follow the development of social organization or structure in newly formed or reconstituted groups, as in the case of territory formation at the beginning of the breeding season and flock formation at the end of the breeding season in many species of birds.

Of course it would be a mistake to assume that there are no connections between these various aspects of social development in a species. The different focuses of study which isolate them should be regarded as complementary rather than incompatible; each has its limitations if anything like a total picture of the social behavior of a species is to be hoped for. Nevertheless particular questions have to be studied one at a time, and the concepts and methods appropriate to one may be inappropriate to others. At any rate studies of particular aspects of social development have tended to proceed in isolation from one another; particular phenomena and questions arising from them have emerged to prominence to the neglect of others or their relationship to the total complex of which they are parts. The phenomenon of imprinting, for example, has become the subject of a body of research which in some respects has tended to become progressively esoteric and divorced from questions about how imprinting is integrated with other aspects of social development. Some of this research has been generated by questions that have arisen about details of experimental method and apparatus design, and these questions are remote from similarly self-generated questions in research on, for example, the development of hierarchical organization in groups and territoriality. That rapprochement is possible is indicated by imprinting studies which have attempted to relate imprinting to the broader subject of perceptual learning (e.g., Sluckin, 1962; Sluckin and Salzen, 1961; Bateson, 1966) and other attempts to fit imprinting into broad theories of behavioral development (e.g., Moltz, 1960, 1963; Schneirla, 1965). It is an open question, however, whether the total diversity of social phenomena in even a single species has yet been sufficiently explored for a rigorous comprehensive theory of social development to be built. For each of the aspects of social development that I have listed our knowledge is fragmentary and divided by differences of concept and method. The study of social behavior has yet to receive its first "universally received paradigm" (Kuhn, 1962).

However, to say that the study of social behavior is at present a science of particulars rather than a science of universals is not to say that it goes its way in a theoretical vacuum. No science does at any stage of its history. Every study is informed by some preconceptions about what is worth attending to in the subject of study, what kinds of questions are important and what kinds of answers are to be expected, and what methods of study are appropriate (for a vigorous discussion of this point, see Popper, 1959). But students of social behavior have not all shared the same preconceptions. Differences in preconceptions underlying different studies have contributed to the diversity which is our subject. An understanding of these differences in preconceptions might therefore elucidate some of this diversity. To this end the remainder of this essay will be concerned mainly with such differences of preconceptions and their sources and the kinds of influences on the study of social development that they have had and might still have. Of necessity I shall have to be selective, and I have chosen to confine myself to discussion of some examples from the study of the developmental aspects of social communication.

Conceptions of the development of social communication and conceptions of social development in general will obviously tend to be closely bound to one another. The concepts of communication and sociality can be held apart only in abstraction. Cherry (1957) has defined communication as ". . . the establishment of a social unit from individuals by the use of language or signs"; and Barnett (1967) has pointed out the common etymological root of the words "communication" and "community." Nevertheless the history of studies of social communication shows divergence from as well as convergence or integration with other branches of social behavior study, the direction of the trend depending upon whether the ideas informing the studies were based on conceptions of social behavior (or behavior in general) or on conceptions of communication. I shall attempt to illustrate both types of influence in two very different schools of behavior study: behaviorism and ethology.

By behaviorism I mean the doctrines and practice in animal learning studies that stem from J. B. Watson's behaviorist manifesto of 1913. Watson's doctrines provided the first major influence in this century to affect thinking about the development of social communication; they had repercussions in all parts of psychology. There is no need to go into details about the methodological and conceptual innovations that Watsonian behaviorism brought into vogue. Their influences on the investigations and conceptions of behavioral development, including the development of social communication, are still with us. In fact, however, this behaviorism has not directly inspired very much actual work on the development of communication in animals, apart from its powerful influence in the study of language acquisition in man. At least some behaviorists would probably say that such work is unnecessary for an understanding of how communication behavior develops. If, as they would maintain, all behavior develops according to the same principles—namely the functions relating frequencies and contingencies of stimuli, responses, and reinforcements—then it is immaterial what kind of behavior or what kind of animal one chooses to study to discover these principles. The choice will be a matter of convenience. Even Skinner's book (1957) *Verbal Behavior* is based more on studies of laboratory rats working for food reward in Skinner boxes than on studies of what goes on when people talk to one another (for a critique of the argument of this book, see Chomsky, 1959).

If this behaviorist view were correct, then the scope of my subject would be much narrower than the view I take of it. But diversity and complexity have developed within behaviorism itself. For example, behavioristically informed studies of verbal learning have tended to become progressively esoteric, partly because of increasing involvement with problems peculiar to language (e.g., the meaning of "meaning"), and partly because much of the research consists of variations of a few themes, variations which have become increasingly subtle but the point of which has become increasingly obscure to the uninitiated or uncommitted. In any case the doctrine that differences between organisms and between types of behavior can be ignored in the study of behavioral development, and the doctrine that all behavioral development can be explained as respondent or operant conditioning, have been vigorously challenged by psychologists, linguists, and biologists.

Comparative ethology began taking issue with behaviorism on these points in the late 1930's. Nothing could be more different than the parentages of behaviorism and ethology. Behaviorism was sired by Russian physiology on psychological associationism with some midwifery from positivist philosophy. Ethology came from a union of the comparative tradition in zoology with the amateur tradition in natural history, perhaps with some help from Kant. It is not surprising therefore that ethology has opposed the doctrines of behaviorism with doctrines that are their contradictories (see Lorenz, 1950). From the outset ethology concerned itself with the particular features of the behavior patterns of different species and attempted to account for them in terms of evolutionary adaptation and evolutionary origins. The species-specific and stereotyped character, narrowly selective responsiveness to stimuli, and involved functional integration of much social behavior in animals, together with the evidence for evolutionary interpretations (see Tinbergen, 1953), implied for the ethologists writing in the 1940's and early 1950's that the development of behavior in most animals must to a large extent be controlled genetically and independently of the vicissitudes of the environment or individual experience. They maintained that the effects of experience, if any, are overlaid on genetically determined structures that develop "maturationally," and that these effects are themselves subject to constraints that the genes impose, e.g., on the kinds of experience that can affect behavioral development and on the stages of development at which they can have their effects (see Tinbergen, 1951). Lorenz (e.g., 1937) wrote of "instinct-training interlocking" to account for the development and integration of variable and rigid components of behavior patterns, but the role he assigned to training was played on a stage directed by the genes. Likewise Tinbergen's hierarchical theory of instinct (Tinbergen, 1951) was to a large extent preformationistic in its implications about behavioral development.

Like behaviorism, however, ethology, in its early years, appears to have been less inclined to do research on questions of behavioral development than to draw conclusions about them from indirect arguments or general principles. For instance, although there was some investigation of developmental aspects of social communication—some of Tinbergen's work on "releasers" for example (e.g., Tinbergen and Kuenen, 1939)—one looks in vain for even a single descriptive study of the whole course of development of a display pattern, let alone experimental study of the processes molding the transitions from stage to stage in such development. It appears that facts about the taxonomic distribution and adaptive correlation of variety in social behavior patterns, and so on, were regarded as sufficient premises for the inference that in their essential organization social communication patterns are innate in the sense that their development is controlled by genetic processes, the environment providing only the conditions in which these processes can operate. And there, for the most part, the matter was left.

The argument from facts pertinent to questions about the evolution and adaptiveness of behavior—even facts about the heredity of behavior patterns—to conclusions about individual behavioral development is weak however. Part of its persuasiveness depends upon ambiguity in the notion of innateness: "innate" is used in the sense of genetically inherited (when the distribution among individuals of the variations of a character are believed to reflect the distribution of genetic variations rather than variations of environment) and in the sense of genetically controlled (when it is believed that the processes of development in an individual are caused and patterned entirely by the genome without any contribution from or interaction with the environment, apart from its role in providing the conditions in which these processes can take place). It has been pointed out in numerous criticisms of the early ethological position on questions of behavioral development that facts about heredity do not carry any precise entailments about processes of development (for a recent discussion, see Lehrman, 1970). Initially such criticisms tended to be interpreted by ethologists as arguments for the behaviorist position that all behavior is learned. In fact Beach (1955), Hebb (1953), Schneirla (1956), and Lehrman (1953) were arguing against both sides of the nature–nurture question; their position was that thinking of individual development in terms of an exclusive dichotomy between instinct and experience is logically dubious and heuristically constraining. In their view the way to knowledge about the processes of behavioral development can only be through study of behavioral development, not through study of heredity, adaptation, evolution, or even motivation.

This point is now accepted by many, if not most, ethologists (however, see Lorenz, 1961, 1965). Ethological studies of development of social communication patterns are multiplying, although there are still too few for any synthesis of facts and ideas to have emerged in a generally accepted comprehensive theory. The work so far has revealed complexities which the older ideas about the instinctual component of development did little to prepare one for. I shall describe a recent example to illustrate the kind of work that is being done and the kinds of results that are being obtained.

Marler and a group of students at Berkeley studied song development in the white-crowned sparrow *Zonotrichia leucophrys* (the work is summarized in Marler and Hamilton, 1967). The study began with the observation that different populations of the sparrows have discernibly different song dialects (Marler and Tamura, 1962). This observation posed the question of how a sparrow develops the song type of the population from which it comes. Marler and his associates pursued the question by hand raising birds taken from the parents as nestlings and manipulating their auditory experience. Some of the birds were raised, either singly or in small groups, in acoustic isolation from all sounds except those they themselves produced. The period of acoustic isolation was varied, in duration and timing with respect to the developmental age of the birds, between different groups. Other birds were subjected to playback of "tutoring" sounds, either recordings of the dialect of the population from which they came or recordings of the dialect of another population or recordings of the song of a different species, and again the time when these sounds were presented, was varied between experimental groups. Finally, some birds were surgically deafened, the operation being performed at different stages of song development, or after different types of auditory experience, in different birds.

The results of these experiments showed that no simple answer can be given to the question of whether the song of the white-crowned sparrow is innate or learned. The dialect that a bird acquires depends upon what white-crowned sparrow dialect was sung to it between the age of about 2 weeks and the age of about 2 months. If a bird is kept alone in continuous acoustic isolation until song develops, the song that then emerges has certain features that identify it as white crowned-sparrow song, but it lacks the kind of detail that distinguishes one dialect from another. Birds deafened early in life develop songs which are highly variable and which possess little that would enable one to recognize them as productions of a white-crowned sparrow. So, clearly, experience plays a profound role in song development in these birds, experience of the sounds they hear the birds around them making and experience of hearing their own voices. Yet tutoring with songs of species other than the white-crowned sparrow had no influence on song development in Marler's birds, even when the tutoring song was one very like that of a white-crowned sparrow (the song of Harris' sparrow *Zonotrichia querula*). Apparently, there are quite specific constraints on the learning process here which prevent acquisition of any but the species-specific song type. The deafening studies (Konishi, 1965) revealed something about how experience of song during the first 2 months of life has its effect on song development. If the deafening is effected after appropriate auditory experience during the first 2 months but before the bird itself begins to sing, the song that eventually emerges is as poor a version of white-crowned sparrow song as that of birds deafened early in life without any training experience. If, however, the deafening is carried out after a bird has developed a full species-specific or population-specific song, it continues to produce this song and the effects of the deafening appear only gradually, after some weeks or months, and then only as slight deviations from the acquired pattern.

These results have given rise to the idea that during its first 2 months a sparrow acquires an auditory "template" of the song dialect of its social group and learns to produce this song itself by matching and correcting its own vocalizations against the "template" as its voice matures. After full song has developed in this way, either further "template" matching is unnecessary for its preservation or the function of the auditory "template" can be taken over by a proprioceptive "template" acquired by a bird in the practice of singing its own song. This theory is an elegant application to development of some of the features of the reafference principle of von Holst (von Holst and Mittelstaedt, 1950; von Holst, 1954). The notion of a "template" is, of course, an open one which must wait neurophysiological study to acquire closure (cf. Kaplan, 1964).

This story about song development in the white-crowned sparrow cannot, however, be generalized to other species. Similar studies of other species have revealed exceptions to each of its particulars. Many birds develop normal song even when raised alone in acoustic isolation from all sound except those they make themselves (for examples, see Thorpe, 1961; Marler, 1963; Marler and Hamilton, 1967; however, some of the evidence has recently been called into question by Konishi and Nottebohm, 1969). In some birds the period during which effects of heard song on song development can be demonstrated extends through the first year of life [e.g., the chaffinch *Fringilla coelebs* (Poulsen, 1951; Thorpe, 1958)] or throughout life [e.g., the canary *Serinus c. carnarius* (Poulsen, 1959) and the European blackbird *Turdus merula* (Thielke-Polz and Thielke, 1960)]; and in some cases the sounds imitated can be those of other species of birds [e.g., the bullfinch *Pyrrhula pyrrhula* (Nicolai, 1956, 1959)] or a wide range of other sounds (for chapters on vocal mimicry in birds, see Armstrong, 1963; Thorpe, 1961). The effects of early deafening on vocal development have been found to be much less pronounced in some species [e.g., Oregon juncos *Junco oreganus*, Mexican juncos *Junco phaeonotus*, and domestic fowl *Gallus domesticus* (Konishi, 1963, 1964)] than in the white-crowned sparrow.

Such variation in the details of song development in birds illustrates the difficulties in the way of explaining all social behavior in terms of a single developmental theory, and the need for observation and experiment on many species before such explanation is attempted. Indeed it may be that only an evolutionary approach can provide a synthesis of all the facts about song development in birds since it is conceivable that evolution may have given rise to several fundamentally different types of developmental process which can be collectively explained only in terms of phylogenetic origins and natural selection. But even this approach requires more knowledge of how development proceeds in different species, and how it is related to species ecology and life history, than we at present possess.

The limitations of these studies of song development for broad generalizations about the development of social communication can be seen from another viewpoint. The studies of song development I have referred to were directed at only one kind of question about the development of vocal communication in birds, namely: what determines the development of the motor patterns manifest in the production of song? But song serves as a medium of social communication, which implies that its employment conveys information about the singer to a recipient which acts upon the information. So a complete account of the developmental aspects of bird song would have to include consideration of how a bird comes to produce its song only when it is in a certain state or in a certain situation, and also consideration of how birds come to respond to the song in the specific ways in which they do.

These aspects of the development of vocal communication in birds have been studied in a variety of ways and in a variety of species. Descriptive studies have attempted to trace the developmental history of vocal and other communication patterns by observation of individuals from nestling stages to adulthood and to correlate this developmental history with evidence of the development of motivational systems [e.g., Moynihan on gulls (1959) and Kruijt on jungle fowl (1964)]. Experiments in which juvenile birds were treated with sex hormones have provided evidence that changes in the concentration of sex hormones in the blood are implicated in the development of calls and other displays that serve communicatory function in reproductive behavior [e.g., Boss (1943) on the herring gull *Larus argentatus* and Hamilton (1938) and Andrew (1963, 1969) on domestic fowl)]. Effects of early auditory experience have been demonstrated in studies of the development in young birds of approach responses manifesting species or individual recognition of parental calls (e.g., Gottlieb, 1966; Tschanz, 1968).

Important as such studies as these are within their particular contexts of research, however, they have not provided anything like a full understanding of the developmental processes underlying vocal communication in any species. Indeed there may be some students of social communication in animals who are of the opinion that in just those respects in which the vocal and other social behavior of a species can be said to constitute a communication system (e.g., in the extent to which it involves the encoding and decoding of content in signals), it has escaped close analysis from a developmental point of view. However, there might also be some disagreement about what the objects of such analysis should be. For the questions we ask about the development of a social communication system are predicated on our conception of that system. Conceptions of social communication systems have changed as new facts and new ideas have come to light, and the issues that have arisen seem far from being settled. To illustrate what I have in mind I shall return to the matter of preconceptions with some remarks about different conceptions of communication systems and how they pose different questions for a developmental approach to social communication.

The instinct theories of Lorenz and Tinbergen pictured social communication in animals as essentially a system of displays and responses innately tuned to one another: performance of a display by one animal acts as a "releaser" for the "innate releasing mechanism" for a specific response pattern in the recipient. Variations of "motivational state" could modulate the form or intensity of a display or the output from an innate releasing mechanism so that a certain amount of variability in social interactions was allowed for. However, the conception of this system was based largely on observations of rigidly stereotyped and species-characteristic types of social interactions, and assumptions of innateness and endogenous control. Hence, the developmental and motivational aspects of social communication tended to be viewed through the idea of instinctual fixity.

Later ethological studies of social interactions have shown that fixity in the sequential patterning of social interactions is by no means the rule. A particular display or display component in the repertoire of an animal may enter into a variety of combinations with other displays or components, and each combination may enter into a variety of interaction sequences [e.g., in the agonistic behavior of titmice (Stokes, 1962a,b)]. To cope with the variety and complexity that observation of interaction sequences has brought to light, ethologists have turned to such procedures as factor analysis (e.g., Wiepkema, 1961; Baerends *et al.,* 1962) and the mathematics of stochastic processes (e.g., Nelson, 1964; Altmann, 1965; Hazlett and Bossert, 1965).

The stochastic approach reflects part of the influence on animal behavior studies of information theory of the type developed by Shannon and Weaver (1949). The social behavior of a species is treated as if it consisted of the transitions between the items of a finite set of discrete events or states. One has first to sort out the items constituting the set of events or states and then estimate the transition probabilities for all ordered pairs or longer permutations of the items. The statistical properties of the communication system can then be further analyzed, for example for the presence of first- or higher-order Markov chains, the "quantity of information" conveyed by each item or sequence of items, and the degree of "redundancy" in the system. "Quantity of information" and "redundancy" here are used in the highly technical senses that have been attached to them in information theory. Measurement of these quantities has proved useful in some studies of animal communication, e.g., in the making of precise quantitative comparison between bees and ants as transmitters of information about direction and distance (Wilson, 1965).

The conception of social communication that is implied by and which emerges from stochastic analysis of behavior sequences sets what from other viewpoints must seem limited and narrow questions for the student of social development, however. Developmental study informed by this approach would, presumably, be concerned with the emergence, during individual ontogeny or during the formation of social groups, of the discrete items constituting the finite set of social signals and responses and the establishment of the contingencies in the temporal patterning of mature social interactions. To my knowledge, the stochastic approach has not yet inspired such study. In any case there are problems about social communication and its development that the stochastic approach by itself does not touch but which are matters of concern for other approaches.

It has been remarked that information theory has nothing to do with information and is not a theory. At least the suggestion has been seriously made that "the phrase 'theory of information' . . . is perhaps a somewhat misleading one . . . a more reasonably descriptive name for this field of study might be 'statistical theory of signal transmission'" since "the semantic aspects of information are irrelevant" to it (Sluckin, 1954). The semantic aspects of information are relevant to the broader approach to communication that describes itself as the theory of signs or semiotic. According to Sebeok (1968), the American philosopher C. S. Pierce was "the real founder and first systematic investigator of semiotic"; but much of the recent application of the ideas of semiotic to the study of animal communication stems from the writings of Charles Morris (1938, 1946) and Colin Cherry (1957). For example, Morris introduced the division of semiotic into syntactics, semantics, and pragmatics which has been utilized by a number of students of animal communication (e.g., Marler, 1961; Smith, 1963, 1965, 1968). But semiotic and that part of it which deals with animal communication—zoosemiotic (Sebeok, 1965)—are still concerned mainly with matters of classification and conceptual framework; new terms and systems of categories have proliferated, but their scope has yet to be settled, and whether they will lead to a unified theory of social communication in animals remains to be seen. In the meantime we can expect that questions about the development of social communication will vary according to the conceptual framework of semiotic adopted and the scope that the elements of this framework are given.

Marler (1961) was perhaps the first ethologist to apply ideas from semiotic to the study of animal communication. He provided examples of how pragmatics and syntactics can be applied to animal communication: by observing the effect of a signal on the behavior of a recipient, one can observe the function that a signal serves in the communication system (pragmatics); and by investigation of the physical nature of signals, their temporal relationships to one another, and their accompaniments, one can work out the structural features of the communication system (syntactics). (Stochastic analysis of communication sequences obviously belongs in syntactics. However, Marler's discussion of the degree to which some signals are continuously variable suggests that the stochastic approach may have limited application even in this field.)

Marler also showed how facts about the function of signals and facts about their physical nature can be related to one another in ways that make sense from an evolutionary point of view. However, he declined to discuss semantics, except to comment that "semantics are of doubtful value in animal studies."

Marler did not concern himself, in this paper, with developmental aspects of animal communication. If he had he no doubt would have directed attention to questions about how specific responsiveness to signals develops, and questions about how the physical forms and syntactic connections of a signal emerge and are molded during development (cf. his work on song development discussed earlier); but since semantics appeared to him dubious in animal studies, he presumably would have ignored questions about the development of the connections in an animal between the signal it transmits and the state or situation it is in or whatever else it encodes in the signal.

Smith (1963, 1965, 1968) has attempted to study a semantic dimension in animal communication, although his conception of semantics may seem odd to a linguist. According to general usage, semantics is the study of meaning. But Smith, following Cherry (1957), has adopted the operational move of determining the meaning of a signal by observing the response of a recipient and so locating meaning in the pragmatic domain. The scope of semantics is restricted to what is encoded in a signal by its sender, and this (what is encoded) Smith has chosen to refer to as the message of the signal. According to Smith's conception of communication, the sender of a signal and its recipient must share a code in which the sender can encode a message and from which the recipient can extract a meaning. The message is "considered to represent some aspect (s) of the state (or central nervous state) of the communicator" (Smith, 1968, p. 46). But the meaning that a recipient extracts from a signal may be more than the sender puts into it. Smith has suggested (1968, p. 48) that meanings, in his sense, are not "derived simply from messages, but from messages *in contexts*."[1] Context here includes anything accompanying or present with the message that affects the receiver's reception of it, e.g., the receiver's state or status (e.g., its sex), and the circumstances in which communication is taking place. In this way Smith has provided a theoretical framework for such well known facts as the fact that the song of an unmated but territory-holding male bird can serve both as an attractant to an unmated female in reproductive condition and as a repellent to a territory-seeking male. He has investigated the communication patterns of tyrannid flycatchers in some detail and found numerous

---

[1] My emphasis.

instances of displays that he believes encode a single message but which occur in a variety of contexts and, hence, convey a variety of meanings. The "kitter" call of the eastern kingbird (*Tyrannus tyrannus*) for example is used in five different kinds of situation, and this variation of context together with variation in the motivational states and so forth of recipient birds provides the call with a considerable variety of different meanings (for details see Smith, 1966). The call itself is variable in form (i.e., syntactically), but there appears to be little correlation between this variability and differences of situation or motivation of the calling bird. Smith has argued (1968, p. 52) that all occurrences of the call have one feature in common: the calling bird "is experiencing some internal conflict with a tendency to locomote," and this common feature he has taken to be the message of the display. In general, he has maintained, when a display occurs in more than one context and hence can convey more than one meaning, a "common denominator" can be found which is the message of the display. The range of messages encoded in the display repertoire will therefore be narrower than the range of meanings extracted from the displays.

Smith has not concerned himself with developmental aspects of communication, but his conception of communication systems obviously carries implications about what the questions for developmental study are. Investigation of the development of a social communication system will be divided between investigation of how messages are associated with signals and investigation of how meanings are associated with signals in contexts. Considerations of context will be relevant to the developmental study of the pragmatic aspect of the communication system but not to developmental study of the semantic aspect.

This last point may be questioned, however. Smith's notion of context includes so much that I think it can be applied to messages as well as meanings (in his senses of the terms). Consider the following example from my own studies (Beer, 1969). The "long-call' of the laughing gull (*Larus atricilla*) typically consists of at least four sections: one or two introductory disyllabic notes ("ke-hah"), a series of "short notes," a series of "long notes," and a series of "head toss notes." The numbers of each of these different types of notes vary from long-call to long-call: the number of "short notes" is more or less constant for an individual, and appears to be involved in the conveying of the identity of the calling bird; but the numbers of the other types of notes appear to depend upon the situation in which communication is taking place. For example, the longest strings of long notes are uttered when the mate or potential mate is coming in to land or has just landed beside the calling bird. In addition to their occurrence in the long-call, each of these different types of notes can occur in isolation from the others or in various other combinations with them. These calls of the laughing gull have not yet been subjected to the kind of detailed message-meaning analysis that Smith has given to his flycatchers, but they clearly provide material for such analysis. I suspect that such analysis will show that context will have to be taken into consideration in the investigation of the semantics as well as the pragmatics of the calls. If we suppose it to be the case that each of the types of notes in the long-call has associated with it a particular message, and that this message is the same whether it occurs as part of a long-call or not, then we shall have to consider the long-call as a string of messages or as a compound message. Either way, if we follow Smith, we shall have to assume in the long-calling bird a variety or complex of states (corresponding to the several messages ordered or compounded in the long-call); and the state corresponding to each message in the string or compound of messages expressed in the long-call can be considered as being in the context of the states corresponding to the other messages, in essentially the same way as the signal occurs in context for a recipient by virtue of the fact that "the signal comes as one of many simultaneous sensory inputs to the CNS" (Smith, 1965). Of course talk about "the state of the central nervous system" conveys little useful information here; indeed, it perhaps exposes one to the possibility of circular argument. In any case the notion of context can be usefully employed in discussion of social communication without raising neurophysiological hares.

At least in the case of the social displays of gulls I think there are two ways in which the notion of context can be applied to the behavior of the displaying bird. In the first place there are numerous displays which occur in a variety of sequences or combinations with other displays by the displaying bird and hence the meanings of which may be determined in part by the behavior of the displaying bird—the syntactic structure of its display sequences and compounds. The code that Smith assumes must be shared by the sender and receiver of a communicating pair may thus contain something analogous to the syntactic and semantic rules of a language. If such is the case then in this respect one will have to deal with contextual features in the production of a signal as well as with the contextual features that influence its reception. In the second place the selection by a displaying bird of the display, display sequence or display compound that it performs on any occasion will presumably be determined by much the same sorts of situational, motivational, and other contextual features that determine the response of a recipient: the display will be "context determined" (Manley, 1960) for the displayer, just as it is "context interpreted" by the recipient.

The study of the development of social communication may, therefore, at least in some cases, have to include concern with contextual features in the production of displays as well as with contextual features in response to displays, and with the degree to which and the manner in which these contextual features are shared by both senders and receivers of the displays.

I have mentioned the possibility that analysis of animal communication, at least in some species, might reveal a structure of syntactic and semantic rules analogous to those of langauge. Both linguists and zoologists have concerned themselves with comparison of human language and animal communication in efforts to decide the question of whether the differences are differences of kind or degree (for example see de Laguna, 1963; Sturtevant, 1947; Hockett, 1960a,b; Altmann, 1967; Hockett and Altmann, 1968). Some support has been found for the view that no feature of human language is unique to it, which is perhaps not surprising since structural linguists and students of animal communication have to some extent approached their subjects with similar preconceptions about the organizations of the systems they study and the methods of analysis appropriate to them (for example stochastic analysis has been applied in the study of language and in the study of animal communication; cf. Hockett, 1955; Altmann, 1965).

However, the dominance of the structural approach in modern linguistics has been challenged. Approaches to language which went out of fashion toward the end of the 19th century have been revived or rediscovered by a group of scholars who describe their work as transformational linguistics, and this group has attacked some of the basic premises of structural linguistics (for a discussion of the differences between structural and transformational linguistics see Chomsky, 1964). Whereas structural linguistics regards the study of language as the working out of the inventory of elements of which a language consists and the assigning of these elements to categories corresponding to their phonetic, syntactic, and semantic functions, transformational linguistics approaches language from the point of view (Chomsky, 1964, p. 61) that

> serious investigation of language use and acquisition presupposes a study of underlying generative processes (for which, to be sure, actual performance will supply evidence), and that very little is to be expected of direct operational analysis of "mentalistic" terms or radical behavioristic reduction of the sort that has been so dominant in modern speculation on language and cognition.

This is not the place to go into the details of the issues that divide structural linguists and transformational linguists, but the differences of views about language acquisition are obviously relevant to our subject and so perhaps warrant brief comment.

The view of structural linguistics on language acquisition appears to be that a child learns a language by "some sort of process of stimulus–sentence conditioning or sentence–sentence association" (Chomsky, 1964), from which it should follow that language utterances and responses to language constitute a finite set for each individual determined by his or her experience. Opposing this view Chomsky has emphasized the "creative" aspect of language: the fact that I may now be uttering a sentence which neither I nor anybody else has uttered before and which you nevertheless have no difficulty understanding. According to Chomsky, this openness in the expression and comprehension of language transcends the limitations of the kind of linguistic behavior that any of the processes envisaged by behavioristic learning theories could conceivably establish, at least if anything like the putative operational meanings of the terms in these theories are preserved. Chomsky argues that the acquisition of language must depend upon the possession of some form of species-specific innate organization which interacts with the linguistic experience of the child to produce a system of rules in the mind, a generative grammar by means of which thought can be transformed into utterance and heard speech comprehended. The rules of this grammar are finite, but the faculties of expression and understanding which depend upon them are infinite in their capacities. In their research into linguistic structures Chomsky and the other transformational linguists have built a strong case for the existence of such a grammar underlying linguistic performance. The arguments that Chomsky brings against the adequacy of behavioristic learning theory to cope with language acquisition also seem to me to be sound. Whether he proposes a clear and positive alternative account of language acquisition, however, is another matter.

Chomsky's use of the term "innate" in his discussions of language acquisition appears to be no less ambiguous and no less open to criticism than Lorenz's. His argument for the innate basis of language, like those of the "Cartesian linguistics," in which he has found anticipations of the central themes of transformational linguistics (Chomsky, 1966), does not distinguish clearly between epistemological problems, ontogenetic problems, and problems having to do with the uniqueness of man. The relationships between these different kinds of problems are obscure, and, consequently, the notion of innateness that emerges from the argument is obscure. At least it can be said that it has not contributed anything positive to our understanding of linguistic development. If the transformational linguists are right in their conceptions of the structure of language and the generative processes that operate it, then only by developmental study will it be discovered how this structure and these processes arise during the life of an individual. Indeed Chomsky himself has said as much, although in the context of a criticism of a position other than his own (Chomsky, 1959, p. 43):

> The manner in which . . . factors operate in language acquisition is completely unknown. It is clear that what is necessary in such a case is research, not dogmatic and perfectly arbitrary claims, based on analogies to that small part of the experimental literature in which one happens to be interested.

The ideas of transformational linguistics should thus lead to some reorientation in the study of language acquisition. Indeed, such influence is already clear, for example in the work of Brown *et al.* (1968) and McNeill (1966a,b). These ideas may also lead to some reorientation in the study of the development of social communication in animals other than man, although Chomsky would apparently regard this suggestion with scepticism. Contrary to many other linguists, he has emphasized the distinctness of language from any known form of animal communication (Chomsky, 1966, p. 78):

> Each known animal communication system either consists of a fixed number of signals, each associated with a specific range of eliciting conditions or internal states, or a fixed number of "linguistic dimensions," each associated with a nonlinguistic dimension in the sense that selection of a point along one indicates a corresponding point along the other. In neither case is there any significant similarity to human language.

But I think it is true to say that the only kinds of "semantic" systems that have been sought in the social communication of animals are those that Chomsky mentions. It is at least possible that if the notions of deep and surface structure, generative and transformational processes, and so on, were applied to the analysis of some animal communication systems, our conceptions of these systems would be changed just as profoundly as the conception of language structure has been changed from the transformational viewpoint. My studies of the vocal behavior of the laughing gull have indicated complexity that neither of the kinds of system mentioned by Chomsky can accommodate easily but which might be accommodated by a system of rules at least analogous to those of a transformational grammar.[2] Such a reorientation would obviously affect the form that questions about the development of this behavior would take.

In this essay I have tried to show that the study of social develop-

---

[2] I am grateful to Mr. Max Snodderly of Rockefeller University for having drawn my attention to this possibility.

ment in animals is not a science unified by theory or even agreement about its subject matter. The diversity of social phenomena is vast and so, consequently, is the diversity of questions about social development which are presented for study. But our knowledge of this diversity is fragmentary. A reviewer of present knowledge finds himself reiterating a plea for more research. However, the diversity in the study of the development of social behavior in animals is a reflection of more than the fact that the social behavior of a particular species has many aspects, or the fact that the social patterns of different kinds of animals are as various as their patterns of anatomical structure. Different scientists view social behavior and its development in different ways. The differences dividing viewpoints have been deep, even to the point of involving questions of a philosophical or metaphysical nature. How, for example, is it to be decided whether the developing organism should be regarded as a stimulus–response machine, a stochastic process, or an agent whose actions are the expressions of intention (cf. Taylor, 1964)? Yet decisions on such questions must be at least tacitly made, and they will affect the kind of description we make of behavior and hence what we see to study in it.

The history of science suggests that the rightness of such decisions can be judged only in retrospect. The study of social behavior in animals is still in such flux that it would be foolhardy to be dogmatic about how we should view our subject. There is no formula for scientific discovery. Contrary to what Francis Bacon hoped, science is still dependent on "the sharpness and strength of men's wits"; but surely that is part of its fascination and challenge.

ACKNOWLEDGMENTS

I am grateful to Professor R. A. Hinde for his comments on the manuscript. The unpublished gull work referred to was supported by Grants GM 12774 and MH 16727 from the U. S. Public Health Service and a grant from the Rutgers University Research Council (07-2208) and was dependent upon the cooperation and hospitality of the U. S. Fish and Wildlife Service and the personnel of the Brigantine National Wildlife Refuge.

REFERENCES

Altmann, S. A. (1965). Sociobiology of rhesus monkeys. II. Stochastics of social communication. *J. Theor. Biol.* Vol. 8, 490–522.
Altmann, S. A. (1967). The structure of primate social communication. *In* "Social

Communication among Primates" (S. A. Altmann, ed.), p. 325. Univ. of Chicago Press, Chicago, Illinois.

Andrew, R. J. (1963). Effect of testosterone on the behavior of the domestic chick. *J. Comp. Physiol. Psychol.* Vol. 56, 933–940.

Andrew, R. J. (1969). The effects of testosterone on Avian vocalizations. In "Bird Vocalizations" (R. A. Hinde, ed.), p. 97. Cambridge Univ. Press, London and New York.

Armstrong, E. A. (1963). "A Study of Bird Song." Oxford Univ. Press, London and New York.

Baerends, G. P., and van der Cingel, N. A. (1962). On the phylogenetic origin of the snap display in the Common Heron (*Ardea cinerea* L.). *Symp. Zool. Soc. London* Vol. 8, 7–24.

Barnett, S. A. (1967). "Instinct and Intelligence." Prentice-Hall, Englewood Cliffs, New Jersey.

Bateson, P. P. G. (1966). The characteristics and context of imprinting. *Biol. Rev.* Vol. 41, 177–220.

Beach, F. A. (1955). The descent of instinct. *Psychol. Rev.* Vol. 62, 401–410.

Beer, C. G. (1969). Unpublished studies.

Boss, W. R. (1943). Hormonal determination of adult characters and sex behavior in Herring Gulls (*Larus argentatus*). *J. Exp. Zool.* Vol. 94, 181–209.

Brown, R., Cazden, C., and Belluga-Klima, V. (1968). The child's grammar from I to III. In "Minnesota Symposia on Child Psychology" (J. P. Hill, ed.), Vol. 2, pp. 28–73.

Cherry, C. (1957). "On Human Communication." Wiley, New York.

Chomsky, N. (1959). A review of B. F. Skinner's "Verbal Behavior." *Language* Vol. 35, 26–58.

Chomsky, N. (1964). Current issues in linguistic theory. In "The Structure of Language" (J. A. Fodor and J. J. Katz, eds.), p. 50. Prentice-Hall, Englewood Cliffs, New Jersey.

Chomsky, N. (1966). "Cartesian Linguistics." Harper, New York.

de Laguna, G. A. (1963). "Speech: Its Function and Development." Indiana Univ. Press, Bloomington, Indiana.

Gottlieb, G. (1966). Species identification by avian neonates: Contributory effect of perinatal auditory stimulation. *Anim. Behav.* Vol. 14, 282–290.

Hamilton, J. B. (1938). Precocious masculine behavior following administration of synthetic male hormone substance. *Endocrinology* Vol. 23, 53–57.

Hazlett, B. A., and Bossert, W. H. (1965). A statistical analysis of the aggressive communications systems of some hermit crabs. *Anim. Behav.* Vol. 13, 357–373.

Hebb, D. O. (1953). Heredity and environment in mammalian behavior. *Brit. J. Anim. Behav.* Vol. 1, 43–47.

Hockett, C. F. (1955). "A Manual of Phonology," Mem. II. Indiana Univ. Publ. Anthropol. Linguistics, Bloomington, Indiana.

Hockett, C. F. (1960a). Logical considerations in the study of animal communication. In "Animal Sounds and Communication" (W. E. Lanyon and W. N. Tavolga, eds.), p. 392. Am. Inst. Biol. Sci., Washington, D. C.

Hockett, C. F. (1960b). The origin of speech. *Sci. Amer.* Vol. 203, 89–96.

Hockett, C. F., and Altmann, S. A. (1968). A note on design features. In "Animal Communication" (T. A. Sebeok, ed.), p. 61. Indiana Univ. Press, Bloomington, Indiana.

Kaplan, A. (1964). "The Conduct of Inquiry." Chandler, San Francisco, California.

Konishi, M. (1963). The role of auditory feedback in the vocal behavior of the domestic fowl. *Z. Tierpsychol.* Vol. 20, 249–267.

Konishi, M. (1964). Effects of deafening on song development in two species of juncos. *Condor* Vol. 66, 85–102.

Konishi, M. (1965). The role of auditory feedback in the control of vocalization in the white-crowned sparrow. *Z. Tierpsychol.* Vol. 22, 770–783.

Konishi, M., and Nottebohm, F. (1969). Experimental studies in the ontogeny of avian vocalizations. *In* "Bird Vocalizations" (R. A. Hinde, ed.), p. 29. Cambridge Univ. Press, London and New York.

Kruijt, J. P. (1964). Ontogeny of social behavior in Burmese Red Jungle fowl. *Behaviour* Suppl. 12.

Kuhn, T. S. (1962). "The Structure of Scientific Revolutions." Chicago Univ. Press, Chicago, Illinois.

Lehrman, D. S. (1953). A critique of Konrad Lorenz's theory of instinctive behavior. *Quart. Rev. Biol.* Vol. 28, 337–363.

Lehrman, D. S. (1970). Semantic and conceptual issues in the nature-nurture problem. *In* "Development and Evolution of Behavior" (L. R. Aronson *et al.*, eds.), p. 17. Freeman, San Francisco, California.

Lorenz, K. Z. (1937). Uber die Bildung des Instinktbegriffes. *Naturwissenschaften* Vol. 25, 289–300, 307–318, and 324–331.

Lorenz, K. Z. (1950). The comparative method in studying innate behavior patterns. *Symp. Soc. Exp. Biol.* Vol. 4, 221–268.

Lorenz, K. Z. (1961). Phylogenetische Anpassung und adaptive Modifikation des Verhaltens. *Z. Tierpsychol.* Vol. 18, 139–187.

Lorenz, K. Z. (1965). "Evolution and Modification of Behavior." Chicago Univ. Press, Chicago, Illinois.

McNeill, D. (1966a). The creation of language. *Discovery* Vol. 27, 34–38.

McNeill, D. (1966b). Developmental psycholinguistics. *In* "The Genesis of Language" (F. Smith and G. A. Miller, eds.), p. 15. M.I.T. Press, Cambridge, Massachusetts.

Manley, G. H. (1960). The agonistic behaviour of the Black-headed Gull. Unpublished Ph.D. Thesis, Oxford, University.

Marler, P. (1961). The logical analysis of animal communication. *J. Theor. Biol.* Vol. 1, 295–317.

Marler, P. (1963). Inheritance and learning in the development of animal vocalizations. *In* "Acoustic Behavior in Animals" (R. G. Busnel, ed.), p. 228. Elsevier, Amsterdam.

Marler, P. R., and Hamilton, W. J. (1967). "Mechanisms of Animal Behavior." Wiley, New York.

Marler, P., and Tamura, M. (1962). Song 'dialects' in three populations of white-crowned sparrows. *Condor* Vol. 64, 368–377.

Moltz, H. (1960). Imprinting: Empirical basis and theoretical significance. *Psychol. Bull.* Vol. 57, 291–314.

Moltz, H. (1963). Imprinting: An epigenetic approach. *Psychol. Rev.* Vol. 70, 123–138.

Morris, C. W. (1938). Foundations of the theory of signs. "Encyclopedia of Unified Science," Vol. 1, No. 2. Univ. of Chicago Press, Chicago, Illinois.

Morris, C. W. (1946). "Signs, Language and Behavior." Prentice-Hall, Englewood Cliffs, New Jersey.

Moynihan, M. (1959). Notes on the behavior of some North American gulls. IV. The ontogeny of hostile behavior and display patterns. *Behaviour* Vol. 14, 214–239.

Nelson, K. (1964). The temporal patterning of courtship behavior in the glandulo-caudine fishes (Ostariophysi, Characidae). *Behaviour* Vol. 24, 90–146.

Nicolai, J. (1956). Zur Biologie und Ethologie des Gimpels (*Pyrrhula pyrrhula* L.). *Z. Tierpsychol.* Vol. 13, 93–132.

Nicolai, J. (1959). Familientradition in der Gesangsentwicklung des Gimpels (*Pyrrhula pyrrhula* L.). *J. Ornithol.* Vol. 100, 39–46.

Popper, K. R. (1959). "The Logic of Scientific Discovery." Basic Books, New York.

Poulsen, H. (1951). Inheritance and learning in the song of the Chaffinch (*Fringilla coelebs*). *Behaviour* Vol. 3, 216–228.

Poulsen, H. (1959). Song learning in the domestic canary. *Z. Tierpsychol.* Vol. 16, 173–178.

Russell, E. S. (1916). "Form and Function." Murray, London.

Schneirla, T. C. (1956). Interrelationships of the "innate" and the "acquired" in instinctive behavior. *In* "L'instinct dans le comportement des animaux et de l'homme," p. 387. Found. Singer Polignac, Paris.

Schneirla, T. C. (1965). Aspects of stimulation and organisation in approach/withdrawal processes underlying vertebrate behavioral development. *In* "Advances in the Study of Behavior" (D. S. Lehrman, R. A. Hinde, and E. Shaw, eds.), Vol. 1, p. 1. Academic Press, New York.

Schneirla, T. C., and Rosenblatt, J. S. (1961). Behavioral organization and genesis of the social bond in insects and mammals. *Amer. J. Orthopsychiat.* Vol. 31, 223–253.

Sebeok, T. A. (1965). Animal communication. *Science* Vol. 147, 1006–1014.

Sebeok, T. A. (1968). Goals and limitations of the study of animal communication. *In* "Animal Communication" (T. A. Sebeok, ed.), p. 3. Indiana Univ. Press, Bloomington, Indiana.

Shannon, C. E., and Weaver, W. (1949). "The Mathematical Theory of Communication." Univ. of Illinois Press, Urbana, Illinois.

Skinner, B. F. (1957). "Verbal Behavior." Appleton, New York.

Sluckin, W. (1954). "Minds and Machines." Penguin, London.

Sluckin, W. (1962). Perceptual and associative learning. *Symp. Zool. Soc. London* Vol. 8, 193–198.

Sluckin, W., and Salzen, E. A. (1961). Imprinting and perceptual learning. *Quart. J. Exp. Psychol.* Vol. 13, 65–77.

Smith, W. J. (1963). Vocal communication of information in birds. *Amer. Natur.* Vol. 97, 117–125.

Smith, W. J. (1965). Message, meaning and context in ethology. *Amer. Natur.* Vol. 99, 404–409.

Smith, W. J. (1969). Communication and relationships in the genus Tyrannus. *Publ. Nuttal Ornithol. Club* No. 6.

Smith, W. J. (1968). Message-meaning analysis. *In* "Animal Communication" (T. A. Sebeok, ed.), p. 44. Indiana Univ. Press, Bloomington, Indiana.

Stokes, A. W. (1962a). Agonistic behaviour among blue tits at a winter feeding station. *Behaviour* Vol. 19, 118–138.

Stokes, A. W. (1962b). Comparative ethology of great, blue, marsh and coal tits at a winter feeding station. *Behaviour* Vol. 19, 208–218.

Sturtevant, E. H. (1947). "An Introduction to Linguistic Science." Yale Univ. Press, New Haven, Connecticut.

Taylor, C. (1964). "The Explanation of Behaviour." Humanities Press, New York.

Thielke-Polz, H., and Thielke, G. (1960). Akustiches Lernen verscheiden alter schallisolierter Amseln (*Turdus merula* L.) und die Entwicklung erlernter Motive ohne und mit künstlichen Einfluss von Testosteron. *Z. Tierpsychol.* Vol. 17, 211–244.

Thorpe, W. H. (1958). The learning of song patterns by birds, with special reference to the song of the chaffinch *Fringilla coelebs. Ibis* Vol. 100, 535–570.

Thorpe, W. H. (1961). "Bird Song: The Biology of Vocal Communication and Expression in Birds." Cambridge Univ. Press, London and New York.

Tinbergen, N. (1951). "The Study of Instinct." Oxford Univ. Press, London and New York.

Tinbergen, N. (1953). "Social Behavior in Animals." Methuen, London.

Tinbergen, N., and Kuenen, D. J. (1939). Uber die auslösenden und die richtunggebenden Reizsituationen der Sperrbewegung von jungen Drosseln (*Turdus m. merula* und *T. e. ericetorum*). *Z. Tierpsychol.* Vol. 3, 37–60.

Tschanz, B. (1968). Trottellummen. *Z. Tierpsychol.* Suppl. 4.

von Holst, E. (1954). Relations between the central nervous system and the peripheral organs. *Brit. J. Anim. Behav.* Vol. 2, 89–94.

von Holst, E., and Mittelstaedt, H. (1950). Das Reafferenzprincip. *Naturwissenschaften* Vol. 37, 464–476.

Vowles, D. M. (1961). Neural mechanisms in insect behaviour. *In* "Current Problems in Animal Behaviour" (W. H. Thorpe and O. L. Zangwill, eds.), p. 5. Cambridge Univ. Press, London and New York.

Watson, J. B. (1913). Psychology as the behaviorist views it. *Psychol. Rev.* Vol. 20, 158–177.

Wiepkema, P. R. (1961). An ethological analysis of the reproductive behaviour of the Bitterling (*Rhodeus amarus* Bloch). *Arch. Neer. Zool.* Vol. 14, 103–199.

Wilson, E. O. (1965). Chemical communication in the social insects. *Science* Vol. 149, 1064–1071.

V. CONTEMPORARY ISSUES IN THE STUDY OF BEHAVIOR

BEHAVIORAL SCIENCE, ENGINEERING, AND POETRY[1]

DANIEL S. LEHRMAN

This paper was prepared for a meeting in the American Museum of Natural History, where T. C. Schneirla was Curator of Animal Behavior. Schneirla, who conceived the meeting before his untimely death, was my teacher, and I did my doctoral thesis research in the Museum.

The feelings that attracted many of us to the study of animal behavior in the Museum, and the orientation toward that study that we learned, are quite different from those that characterize the mainstream of American behaviorist psychology, as currently exemplified, for example, by the work of B. F. Skinner, the most influential source of, and the most eloquent spokesman for, its ideas. I should like to try to describe some of the ways in which the study of animal behavior by Schneirla and his students expresses values and orienting attitudes different from those ordinarily associated with the use of animals as subjects for psychological research.[2]

In speaking of the behavior of either lower animals or human beings, Skinner has repeatedly said that the basic aim of the study of behavior is to understand how it is shaped and controlled by contingencies of reinforcement—that is, to understand the probabilistic relationships between the performance of acts by the animal, the ways in which it is reinforced (or rewarded), and the changes in probability that the acts will occur again. Although these ideas are intended to apply to all behavior, including human, a great deal of the research on which they

[1] I am indebted to Dorothy Dinnerstein, Max Hertzman, and Jay S. Rosenblatt for many helpful discussions of the matters discussed in this paper.

[2] Schneirla was not the only nonbehaviorist student of animal behavior of his generation; nor is animal behavior the only field of psychology in which counterstatements to behaviorism have been made. For example, such disparate disciplines as psychoanalytic psychotherapy and Gestalt-oriented cognitive psychology have in common the fact that they attempt to formulate psychological processes in terms that are isomorphic with the experience of the subject, rather than with the operations of the observer.

are based has been done with various kinds of lower animals—rats, pigeons, monkeys, etc. The popular image of the experimental psychologist busily following a rat in a maze has been changed to the image of a pigeon in a Skinner box through the practically single-handed efforts of Dr. Skinner.

Not everybody, of course, agrees with this formulation of the basic aim of the study of behavior. In recent years, Skinner and his colleagues have applied the ideas of behavior control to basic problems of human psychology in two related ways: by stating that the processes of education and of the management of social relations can be understood as the "shaping" of behavior by controlling contingencies of reinforcement, and by developing clinical methods which imply that the behavioral control of symptoms constitutes the cure of psychological illness. Such extensions of behaviorist assumptions and techniques to the engineering of human personal relationships has naturally aroused criticism from clinical and social psychologists. Carl Rogers, for example, in a debate with Skinner, pointed out that to control a symptom is not necessarily the same thing as to eliminate the internal difficulties which gave rise to it; and that there is no way to be sure that the motives and values of the person who is doing the controlling are the same as, or consistent with, those of the individual who is being controlled.

Debates like these express disputes about the philosophy, values, ethics, and techniques of psychotherapy. They do not deal with the problems of animal behavior at all; when Carl Rogers disputes Skinner's assertions that the major goal of behavioral science is to know how behavior patterns are shaped by the contingencies of reinforcement, and that the only statements about behavior which have any scientific content or scientific validity are those that summarize what we have to do to control behavior, Rogers implies that what he objects to is the application to human beings of concepts and techniques derived from, and appropriate to, the study of the behavior of animals.

I would like to suggest that, for at least some students of animal behavior, the monolithic theoretical systems of behaviorist psychology, and the rigidly operationist methodologies upon which they are based, are no more appropriate to the study of the lives of animals than they are to the understanding of the lives of people.

Why Study Animals?

Why would a scientist elect to spend his time, his energy, and his feelings in the study of the behavior of animals? I think that there are, in the feelings of people who devote themselves to the investigation of animal behavior, two broadly different classes of orienting attitudes, which have different sources, and which lend different expressive qualities to the scientific work. These are not totally mutually exclusive; they doubtless do not exhaust the whole field of possibilities; and they can coexist in the same personality. One can, nevertheless, distinguish two quite different types of justification for the study of animals.

THE BEHAVIORIST ORIENTATION

Most of the American experimental psychologists who use animals as their research subjects do so on the assumption that what they are doing is to elucidate the general laws of behavior—laws whose character does not depend upon the particular kind of animal that is used for their study—laws that are addressed to problems not specific to the life of the particular animal studied. Thus, the problem to which an experiment is addressed exists, or can exist, in the mind of an experimenter before he makes a decision about what kind of animal to use. The choice of species for the subject is then a matter of convenience—of technological convenience. Thus, the same techniques and the same formulations of problems can very readily be applied, with the same quantitative methods and sometimes with the same instruments, to studies of rats, of pigeons, of monkeys, of psychotic human beings and of normal human beings.

It is an old cliché that the principal subjects of psychological experiments are rats and college sophomores. And it is true that many experimenters can and do shift readily from rats (or pigeons) to sophomores, without any change in the nature of the problems on which they are working.

I think that in these cases it would not be too unjust to say that the rat and the college sophomore are to some degree, or in some respects, equivalent to each other for the experimenter. The experimenter does not mean to insult the college sophomore, or even the rat, by implicitly or explicitly making that assumption. He is merely expressing his feeling that the choice of the subject is a matter of technique, and that the laws of behavior which he wishes to understand are important and interesting to the extent that they apply to many different kinds of subjects. The background assumption, often made explicit, is that what we are really after, and what makes our efforts defensible, is to understand the behavior of man.

Of course, no scientist is so naïve as to think (or at least so unsophisticated as to admit he thinks) that a white rat and a college sophomore are identical with each other. But the tradition of American behaviorism is that "comparative" psychology is the search for laws that cut across species differences, that what is sought in the study of the behavior of one species is, in part, clues to what is going on in another, and that eventual relevance, no matter how remote, to the understanding of man is the ultimate test. I think it is an entirely accurate and just perception of my colleagues who work on problems of learning, motivation, sensation, social dominance, etc., in the laboratory rat to say that virtually none of them would feel fully justified in devoting their energy to its study if they were deeply convinced that the rat was so fundamentally different from man that they would have to regard it as a separate living creature rather than as an arena for the testing of psychological hypotheses, or an exemplification of psychological theories.

Also basic to what I here call the "behaviorist orientation" is the idea that scientific explanations of, and statements of scientific insights into, behavior, *consist of* statements about how the experimenter gains control over the behavior, or about how the actions of the subject can be predicted from the actions of the experimenter. For Skinner, statements of relationships between schedules and contingencies of reinforcement, on the one hand, and frequencies of performance of acts, on the other, are the total substance of psychological analysis. For Hull, prediction, by quasi-mathematical techniques, of how the behavior of the subject is altered by the operations of the experimenter, constituted the totality of psychological explanation. Both of these versions of modern behaviorism insist that questions about the processes internal to the subject that give rise to the observed behavior are unnecessary, misleading, nonscientific, and/or irrelevant to an inclusive system of behavior analysis. For Skinner, questions about the subject's feelings or other aspects of his subjectivity, or about internal reorganizations in the subject which might mediate the changes in his behavior which follow upon reinforcement, are nonscientific distractions from rigorous analysis of the provenance of behavioral organization. For Hull, the unitary "intervening" variables which he introduced into his predictive equations gained their validity solely from their ability to simplify and unify the process of predicting the subject's actions from the experimenter's operations; it was irrelevant to ask whether these "variables" corresponded to anything in the actual organization of any actual animal or person. Physiological analysis, or physiological inquiry into behavioral processes, or attempts to verify the physiological existence of events implied by behavioral descriptions, or to determine the physiological substrate of hypothesized processes, also seem essentially irrelevant to the schemata provided by

Skinner and Hull (especially in the version of Hullian theory provided by Kenneth Spence).[3]

It is not only the subject that is denatured by behaviorist psychology; the experimenter himself is not permitted to be entirely human. Rigorous adherence to the notions of operationally defined prediction and/or control as criteria for evaluation of scientific work exclude any formal or significant recognition of important aspects of the experimenter's own subjectivity. The experimenter's creative integration of materials from different levels, from different contexts, of different degrees of relevance, to produce the inductive leap which is the formulation of a new problem; his anxious shifting of his angle of view of concepts, categories, and data with which he cannot feel satisfied; his "aha!" experience when his cognitive field reorganizes itself so that he sees things in a new relationship which seems explanatory to him—none of these essentials of the activity of a scientist are accepted, in behaviorist circles, as relevant either to the choice of terms for the description of behavior or to the mode of describing scientific work for its public. Skinner, who often discusses important human problems with humane sensitivity, equally often insists that the psychologist's own perception of reality is irrelevant to the analysis of behavior. And Howard Kendler, in a defense and extension of Hullian theory, once remarked that considerations of this kind were relevant to understanding a scientist's thinking but not his theory!

An observer with a sufficiently jaundiced eye can see these trends as resulting in a vast psychological literature from which the reader can find out neither what happens in the subject nor what happens in the experimenter, and in the training of psychologists (of *psychologists!*) who gather from their surroundings that emotional detachment from the material with which they work is a prerequisite for success.

THE NATURAL-HISTORY ORIENTATION

There is a second, and quite different, sort of attitude from which an investigator can arrive at the feeling that his time and energy could be spent profitably and usefully by studying the behavior of animals.

The animal itself, and the behavior by which it lives its natural life,

---

[3] I exclude a good deal of physiological psychology from what I call the "behaviorist orientation." A great many investigators of such problems as the physiological basis of hunger, thirst, sexual behavior, sensation, etc. are led by their physiological orientation to work on what I consider natural units of behavior, and to make fundamental contributions to what I call the "natural-history orientation," even when (like Neal Miller) they consider themselves to be exploring behaviorist theories.

can seem to a human observer like a mysterious and attractive part of the world around him. The interest of the investigator in understanding the life of the animal can have a direct character—can carry an immediate emotional charge of curiosity and fascination, and of apprehension of the animal as a subject that has an existence of its own, independently of whether it is serving as an object for a human experimenter. Feelings of this kind have, for the observer, more in common with the feelings involved in watching a sunset or reading a poem than they do with those involved in solving engineering problems, or in abstracting formalized general relationships from narrowly defined operations of experimenter and subject.

What I here call the "natural-history orientation" to animal behavior implies primary attention to the behavior of the animal considered as an aspect of the way the animal is related to its natural environment, including other members of its species. One aspect of this orientation is the concentration on questions arising from the natural life of a particular species (rather than questions applied to an arbitrarily selected species from a generalized theoretical framework): questions about habitat selection and the formation of mating pairs, about the mechanisms of sexual behavior, about nest building and care of the young, about migration, about food selection, about social relationships, etc.

It is almost never true of behaviorist "rat psychologists" that they regard rats with particular affection, or consider them more interesting than other kinds of animals, or entered the academic profession of psychology because of a preexisting adolescent interest in the behavior of rats. On the other hand, it is absolutely commonplace (although not universal) among natural-history-oriented students of animal behavior that they entered the scientific profession as the continuing expression of a boyhood or girlhood fascination with the behavior of particular kinds of animals.

The differences between the "behaviorist" and the "natural-history" orientation, as I have been describing them, certainly do not imply that all behaviorists, or all natural-history-oriented students of animal behavior, agree with each other about matters of theory or interpretation. The differences among such behaviorist thinkers as Skinner, Hull, and Tolman run wide and deep, but all share the orienting attitudes that prediction and control are the aims of behavioral science, and that the justification for experimenting with animals is to provide insights for the understanding of the behavior of human beings. Schneirla and Konrad Lorenz have fundamental and irreconcilable differences of opinion about many basic problems in the interpretation of the organization and development of animal behavior, but they share the orienting attitudes that the life of the animal itself poses problems to the investigator, that the units of behavior studied should be natural units evolved through natural selection, and that the contemplation and appreciation of the complexities of nature are valuable human aims, independent of their usefulness in understanding human life (a problem to which both addressed themselves).

I describe natural-history-oriented students of animal behavior as scientists for whom the enjoyable act of watching the animal do what comes naturally to it in its natural (or quasi-natural) environment is the starting point for asking questions that can be transformed into scientific problems. In doing this, I am not by any means implying that questions arising from the investigator's passion are necessarily less significant than those arising from a concern for social utility; the questions aroused in the mind of an investigator simply by watching a freely moving animal need not necessarily be trivial questions, any more than the questions dealt with by running rats in mazes or Skinner boxes need necessarily be important questions.

A newborn kitten can withdraw from an electric shock, and it can show a motor response to a tone; but attempts to develop a simple conditioned association between the tone and the withdrawal to shock fail until the kitten is a couple of weeks old. It would, however, be premature to conclude from this that the kitten cannot learn very much during its first 10 days. My colleague Jay Rosenblatt, while watching kittens with their mothers, noted that by the time the kittens are 2 or 3 days old each kitten is feeding from a particular nipple of the mother and has developed a particular route for getting to that nipple. Under some circumstances it can be demonstrated that by the time the kitten is 7 or 8 days old, it has even developed what looks like territorial rights to the nipple; it shows a tendency to cling to its "rightful" nipple when challenged by a sibling, while being willing to give up a "wrong" nipple if it has latched onto one.

Now, that is a rather important, and rather complex, kind of learning that can be seen in the kitten during its first few days of life. The difference between the scientist who cannot demonstrate learning in a kitten until it is more than 10 days old, and the one who can show it when the kitten is 3 days old is, I think, the difference between the investigator who is trying to find out when the kitten can learn something that the *experimenter* wants it to learn and one who is trying to find out when the kitten can learn something that the *kitten* wants to learn![4]

---

[4] Walter Stanley has also recently demonstrated very early learning in puppies, using the puppy's reaction to an artificial nipple as the starting point.

That observation could not have been made except by someone with a great deal of patience in watching kittens and a great deal of interest in what goes on between kittens and their mothers. But I submit that the observation does not seem, on that account, trivial or uninteresting to psychologists or zoologists, or even people, who do not themselves have that kind of patience or that kind of interest. The fact that I am talking about an orientation toward problems that arise from an interest in the animals themselves does not mean that the answers to the problems do not provide information and insights that are valuable and interesting to other kinds of people as well.

It is, no doubt, nothing more than a personal prejudice of mine that I think that most natural-history-oriented papers contain facts or insights that are interesting and memorable, independently of whether I am or am not interested in the theoretical point made by the paper, and independently of whether I do or do not agree with the conclusions or interpretations of the author; while most papers published in the behaviorist tradition seem to be written on the assumption that their empirical contents exist only as support for a particular argument, or as an extension of a particular point of view, and have no character or memorability in any other context.

It is, I think, a matter of fact that most natural-history-oriented students of animal behavior are aware that investigators with points of view incompatible with their own often investigate interesting areas to which their own theories would not lead them, and produce interesting bodies of fact and interpretation that deserve respect; while most behaviorist-oriented students of animal (and human) behavior, faced with apparently indigestible new formulations by an opposing theorist, are satisfied to demonstrate that they can explain the new facts within their own theoretical framework, without assimilating the fact that the opposing or irrelevant ideas of their colleagues have opened new problems which their own theories did not, in fact, lead anybody to.

COMPARATIVE PSYCHOLOGY

The behaviorist and the natural-history orientations imply quite different attitudes toward the definition of "comparative" psychology and toward the role of species comparisons in psychological thinking.

If an investigator regards animal subjects as useful primarily to the extent to which they exemplify general laws whose importance derives from their applicability to many species, including man, then he will naturally tend to be encouraged by, and interested in, discoveries of common behavioral features in different species, and discouraged by the discovery of species idiosyncrasy. A technique or concept that yields the same results in many different species will be regarded as more "generally applicable" and, consequently, more "powerful" than one that depends upon the peculiarities of the behavior of a few species. There thus occurs a sort of "natural" selection process, by which the attention of investigators drifts away from any sorts of behavior that do not lend themselves to cross-species generalization in their raw form, and a few "powerful" techniques become increasingly dominant, increasingly pervade the training of new generations of students, and thus increasingly dictate the form and content of new research.

Clark Hull regarded it as a great strength of his behavior theory that it provided mathematical equations for describing the rates of acquisition and performance of habits that could be applied to the behavior of many different species of animals simply by changing the constants. It is a remarkable and well-known characteristic of Skinner's operant conditioning method that the relationships between schedules of reinforcement and frequencies of performance of acts have the same pattern, and sometimes the same quantitative parameters, in the widest variety of animal species, including man. This is widely regarded as evidence that the technique, and, consequently, the philosophy which it expresses, gives access to the most basic, fundamental, and widely relevant materials for the understanding of behavior. An alternative view is, however, possible.

I vividly remember the occasion, some 15 or 20 years ago, when I first visited a major operant conditioning laboratory (which, as it happened, was the archetypal one). My host showed me a pigeon in a chamber, and a button which I could press to present the pigeon with a reinforcement which, to my untutored eye, looked like a piece of ordinary pigeon food, but which I was assured had magical properties. Following instructions, I spent a happy hour teaching the pigeon to turn around in a circle and then stand for 2 seconds with its side toward the food dispenser, before looking in the dispenser for the food. Suddenly, I was visited by a dazzling revelation. If *any* behavior could be shaped up in this chamber, perhaps I could teach a domestic pigeon to perform the courtship bow of the ringdove, which is quite different from that of the domestic pigeon; perhaps I could teach the bird to court when it was immature, or not in breeding condition; perhaps I could alter the frequency of occurrence of bowing and other instinctive behavior patterns, or cause them to be performed in other than the natural situation, and omitted in the natural situation. In short, I could use the operant conditioning technique to elucidate the origin and internal organization of instinctive behavior patterns! Eureka! Oh, wow!

I explained these plans to my host, who quickly disillusioned me by saying, "Well, I don't think that will work. We've tried that kind of thing a little, and this technique doesn't work too well with what you might call 'bird behavior.' " At that moment, a heretical suspicion entered my soul, which I have never been able fully to exorcise. Is it possible, I wondered, that the remarkable uniformity of the behavior in the operant conditioning situation of rats, guinea pigs, rhesus monkeys, pigeons, and people depends partly upon the fact that the technique, and the philosophy which it expresses, carefully avoid a good deal of what makes a guinea pig a guinea pig, and a pigeon a pigeon—to say nothing of what makes a person a person?

By contrast, for the natural-history-oriented investigator, the ways in which different animals have evolved different modes of adaptation to different environments is itself a central interest. This applies not only to the enormous variety of species-specific unlearned behavior patterns but also to the modes of learning. Animal species differ with respect to the importance of individual experience in their lives, with respect to the relative ease with which they learn different kinds of things, and with respect to the modes of learning itself. A bird may learn to sing the typical song of its species by hearing it when it is still too young to be able to practice it, while a bird of a related species may require no early tuition to sing its typical song; a particular species of fish may learn the topography of tidal pools, by swimming over them at high tide, well enough to jump from one to another when the spaces between them are dry; one species of mammal may require sexual experience for the full development of its sexual behavior, while in another species the relevant experience is preadolescent social experience, and in still another, early experience seems to be of little or no importance; an ant may learn a maze as rapidly as a rat, but changing one choice point in the already-learned maze may drastically disturb the rat's performance, while the ant will quickly adjust to the change; a rat that learns a maze pattern to get to food will be able readily to use the same pattern to get home, but an ant will have to learn this problem as two separate tasks. All these observations seem anomalous from the point of view of any of the conventional behaviorist learning theories, but all illuminate ways in which different animals adapt to their different environmental requirements, and each is consonant with other features of the species in question.

For the natural-history-oriented comparative psychologist, comparison of species means to consider simultaneously similarities and differences between species so that each illuminates the other. The value of comparison comes not from the merging of different levels into a misleadingly unified conception of behavior but from the development of an evolutionary perspective which enables us to appreciate the emergence of new qualities without neglecting the underlying continuities and their transformations.

THE BEHAVIORAL SCIENTIST AND HIS MATERIAL

The fact that different sorts of questions are raised from the behaviorist orientation and from the natural-history orientation reflects, to some degree, the fact that the two orientations imply different sorts of emotional and intellectual relationships between the investigator and the animals which are his subjects.

The experimenter and the animal are both living things, and the scientific investigator of behavior cannot escape the fact that his work expresses a relationship to a part of the living world, of which he is also a part. If the scientist's feeling about his animal subjects, which keeps him in touch with them, is primarily a feeling of being in control of them, or of knowing how to control them, then he is expressing a very different relationship to them than will be the case if his primary feeling is what I might call an affectionate respect for what the animals are doing when he is not controlling them.

Of course, control is of the essence of the experimental method, and is exerted by all scientific investigators. Every scientist finds out what is going on in an animal, or in any material with which he works, by altering it or interfering with it, and observing the result of his intervention. I think there is, however, a difference between, on one hand, systematic, monolithically organized, comprehensive control, with statements about the manner of exercising control constituting the central features of explanation of the animal's behavior and, on the other hand, interference with the behavior of the animal with the purpose of gaining comprehension of what is going on in it when it is freely performing the behavior that is natural to it.

Schneirla spent thousands of hours watching army ant colonies in jungles and deserts, and carrying out experiments in the laboratory to illuminate various aspects of what he saw in the field. His central interest was the nature of social integration in the colony, and the regulation of the colony's behavioral relations to its environment. In pursuing this interest, he explored, and assimilated from the work of others, the widest possible range of aspects of the army ant's nature and existence: its external morphology, its use of individual experience, its sensory capacities, its learning abilities, its modes of neural integration, its behavioral ontogeny, its reproductive physiology, its ecological relationships to the environment, the functional accomplishments of its behavior, its evolutionary relationships to other kinds of ants and other families and phyla of animals. He integrated all these considerations into a marvelously detailed, richly articulated, deeply explanatory picture of the behavioral events in the life of this creature. His writings reverberate with explicit and implicit significance for the student of learning theory, of motivation, of social relations, of behavioral development, of instinct theory, as well as for those of ecology and evolution.

This ability to integrate material from different levels and sources into a pattern which illuminates and explains the behavior of the animal while maintaining an appreciation of the diversity of the processes involved, and of the diversity of the lives and natures of different animals, is the highest development of the natural-history orientation to the study of animal behavior and is usually regarded as a high talent by natural-history-oriented investigators when they recognize it in a colleague. The ability most valued in behaviorist-oriented scientists of equivalent talent and stature is the ability, when faced with an apparently qualitatively new or unexpected behavioral event or phenomenon, to demonstrate that it can be assimilated into an already-existing theoretical framework, and is therefore not really new or interesting or disturbing to the *status quo*.

As indicated by the expressive quality of the research and of the writing about the research, the relationship of the investigator to his material is, in extreme examples of the behaviorist and of the natural-history orientation, strikingly different. The behaviorist orientation expresses detachment, lack of interest in the inner nature of the animal, and stress on control and/or prediction of behavior as the aim of professional effort; the natural-history orientation expresses a feeling of continuity between investigator and subject as parts of nature, interest in all data that illuminate that inner organization of the animal from which its behavior emerges, and stress on understanding and appreciation of the animal as the goal of research.

European ethologists, most of whom are zoologists who have a rather undifferentiated and poorly informed conception of the field of psychology, are often heard to say that the difference between themselves and "animal psychologists" is that they love their animals. Investigators of animal behavior who spontaneously describe their attitude to their subjects in terms of love, and those who spontaneously describe their aims in terms of control, speak as clearly as possible about the differences between them.[5]

[5] This discussion characterizes contrasting sets of attitudes toward a specific realm of activity and of subject matter, and should not be interpreted as a romantic view of good guys and bad guys. The way in which these attitudes are isolated from, or integrated with, other aspects of the scientist's life is a very complex problem, which I have not discussed here. Behaviorist-oriented and natural-history-oriented students of animal behavior both include arrogant and respectful teachers, task-oriented and status-oriented workers, good and bad experimenters, faithful and unfaithful spouses, theorists and empiricists, convivial souls and wet blankets, gourmets and ascetics.

Engineering and Poetry: Functions of Science

The function of control, of mastery over the environment, of creating improvements in the practical conditions of life, is widely regarded as the essential social function of science, and as the justification for its support by society. The study of behavior shares with other sciences this perspective: the prospects, however remote, of eliminating mental illness, controlling aggression, improving education, understanding psychosomatic diseases, etc., seem to many people like the central justifications for the activities of behavioral scientists.

Without disputing these justifications for science, or these conceptions of the function of science, which everybody recognizes, I should like to point to another kind of role which science plays in human life, although not to the extent that it could.

The "practical" function of science has much in common with technology. A scientist, like an engineer, is engaged in trying to understand the world, partly for the purpose of gaining control over it and being able to manipulate it, partly to make it over into the image he has of bettering the conditions for human life.

But there is another aspect of the activity and the life of a scientist, and another function for science, which is not often enough stressed. In addition to (or instead of) serving a function like that of an engineer, the scientist can also serve a function like that of an artist, of a painter or poet—that is, he sees things in a way that no one has seen them before and finds a way to describe what he has seen so that other people can see it in the same way. This function is that of widening and enriching the content of human consciousness, and of increasing the depth of the contact that human beings, scientists and nonscientists as well, can have with the world around them. This function of arousing and satisfying a sense of wonder and curiosity about the riches of the natural world, and of strengthening the civilized human being's weakened feeling of being part of the world around him, is a function which you can see being served in any hall or gallery of the American Museum of Natural History. It is a function which was characteristic of the work of T. C. Schneirla and the scientists influenced by him.

Young people today express widespread revulsion against science because of the presently destructive, and ultimately threatening, effects of technology on the quality of life. The kind of science of which I speak is one expression of an attitude toward life that could save us from technology.

THE DEVELOPMENT OF HUMAN BEHAVIOR: THEORETICAL CONSIDERATIONS FOR FUTURE RESEARCH

DALE B. HARRIS

The psychologist's approach to problems of development now has a respectable history. Known first as "genetic psychology," the family line has grown in several directions by intermarriage from time to time with many different aspects of behavioral and biological science. Indeed, the field of child development research, funded by the Laura Spellman Rockefeller Fund in the 1920's and encouraged by the National Research Council in the 1930's, which sponsored the Society for Research in Child Development, was explicitly designed to be multidisciplinary in character. If it has remained somewhat varied, it has nevertheless developed a characteristic viewpoint—concern with structural and behavioral growth and change from conception to death, and a unique method—the longitudinal study—usually applied to a fairly broad spectrum of variables, measured in a small but faithfully followed sample. If it lacks a unified comprehensive theory, it has produced many studies—descriptive, normative, cross-sectional, comparative, and experimental—and many speculations and minor theories.

Differing Approaches in Developmental Psychology

As psychologists have become more and more active in this broad forum, they have brought with them the major split which has haunted American psychology for more than 70 years. Those interested in measurement, in hypothesized abilities and traits, in human variability, took to the study of children readily and absorbed the biologically oriented theories or viewpoints concerning the growing organism which came down from child development's early beginnings. Those in the behaviorist and neobehaviorist camp followed a somewhat different course.

True, J. B. Watson and A. P. Weiss, the founders of American behaviorism, both used the observational method with infants quite as much as the experimental. But as behaviorism became theoretically sophisticated in the late 1930's, instrumenting its laboratories, adopting positivism, and emphasizing the hypothetico-deductive strategy and the crucial experiment with its concern for elegant design, it exerted a strong influence on the area of child development (e.g., McCandless and Spiker, 1956). Observations occurred less and less in the natural setting. Behaviorism's concern with the analysis of causation via the identification and control of stimulus variables led it to attend primarily to variation in the stimulus, usually quite specifically defined.

Those who followed the tradition of child study continued to be concerned with the child in his natural setting. Their experiments were designed within nursery or elementary schools, children's clubs or other "natural" groupings, or in small groups artificially contrived in the spirit of play or other spontaneous or assigned activities. Their interest focused more on observing the variability of response under conditions of complex stimulation. Gesell's systematic observations of infants' spontaneous behavior generally used naturally occurring objects as stimuli and likewise attended to the emerging varied behavior as evidence of "intrinsic growth."

In recent years many in the behavioristic tradition have designated their field as "experimental child," confining themselves to special problems and experimental settings suitable to the instrumented laboratory. They have freely admitted that at present their work has little to do with practical problems of the care, rearing, and education of children. However, in late years some proponents of "behavior shaping" have turned from pigeons to children and have taken their techniques into the clinic and nursery schools with dramatic results in individual cases. Prominent among the spokesmen for this methodology are Bijou and Baer (1961, 1965).

Of those who have remained in the more traditional stream of observation, description, and concern with the variability of response, given a stimulus situation, perhaps the most extreme are Barker and Wright (1954). Their attention to the stream of behavior characterizing the individual in a complex social environment has led them to identify behavioral units known as episodes and environmental units known as "settings." They have generated an ecological view of the organism, one which clearly points toward a kind of systems theory. Just as organs within the body are complexly interrelated as an integrated series of physiological systems to form a functioning individual, so may any environment be viewed as an integration of many complexly related ecological units, and the behavior of a group be viewed as an ecological system embracing the interrelated behaviors of individuals. Individuals relate to their environments in complex ways that can also, it seems, be described as a *system* of relationships. Just so may the behavior of any one person be viewed as an ecological system, if that behavior be observed at the molar level and across a period of time. This is a far cry from lever pushing in a two-light or even a complex three-light choice situation where the reward is an M & M candy! Yet both these positions, and many more, are encompassed within the legitimate concerns of the Division on Developmental Psychology of the American Psychological Association.

The perennial division of the scientific approach to phenomena into science versus technology, or basic versus applied, however convenient for forensics, seems to have served chiefly as a device for some to put down others. This argument exists in child psychology no less than in other fields of science. The fact remains that the general public, which ultimately foots the bills for science, is interested in improving its lot. Sooner or later the question gets asked, "What good is it for us?" The result of all of this has been to create a myth concerning science, a myth that has very probably vastly overvalued science. Indeed, there seems to be something of a reaction setting in in these latter days against science and perhaps against all intellectualistic approaches to human experience. The back-to-simplicity movement of the hippies, the back-to-nature movement of hundreds of thousands of vacationing Americans, the burgeoning reaffirmation of fundamentals by the very large middle segment of so-called forgotten Americans so graphically demonstrated by the recent *Newsweek* survey (October 6, 1969) are all perhaps evidences of this trend. Science, perhaps not surprisingly to scientists themselves, has not brought the millennium. It has simply opened up many more questions, puzzles, and, indeed, threats to man's welfare.

Differing Conceptual Modes

One by-product of this history has been to divide people into patterns of thinking, or ideology. The crude dichotomy, we say, creates an unnecessary or false problem. But dichotomies often highlight persistent issues, the more troublesome because their roots are implicit and unrecognized. One common division of thinking can be noted among scientists and can also be found in the thinking of men on the street. Thus it seems possible to divide mankind into "engineers" and "ecologists." The engineers see the world as a challenge to their fabricative and manipulative ingenuity. They would fit the world to man. The ecologists see the world as a complexly balanced system of interlocking subsystems, a challenge to their comprehension and understanding; they would have man fit into the world. The ecologist points with alarm to the man-caused death of Lake Erie, while the engineer points with pride to man-made lakes flooding former woodlots and farmlands. Child psychology has always had a close affiliation with the education of children and this polarity in viewpoint becomes particularly clear in viewpoints concerning the child and his training and education. The one would shape behavior toward desired patterns; the other seeks to provide conditions maximally supportive of growth trends in the organism.

Indeed, it is difficult to regard these contrasted viewpoints without concluding they lead to (or do they spring from?) differing value systems. The "engineer" of human behavior shapes behavior according to the model wherein the behavior is directed toward a predetermined end state. The ecologist, considering man as adapting himself according to an open-system model within interlocking environmental–organismic systems, implies some potential for self-direction in that transactive process.

Another expression of these two modes of construing the organism—for the ideas reach far beyond the human child—is found in the nature–nurture controversy. Seventy years ago man's behavior was seen clearly as part of the natural world, and civilization was bent toward curbing and directing through cultural mechanisms such inborn behavioral dispositions as man shares with his animal relatives. Since the advent of behaviorism in American psychology, behavior is seen to be largely if not wholly shaped by external contingencies. Both practice (repetition) and reward (reinforcement) have been variously construed as significant in this behavior modification or learning. Of late, even the concept of inner "drive," the last stronghold of a "nature" man might share with the animal world, has been reduced to strong stimulus.

Most behavioral scientists manage with the position that behavioral development is unthinkable without genetically derived structures and the stimuli of a complex environmental system which maintain and, indeed, initially evoke the structure. This model is applied to behavior also; the capacity for the simplest reflexes is part of the organism's nature, yet even these reflexes require stimuli for their evocation, and their first few manifestations are usually imperfect examples of their final form. A necessary interaction or transaction among these sets of forces is now generally accepted.

Human geneticists and many comparative psychologists do not balk at the notion that behavior patterns are genetically linked. Some claim the greatest discovery in the century was the successful analysis of DNA.

With our rapid advances in knowledge of environmental control we become able to shape the perfect environment (if we ever do apply what we already know) and face up to what we can or cannot do about ourselves. Now the engineering-minded biologists talk of the possibility of reassembling the double helix along more desirable lines. If so, natural evolution is succeeded, and man's future truly lies in his own hands. More than ever, then, his future development will depend on the ideas, institutions, and personal commitments men make. And though these are social and psychological in nature, they lie beyond the realm of the laboratory; their content and specifications are not to be found empirically.

But this possibility lies in the future. At present many psychologists insist that the organization of all animal behavior must be reduced to one learning principle. In their effort to study learning in its simplest, "purest" form, some behaviorists have pushed behind complex learning to the earliest reflexive movements, and behind the young organism to the fetus. To avoid the complications of language, some prefer to study learning in various subhuman species. Yet few besides Skinner (1953) have been able consistently to maintain the monistic position. Others have had to readmit the concept of biological need or drive in some form, maintaining one mechanism (classic conditioning) by which resultant behaviors are changed and attached to various stimuli. Mowrer (1960a) speaks of two kinds of learning. Recently Gagné (1965, 1968) has posited no less than eight types of learning, hierarchically related. Indeed, whether learning is the same at different phyletic and ontogenetic levels or whether different learning principles must be invoked at these levels to account for the origin and modification of behavior seems to be a central issue in much of psychology's travail with theory.

But social and behavioral science generally finds dual or multiple principles offensive, the genetic relatedness of behavior untenable, and seeks to unify pluralisms. For example, the nature–nurture controversy concerning the development of behavior has repeatedly been swept under the rug, reasoned away, declared a pseudo-problem, and otherwise disposed of.[1] But whenever an important (or value-laden) issue develops in social life, the problem usually recurs in its sharply dichotomous form. We want to know what we can readily modify, and to what extent. The recent discussion by a scholarly educational psychologist, that racial groups appear to differ in certain kinds of educability because of intrinsic characteristics, has brought a storm of learned protests. The opposi-

---

[1] The persistence of this issue throughout this volume, despite many irritated dismissals of it as unnecessary and trivial, is evidence that a real discontinuity troubles our thinking.

tion has argued the compromise position less than it has appealed to manifest behavioral differences as evidence of differences in learning opportunity.

Even though at present it seems more proper to ask what happens developmentally when a particular environmental event does or does not occur at one or another time in growth, we still find ourselves asking the question we have tried to lay aside—what part of the behavior product is organized intrinsically, and what part is learned? Thus our emphasis is still on outcomes rather than on process. Surely, then, one of the fundamental considerations for future research along present behavioral principles consists in resolving or reconciling this issue of process versus outcome in behavior.

It may well be argued that this emphasis on polarized viewpoints in the study of behavioral development is unjust. There have been numerous attempts to show that such division is more apparent than real (e.g., Zigler, 1963). For example, the language of Piaget (1953, 1954) has been restated in behavior theory terms (Stevenson, 1962). What has been called social learning theory seems to reconcile the shaping forces of the environment with the active qualities of the organism via concepts of social models and imitation (Bandura, 1969). The inadequacies of appetitive drive theories have been supplemented by emphasis on positive but complex motivational factors (e.g., White, 1959; Berlyne, 1960; Hunt, 1960). The inadequacies of the chain linkage sequencing hypothesized by strictly behavioristic interpretations of language formation (e.g., Skinner, 1957) have been modified by the theory of symbolic mediators (G. Miller, 1965; Mowrer, 1960b; Osgood, 1952; Kendler, 1963; Jenkins and Palermo, 1964). The concept of reaction has increasingly been supplanted by concepts of dyadic interaction (Sears, 1951) or, in more complex paradigms, by a transactive relationship between a complex organism and a complex environment. Such a transactive relationship is clearly the position of Piaget. These may, in time, prove to be positions of greater power in reconciling the grossly drawn antithetical positions.

But possibly this effort for reconciliation is for psychology, after all, in vain. One of the most serious students of psychological theories in their manifold aspects, Sigmund Koch, has reluctantly concluded (1969) that "whether as 'science' or *any* kind of coherent discipline devoted to the empirical study of man, psychology has been misconceived." Its few genuine discoveries, he says, are "heavily overbalanced by the pseudoknowledge that has proliferated," taken all too seriously by people because of the contemporary overvaluation of science generally, and, as a consequence, biasing "the deepest attitudes of man toward Man." In an excoriating statement he goes on to point out that the behavioral sciences were created by fiat in the 19th century in emulation of the natural sciences, which had come into being through several hundred years of discovery and refinement of their findings. J. S. Mill's hypothesis that the backward state of the social sciences could be improved by applying to them the methods of physical science, says Koch, has been "fulsomely disconfirmed." He entertains a faint hope that the analytical methods of science may apply with some success in biological science, but that even here "insufficient concern has been given to the strong chance that at some critical point of system-openness, boundary-weakness, or mere internal complexity, the definitive analytic pattern may no longer apply."

Nor does Koch believe that protest movements within psychology, such as various forms of return to phenomenology, existentialism, or humanistic psychology, though they are attempts to correct "a-meaningful inquiry," offer any hope. Koch's solution is radical; replace Psychology with "psychological studies" and let them spin off into a number of fields which may explore the many and varied concepts more fruitfully—biology, linguistics, the various humanities.

A more characteristic solution is offered by Spiker (1966). He dismisses the need for any mediation between camps. There are only two relevant issues—the definition of development, which he is willing to use descriptively, and the nature of empirical laws and the kinds of explanations of these laws. In the former he sees no problem; so used, the term "development" is convenient. Yet it could be argued that one's definition of development determines the phenomena he will observe and the data he will collect; the matter of definition may be more crucial than Spiker recognizes.

The second issue Spiker holds to be more crucial, and he affirms unqualifiedly the empirical positivistic stance of the rigorous behaviorist. All other issues, such as those of preferences for logic and form of theory, epistemological assumptions, the construing of "purpose" and "cause," the question of reductionism, research method, molar versus molecular analysis, and the social or human relevance of issues—all these are declared irrelevant. In the same symposium, Berlyne (1966) takes an even stronger view of these matters. Yet these problems persist in discussions of development, whether in biology or psychology. I fear it is too cavalier to wave them aside; such issues must be considered seriously in the concept of *development*.

Psychology and the Philosophy of Science

The root significance and deterministic character of epistemological assumptions, whether implicit or explicit, are discussed trenchantly by

Kessen (1962). Certainly, how we state the basis of our belief in the stable characteristics of reality will influence what phenomena we observe and how we observe them. Moreover, it is well to remember that such realities are constricted, not immanent in the organism or in the stimulus. A current paper in psychology reemphasizes the subjective character of initial assumptions and, indeed, of the scientific enterprise; the empirical basis of science, the autonomy of facts, is challenged (Kessel, 1969). Differences in such assumptions appear to be fundamental to the distinction I have drawn (perhaps in overdramatic terms) between experimental child psychologists of the behavior theory tradition and developmental psychologists who draw more heavily on biological or organismic models. Very likely such differences also occur in other disciplines related to human behavior. Though we ignore them, there are different assumptions about the nature of human nature. There are different interpretations of how theory is to be constructed. Intellectual predilections for different concepts or constructs which are formulated to provide theory play their part. Indeed, there may be personal predilections for *method* which enter this picture. Some prefer graphics, or what might be called a mapping approach to observed behavior; others prefer the identification and manipulation of quite explicitly defined environmental variables and their equally explicitly defined behavioral responses.

Further research in human development, then, requires reconsideration of issues in the philosophy of science. We have listed epistemological assumptions; these must be acknowledged and better understood. We know the different modes of theory construction, deductive and inductive, but are we fully aware of the complex interactions of intellectual strategies and our operational procedures and methodologies?

What about our interpretation of *explanation?* There is the constructive type of explanation, in which theory is built around concepts and constructs of successive orders of generality. This strategy, favored by many psychologists, runs the danger of spinning off into specialized and esoteric vocabularies, insufficiently defined operationally. Others, including some contributors to this volume, clearly favor a reductive strategy, wherein behavioral data are referred to physiology, physiological data are referred to biochemistry, and so on. But this strategy runs the danger of accepting as explanatory descriptions at the next lower level of phenomena. Claims are made that each type of explanation is fundamental—for the one, that only after a certain amount of concept and construct sophistication is attained at each phenomenal level can the descriptive levels be interrelated successfully; for the other, that science seeks to be reductionist in an ultimate sense. Both strategies must be utilized; though a particular investigator may work more comfortably in one rather than the other, he must see them as complementary, not competitive.

There are the other persisting philosophical issues in science—those of reductionism and determinism as related to the development of behavior. No one seriously denies that living matter is comprised of the same elements as inert or physical matter. No one seriously affirms an *élan vital* which speaks for the distinctions attributed to life—responsiveness to stimulation, self-movement, self-regulation and repair, and reproduction. Yet there are major qualitative differences between the relatively simply structured earthworm and the soil through which it burrows.

Likewise the problem of determinism. No scientist considers *causa finalis;* rather he consistently thinks in terms of *causa efficiens*. Yet in a thousand ways the behavioral scientist allows himself to traduce this basic principle. His language as well as the phenomena of his experience betray him into speaking of purpose and goal.

Finally, when one considers the development of behavior, there remain many paradoxes. A greater differentiation of the organism is accompanied by greater integration and organization of the parts. The more the organism reduces random activities to skill or habits, the freer it becomes to formulate new patterns of behavior. In the development of the individual case we are confronted with continuous change and also with undeniable continuities or rigidities. These are but some of the seeming paradoxes which beset developmental studies. If a paradox means that we have failed to make a necessary distinction, then we must work out these distinctions for future research to be fruitful.

In an interdisciplinary approach it is well to remember also that our concepts and constructs are phrased in language into which are fused common meanings or usage, technical meanings from our several disciplines, and personal or private meanings idiosyncratic to the experience of each of us. In addition our metrics differ. And there are some phenomena to which we may react meaningfully and reliably but which defy any metric; they are intersubjective. Issues such as these are sometimes insufficiently recognized.

Structure and Function

Another theoretical consideration to be resolved for furthering future research is found in the relation of phylogeny to ontogeny. There is a very real reason why the study of development in the individual leads the investigator inevitably to reflect on the study of evolution, and the problem is far more complicated than the simple recapitulation theory long ago advocated by Haeckel and by G. Stanley Hall. It is, of course, unquestionably accepted that any organism is the product of a long evolutionary process. This is certainly acknowledged to be true in form or structure and rather widely held to apply also to behavioral forms, at least up to the level of *Homo sapiens*. We recognize that man has evolved certain unique form characteristics—upright posture, eyes frontally positioned and bifocal, opposed thumb, complicated larynx, and uniquely developed and convoluted brain tissue. We recognize that he is certainly the least specialized in behavior, and consequently has greater adaptability than other forms. Nevertheless he does have a unique and ubiquitous form, and this structure enhances certain behavioral probabilities and reduces other behavioral probabilities. For example, the structure which opposes the thumb to the fingers opens to him a host of activities denied those lower primates. His erect posture condemns him to an unusual amount of lumbar and sacroiliac difficulties seemingly not found in other animals but frees his forelimbs for the most prodigious feats. His frontal vision allows complex, analytical perceptions, his complex larynx and elaborated brain, speech and thought.

The fact remains that in behavior, as in form and structure, there are gross limits to the variability of the mature organism which can generally be stated. Parameters for the *individual* can be stated only in a very general way and for selected characteristics, even when parental characteristics are known. But for groups—species, and to some extent, for family lines—prediction of the limits of adult variability can be made somewhat more specifically. Clearly, then, there are problems inherent in the relationship of phylogeny to ontogeny and of form to structure which, however they are construed on the abstract level and in the philosophy of science, have very practical consequences for the behavior of man.

The Problem of Behavioral Units

We have listed a number of considerations in the philosophy of science—matters of epistemological assumptions, predilection for a particular mode of theory construction or of scientific explanation, the relation of the phylogenetic and ontogenetic as these relate to behavior development, and the paradoxes which confront us in behavioral development. Theoretical considerations become complexly intertwined with methodological issues. But before considering certain of these, as they relate to the study of human behavior, it may be appropriate to make a further observation on the development of psychology as a science, one of the reasons for Koch's great pessimism about the field. As we have noted, psychology has abandoned a search for the grand encompassing theory or system and has progressed by attacking small problems and developing miniature or micro theories to handle these specific problems. It has frequently been said that the attempt to contrive any grand theory of development is foredoomed to failure (e.g., Zigler, 1963); we must find refuge in a variety of theories dealing with aspects of behavior or possibly of development.

With respect to psychology's inclination for limited theory, two observations may be made. The physical sciences long ago accepted the principle of complementarity—that seemingly contradictory theories may be true under appropriate circumstances; both may have their place in the development of science. Psychologists seem not to be quite so relativistic; in the bifurcation I have described of viewpoints concerning the nature of behavioral development, the behavior theorists, espousing a more mechanical view of the organism, and oversimplifying the behavioral situation by laboratory elegance, are particularly aggressive in asserting that theirs is the only proper stance to take. It seems to me that those who follow the more organismic model in their thinking are more faithful to the principle of complementarity. They readily admit the effectiveness of classic and operant conditioning, and the shaping of specific behaviors. Indeed they use these concepts at many points in their discussions and treatment of behavior, yet they insist with equal vigor that when behavior systems are looked at more broadly, the additive principle implicit in the behavior theory concept simply is inadequate to account for many observed phenomena.

The other point is that behavior, necessarily fragmented by the particularistic approach required by limited theories, must somehow be reassembled, reintegrated into the functioning organism, returned to its usual behavioral habitats. For it is here that scientific understanding and the application of laws are ultimately validated if effects significant for man are to be obtained.

The critics of a narrowly conceived behavioristic psychology are fairly numerous and well known (e.g., Wann, 1964). From philosophers of science to general psychologists, to clinicians, to personality theorists, they cover a broad range. Most of them are in one way or another concerned with problems of complex behavior, with man behaving as a unity—an integration of many part functions and subsystems.

It is my contention that the study of part-behaviors, and the construction of miniature theories appropriate to these limited areas of behavioral research, is entirely proper and very necessary. Nor are the results purely esoteric; their practical utility has been demonstrated again and again. However it does seem that the study of molar behaviors, as they occur in natural settings, is also entirely appropriate. We must deal with behavior changes over the life-span as well as the changes wrought under special conditions of training during more limited time intervals. Indeed, it is only in viewing such molar behaviors in natural and functional man-made environments, over long spans of time, that the peculiarly developmental characteristics of man's behavior may be found.

The concept of time, so often stressed by the developmentalist, may bear a crucial relationship to the difference in the views of development as held by the experimentalist and by the developmentalist. The experimentalist seeks to produce changes during quite short intervals. The developmentalist who, like the ethologist, goes to the natural setting, views time as more than a mere measure of environmental contact. Growth and change, developmentally considered, require a process of *nurturance*. And nurturance has a durational dimension not measured in trials or brief encounters. It is similar to the point made by the psychoanalyst Wheelis (1969) that in psychotherapy little by little the person comes to see himself as a different kind of self than he had conceptualized, supported all the while by nurturance, both emotional and insightful, supplied by the therapist. Thus therapeutic change in behavior occurs developmentally, as it were.

Moreover, the study of behavioral development, when it is applied to the human species, focusing on molar behavior, and using the comparative as well as ontogenetic approaches by the nature of the cultural imperative, will inevitably study problems intimately involved with human values. Values are always invoked in, and sometimes trigger, social and political action. And, we are repeatedly assured, the issue of values is of prime importance to man's chance for survival. Problems of radical environmental change, whether from nuclear or pollutant causes, may be more urgent than the issues considered in this volume.

Throughout this volume the issue of observation under rigorously controlled conditions versus "natural" conditions has persisted. There may be good reason for this, despite the laboratory experiment's central place (quite properly) in science. The issue may be less the experiment per se than the type of stimuli selected for experimental control. Few animals, including humans, experience many electric shocks during development in their usual habitats. It seems unlikely that such shock played any significant role in the evolution of most species. Hence the use of such shock in a learning experiment may be inappropriate and produce misleading results. Shock appears phenomenally to be a disruptive stimulus; it may confuse data rather than lead to understanding. For example, in one seminal program of research on infant learning, shocks applied to the sole of the foot (was this an example of perseveration of laboratory habit?) gave ambiguous results. After some fruitless months it occurred to the experimenters that a biologically relevant response, sucking, might be more profitable. It was! Thus the concept of behaviorally relevant information regularly available in the environment is important, as contrasted with the sensory discriminations possible under artificial or idealized conditions.

Problems of Methodology

A significant consideration for scientific methodology, then, is that behavior thus broadly construed cannot completely be subjected to the disciplines of the laboratory. A science of behavioral development may have to "soften" itself a bit. Our ethical standards will not permit certain deliberate alterations, such as conditions of deprivation which might permanently limit or debilitate the human subject. Moreover, rigorous control will not be feasible because of necessary time intervals for certain important human problems. Man is a notably curious, mobile creature, interacting with his complex changing environment, and simply cannot be contained uncontaminated under true experimental control for any long period of time. In addition, experimental designs permit us to handle only two, three, or possibly four independent variables; beyond this number of supposedly antecedent conditions our usual statistical procedures and their logic cannot readily go.

The experiment offers a problem which takes on special significance when complex symbolic behavior is studied. In the well-designed study the experimenter determines the response the child is to make and establishes the rules or conditions under which he makes it. If the child succeeds, the experimenter accepts the result. If he fails completely, the subject may be (and often is) discarded. Yet if child study has shown us only one important fact, it is that a subject, allowed to give a response or make a discovery in his own way, often is successful. The point is that learning experiments commonly focus on discrimination made under conditions experimentally proposed, not on the organism's perceptually guided behaviors under conditions other than the experiment. All this is not to discredit the experiment, which is the all-powerful tool of science. It is merely to suggest that experiments can be more intelligently designed when based on a rich fund of information concerning the organism's repertoire of responses outside the laboratory. All too often the graduate student and future scholar, trained principally within the laboratory, remains unaware of environmentally "normal" behavior and is the captive of his limited knowledge.

Longitudinal method, a special tool of developmental psychology, is not an experimental design, not even a quasi-experimental design (Campbell and Stanley, 1963). Kessen's discussion of the method (1960), seeking to incorporate the S–R paradigm, makes age the independent variable when any response is studied quantitatively. But this will not do for Kessen or anyone else who considers time alone an insufficient antecedent condition or "cause" of behavioral change or development.

True, the longitudinal method is descriptive, but we have already acknowledged that the strict positivistic viewpoint may be too limited in its characteristic view of man as object rather than agent. The longitudinal method, of course, comes within the purview of the measurement of change, the best statistical overview of which is the collection of papers edited by C. W. Harris (1963). It has a number of serious drawbacks which include high money and time costs, selective sampling, and complex problems relating to the effects of the changing social milieu. Compromises with this costly method have been suggested by Bell (1953, 1954), Schaie (1965), and Baltes (1968), among others. Yet multiple measurements of the same cases remain our best way of getting at development considered as *process*. Shuttleworth's discussion (1939) of the longitudinal method, its advantages and disadvantages, remains a classic too little known today.

Multivariate concepts and methods must be developed and used if the complex causal networks operative in development are to be analyzed. A possible but largely untried approach has recently been suggested by Van den Daele (1969) as "set-theoretical" models which allow for the treatment of multidimensional development wherein relatively different levels of maturity may coexist at the same period. This fact has long been recognized in child study, but never very successfully handled, although Olson (e.g., 1957) has advocated a multifactorial, "organismic age" as a developmental measure.

Another method, eschewed by the hard-nosed or entered reluctantly because of its post-hoc character, is the old individual differences approach to the contrasted group or the "experiment of nature." True, this type of research is hypothesis-generating rather than hypothesis-testing, but rigorously conducted, with adequate regard for the identification of conditions, selection of samples, and precision of instruments, we can get socially and scientifically useful information. With such research we can make informed statements of a probabilistic character; without it we can make only hortatory or purely political statements.

Developmental studies of human behavior, then, will be experimental whenever possible and wherever human ingenuity can break up problems to manipulable experimental units without destroying the original meaningful issues. But developmental studies of behavior must also incorporate animal research, make use of inferences from comparative studies, utilize *ex post facto* designs with caution, multivariate methods and "experiments" of nature as well as so-called quasi-experimental designs, if they are to come to grips with major *developmental* issues in future research.

Ubiquitous Problems of Development

In addition to its scientific methodology, there are a number of special problems which beset the study of human behavior, especially when viewed developmentally. There is its characteristic *complexity* and *organization*, its apparent *directionality*, its *process* nature, the problem of *stages*, the question of *hierarchical relationships*, and finally the concept of *potential*. All these are important considerations for future research on human development. Each of these problems has its parallel in aspects of the development of physical structure; indeed, a useful analogical model for behavioral development may come from that of structural growth.

First is the problem of complexity. This was identified a number of years ago as *organized complexity* by Warren Weaver (1967, pp. 31–33). For long the behavioral scientist has looked at behavior dimensions one or two at a time. Yet it seems necessary to consider the organization of multiple factors in some organismic fashion. Causation is never simple; it is complex, and interactions among identifiable variables themselves have effects on development that apparently cannot be told from the individual variables taken singly. From physiology we can find a crude analogy. One can study the action of the heart and of the lungs quite separately, yet to understand the organism one must know something of how the functions of the circulatory and respiratory systems are integrated in the process of maintaining life.

Any study of the factor of complexity must take into account the fact that over time development shows a *directionality*. Now it is quite clear that chronological time itself is merely incidental and not always an adequate measure of the directional change which occurs even when that is linear. We have long been accustomed to calendar time and to physiological time. There may be other distinctions which we must yet fathom. The scientist of the behavioral theory persuasion frequently uses the number of organism–stimulus contacts, the number of trials, as the important measure. This measure is scarcely related to time, developmentally considered. Yet in physical growth processes changes are sufficiently correlated with time so that time or age becomes a convenient measure of the change.

Nevertheless the direction of development in general is from simple to more complex, from low organization to more complex organization. In structure the ultimate form and size is predictable from quite early ages. In behavior the range of possible limits is similarly predictable, though with less precision. Man also characteristically projects himself into the future through goals and purposes. Through his intricate symbolizing apparatus he can construe the possibilities of events that have not yet occurred. He projects himself into his imagined, anticipated, or hoped-for future; he sets goals. And this future, these goals, as well as his past learnings, exert constraint on his present behavior. Moreover the point is often made that what is "real" for the individual is *his* perception, *his* construction, of an event. Hence his psychological sets, however acquired, have a certain teleological significance.

If one adamantly rejects this consideration, let us recall the view of Kurt Lewin, a thoroughly behavioral psychologist, who insisted that behavior is a function of the environment of the moment and capable of reduction to mathematical equations. He accommodated the undeniable importance of the organism's past history as one factor in his equation. Similarly one might include the conceptualized future goal as another factor in the equation.

But what about the *organization* of behavior? Since the days of Spencer it has been clearly recognized that the organism maintains an equilibrium with its environment; when it fails to maintain this equilibrium it dies. In the state of equilibrium organisms show variability, spontaneity, indeed "purposiveness," in their behavioral responses. These responses show coordination, organization. In other words the organism adapts to environmental disturbances. It uses energy from outside to counter such disturbances, even while they are acting. Thus the organism works counter to the physical principle of the degradation of energy. Its capacity to store energy introduced from outside makes possible complex and flexible behavior. It is an open system.

Many organismic characteristics can be simulated in the electronic computer, which also has sensory, storage, connective, and effect-on devices. The neural tissue in the organism and the circuits in the machine enable both to make the correct response. Living tissue has the property of "irritability"; that is, it is capable of quick and vigorous response; a small disturbance may produce a large, often variable effect. Thus the reaction is equal to or greater than the disturbance.

Also, the organism possesses the property of negative feedback. The input to the motor effort depends in part on its own output as well as on the disturbance. As the output is effective, the output reduces itself. Thus the system is capable of self-modification. Thus far the computer possesses this characteristic when specific disturbances are anticipated and planned for.

Computers clearly have the reverse capability—output can continue to stimulate itself. Such positive feedback likewise seems to appear under certain conditions in man, as in "emotional" states. For example anger or rage seems to feed on itself, but only for a time. Successful and pleasant activities similarly seem to exert a similar positive reinforcement function. Olds (1955) has, indeed, located a center in the brain septal area of the rat which seems to control pleasant sensations; we have the demonstration of animals continuing self-stimulation by bar pressing, which sends minute electrical stimuli to electrodes implanted in this center.

Another function noted in man is the function of time in the searching and control procedures. The influence of the output on the input appears to decrease exponentially with time. The phenomenon is well illustrated in learning curves and certainly attested by experience, subjectively noted or objectively measured. Computer simulation of human learning is being explored, and computer simulations of the complex processes of development should be fruitful.

Man, however, has a particular "sign-making" capacity. He can and does group stimuli into classes to which he makes appropriate and uniform response. We call this "generalization." While stimulus generalization is disputed by some learning theorists as merely deficient discrimination, an active generalizing function is important in cognitive theory and in a number of theories of language development. Computer simulation of so-called cognitive processes has been accomplished, though the limits of such simulation are still debated.

The English psychologist Craik (1966, pp. 17–18) makes a distinction between quantitative feedback and "qualitative feedback," wherein the organism is actuated by results to make new, distinctive, often unanticipated connections in its nervous system. By these new connections the organism is enabled to explore the possibilities of varied response to stimuli. Curiosity, exploration, and manipulation noted especially in primates, and emphasized recently by Harlow (1953), Berlyne (1960), and Montgomery (1953), come to mind at once. Computers similarly can be so programmed, although their ultimate variability or "ingenuity" has not yet been fully explored.

The *process* character of development was first experienced in the growth area by fitting mathematical curves to empirically determined data. Shuttleworth (1939), Shock (1951), and others have emphasized that we cannot measure the growth process directly, only its residue, through the determination of increments. The mathematics of the calculus and the statistics of time series have proved useful. Similar applications have been made to data derived from learning studies, resulting in learning curves based on number of trials generally extending over a limited time period. Learning curves have been discussed succinctly by Hilgard (1951), and their similarity mathematically to growth curves, in some instances, is apparent.

The application of curve fitting to psychological data gathered longitudinally on the same individuals has been limited by the paucity of such data but even more by the character of the instruments available in many "psychological" areas, such as social skill, personal adjustment or adaptation, motivation and the like. Such instruments as exist are not scaled in such fashion as to permit the derivation of increments and their mathematical manipulation. Moreover, the character of these important areas of human development and adaptation is so general that elements of appropriate scales suitable for one age have no relevance to similar domains at another age. Even in the much-researched and quantified area of mental skills and abilities, the content and character of tests changes considerably over the first two decades, and the equivalence of growth units has consequently long been a problem. We say that qualitative changes occur; perhaps this is the best that can be said at present. When we define such phenomenological developments so precisely that we can develop scalable instruments, the domain often ceases to be recognized in the human terms that gave it meaning originally.

Experimental studies generally stress the tracing of effects into differences between means in the dependent variable. Consequently curve fitting and time series statistics are generally neglected in psychological statistics courses. In the future, developmental studies must give attention both to calibrating instruments and to appropriate methods for mathematically expressing process functions.

Stages in development are usually identified as segments of the age continuum. Often they are seen so distinct from one another as to be considered qualitatively different. But psychology quite generally disclaims the notion of discontinuities. Whenever we study closely (i.e., measure frequently) the course of change in a behavioral variable, whether occurring in nature or manipulated in the laboratory, we generally find increments so small as to be considered continuous. Often these changes, measured over short time intervals, occur within the error of our measuring instruments.

It seems that when we observe behavior in its gross manifestations, we note stages. When we measure closely, we find continuity. Yet when we look at long-continued measurements of variables, particularly skills, we note a progressive process in which fairly long intervals of gradual change are followed by shorter intervals of more rapid change. While one might view the periods of rapid change (perhaps periods of reorganization?) as stages, it has been customary to view the periods of gradual change characterized by distinctive behavior properties as the stages, and the periods of rapid change as the transitions.

Thus inevitably the stage concept must accommodate the further concept of transition. It must also accommodate the undeniable fact of change by small, sometimes seemingly erratic increments. In a classic paper on the stage problem, Kessen (1962) has made a signal contribution to the analysis of these problems. He has observed that traditional learning theory really concentrates on a transition process between "states," which are momentary, and arbitrarily selected, thin time-slices of continually changing behavior. He notes the recent attempts of developmental psychologists in the American learning theory tradition to write general and inclusive formulas for behavioral change involving factors for stimulus input, and for behavioral responses, which will hold for all behavior and, indeed, for all organisms. He recognizes that in such a formulation a stage as a qualitative event has no place; stage becomes merely a parametric variation in the general formula. Thus in these formulas demonstrable age changes in behavior are accounted for by values which modify the generalized constants so as to predict the age variations.

He recognizes that stage is a persistent idea, however, and suggests that computer simulation of complex behaviors may validate the notion of stages. If, as noted above, we manage to write a precise rule system which accounts for a behavioral event, but find that we must write different programs, involving modifications in the rule systems, to simulate behavior at different ages, we will have a precise basis for defining stages. Such stages are, however, empirically rather than theoretically based. This idea is a new departure, and although it appears promising, its fruitfulness is yet to be demonstrated.

Kessen's admirable paper demonstrates the difficulties of the stage concept for scientific purposes. The simple statement of successive stages cannot lead to a general theory. By its very nature, a stage theory cannot turn up negative instances to compare with the universal case. Only a truly experimental science can test the consequences of introducing or withholding variables into a sequence of events.

At the Dedham Conference where Kessen's paper was presented, there was a persisting and unresolved divergence between those preoccupied with transitions and those who insisted that transitions were from one state of affairs to another state of affairs. The latter often refused to accept the infinitely brief time-slice manner of establishing "states," and preferred to talk of *periods* of time, or stages. Further, they noted that the field of developmental psychology presents many problems which cannot, for strategic or ethical reasons, be put to experimental test.

One solution to this old problem, as we have noted, is to withdraw to those problems which can be examined in the rigorous experiment. While this withdrawal may be deplored in the short run (as appears to be happening in society at present), it may prove profitable in the long run, particularly when the investigator maintains a steady eye on larger issue while engaging the methodological minutiae of his area. An example is the study of perceptual development by Eleanor Gibson (1969). Although she opts for *trends,* not stages, she fully recognizes the increasingly hierarchical character of behavioral organization with age and experience. Her book is a magnificent example of how one specific function of organism can be studied in a basic way, yet related to other functions, and shown to have major social meaning and utility.

The *hierarchical* character of development has long been implicitly recognized in the concepts of differentiation and integration, first applied to embryonic structure and then to the ontogenesis of fetal movement. More recently, the organization of behavior into hierarchies of superordinate and subordinate categories has been recognized and increasingly appealed to in theory. Piaget's use of this principle in his developmental theory of intelligence is well known. The processes of assimilation and accommodation result in an organized cognitive structure of ever-increasing complexity. His position also readily accommodates the previously mentioned issue of apparent qualitative change when the content and character of different points or zones in development are compared. The related, hierarchical character of development is apparent most clearly when the process is traced through its entire course. In the field of complex human learning and concept formation, Ausubel (1968) has made significant and central use of the concept of "organizers," which clearly has a hierarchical character.

Recently, behavioristically oriented psychologists have appealed to similar principles. Gagné (1965) identifies eight kinds of human learning, from signal learning (the conditioned reflex) to problem solving. These are clearly arranged in a series; each succeeding type subsumes the preceding type; and the eight types parallel ontogenetic development in their appearance, though as yet in no precisely determined age-relatedness. He specifically utilizes such a concept in his later discussion of learning and developmental theory (1968); though he treats it as "cumulative learning," it has the complex, branching character of a hierarchy of superordinates and subordinates. Students of verbal behavior, especially language development, utilize hierarchical concepts freely (e.g., Bellugi and Brown, 1964; Brown and Bellugi, 1964; W. Miller and Ervin, 1964), as do those working on concept formation (e.g., Bruner et al., 1966). The rigorous chaining theory of language learning held by Staats (1968), however, continues to treat the organized, hierarchical character of sequentiality as a sequential, cumulative process; his diagrams lack the branching superordinating–subordinating character of those of Gagné. Berlyne (1965) is much more successful in relating stimulus–response language and concepts to the hierarchical feature of behavior as emphasized by the less behavior-theory-minded developmentalists.

We earlier noted that certain teleological implications seem to intrude themselves inevitably in discussions of human behavioral development, especially through the concepts of goal or objective. The concept of end-state, whether conceived as mature structure or as behavioral goal, also involves the concept of *potential,* another of the aspects peculiar to behavioral development.

In physical growth we know full well that environmental nurturance is necessary to call forth and to realize the size and form of the mature organism. We know that environmental circumstances must support the character of that development or anomalies will result. Yet we also know that there are definite limits to the size and form which that ultimate state will achieve, even within widely varying conditions or environment. Potentiality may be a range, not a point or a state, but it nevertheless has reasonably clear-cut parameters.

Similar concepts may apply to the development of behavior. In a given individual certain parameters may prescribe the range of ultimate attainment possible. Circumstances of behavioral support (i.e., stimulation which leads to learning) will determine the level of achievement within this range of potential.

For so long has behavioral science in the United States been dominated by the completely environmentalistic viewpoint that it is almost heresy to make such a statement regarding behavior. We recognize it in physical qualities, but are loath to believe there are individual differences in behavior potential. When behavior falls short of what is desired we invariably lay the blame on the conditions of nurture, yet it is clear that in many forms of animal life some behaviors are more readily modifiable or conditionable than others. Could it not be true that something analogous to this obtains in the human being as well? Any number of infant studies have shown that certain behaviors respond to conditioning more readily than others.

Moreover it is increasingly noted that particular stimulation is more potent in influencing behavior during certain developmental time intervals or "stages" than at others. Indeed, after certain periods in development, virtually no amount or kind of environmental "enrichment" seems to make a difference. This familiar concept of "critical periods" is demonstrable in various species, and analogies have been drawn to human development. Whether in man this changing susceptibility is a necessary characteristic of development or enforced by social constraints on an organism growing in complexity and social responsivity remains a question. Yet it is an important issue, socially, as the debates over educational curricula, enrichment experiences, and the like attest.

Moreover the concept of potential has no meaning apart from the projection into the future which we mentioned earlier. Actualization of potential implies a goal, that which it will be actualized into. Here again, this matter skirts dangerously on the forbidden territory of teleology. But the concept of potential has no meaning when restricted solely to the present.

In discussing the meaning of potential it is perhaps apropos to mention once more the almost forbidden topic of volition or will. William James took the phenomenological position that "desire, wish, will are states of mind which everyone knows, and which no definition can make plainer" (1890, Vol. II, p. 486). He made the distinction between wish and will as that between the perception of the impossibility or possibility of one's attainment of a goal. Volition, or acting upon the possibility of goal attainment, rests on the voluntary movements of the body. These movements depend in their turn on mental conceptions made up of memories or memory images of perceptions and sensations; these in turn reduce to efforts of attention. At the center of attention is the idea or concept.

Clinical and counseling psychology both utilize concepts of potential and development. It is interesting to note that whatever the philosophical considerations of will or "free will," there is a strong movement among some psychotherapists toward a concept of volition. So-called "rational therapy" appears to rest on such assumptions. Allen Wheelis (1969), a psychoanalyst, presumably trapped by the id and the unconscious, insists that while behavior or personality change is very difficult, "within us lies the potential for change, the freedom to choose other courses." He insists freedom is "the awarenesss of alternatives and the ability to choose." In his therapy, insight is not enough; "effort and will are crucial." Indeed, he argues that we place our own restrictions on ourselves, creating the necessities which we believe constrain us. Personality change, when it occurs at all, follows long and arduous effort. A similar plea for the recognition of volition, the will, in psychotherapy and in the conduct of healthy personal life occupies half of Rollo May's recent book (1969).

However troublesome to science, the developmental concepts of organization, directionality, process, potential, and stages have a humanistic and qualitative component resulting from viewing man as Man, and not as a collection of part processes. The phenomenon of man's development, studied according to scientific canons of objectivity, parsimony, replicability, and the like may lead us through concepts of organized complexity to a humanly meaningful view as well as scientific understanding of behavior process. Perhaps we may be cautioned as well as take heart from a comment by the Nobel prize-winning physicist Richard Feynman (1967). Noting that the biggest mysteries in his science occur precisely "where the laws are known but we don't know exactly what's going on," he adds, ". . . we get reports from the experimentalists, the watchers of the chess game, and we try to analyze the information. We may even suggest new experiments. But we're still waiting and hoping for the big strategy. Then maybe we'll really understand how wonderful is nature." Developmental embryologists seem invariably to gain a similar sense of wonder as they advance knowledge in their field. Why do psychologists remain so pedestrian when confronting the processes of behavioral change and adaptation? Is it because they have not yet recognized the human aspects of the really big issues of development?

REFERENCES

Ausubel, D. P. (1968). "Educational Psychology, A Cognitive View." Holt, New York.

Baltes, P. B. (1968). Longitudinal and cross-sectional sequences in the study of age and generation effects. *Hum. Develop.* Vol. 11, 145–171.

Bandura, A. (1969). "Principles of Behavior Modification." Holt, New York.

Barker, R. G., and Wright, H. F. (1954). "Midwest and its Children." Harper, New York.

Bell, R. Q. (1953). Convergence: An accelerated longitudinal approach. *Child Develop.* Vol. 24, 145–152.

Bell, R. Q. (1954). An experimental test of the accelerated longitudinal approach. *Child Develop.* Vol. 25, 281–286.

Bellugi, U., and Brown, R., Eds. (1964). The Acquisition of Language. In *Monogr. Soc. Res. Child Develop.* Vol. 29, Ser. No. 92, 5–191.

Berlyne, D. E. (1960). "Conflict, Arousal and Curiosity." McGraw-Hill, New York.
Berlyne, D. E. (1965). "Structure and Direction in Thinking." Wiley, New York.
Berlyne, D. E. (1966). Discussion: The delimitation of cognitive development. *Monogr. Soc. Res. Child Develop.* Vol. 31, No. 5, Ser. No. 107, 71–81
Bijou, S. W., and Baer, D. M. (1961). "Child Development," Vol. I. Appleton, New York.
Bijou, S. W., and Baer, D. M. (1965). "Child Development," Vol. II. Appleton, New York.
Brown, R., and Bellugi, U. (1964). Three processes in the child's acquisition of syntax. *Harvard Educ. Rev.* Vol. 34, 133–151.
Bruner, J. S., Olver, R., and Greenfield, P. (1966). "Studies in Cognitive Growth." Wiley, New York.
Campbell, D. T., and Stanley, J. (1963). Experimental and quasi-experimental designs for research on teaching. *In* "Handbook of Research on Teaching" (N. L. Gage, ed.), pp. 171–246. Rand McNally, Chicago, Illinois.
Craik, K. J. W. (1966). "The Nature of Psychology." Cambridge Univ. Press, London and New York.
Feynman, R. (1967). Quoted by Lee Edson, *in* "Two Men in Search of the Quark." *N. Y. Times Mag.* Oct. 8, VI, 55ff.
Gagné, R. M. (1965). "The Conditions of Learning." Holt, New York.
Gagné, R. M. (1968). Contributions of learning to human development. *Psychol. Rev.* Vol. 75, 177–191.
Gibson, E. (1969). "Principles of Perceptual Learning and Development." Appleton, New York.
Harlow, H. F. (1953). Motivation as a factor in the acquisition of new responses. *In* "Current Theory and Research in Motivation: A Symposium" (M. R. Jones, ed.), pp. 24–49. Univ. of Nebraska Press, Lincoln, Nebraska.
Harris, C. W. (1963). "Problems in Measuring Change." Univ. of Wisconsin Press, Madison, Wisconsin.
Hilgard, E. R. (1951). Methods and procedures in the study of learning. *In* "Handbook of Experimental Psychology" (S. S. Stevens, ed.), pp. 517–567. Wiley, New York.
Hunt, J. McV. (1960). Experience and the development of motivation: Some reinterpretations. *Child Develop.* Vol. 31, 489–504.
James, W. (1890). "The Principles of Psychology," Vols. I and II. Holt, New York.
Jenkins, J. J., and Palermo, D. S. (1964). Mediation processes and the acquisition of linguistic structure. *Monogr. Soc. Res. Child Develop.* Vol. 29, No. 1, Ser. No. 92, 141–169.
Kendler, T. (1965). Development of mediating responses in children. *Monogr. Soc. Res. Child Develop.* Vol. 28, No. 2, Ser. No. 86, 33–48.
Kessel, F. S. (1969). The philosophy of science as proclaimed and science as practiced: "Identity" or "dualism?" *Amer. Psychol.* Vol. 24, 999–1005.
Kessen, W. (1960). Research design in the study of developmental problems. *In* "Handbook of Research Methods in Child Development" (P. H. Mussen, ed.), pp. 36–70. Wiley, New York.
Kessen, W. (1962). "Stage" and "structure" in the study of children. *Monogr. Soc. Res. Child Develop.* Vol. 27, No. 2, Ser. No. 83, 65–82.
Koch, S. (1969). Psychology cannot be a coherent science. *Psychol. Today* Vol. 3, No. 4, 14ff.

McCandless, B., and Spiker, C. C. (1956). Experimental research in child psychology. *Child Develop.* Vol. 27, 78-80.

May, R. (1969). "Love and Will." Norton, New York.

Miller, G. (1965). Some preliminaries to psycholinguistics. *Amer. Psychol.* Vol. 20, 15-20.

Miller, W., and Ervin, S. (1964). The development of grammar in child language. *Monogr. Soc. Res. Child Develop.* Vol. 29, No. 1, Ser. No. 92, 9-34.

Montgomery, K. C. (1953). The effect of the hunger and thirst drives upon exploratory behavior. *J. Comp. Physiol. Psychol.* Vol. 46, 315-319.

Mowrer, O. H. (1960a). "Learning Theory and Behavior." Wiley, New York.

Mowrer, O. H. (1960b). "Learning Theory and the Symbolic Processes." Wiley, New York.

Olds, J. (1955). Physiological mechanisms of reward. *In* "Nebraska Symposium on Motivation" (M. R. Jones, ed.), pp. 73-139. Univ. of Nebraska Press, Lincoln, Nebraska.

Olson, W. E. (1957). Developmental theory in education. *In* "The Concept of Development" (D. B. Harris, ed.), pp. 259-274. Univ. of Minnesota Press, Minneapolis, Minnesota.

Osgood, C. E. (1952). The nature and measurement of meaning. *Psychol. Bull.* Vol. 49, 197-231.

Piaget, J. (1953). "The Origin of Intelligence in the Child." Routledge & Kegan Paul, London.

Piaget, J. "The Construction of Reality in the Child." Basic Books, New York.

Schaie, K. W. (1965). A general model for the study of developmental problems. *Psychol. Bull.* Vol. 64, 92-107.

Sears, R. R. (1951). A theoretical framework for personality and social behavior. *Amer. Psychol.* Vol. 6, 476-482.

Shock, N. W. (1951). Growth curves. *In* "Handbook of Experimental Psychology" (S. S. Stevens, ed.), pp. 330-346. Wiley, New York.

Shuttleworth, F. K. (1939). The physical and mental growth of girls and boys age six to nineteen in relation to age at maximum growth. *Monogr. Soc. Res. Child Develop.* Vol. 4, No. 3, Ser. No. 22, vi-291.

Skinner, B. F. (1953). "Science and Human Behavior." Macmillan, New York.

Skinner, B. F. (1957). "Verbal Behavior." Appleton, New York.

Spiker, C. C. (1966). The concept of development: Relevant and irrelevant issues. *Monogr. Soc. Res. Child Develop.* Vol. 31, No. 5, Ser. No. 107, 40-54.

Staats, A. W. (1968). "Learning, Language, and Cognition." Holt, New York.

Stevenson, H. W. (1962). Piaget, behavior theory and intelligence. *Monogr. Soc. Res. Child Develop.* Vol. 27, No. 2, Ser. No. 83, 113-126

Van den Daele, L. D. (1969). Qualitative models in developmental analysis. *Develop. Psychol.* Vol. 1, 303-310.

Wann, T. W., ed. (1964). "Behaviorism and Phenomenology." Univ. of Chicago Press, Chicago, Illinois.

Weaver, W. (1967). "Science and Imagination." Basic Books, New York.

Wheelis, A. (1969). How people change. *Commentary* Vol. 47, No. 5, 56-66.

White, R. W. (1959). Motivation reconsidered: The concept of competence. *Psychol. Rev.* Vol. 66, 297-333.

Zigler, E. (1963). Metatheoretical issues in developmental psychology. *In* "Theories in Contemporary Psychology" (M. H. Marx, ed.), pp. 341-369. Macmillan, New York.

Discussion

L. P. Lipsitt: As an experimental child psychologist, I speak from a somewhat different point of view of the field than Dr. Harris represents, for my work on neonatal behavior and learning processes of the infant tends to be of an experimental manipulative sort which explores behavior processes under laboratory conditions, usually using physically specifiable stimulating conditions and recording fairly objective response measures. The style of this work and that of some of my closest colleagues is designed to enhance the probability of documenting replicable functional relationships which will illuminate the manner in which behavioral consequences are determined by documented antecedent conditions. We aim, for example, to be able eventually to describe the behavioral repertoire of the young and growing organism in terms of experiential conditions required to call forth or make manifest the behavioral capabilities of children at different ages. It is this sort of orientation to the study of children's behavior that has come in for some rather well-controlled kicks in the tail in Dr. Harris' presentation, largely on grounds that the laboratory approach tends to preclude the "naturalistic" study of child behavior and perhaps misses out in the documentation of psychological development which emphasizes the whole child—his uniqueness, his "organization," his organismic integrity, in short, his humanity.

The fact of the matter is that the study of children through the utilization of sophisticated equipment, good stimulus control, and sound response measurement—all of the characteristics which Dr. Harris suggests typify "laboratory elegance"—do not signify disinterest, aloofness, or insensitivity on the part of the developmental scientist. The experimental child psychologist simply seeks to study development under conditions that will enable him to explain and predict behavior in situations where he was not previously able to do so, or, at least, not quite so precisely. All of the infant experimenters that I know are creatures of humanity themselves and have a deep and abiding interest in and respect for the beauty of development unfolding and the worth and dignity of the individual. Moreover, many recent studies of infant behavior have sought to document individual differences in response attributes and to study the persistence of these with time. Additionally, laboratory behavior does bear a relationship to behavioral phenomena in "real life."

The very study of psychological processes, which Dr. Harris admires, is actually the hallmark of experimental psychology. While the notion of processes can be diversely interpreted to include or exclude whatever type of studies one wishes, the experimental child psychologist who concentrates on the study of learning processes seeks to examine the multitude of stimulus and organismic conditions which facilitate learning. It would seem to me that, empirically, the most profitable approach to the study of behavior processes would be through the avenue of documenting the relationship between precursor circumstances, on the one hand, and developmental outcome, on the other. Unfortunately, the term processes is too often used by propagandists on behalf of one scientific methodology or another to elevate one method while denigrating another.

I would like to suggest that the field of child development, which includes the discipline of child psychology, has been hung up for a number of years on the study of what might be termed the emerging milestone-behaviors of infants and children. The organic anthropometric model served respectably, and still does so, in the study of certain kinds of organismic variables such as height and weight and other physical dimensions, but its wholesale adoption as a model for the study of behavior has sometimes made the field of child development look as though the only kinds of functional relationship which are of interest to the child developmentalist are those which plot the emergence of some behavioral attribute as a function of age. The classic studies of Gesell and his colleagues follow pretty much the anthropometric model, and child developmentalists have spent a good deal of time searching after the typical age at which the normal child first achieves the pincer grasp, first says three meaningful words in association with one another, first pulls himself to standing, first walks, and so on. It was an easy step for the child psychologist of 40 years ago to simply begin the study of mental phenomena in roughly the same way. When the fact emerged that infants and children are quite consistent with respect to the age of emergence of these milestone-behaviors, the quantification and comparison game began which capitalized upon the norms to create the concept of mental age. Mental age was the behavioral equivalent of physical measurement, like the study of weight and height as a function of chronological age. I think that what happened is that through the developing interest, especially in this country perhaps, in psychometrics and the gathering of norms, the developmental testing approach found a ready audience among professionals interested in helping to discern whether given individual children matched properly with their peer groups in terms of behavioral performance. It is only now, although much evidence was around to this effect even 20 years ago, that we are fully appreciating that the mental age measurements which these norms provided on infants do not predict the behavior of the child at successive ages very well, particularly over the long term. More importantly, the obsessive amassing of extensive descriptive norms relating to the appearance, at successive ages, of milestone-behaviors did not enable the serious student of development to grasp the processes through which these behaviors emerged. While we know the age at which chlidren typically begin to walk, the age at which they first utter words, the age by which they engage in detour behavior to attain a partially hidden object, and while we even have extensive information relating to the variability of appearance of such behaviors and the differences among subcultures with respect to them, we have very little information indeed as to how these transitions, these acquisitions, and these transactions come about.

I do not know of a single study in the developmental literature which would illuminate the learning mechanisms which are obviously present and by which walking behavior is acquired, even though I don't believe that any of us would doubt that there are learning processes involved, regardless of where we sit on the nature–nurture continuum. Every one of us who has ever had a child or who has watched a child begin to walk has observed that usually the parents stand face to face and about a foot apart from one another, holding the child on the floor upright on his legs, and flopping the child from one parent to the other. When the child flops easily the one-foot distance, the parents or other adults back up to about two feet and again do the same. The child gradually takes one step, then two, then three, and so on, catching himself in the arms of the parent as he falls that last step each time. Sometimes infants can be seen to administer this experience to themselves as they flop from one side of a playpen to an adjacent perpendicular side. All of this involves a shaping-up process which is to some unknown extent experienced by the child who is "ready" (i.e., has the potential) to walk. Whatever one might say about the genetic built-in-ness of walking behavior, that is, whatever one might say about the pre-programmed potential for the two-legged stance and for walking, one has to admit that there is learning involved in the acquisition of this and other milestone-behaviors, and there is much that we have yet to discover about the manner in which the age of onset of these milestone-behaviors can be pushed around, for better or worse, by facilitative or deleterious training. I would say, therefore, that what we need to do, and I think I'm in agreement with Dr. Harris in at least this, is to have more studies of processes—that is, of the relationship between precursor events and behavioral consequences—and I believe that in order to illuminate such processes we must know more about specific learning mechanisms. This is what the experimental child psychologist is after—learning mechanisms, learning processes, perceptual phenomena, response-reinforcement contingencies, and so on. The experimental child psychologist is seeking to delineate the stimulus conditions under which behavior is controlled.

Now I think that when one fully appreciates that, he has little further trouble (even if he is a learning psychologist) with the heredity-environment or maturation-learning dichotomies. These dichotomies break down, because a complete specification of the stimulating circumstances by which the organism is controlled must include both congenital and learned stimulation. Behavior is obviously both hereditarily and environmentally controlled. All learning proceeds on the basis of congenital dispositions, and no organism can exceed its hereditary potential. As Dr. Eisenberg said previously, nothing can be accomplished which is not possible. Therefore learning is inextricably tied to and restricted by hereditary potential or congenital permission. It takes a certain kind of protoplasm, a certain kind of genetic structure, for a walking infant to emerge from a nonwalking condition, or for a certain species to talk with syntax, and that's perfectly all right with the learning psychologist!

I really think, then, that because all learning processes must capitalize upon hereditary givens, the learning-heredity issue is a kind of straw man. I think that there is all too often the spurious assumption made on the part of scientific investigators and spokesmen who are more disposed toward the study of genetically controlled behavior (those who happen to be more over on the constitutional side of the worn-out continuum) that behavior investigators like Pavlov and Watson and Hull, and even Skinner, have no respect for constitutional attributes and individual differences in the determination of environmentally potentiated behavior. The fact of the matter is, however, that Pavlov was a physiologist and knew very well, as did Watson, one of his successors, that you can't get conditioning unless you first have an unconditioned response repertoire. There has to be a congenital response system present in order for any kind of conditioning to occur, whether it be classical or operant.

Learning, then, is innate. This stems from the dependency of learning processes on congenital, reflexive, and endogenously stimulated behavior. I think that this is the only solution to this dilemma that the learning psychologist seems to get forced into, usually by unanswerable questions concerning the relative importance of nature and nurture variables. Learning is, after all, a natural phenomenon!

I would not want anything that I said to be construed as suggesting that unconditioned responses are not modifiable. They definitely are! Habituation phenomena have been well studied, wherein a particular unconditioned response is first elicited by some stimulus. With repeated elicitation, the response wanes in strength and is sometimes caused to disappear entirely. Then if you wait a while and stimulate again, recovery of the response can be seen to occur. Similarly, if the stimulus is changed somewhat from the habituation stimulus, recovery will also occur, apparently to an extent commensurate with the distinctiveness of the recovery stimulus.

Definitely, unconditioned responses are experientially modifiable, but this does not detract in my opinion from the interpretation that, in classical conditioning, there must be an unconditioned response there for behavior modification or learning to commence and progress. Similarly, in operant conditioning, the pigeon must have the pecking response, or some other congenital substitute, which he has simply by virtue of membership in a particular species, which can be shaped for learning of that sort to occur.

That is to say, the congenital response repertoire is absolutely necessary for conditioning. It is in this sense that I insist on learning as an innate attribute. It does not make sense to me for response systems or patterns to be classified distinctively as either learned or innate.

Finally, I would like to add this statement. Much has been mentioned about the contributions of Dr. Schneirla. I think it was said that Schneirla once had a useful theory and orientation, particularly with regard to the assumption about the importance of the stimulus intensity continuum in determining approach and withdrawal behavior, but that the theoretical proposition had now outlived its usefulness. It so happens that within the field of experimental child psychology, particularly among those now studying infant behavior, there is a current rejuvenation of the notion that high stimulus intensities promote withdrawal and milder stimuli instigate approach behavior. The line of research to which I am alluding has actually been brought back into American infant laboratories through the work of Sokolov and other Soviet investigators rather than from the writings of Schneirla himself. Sokolov and his followers, such as Lacey and Graham in this country, both of the latter dealing with children, have begun to contrast orienting behavior with defensive reflexes and have remarked on how defensive responding is a casting off of stimuli whereas orienting behavior sets the organism up for further intake and assimilation of stimuli. These researchers have been working with heart rate in the newborn and older child, and they have equated cardiac deceleration with the orienting response, and cardiac acceleration with the defensive reflex. There is really a very active area of research here with children, in which I am myself involved, that I think has a considerable relationship to the thinking of Schneirla.

LEVELS, CATEGORIES, AND METHODOLOGICAL ASSUMPTIONS IN THE STUDY OF BEHAVIORAL DEVELOPMENT

HERBERT G. BIRCH

Two statements that Dobzhansky has made in the past (1969), focus on some of the issues relevant to the study of behavioral development in rather direct ways. The first is his statement on the issue of "typological thinking." He says that there is a habit of thought, perhaps as old as language itself, that keeps getting in the way of our understanding of the history and nature of the processes of life, that is, the habit of thinking in terms of static types.

Of course, we must sort out the overwhelming diversity of phenomena we perceive and experience into categories, and we do so in words like "man," "cat," or "dog." Such words do not refer to particular persons or animals but to abstract representatives of mankind, catkind, and dogkind. Also, such words emphasize differences between kinds, as if there were rigid boundaries. They give no hint of what the "kinds" may have in common, nor do they take into account, or even suggest, the diversity within kinds—the diversity of persons, of cats, and of dogs.

I think that in a considerable portion of the discussion about behavioral development, we have been victims of this tendency that Dobzhansky speaks of as a "natural human tendency." In this sense, we may view ourselves as human beings. However, if we recognize the dangers that are inherent in such categorization, we realize that we must be careful in our use of special separate categories, such as nature, nurture, heredity, environment, learned, acquired, and so on, as though these were entirely independent events or events that were not related to one another in important systematic ways.

The second thing that Dobzhansky warns us about is that we often speak most loosely about such things as "inherited behaviors" or "inborn behaviors" or "genetically determined behaviors." In one of his papers (Dobzhansky, 1969) he says that the geneticists are constantly forced to remind their colleagues, especially those in the social sciences, that what is inherited is not this or that particular phenotypic trait or character but "a genotypic potentiality for an organism's developmental response to its environment."

> A genotypic potentiality for an organism's developmental response to its environment, given a certain genotype and a certain sequence of environmental situations, the development follows a certain path. . . . The carriers of other genetic endowments in the same environmental sequence might well develop differently, but, also, a given genotype might well develop phenotypically along different paths in different environments (Dobzhansky, 1969).

What he means is that identical genetic constitutions will result in different products when their development takes place under different environmental conditions and in different circumstances. Anything we know about genetic endowment is based upon our consideration of particular phenotypic distributions in particular sets of environments under particular conditions for development. This is a *sine qua non* of genetic analysis, and it necessarily leads us to develop a fundamental confusion around three very important points.

One point of confusion is that development takes place independently of environment and is genically determined. This cannot be the case!

The second point, and this is much more important from an investigative and scientific point of view, is that ubiquity is confused with absence. We confuse the continued presence of a set of buffered or standard environmental circumstances upon which the development of a given genotype is determined with the absence of appropriate environmental circumstances and the dependence of development upon this. This confusion of ubiquity with absence or of constancy with absence has permeated in an open or hidden way many features of the discussion of behavioral development. I think that it is necessary to consider this matter in a straightforward and simple manner.

The third point that emerges from a population geneticist's consideration of problems of genetic development is that it is absolutely correct to say that every characteristic of the organism is genetically determined. Benson Ginsberg (1958) has expressed this proposition in what I think is a correct scientific form. He says: "All aspects of our organisms may be thought of as 100 per cent genetic, but not as 100 per cent determined." He makes a distinction between the universal importance of genetics or ancestral influence in the development of any organism and the particular phenotype which is going to emerge. The nature of the structures and the ways in which they will be determined for any genotype are dependent upon the particular conditions in which they are developing. In this sense, then, our problem in the genetic analysis of behavior is in understanding not only the genotype but the particular circumstances in which this genotype operates for the species or for the individual. This is not an unexaminable question nor is it an unimportant question. I'd like to approach it for just a moment by playing with mathematics.

Let us consider a simple organism like the *Drosophila*, a relatively simple organism from the point of view of its genetic constitution as compared with a human being. We find that *Drosophila* has a gamete in which we can, in fact, identify at least ten-thousand gene locations with a minimum of two variants for each of these genes. We then would have two to the ten-thousandth possible gametes and variants of this particular organism. If we turn to the zygote, add one to our base, we could expect potentially three to the ten-thousandth variants.

In actual fact, in any study of a group of *Drosophila* that have developed we find that the number of two variants that were produced, and the number of potential variants that could have emerged from this sexual combination, differ from one another astronomically. This is so although we get a large number of variants and a large number of combinations that emerge as individuals. Therefore, not only are genes inherited but there need also to be particular conditions for the survival of particular combinations that occur with direct continuous dependence in the process of genetic selection upon the circumstances in which the development is taking place.

If we recognize that fact, what do we mean when we speak about a given set of behaviors being genetically determined? To what extent are the given behaviors, or the given characteristics that we observe, dependent upon the particular developmental opportunities that are present in this species, or in this organism, for the manifestation and organization of the genetic information as phenotype for this organism? I would submit that most of our analyses of behavior genetics have, in fact, not concerned themselves with this issue in a fully systematic way. In the main, our analyses of the genetics of behavioral organization have tended to be analyses in which we have asked the extent of the transmission of some behavior from parent organism to offspring, and the degree of species-typicality and species-specificity of behavioral patterns. Once one has this information, one can, indeed, say that the behavior is likely to be related to the genetic background of the organism. But, what is it that is genetically transmitted? Is it the behavior pattern?

A beautiful example of such an analysis of behavior is the work of King and Shea (1959) with the deermouse (*Peromyscus*). They put the subspecies *bairdii* and *gracilis*, the forest-living and the field-living variety of the fieldmouse, on elevated mazes. These subspecies of the genus behave remarkably differently on the elevated maze. One can say that there are, in fact, species differences of a truly defined and heritable kind existing between these two subspecies of the deermouse.

However, King and Shea took their analysis one step further. They examined the developmental sequence of locomotor and clinging responses in these two subvariants of deermice. They found that *bairdii* locomotor responses, that is, running responses, emerged and matured well in advance of the clinging response, whereas in *gracilis* the locomotor response and clinging response emerged simultaneously.

Then they ask: With respect to the behavior of the subspecies on the elevated maze, is it different behavior that is inherited, or is the difference in maze behavior a consequence of the different rates of development and the degree of coordination or separation of particular responses involved in the relevant pattern? They argue that this kind of detailed consideration of the elements of the organism's response is needed if we are to have some insight as to what it is that is being transmitted.

In contrast, some people continue to do the Tryon kind of experiment on the inheritance of "intelligence" in animals (Tryon, 1940). They have repeated the same erroneous form of analysis. Tryon selectively bred successive generations of individuals that performed well or poorly on a particular complex task. The result was that one strain of rats was good at learning such a task and another strain was really incompetent at the task. It was then argued that the inheritance of intelligence was demonstrated, that there are bright and dull strains of rats. However, if we confront these same strains with different learning tasks, that is to say, a task other than that on which they had been selected, we find little or no difference between the two groups in regard to the ease with which they learn. For example, if we move to an elevated maze of the same pattern as the alley maze on which they have been selected, we lose this distinction between the two Tryon strains of rat. When we turn to other tasks, we find this distinction absent as well.

It appears that what has been selected for inadvertently was not some general property such as "intelligence" but, rather, a much more explicit property, namely, the tendency of one of the strains to be responsive to proprioceptive stimulation, and the other to be responsive to visual stimulation, as the primary information to which each responds in its environment. Also, certain temperamental attributes were inherited, such as the tendency to be easily excited on an unstable substrate.

It is these kinds of properties that appear to be transmitted. The relation of such systems to the competence of the organism as a learner or as a performer has to be understood in terms of the ways in which the particular environment in which he is functioning presents alternative opportunities for the utilization of one or another system in the development of competence of function. In pointing to these considerations, I am saying that we have the task of defining precisely how mechanisms that affect the growth and development of organisms at the genetic level affect behavior, either in its development or in any of the aspects that we may be analyzing.

If we take this approach to the problem of behavioral development, I think we can deal with an issue that has been implicit in many of the discussions, that is, the concept of levels of organization. For example, I have been struck by two general ideas that have been advanced repeatedly. They have been presented without reference to the concept of levels of organization; in fact, they cut across levels of organization. One of these ideas was presented by Professor Skinner: a general concept of the ways that reinforcement contingencies modify behavior (Science, 1964). Skinner applies this concept to organisms at the level of the bird, the lower mammals, the higher mammals, and the human being.

A second concept, which some people think is polar to this one, is the concept of approach–withdrawal (Schneirla, 1965). It, too, has been used as a concept that is not based on levels of organization. The concept of levels of organization deals with the properties of different levels, the ways to look at organisms at different levels and at the characteristic differentiation of behavior.

Schneirla's thinking differs from Skinner's thinking in that it included the ideas that the particular mechanism that mediates approaches or withdrawals varies systematically across phyletic lines and that the task is to identify the nature of the mechanism that contributed to the responses of an organism at any particular level of organization. At the level of unicellular organisms, for example, he was concerned with the problem of metabolic gradients, of the existence of sol–gel conditions in protoplasm that result in a given ameboid movement toward or away from the source of stimulation.

At another level, such as the *Poriphera,* he was concerned with neuroidal conduction, with the degree and the manner in which the force of one cell acting upon another could mechanically transmit the influence of stimulation decrementally and so result in given differentiated patterns of approach or withdrawal. At the level of mammalian organization, he was primarily interested in the problems of sensory control in behavior. He was interested in the nature of the effective environment for an organism and was concerned at every point with defining the particular level of organization and the mechanisms through which approaches, withdrawals, and organization of responses were mediated.

These examples of Schneirla's application of the concept of levels of organization make clear that when dealing with processes or behavior patterns that have a general phenomenal similarity, one has to be concerned with the possibility that what is similar at a phenomenal level is, indeed, different as to mechanism, and as to the level which that particular process or behavior represents for the phyletic level of the organism under consideration. His comparative analysis of behavior and learning in the ant as contrasted with that in the mammal is perhaps one of the finest examples of that kind of recognition (Schneirla, 1933).

Concepts cannot be criticized because they cut across levels of organization or because they cut across different phyletic classes but rather because they cut across them without a consideration of the fact that phenomenally similar behavior may be mediated and underlaid by different mechanisms at each particular level.

This consideration leads us to a question with respect to other kinds of levels that have been exercising the discussion of behavioral development, that is, the question of the biochemical level, the physiological level, the morphological level, and the behavioral level.

I have always been impressed by the elegance of Dr. Sperry's investigations and the beauty with which he has been able to demonstrate the explicitness of growth and connections in complex organisms when they have been subjected to injury or a variety of altered conditions and states during development. I have not the slightest doubt that these organizations of neural structures are produced independently of function and independently of any specific, explicit experiences that the organism may have had in a "psychological" sense, but I do have two questions in respect to these phenomena:

First, I do not think that either he or anyone else knows the mechanism through which this explicitness is mediated. I think that we have the problem of understanding the particular responses of these disordered cells to the environment in which they are growing. We have to find out the kind of information they are responding to that leads to a given growing neuron attaching to another point in the nervous system. It is this kind of question that has exercised the people working on the growth of single nerve cells in tissue cultures and in other kinds of circumstances. Until we begin to get a fuller understanding of the kinds of processes that Crain and his associates have been concerned with (1967, 1968, 1969), we will be at a loss to understand the nature of the environmental information to which the growing neurofibrils are responsive in the Sperry situation. Crain and his colleagues are seeking to define the conditions that determine the particular growth of neural elements in respect to one another. Most certainly, these are not at the level of psychological experience. But most certainly, and I think that Sperry would agree, these connections are not occurring in any mysterious way but are responsive to the particular conditions in which this growth is taking place.

Second, to what extent does the existence of a given structure or a given connection between structures permit us to draw any kind of explicit conclusion about function? I would submit that it tells us very little! I think this is an important issue.

Explicitness in growth occurs not only in amphibians but in mammals as well. In mammals, however, this growth occurs in an organism in which there is an intimate relation among sensory systems with the opportunities for integration among them, for the patterns of afferent organization to be reorganized and for modifiability of a variety of behaviors to take place. Equal explicitness in growth in the amphibian is accompanied by rigidity, nonplasticity of behavior, and relative unmodifiability of responsiveness.

I think that Aristotle thought, as did a number of other Greeks, that looking at structure as such in an attempt to determine the functional attributes of this structure can sometimes be misleading. The brain is not a refrigerator, and we should remember that this was once a hypothesis with respect to its function.

We can, indeed, ask questions with respect to the ways in which physiological events underlie behavior, but we should not be so overwhelmed by data that indicate that under given conditions of stimulation there are alterations in the biochemistry of the brain that we make dashing, adventurous, and leaping assumptions about the relevance of such findings to behavior.

For example, one of my projects is deeply concerned with the effects of nutritional adequacy or inadequacy at a given point in time in the organism's development, upon the growth of its nervous system, for example, upon its myelination and upon the completeness of its cell division. I do not know what the different conditions of enriched or impoverished environment do to the nutritional state of the organisms, what they in fact ingest and what they utilize under these conditions. I do not know what the intermediate or the mediating steps are with respect to any of a number of these relations. I would like to submit that it may well be that animals growing up in an enriched environment have thicker coats than do the animals that are growing in an unenriched environment. I do not know the association between coat depth and thickness and other events. What we need are not mere statements of association and a suspension of critical disbelief but some hypothesis that states: Through these mechanisms, stimulation affects the nervous system by a particular structural modification or by a particular alteration of responsiveness. Until we test such hypotheses, we will have great difficulties in understanding precisely what these biochemical changes may mean for the behavior that we are studying.

Another problem with respect to level has been raised in considering problems of behavioral development. Dr. Purpura is correct in suggesting that the reason young children select one kind of matching object, a circle and red match box, rather than another, a white dress, is based upon the degree to which one or another attribute of the objects produces either massive excitation or inhibition, or some combination of these effects. I would disagree, however, that this is so simply on the basis of his findings with respect to inhibitory processes in young organisms. On the basis of his work, he could not predict which stimuli would be most readily responded to. His study suggests an underlying mechanism that may be contributing to the organization of behavior as I analyzed it, but in and of itself, his finding does not permit us to make any precise statements about the nature of the behavioral organization responsible for the choice. The concept of levels proposes that we cannot predict the properties of sodium chloride from the properties of sodium and chlorine. We cannot predict specific behaviors by looking at underlying structures or by defining the specific patterns of underlying neurophysiological organization.

The concept of levels engenders a respectful concern that, although we recognize that accurately described behavioral organizations have an underlying physiological base, and that our task is to identify this base, we need to be skeptical about what the physiologists of a particular decade are going to say about the role of a physiological fact in behavior. I am old enough to remember that one set of physiologists argued that you could account for all behavior in terms of telephonic analogies. I have read sufficiently to know that other kinds of physiologists at a slightly earlier period argued that one could account for all of these behaviors on the basis of particular kinds of chemical attributes. I am at least old and young enough to recognize that neurophysiology will advance. In the course of its advance, it will give us a precise understanding of the underlying mechanisms of behavior to the degree that it is tied to a concern for the understanding of behavior and its mechanisms. We should not be naïve enough at any point to accept the contemporary stage of physiological data as a sufficient explanation for behavioral phenomena.

Let us look at Dr. Purpura's suggestion for a moment. I find myself in empathy with it. Let us say that we seek to account for the behavior of the children choosing one or another object in terms of a given pattern of excessive inhibition. How do we account for changes in the behavior? Through what mechanism does this inhibition, if we are to accept it as the mechanism, change in its ease of occurrence so that at a later stage of development it is the circle and the red match box which is inhibited rather than the white dress? This is the problem that I would have to deal with if I were to understand the developmental process or the physiological events that underlie the developmental process. At the moment, I do not have such an understanding and I do not know who does. Psychologists are not going to have the problem of understanding the organization of behavior solved by the presence of a detailed body of physiological information. In order to define which physiological information is relevant and which is noise, one has to engage in behavioral analysis with the same degree of intensity and rigor as occurs in physiological, biochemical, or any other kind of investigation.

The final question, then, concerns the way in which we look at development. Two problems arise in this regard. In most of our studies we deal with cross-sectional analyses of organisms that are of different ages. This is convenient, and we rarely engage in detailed longitudinal analyses of populations of organisms. If we are going to answer developmental questions, we must look at populations longitudinally. A recent series of psychological studies illustrates this need very well.

For years people have been arguing that the IQ's of children living in disadvantaged environments become lower in successive years of age. Now the angels among us, those who are on the side of good, have argued that this kind of finding suggests very strongly that there is a cumulatively depressing effect on the intellect of children in a cumulatively defective environment. Those who seek to interpret this behavior in another way have argued that this decline in intelligence with age in Negro children, for example, in the Southern United States is an expression of the fact that sensory–motor function is fine in Negro children, but at higher levels of intellectual achievement they show a deficit. On the basis of the same body of cross-sectional data, both of these conclusions have been argued with great force. However, the first question is, can one conclude from these cross-sectional studies of Negro children in these communities that there is a decline of IQ with age? The answer is "No. You cannot!"

One person, Kennedy (1966) for example, has recently reexamined his own populations and studied one segment of it longitudinally rather than cross-sectionally; he found no such decline. The declines that have previously been reported are more parsimoniously interpreted as sampling effect rather than as the expression of a deteriorating developmental process. Strong political or ideological convictions in one direction or another that permit you to draw conclusions from cross-sectional data as though they were longitudinal data give you a set of issues and problems that may have nothing to do with development but may be relevant to the faultiness of experimental design and data collection in population studies.

Although I cited research with the IQ, I suggest that there are other examples of developmental phenomena that have been described on the basis of cross-sectional data but which would appear to be different if they were looked at longitudinally. I am concerned that one cannot infer longitudinal developmental conclusions from serial cross-sectional data without danger of serious error.

Finally, I have become increasingly sensitive about the need to recognize long-delayed effects upon development in human populations that we know so well exist in nonhuman groups. Events which occur at a given point in the life of an organism may not be manifested as significant until a considerably later point in time. We recognize this with respect to certain characteristics of neurological damage and endocrine phenomena. We should also recognize that there may be intragenerational effects of a non-Lamarckian kind which manifest themselves across generations, at least in humans, as a body of epidemiological data that I have recently been considering would indicate. I would infer this to be true in nonhuman populations as well.

We increasingly find that the characteristic physical growth rate of children, both *in utero* and during the first years of life, regresses far better upon the mother's conditions of life when she was a young child than they do upon the particular circumstances of her pregnancy or particular life circumstances of the child being studied. Effectively, conditions for intrauterine growth and development may be affected by the maternal experience at a considerable distance in time, perhaps by the early life conditions resulting in different pelvic attributes, in a different uterine efficiency, etc.

In looking at birth weight data in North Carolina, for instance, I found surprisingly, that the order of low birth weights, mortalities, and morbidities are lowest for the white middle class, next lowest for the white lower class, next for the Negro middle class, and worst for the Negro lower class. Why was the socioeconomic gradient not expressing itself? I then divided the middle-class Negro women into those who came from middle class backgrounds and those who came from backgrounds that were equivalent to working class or to the poor farming class, sharecrop farming backgrounds. When I did this, the Negro middle class-middle class women were very much like the white middle-class women, whereas their sisters who had risen to the middle-class position from lower-class positions were more like white women in lower-class circumstances. Thus, the conditions under which the growth of the mothers took place may well affect the characteristics of the offspring that they produce. I think that the British data (Baird and Illsley, 1953) on this question point precisely in this direction. We must expand our concepts of development from a concern with immediate circumstances within single generations and begin to look more broadly at intergenerational effects and the mechanisms through which they are mediated.

REFERENCES

Baird, D., and Illsley, R. (1953). Environment and childbearing. *Proc. Roy. Soc. Med.* Vol. 46, 53–59.

Crain, S. M. (1969). Electrical activity of brain tissue developing in culture. In "Basic Mechanisms of the Epilepsies" (H. H. Jasper, A. A. Ward, and A. Pope, eds.), pp. 506–516. Little, Brown, Boston.

Crain, S. M., Bornstein, M. B., and Peterson, E. R. (1968). Maturation of cultured embryonic CNS tissues during chronic exposure to agents which prevent bioelectric activity. *Brain Res.* Vol. 8, 363–372.

Crain, S. M., and Peterson, E. R. (1967). Onset and development of functional interneuronal connections in explants of rat spinal cord-ganglia during maturation in culture. *Brain Res.* Vol. 6, 750–762.

Dobzhansky, T. (1969). Introduction. In "Science and the Concept of Race" (M. Mead, T. Dobzhansky, E. Tobach, and R. E. Light, eds.), pp. 77–79. Columbia Univ. Press, New York.

Ginsberg, B. E. (1958). Genetics as a tool in the study of behavior. *Perspectives Biol. Med.* Vol. 1, 397–424.

Kennedy, R. F. (1966). Address at the University of Capetown, June.

King, J. A., and Shea, N. J. (1959). Subspecific differences in the response of young deermice on an elevated maze. *J. Heredity* Vol. 50, 14–18.

Schneirla, T. C. (1933). Some comparative psychology. *J. Comp. Psychol.* Vol. 16, 307–315.

Schneirla, T. C. (1965). Aspects of stimulation and organization in approach/withdrawal processes underlying vertebrate behavioral development. In "Advances in the Study of Behavior" (D. S. Lehrman, R. A. Hinde, and E. Shaw, eds.), Vol. 1, pp. 1–71. Academic Press, New York.

Skinner, B. F. (1966). The phylogeny and ontogeny of behavior. *Science*, Vol. 153, 1205–1213.

Tryon, R. C. (1940). Genetic differences in maze-learning ability in rats. *Yearbook Natl. Soc. Study of Educ.* Vol. 39, 111–119.

PERSISTENT PROBLEMS IN THE STUDY OF THE BIOPSYCHOLOGY OF DEVELOPMENT

LEON EISENBERG

From the standpoint of the clinician, namely, from a pragmatic viewpoint, I should like to propose that the following points need to be incorporated in any discussion of the biopsychology of development.

First, permit me a comment on the danger of attempting to deal with diverse levels of organization and integration in the consideration of any phenomenon. Though each of us is quite aware of the murky state of his own field, each of us approaches such a task with the soon-to-be-dashed hope that clarity exists elsewhere. One hopes as well for a set of free ideas that can be borrowed to bring order into the chaos that beclouds his own specialty. He discovers that all is not as well elsewhere as he'd hoped, especially if the representatives of other disciplines are thoroughgoing scholars. He can draw some limited comfort from this, since misery does love company. Yet, there inevitably appear to be a few concepts worth "borrowing." All too often, they appear so only because he regards these concepts as better established in the field unfamiliar to him than they are in fact regarded by the people within that field. This is really quite a serious danger. I would caution all of us to question how transferable concepts are across levels of organization and, certainly, across developmental stages.

What we need and do not have is the equivalent of the Lorentz transformation equations in relativistic physics that apply in moving from one inertial field to another. One must take into account phyletic and developmental "inertial fields." Those of us who are clinicians, I think, are particularly vulnerable to hasty translations.

Behaviorists tend to be insecure about the reality of their concepts. A term from genetics, like "coding" or "programming," just reeks of science. If you're working in a clinical field, an ethological term like "imprinting" is too readily seized upon and reified to give an explanation for phenomena to which, as I shall suggest, it doesn't really apply.

One additional general comment about the discussion presented here is offered from the standpoint of a participant observer. Pupils tend to be touchingly loyal to their teachers. This is a moving tribute in an era in which loyalty is uncommon. Yet, the very loyalty may betray the major contribution of the teacher. From his writings and the comments I have heard from his students, Schneirla was a great man—great because of his capacity to inspire extremely significant work from his students, who are among the people I most admire. That does not mean that one has to hold onto an idea, like approach–withdrawal in response to stimulus intensity, as a concept any longer than it is useful, even though it may have been an important idea historically in the late 1930's, when some general theory was needed as a starting point. Dr. Hamburger, in a side discussion, compared the approach/withdrawal (A/W) theory to Childs' gradient theory in embryology, which was "exciting" at one time. However, Childs felt obliged to make it a single explanatory mechanism for all of embryology. The broader it got, the less useful it became.

Thus, it seems to me appropriate to examine briefly some of the implicit and explicit meanings of the terms that originate on one level of organization and are shifted to another, thus losing their sharp definitions.

One such is the concept used by Professor Rosenzweig: "impoverished" versus "enriched" in respect to the environment—terms derived from the level of human social organization. He himself has raised the issue: "impoverished" or "enriched" in relationship to "what," in the course of the Conference.

The question is important not only in respect to the natural environment for the rodent studies, but also, of course, in relationship to the *potential* behavioral repertoire of the animal which is being placed in one or another environment. The very same problem arises in child development. It is one of the issues most exercising those educators and psychologists who are concerned with early development. One has to ask: "What is the behavior that is defined as intelligent that one wishes to induce by one or another kind of environment?"

If an urban midde-class environment is taken as modal, as so often it is, it is because we assume its product is what we want to emerge out of experience. Therefore, one looks at the discrepancy between the lower-class environment and the urban middle-class environment in order to find out how to "enrich" the former. If some other kind, or class, of child or adult is what we would like to see emerge, other definitions of the "desirable" environment would be sought. Here, of course, we must make value judgments explicit rather than implicit.

Furthermore, can we define the characteristics of the "ideal" environment without specifying the constitution of the child placed in it? If our goal is to augment the diversity inherent in individual differences, as Dr. Mead stressed, a narrow, standard environment would hardly be our aim. One would want an environment with that degree of richness which would enable children with a variety of initial dispositions to thrive most readily.

More to the point, however, is the fact that before we can design an environment, we need to know much more about its interaction with the child in ontogenesis than we know now. Today, we can only specify such crude factors as "social class," some aspects of the "linguistic environment," some aspects of the "general characteristics of family structure," and so on. We lack what a number of our participants have called for, namely, detailed ontogenetic studies of the relationships among the factors acting on the child, the stage of the child at the time, and the individual characteristics of the child who is being acted upon. We also need to know how these relationships change from stage to stage. Without such information, we are in serious difficulty in attempts to specify therapeutic interventions. Another persistent question in understanding the effects of experience is that of transfer of training. How do we foster a problem-solving orientation that transfers from one learning situation to another, which in some way fits the notion of general intelligence? All of us know students who have done well in a course, say, calculus, and yet tend to be baffled when the application of that mathematical knowledge is called for in a course in physics. Very often, the student has to relearn his calculus in a new setting in order to understand its relationship to the problems he's called upon to solve.

Given this uncertainty about transfer effects in university education, how much more wary must we be in drawing conclusions about something akin to "intelligence" from the specific performances (maze-learning, aversive conditioning, etc.) induced in lower animals! In the end, the adaptability of those animals must be judged against the evolutionary criterion of producing surviving offspring. We aim at the ultimate goal of greater understanding of the human condition. But, our zeal may lead us to confound analogies with homologies and to mistake similarities for identities by looseness of language usage.

The second concept too readily embraced by developmental psychologists is that of the critical period. This is rather well established in experimental embryology and can be precisely defined. The skin overlying the optic cup can be determined to become lens only within some sharply restricted period of time. Once determination has occurred, differentiation typical of the phyletic level of the organism cannot be reversed.

To what extent does this concept accurately apply to other levels of organization, particularly at the behavioral and psychological levels?

The embryological notion of critical period is implicit in the concept of imprinting in ethology. As other participants have noted, particularly Dr. Beer and Dr. Hinde, imprinting is not such a qualitatively different kind of learning as it was originally touted to be. Despite this, and despite its demonstration in only a few species, most notably birds, it has invaded the clinical literature in rampant fashion. It was welcomed with joy by those preoccupied with early influences on late behavior. With excitement, they exclaimed: "It's what happens in the first 6 months that really matters!" Perhaps, if you are a bird, and even not so well for birds! But, I have not seen any data that suggest anything comparable for the human species.

There may indeed be sensitive periods (relatively critical periods) but for the human being, the time intervals are so very much longer, the variability of response so much greater, and the "repairability" (that is, the chance of making up for it later) so very much more possible, that the use of the term "critical period" is more likely to be misleading that it is to be helpful. In some respects it is even dangerous, for it suggests the inutility of attempts at making up for past misfortune and so discourages efforts at repair. In the field of "cultural deprivation" and educational intervention, there is only one step from "it's all determined genetically" to "it's only what happens in the first 6 years of life that matters." But, if it is either, then it clearly is a welcome piece of news for the taxpayer because you don't have to bother building better elementary schools if the child's teachability is determined before he arrives. This very argument has been used by opponents of increased support for public education and against attempts at accountability for educational outcome. It makes failure the fault of the child or his family, rather than the fault of the system.

If the concept of imprinting is to have any value at all, independent evidence of its existence in a particular species must be documented before its applicability as a general phenomenon is *assumed* to be correct.

A third issue is the assumption of the consistency of the mature or adult behavioral characteristics, whose origins we attempt to discern in earlier developmental stages. We have focused on the problem of "how you go" from the newborn organism to the adult, assuming that the behavioral characteristics of the adult are more sharply fixed or clearly understood than I would suggest is really the case.

If we look at our friends or ourselves or our patients, we observe a complex repertoire of behavior with a style or central disposition to respond that we may call for the moment "personality." That people fit into personality types provides an interesting clinical problem . . . how did they get to be what they are from where they began? Students of human development are all too ready to assume that these personality characteristics represent differentiated traits similar to the *structures* which morphologists might view as an outcome of earlier genetic and experiential determinants. I raise the question: To what extent is the apparent consistency of the adult personality a built-in *characteristic of the organism,* and how much is it a result of *currently* acting social influences that *maintain* the apparent consistency which is not at all an invariant characteristic *of* the adult?

Whether one prefers the concept that the social field determines behavior, or whether one believes that reinforcement contingencies maintain behavior, I would suggest that one must consider the possibility that the behavior of the human adult is much more modifiable than is usually believed.

Therefore, viewing personality as an end point is misleading because, in fact, the same individual placed in different environments (as one might do if searching for genetic influences) would become a differently behaving person in response to new social constraints (or reinforcement contingencies). The developmental problem may be misperceived from the outset if we *assume* fixity of the adult behavior whose genesis we seek to understand. What makes each of us pretty much the same person tomorrow that we were yesterday is the fit between us and the environments that we select for ourselves or that society permits or constrains us to chose among. Put out of our comfortable ecological niche and placed elsewhere by harsh necessity, each of us, I suspect, would become over time very different from what he is now. If that is correct, then the "end point" in adulthood is something that has to be examined closely, and seen as a *potential* for behavior, just as one views the potential precursors in infancy. The developmental issues to be understood if we recognize the variability in the adult behavioral repertoire are far different from those we confront if we accept adult personality as a fixetd end point.

I would like to turn now to the recurrent issue within the discussion of the biopsychology of development, namely, the nature–nurture controversy.

The extreme positions on this issue at this point in history are so ludicrous that no serious scholar would advance either. In fact, by adopting the formulation offered by Lehrman, or by working one out as a group, we could readily get everyone to agree on a general statement about heredity and environment. And yet, we continue to argue from one position or another when it comes to interpreting facts. I suspect that this is so because of the *political* connotation of each position. I suggest that theory in biology has been influenced by the social role of science, and by the society in which a science exists at any point in time. That is, having come to a particular view of man in nature as a function of one's own social setting, one reads that view into biology as though it arose from independent scientific study. Then, one returns to the political arena with *apparently* independent scientific evidence for the validity of one's preconceptions.

Permit me a moment to trace for you some of the ancient philosophical antecedents of the very issues that agitate our society today.

In Plato's *Republic,* Socrates first attests to the value of truth, but then goes on to say, in discussing the ideal state: "If anyone at all is to have the privilege of lying, the rulers of the state should be those persons." Glaucon asks: "How may we devise one of these useful falsehoods?" and this is Socrates' response; "Citizens, we shall say to them in our tale, you are brothers, yet God has framed you differently. Some of you have the power to command, and in the composition of these he has mingled gold, wherefore also they have the greatest honor. Others he has made of silver, to be auxiliaries; and others again who are to be husbandmen and craftsmen he has composed of brass and iron; and the species will generally be preserved in the children." In a later passage, he adds: "Any meddlesome interchange between the three classes would be most mischievious to the state and could possibly be described as the height of villainy."

Once the power of science was available to them, men managed to see in nature that which they had deduced from society. Once perceived in the state of nature, with the "apolitical" force of a "scientific" generalization, the very same concept can be reintroduced into politics as something "real," convincing because it is inherent in the world outside of man.

It didn't take Herbert Spencer long to recognize the implications of his view of Darwinism for the society of his time. He used the notion of "survival of the fittest" in a far more restricted sense than Darwin did. Be that as it may, the point is the social use of an ostensibly biological concept. Spencer wrote: "The poverty of the incapable, the distresses that come upon the imprudent, the starvation of the idle, and those shoulderings aside of the weak by the strong . . . are the decrees of a large, farseeing benevolence. We must call those spurious philanthropists who, to prevent present misery, would entail greater misery upon future generations. . . . All defenders of the poor law must be classified among such. The rigorous necessity which, when allowed to act upon them, becomes so sharp a spur to the lazy, and so strong a bridle to the random, these paupers' friends would repeal, blind to the fact, that under the natural order of things society is constantly excreting its unhealthy, imbecile, slow, vascillating, faithless members. These . . . unthinking men advocate an interference that not only stops the purifying process, but even increases the vitiation."

Now, political scientists and philosophers, of course, have advocated quite other points of view as "natural"! To take but one quotation to illustrate the environmentalist hypothesis, Helvetius wrote: "Two opinions today divide scientists on this subject. One group says: The mind is the effect of a certain kind of temperament and internal organization, but no one has yet been able by any observations to determine the kind of organ, temperament or nurture that produces the mind. This vague assertion, destitute of proofs, is reduced to this statement: The mind is the effect of an unknown cause or an occult quality.

"Quintillian, Locke and I myself say: The inequality of minds is the effect of a known cause, and this cause is the difference of education. . . .

"If I could demonstrate that man is indeed but a product of his education, I should undoubtedly have revealed a great truth to the nations. They would then know that they hold within their own hands the instrument of their greatness and their happiness, and that to be happy and powerful is only a matter of perfecting the science of education."

I do not mean to imply that such opinions are necessarily the political views of those who choose one or the other emphasis in the nature–nurture controversy, but these issues are still very much with us in both the scientific and societal arenas today; witness, Shockley and Jensen. The dual aspect of these issues confounds attempts by people who believe themselves to be talking only about embryology or ringdove behavior to limit themselves to dispassionate analysis of what appear to be scientific issues. Rather than force me to make a choice between the two, let me take the pragmatic approach of the clinician. If I am asked why I am interested in understanding development, I have to answer, "In order to be able to influence it."

Dr. Harris contrasts the "engineering" and the "ecological" view. But, whether I'm an engineer who wants to change people to some ideal type, or an ecologist who wants to create conditions to permit the "flowering" of individuals, my understanding is in the service of *change*. Thus, the study of the development of behavior in animals, whatever intrinsic or poetic value it may have for its student (and I won't deny him his pleasure), matters to me *primarily* as it sheds light on the human condition. What I seek and what I contend clinicians seek is a *powerful* theory; that is, one that specifies the mechanisms of process and hence the points of potential intervention. In my view, only an epigenetic theory has such value (I spare you the appropriate quotation from Aristotle).

I would argue that there is no *behavior,* certainly nothing like intelligence, or mating behavior, or display patterns, or even stature, in the zygote. Such notions are utterly absurd carryovers from performationism. What the DNA specifies are chemical constituents. These constituent enzymes and substrates interact with one another and with the internal and external environment of the developing organism to produce successive stages of ever greater complexity with the sequential emergence of new properties at each succeeding stage of development. It is the nature of the interactions that must concern us, not so that we can disregard the genetic code, but so that we can understand it and its environmental dependency.

The code, for example, may specify galactosemia in a newborn, but the galactosemic infant is distinguishable from his genetically unmarred brother only in an outer world in which his diet contains milk. Remove the offending disaccharide, the development of the infant is phenotypically normal. Or, it may dictate, as it did in all of us, the capacity for language *acquisition,* something that I would argue is specifically human, but that language acquisition occurs *only* in a verbal environment. Remove the speakers, no language appears.

I suppose that, in principle, language could be encoded; that is, the words, the grammar, and everything else. But, what a waste of eons of time to achieve "language" by biological selection, when it can be acquired via a predictably available environment for each human infant. In general, what is in the genetic code is an efficient packaging of that which is not *dependably* available in the average expectable environment of the organism. After all, unless one invokes divine creation, life began at some point as a random aggregation of molecules. In principle, what has been done in the course of evolution can be done in the laboratory, but what can be done in principle isn't necessarily easy to carry out in fact. But, how cumbersome and complex the process if natural selection had to be recapitulated each time a new organism was created. In similar fashion, the genetic code takes advantage of that which is at hand in the environment, as well as that which emerges from the synchronous chaining of processes in which interaction need not be specified as such.

Recall the example of spontaneous motility in the chick embryo. I am not suggesting that the motility was "designed" in order to keep the joints flexible, but if paralysis is induced, the joints ankylose.

"Nature" didn't have to design a joint that wouldn't freeze in the absence of movement precisely because motility arises from independent neuromuscular development. The synchronous relationship of these two processes avoids the necessity for a complex developmental chemical sequence simply because of the interrelationship between organ systems. "Joint mobility" isn't coded in the genes as such; it is determined by the relationship between elements in the developmental processes, each of which in turn is influenced by genetic constituents.

Is the fact that spontaneous motility occurs and therefore "prevents" ankylosis an environmental influence? . . . Is it learning? . . . Is it coded? Such semantic arguments are irrelevant to the understanding of development. The point is to recognize that articular embryogenesis is influenced by events occurring coterminously in the motor system; that is an important step in understanding the evolution of the joints. Dr. Hamburger may have been studying spontaneous motility, but he has also been, unwittingly, a student of orthopedics!

The challenge in understanding such interactions lies in overcoming the limitations of our own ingenuity in recognizing those aspects of the ubiquitous environment that we fail to see *precisely* because they are ever present. If a behavior emerges in the adult organism without having been learned (learned in the sense of having a clearly *isomorphic* earlier anlage), the conclusion that experience is unnecessary is not at all compelling. The relevant experience may not be at all where we have searched for it. Nor, I would add, can behavior in any sense be considered *simply* learned just because we can trace its genesis from sequential experience. That learning has taken place in an organism whose structure and function, and yes, spontaneous motor activity, provided the "ground" upon which the "figure," i.e., the "learned" behavior, later emerged. Thus, language can be said to be inherited or innate in the sense that only man can learn it. But, the simple statement that language is unique to man has said as much already; we haven't added anything more when we say it is "innate." The danger is that we fool ourselves into thinking we are wiser than we are by a term that implies mechanism—occult and unknown in Quintillian's terms.

The experimental embryologist, I would point out, doesn't invoke genes in the course of his experiments in development. He understands perfectly well that they're there; if he's doing breeding experiments, he'll be looking for them, but if he's studying experimental embryology, he doesn't use them as a god out of a machine to "explain" the phenomena he's concerned with. Rather, he tries to understand what it is about the cells that will become pancreas when they are in the presence of mesenchyme, what gets altered or determined, so that at a point later in time, those cells will become identifiable as demonstrated by prozymogen granules. If cells that would have become pancreas are removed from the surrounding mesenchyme too soon, they never become pancreas. If one waits an appropriate period of time, he can remove the mesenchyme, and the pancreatic rudiment goes on, in a primitive sense, to become pancreas. Something has happened in the interrelationship between two tissues. The "information" coded in pre-pancreas is insufficient to determine outcome in the absence of "information" supplied by adjacent tissue.

In this sense I would suggest to you that the dichotomy between learned and innate is not only useless but harmful to the student of behavior. The task before us is to identify the biochemical, physiological, structural, behavioral, and social elements in which interactions in various manners and proportions catalyze the emergence of organized behavior.

Consider only viral transduction. One has a bacterium following its own life course (happily perhaps). It gets infected with a bacterial virus. The virus leaves behind part of its genome in the bacterium. From then on, the bacterium breeds true to new genetic specifications. Clearly, that's an environmental change! And yet it is no argument for Lamarckianism. In fact, this environmentally induced change shows the beauty and power of genetic theory itself. In this case, it is an environmental event actually capable of influencing the genome. If we're to believe the predictions of the geneticists who are eager to try to influence the human genetic constitution, they are anticipating experiments with viral transduction in the effort to leave behind that part of the genetic code necessary to repair an otherwise damaging defect.

I would suggest again that the student of behavior must examine in detail the steps in the evolution of structure or function which includes attending as well to the nonsensory input, to the internal input within the organism, as well as the sensory input from the outside world. For some questions, sensory input may be utterly irrelevant, but that is not equivalent to saying that the characteristic under study is preformed. Only that can happen which could have happened . . . by definition. Only that can emerge which the "genetic potential" permitted to emerge. At that level of "explanation," one has said nothing! The salient issue is one of studying the process of development, whether from the zygote to the blastomere, the embryo to birth, or the course from birth to adolescence, in order to understand *in detail* the interrelation between the state of the organism at a point in time and the influences acting upon it that can account in a precise way for the behavior one wishes to understand. And understanding, from the clinical tradition, should be in the service of assisting the flowering of that which is healthy and of inhibiting that which is self-destructive.

It is for this reason that general statements about "innate" or "species specific" behavior are of no utility. It is only when one acquires knowledge of the epigenetic *mechanism* of developmental process that undertanding in the sense of being able to help has been advanced.

REFERENCE

Eisenberg, L. (1965). A developmental approach to adolescence. *Children*, Vol. 12, 131–135.

Eisenberg, L. (1967). Clinical considerations in the psychiatric evaluation of intelligence. *In* "Psychopathology of Mental Development" (J. Zubin and G. A. Jervis, eds.). Grune and Stratton, New York.

Eisenberg, L. (1969). Child psychiatry: The past quarter century. *Amer. J. Orthopsychiat.* Vol. 39, 389–401.

Grobstein, C. (1964). Cytodifferentiation and its controls. *Science*, Vol. 143, 643–650.

Spencer, H. (1902). "Social Statics." Williams and Norgate, London.

Wiesel, T. N., and Hubel, D. H. (1963). Single cell responses in striate cortex of kittens deprived of vision in one eye. *J. Neurophysiol.* Vol. 26, 1003–1017.

Winick, M. (1968). Nutritions and cell growth. *Nutr. Res.* Vol. 26, 195–197.

Discussion

L. R. Aronson: Although Dr. Schneirla spoke of the approach/withdrawal (A/W) theory as far back as 1939, the A/W theory was not clearly formulated until 20 years later when Schneirla wrote his first definitive paper on the subject. Moreover, his major A/W paper was written just a few years ago. It is not correct, therefore, to consider approach/withdrawal as an old, outmoded theory having only historical interest. In fact, it is a very new theory and its validity is first being examined and its value appreciated.

Dr. Rosenblatt used this theory to good advantage in his study on the ontogeny of nursing behavior in kittens. It was quite apparent that mild, approach-type stimuli guided the kittens to the nipples. Alternatively, stimuli of high intensity caused withdrawal movements, and efforts were made to avoid these in the design of his experimental situations.

Good theories—those that withstand the test of time—are developed to explain fundamental processes and are, therefore, likely to be broad and all inclusive. This, I consider a virtue of good theory and certainly not a weakness.

M. R. Rosenzweig: I think it is quite proper to put emphasis on the dangers of reification, the difficulties that we have when we listen to each other and take the concepts beyond the area for which they were intended. We have difficulty with each other as scientists, and the difficulties are compounded when what we are talking about gets out into a more general public even less acquainted with these difficulties of translation and translocation.

You mentioned the reification of terms such as "encoding" or "enriched" and "impoverished" or "imprinting." I think that we have a real dilemma. We can try to put fences around what we are to talk about. We can issue a *caveat lector*, a *caveat auditor*, but we know very well that as soon as we use a term, as soon as we mention some research which conceivably might be applied to human behavior, the term will be used in public discussions. It's very hard to know what to do in dealing with this problem because we have to communicate, and we know that as the communications are repeated, they are going to be abridged, smoothed-off, altered, transformed. The term may end up in the public property as being something very different from what we intended.

Let me comment on the example of imprinting that you mentioned. The first time that the concept of imprinting was presented at a meeting of the American Psychological Association was, I believe, in a talk that Eckhard Hess gave in 1954 in New York City. He gave a dramatic presentation of the phenomena of imprinting and then there was a question period. One of the questioners immediately began making some comments in which he attempted to apply the concept of imprinting to the first years of human life and made many of the types of wide-ranging interpretations that we've seen. I can still recall Eckhard Hess jabbing at this person with his ever-present cigar and saying: "Well, that's just why I thought I probably shouldn't give this talk here. I realized that some damn fool clinician would take the concept and run."

Eisenberg: You raise a problem that one must face; namely, science for public consumption. Up to a few years ago what scientists said was by definition hailed as true and, therefore, too readily believed. There has been a marked change—perhaps not all to the bad, but surely not all to the good in the public view of science. We no longer have the problem of people being too ready to listen, but of their being not willing to listen at all, particularly the young.

But even in the field of one's own experimental interest, terms can be misleading.

If your rats had been trained in a Skinner box to chain elaborate behavior sequentially, so that the rat was behaving as no rat had ever before, I would have been utterly amazed if a morphologically detectable change had been produced in its brain. It is not because I do not believe that brain has been altered by that experience, but I doubt indeed that something that has been trained in such a limited way could make itself visible morphologically. The point is that the rat that is trained to do something in a Skinner box is not necessarily a "more intelligent" rat.

In fact, I have difficulty in comprehending, given the necessary imprecision of the measures employed, how brain weights can have been changed by "the enriched environment." This is the more difficult to understand, given your data on increased size in occipital cortex in blinded rats reared in the special environment when contrasted with the controls. How do you decide what is enrichment in the case of the rat in an environment with opportunity for exploration when we lack behavioral output measures with biological meaning to detect change in performance?

If the bit of history that I'm about to state is correct, then it illustrates the dilemma.

I am told that in the early part of this century, psychologists were concerned with the question of visual discrimination by rodents. I believe the early experimental apparatus was similar to a T-maze. The rats just never learned. Even after some modification of the apparatus, it took the animals many trials to learn the discrimination. The conclusion was, at least in respect to this attribute, that the rat was stupid! When Lashley mounted the rat on a platform and forced him to jump so that the direction of jump had differential consequences with respect to the distinguishing signal lo and behold! The rat learned.

The conclusion from the experiment is that the psychologists were stupid, or the psychiatrists or the scientists, not the experimental animal.

The dilemma is the choice of outcome measure and its legitimate relationship to the earlier input effects; or, conversely, if we have an outcome we're interested in, our ingenuity in deciding what kind of developmental inputs may influence that kind of outcome.

R. W. Sperry: Just a short point about your passing reference to how the first six years of life pretty much determine human nature: This idea has come down through psychiatry and psychology and many draw the conclusion that this is true because of the way in which the fetus or the infant has been treated.

The commonly drawn inference in this connection is that the experiences to which the infant is subjected during these years are primary. I would like again to suggest that there might be another interpretation here, namely, that it is the developmental and maturational processes primarily that make these years so determinative.

During the first few years, the maturational program is unraveling at great speed. A lot of this determination seems to be inbuilt in nature; this is becoming increasingly clear from current infant studies. I think that we ought to keep our minds open to the possibility that the impression these first years are so critical is based to a considerable extent on the rapid unraveling of the individual's innate character.

Now this, of course, is within the great spectrum of ordinary experience and excludes extremes. The extremes of experiences, of course, can seriously shape the person, and again, I have to say that we're talking here really about differences in emphasis. I suspect that the emphasis has been a little off in psychiatric theory in thinking that it is what the mother has done to her infant that has made this dramatic effect in the first six years.

. . . I've said too much already!

Dr. Eisenberg: Dr. Sperry, I think you've managed entirely to misconceive what I've said.

Yes, it has been argued that the first 6 years of life are determinative. I'm not aware of any evidence that really supports that generalization. I question its truth. What impresses me is the *modifiability* of human behavior and the fact that the content that goes into the head has a lot to do with what happens to the person, even when the neural network seems to be, more or less, anatomically quite satisfactory, so far as we now can judge.

You made the point in your last presentation that if an experienced neuroanatomist looks at brain sections, he's impressed with the individual differences between them, perhaps more marked than those of fingerprints. Without denying the observation that the differences are striking, so are the differences between any two forests; yet, no one argues that such differences reflect determinative processes; purely random events, subject to the general laws of nature, suffice to produce "individuality." Indeed, anatomical differences *may* be genetically determined, but the mere *existence* of difference constitutes no proof thereof. However precise the arrangements in the adult brain, unless one has systematically studied the process along the course of time and attempted to intervene as an experimentalist to see what various interventions do to the end process, one has no evidence as to how it came about.

The evidence for plasticity within the adult central nervous system is indeed sparse but I, at least, was impressed very much by the work of Rose and his co-workers (1960). By using heavy particles, they were able to produce thin layers of cell and fiber dissolution and to demonstrate that 6 weeks later, in a similarly lesioned littermate, if the lesion had not produced a cyst, there were now fibers growing across a zone previously translucent. Rose takes the position that this doesn't represent new growth, but merely the making visible (by pruning the jungle of fibers) of growth that's occurring all the time. Whatever the interpretation, here we see that even the adult rabbit is not fixed, but in fact is one in which some sort of growth process continues. That's far and away from being able to indicate functional consequences of this growth. Indeed, if we had to begin with a retina that was random and get it shaped by the environment, that would be a hell of a way to acquire vision!

I guess the great difficulty is the way you interpret experiments and here I would like to borrow a story from Neal Miller. It has been demonstrated that if you yoke rats so that each of them has an electrode on his tail and you allow one rat to push a button following a signal so that he can avoid the shock for both, whereas the other rat is simply a slave and has no control, the rat who is in the unhappy circumstance of being shocked and unable to control it develops stomach ulcers, whereas the rat who is in control of the button, both having gotten the same amount of electric shock, doesn't have stomach ulcers. This experiment with rats has to be compared with the Brady experiment with the "executive" monkey in which the executive monkey, the one who presses the lever, compared to the slave, is the one who gets the ulcers. The obvious conclusion from this experiment is that if you're going to be an executive, you'd better be a rat!

REFERENCE

Rose, J. E., Malis, L. I., Kruger, L., and Baker, C. P. (1960). Effects of heavy, ionizing, monoenergetic particles on the cerebral cortex. II. Histological appearance of laminar lesions and growth of nerve fibers after laminar destructions. *J. Comp. Neurol.* Vol. 115, 243–255.

P. H. Wolff: It seems to me that it does make a difference what you decide on some of the issues. Namely, you either have an explicit or an implicit way of looking at the facts; the facts do not speak for themselves.

Therefore, I will bring it back to Chomsky. If you take one or the other position on this, I think you will study the problem of language, or any other problem that was raised here in quite different ways. The facts you obtain may then be interpreted in quite new ways, but, you look for different kinds of questions when you raise them within a framework. I think this is also Lettvin's approach to the problem, that it is the frame of reference from which you start that determines to some degree what you look for and probably, to some extent, what you find.

I think you cannot *not* have a theory, and if you call it stimulus and response, you also have a theory. Even a nontheory is a theory!

Eisenberg: I don't see any dispute between us. Indeed, theory guides observation. One sees only what one looks for. In the days of preformationism the introduction of the microscope was followed by diagrams of the expected homunculus "seen" inside the head of the sperm. Given the chromatic and other aberrations of the lenses then used, the rather blurred images, it was not at all difficult to see what was expected. Similar, if more sophisticated, illustrations can be given from contemporary science.

If we come back to the Chomsky formulation, I think he is right in contending that human language is qualitatively different from forms of communication in other species. One can deny qualitative differences, but if you accept them, that will lead you to study human speech in a different way from those who regard it as the chaining of operant response behavior. Once one says that human language is qualitatively different, then one is already saying as much as is given by the statement that language rules are "innate," namely, that it is only the human nervous system that has the capacity to generate linguistic rules from verbal stimulus input. Whether or not language acquisition does follow the Chomsky model depends upon empirical studies for verification, studies which he himself is not—and need not be—interested in doing.

VI. SOCIETAL IMPLICATIONS OF THE STUDY OF BEHAVIORAL DEVELOPMENT

OPTIONS IMPLICIT IN DEVELOPMENTAL STYLES

MARGARET MEAD

The rat model, which had considerable influence on anthropology in the 1940's and 1950's, emphasizes the ways in which rats learn such skills as running mazes. This has been generalized to human behavior so that culture itself has been spoken of a maze which the child learns to run, or culture patterns have been spoken of as maze ways. With such a model it was possible to look at human culture as a maze through which human beings found their way, with some of their behavior reinforced and some unreinforced.

One of the difficulties of this model is that man, experimenting with rats, was always in control. No account was taken of the species characteristics of the rat; in fact the rat's principal virtue as an experimental animal was that it could be fitted into such generalized man-made models. A by-product of this attitude was, of course, that the experimenter, instead of observing the rats, often only observed the record. One of our cherished oral traditions is the story of the anthropologist who was taken to see the rats running mazes at Yale and remarked, to the expressed amazement of the experimenter, that one of the rats had a broken leg.

It was a good many years after the choice of the rat as the ideal experimental animal that attention began to be paid to the species characteristics behavior of the Norway rat. By that time it was rather late to break away from the rat model which led to human cultures being seen as mazes and human beings as generalized creatures who were conditioned—by someone unknown, or by something called "the culture"—to culturally characteristic forms of behavior. It was a model which expectably resulted in ignoring hereditary individual differences among human beings.

Other models have recently been imported into the thinking of anthropologists, the stickleback fish model, the graylag goose model, etc., and we have to spend a considerable amount of time trying to refute models based on a miscellaneous assemblage of creatures, invoked to generate theories about aggression or territoritality. It is also, I believe, important to stress, in this context, that anthropology is not an experimental science. We do not experiment with human beings. We study natural experiments that come about within the historical process, and we use these carefully observed complex events as living models for generating hypotheses about human behavior, or for the first testing of hypotheses that have already been generated. The material that we work with is too complex to replicate. We have to depend upon recordings by film and tape. This method does not make it possible to replicate the experiment, but it does permit us to replicate the situation in which different analysts work with identical materials in the light of changing frames of reference. We consider that the types of experiment which can be replicated in the laboratory, using human subjects, will never produce answers to the kinds of problems with which we are concerned.

This difference between cultural anthropology and the laboratory sciences has to be made clear here because of the dominance of experiments on rats in the study of behavioral development.

We are honoring here the memory of Theodore Schneirla, and this carries me back to the first paper I ever heard him give—at a conference on topological psychology. He spelled out, in fine detail, the way in which at a certain phase of the life cycle the young ants evoked special responses from the whole colony. This was in the period just at the beginning of World War II, when we were still extraordinarily influenced by the kinds of thinking that were closely related to seeing cultures as mazes, as systems that were already set up in which adults treated children in such a way that the children would replicate the behavior of the adults. This did not mean that we thought of human children as complete blanks, but it did mean that we tended to think of a one-way process. As the children grew, the adults intervened; they beat them or praised them or hugged them or refrained from hugging them. Whatever they did to the children, the children became an exact representation of the adults who had reared them.

That lecture of Schneirla's, his vivid description of the evocation of adult behavior by the state of the young, was one of the things that touched off an understanding of the circularity of the process. As we came to use cybernetics as a cross-disciplinary form of thinking—and Ted Schneirla was a member of that series of conferences, too—we came to realize that the model which saw the acts of adults as the sole agency for producing the character of the growing children was far too simple (von Foerster, 1950–1956). What we had to recognize was that in human culture we were dealing with a process in which each change in the child evoked behavior in the adult which in turn evoked further behavior in the child. As the adult acted, to hold, or suckle, or tease, or lull the child, in culturally characteristic ways, the child responded with behavior which evoked the next response from the adult, which in turn evoked a new response from the child. An inexperienced woman from one culture, given a baby from another culture to care for briefly, would not develop culturally regular responses. You can see how faulty, how essentially inappropriate a manmade maze, run by rats, whose responses are mechanically recorded and statistically analyzed, is for the understanding of human culture.

As I discuss this, I realize that for the younger readers what I am saying may be almost unintelligible because cybernetic thinking has been part of their way of thinking all their lives. But if you look at rat psychology, and theories of human behavior based upon it, you will see what a discrepancy there is between the recognition of the circularity of human transactional systems and the image of the fully constructed maze upon the form of which the running rats can have no influence except the mechanical one of wearing it out.

Another aspect of discussions about the biopsychology of development is that people get upset whenever any genetically governed human behavior is mentioned. I have been wondering for some time why every single attempt to delineate a genetic pattern is regarded as reactionary. If, for example, we have a discussion of aggression, like that of Konrad Lorenz (1966), this conveys to people that if aggression is innate, then man is helpless to do anything about it, and this in turn is regarded as a fascist conclusion. If, however, somebody suggests that someday we will be able to replicate individuals, and possibly replicate Winston Churchill, as a superior human being, this disturbs people even more. Whichever way the statements are made—that some types of behavior are genetically determined in man as a species, or that some genetic behavior is peculiar to only one or a few members of the species—people find it disturbing.

Now it is true that today we have some extraordinary misuses of the science of genetics. Dr. Arthur Jensen, for example, has lumped together the entire group of people in the United States who are classified as American Negroes, as having special genetic traits (Jensen, 1969). This classification includes any individuals of any known African ancestry, which may mean one known Negro ancestor four generations back who may not himself or herself have had only African ancestry. He treats a social classification of this sort, which carries with it systematic discrimination at every socioeconomic level, as if it were genetic. He then places side by side evidence on the importance of genetic traits derived from the study of twins and the fact that "Negroes" score lower on intelligence tests, tests that are themselves validated by school achievement, than do "whites." He further suggests that because tests show a greater proclivity for "concrete thinking," separate kinds of schools would give "Negro" children a better chance. The suppression of the most elementary recognition of the difference between a genuine Mendelian population and the mixed multitudes classified as American Negroes is, of course, a tremendous stimulus to shuddering away from the introduction of genetic arguments when we are dealing with the education of American children.

Also, when we look at the practices of human cultures through time, we find that societies have always made a series of assumptions about human nature on which their informal or formal educational practices were based. Many of these assumptions have been articulate, others have been inarticulate. For example, in Samoan traditional culture (Mead, 1949) children were classified in four groups: those whose ears were open and whose throats were open, so they could both learn well and express what they had learned; those whose ears were open but whose throats were closed, the shy; those whose ears were closed but whose throats were open, the foolish; and those whose ears and throats were both closed, the hopelessly stupid. Decisions were made very early as to which group a child belonged, and subsequent treatment reinforced the imputed "innate" behavior.

The Mundugumor of the Sepik area of New Guinea (Mead, 1935) believed that only male children born with the cord around their necks could be artists. So if a man had not been born so, nearly strangled at his birth, he could never play the role of a master painter. Such assumptions are, of course, self-fulfilling prophecies, and people who were not born with cords around their neck, no matter how gifted they were and how much they wanted to be artists, were not artists. At best they were permitted to prepare the master painter's pigments by chewing them!

The Balinese (Mead, 1955) observe infants carefully to decide whether they are serious or naughty. Having made their decision, they categorize each baby as serious or naughty for the rest of his or her life, right into old age when, as doddering old men and women, they are too old to get into mischief themselves but not too old to relish gossip.

Or, we may turn from such imputed behaviors and their consequences to another mechanism for standardizing individuals in primitive and peasant societies—breast feeding. When mothers had to breast feed their infants because they had no form of artificial feeding, the mother–child pair became a self-regulating survival selection mechanism (Mead,

1967). If baby and mother were a good fit, the child thrived and the mother kept her milk, but if the baby did not thrive, the mother in turn began to lose her milk, and a vicious circle of loss of weight and loss of milk ensued, until the baby died. Way was made for another infant to be born who might be a better fit, and so thrive. The babies who survived were the result of this self-selective process which over many generations could have a great deal of importance. This kind of mechanism in which there is an individual, vitally significant tie between a nurturing adult and a growing baby is one of the ways in which individual differences and ranges of temperament have been narrowed in small inbred societies.

As societies become larger and more complicated, equipped with calendars and scales, it is possible to make other kinds of assumptions, such as that children should begin school at age 6, and then further complicate the matter by setting an arbitrary date as a cutoff point so that a child who turns six after that date will have to wait another year to enter school. This is definitely an unfair deprivation, although it is not clear in which direction!

We have made the assumption that 6 is a good age to begin school. However, some specialists in child development feel it is the worst possible age. They have had a system in New Zealand by which a child could enter school at age 5 and complete the beginning grade in any fraction of 3 years, without prejudice. By the time these children reached the fifth or sixth grade, you could tell something about how they were going to fit into society because they had been permitted to set their own pace.

Today we artificially feed many infants that no breast-feeding mother could keep alive, because where a mother's milk supply would be impaired by the experience of a baby that did not thrive, a formula is not responsive to apparent rejection and failure. We also put babies in hospitals and keep them calm with a simulation of the maternal heartbeat.

We have method after method of standardizing individuals in terms of such criteria as weight at birth, chronological age, and IQ tests which are designed to predict how a child will fit into the school system on which the tests have been validated. Such predictions are self-fulfilling and discriminate heavily against the children who fail to match the assumption, such as tiny postmature babies, children who can read at age 4 or prefer to wait until age 8, and children whose minds have a different cast from the skills stressed in a particular school. Within systems of classification of this kind it is no wonder that people become restive when hereditary qualities are invoked.

But if we can take more account of individual differences, and if we can begin to build a system which can take individual differences into account—the tempo of individual learning, the salience of one form of imagery, or of one sensory mode over another, the configuration of each individual's distinctive abilities—there is a possibility of so elaborating on such individual possibilities that we will have differences that are as great as the learning styles of species of songbirds are found to be when they are studied carefully.

Ethologists have identified the differences between songbirds who have different species-characteristic ways of learning their own and sometimes other birds' songs. Differences between individual human beings are much greater, but we have not as yet been able to do very much with such differences. We have devised oversimplified classifications—as if all species of songbirds learned to sing the same way—and then classified those individuals who did not fit as failures. Today the average pediatrician does not look at the baby but asks the mother how old the baby is. We ask a child, "How old are you? What grade are you in? What does the teacher teach you?" The whole adult world responds to children in highly standardized ways instead of finding ways to cultivate complex individual differences.

But in spite of our staggering educational problems, brought upon us partly by the population explosion and partly because the system itself is obsolete, we do have the technology to begin to treat individual children as individuals. Here I strongly agree with Dr. Skinner, that we should use all the technology we have and that technology is not the enemy of man unless man makes it his enemy. With existing technology it is possible, for example, to make far more delicate diagnoses than we do, and then to devise teaching methods that are appropriate. It is possible, for example, to recognize the point at which a child makes a first major generalization, and the recognition, by the parent, may make a difference in the child's thinking for the rest of its life.

Such recognitions can be combined with our present style of upbringing in which educated men, as well as educated women, spend a great deal of time with their young children. Throughout history, the higher the rank, education, and ability of the father, the more likely it has been that the children would be turned over to subordinates who were interposed to some extent even between mother and child, and almost completely between father and young child. The last 20 years has been the first time in recorded history in which educated elite males have paid systematic attention to the development of their young children (Mead, 1947).

Take, for example, a child playing on the kitchen floor with mixed cutlery. The child puts two spoons side by side; the sensitive parent, educated mother or educated father, watching the child as the child reaches for a third spoon, dumps a lot of extra spoons on the floor, recognizing that the child is building a category. But the uneducated adult is more likely to say, "No, dear, you don't want three spoons, you want a knife and a fork and a spoon." Later, when the child is tested by being asked to sort a mixed lot of objects, it will make selections like a knife and fork and spoon when asked for similarities and be labeled a concrete thinker. Gesell and Ilg worked out a spiral of recurrent growth which showed how, if a child failed to learn something the first time it was ready to learn it, it might be quite a long time before there was a chance to learn it the next time. When a child learns at a second or third point of readiness instead of a first time, it will learn differently, in combination with a different set of skills, and this may make a major difference in what that particular child will be able to do with its innate potentialities. With the technical capabilities that we have today there is no reason why we cannot devise an educational system that is able to diagnose the peculiar style of perception of each child and its own peculiar rhythm of growth as carefully as the ethologists have delineated the styles of different species.

It is one of the glories of humankind that each individual can draw both on innate potentialities and upon his entire cultural tradition. Innate characteristics need not be seen as limiting and restrictive, either to those who possess them or to those who do not. A child may be keenly sensitive to sound and not very sensitive to vision. Or he may be keenly sensitive to what he sees and dull in relation to what he hears. Such differences need be arranged in no hierarchy. Instead we can consider each configuration given by heredity and treat them all as potentialities which, if duly allowed for and cultivated, may give distinctive and valuable results. Dullness of one sense is often accompanied by extra sensitivity in another. We can take the complimentaries, the compensations, the peculiarities, and the idiosyncracies of each child as positive. We no longer need to greet every discussion of difference as essentially undemocratic, or limiting, the recognition of which is to be avoided at all costs. We can emphasize instead the enormous possibilities for each individual if we do not treat them like rats running manmade mazes which disregard their individual differences, and so try to make them all alike and penalize someone, either he who is different or he who is not, because he differs from his fellows. Small societies were able to do this unsystematically because there were so few children and it was easy to distinguish among them. But we have seen that even they forced their children into artificial categories.

I should like to close by returning to the model provided by breast feeding because it is one of the best models we have at present. The primitive mother breast fed her baby, and if she and the baby were a good fit, the baby thrived and lived; if they were not, the baby died. Then, when bottle feeding was invented, it was realized by pediatricians that infants' stomachs were limited in size, that it was one thing to have an infant and mother attached to each other in a self-regulatory system and quite another to have the baby attached, potentially, to a whole dairy. And so a few babies were studied, their stomach capacity was established, and feeding schedules were arbitrarily set up based on standard-size stomachs, standard-size bottles, and standard amounts of milk for babies of different ages. Where the schedule times were altered, it was to fit them into the convenience of the outside system, the call of the Fuller brush man, or a given radio serial, rather than out of any consideration for the needs of particular babies.

The next step forward—not back, as some commentators have represented it—is self-demand feeding, in which the mother, equipped with a clock and calendar, plots the individual rhythm of her particular baby as it begins its extrauterine life. Then she makes a schedule which assures herself and the child of some manageable regularity around which the other demands of life can be fitted and that, nevertheless, is adapted to that child's rhythm. This makes it possible for the infant's initial experience to be that of moving in step with the outside world instead of being submitted to an artificial and arbitrary pattern imposed upon it, based, not on its needs, but on a standard conception of what all babies need.

This is no return to primitive behavior, no simple feeding the baby when it cries, as mothers have done for thousands of years. This self-demand schedule would not be possible without the sophisticated records made possible by calendar and script and timepiece. With these, and our new conceptions of the circularity of relations between mother and child, we can individualize each baby, and give it a far better chance to develop its own distinctive style. Where with fixed schedules—and such fixed schedules were in many cases imposed back upon breast feeding when breast feeding was resorted to after bottle-feeding standards had been developed—each baby was either a good baby or a bad baby in terms of how well it fitted the arbitrary rhythm. With self-demand feeding, there are no good babies or bad babies, no babies that are always hungry too soon or sleep too long when it is feeding time. There are only different babies. And this appreciated difference, more vividly recognized by the breast-feeding mother, can in turn be adapted to bottle feeding when bottle feeding is necessary.

What can be done with an infant's pattern of hunger, as it is transformed into orderly appetite, can be done with learning to read and learning mathematics, with learning to observe and learning to remember. So we can move to another level of acceptance of genetic differences by recognizing and building upon the unique and innate patterns of each child and its unique contribution to the world.

REFERENCES

von Foerster, H., ed. (1950–1956). "Cybernetics," 5 vols. Josiah Macy, Jr. Found., New York.

Jensen, A. R. (1969). How much can we boost IQ and scholastic achievement. *Harvard Educ. Rev.* Vol. 39, No. 1, 1–124.

Lorenz, K. (1966). "On Aggression." Harcourt, Brace, New York.

Mead, M. (1928). "Coming of Age in Samoa." Morrow, New York (reprinted, Mentor MP 418. New American Library, New York, 1949). Laurel Edition 1465. Dell, New York, 1968.

Mead, M. (1935). "Sex and Temperament in Three Primitive Societies." Morrow, New York (reprinted, Mentor MP 370. New American Library, New York, 1950). Laurel Edition 7777. Dell, New York, 1968.

Mead, M. (1947). On the implications for anthropology of the Gesell-Ilg approach to maturation. *Amer. Anthropol.* Vol. 49, No. 1, 69–77.

Mead, M. (1955). Children and ritual in Bali. *In* "Childhood in Contemporary Cultures" (M. Mead and M. Wolfenstein, eds.), pp. 40–51. Univ. of Chicago Press, Chicago, Illinois.

Mead, M., and Newton, N. (1967). Cultural patterning of perinatal behavior. *In* "Childbearing: Its Social and Psychological Aspects" (A. F. Guttmacher and S. A. Richardson, eds.), pp. 142–245. Williams & Wilkins, Baltimore, Maryland.

A BEHAVIORAL ANALYSIS OF VALUE JUDGMENTS

B. F. SKINNER

The levels approach to development follows an orderly progression. It begins with the molecule, moves on to the cell, then to the organ and the organism, and through evolution to the development of the human species. Man himself did not move so swiftly. It was only through a very long process of evolution that he advanced to his present condition. Near the end of that advance he began to develop cultures which have greatly extended his capacities. Some of these cultures have produced a subculture we call science, and scientific cultures have come at last to include a science of behavior. This was, perhaps, an inevitable step, and it may lead to the greatest of human achievements. Beyond the extraordinary accomplishments of physical and biological technology may lie man's greater achievement in coming to understand himself and learning how to control himself.

We have reached a point at which the genetics of the human species may be manipulated. Something can already be done through breeding, but geneticists are now talking about changing chromosomes directly. We have already reached a stage at which we can change man as a physiological organism, for example, through surgery or drugs.

We have long been able to change man's behavior by changing the world in which he lives, including the culture of which he is a part, but new methods are becoming available. An extensive technology is already in existence. It is high time. Everyone is aware of the serious problems we face today—an exploding population, the threat of nuclear war, pollution, and so on. We naturally try to solve such problems by playing from strength. We try to deal with them through highly developed physical and biological technologies. To control population, we search for new methods of contraception. To prevent nuclear war, we build a deterrent force or a foolproof ABM system. To control pollution, we design new ways of disposing of wastes. The trouble is that all these problems demand a behavioral technology. How can we induce people to use contraceptives? How can we convince the people of the world that war is always worse than the problems it seems to solve? How can we induce people to avoid polluting the environment? To answer questions of this sort, we need a technology of behavior comparable in power with physical and biological technology. It is possible that a technology of behavior is becoming available just in time.

But not everyone views such a technology with equanimity. On the contrary, it is openly opposed. A common tactic is to ask certain standard questions about the uses to which a science of behavior and its related technology will be put. We say we want to use such a science to better the human condition, to improve our way of life, to progress toward a better world. But what do we mean by better? What is good about the good life? What is progress? These are said to be questions about "value judgments." They are questions not about facts but about how we feel about facts.

The answers to these questions are also said to be beyond the reach of science. Somehow or other, it is felt, a different kind of wisdom is needed. Science may tell us how to do things, but it cannot tell us what to do. Physicists and biologists have often agreed, but it would be a great mistake for the behavioral scientist to join them. Questions about values are really questions about human behavior—about those who undertake to do something about their culture. People who act to promote what they call progress or to better the human condition or to build a good life do so for good reason, and we ought to be able to analyze their reasons. In doing so we should come up with an answer to questions about values.

We can begin in a simple way. There are some things that everyone calls "good." Food is good to a hungry person, a warm fire is good to someone who is cold. These things are, as we say, "reinforcers"—they are things which have the effect of strengthening the behavior which produces them. A hungry person eats because food is reinforcing. A cold person approaches a warm fire because escaping from cold is reinforcing. We are likely to ask how such things feel, and we shall be told that they feel good. But feelings are incidental and irrelevant. The important fact about these things is that they make the behavior which leads to them more probable, and that fact is important because it explains why in the evolution of the human organism food should become good. When a man came upon a supply of food, it was important that he learned quickly to do so again. When a man escaped from extremes of cold or heat, it was important that he learned to do so upon future occasions. Man has evolved a structure, a human nature, if you will, with respect to which certain things are good in the sense that they make him more likely to behave in given ways when such things follow. These things also "feel good," but that is not why they are reinforcing. Much of our physical and biological technology is devoted to maximizing goods of this kind—creating more food which tastes good, providing more opportunities for sexual contact, escaping from extremes of temperature, and so on. Let us call things which are immediately reinforcing in this way "personal goods."

The goods of others quickly come into the picture. As soon as food, sex, water, and so on became reinforcing, they must almost immediately have been used in the control of human behavior. People begin almost immediately to use the genetic endowment of the individual in this way. One man pays another for working for him. The pay is a conditioned reinforcer exchangeable for food, sex, or some other immediate reinforcer, and it explains why the second person works for the first. His behavior is primarily for the good of the first person. Something of this same sort happens when we admire people when they do things which reinforce us. In the act of admiring them we make them more likely to do those things again. In a sense they work for us to achieve our admiration, as an employee works for an employer to be paid.

Whether there is any inherited disposition to act for the good of others is questionable. In the lower species we have conspicuous examples in which one individual acts for the good of another. Maternal behavior is an example. The mother takes care of her young—primarily for the sake of the young. It may be that there is a small amount of innate altruistic behavior in the human race, but most of what we do for others we do because we are reciprocally reinforced by them. Other people use personal goods to induce us to work for their good.

The goods of others may actually in the long run override personal goods. They may, in fact, lead to death. Take for example, the classic hero. A group is threatened by a predator or enemy. A strong member drives the predator or enemy away and is wildly admired by all those who have gained from his behavior. He is thus induced to do the same thing again. The curious thing about these contingencies of reinforcement is that the greater the danger, the greater the admiration. By a process of escalation this may reach the point at which the hero goes out and gets killed. A process designed with respect to the preservation of the individual has actually worked toward his destruction.

The goods of others become particularly powerful when the "others" are organized. We control each other ethically with mild reinforcers of approval, disapproval, criticism, blame, and so on. When a government takes over, the control becomes more explicit. A government codifies its activities. It organizes agents to impose sanctions. It uses insignias, flags, and other devices to identify itself and its members. The result is a much more powerful control than that exerted by the ethical group. Organized religion follows a similar pattern. Principles are codified, people are appointed to impose sanctions, and rituals and insignia are elaborated. Governments and religions may work in the same direction as the ethical practices of the group, but they do so much more powerfully.

Economic control also becomes especially powerful when organized. We may induce a neighbor to do something for us by giving something in return. But the practice becomes much more explicit in industry and commerce. Money is invented, values are codified, procedures of exchange are ritualized. Economic control, therefore, becomes more powerful. The educational establishment follows a similar pattern. We teach each other various things; we tell each other what we know, we teach each other minor skills, and so on. The establishment sets up regimes of daily instruction, creates textbooks and other instructional materials, and trains specialists. Something of the same sort occurs in organized psychotherapy.

All such institutions use personal reinforcers to achieve their appropriate effects. A city government may induce its citizens to stop at intersections by fining those who do not stop. Teachers use failure or the birch rod, on the one hand, or grades, diplomas, and prizes, on the other, to induce students to study. Economic systems use money which is exchangeable for personal reinforcers. But these institutions also claim a more general return. They justify themselves by pointing to certain entities long associated with value systems. Governments are said to promote justice, security, and peace, religious piety and salvation, economic wealth, educational knowledge and skills, and psychotherapeutic mental health. These are some of the values often cited when people raise questions about values. And they are the kinds of values which are now being strongly challenged.

Young people in particular are beginning to ask some embarrassing questions:

Why should I serve my fellow man?

Why should I seek to be admired by other people?

Why should I avoid censure or criticism?

Why should I die for my country?

Why should I follow the precepts of a religion?

Why should I let the incentives of an economic system convert me into an eager beaver?

What is so wonderful about the things a school or college wants to teach me?

What is wrong with being a little psychotic?

A BEHAVIORAL ANALYSIS OF VALUE JUDGMENTS 547

We cannot answer these questions by pointing to absolutes. There is no absolute truth in value judgments. No one has that kind of truth or can answer questions by appealing to it. It is not a question of what people should do or ought to do, or what is right. The question is why certain cultures have made certain things reinforcing or have failed to do so. If these values are now being challenged, it is presumably because the culture has engineered them badly.

It is easy to explain the bad engineering. It is difficult to maintain any kind of economic balancing when personal goods are used to promote the goods of others. What the employee does may be quite out of line with what the employer pays him. What the citizen gains in terms of order and justice may be out of proportion with what it costs him to obey the law. Organized institutions tend to produce fat cats who thrive at the expense of those they control. Hence, there is a lack of balance between what the individual gives to the institution and what he gets from it.

Moreover, the reciprocal values of justice, piety, knowledge, wealth, and mental health, whatever their magnitude, are mostly deferred reinforcers. Nothing happens immediately when a man conforms to the sanctions of an agency. He works now and is paid later. He respects religious sanctions now and is reinforced in what is significantly called an afterlife. He obeys the law but receives no sudden increase in justice or security.

When the goods of others are not effectively engineered, the individual attempts to return to personal goods, to immediate reinforcers such as food, sex, drugs, alcohol, and so on. He moves away from social control through amorality or anomie. But the move may go too far, for without the mediation of others, the individual would be nothing but a feral animal—that animal epitomized, probably erroneously, by those children who were said to have been raised by wolves. It is only when other people mediate some of the consequences of a man's behavior that he comes under the control of remote consequences. And these are often important.

A culture, with its mediated reinforcers, produces much more effective behavior than a nonsocial environment. Verbal behavior is an example. It arises in the individual, and must have arisen in the culture of the species, for social reasons. Practical activities are coordinated when the vocal responses of one man serve as important stimuli to another. But once verbal behavior has been elaborated, then the individual (as combined speaker and listener) begins to talk to himself in productive ways. One acquires behavior as part of a social system which becomes extremely advantageous to one as an individual. Economic arrangements lead to the production of wealth far beyond anything possible to an individual alone. Education transmits important features of the culture, teaching new members what other members have already learned, and thus vastly extending the experience of the individual. Effective governments produce security and justice, freeing the individual for many other kinds of activities.

But how shall we strike a balance between the extent to which one's life should be controlled by personal reinforcers and by the goods of others? Must we continue to oscillate between social control at the expense of the individual or individual gratification with the loss of the benefits of social control? These two sets of values offer little promise as guides to the behaviors of those who do something about their cultural practices.

A third kind of value has to do with the strength of a culture. A culture has been defined as a system of ideas with its associated values. If we take ideas to mean cultural practices, then values may be taken to mean what we are discussing here: the reasons why practices are indeed practiced. In any given culture people engage in agriculture, commerce, child rearing, warfare, government, and so on. They exhibit family structures and kinship systems. These are the customs of a culture. They are followed, not because it is customary to follow them, but because something happens when they are followed. What happens is mainly due to the behavior of other members of the group.

At any given time we can look at a culture as an ongoing system. We can observe what things are important to the people in it—what their values are. We can take the position of "relativism" and argue that there is no disputing values. What is good for the Hottentot is good for the Hottentot, and that is that. The values in a given culture are what make the culture function. But we can ask something else about a culture. Is it conserving or using up its natural resources? Is it building good or bad relations with its neighbors? Is it transmitting or failing to transmit important parts of itself to its new members? Questions of this sort emphasize the fact that a culture may be maintaining itself, increasing its strength, or growing weak.

A parallel has often been pointed out between the evolution of a culture and the evolution of a species. Up to a point the parallel is useful. The culture represents a species. It is defined as an assemblage of practices representing the traits of a species. New practices arise for many reasons (they may be invented or they may come about by accident), and these are mutations to be tested by their contribution to the strength of the culture. The parallel breaks down at the critical point of transmission of practices. Cultural evolution is not only Lamarckian; an acquired characteristic may be taken up by other "species" as well.

The concept of cultural evolution is important because it leads us to evaluate the strength of our own culture. Is a given form of government actually maintaining peace and security, domestically and internationally, in an effective way? Does it give its citizens freedom from attack by others? Is an economic system producing what the culture needs? Is education making the most of the genetic material born into the culture? Are psychotherapeutic practices and institutions maintaining some kind of stability? And so on.

When we look at our culture in that way, we may be inclined to act. We may see changes which will lead to reinforcing consequences. The redesign of a culture is commonplace. Men invent new ways of teaching, new ways of raising children, new ways of collecting taxes, new ways of producing goods, and so on. Most of these changes can be traced to personal goods or the goods of others, which we have already examined. But some of them may arise from a concern for the survival of the culture. But why should men be concerned about the survival of their culture? What difference does it make to young people in the last third of the twentieth century what the people who live in the last third of the twenty-first century will look like, what forms of government they will follow, what their literary or artistic interests may be? Certainly, no current goods in the sense of reinforcers can be derived from remote events of that kind. We are talking now not about what is good for the individual but about what is good for the culture. But how can the good of the culture be made good to the individual?

When young people ask, "Why should I care whether my culture survives?" the only honest answer seems to be this: There is no good reason, but if your culture has not convinced you there is, so much the worse for the culture. Somewhere in the process of the evolution of a culture, possibly for quite accidental reasons, the culture has begun to encourage its members to work for its survival. The sources of practices, as mutations, like the sources of biological mutations, are irrelevant. The important fact is the contribution to the strength of the culture. Those cultures which induce their members to work for their survival are, other things being equal, more likely to survive.

To change a culture, to increase its survival, one must answer three questions: (1) What are the conditions the culture must meet in order to survive? No one has formulated the answer in very clear terms. Even the emergencies to be met by a culture in the fairly near future are hard to predict. Tentative answers at least are, however, necessary. (2) What kinds of behavior on the part of the members of the culture will be most effective in meeting these conditions? (3) What kind of social environment will produce such behavior?

We have made some progress in answering the last two questions. It is not impossible to identify kinds of behavior relevant to the solution of problems likely to be met by a culture and to design an environment likely to generate that behavior.

We are most likely to view the survival of a culture in competition with other cultures. We can visualize future emergencies in the form of the domination of world markets, military conquests, or the spread of a religion or economic system. When the Russians sent the first artificial satellite around the earth, it was not difficult to visualize a war in which a new technology might decide the issue. That was America's answer to question 1. What was needed in America was a comparable technology, and that was the answer to question 2. Better scientific education and training was the answer to question 3, and fairly substantial changes were made in support of scientific teaching. The unfortunate thing is that jingoistic nationalism, revealed religious truths, a commitment to historical determinism, or social Darwinism lead to narrow definitions of survival value and, therefore, a necessarily limited social design. They recognize only one of the contingencies of survival to be faced by a culture—namely, struggle to the death with other cultures. As a result, in the very act of strengthening a culture one emphasizes and even encourages the kinds of activities which may lead to its destruction.

Will any culture eventually be affected by a mutation which will make its members interested in the survival of the human race? Can men be induced to work for the strength of humanity as a whole? There have been moves in that direction. To convince the individual that all men are brothers leads to a different kind of action "for the good of others." To argue that no man is an island and that the good of others necessarily affects his own good is a similar line. If any part of the human race eventually engineers a culture which powerfully supports activity for the sake of the human race, we may see new cultural designs of surprising power.

It would be a mistake, however, to try to justify them in any absolute sense. There is nothing fundamentally right about the survival of a culture, any more than there is something fundamentally right about the set of traits which define a species. Those who are induced by their culture to act in its service will do so, and the culture will benefit. They will not do so because of any certain knowledge in advance of where the culture is going. Those who want to know now what will be right in the future miss the whole point of evolution. Although we are now at the point at which we can design new mutations, by inventing new cultural practices, we do not know where other mutations will come from, nor can we surely predict their survival value. There is no way in which one can predict later stages in an evolutionary history. It is not in the nature of evolution that this should be possible.

We do not even know what man will be like in the future simply as an organism. The processes of mutation and selection which have brought the species to the present point will continue, but of course slowly. The process can be accelerated or retarded by changing the conditions under which members of the species survive and breed. If we can begin to change the genetic constitution of man, the process may be greatly accelerated, but we cannot now say in what direction.

Nor can we now tell what future cultures will be like. Those who work for the survival of their culture may solve fairly immediate problems and make reasonable guesses about a longer term. As our knowledge of human behavior improves, we shall no doubt design more effective practices and be able to induce the members of a culture to observe them. But many so-called mutations will be out of our control, as in the long run are the conditions of selection.

We shall work for the survival of our culture, if at all, because of the personal goods which are effective because of our genetic endowment, as these arise naturally or as part of our cultural environment. These are our values, and there are no alternatives. The culture will be strongest whose members are not deterred from acting in its interests by those who cite opposing values and claim a more imposing authority.

IN DEFENSE OF BIOLOGICAL FREEDOM

RENÉ DUBOS

The title "In Defense of Biological Freedom" is intended to convey two different but related meanings. On the one hand, I want to affirm my belief that there is such a thing as biological freedom. By this I mean that irrespective of the organism's biological past and of the circumstances that prevail at the moment of decision, men and animals can exercise free will in making choices. On the other hand, I also want to emphasize that the existential manifestations of freedom are always conditioned, and often extremely limited or distorted by biological antecedents and by environmental factors. The phrase in defense of biological freedom is a plea for the establishment of social conditions favorable to the full expression of free will.

In the preceding paragraph, I have given simultaneous allegiance to two concepts—determinism and free will—which appear incompatible. This intellectual inconsistency does not disturb me. Determinism and free will are biological illustrations of the complementarity principle that Niels Bohr made popular a generation ago in an attempt to reconcile the particle and wave theories of the electron.

When the process of decision making is analyzed in such detail that each step is traced to its ultimate causal connections, freedom seems to disappear because all aspects of behavior are conditioned by genetic and environmental factors. Yet, the awareness of personal freedom in making decisions is a straightforward experience. Just as the physicist studies the electron as a wave or as a particle, depending upon the type of observations and calculations with which he deals, so shall I assume that human behavior can be studied as an expression of determinism or of free will, depending upon the point of view of the observer.

If this book had been written in the 16th century, most contributors would have made reference to the determination of human characteristics by astrological influences. They would have assumed, for example, that persons born under the sign of Jupiter, Saturn, or Mercury tend to be, respectively, of a jovial, saturnian, or mercurial temperament. Because the contributors would have been familiar with Greek medical science, they would have believed that the four humors of the body—blood, phlegm, yellow bile, and black bile—account, respectively, for the sanguine, phlegmatic, bilious, and choleric qualities of the person. In the light of this Hippocratic doctrine, they would have taken for granted that the physician can control temperament by manipulating the relative proportions of the four humors. Since most of our 16th century ancestors would have been orthodox Christians, they would have believed that man is responsible for his actions. In other words, they would have implicitly accepted that astrological and humoral determinism is not incompatible with free will.

Today we have moved far beyond this ancient biology. Instead of believing in astrological influences, we know that the hereditary endowment is transmitted from one generation to the next by chemical mechanisms located chiefly in the cell nucleus. Instead of identifying temperament with the relative proportions of the four body humors, we know that the phenotypic expressions of the genetic endowment and, consequently, behavior are conditioned by environmental forces. We summarize our deterministic philosophy by stating that, at any given moment, all developmental and behavioral expressions of the phenotype are the consequences of the interplay between the genotype and environmental forces. And yet: few are those among us who really believe, deep in our hearts, that the orthodox concepts of determinism—as presently formulated—are sufficient to account for human life.

Whatever their philosophical, scientific, or religious allegiance, practically all human beings accept as a primary datum of experience that they have at least some degree of freedom in their decisions and choices. In fact, it is my impression that many students of behavior acknowledge the existence of biological freedom in animals. According to George Wald, the unpredictability of animal behavior led an exasperated physiologist to state what has come to be known as the Harvard Law of Animal Behavior: "Under precisely controlled conditions an animal does as he damn pleases." In Wald's words, "Could one ask more free will than that?"

Granted that human beings—and probably animals—are not the passive products of genetic and environmental forces, it is at present impossible to account scientifically for either the nature of free will or the manner in which it intervenes in development and behavior. The reason for this failure may be that the scientific method—as we know it—has been developed to deal with purely deterministic processes and that, for this reason, the experimenter excludes from his observations all the phenomena that involve free will. Even though the existence of these phenomena is widely acknowledged, their manifestations are removed from analysis by the artifice of statistical manipulation. The limitations of the experimental approach to the study of behavior may precisely come from the fact that the methods of science apply only to deterministic processes.

What experimental science can do, however, is to study how the influences that impinge on the person affect the manifestations of his free will. Among these influences the most obvious are those which act on the organism at the moment of decision—confidence or fear, the state of health or disease, the social pressures, and practically all environmental factors. More important, probably, even though less obvious, are the effects of past experiences which have become incorporated in the biological makeup of the organism. The most extensively studied among these are the genetic factors which condition all behavioral responses. I shall not discuss these genetic factors but shall emphasize instead the influences of early life. My reasons for this choice are that (1) early influences exert a profound and lasting influence on all the biological and mental characteristics of the adult; (2) they can be manipulated and can, therefore, provide a tool for effective social action.

Experiments in animals and epidemiological observations in man have demonstrated that anatomical characteristics, adult body size, and physiological functions, as well as learning ability and behavioral patterns, are lastingly affected by the environmental conditions which the organism experiences during prenatal and early postnatal life. Innumerable aspects of the total environment have been shown to play a role in this early conditioning. Nutrition, infection, temperature, humidity, type of caging, intensity and variety of stimuli, degree of crowding, and association with animals of the same or other species are among the many environmental factors of early life that have been manipulated experimentally to shape the biological and mental characteristics of the adult.

The experiences of early life are of special importance in man because his body and especially his brain are incompletely differentiated at the time of birth and complete their development while responding to environmental stimuli. Information concerning the effects of early influences is readily obtained from the study of experimental animals and can be documented also in the case of human beings. For example, Japanese teen-agers are now much taller than their parents and differ in behavior from their prewar counterparts, not as a result of genetic changes but because the postwar environment in Japan is very different from what it used to be. A similar phenomenon is observed in the settlements of Israeli kibbutzim. The kibbutz children are given a diet and sanitary conditions as optimum as can be devised and are brought up in an intellectually stimulating environment. Early in their teens, they tower over their parents who originated from crowded and unsanitary ghettos in central and eastern Europe.

The acceleration of growth in Japan and in the Israeli kibbutzim constitutes but a particular case of a trend toward earlier maturation of children in Westernized countries. This is evidenced by greater weights and heights of children at each year of life, and by the earlier age of the first menstrual period. During the past hundred years, the mean age of menarche has fallen from 16–17 years to 12–13 in many parts of the world that have adopted the ways of Western civilization. Growth is not only being accelerated; the final adult heights and weights are greater as well as attained earlier. Some 50 years ago, maximum stature was not being reached in general until the age of 29; commonly now it is reached at about age 19 in boys and age 17 in girls.

The factors responsible for these dramatic changes in the rate of physical and sexual maturation are not completely understood. But improvements in nutrition and the control of childhood infections have certainly played a large part; however, other forces—such as wider social contacts—may have also been influential.

There is no doubt, in any case, that development is handicapped both quantitatively and qualitatively by certain toxic conditions, nutritional deficiencies, infectious processes, and sensory and emotional deprivations experienced during the prenatal and early postnatal phases of life. This well-established fact poses a number of grave social dilemmas, especially in the formulation of medical programs for the underprivileged groups, both in this country and abroad.

Little if anything is known of the long-range consequences of changes in the rate of maturation, but it can be assumed that the fact of being early or late in development exerts an influence upon many aspects of behavior, such as self-confidence, social success, and, more generally, the ease of finding one's place in the social order. In this regard it is rather disturbing that our society increasingly tends to treat young men and women as children and to deny them the chance of engaging in responsible activities, precisely at a time when their development is accelerated.

In man, the most crucial stages of physical and mental development occur very early in life. By age 6 the brain is three times larger than it was at birth; its cytoarchitectonic structure has been essentially completed through an elaborate sprouting of dendrites and immense proliferation of synapses. Language, thought, imagination, and the sense of self-identity have reached a high level of development. It is legitimate to assume, therefore, that the very structure of the brain and the fundamental patterns of behavior are conditioned by the early experiences of extrauterine existence, since their development occurs during the period when the infant is first subjected to the stimuli of the total environment.

It has been convincingly demonstrated in animals that malnutrition can result in smaller size of the brain and in abnormalities of its chemical composition. Similar disturbances can be elicited by certain neonatal infections or by placing the experimental subject under conditions of sensory deprivation. It is difficult, however, to extrapolate from animal experimentation to human behavior, because in human life unfavorable biological conditions are always associated with objectionable social environments. It is legitimate to believe, nevertheless, that neonatal malnutrition or infection, as well as behavioral deprivation, commonly interfere with the development of both the body and the brain.

It can be affirmed, furthermore, that this interference has irreversible effects. I use the word "irreversible" to denote that no technique is yet available for reversing certain effects of early influences on the body and the brain. One can anticipate, of course, that some progress in this direction will be made, but it is probable that many effects of early influences will be found to be truly irreversible.

The organism's structure—physical and mental—can be strongly affected only while the processes of organization are actively going on. Furthermore, as the biological system achieves its organization, it becomes increasingly resistant to change. Organization inhibits reorganization. These statements can be most readily documented for anatomical and physiological differentiation, but they are valid also for behavior patterns. In a recent study of Boston slum children, for example, it was found that they continued to conform to the ways of life of their destitute parents, despite intensive efforts by skilled nursery-school workers to change their habits and tastes. As early as 3 or 4 years of age, the children were already victims of environmentally and culturally determined patterns; and there was much reason to fear that they would in turn imprint their own children with these patterns. They were not culturally deprived; they had a culture from which they could not escape. The same could be said, of course, of children raised in carefully manicured, but emotionally deprived wealthy suburbs.

Granted that early influences, both prenatal and postnatal, are the most influential factors in the shaping of personality, it is also true that surroundings and events continue to have formative and repressive effects on its development and expressions throughout the life-span. All biological and mental attributes are constantly being altered by the organism's responses to the total environment. Thus, individuality is made up at any given time of the inherited potentialities that have been made functional by life experiences. Since it changes continuously in response to environmental stimuli, it might be defined as the continuously evolving phenotype. It represents the incarnation of the genetic and experiential past.

The persistence of the past in the body and brain of the organism imposes biological constraints on its freedom of behavior. The origin of these constraints can best be understood by following chronologically the various steps of mental development.

From the very beginning of his life, the child responds to environmental stimuli, stores information about the environment, and develops adaptive patterns of responses to it. This initial process of coping with the environment is largely unconscious, but it is soon followed by a more active and conscious process during which the child attempts to create his individuality by integrating his genetic endowment with the biological and mental memories of his early experiences.

From a very early age, the child thus begins to "imagine" a world of his own in which he can act out his individuality. I have used the word imagine in its strong etymological sense, namely, "to create an image." This is what Shelley had in mind when he wrote in "Defence of Poetry": "We want the creative faculty to imagine [to create an image of] that which we know." For the child, the actualization of free will is the creative imagining of a world that he constructs mentally.

In normal adult human beings, behavior ideally reflects an increasing degree of freedom in making decisions. Nevertheless, each person continues to be influenced by his past experiences, which provide the material out of which his decisions are made. Man is the creature who creates by choosing, eliminating, and organizing. All these activities have roots in the past and are conditioned at each moment by environmental forces, but they also involve anticipations of the future that are, in the final analysis, the creations of free will.

Under usual circumstances, the organism exists as a functioning structure made up of inherited and acquired characteristics that are organically integrated. This integrated structure is more or less enduring and remains effective long after the conditions that have brought it into being have disappeared. Since each person develops such a unique, integrated, and enduring structure which is largely of his own making, his responses to environmental stimuli eventually acquire much independence of his evolutionary past and even of the culture to which he belongs. Irrespective of theories concerning the fundamental nature of free will, this independence enables man to create a future of his own choice. By the exercise of free will each person selects the set of conditions under which he operates and which thereby influences his further development by eliciting responses that become lastingly incorporated in his physical and mental constitution.

In the light of the preceding remarks, man is as much the product of his environment as of his heredity and his free will. There is not much of anything that can be done about changing heredity, and free will is an exclusively personal matter. But society can manipulate the environmental forces and in fact does it constantly. Hence, large social responsibilities are involved in maintaining an environment suitable for the development of human beings and especially of children.

The crucial factor in this regard is to provide the opportunity for a wide range of experiences so that each person can select those most favorable for the full expression of his individuality. If the surroundings and ways of life are stereotyped, the only components of the genotype that can develop adequately are those adapted to the narrow range of prevailing conditions. This is as true in economic prosperity as in poverty, and it is for this reason that the child raised in a bland even though wealthy environment may be as handicapped as the slum child. The lack of stimulating experiences at a critical stage in development constitutes a limitation for the exercise of free will later in life.

In social planning, we must therefore shun uniformity of surroundings as much as absolute conformity of behavior. Diversity is vastly more important than efficiency because it is essential for the expression of human potentialities.

However, no population can survive without some form of hierarchy that integrates its component parts into a coherent social structure. The social need for unity and stability limits the exercise of freedom because it requires that individual persons adapt their values to those of the group in which they function. Just as the body and the brain cannot escape the shaping influences of the place in which the organism develops, so is the exercise of free will limited by social constraints.

The viability of any biological system requires the acceptance and, indeed, the deliberate choice of certain personal and social constraints. These constraints are deterministic to the extent that they derive from past experiences and from the interplay with the other components of the system. But they are also an expression of free will because man at each moment of his life uses the raw materials that he derives from his past experiences and from present environmental conditions to make himself according to value judgments based on anticipations of the future.

In theory there is no such thing as biopsychology, because all aspects of psychology are expressions of biological forces. In practice, however, the choices that the person makes determine the kind of experiences to which he is exposed and, consequently, give a direction to the development of his attributes. As a result, psychological attitudes progressively depend more on the choices of free will than on purely biological forces. This is symbolized by the statement, attributed to Albert Camus, that after the age of 40 a man is largely responsible for his face.

To the extent that psychological attitudes determine the surroundings and events that impinge on the person and thereby shape his biological and mental characteristics, they affect all aspects of development. But while man truly makes himself in the course of his daily life through the exercise of free will, he can do it only with materials provided by his heredity, his experiential past, and his environment. Existential life takes place at the obscure interface where determinism and free will interplay.

AUTHOR INDEX

Numbers in italics refer to the pages on which the complete references are listed.

A

Abderhalden, E., *125*
Abbott, L., *342*
Acevedo, H. F., 198, *221*
Ader, R., 182, *189*, 240, *247*
Adler, J., 11, *13*
Adler, N. T., 291, *293*
Agrawal, H. C., 177, 178, 188, *189*, 190, *191*
Ainsworth, M. D. S., 418, *430*
Akelaitis, A. J., 33, *39*
Alexander, G., 371, *407*
Alford, B. R., 78, 79, 81, *121*
Allfrey, V. G., 6, *13*
Allinsmith, W., *432*
Alonso, C., *223*
Altman, J., 311, *338*
Altmann, S. A., 443, 448, *451*, *452*
Anchel, H., 307, *340*
Anděl, J., *247*
Anderson, G., *408*
Anderson, W. J., *338*
Andrew, R. J., 442, *452*
Angervall, L., 200, *221*
Angevine, J. B., Jr., 129, *166*
Änggård, L., 79, 84, 85, 101, *121*
Angulo y González, A. W., 46, 59, 64, 75, 77, *121*
Anokhin, P. K., 28, 39, 52, *64*, 66, 107, 119, *122*, 176, *190*, 370, *407*
Aprison, M. H., *190*
Arai, Y., 240, *247*, 263, *293*
Arden, G. B., 184, *190*
Aren-Engelbrektsson, B., 266, *293*
Armstrong, E. A., 441, *452*
Armstrong, G. B., 11, *13*
Arnold, W. J., 297, *302*
Aronson, L. R., 122, 298, *302*, *453*, *525*
Åström, K.-E., 100, 101, 102, *122*
Attardi, G., 30, *40*
Atz, J. W., 108, 119, *122*
Austin, M. F., 164, *167*
Ausubel, D. B., 492, *495*

Avery, G. T., 93, 95, 96, 97, 99, 100, *122*
Axelrod, L. R., *221*

B

Babák, E., 233
Babický, A., 239, *247*
Bacon, W. E., *409*
Baer, D. M., 474, *496*
Baerends, G. P., 443, *452*
Baird, D., *513*
Balaban, M., 55, *64*
Baker, C. P., *528*
Bagnara, J. T., 116, *122*
Balázs, R., 331, *338*
Ball, J., 291, *293*
Balsmis, M., *340*
Baltes, P. B., 486, *495*
Bandura, A., 478, *495*
Banks, E. M., *407*
Barcroft, J., 100, 101, 102, *122*
Barker, R. G., 474, *495*
Barnett, S. A., 436, *452*
Barraclough, C. H., 267, *293*
Barraclough, C. A., 237, 240, *247*
Barron, D. H., 28, *40*, 100, 101, 102, *122*
Bartelmez, G. W., 133, *166*
Bateson, P. P. G., 416, 419, 429, *430*, 435, *452*
Bauer, J., 412, *430*
Baxter, B. L., 306, *338*
Baxter, R. E., 47, 59, *65*
Beach, F. A., 249, 253, 254, 256, 257, 260, 261, 263, 265, 269, 270, 271, 272, 277, 278, 279, 288, *293*, *294*, *295*, 298, *302*, 315, *338*, 439, *452*
Bearn, J., 200, *221*
Beer, C. G., 433, 446, *452*, 518
Beermann, W., 6, *13*
Beidler, L., 43, *44*
Bell, D., 291, *293*
Bell, R. Q., 486, *495*
Bellairs, A., *65*

AUTHOR INDEX

Belluga-Klima, V., *452*
Bellugi, U., 493, *495, 496*
Bencosme, S. A., 202, *221*
Benzer, S., 11, *13*
Benirschke, K., *222*
Bennett, E. L., 306, 307, 308, 309, 310, 312, 317, 326, 327, 337, *338, 339, 340, 341*
Bennett, T. L., 327, *338*
Bergström, R. M., 93, *121, 122*, 165, *166*
Berk, T. J. C., *191*
Berl, S., 183, *190*, 193
Berlyne, D. E., 478, 479, 489, 493, *496*
Berman, S., *125*
Bernard, G., 201, *223*
Bernhard, C. G., 100, 102, 103, *121, 122*
Bernstein, I. S., 423, 424, 425, *430*
Berrington, E. J. W., *296*
Bethe, A., 28, *40*
Bibr, B., *247*
Bijou, S. W., 474, *496*
Bingham, W., 319, *338*
Birch, H. G., *127*, 503
Bitterman, M. E., 325, *338*
Blandau, R. J., *294*
Bloch, E., 199, *221, 222*
Block, J. R., 325, *338*
Bobbitt, R. A., *431*
Bodian, D., 46, 47, 48, *64*, 106, *122*, 129, *166*
Bogdanov, O. V., 114, *122*
Bogen, J. E., 35, *40, 41*
Boggan, W. O., *15*
Bogoch, S., *191*
Bok, S. T., 164, *166*
Boling, J. L., 271, 277, *294*
Bonner, J. F., 6, *14*
Bornstein, M. B., 66, *122, 513*
Boss, W. R., 442, *452*
Bossert, W. H., 443, *452*
Boucher, D., 196, 209, *222*
Bouhnik, J., 200, *227*
Bounds, T. W., *294*
Bowlby, J., 418, 419, *430*
Bowling, D. M., *342*
Boyd, E., *192*
Brackbill, Y., 419, *430*
Bradbury, J. T., 237, *247*
Bredberg, G., 90, 94, *122*
Bresler, D. E., 325, *338*

Bridgman, C. S., *124*
Bridson, W. E., *294*
Brink, R. A., *14*
Brockway, B. F., 117, *122*
Bronson, F. H., 375, *409*
Brookhart, J. M., *191*
Brooksbank, B. W. L., *338*
Brown, R., 450, *452*, 493, *495, 496*
Bruner, J. S., 493, *496*
Bryant, J. W., 112, *121, 124*
Bryant, S., 65
Budtz-Olsen, O. E., *342*
Burke, C. J., 424, *431*
Burns, R. K., 211, *222*
Bursian, A. V., 69, *121, 122*

C

Callison, D. A., 176, *190*
Cammermeyer, J., 176, *190, 192*
Campbell, B. A., 324, *338*
Campbell, C. B. G., 68, *124*
Campbell, D. T., 486, *496*
Cannon, D. J., 346, *408*
Carmichael, L., *66*, 93, 95, 97, 99, 100, 110, *122, 124, 126*, 350, *407*
Carteret, P., 196, 205, 206, 207, *222*
Casamajor, L., 88, *127*, 353, 371, 398, *409*
Caspari, E., 3, 9, *14*
Cassmer, O., *223*
Cazden, C., *452*
Chaffee, E. L., *124*
Chagas, C., *226*
Chaikoff, I. L., *229*
Chanda, S., 178, *190*
Changeux, J. P., *14*
Chargaff, E., 173, *190*
Chesler, A., 175, *190*
Cherry, C., 436, 444, 445, *452*
Chester-Jones, I., 199, *222*
Chodynicki, S., 95, 96, 99, *122*
Chomsky, N., 437, 448, 449, 450, *452*, 528, 529
Chow, K. L., *40*
Clark, L. D., 321, *339*
Clemens, L. G., 268, *294*
Clemente, C. D., *407*
Clendinnen, B. G., 116, *122*, 325, *338*
Clouet, D. H., 188, *190*
Coghill, G. E., 46, 51, 53, 59, 60, 63, *64*, 65, *66*, 106, *122*

Cohen, A., 199, *222*, *226*, 229
Coleman, F. N., *126*
Coleman, P. D., 306, *339*
Collins, R. L., 43, *44*
Comline, R. S., 200, *222*
Connolly, M. T., 216, *224*
Cooper, R. M., 316, *339*
Cornwall, A. C., 346, *407*
Cornwell, A. C., *127*, *409*
Coronios, V. D., 84, 88, *122*, 350, 397, 398, 405, *407*
Cowdry, E. V., 132, 164, *166*
Craik, K. J. W., 489, *496*
Crain, S. M., 43, 59, *64*, *65*, *66*, 109, 110, *122*, 508, *513*
Crain, W. M., 324, *339*
Cravioto, J., 325, *339*
Crook, J., 427, *430*
Crossley, D. A., 278, 279, 280, 281, *296*
Crowley, D. E., 75, 77, *123*
Crozier, W. J., 76, 77, 78, 80, 81, *123*
Cummins, R. A., *342*
Currie, A. R., *224*, *226*, 228

D

Daniel, R. S., 105, *127*
Das, G. D., *338*
Davidson, J. M., 266, 267, 268, 290, *294*
Davis, J. M., 176, 178, *189*, *190*, *191*
Davis, L., 28, *40*
Davison, A. N., *338*
Dawes, G. S., 201, *222*
Deanesly, R., 201, *222*
de Beer, G. R., 106, *123*
Decker, J. D., 55, 57, 58, *64*
Deag, J., 427, *430*
Deets, A. C., 372, *407*
De Groot, J., *407*
DeHann, R. L., *41*, *65*
Dekaban, A. S., 133, *166*
de Laguna, G. A., 448, *452*
Delost, P., 195, 203, 205, 207, 208, 209, 211, 213, 214, 216, *222*, *223*, *224*, *225*, 230, 237
Dempsey, E. W., *296*
Denenberg, V. H., 236, *247*
Denisova, M. P., 92, *123*, *126*
De Robertis, E., 174, 186, *192*
Detwiler, S. R., 49, *66*, 77, 78, 110, *123*, *125*, *408*

De Vore, I., *431*
Diamond, M. C., 272, 285, 292, *294*, *296*, 308, 309, 312, 337, *338*, *339*, *341*
Diczfalusy, E., 196, 199, 200, 201, 202, 203, 204, 205, *223*
Dieterlen-Lievre, F., 201, *223*
Di Perri, R., *191*
Dlouhá, H., *247*
Dobzhansky, T., 503, *513*
Doisy, E. A., 177, *191*
Donovan, A., 89, *123*
Donovan, B. T., *226*
Dornhorst, A. C., 201, *223*
Drachman, D. B., 56, *64*
Dravid, A. R., 178, 179, *190*, *191*
Dubos, R., 553
Dupouy, J. P., *226*

E

Easler, C. A., *407*
Eaton, G., 279, 281, *294*
Eayrs, J. T., 116, *122*, 202, *223*, 325, 331, *338*, *339*
Edwards, D. A., 263, 265, 268, *296*
Eguchi, Y., 200, *223*
Eichenwald, H. F., 325, *339*
Eisenberg, L., 500, 515, *525*, 526, 527, 528
Elger, W., 263, 264, *295*
Ellingson, R. J., 70, 87, 88, 91, 94, *123*, 182, 184, 188, *190*, *192*, 373, *407*
Ellis, H. C., 327, *338*
Emerson, P. E., 418, 419, *431*
Engel, L. L., 229
Engel, R., 91, 94, *123*
English, H. B., *294*
English, A. C., *294*
Ervin, S., 493, *497*
Essman, W. B., 325, *338*
Ewbank, R., 372, *407*
Ewer, R. F., 346, 347, 348, 352, 353, 370, *407*

F

Faltin, J., *247*, *248*
Faulkner, R., *13*
Fazekas, J. F., 174, 175, *191*
Feder, H. H., 263, 265, 268, *294*
Fehr, C., *409*
Feind, C. R., 90, *125*

Fernandez, C., 73, *126*
Feynmau, R., 495, *496*
Fifková, E., 307, *339*
Figurin, N. L., 92, *123*, *126*
Filmer, D., *14*
Fish, I., 178, *190*
Fish, M. W., 84, 88, 100, *123*
Fischer, E., 28, *40*
Fischer, J., 175, *190*
Fitz-Gerald, F. C., 322–*341*
Fitzgerald, J. E., 89, *123*, 148, 149, 154, 159, 161, 165, *166*, *167*
Fitzgerald, P., *228*
Flandera, V., *247*, *248*
Fleischer, K., 90, 94, *123*
Fodor, J. A., *452*
Forgays, D. G., 317, 319, 320, *339*
Forgays, J. W., 320, *339*
Forgus, R. H., 320, *339*
Foss, B. M., *407*
Fox, J., 320, *341*
Fox, M. W., 65, 184, *190*, 374, *407*
Fourment, A., 306, *342*
Friedman, A. H., 182, *190*
Frilley, A., 197, *227*, *228*
Fromme, A., 110, *123*
Fry, P. C., 325, *339*
Fujita, S., 49, *64*
Fuller, J. L., 37, *40*, 321, *339*, 346, *407*

G

Gage, N. L., *496*
Gagné, R. M., 477, 492, 493, *496*
Gaito, J., 309
Gaitonde, M. K., 188, *190*
Galebsky, A., 90, 92, *123*
Gardner, B. T., 35, *40*
Gardner, L. I., 199, *223*
Gardner, R. A., 35, *40*
Garma, L., *192*
Garrigan, O. W., 173, *190*
Gartlan, J. S., 423, 424, 425, *430*
Gaze, R. M., 29, *40*, 50, *64*
Gazzaniga, M. S., *41*
Geloso, J. P., 201, 202, 204, 205, *223*
Gerall, A. A., 252, 262, 265, 267, 270, 274, 282, *294*, *295*
Gerhard, J. C., 4, *14*
Geschwind, N., 35, *40*
Ghilain, A., 200, *223*

Gibson, E., 492, *496*
Gibson, E. J., 327, *339*
Ginsberg, B., 504, *513*
Giroud, C. O. P., *224*
Glassman, E., 12, *15*, 327, *339*
Globus, A., 307, 311, *339*
Godwin, J. T., *228*
Goldfoot, D. A., 262, 276, 277, *294*
Goldring, S., 85, *124*
Golosow, N., 202, *223*
Goldschmidt, R., 6, *14*
Gold, P. S., 115, *123*
Goldstein, K., 28, *40*
Gonet, A., 203, *223*
Goodman, D. C., 39, *40*
Gorbman, A., 201, *223*, 229
Gordon, B. N., *431*
Gordon, J. B., 3, *14*
Gordon, J. E., 325, *342*
Gorski, R. A., 237, 240, *247*, 267, *293*, *294*
Gottlieb, G., 53, 61, 62, 64, 66, 67, 69, 70, 80, 92, 116, 117, *123*, 324, 442, *452*
Goy, R. W., 273, 274, 282, *294*, *295*, *296*
Grady, K. L., 265, 266, 267, *294*
Graham, L. T., Jr., 174, *190*
Grant, J. K., *224*, *226*, *228*
Graziani, L. J., 91, 94, *127*
Gregory, E., 375, *407*
Green, M. M., 6, *14*
Green, J. D., 391, 393, *407*
Greenberg, R. E., 200, *223*
Greenfield, P., *496*
Griffin, A. M., 84, 88, *127*
Griffin, G. A., 322, *339*
Griffiths, W. J., 319, *338*
Grobstein, C., 202, *223*, *525*
Grumbach, M. M., *223*
Grunt, J. A., 274, *295*
Gunther, M., 346, *407*, 411, *430*
Gyllensten, L., 80, 81, 113, 114, *123*, 306, 307, *340*

H

Haddad, R. K., 325, *340*
Hagquist, C. W., *296*
Hahn, P., 235, 247, *248*
Halberg, F., 182, *190*
Hamburg, D. A., 428, *430*
Hamburgh, M., 202, *223*, *224*, *296*

Hamburger, V., 45, 48, 52, 56, 57, *64*, *65*, *66*, *124*, 516, 523
Hamilton, W. J., 439, 441, 442, *452*, *453*
Hansen, E. W., 420, *430*
Hard, E., 297, *302*
Hard, W. L., 202, *224*
Harlow, H. F., 322, 324, 325, *339*, *340*, *342*, 346, 372, *407*, *408*, 411, 412, 414, 417, 419, 420, 426, 428, *430*, 489, *496*
Harlow, M. K., *340*, 412, 414, 417, 420, 426, 428, *430*
Harris, C. W., 486, *496*
Harris, D. B., *409*, 473, *497*, 498, 500, 521
Harris, G. W., *226*, *247*, 252, 254, 255, 263, 265, 267, 268, 270, *295*
Harrison, R. G., 49, *66*, 110, *124*
Hartelius, H., 174, *191*
Hartman, C. G., 71, 74, *124*
Hartman, P. E., 5, *14*
Haugen, F. P., *191*
Hayes, C., 419, *430*
Haynes, H., 92, *124*
Hazlett, B. A., 443, *452*
Heaton, M. B., *121*
Hebb, D. O., 315, 320, *340*, 439, *452*
Heck, W. E., 90, *124*
Heggestad, C. B., 203, *224*
Hediger, H., 393, 404, *408*
Hein, A., 301, *302*
Held, R., 32, *40*, *124*, 301, *302*, 412, *430*, *432*
Helfenstein, M., 57, *64*
Hellström, P. E., *122*
Hemon, P., *223*
Hendricks, S. E., *294*
Hepp-Reymond, M.-C., 75, 77, *123*
Heron, W., 307, *340*
Herrick, C. J., 60, *64*
Hertz, R., 271, *295*
Hess, E., 30, *40*, *408*, *431*, 526
Hibbard, E., 29, *41*, 43, *44*, 105, *124*
Hilgard, E. R., 490, *496*
Hill, R. M., *190*
Hillman, D. A., 199, *224*
Himwich, W. A., 173, 174, 175, 176, 177, 178, 179, 180, 181, 186, 187, 188, *189*, *190*, *191*, *192*, 193, 330, *340*
Hinde, R. A., *409*, 411, 412, 413, 422, 426, *430*, *431*, *432*, *452*, *453*, *454*, *513*, 518

Hines, M., 411, *430*
Hiroi, M., *294*
His, W., 129, *166*
Hochhauser, S., 116, *126*, 325, *341*
Hochsletter, F., 151, *166*
Hockett, C. F., 448, *452*
Hodos, W., 68, *124*
Hofer, M. A., 397, *408*
Hoffer, B. J., *127*
Hoffmann, F., 199, *224*
Hogg, I. D., 112, 121, *124*
Hokfelt, B., 200, *224*
Holsten, R. D., *15*
Holz, A. M., 256, 258, 260, *294*
Hooker, D., 63, *64*, 89, 90, 94, 95, *124*, 149, 165, *166*
Horel, J. A., 39, *40*
Hoshino, K., 212, 216, *224*
Hubel, D. H., 113, *127*, 300, 301, *302*, 307, *340*, *342*, 525
Huffman, B. J., *126*
Hughes, A., 58, *65*
Humphrey, T., 46, 47, *65*, 89, 90, 91, 94, 95, 112, 121, *124*, 148, 165, *166*
Hunt, J. McV., 478, *496*
Hunt, W. E., 85, *124*
Hydén, H., 12, *14*, 174, *191*
Hymovitch, B., 317, 319, *340*

I

Ikeda, H., *190*
Illsley, R., *513*
Imberski, R. B., 9, *14*
Inhelder, B., 412, *431*
Isakson, S. T., *126*
Ishikawa, E., *221*
Ivanitskii, A. M., 346, 355, *408*

J

Jackson, J. H., 174, 175, *191*
Jacob, F., 4, 5, 6, *14*, 18
Jacobson, M., 29, *40*, 43, *44*, 50
Jacquot, R., 200, 204, *224*, *226*
James, Wm., 494, *496*
James, W. T., 346, *408*
Jarrett, I. G., *222*
Jasper, H. H., *66*, 98, *124*, *513*
Jay, P., 426, *431*
Jaynes, J., 315, *338*

Jean, Ch., 196, 203, 204, 205, 207, 210, 211, 216, 220, *222, 223, 224,* **225**
Jean, Cl., 196, 206, 208, 209, 210, 211, 212, 213, 214, 218, *222, 223, 225*
Jenkins, J. J., 478, *496*
Jensen, A. R., 535, *541*
Jensen, G. D., 412, 413, *431*
Jilek, L., *123, 124, 166,* 175, *190*
Johnson, L. L., *294*
Jones, M. R., *409, 497*
Josimovich, J. B., 203, 204, *226*
Jost, A., 196, 197, 198, 199, 200, 201, 202, 203, 204, 205, 207, *223, 225, 226*

K

Kaiser, I. H., *122*
Kamoun, A., 199, *226*
Karmel, B. Z., 373, *408*
Kasatkin, N. I., 92, *124*
Kang, B. S., *125*
Kaplan, A., 440, *452*
Katz, J. J., *452*
Kavanau, J. L., 315, *340*
Kaye, H., 92, *125,* 346, *408*
Keeler, C. E., 80, 81, *124*
Keibel, F., 129, *166*
Kendler, T., 478, *496*
Kennedy, R. F., 511, *513*
Kent, A. E., *15*
Kerpelman, L. C., 327, *340*
Kessel, F. S., 480, *496*
Kessen, W., 346, *408,* 480, 486, 491, *496*
Keston, W. L., *228*
Kimmel, D., 140, 164, *166*
King, D. L., 83, 116, *124*
King, J. A., 82, 83, *124, 125, 127,* 233, 234, *247,* 505, 506, *513*
Kislak, J. M., 278, *294*
Kling, A., 347, 348, 349, 350, 353, 356, 357, 358, 365, 366, 367, 368, 370, 392, *408*
Klinghammer, E., 417, *431*
Klyazina, M. P., 84, 85, *124*
Knobil, E., 203, 204, *226*
Kobayashi, F., 211, *226*
Koch, S., 478, 479, 483, *496*
Koepke, J. E., 397, 406, *408*
Köhler, W., 32, *40*
Kohn, A., *231*
Kolář, J., *247*

Koldovský, O., 235, 237, 240, 247, *248*
Kolmodin, G. M., *122*
Kouishi, M., 440, 441, *453*
Koshland, D. E., 4, *14*
Koster, R., 268, 270, *295*
Kovach, J. A., 347, 348, 349, 350, 353, 356, 357, 358, 365, 366, 367, 368, 370, 392, *408*
Kraus, M., 237, 240, 241, 242, 243, *247, 248*
Krzalić, L. J., *193*
Křeček, J., 233, 236, *247, 248*
Krech, D., 187, 306, 307, 309, 313, 317, 326, *338, 339,* **340,** *341*
Křečková, J., *247*
Kruivt, J. P., 442, *453*
Kruger, L., *528*
Kubát, K., *247*
Kuenen, D. J., 438, *455*
Kühn, A., 7, 8, *14*
Kuhn, T. S., 435, *453*
Kummer, H., 427, 428, 429, *431*
Kuriyama, K., 174, *192*

L

Lane, H. H., 75, 77, 92, *124*
Lange, P. W., 12, *14*
Langworthy, O. R., 68, 71, 73, 74, 92, 94, *125,* 353, 371, 398, *408*
Lanyon, W. E., *452*
Lapham, L. W., *127*
Laqueur, G. L., *340*
Larsell, J. F., *125*
Larsell, O., 73, 74, 112, *125*
Larsson, K., *293,* 297, *302*
Lashley, K. S., 28, 33, *40,* 526
La Torre, J. C., 312, *340*
Lauber, J. K., 115, 116, 121, *125*
Law, F., *339*
Lawrence, M. M., 90, *125*
Layne, J. N., 82, 83, *125*
Leathem, J. H., *247*
Lecours, A. R., 92, *128*
Legrand, C., *223*
Legrand, J., 202, *223, 226*
Lehrman, D. S., 297, 298, *302, 409, 431,* 439, *453, 454,* 459, *513,* 519
Leiderman, P. H., *409*
Lemmon, W. B., 103, *125*
Lemmon, W. S., *432*

AUTHOR INDEX 567

Lesinski, J., 206, *226*
Lessac, N. S., 313, 321, *340*
Levikova, A. M., 92, *124*
Levina, S. E., 201, *226*
Levine, S., 236, *248*, 252, 255, 263, 265, 267, 268, 270, 271, *295*, *409*
Levowitz, A., 320, *340*
Levy, J., 35, *40*, *41*
Levy, L., *127*
Lewis, D., 424, *431*
Lewis, G. W., 236, *248*
Leyhausen, P., 391, 393, *408*
Light, R. E., *513*
Lillie, F. R., 253, *295*
Lind, J., 200, *223*
Lindner, B., *339*
Lindsley, D. B., *41*, 87, 88, 89, *126*, 373, *408*
Lipsitt, L. P., 92, *125*, 346, *408*, *409*, *410*, 498
Lishman, W. A., 325, *339*
Lissitzky, S., *223*
Liu, N., 196, 204, 205, *226*
Livingston, W. K., 175, *191*
Lobo, L. C., *226*
Locke, M., *14*, *15*
London, W. T., 205, *226*
Loraine, J. A., *228*
Lore, R. K., 320, *340*
Lorenz, K., 416, *431*, 437, 438, 439, 442, 449, *453*, 535, *541*
Loring, J. M., *229*
Love, W., *341*
Lundin, P. M., 200, *221*
Luttge, W. G., *296*
Lyon, M. F., 6, *14*

M

MacArthur, C. G., 177, *191*
MacNeill, M., 307, *340*
McCandless, B., 474, *497*
McBride, G., 351, 371, *408*
McClearn, G. E., 37, *40*
McClintock, B., 6, *14*
McCrady, E., *125*
McGill, T. E., 43
McGraw, M. B., 90, *125*
McLaughlin, A., 93, *126*
McNeill, D., 450, *453*
Magoun, H. W., 175, *191*

Maletta, G. J., 113, *125*
Malis, L. T., *528*
Mall, F. P., 129, *166*
Malmfors, T., 113, *123*, *340*
Manley, G. H., 447, *453*
Mann, I., 92, *125*
Maper, M. O., *15*
Marcaud, L., 5, *14*
Marler, P., 439, 441, 444, *453*
Marty, R., 70, 79, 84, 85, 87, 88, 92, *125*, *126*
Marx, M. H., *497*
Mason, W. A., 322, *341*, 346, *408*, 419, *431*
Matthews, S. A., *66*, 110, *125*
May, R., 495, *497*
Mead, M., *513*, 517, 533, 536, 538, *541*
Means, L. W., *126*
Meidinger, R., 273, 277, *295*
Meier, G. W., 414, *431*
Mela, P., *193*
Melby, E. C., *64*, *166*
Mercier-Parot, L., 200, 203, 207, *226*, *228*
Meredith, W., 37, *40*
Meyer, R. K., *295*
Meyerson, B. A., 100, 102, *122*, *125*
Mialhe-Voloss, C., *226*
Michael, R. P., 291, *295*, 391, 393, *408*
Michel, O., *223*
Michel, R., *223*
Mikaelian, D., 79, 80, 81, 112, *125*
Miller, G. A., *453*, 478, *497*
Miller, P. H., *408*
Miller, W., 493, *497*
Miner, N., 33, *41*
Minkowski, A., *128*, *191*
Minkowski, M., 89, 94, *125*
Minot, C. S., *129*, *167*
Miquel, M., *223*
Mirsky, A. E., *13*
Mittelstaedt, H., 440, *455*
Mizusawa, S., 201, *227*
Molliver, M. E., 100, 102, *125*
Moltz, H., 435, *453*
Monchamp, A., *226*
Money, W. L., *226*, *228*
Monod, J., 4, 5, 6, *14*, 18
Montgomery, K. C., 489, *497*
Moore, C. R., 196, *227*
Moore, C. S., 254, *295*
Moreau, T., *127*

Morimoto, H., 331, *341*
Morris, C. W., 444, *453*
Morris, D., *410*
Moruzzi, G., 175, *191*
Mosley, J., *128, 342*
Moth, W., 9, *14*
Mott, J. C., 222
Motulsky, A. G., 5, *14*
Moulton, D. G., 371, 383, *408*
Mowrer, O. H., 477, 478, *497*
Moynihan, M., 442, *453*
Mullins, R. F., Jr., 252, 263, 265, 268, 271, *295*
Murphy, K. P., 90, *125*
Mussen, P., 314, *341, 496*
Myant, N. B., 201, 202, *227*
Myers, H. I., *296*
Myers, R. D., 320, *341*
Myers, R. E., 34, *40, 41*
Myslivecek, J., 184, *191*

N

Nadler, R. D., 256, 263, 264, 267, 268, 270, *295, 296*
Narayanan, C. H., 55, 57, 59, 62, *64, 65*
Nataf, B. M., 202, *227*
Nauta, W. J. H., 39, *40*
Nelson, K., 443, *454*
Nemethy, G., *14*
Neumann, F., 263, 264, *295*
Newton, N., *541*
Nichols, C. W., 229
Nicolai, J., 441, *454*
Noble, R. G., *294*
Noell, W. K., 80, 81, 85, 116, *125*
Nur, U., 6, *14*
Norrlin, M. L., *123, 340*
Nottobohm, F., 441, *453*
Novák, V., *247*
Nyman, A. J., 317, *341*
Nováková, V., 237, 240, 245, 246, *247, 248*
Nucci, L. P., 278, 279, *295*

O

Obika, M., 116, *122*
Obraztzova, G. A., 83, 84, 85, *124*
Olds, J., 489, *497*
Olson, W. E., 486, *497*
Olver, R., *496*

Oppenheim, R., 42, 55, 56, 61, *64, 65, 121, 124*
Orndoff, R. K., *294*
Osgood, C. E., 478, *497*
Osťádalová, I., 245, *247, 248*

P

Palatý, V., 240, *248*
Palermo, D. S., 478, *496*
Pankratz, D. S., 83, 85, *126*
Papas, G. D., 178, *192*
Pardee, A. B., 4, *14*
Parizek, J., *247*
Parke, R. O., 374, *410*
Parkes, A. S., 198, *227*
Pascoe, E. G., 183, *192*
Patterson, G. H., 103, *125*
Pauker, R. S., 279, *294*
Paulson, G. W., 115, *126*
Pearson, A. A., 164, *167*
Peiper, A., 89, *126*
Pennelle, D. K., *191*
Penny, J. E., *342*
Persson, H. E., 100, 102, *125*
Peters, J. J., 115, *126*
Petersen, J., 184, *191*
Peterson, E. R., *66, 122, 513*
Pfaff, D., 375, *407*
Pfeiffer, C. A., 240, *248*, 254, *295*
Phoenix, C. H., 251, 252, 253, 255, 272, 273, 276, 277, 285, 288, 291, 292, *294, 295, 296*
Piaget, J., 412, *431*, 478, 492, *497*
Pickering, D. E., 205, *227*
Picon, L. O., 200, 202, *226, 227*
Pincus, G., 76, 77, 78, 80, 81, *123*
Pitts, F. N., Jr., 182, 188, *192*
Poggiani, C., *409*
Pollock, L. J., 28, *40*
Ponse, K., 197, *227*
Pope, A., *66, 513*
Popp, M., *248*
Popper, K. R., 436, *454*
Porter, R., *431*
Potter, K., 222
Poulsen, H., 441, *454*
Powers, T. H., *126*
Prater, L., 325, *342*
Prechtl, H. F. R., 371, *408*, 411, 412, *431*

Preyer, W., 51, 53, 54, 55, 56, 59, 65, 93, 96, 99, 106, *126*
Pribram, K. H., 397, 406, *408*
Provine, R. R., 57, 58, *65*
Pujol, R., 70, 79, 87, 88, *126*
Purpura, D. P., 66, 178, 183, *190, 192,* 193, *510*

Q

Quick, C., 182, 188, *192*

R

Ramón y Cajal, S., *167*
Rankin, R. M., 201, *227*
Ransom, B., 427, *431*
Ransom, T., 427, *431*
Rasmussen, G. L., 140, *167*
Rasquin, P., 269, 270, 288, *294*
Rave, A., *340*
Rawdon-Smith, A. F., 95, 96, 97, 99, *126*
Rawson, R. W., *226*
Ray, O. S., 116, *126,* 325, *341*
Ray, T. S., *432*
Raynaud, A., 197, 198, 202, 205, 206, 210, 211, *227, 228*
Raynaud, J., *228*
Razran, G. H., 92, *123, 126*
Read, J. M., 317, 319, *339*
Reese, E. P., 416, 419, *430*
Rennik, B. R., *222*
Resko, J. A., *295*
Reynolds, H. C., 73, 75, *126*
Rhines, R., 132, 134, 150, 161, *167*
Rheingold, H. L., *408, 431*
Rhodes, H., *339*
Riege, W. H., 331, *341*
Riesen, A. H., 306, *339, 341*
Rinaldi, F., 176, *192*
Riss, W., 274, 275, 276, *295*
Roberts, A., 120, 121, *126*
Roberts, E., 174, *192*
Roberts, W. W., 75, *126*
Robertson, H. A., *228*
Robertson, R. I., 271, *296*
Roche, J., *223*
Roe, A., *41*
Roffi, J., 200, *228,* 229, 230
Rokos, J., *247*

Romer, A. S., 104, *126*
Rosa, P., 198, 203, *228*
Rösch, G. A., 10, *14*
Rose, G. H., 77, 87, 88, 89, *126,* 182, 184, 188, *190, 192,* 373, *408,* 527, *528*
Rose, S. P. R., 174, *192*
Rosen, M. G., 93, *126*
Rosenberg, E., *222*
Rosenblatt, J. S., 298, *302,* 345, 346, 347, 356, 357, 359, 365, 366, 367, 369, 370, 373, 375, 383, 390, 391, 393, 397, 406, *408, 409, 410,* 411, 417, *431,* 434, *454,* 465, 525
Rosenblith, J. F., *432*
Rosenzweig, M. R., 186, 303, 306, 308, 309, 310, 312, 317, 326, 327, 328, 329, 330, 331, 332, *338, 339,* 340, *341,* 517, 525
Rosett, J., 177, *192*
Ross, M. H., 199, *228*
Rothenbuhler, W., 11, *14*
Rouger, Y., 375, *409*
Rowell, T. E., 414, 422, 427, *431*
Rowland, J. L., 322, *341*
Rubel, E. W., 89, *126*
Ruben, R. J., 78, 79, 80, 81, 112, *121, 125*
Ruckelahaus, S. I., *342*
Rundlett, B., 272, *296*
Russell, E. S., 434, *454*

S

Sackett, G. P., 417, 428, *431*
Saffron, E., *341*
Sak, M. F., 203, *228*
Salganicoff, L., 174, 186, *192*
Salk, L., 372, *409*
Salzen, E. A., 435, *454*
Sandel, T. T., 57, *65*
Sandritter, W., *248*
Saul, R., 38, *40*
Saunders, V. F., 186, *192*
Saxonova, N. S., *231*
Scammon, R. E., 177, *192*
Schadé, J. P., 183, *192,* 324, *341*
Schaffer, H. R., 418, 419, *431*
Schaie, K. W., 486, *497*
Schapiro, S., 231, 329, *342*
Schatz, A., 209, *228*
Schatz, V., *228*

AUTHOR INDEX

Scheibel, A., 183, *192*, 324, *339*, *342*
Scheibel, M., 183, *192*, 307, 324, *342*
Scherrer, J., 67, 84, 85, 87, 88, 92, *125*, *126*, 188, 189, *192*, 306, *342*
Scherrer, K., 5, *14*
Schlesinger, K., *15*
Schlscha, E. B., *228*
Schlütter, G., *248*
Schmidt, R. S., 73, *126*
Schneider, G. E., 39, *40*
Schneirla, T. C., 345, 347, 350, 357, 359, 365, 367, 369, 370, 406, *408*, *409*, *410*, 411, 416, 417, *431*, 434, 435, 439, *454*, 459, 469, 471, 501, 507, 508, *513*, *525*, 534
Schrier, A. M., *430*
Schuller, E., *128*, *342*
Schwartz, I. R., 178, *192*
Scott, J. P., 233, 234, *248*, 346, 375, 406, *409*
Scrimshaw, N. S., 325, *342*
Schwers, J., 200, *228*
Sears, R. R., 478, *497*
Sebeok, T. A., 444, *452*, *454*
Semmes, J., *40*
Shank, R. P., *190*
Shannon, C. E., 443, *454*
Shapiro, D., *409*
Sharma, S. C., 57, 58, *65*
Sharpe, L. G., 423, 424, 425, *430*
Shaw, E., *409*, *431*, *454*, *513*
Shea, N. J., 505, 506, *513*
Shepherd, D. M., 200, *228*
Shock, N. W., 490, *497*
Shuttleworth, F. K., 486, 490, *497*
Shutze, J. V., 115, 121, *125*
Sidman, R. L., 89, *126*
Silver, M., 200, *222*
Siegel, P. B., 115, *126*
Simpson, G. G., *41*
Singh, S. D., 322, 323, *342*
Sinks, J., *295*
Siqueland, E. R., 346, *409*
Skinner, B. F., 437, *454*, 459, 460, 462, 463, 477, 478, *497*, 500, 507, *513*, 538, 543
Slagle, R. W., *341*
Sluckin, W., 416, *431*, 435, 444, *454*
Smallman, R. L., *44*
Smith, F., *453*

Smith, K. U., 87, 88, 105, 114, *127*, 373, *410*
Smith, W., *409*
Smith, W. J., 444, 445, 446, 447, *454*
Smyth, C. N., 90, *125*
Snoeck, J., 196, 204, 205, *228*
Sodersten, P., *293*
Sokoloff, L., 56, *64*
Solomon, R. L., 313, 321, *340*
Sonenberg, M., *228*
Spatz, M., *340*
Spemann, H., 252, *296*
Spencer, H., 520, *525*
Spencer, J. W., 176, *190*
Spencer-Booth, Y., 413, 422, 426, 428, 429, *430*, *431*, *432*
Sperry, R. W., 27, 28, 29, 30, 31, 32, 33, 34, 35, 38, 39, *40*, *41*, 43, *44*, 50, 51, *65*, 283, *296*, 300, 302, 304, 306, *342*, 508, 527
Spielman, M. A., *295*
Spiker, C. C., *410*, 474, 479, *497*
Staats, A. W., 493, *497*
Stachenko, J., *224*
Stanley, J., 486, *496*
Stanley, W. C., 346, 361, 364, *409*, 465
Stavsky, W. H., 356, *409*
Stebbins, G. L., 8, *114*
Steinach, E., 254, *296*
Steinberg, M. L., *126*
Stenberg, D., *122*
Stephenson, H. W., *408*
Stern, J. J., 262, *296*
Stevens, S. S., *41*, *65*, *496*
Stevenson, H. W., *431*, 478, *497*
Steward, F. C., 3, *15*
Stokes, A. W., *454*
Stollnitz, F., *430*
Stone, C. P., 254, 263, 277, *296*
Storrs, E. E., 109, *126*
Stossberg, M., 8, *15*
Streeter, G. L., 129, 141, *167*
Strong, R. M., *167*
Sturtevant, E. H., 448, *454*
Stutinsky, F., *226*
Sutcliffe, E., *124*
Sviderskaya, G. E., 69, *127*
Swank, R. L., 176, *190*, *192*
Swanson, H. H., 278, 279, 280, 281, *296*
Symington, T., *224*, *226*, *228*
Székeley, G., 29, *41*, 50, *65*, 305, *342*

T

Takari, F., *221*
Tamura, M., 439, *453*
Tansley, K., 73, 78, *127*
Tavolga, W. N., *452*
Taylor, C., 451, *454*
Taylor, N., *64, 166*
Taylor, N. R., 200, *228*
Tello, J. F., 144, 164, *167*
Thielke, G., 441, *454*
Thielke-Polz, H., 441, *454*
Thoman, E. B., 297, *302,* 346, 368, 369, *409*
Thompson, W. R., 37, *40*
Thorpe, W. H., 415, *432,* 441, *455*
Tice, A. A., 199, *223*
Tiefer, L., 278, 279, 280, 281, *296*
Tighe, T. J., 327, *339*
Tilney, F., 88, *127,* 177, *192,* 353, 371, 398, *409*
Timaras, P. S., 113, *125*
Tinbergen, N., 437, 438, 442, *455*
Torok, A., *342*
Tobach, E., *409, 513*
Toropova, N. V., 346, 361, *410*
Tracy, H. C., 51, 59, *65,* 106, *127*
Trattner, A., *409*
Trojan, S., *123, 124, 166, 191*
Tryon, R. C., 506, *513*
Tschanz, B., 442, *455*
Tuchmann-Duplessis, H., 200, 203, *228*
Tucker, B. E., *191*
Tuge, H., 105, *127*
Turkewitz, G., 92, *127,* 345, 397, *408, 409, 410*
Tusques, J., 206, *228*

U

Urspring, H., *41, 65, 342*

V

Valenstein, E. S., *295*
Valverde, F., 183, *193*
Van den Berg, C. J., 186, *193*
Vandenberg, S. G., 314, *342*
Vandenbergh, J. G., 117, *127*
Vanden Daele, L. D., 486, *497*
van der Cingel, N. A., *452*
Van Lawick-Goodall, J., 372, *410*

van Marthens, E., 325, *342*
Van Wyk, J. J., *223*
Verain, A., 201, *228*
Verain-Pinoy, A., 201, *228*
Verley, R., *192*
Vestal, B. M., 82, *127*
Vigouroux, E., 201, *226*
Villee, C. A., 199, *229*
Villee, D. B., 199, *229*
Vinson, G. P., *222*
Vogt, O., 176, *193*
Vokaer, R., 206, *229*
Volokhov, A. A., 67, 75, 77, 83, 85, 87, 88, *127,* 346, *410*
Vonderahe, A. R., *126*
von Foerster, H., 534, *541*
Von Holst, E., 440, *455*
Von Soemmering, S. T., 305, *342*
Vowles, D. M., 434, *455*
Vukovich, K. R., 329, *342*

W

Wada, J., 35, *41,* 75
Wada, T., 77, *127*
Waddington, Ch., 7, *15,* 17
Waelsch, Heinrich, 186, *193*
Waisman, H. A., 325, *342*
Walk, R. D., 327, *339*
Walker, C. A., 182, *190*
Walker, V. S., *125*
Wallace, R. B., *338*
Walls, G. L., 30, *41*
Walsh, R. N., 308, 312, *342*
Waltan, O., *127*
Walters, R. H., 374, *410*
Wann, T. W., 483, *497*
Ward, A. A., 66, *513*
Ward, I. L., 267, 270, 271, *294, 296*
Warkentin, J., 83, 85, 87, 88, 114, *127,* 373, *410*
Warren, J. M., 319, *342*
Warriner, C. C., 417, *432*
Waterman, A. J., 201, *229*
Watson, J. B., 27, 436, *455,* 474, 500
Waugh, M., 56, *64*
Weale, R. A., 97, *127*
Weaver, W., 443, *454,* 487, *497*
Wedenberg, E., 90, 94, *127*
Weisman, R., 374, *407*
Weiss, P., 29, 31, *42,* 51, *65*

Weitzman, E. D., 91, 94, *127*
Wellman, B., *126*
Wells, L. J., 197, *229*
Wenger, E., 55, *64*, *124*
Werman, R., *190*
Wertheimer, M., 92, *127*
West, G. B., 200, *228*
Weston, E., 393, 404, *410*
Wetzel, A., *409*
Whalen, R. E., 263, 265, 268, 271, 284, 288, *294*, *296*
Wheelis, A., 484, 494, *497*
White, B. L., 113, *124*, 412, *432*
White, R. H., *127*
White, R. W., 478, *497*
Whittaker, V. P., 174, *193*
Wiepkema, P. R., 443, *455*
Wiesel, T. N., 113, *127*, 300, 301, *302*, 307, *342*, *525*
Wiesner, B. P., 198, *229*
Wilcott, R. C., 70, 87, 88, *123*, 373, *407*
Wilhelmsson, M., *293*
Wilkins, L. J., 202, 220, *223*, *229*
Williams, D., 371, *407*
Williams, R. J., *44*, 109, *127*
Willier, B. H., *65*
Wilson, C., 393, 404, *410*
Wilson, D. A., *338*
Wilson, E. E., 147, 148, *167*
Wilson, E. O., 443, *455*
Wilson, J. E., *15*
Wilson, M., 319, *342*
Wilson, R. G., *294*
Wimer, C., 325, *342*
Windle, W. F., 46, 47, 59, *65*, 84, 88, 89, 100, *123*, *127*, 129, 132, 134, 141, 142, 148, 149, 150, 154, 159, 161, 164, 165, *166*, *167*, 353, 398, *410*
Winick, M., 177, 178, *190*, *192*, *525*
Wislocki, G. B., 89, *126*
Wodinsky, J., 346, 352, *410*
Wolff, J., 201, *229*
Wolff, P. H., *528*
Wolff, R., 391, 393, *408*
Woll, R. J., 345, 359, 360, 363, 397, *410*
Woods, P. J., 320, *342*
Woodward, D. J., 112, *127*
Wortis, J., *191*
Wortis, R. P., 298, *302*
Wright, H. F., 474, *495*
Wu, S-Y., *341*
Wyman, J., *14*

Y

Yakovlev, P. I., 92, *128*
Young, F. A., *41*
Young, I. M., *223*
Young, W. C., 197, 201, *229*, 252, 253, 270, 271, 272, 274, 292, *294*, *295*, *296*, 297, *302*
Youngstrom, K. A., 105, *128*

Z

Zamenhof, S., 116, *128*, 325, *342*
Zangwill, O. L., *455*
Zemp, J. W., 12, *15*
Zetterström, B., 88, 89, 92, 113, *128*
Zeigler, E., 478, 483, *497*
Zimmerman, A. A., *125*
Zimmerman, R. R., 411, 419, *430*
Zubek, J. P., 307, 316, *339*, *340*

SUBJECT INDEX

A

Abortion, produced by exogenous hormones, 206
Accommodation, in human infant, 92
Acetylcholinesterase, 186
  enriched environment and, 308, 336
  light deprivation and, 113
  visual impoverishment and, 307, 336
Acoustic isolation, in song development in sparrow 439–441
ACTH, see Adrenocorticotropic hormone
Adrenal cortex, fetal, 199–201
Adrenal glands, premature weaning and, 240, 241, 243–244
Adrenal medulla, pituitary gland and, 229
Adrenalin, transplacental passage of, 205
Adrenocortical hormones, fetal, 199–201
Adrenocorticotropic hormone, 204–205
  epinephrine and, 229
  hypophysis and, 200
  premature weaning and, 241
Adrenomedullary hormones, see also Epinephrine
  fetal, 200–201
Adulthood, 233–235
Age
  anthropometric model and, 499–500
  critical periods and, 233–235
  of human embryo, 130–132
  in longitudinal method, 486
  mental, 499
  mother-infant relations and, 422
  roles and, 423–424
  stages in development and, 490–492
Agonistic behavior, in titmouse, 443
Aldosterone, pinealectomy and, 242–244
Algae, pattern formation in, 7
Allosteric proteins, 4
Ambystoma, motility in, 46, 59–60
Amino acids, see also *specific compounds*
  in brain, 177, 178, 179, 180, 186, 187, 193–194
  gene regulation and, 4, 5

γ-Amino-butyrate, in brain, 178, 179, 186, 193–194
  compartmentalization of, 186
Amnion
  estrogen in, 198
  motility in, 52, 53, 61–62
Amniotes, motility in, 58–59
Amphibians
  chronic anaesthesia in, appearance of normal behavior and, 66
  motility in, 65–66
    as integrated performance, 52
  motor primacy in, 106
  nerve-endorgan rearrangement in, 28
  optic tract in, 283
  regeneration in, 50
    cell differentiation in, 42
  respiration in, 165
  retina in, 300
  Rohon-Beard cells of, 48
  selectivity in growth of nerve connections in, 29
  sensory development in, 105
    light sensitivity and, 116
  sensory input and, 51
  swimming in, absence of prior muscular movement and, 110
Anesthetics, chronic, appearance of normal behavior and, 66
Anamniotes, motility in, 58
Androgens, see also Testosterone
  congenital malformations and, 211
  copulatory behavior and, organization of brain mechanisms for, 250–255, 282–283, 284, 287–291
  disorders of fetal growth and, 207
  fetal testicular secretions and, 198
  premature weaning and, 240, 241
  reproductive function and, 237
  sexual differentiation and, 251
  synthesis of, in human fetus, 199
  transplacental passage of, 204, 205
Androstenedione, 198
  copulatory behavior and, 262

573

SUBJECT INDEX

Anoxia, 175
Ant(s), behavior and learning in, 443, 469, 508, 524
Antiandrogen, see Cyproterone
Antibiotics, postnatal growth disorders and, 209
Approach-withdrawal theory, 507–508, 516, 525
Armadillos, intrastrain differences in, 44
Arousal, suckling and, 393, 394, 395, 397–398, 406
Arthropods, evolution of, 434
Artiodactyls, 68
  evolution of, 103–104
Aspartic acid, in brain, 179
Atropine, visual sensitivity and, in guinea pig, 96–97
Auditory system, see also Sensitivity, auditory
  acceleration of maturation in, 116–117
  deceleration of maturation in, 116
  function of prior to complete maturation, 112
Axon, outgrowth from embryonic nerve cell, 49

B

Baboon(s)
  dominance in, 414, 422, 427
  protection in, 428
  tripartite relations in, 429
Bacteria, chemotactic behavior of, 11
Barbiturates, dog brain and, 176
Beagle(s), differential environment and baseline for, 313
  learning ability and, 321–322
  problem solving and, 321
Bee(s)
  social activity of, 10–11
  transmission of information in, 443
Behavior, 10, see also specific behaviors
  capacity for, differentiation and, 46
  changing, 521
  consistency of, 518–519
  control of, 500, 543–544, 559
    value judgments in, 544–551
  determinism in, 553–560
  embryonic brain and, 164–165
  environment and heredity and, 34–37

field, 22
free will in, 553–555, 558–560
functional activity and differentiation and, 10–11
genetic analysis of, 11
genetic determination of, 535–536
  individual differences in, 538–541
genetic transmission of, 504–507
homology and, 108
modifiability of, 11–13
in natural environment
  in animals, 464–466, 468, 469–470
  in humans, 474–475
plasticity of, 27–28
premature weaning and, 237
study of
  approaches to, 473–475
  behavioral units in, 482–485
  conceptual molds for, 475–479
  experimental, 498–501
  levels in, 507–511
  methodology for, 485–487
  natural history approach to, 459, 463-466, 534
  organization in, see Organization
  philosophy of science and, 479–481
  problems of development in, 487–495
  structure and function in, 481–482
testosterone and, 245–246, 272
verbal, 437, see also Communication
Behavioral testing, 183
Behavioral units, 482–485
Behaviorism, 459–460, 476–477, 492
  in child development, 473–474, 498–501
  in study of animals, 461–463, 466, 469, 470
    comparative, 466–468
  in study of social behavior, 436–439
    communication, 436–437
Behavior shaping, 474
  heredity and, 34–37
Binocular interaction, visual experience and, 307
Bird(s), see also specific birds
  approach to conspicuous objects in, 416
  conditioning in, 467–468
  evolution of, 104, 118
  imprinting in, 415–416, 417, 418–419, 518
  nonvisual photic sensitivity in, 80
  optic tectum of, differentiation in, 49

previous breeding experience in, 298, 299–300
roles in, 424
selectivity in growth of nerve connections in, 30
sensory development in, 67, 69, 92, 103, 109
  evolutionary pathways and, 68
song development in, 439–441
vocal mimicry in, 441
Blindworm, thyroxine in, 210
Blood, see also Hemoglobin; Plasma
vasopressin in, 239
Bone
  metabolism in, 245
  thyroid hormones and, 202
Brain, see also specific structures
  differential environment and, see Environment
  direct modification of, 324–326
  individuality of, 33, 527
  lateral specialization of function in, 35
    in twins, 37
  mammalian, 11, 164–165
  measures of development of, 177–178
    anatomical, 183
    behavioral testing, 183
    chemical, 186–187
    electrophysiological testing, 183–185
    multidisciplinary, 187
    validity of, 178–179, 181–182
  mediation of copulatory behavior in, 250–255, 264, 278, 282–283, 291–293
  methodology for fractionation of, 173–174
  methodology of neuroembryology and, 129–133
  motor system paralysis and, 114–115
  oxygen consumption of, 174–175
  plasticity of, 38–39, 42–43
    behavioral, 27–28
  ribonucleic acid in, see Ribonucleic acid
  selectivity in growth of nerve connections in, 29
    molecular identification and, 30–31
  sequence of differentiation in, 49
  size of, 183, 325, 526
  species differences in development of, 188
  spontaneous motility and, 57
    electrical activity and, 59
  synaptogenesis in, 193–194
  theories of development of, 174–176
Brain stem, 175
  in human embryo, 163
Breast feeding, see also Suckling
  individual differences and, 540–541
  survival selection by, 536–537
Breathing, see Respiration
Breeding, in opossum, 75
Breeding experience, 298–300
Budgerigars, testicular activity in, 117
Bullfinch, song development in, 441

C

Calf, thyroid in, 201
Canary, song development in, 441
Carbon dioxide, motility and, 59, 60
Carnivores, 68
  evolution of, 103–104
Castration
  copulatory behavior and
    in cat, 298
    in dog, 298
    in guinea pig, 274–276, 277–278, 298
    in hamster, 279–281
    in rat, 258–262, 263, 265–267, 288
  penis growth and, 256–258
  sexual differentiation and, 197–198
Cat(s)
  attachment to familiar area in, 391, 393
  auditory evoked response in, 188
  brain of, 150, 154
    amino acids in, 193–194
    synaptogenesis in, 193–194
  copulatory behavior in, 298
  electroencephalogram in, 324
  eye in, 300–301
  home orientation in, see Home orientation
  learning in, 465
  light deprivation in, 113, 306–307
  motility in, onset of, 46, 47
  myelinization in, 68
  neurofibrillar differentiation in, 132, 134
  sensory development in, 67, 70, 80, 84, 86–89, 103, 118

SUBJECT INDEX

suckling in, see Suckling
visual evoked potential in, 184
Cell differentiation, see Differentiation
Cell division, unequal, in pattern formation, 7, 8
Celloniella palensis, environment of, 8
β Cells, 203
Central nervous system, 10, 250, 447, see also Brain
   of *Drosophila,* 11
   estrogens and, 210
   hormones as organizers of, 251–255, 267
   inhibitory systems and, 66
   interaction in, structuration and, 49–50
   organization of behavior and, 300
   plasticity in, 42–43
      cell differentiation and, 43
   spontaneous motility and, 57
   thyroid hormone deficiency and, 202
   vertical development of, 175–176
Cercopithecus aethiops, roles in, 423–424
Cerebellum
   neural connections to, in rat, 75
   training and, 305
Cerebral cortex, 174, 175, 325
   synaptogenesis in, 193–194
   visual impoverishment and, 307
Cerebral dominance, 35
   determination of, 44
   in twins, 37
Chaffinch, song development in, 441
Chelydra, motility in, 58
Chemoaffinity, selectivity in growth of nerve connections and, 30–31, 49–50, 120
Chemotaxis, 31
Chick (s)
   brain of, motor paralysis and, 114–115
   discontinuity of behavior in, 52
   motility in, 54, 59, 63, 65–66, 115, 121
      differentiation and, 48
      electrical discharge and, 57–58
      onset of, 46, 47
      prereflexogenic period in, 55–57
   motor primacy in, 106
   neurofibrillar differentiation in, 132, 164
   sensory development in, 69, 118
      augmented light stimulation and, 115, 116
Chimpanzee, training, 35–36
Cholesterol, in human fetus, 199

Cholinesterase
   enriched environment and, 308, 336
   visual impoverishment and, 307, 336
Chreods, 20, 23
Chromosomes
   chemotactic behavior of bacteria and, 11
   heterochromatic regions of, genic activity in, 6
Circulatory system, 235
Citric acid, 240
Classification
   of individuals, 538
   of social behavior, 412–415, 429
CNS, see Central nervous system
Colchicine, reduction of plasticity by, 43
Commissures, identified in human embryos, 163
Communication, 442–445, 451, 528,
   behaviorism and, 436–437
   definition of, 436
   ethology and, 437, 439–443
      stochastic processes in, 443–444
   language, 448–450
   semantics in, 445–448
   song development in birds, 439–442
Communication systems, 442
   statistical properties of, 443
Complexity, in development, 487
Concept formation, 493
Conditioning, 69, 437, 477
   age and, 324
      critical periods, 346–347
   by culture, 533
   failure of, 346, 347, 465
   generality of, 467
   in home orientation, 398–399
   potential and, 494, 500–501
   premature weaning and, 245–246
   ribonucleic acid synthesis and, 13
   sensory development and, 92
   in suckling and home orientation, 394, 395, 399
Congenital malformations, prenatal hormone treatment and, 210–221
Contact comfort, 414, 426
   monotropy and, 417, 419
Context, meaning of communications and, 445–448
Contrast, visual cortex and, 184

Copulatory behavior
  in guinea pig
    experience and, 298
    female, 271–274
    male, 274–278, 298
  in hamster
    female, 278–279
    male, 279–281
  in rat, 254–255
    female, 267–271
    male, 258–267, 297
    mediation of, 250–255, 282–283, 284, 287–291
Corn, gene regulation in, 6
Corpus callosum, 35
  nerve connections and, 33–34
  plasticity and, 38–39
Cortex, 100–101, 174, 175, 325
  adrenal, 199–201
  compounds responding to stress in, 186
  differential environment and, see under Environment
  growth hormones and, 116
  lack of function and stimulation and, 110
  negative phototropism and, 80
  organization of, 301
  ribonucleic acid in, learning and, 12
  separation from white matter, 309–310
  synaptogenesis in, 193–194
  vertical development and, 176
  visual sensitivity and, 78, 184
Corticosteroids, 203, see also Corticosterone; Cortisol; Cortisone
  transplacental passage of, 204, 205
Corticosterone, premature weaning and, 241, 242, 243
Cortisol
  epinephrine and, 229
  in fetal adrenal cortex, 199
Cortisone
  congenital malformations and, 210
  disorders of gestation and fetal growth rate and, 206
  disorders of neonatal and postnatal growth and, 207
Cretinism, 202, 237
Critical periods, 9, 233–237, 415–416, 517–518
  endocrine function and, 237–247
  learning and, 346–347, 350, 358, 365, 406–407
Cultural evolution, 548–551
Culture, 534, 543
  conditioning by, 533
  control of behavior in, 543–551, 559
  effect on education, 536–537
Crocodilians, 118
  evolution of, 104–105
Cryptorchidism, 212, 213
Cyproterone, copulatory behavior and, 262–263, 264–265, 276–277
Cytoplasmic inheritance, 109, 119

D

Dark-rearing, see Light deprivation
Deermouse
  differential environment and, 315, 337
  sensory development in, 82–84, 103, 118
  species differences in, 505–506
Dehydroepiandrosterone, 198
Dendrites, arborization of, 183
Deoxyribonucleic acid, 12
  in brain, 178, 325
  5-fluorouracil and, 9
  gene regulation and, 5
Determinism, 481
  in human behavior, 553–560
Diabetes, 237
  maternal, 203
Dialect, in song of sparrow, 439–440
Didelphys virginiana, sensory development in, 71–75
Diencephalon, in human embryo, 136, 151, 152, 153, 157, 158, 159, 163
Differentiation, 111, 120, 492
  behavioral, 10
    capacities, 46
    nerve nets, 31–32
  in critical periods, 9, 517
  distinguished from pattern formation, 7
  early environment and, 555
  functional activity and, 51
  gene regulation and, 3–6
  of islets of Langerhans, 202
  learning and, 12–13
  of left and right hemispheres, 35
  morphology and, 3
  motor, 106
    precedence over sensory, 48–49, 63

neurofibrillar, 132–133, 134, 142, 143, 145, 146, 150, 154, 160, 163, 164
onset of motility and, 47, 55
of organ of Corti, 95
plasticity and, 43
of Purkinje cells, 112
in regeneration, 42
in retina, 92
of roles, 423–425
schedule of, 49–50
in secondary nuclei and tracts, 162–163
sexual, 197–199, 255, 285
  in ramstergig, 250–252
of thyroid, 201, 202
Digestive system, 235
Diiodothyronine, 206
Diiodotyrosine, 201
Diptera, salivary glands of, gene regulation in, 6
Directionality, in development, 487–488
DNA, *see* Deoxyribonucleic acid
Dog (s), *see also* Beagle (s)
  amino acids in brain of, 179
  barbiturates and, 176
  behavioral development in, 346
  copulatory behavior in, 298
  effects of phenylalanine on, 178–179, 180
  home orientation in, 375
  oxygen consumption in brain of, 174–175
  parathyroid hormones in, 202
  picrotoxin in, 176
  sensory development in, 67
  suckling in, 346, 364
  testosterone in, 288
  visual evoked potential in, 184, 185
Domestic fowl, communication in, 442
  song development, 441
Dominance, in social development, 414, 420–421, 422, 423, 424, 427
Dorsal alar plate, differentiation in, 48
Drive, 478
Drosophila
  gene regulation in, 6
  inheritance in, 505
  phototactic behavior of, 11
Drug (s), excitant and depressant, brain development and, 335
Duck (s)
  erythroblasts of, information transfer in differentiating cells of, 5
  sensory development in, differential environment and, 115, 116–117
Duckbill, 104

E

Ear
  of guinea pig, 96
  of rat, 75–76
E. Coli, genic regulation in β-galactosidase system of, 4, 6
Education, 548
  critical periods and, 518
  cultural influence on, 536–537
  individual differences and, 538–539
  transfer of training in, 517
EEG, *see* Electroencephalogram
Ejaculation, *see* Copulatory behavior
Electrical activity
  function and stimulation and, 109–110, 111–112, 114–115
  light deprivation and, 306
  measurement of brain development and, 184
  motility and, 62–63
    spontaneous, 57–58, 59, 60, 66
  sensory development and, 70, 120–121
    in cat, 87, 89
    in guinea pig, 95, 96, 97–98
    in house mouse, 78–80
    in man, 91–92
    in rabbit, 84
    in rat, 78
    in sheep, 100, 101
  species differences in, 188
  synaptogenesis and, 193, 194
Electric field theory, nerve connections and, 32–33
Electrodes, measurement of brain development and, 184
Electroencephalogram
  changes in, 183–184
  light deprivation and, 306
  maturity of, 324
Electron microscopy, demonstration of synaptic contacts using, 47–48
Electroretinogram
  in cat, 89, 113
  in duck, 115
  in man, 92
Embryonic field, 7

Emotional disturbance
  at removal from home area, 383–389, 394, 395, 398, 401, 403
  at separation from mother, 397–398
Endocrine function, critical periods and, 237–247
Endocrine glands, 10, see also specific glands
Endocrine mechanisms, handling and, 236
Environment
  dependency of behavior on, 522–524
  differential, 509, 516–517
    baseline for, 313–315
    effects on brain development, 113–114, 304–313, 323–337, 526
    effects on problem solving, 315–323, 337
    learning and, 327–336, 337
    relationship of behavioral and cerebral effects, 323–327
  earlier maturation and, 555–557
  measurement of brain development and, 178–179, 181–182, 184–185, 186, 187
  pattern formation and, 7, 8–9, 13
  natural, see also Ethology
    study of behavior in, 464–466, 468, 469–470, 474, 484, 534
  potential and, 493, 504, 516, 519, 524
  shaping of behavior and, 34–37
  social development and, 412, 413–415, 416
Enzymes, see also specific enzymes
  endocrine glands and, 229
  in end-product inhibition, 20
  in mitochondria, 21
Enzymic systems, 199
Ephestia, effect of 5-fluorouracil on, 9
Epilepsy, 175
Epinephrine, 200
  congenital malformations and, 210
  corticoids and, 229
Epithelium, in human embryo, 146
Erythroblasts, information transfer in differentiating cells of, 5
Estradiol, 206
  congenital malformations and, 212–220
  copulatory behavior and
    in female guinea pig, 287
    in female rat, 271
    in male guinea pig, 277
    in male rat, 265, 266–267

Estrogens, see also Estradiol; Progesterone
  congenital malformations and, 210, 212–220
  copulatory behavior and, 255, 289–291
    in female guinea pig, 271–274
    in female hamster, 278
    in female rat, 267–268
    in male guinea pig, 276–277, 278
    in male hamster, 280–281
    in male rat, 263, 264–267, 288
  disorders of fetal growth rate and, 207
  disorders of gestation and, 206
  disorders in neonatal and postnatal growth and, 208–209, 210
  in female fetus, 198
  reproductive function and, 237
  synthesis of, in human fetus, 199
  transplacental passage of, 204, 205
Estrus, see also Copulatory behavior
  permanent, 211
Ethology, see also Environment, natural
  neurogenesis and, 32
  in study of social behavior, 437–439
    communication, 438, 439–443
    stochastic processes in, 443–444
European blackbird, song development in, 441
Evolution
  comparative study of social behavior and, 433–434, 441
  cultural, 548–551
  ethology and, 437
  of man, 482, 543
    control of, 477
  sensory development and, 68, 103–105, 106, 118–119
Experience, 301–302, 411, see also Environment
  ethology and, 438
  in song development of sparrow, 439–442
  free will and, 558–560
  home orientation and, 381
  sexual behavior and, 297–300
  suckling and, 366–370, 374, 395, 400
    nipple location in, 350, 356–362
  visual response and, 301
Explanation, in human behavior development, 480–481
Eye, see also Retina; Rods; Visual system
  of deermouse, 82

580 SUBJECT INDEX

functional activity in, 10
of guinea pig, 96
of opossum, 73
organization of visual cortex and, 301
of rat, 76, 78
surgical rotation of, 29-30, 50

F

Fallopian tubes, see Genital tract
Feedback, 489
  negative, 489
    allosteric proteins and, 4
    in genetic regulation, 19
Fetal morphogenetic testicular substance, 250, 251
Fetal position, 412
Fetoplacental unit, 196, 221
  metabolism of hormones by, 196, 204-206
Fetus
  externalized, technique for study of behavior in, 93
  intrauterine electrophysiological study of, techniques for, 93
Fish
  motor primacy in, 106
  problem solving in, 325
  respiration in, 165
  Rohon-Beard cells of, 48
  selectivity of growth of nerve connections in, 29
Flowering, environmental stimuli and, 8-9
5-Fluorouracil, in development of *Ephestia*, 9
Forebrain
  in human embryo, 163-164
    in fifth week, 150-153
    in sixth week, 156-158
Fornix, in human embryo, 157
Foulbrood, resistance to, 11
Freemartinism, hormones and, 197, 253
Free will
  in human behavior, 553-555, 558-560
  potential and, 494-495
Fringilla coelebs, song development in, 441
Frog(s)
  cell nuclei from larval intestine of, 3
  motility in, onset of, 46

optic nerve transection in, regeneration and, 50
sensory development in, 105
stimuli in visual field and, 184
Fucus, environment of, 8
Function, 10
  lateral specialization of, 35, 37
  relation of measures of brain development to, 183
  sensory development and, 109-110, 119-121
  sequence of, 110-117
  in study of behavior, 481-482

G

GABA, see γ-Amino-butyrate
β-Galactosidase system, gene regulation in, 4, 6
Gallus domesticus, song development in, 441
Gastric mucosa, premature weaning and, 240-241
Generalization, 489
Gene regulation, cell differentiation and, 3-6
Genetic inheritance, see Inheritance
Geniculate bodies, vertical development and, 176
Genital tract, see also Gonads
  congenital malformations of, 211-220
  differentiation of, see Differentiation
Geotropism, negative, 73
Gerbil(s), brain of, differential environment and, 312-313, 336
Gestation, disorders in produced by exogenous hormones, 206-207
Gestation period
  in cat, 84, 88, 106
  fetal thyroid tissue in, 201
  in guinea pig, 93, 99
  hormones and, see under Hormones
  in house mouse, 78, 81, 106
  in man, 94, 106
  in opossum, 74
  in rabbit, 85
  in rat, 75, 77, 106
  sensory precocity and, 106
  in sheep, 100, 102
Gibraltar macaque, social interaction in, 427

Glucagon, fetal, 203
Glucocorticoids, critical periods and, 242
Glutamic acid, in brain, 178, 179, 181, 186, 193
  compartmentalization of, 186
Glutamine, in brain, 179, 181
Glycogen storage, adrenocortical hormones and, 200
Goiter, in fetus, 201–202
Gonadal hormones, see Hormones; *specific hormones*
Gonadotropins, 198
  transplacental passage of, 204, 205
Gonads, 250
  differentiation of, 197
  premature weaning and, 240
Growth hormone, see Hormones
Guinea pig(s)
  adrenomedullary hormones in, 200, 201
  amino acids in, 181
  androgen in, as organizer, 252–253
  copulatory behavior in
    experience and, 298
    in females, 271–274, 287
    in males, 265, 274–278
  sensory development in, 93, 95–100, 103, 118
  testosterone in, 255
Gulls, communication in, 442, 446–447
Gustation, 73

H

Habituation, 500
Hamster
  copulatory behavior in
    in females, 278–279
    in males, 279–281
  differentiation of β cells in, 203
  motility in, 55
Handedness
  genetic determination of, 43–44
  intelligence scale scores and, 35
  in twins, 37
Handling, 346
  alteration of development by, 236
  brain development and, 329–330, 337
Hemodynamic regulation, 201
Hemoglobin, genetic information and, 4, 5
Herring gull, communication in, 442

Heterochrony, 107–108, 118–119
Hexokinase, enriched environment and, 308, 336
Hierarchies, in development, 492–493
Hippocampus, 177
  effect of environment on, 312
  inhibition in, 193, 194
  premature weaning and, 246
Histones, blockage of genic activity by, 6
Home orientation, 346, 373, 375–379
  disturbance at removal and, 383–389, 394, 395, 398, 401, 403
  functional distinction from suckling, 392, 394, 395, 401–402
  olfaction and, 375, 376, 379–380, 383–387, 389–391, 394, 395, 401, 403
  social isolation and, 380–381
  origins of, 398–399
  spatial orientation in, 392–393, 396, 399, 404
  visual cues for, 390, 391, 395, 402–403, 406
Homochrony, 106–108, 119
Homology, 119
  behavior and, 108
Honeybee, see Bee(s)
Hormone(s), see also *specific hormones*
  chemical measurement of brain development and, 186
  developmental disorders after prenatal treatment with
    congenital malformations, 210–221
    gestation and prenatal growth, 206–207
    neonatal and postnatal growth, 207–210
  gene regulation by, 6
  gonadal, 197–199, 203, 208
    communication in birds and, 442
    copulatory behavior in guinea pigs and, 271–278, 287
    copulatory behavior in hamsters and, 278–281
    copulatory behavior in rats and, 267–271
    genital growth and mating behavior in male rats and, 256–267, 288
    organization of brain mechanisms by, 251–255, 282–283, 284, 291–293

sexual development and, 284–286, 288–291
transplacental passage of, 204, 205
gonadotropic, 198, 204, 205
growth, 203–204
  brain size and, 325
  compensation for lack of thyroid hormones by, 202
  prenatal administration of, 116
  transplacental passage of, 205
metabolism by fetoplacental unit, 196, 204–206
pancreatic, 202–203
parathyroid, 202–203
pattern formation and, 8
pituitary, 116
  brain development and, 331–332, 337
  transplacental passage of, 195, 196, 204–205
Hydrocortisone, disorders of gestation and fetal growth rate and, 206
Hypercalcemia, 202
Hypoglycemia, 175
Hypophysis, 195, 196
  adrenal regulation by, 199–201
  epinephrine and, 229
  fetal hormones and, 204
  gonadotropic function of, 284
  growth-promoting activity in, 203
  hormones of, 116
    brain development and, 331–332, 337
  ovarian transplant and, 254
  sexual development and, 198–199, 244
  thyroid gland and, 201–202
  vasopressin and, 239
Hypothalamus, 283, 284
  adrenal cortex and, 199–200
  critical periods and, 246–247
  in human embryo, 152
  light cycles and, 116
  pituitary gonadotropic function and, 254
Hypothyroidism, 237

I

Identification, see Labels
Imitation, 478
  vocal, in birds, 441
Imprinting, 526
  in birds, 415–416, 417, 418–419, 518
  study of, 435

Individual differences, 539–540
  in education, 538–539
Individuality, 557–559
  of brain, 33, 527
Infantile stage, 233–235
Information storage, 12
Information theory, in study of social behavior, 443–444
Inheritance, 119, 554
  behavioral nerve nets and, 30–32
  behavior shaping and, 34–37
  control of, 543
  cytoplasmic, 109, 119
  determinism and free will and, 554–560
  environment and, 522–524
  ontogeny and, 108–109
  of potential, see Potential
  in study of behavior, see Instinct
Inhibition, 510, 511
  of cell differentiation, plasticity and, 43
  end-product, 20
  in hippocampus, 193, 194
  in learning, 12
  of motor activity, 63–64, 65–66
  in neocortex, 193
  in thymus gland, 200
Innate releasing mechanism, 442–443
Insect (s), see also specific insects
  societies of, 434
Instinct, 34, 438–439
  in learning, 500–501
    langauge, 449
  in song development in sparrow, 439–442
Insulin, 203
  transplacental passage of, 204, 205
Intelligence
  of chimpanzees, 36
  inheritance of, 506
    environment and, 36–37, 511–512, 536
    lateralization of function in brain and, 35
  phenylalanine and, 179
Intelligence scale, 537
  handedness and, 35
Interaction
  of cells, pattern formation and, 7, 8
  social, see Social behavior
Interference, differentiation of left and right hemispheres and, 35
Intromission, see Copulatory behavior

SUBJECT INDEX 583

Iris reflex, 97
Islets of Langerhans, pancreatic hormones and, 202, 203
Isolation
 acoustic, song development and, 439–441
 social, 417–418, 426, 427
  home orientation and, 380–381
  suckling and, 366–370, 374
Isthmus, in human embryo, in fifth week, 154
Iurasequens sexualis, see Ramstergig

J

Junco oreganus, song development in, 441
Junco phaeonotus, song development in, 441
Jungle fowl, communication in, 442
Juvenile stage, 233–235

K

Kidneys, 236
 vasopressin and, 239
Kingbird, communication patterns in, 446
Kitten, *see* Cat (s)

L

Labels, molecular, in neurogenesis, 30–31, 49–50, 120
Lactogenic hormone, 211
Lactose, combination of regulator protein with, 4
Lagomorphs, 68
 evolution of, 103–104
Language
 acquisition of, 449–450, 478, 522, 528–529
 chimpanzees and, 35–36
 compared to animal communication, 448
 hierarchies in, 493
 lateralization of, 35
Langur, social interaction in, 426
Larus argentatus, communication in, 442
Larus atricilla, communication patterns in, 446–447
Lateral geniculate body, light deprivation and, 113
Lateralization
 of function in brain, 35
  genetic determination of, 43–44
  in twins, 37, 44

Laughing gull, communication patterns in, 446–447
Learning, 36, 43, 301–302, 411, 500
 brooder feeding and, 358–365, 373, 400
 developmental status and, 347
 differential environment and, 321–323, 327–336, 337
 differentiation and, 12–13
 growth hormone and, 325
 hierarchies in, 492–493
 imprinting as, 415–416, 435
 individual differences in, 538–539
 innateness of, 500–501
 of language, 449–450, 478, 522, 528–529
 in natural environment, 465–466, 468
 neural connections and, 304–305
 pattern formation and, 12–13
 in song development of sparrow, 439–442
 study of, 477
 to walk, 499
 without experience, 523
Learning curve, 489, 490
Lens protein, 4
Lepidoptera, scale apparatus of, unequal cell division in, 8
Lesions, of corpus callosum, 33–34
Light augmentation, 121
 acceleration of maturation in visual system and, 115–116
Light deprivation, 301, 306, 332, 336
 deceleration of maturation in visual system and, 113–115
Lipid
 in brain, 177, 187
 thyroidectomy and, 202
Liver, glycogen storage in, 200
Lizard, motility in, 58
Locomotion
 brain development and, 330, 337
 patterns of, 395, 396
 in home area location, 384, 386, 389
Longitudinal method, 486, 511–513
Lordosis, *see* Copulatory behavior
Lungs, functional activity in, 10

M

Macaque sylvana, social interaction in, 427
Malnutrition, effect on brain development, 325

584   SUBJECT INDEX

Mammals, *see also specific animals*
  brain of, 11, 164–165, 188
  evolution of, 118
  modifiability of behavior of, 11–13
  motility in, 63
    electrical activity and, 59
    prereflexogenic period in, 58–59
  neurofibrillar differentiation in, 164
  plasticity in, 43
  sensory development in, 67, 92, 103
    evolutionary pathways and, 68
    ontogeny and, 109
  societies of, 434
Mammary gland
  androgens and, 211, 212
  estrogens and, 211, 213, 215–216, 219–220
  somatotropic hormones and, 203, 205
Manipulation, *see* Handling
Markov chains, 443
Marsupials, 68
  evolution of, 103–104
  sensory development in, 73
Mate selection, sensitive period and, 415–416
Mating behavior, *see* Copulatory behavior
Medial lemniscus, in human embryo, 155, 160
Medulla, neural connections to, 75
Memory, 36
  age and, 324
  neural connections and, 305
Meriones unguiculatus, see Gerbil (s)
Meristem, environmental stimuli and, 8–9
Mesencephalon, in human embryo, 136, 146, 148, 157, 158, 159, 163
  in fifth week, 153–154
  in sixth week, 158–159
Mesenchyme, 523–524
  in human embryo, 135, 138, 144, 157
Metabolism
  of hormones, 204
    adrenocortical and adrenomedullary, 200–201
    fetoplacental unit and, 205
  of water and electrolytes, weaning and, 238–239
Metencephalon, in human embryo, 136
  in sixth week, 159–160
Mexican junco, song development in, 441

Micturation reflex, 239
Midbrain, γ-amino-butyrate in, 178
Mimicry, vocal, in birds, 441
Mitochondria, 21
Models, social, 478
Molds, pattern formation in, 7
Monkey (s), *see also* Primate (s); *specific monkeys*
  bilateral brain damage in, 42
  conditioning of, 346
  learning ability in
    age and, 324
    differential environment and, 321, 322–323, 327
  nerve-endorgan rearrangement in, 28
  nipple preference in, 372
  phenylketonuria in, 325
  previous breeding experience in, 298
  reflexes in, 165
  roles in, 423–424, 425
  social behavior of, testosterone and, 288
  social isolation in, 417–418
Monoiodotyrosine, 201
Monotremes, 118
  evolution of, 104
Monotropy, 417–420
Morphogenesis, pattern formation in, 7
Mother-infant relationship, 411, 412, 413–414, 417–420, 421–422, 426–427, 545
  in breast feeding, 536–537, 540–541, *see also* Suckling
Motility
  discontinuity in, 52
  endogenously stimulated, 54, 60–61
  as integrated performance, 52
  onset of, 46–48
    demonstration of, 47
  sources of, 53–54
  spontaneous, 54, 62–63
    electrical discharges in, 57–58, 60
    inhibition of motor activity and, 65–66
    prereflexogenic period in, 55–57, 58–60
  stimulated, 54, 61–63
  systemogenesis in, 52–53
Motivation, 478
  innate releasing mechanism and, 442–443
  meaning of communication and, 446

in suckling and home orientation, 394, 395, 396, 401–402
Motor function
  inhibition of, 63–64, 65–66
  onset of, in man, 143
  ontogeny and, 106–107
  precocity of, 119
Motor system, paralysis of, functional maturation of brain and, 114–115
Mounting, see Copulatory behavior
Mouse, see also Deermouse
  androgens in, 207, 211, 212
  antibiotics in, 209
  brain of, differential environment and, 307, 312, 336
  cortisone in, 210
  estrogens in, 206, 207, 208–209, 210, 211, 212–220
  hypophysis of, 198, 200
  learning in, ribonucleic acid and, 13
  motility in, electrical activity and, 59
  pancreatic hormones in, 202
  paw preference in, 43–44
  sensory development in, 78–82, 112, 118
  sexual maturation in, 117
  somatotropic hormone in, 203, 205
  thyroid hormones in, 206, 207–208
  visual system of, light deprivation and, 113
Movement, visual cortex and, 184
Müllerian ducts, 250
  estrogens and, 211
  testis secretions and, 197, 198
Mus musculus, sensory development in, 78–82
Myelinization, 68, 509
  in auditory system, 92
  in visual system, 92, 113, 114
Myosin, 4
Myostrichomorpha, 249

N

Negro, intelligence in, 511–512, 535–536
Neocortex, inhibition in, 193
Neuroembryology, methodology and, 129–133
Neurogenesis, 508
  electric field theory and, 32–33
  experience and, 304–305

functional activity and sensory input as factors in, 50–51
  functional interchangeability in, 27–29
  interdependency in, 49–50
  lesions in corpus callosum and, 33–34
  molecular labels in, 30–31, 49–50, 120
  onset of motility and, 46–48
  order of differentiation in, 48–49
  selectivity in, 29–30
  vestibular sensitivity and, 75
Neurons, learning and, 12–13
Neurophylogenesis, 174
Nipple, *see under* Suckling
Norepinephrine
  in adrenal glands, 200
  pituitary gland and, 229
Nutrition, see also Malnutrition
  earlier maturation and, 555–556, 557
  sexual maturation and, 244–245
Nystagmus, see Sensitivity, vestibular

O

Object permanence, 412
Odor, see Olfaction
Olfaction, 73
  in home orientation, 375, 376, 379–380, 383, 384–387, 389–391, 394, 395, 398–399, 401, 403
    social isolation and, 380–381
  in nipple location, 354–356, 358, 359–362, 372, 394, 395
  in nipple preference, 353, 354–356
  in sexual maturation, 117
Olfactory tract, in human embryo, 146, 149, 152, 156, 157
Ontogeny
  in designing an environment, 517
  in evolution, 106–108, 118–119, 481–482
  mammalian brain and, 164
  sensory development and, 106–107, 108–111
Opossum (s), 68
  estrogens in, 211
  myelinization in, 68
  sensory development in, 71–75, 103, 112, 118
Optic nerve
  in human embryo, 157
  myelinization of, light deprivation and, 113, 114

regeneration of, 50
surgical rotation of eye and, 29–30
Optic system, *see also specific structures*
  growth of novel connection patterns in, 39
Optic tectum
  differentiation in, 49
  sensory input and, 51
  synaptic connections in, 50
Optic tract, selectivity in growth of, 29
Oregon junco, song development in, 441
Organization, 17, 488–489
  in control of behavior, 545–546, 547
  levels of, 507–511, 515–519
    consistency of behavior in, 518–519
    critical periods in, 517–518
    differential environment in, 516–517
  spatial selectivity in neurogenesis and, 30
Organ of Corti
  in guinea pig, 95
  in house mouse, 79, 80
  in man, 90, 92
  in rat, 75
Orientation, *see* Home orientation
Orienting response, 501
Otocyst, in human embryo, 140
Ovary, 250
  critical periods and, 237
  differentiation of gonads into, 197
  fetal pituitary and, 198
  hormones of, *see specific hormones*
  mediation of copulatory behavior and, *see under* Hormones, gonadal
  testosterone and, 240
Oxygen consumption, of brain, 174–175

P

Pancreas, 523–524
Pancreatic hormones, 202–203
Papio anubis, dominance in, 427
Papio hamadryas
  dominance in, 427
  tripartite relations in, 429
Parakeets, testicular activity in, 117
Parathyroid hormones, 202–203
Pattern formation, 10
  distinguished from differentiation, 7
  environmental stimuli and, 7, 8–9, 13
  gene regulation and, 11
  interaction between cells and cell groups in, 7, 8, 13
  learning and, 12–13
  unequal cell division in, 7, 8
Penicillin, postnatal growth disorders and, 209
Penis, 251, 285
  in female, 270
  lack of development of, copulatory behavior and, 259–260, 261–262, 263, 275, 276, 280
  postnatal growth of, 256–258
Perception, *see also* Sensitivity
  visual, neurogenesis and, 28, 29–30
Perikaryon, 49
Peromyscus stp., *see* Deermouse
Personality, 519
  shaping, 557
Phenylalanine
  in dogs, 178–179, 180
  in monkeys, 325
Phenylethanolamine-N-methyl transferase, 229
Phenylketonuria, 325
Phototropism, negative, 80
Phylogeny, 106, 107, 108, 118, 481–482
  mammalian brain and, 164
Picrotoxin, dog brain and, 176
Pig(s), thyroid in, 201
Pigmentation, in *Ephestia*, 9
Pigtail macaque(s), mother-infant relationship in, 413
Pineal body, light cycles and, 116
Pineal gland, aldosterone production and, 242–244
Pinna reflex, *see* Preyer reflex
Pituitary, *see* Hypophysis
Placenta
  circulation of, 201
  hormones in, 195–196, 203
    estrogen, 198
    metabolism by fetoplacental unit, 196, 204–206
    somatotropic, 204
    thyroid, 201
    transplacental passage of, 195, 196, 204–205
Plants
  pattern formation in, 8–9

stomal apparatus of, unequal cell division in, 8
Plasma, fetal, hormones in, 201
Plasticity, 527–528
 of behavior, 27–28
 of brain, 42–43
  absence of corpus callosum and, 38–39
  corpus callosum lesions and, 33–34
  nerve-endorgan rearrangement and, 28
  neural connections and, 305
Polypeptide chain, translation and, 5
Pons medulla, 174
Poriphera, neuroidal conduction in, 507
Potential, 46
 in development, 493–495, 499, 500, 504
 enviroment and, 504, 516, 519, 524
 in learning, 539
Pragmatics, 444
Pregnancy, *see* Gestation period
Prereflexogenic period, 48, 51
 spontaneous motility in, 55–57, 58–60
Preyer reflex
 in guinea pig, 96
 in house mouse, 78–79
 in rat, 75
Primary afferent ganglia and tracts, in human embryo, 149–150
 in fifth week, 143–146
 in fourth week, 143
 in sixth week and later, 146–149
Primary efferent nuclei, in human embryo, 142–143
 in fifth week, 135, 137–140
 in fourth week, 133–134
 in sixth week and later, 140–142
Primates, 68, *see also specific animals*
 evolution of, 103–104
 motor primacy in, 106
 sensory development in, 118–119
 social development in, 411, 412, 413–414, 419–420, 428
Problem solving, effects of post-weaning environment on, 315–316, 321–323, 337
 specificity of effects, 316–321, 337
Process, in development, 489–490
Progesterone
 copulatory behavior and, 255, 289–291
 in female guinea pig, 271–274, 287
 in female hamster, 278
 in female rat, 267–268
 in male guinea pig, 276–277, 278
 in male hamster, 280–281
 in male rat, 264–266, 288
 previous breeding experience and, 299–300
 transplacental passage of, 204
Prolactin, 204–205
 fetal growth and, 203
Proprioception, 69, 114–115
 in sheep, 101, 103
Prosencephalon, in human embryo, 150
Proteins, 17
 allosteric, 4
 in axoplasmic material, 49
 in brain, 177, 178, 182, 187, 327, 337
 gene regulation and, 3–6
 sensitive periods of, 9
Pseudohermaphroditism, 272–274
 estrogens and, 213
Punishment, ability to form conditioned responses based on, 69
Pupillary reflex, in guinea pig, 96, 97
Purkinje cells
 function in, 112
 premature weaning and, 246
Pyrrhula pyrrhula, song development in, 441

R

Reafference, 440
Rabbit (s)
 adrenal cortex in, 199
  hormones of, 200
 adrenomedullary hormones in, 200, 201
 auditory evoked response in, 188, 189
 cochlear function in, 79
 cortisone in, 210
 hypophysis in, 200
 pancreatic hormones in, 202
 sensory development in, 67, 83–84, 85, 103, 118
 sexual differentiation in, 198–199
 striate cortex in, 307
 suckling in, 346, 355–356
 thyroid in, 201, 206
 visual system in
  amino acids in, 180
  movement and contrast and, 184
Ramstergig, 249, 282–283
 copulatory behavior in, 256, 267, 268

normal development of reproductive system in, 250–253
Rat (s)
  adrenal weight in, 199
  adrenocortical hormones in, 200
  adrenomedullary hormones in, 200
  androgens in, 211, 237
  brain of
    amino acids in, 178
    pleasure and, 489
    protein in, 182
    supernormal growth of, 325
  conditioning in, 324
  control of genital growth and mating behavior in
    in females, 267–271, 288
    in males, 256–267, 288
  copulatory behavior in, 254–255
    experience and, 297
  corticosterone in, 199
  cortisone in, 207, 210
  developmental stages in, 234–235, 236, 239–246
  differential environment and
    effect on brain, 304, 307–309, 328, 329–336, 526
    problem solving and, 315, 316–321, 326, 327
  electroencephalogram in, 324
  estrogens in, 210, 211, 237
  growth hormone in, 203
    brain size and, 325
    learning ability and, 325
    prenatal administration of, 116
  home orientation in, 375
  hypophysis in, 198, 200, 229, 331–332
  inheritance of intelligence in, 506
  intrastrain differences in, 44
  learning in, ribonucleic acid and, 12
  microcephalic, 325
  motility in, 59, 61–62
    electrical activity and, 59
    onset of, 46, 47
  nerve-endorgan rearrangement in, 28
  neurofibrillar differentiation in, 132
  pancreatic hormones in, 202
  pinealectomy in, 242–244
  Purkinje cells of, 112
  retention in, 324

sensory development in, 67, 75–78, 103, 112, 118, 121
  excessive light and, 116
  light deprivation and, 113
suckling patterns in, 346, 368–369
testosterone in, 240
thyroid in, 201
  hormones of, 202, 206, 210
  interference with, 325
transplacental passage of hormones in, 204, 205
use as an experimental subject, 461–462, 464, 533
visual evoked potential in, 184
Recognition of parental calls in birds, 442
Reductionism, 481
Redundancy, in communication systems, 443
Reflex, 412
  conditioned, see Conditioning
  embryonic brain and, 148–149, 165
  growth hormones and, 116
  Preyer, see Preyer reflex
  suckling, see Suckling
Regeneration
  biochemical affinities and, 50
  of peripheral nerves, 29
  redifferentiation in, 42
Regulation, 17–23
  genetic, 17–19
Reinforcement, 507, see also Reward
  in behavior control, 459, 460, 462
  by pleasure, 489
  value judgments and, 544–545
  control of behavior and, 545–548
Reinnervation, 42
  cross-connection of nerves and, 28
Releasers, in communication, 438, 442–443
Reproductive function, see also Copulatory behavior
  androgens and estrogens and, 237, 240
  premature weaning and, 237
Reproductive system
  normal development in ramstergig, 250–253
  sensory stimulation and, 117
Reptiles
  evolutionary pathways and, 68, 104–105, 118
  motility in, 59

Respiration, in human fetus, 165
Respiratory system, 235
Reticular formation, 175, 176
  in human embryo, 155, 160, 161
Retina, 300
  of cat, 89
  excessive light exposure of, 116
  of house mouse, 80
  of man, 92
  of marsupials, 73
  nonneural photochemical processes in, 97
  of rat, 78
  synaptic connections of fibers of, 50
  vertical development and, 176
  visual deprivation and, 113, 306
Retino-tectal system, selectivity in growth of, 29
Reward, see also Reinforcement
  ability to form conditioned responses based on, 69
Rhesus monkey (s), see also Monkey (s)
  mother-infant relations in, 413, 419–420, 421–422, 426–427
  social isolation and, 417–418, 426
  motility in, 46
    onset of, 46, 47
  protection in, 428
  social deprivation in, 428
Rhombencephalon, 132
  in human embryo, 133, 140, 141, 144, 145, 148, 149, 159, 162–163, 164
    in fifth week, 154–156
    in sixth week, 160–161
Rhythms, measurement of brain development and, 182
Ribonucleic acid
  in brain, 178
    enriched experience and, 327, 337
    learning and, 12–13
  gene regulation and, 4, 5
  interference of 5-fluorouracil with, 9
  polydisperse, 5
  premature weaning and, 246
Ribosomes, 5, 12
Righting reflex, see Sensitivity, vestibular
Ringdoves, previous breeding experience in, 298, 299–300
RNA, see Ribonucleic acid

Rod (s)
  of cat, 89
  of house mouse, 80
  of rat, 78
Rodent (s), 68, see also specific animals
  cortex and spinal cord of, 110
  evolution of, 103–104
Rohon-Beard cells, 48
Roles, 423–425, 429

S

Salamander, motility in, 46, 59–60
  onset of, 46
Salivary glands, gene regulation in, 6
Scale apparatus, unequal cell division in, 8
Secondary nuclei and tracts, in human embryo, 150, 162–164
  in fifth week, 150–156
  in fourth week, 150
  in sixth week, 156–161
Selectivity, in growth of nerve connections, 29–30
Semantics, in animal communication, 444, 445–447, 450
Semiotic, in animal communication, 444
Sensitive periods, see Critical periods
Sensitivity
  acoustic, nonauditory, 69
  auditory
    of brain structures, 176
    in cat, 87–89
    in deermouse, 82–83
    evolutionary pathways and, 103, 105
    in guinea pig, 93, 95–96, 97, 99
    in house mouse, 78–80, 81
    in man, 90–91, 92–93, 94
    in opossum, 73–75
    in rabbit, 84, 85
    in rat, 75–76, 77, 78
    in sheep, 102, 103
  elimination of, spontaneous motility and, 56–57
  onset of, differentiation and, 48–49
  photic, nonvisual, 69, 80
  tactile
    blindness and, 307
    in cat, 84, 87–89
    in deermouse, 83
    evolutionary pathways and, 103, 105

590 SUBJECT INDEX

  in guinea pig, 93, 95, 97, 99
  in man, 89, 90, 91, 93, 94, 112, 121
  in opossum, 71, 73, 74, 75
  in rabbit, 83, 84, 85
  in rat, 75, 77, 78, 112, 121
  in sheep, 100, 102, 103
  in toad, 120–121
 vestibular
  in cat, 84, 87, 88, 89
  in deermouse, 82–83
  evolutionary pathways and, 103, 105
  in guinea pig, 95, 97, 99, 100
  in man, 89–90, 93, 94
  in opossum, 73, 74, 75
  in rabbit, 83, 84, 85
  in rat, 75, 77, 78
  in sheep, 101, 102, 103
 visual
  in cat, 87–89
  evolutionary pathways and, 103
  in deermouse, 82–83
  in guinea pig, 93, 96–97, 99
  in house mouse, 78, 80, 81
  in man, 91–93, 94
  in opossum, 73–75
  in rabbit, 83–84, 85
  in rat, 75, 76–78
Sensory function
 evolutionary pathways and, 68
 sequential development of, 68–71, 106–107, 108–111, 118–121
  in birds, 69, 103
  in cat, 67, 70, 84, 86–89, 103
  in deermice, 82–84, 103
  function prior to complete maturation and, 111–113
  in guinea pig, 93, 95–100, 103
  in house mice, 78–82
  light augmentation and, 115–116
  light deprivation and, 113–115
  in man, 89–93, 103, 105, 106
  methodological considerations, 70–71
  in opossum, 71–75, 103
  in rabbit, 83–84, 85, 103
  in rat, 67, 75–78, 103
  in sheep, 100–103, 118
  sound augmentation and, 116–117
  sound deprivation and, 116
Serinus c. carnarius, song development in, 441

Settling reaction, 393, 394, 395, 397–399, 400, 402, 405
Sex, roles and, 423–425
Sex reversal, 254
Sexual behavior, *see* Copulatory behavior
Sexual differentiation, *see* Differentiation
Sexual maturation, 233, 234
 hormones and, 240–245, 284–286, *see also specific hormones*
 prenatal growth, 197–199
Sheep
 adrenal gland in, 199
 adrenomedullary hormones in, 200, 201
 sensory development in, 100–103, 118
Silver-impregnation, demonstration of synaptic contacts and, 47–48
Skeletal maturation, thyroid hormone deficiency and, 202
Sleep, evoked potentials in, 185
Social behavior, 411–412, *see also* Communication; Mother–infant relationship
 analysis and resynthesis in, 415–417, 429
 of bees, 10–11
 changes or differences in, 420–422
 classification of, 412–415, 429
 definition of, 433
 monotropy, 417–420
 roles in, 423–425
 social nexus and, 425–429
 study of, 433–434, 435–436
  behaviorism in, 436–439
  comparative, 434
  ethology in, 437–447
  in single species, 434–435
 in suckling, 392, 395, 396
 testosterone and, 288
Social isolation, *see* Isolation
Social models, 478
Social stimulation
 brain development and, 332–334
 lack of, *see* Isolation
Somatotropin, *see* Hormones, growth
Somesthesia, *see* Sensitivity, tactile
Somesthetic system, function of prior to complete maturation, 112
Song development, acoustic isolation and, 439–441
Sound augmentation, acceleration of ma-

turation in auditory system and, 116–117
Sound deprivation, deceleration of maturation in auditory system and, 116
Spatial organization, selectivity in growth of nerve connections and, 30
Spatial orientation, in home orientation 392–393, 396, 399, 404
Specialization, lateral, *see* Lateralization
Species differences, in brain development, 188
Specificity, in genetic regulation, 18–19
Speech, absence of corpus callosum and, 39
Spinal cord, 175
  differentiation in, sequential order of, 48
  functional maturation of brain and, 114–115
  in human embryo, 135, 143, 144, 146, 148, 155, 163, 164
    in sixth week, 160–161
  lack of function and stimulation and, 110
  molecular labels in, 31
  plasticity of, 28
  selectivity in growth of, 29
  spontaneous motility and
    electrical discharge and, 58, 59
    prereflexogenic period in, 55, 56
Spiny anteater, 104
Stages, in development, 490–492
Startle response, 56
  in deermouse, 82
  in guinea pig, 96
  in opossum, 73
Stimulation, *see also* Environment
  approach to conspicuous objects and, 416
  artificial, 184
  from other animals and inanimate objects, brain development and, 332–334
  hypophyseal, 200
  intensity of, 501, 525
  mechanical, lordosis and, 271
  motility and, 54, 61–63
  neurogenesis and, 50–51
  responsivity to, 188, 506

of self, 61, 489
sensory development and, 109–110, 119–121
  sequence of, 110–117
  spontaneous motility and, 55, 56–57
  to suckle, 393, 394, 395, 397–398, 399, 400–401
  tactile, 61, 399
    nipple location and, 359–362, 364–365, 371, 372, 394, 395
    responsiveness to, 48, 52–53, 55
  visual, *see* Light augmentation; Light deprivation
Stochastic processes, in study of interaction sequences, 443–444, 448
Stomal apparatus, unequal cell division in, 8
Streptomycin, postnatal growth disorders and, 209
Stress, brain development and, 329, 330–331, 337
  chemical measurement of, 186
Substitutions, in social interaction, 426
Suckling, 525, *see also* Breast feeding
  conditioning of, 346
  functional distinction from home orientation, 392, 394–395, 401–402
  initiation of, 370–375, 391, 394–395, 402
    during parturition, 347–348
  nipple grasping and, 362–364, 371, 394
  nipple location in, 364–365, 371, 373–374, 399, 411
    olfaction and, 354–356, 358, 359–362, 372, 394, 395
    tactile stimulation and, 359–362, 372, 394, 395
  nipple position preference in, 350–356, 371–372, 393, 399, 465
  origins of, 393, 397–398
  reflex for, 348–350, 353, 370
    maturation of, 365–368
  social isolation and, 366–370, 374
Superior colliculus
  light deprivation and, 113
  vertical development and, 176
Synaptic contacts, onset of motility and, 47
Synaptogenesis, in cerebral cortex, 193–194
Syntactics, 444
Systemogenesis, 66, 107–108, 176, 188

hippocampus and, 177–178
responses to tactile stimulation and, 52–53

T

Tactile stimulation, see Stimulation
Taste, blockage of, by colchicine, 43
Tectospinal tract, selectivity in growth of, 29
Telencephalon, in human embryo, 146
Teleosts, motility in, 59
  as integrated performance, 52
  prereflexogenic phase in, 51
Template
  in cellular systems, 21–22
  in song development, 440
Teratogeny, 210, 220–221
Terrapin, sensory development in, 105
Testing, 499
  behavioral, 183
  electrophysiological, 183–185
  intelligence, 35, 537
Testis, 250
  androgenic activity of, 198
  differentiation of gonads into, 197
  estrogens and, 211, 213, 214
Testosterone
  behavior and, 245–246
  congenital malformations and, 212
  copulatory behavior and
    in female guinea pig, 272–274, 287
    in female hamster, 278–279
    in female rat, 267–268, 269, 288
    in male guinea pig, 274–276, 277–278
    in male hamster, 279–280, 281
    in male rat, 259–263, 265–271
    organization of brain mechanisms for, 251–255, 282–283, 284
  fetal testicular secretion and, 198
  genital growth and, 256–258
  reproductive function and, 240
  sexual differentiation and, 251
  social behavior in monkeys and, 288
Tetracycline, postnatal growth disorders and, 209
Thalamus, 160, 175
Thermal stimuli, 397, 399
  nipple location and, 353, 394
Thermoregulation, thyroid hormone deficiency and, 202

Thrusting, see Copulatory behavior
Thymus gland, adrenocortical hormones and, 200
Thyroid
  hormones of, 201–202, 203, see also Thyroxine
  transplacental passage of, 205
  interference with, 325
Thyroid stimulatory hormone, 201–202, 204–205
Thyroxine, 201
  congenital malformations and, 210
  disorders of gestation and fetal growth rate and, 206
  inhibition of postnatal growth by, 207–208
  transplacental passage of, 204
Titmouse, agonistic behavior in, 443
Toad(s)
  ectodermal conducting system in, 121
  sensory development in, 105
Tracts, identified in human embryos, 162
Transcription, gene regulation at level of, 5
Transfer of training, 517
Translation, gene regulation at level of, 5
Trigeminal tract, selectivity in growth of, 29
Triiodothyronine, 201, 206
  inhibition of postnatal growth by, 207–208
Turdus merula, song development in, 441
Turtles, 118
  evolution of, 105
  motility in, 58, 61–62
  sensory development in, 105
Twins
  laterality and cerebral dominance in, 37, 44
  mother-infant relations in, 422
Typological thinking, 503
Tyrannid flycatcher, communication patterns of, 445–446
Tyrannus tyrannus, communication patterns in, 446

U

Uracil, 9
Urodeles, motility in, 59

SUBJECT INDEX

Urogenital sinus, estrogens and, 211
Uterus, see Genital tract

V

Vagina, see Genital tract
Value judgments, 544
  in control of behavior, 545–551
Vasopressin
  congenital malformations and, 210
  weaning and, 238–239
Ventral basal plate, differentiation in, 48
Vertebrates, see also specific animals
  evolution of, 434
Vestibular tract, selectivity in growth of, 29
Vision, see also Sensitivity, visual
  suckling and, 394, 402, 406
Visual cortex
  movement and contrast and, 184
  organization of, 301
  vertical development and, 176
  visual impoverishment and, 306–307
Visual cues, home orientation and, 390, 391, 395, 402–403, 406
Visual field, 301
Visual impoverishment, see also Light deprivation
  amino acids and, 180
  effect on brain, 306–307, 336
Visual perception, see also Sensitivity, visual
  neurogenesis and, 28, 29–30
Visual purple, in rat retina, 78
Visual system, see also specific structures
  acceleration of maturation in, 115–116
  deceleration of maturation in, 113–115
  ontogenesis of behavioral nerve nets in, 32
  selectivity in growth of, 29
Vocalization, see also Communication; Language
  testicular activity and, 117
  in ducks, 116–117
Volition, see Free will

W

WAIS, see Weschler Adult Intelligence Scale
Walking, learning of, 499
Water
  in brain, 177
  consumption of, testosterone and, 245–246
  metabolism of, 238–239
Weaning, 233, 234
  differential experience at blinding, 307
  problem solving and, 317–321
  premature, 237
  endocrine function and, 237–247
Weschler Adult Intelligence Scale, lateral specialization of function in brain and, 35
White-crowned sparrow, song development in, 439–442
White matter, 309–310
Wisconsin General Test Apparatus, differential environment and, 323
Withdrawal, 516, 525
  inability to condition, 346, 347
  levels of organization and, 507–508
Wolffian ducts, 250
  estrogens and, 217
  testis secretions and, 197

X

Xenopus, cell nuclei from larval intestine of, 3

Z

Zonotrichia leucophrys, song development in, 439–442
Zonotrichia querula, 440
Zoosemiotic, 444